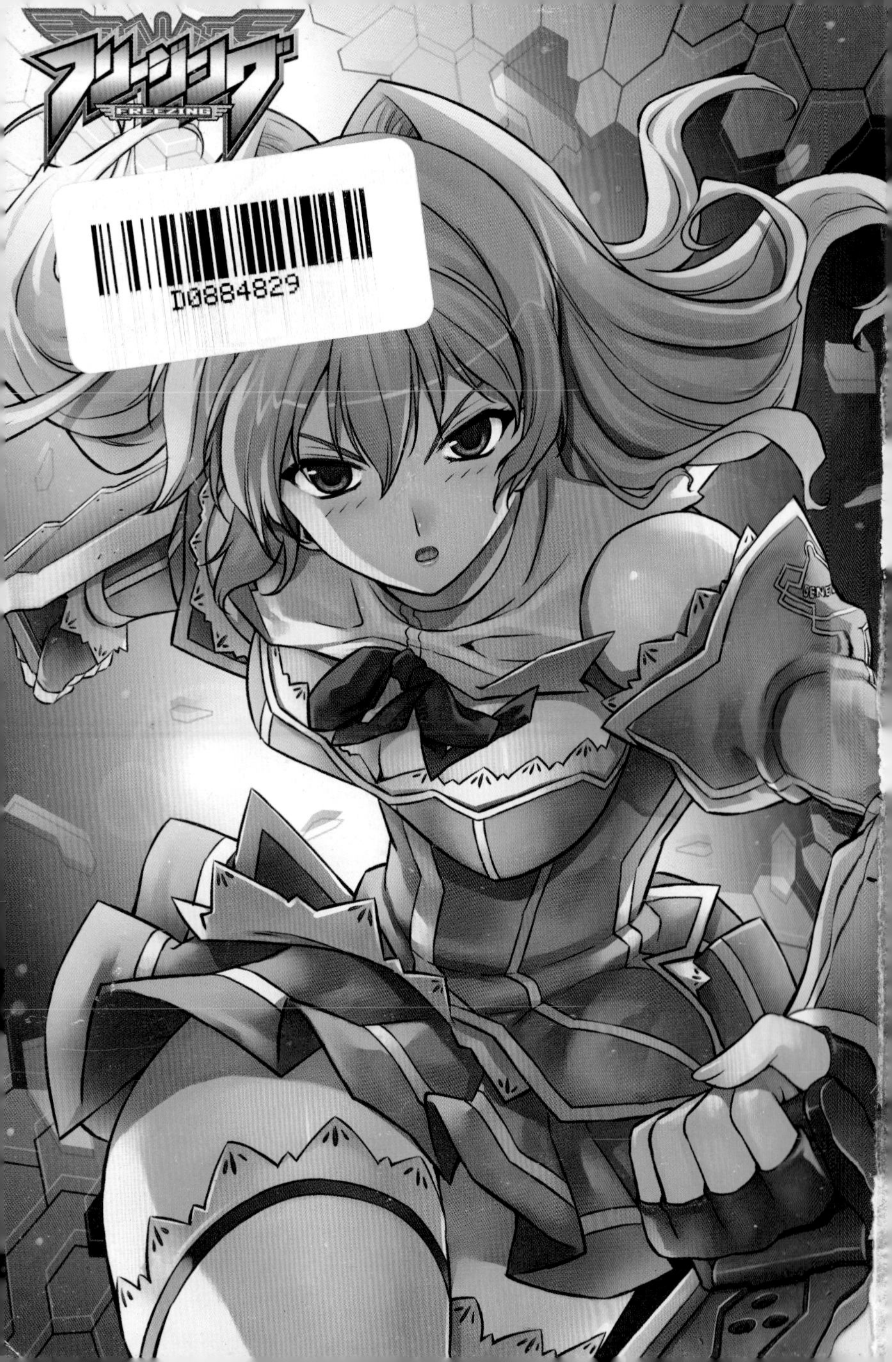
フリージング
FREEZING

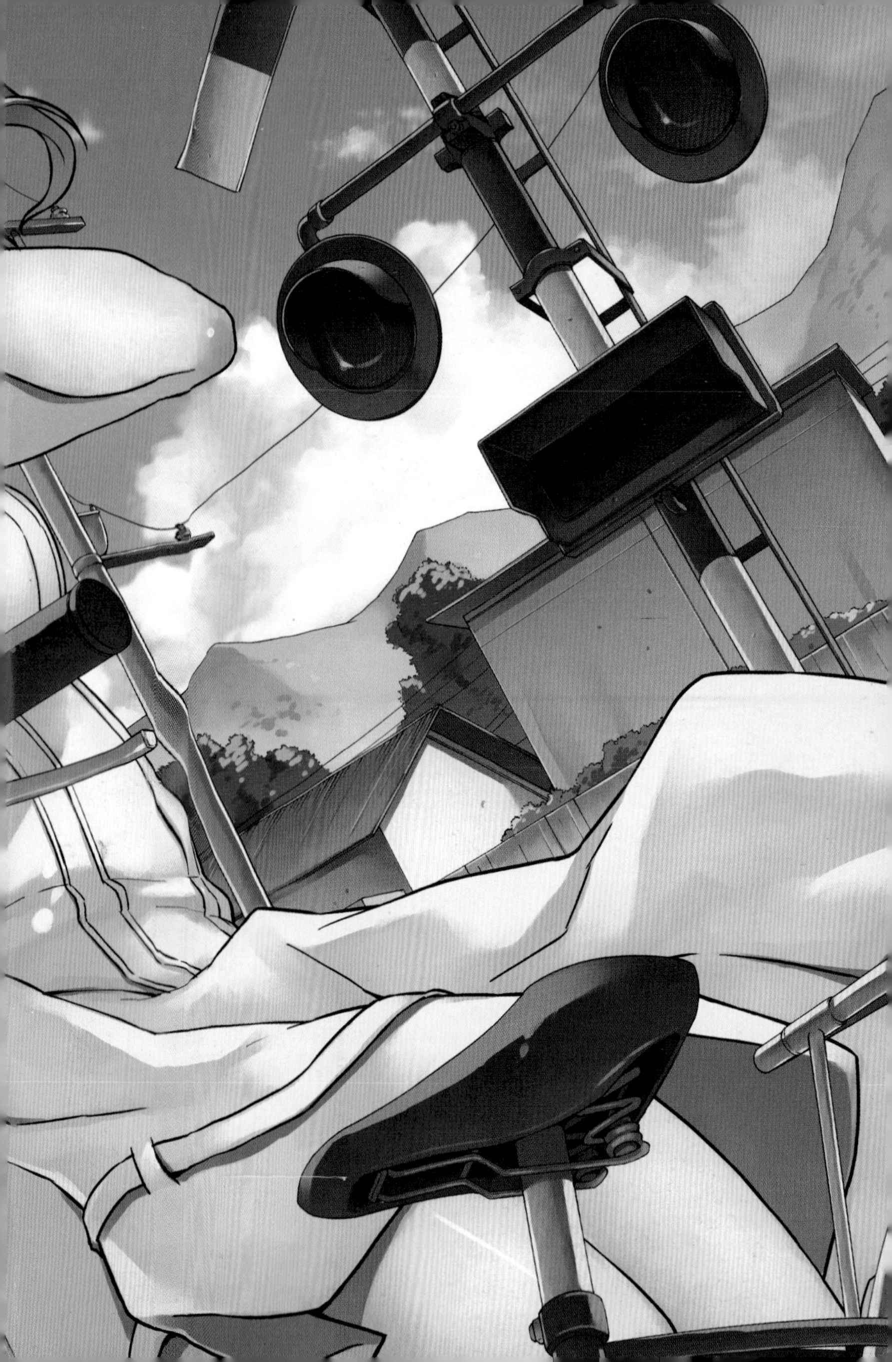

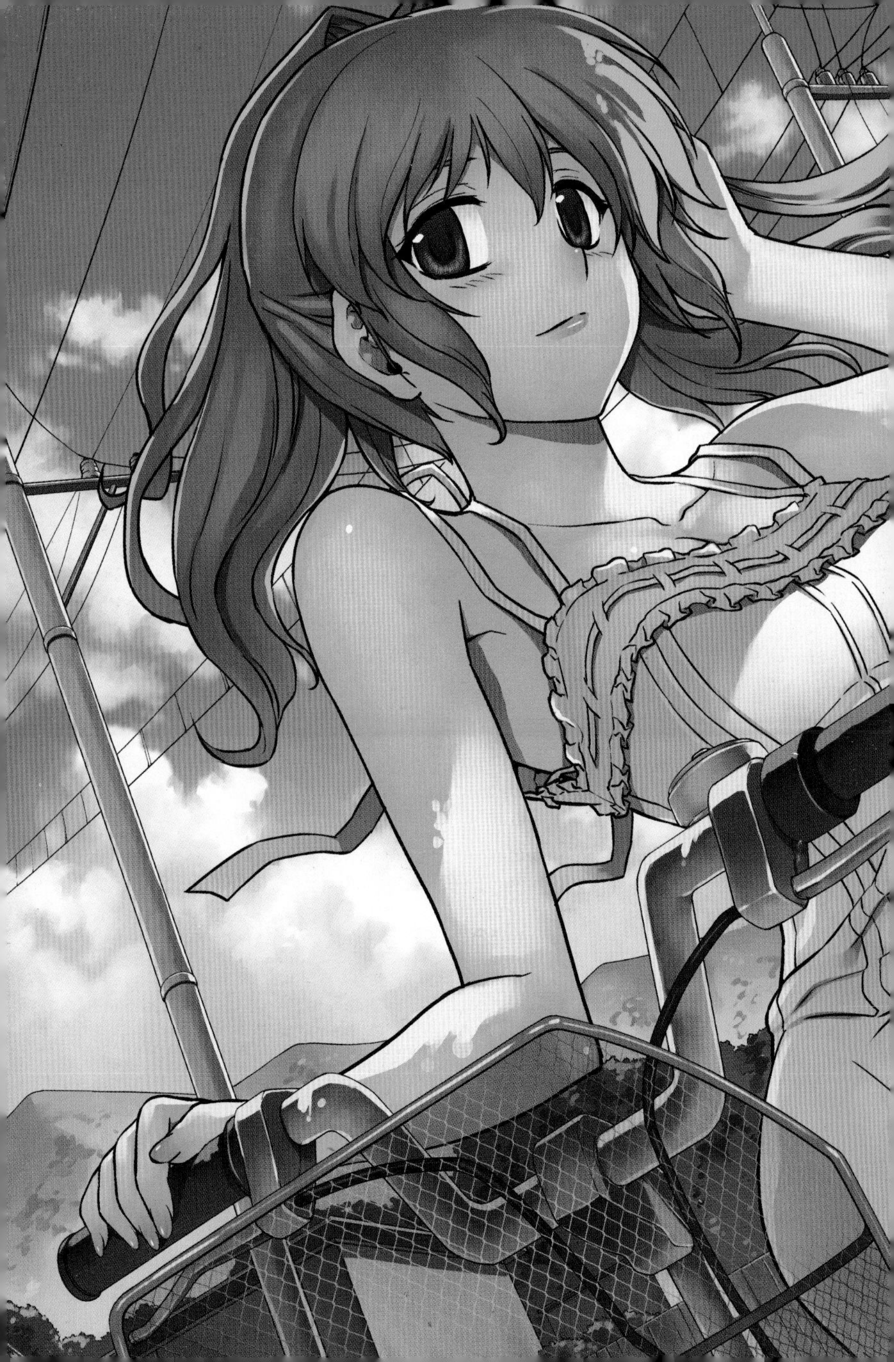

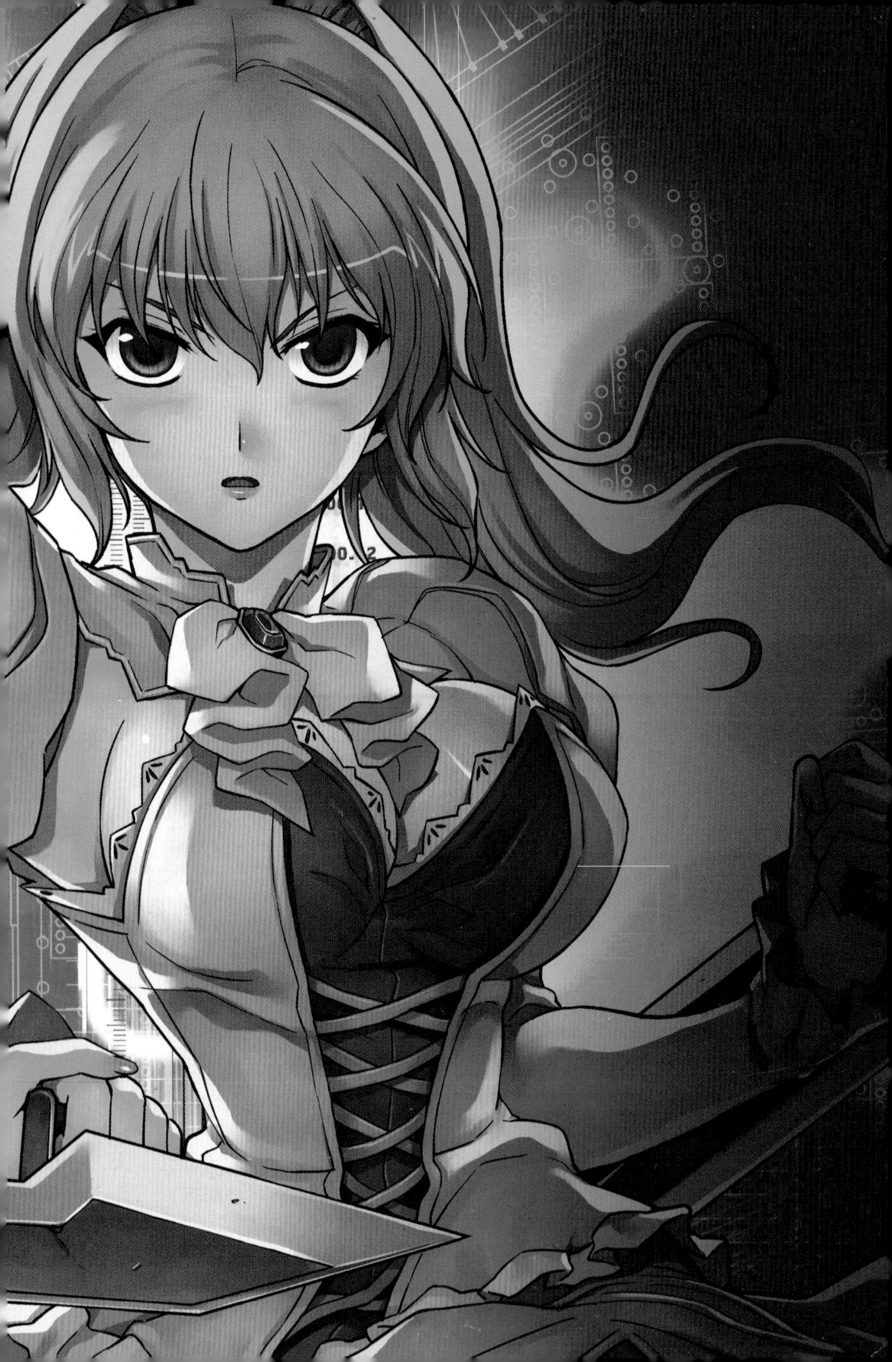

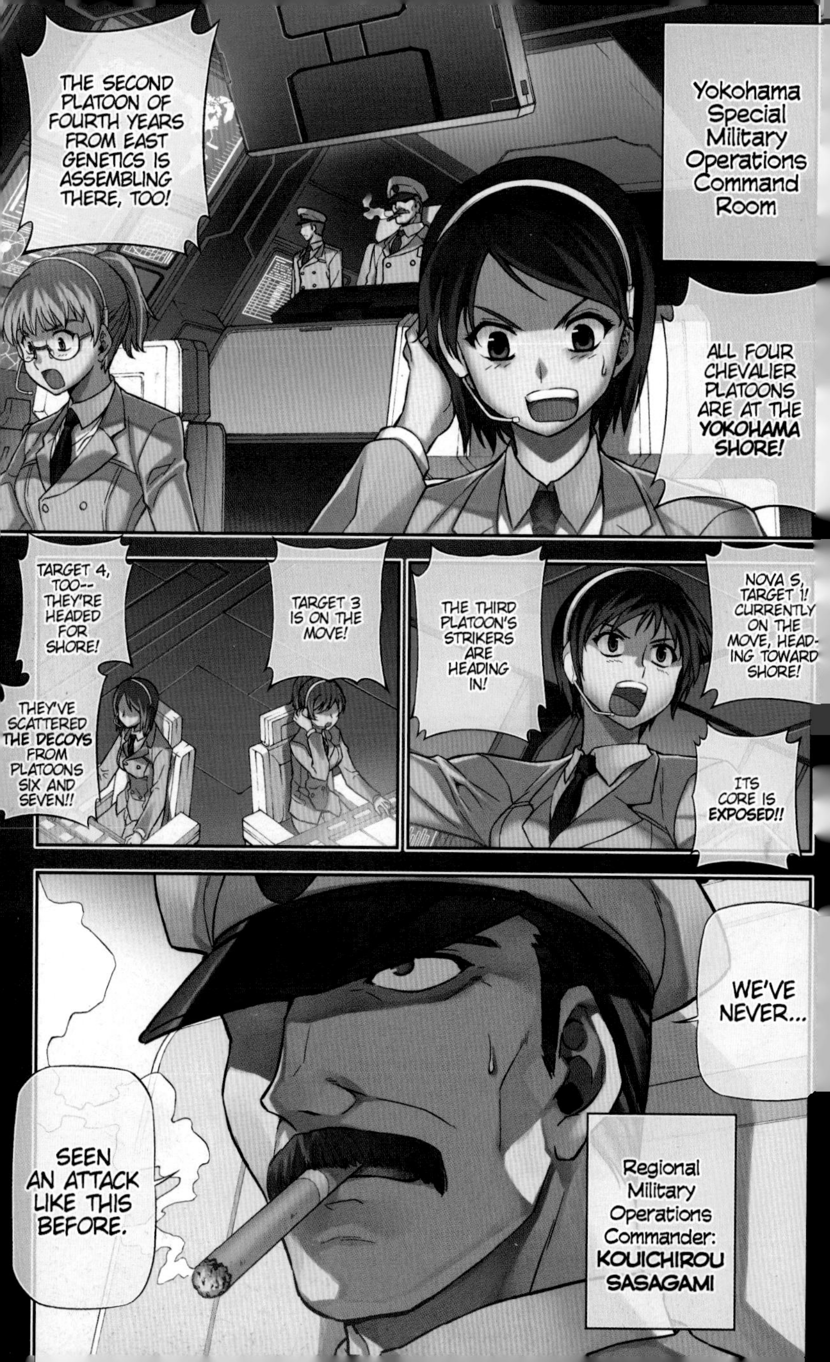
Yokohama Special Military Operations Command Room
ALL FOUR CHEVALIER PLATOONS ARE AT THE YOKOHAMA SHORE!
THE SECOND PLATOON OF FOURTH YEARS FROM EAST GENETICS IS ASSEMBLING THERE, TOO!
NOVA 5, TARGET 1! CURRENTLY ON THE MOVE, HEADING TOWARD SHORE!
THE THIRD PLATOON'S STRIKERS ARE HEADING IN!
ITS CORE IS EXPOSED!!
TARGET 3 IS ON THE MOVE!
TARGET 4, TOO-- THEY'RE HEADED FOR SHORE!
THEY'VE SCATTERED THE DECOYS FROM PLATOONS SIX AND SEVEN!!
WE'VE NEVER...
Regional Military Operations Commander: KOUICHIROU SASAGAMI
SEEN AN ATTACK LIKE THIS BEFORE.

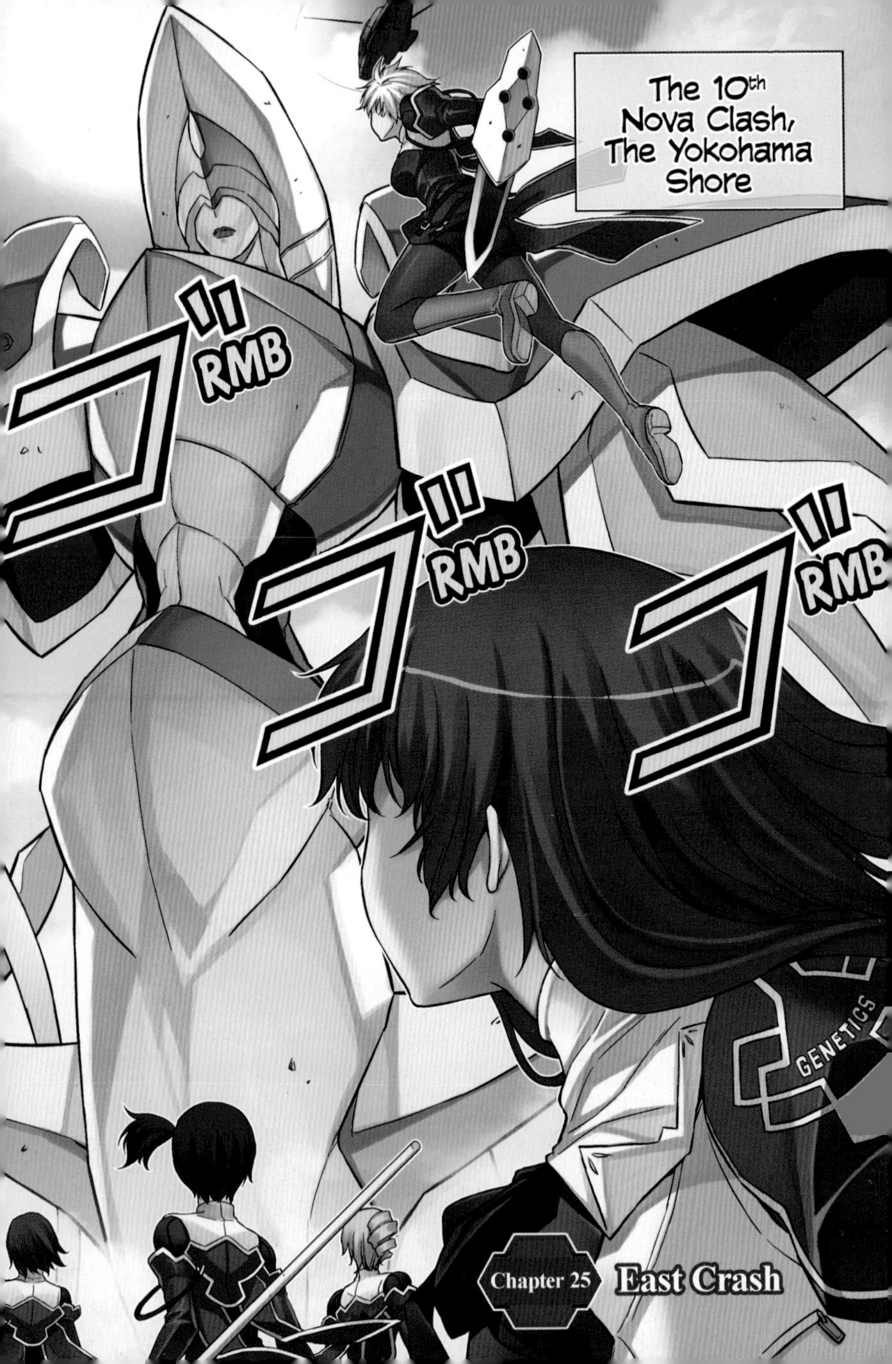
The 10th Nova Clash, The Yokohama Shore
ゴ RMB
ゴ RMB
ゴ RMB
GENETICS
Chapter 25 East Crash

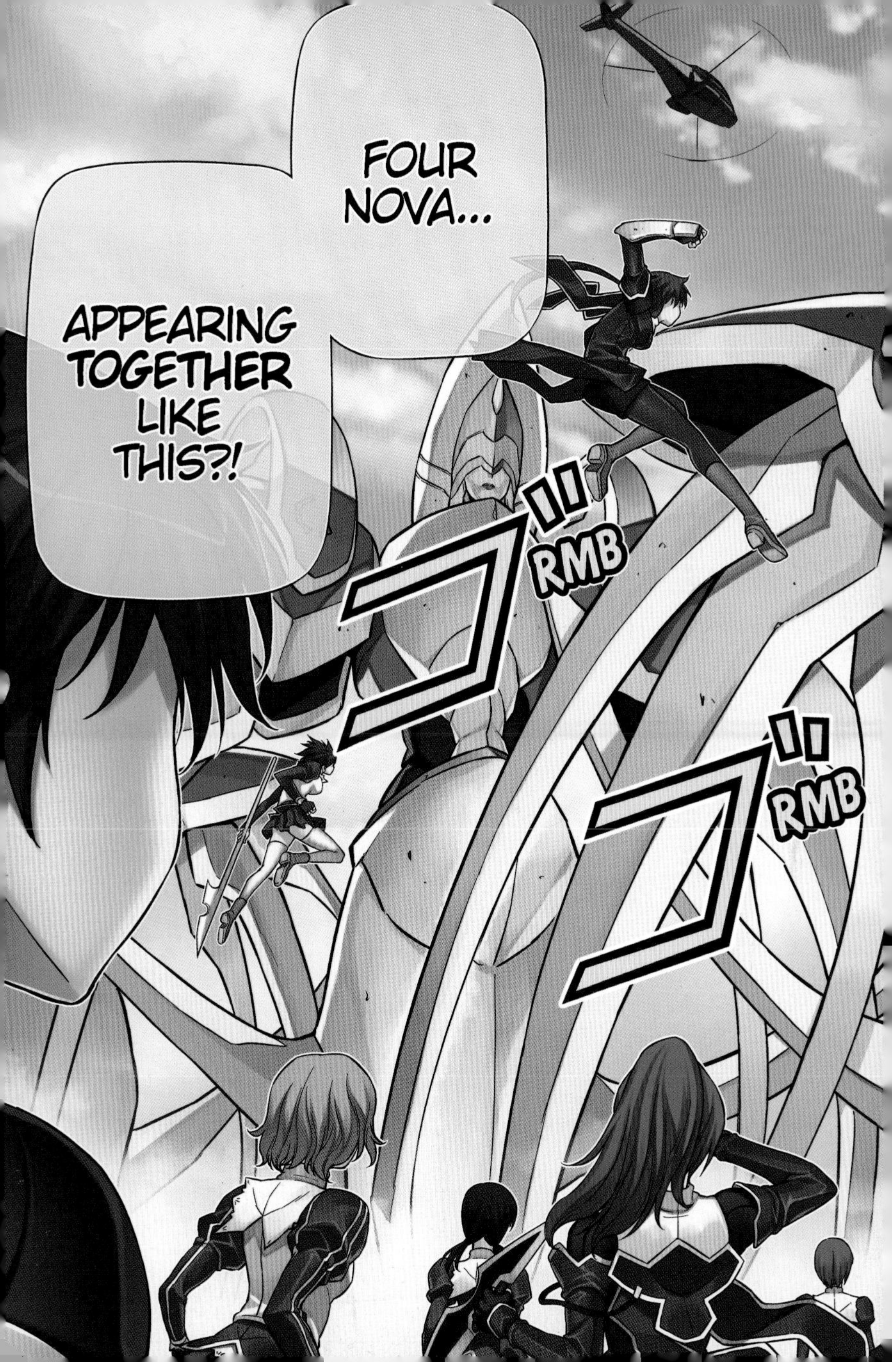
FOUR NOVA...
APPEARING TOGETHER LIKE THIS?!
RMB
RMB

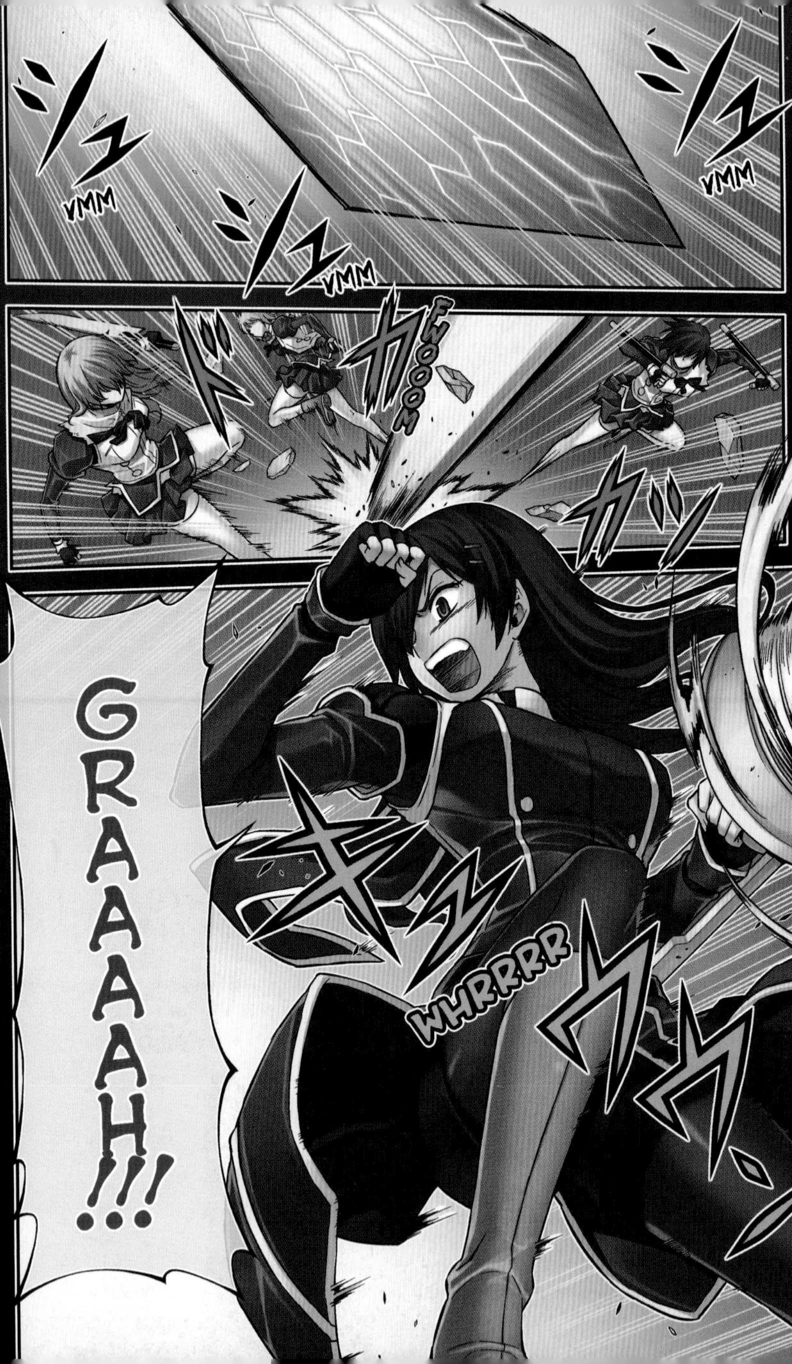
VMM
VMM
VMM
WOOOOM
WHRRRR
GRAAAAH!!!

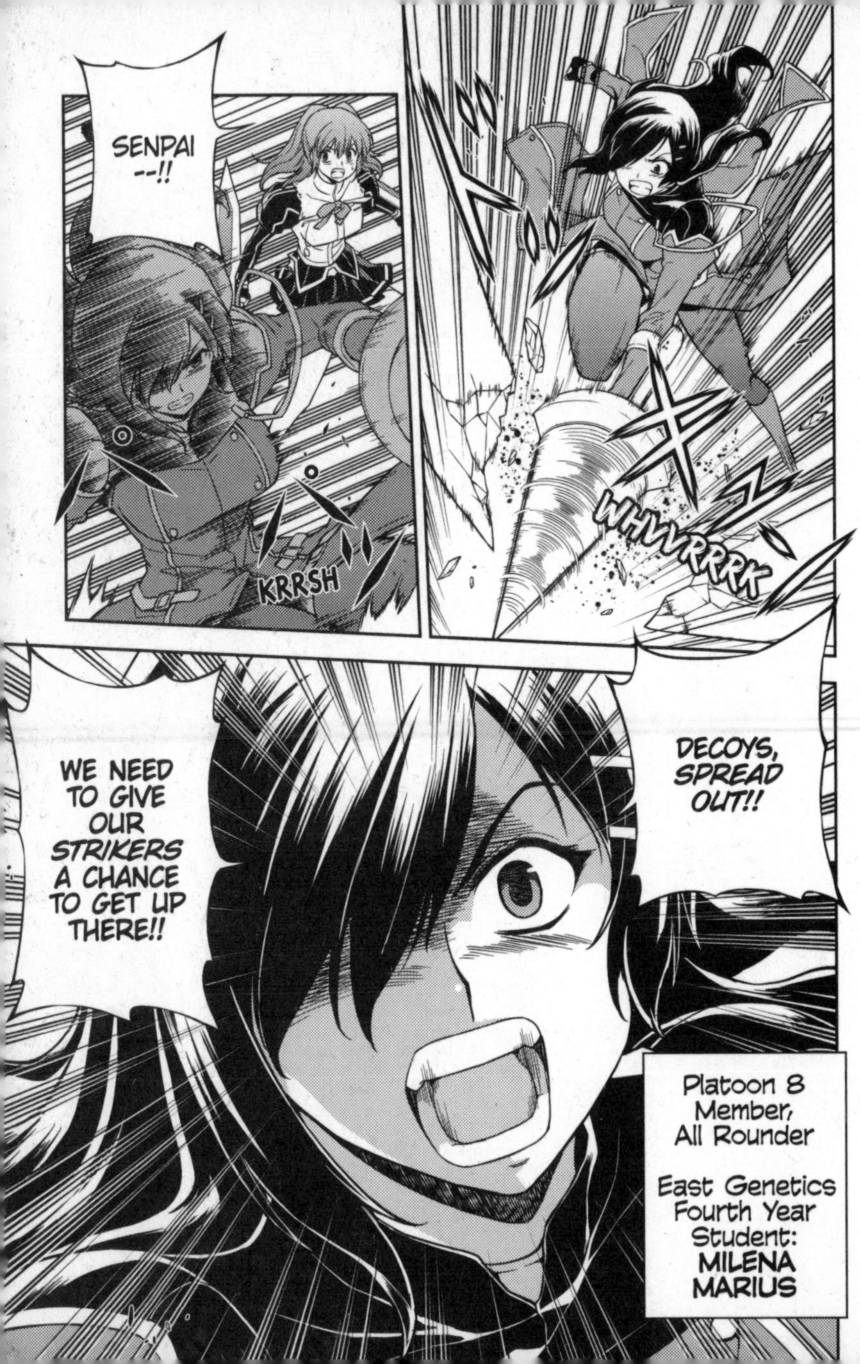
WHVVRRRK
SENPAI --!!
KRRSH
DECOYS, SPREAD OUT!!
WE NEED TO GIVE OUR STRIKERS A CHANCE TO GET UP THERE!!
Platoon 8 Member, All Rounder
East Genetics Fourth Year Student: MILENA MARIUS

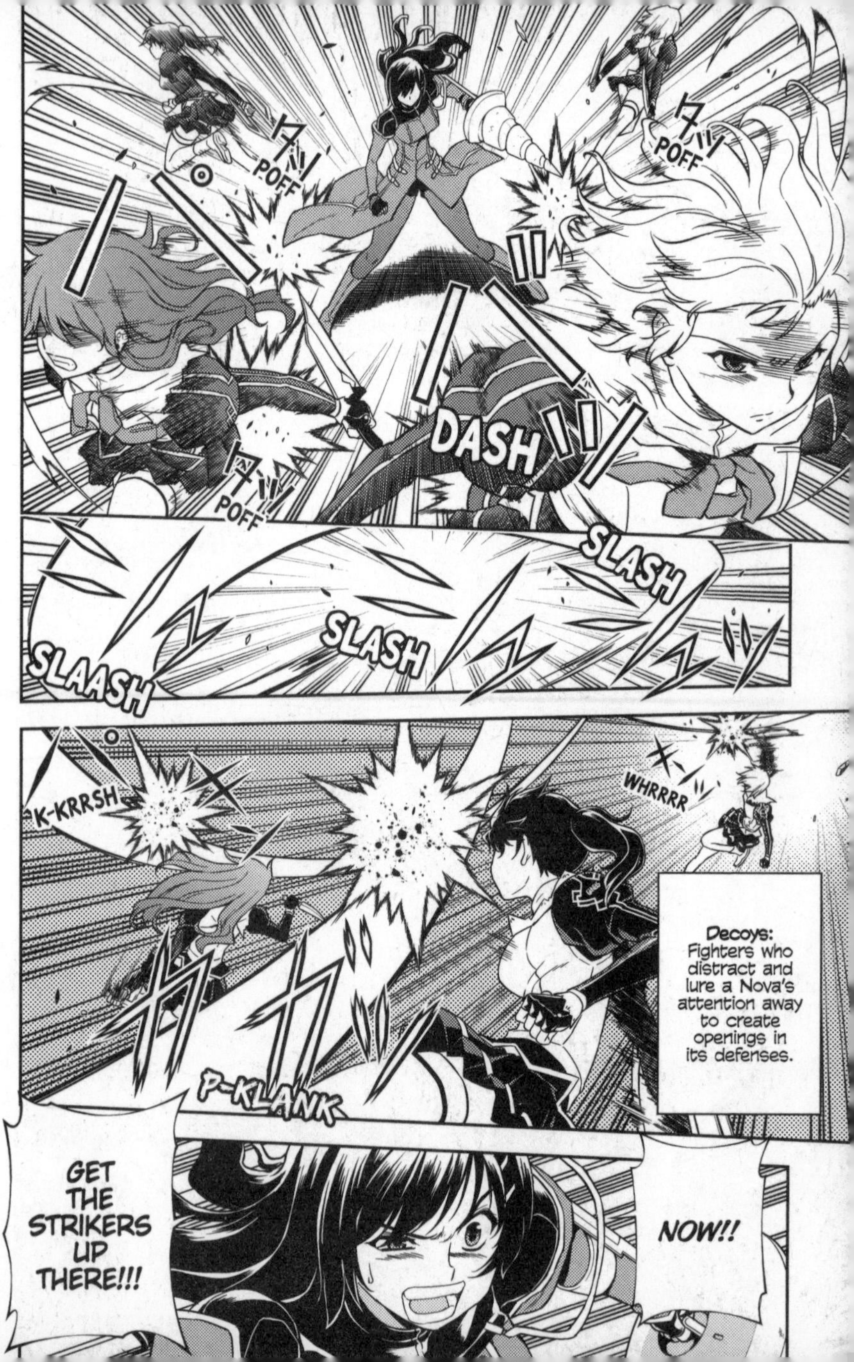
POFF
POFF
DASH
POFF
SLASH
SLASH
SLAASH
WHRRRR
Decoys: Fighters who distract and lure a Nova's attention away to create openings in its defenses.
K-KRRSH
P-KLANK
NOW!!
GET THE STRIKERS UP THERE!!!

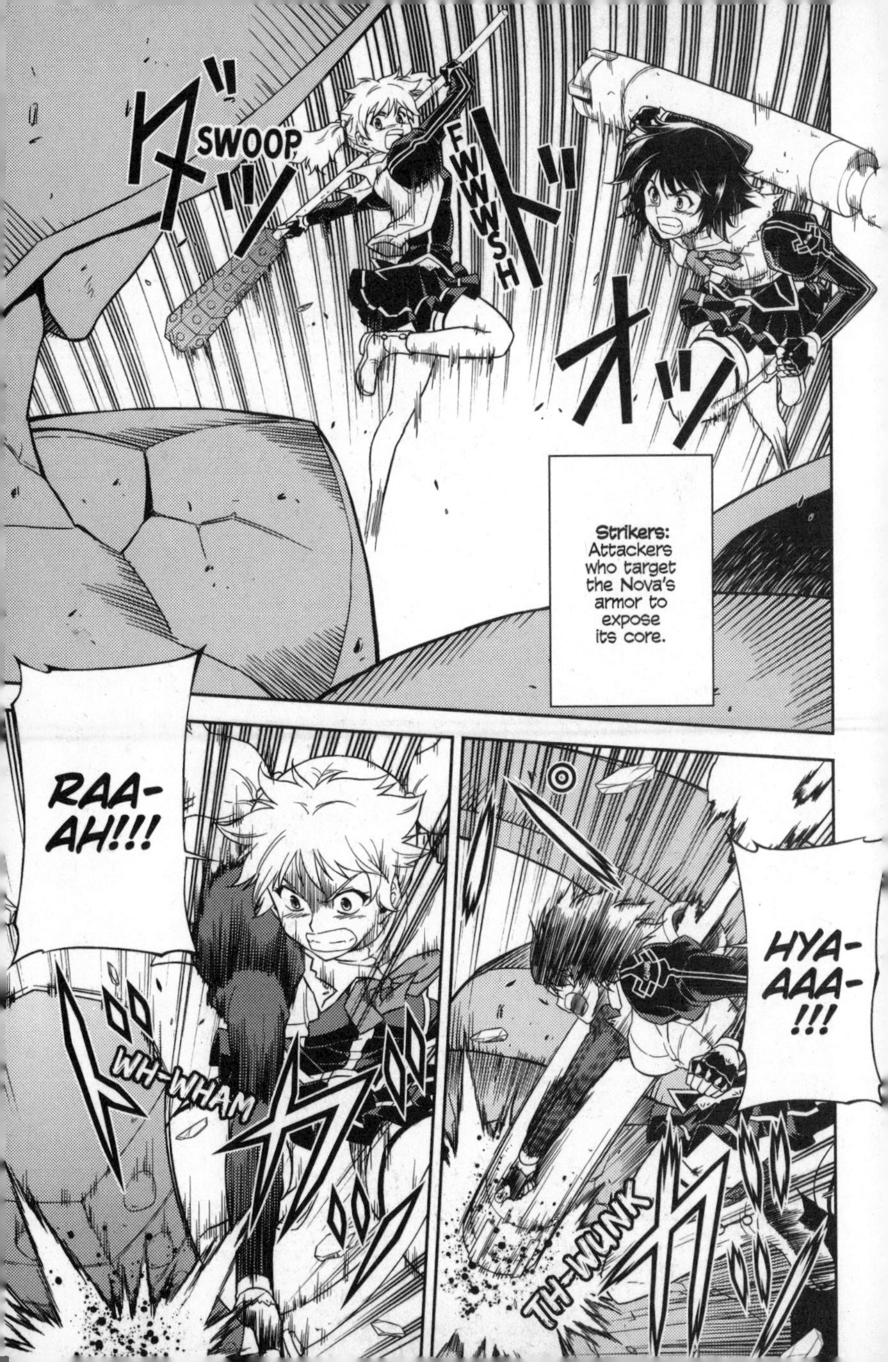
FWWWSH
SWOOP
Strikers: Attackers who target the Nova's armor to expose its core.
HYA-AAA-!!!
TH-WUNK
RAA-AH!!!
WH-WHAM

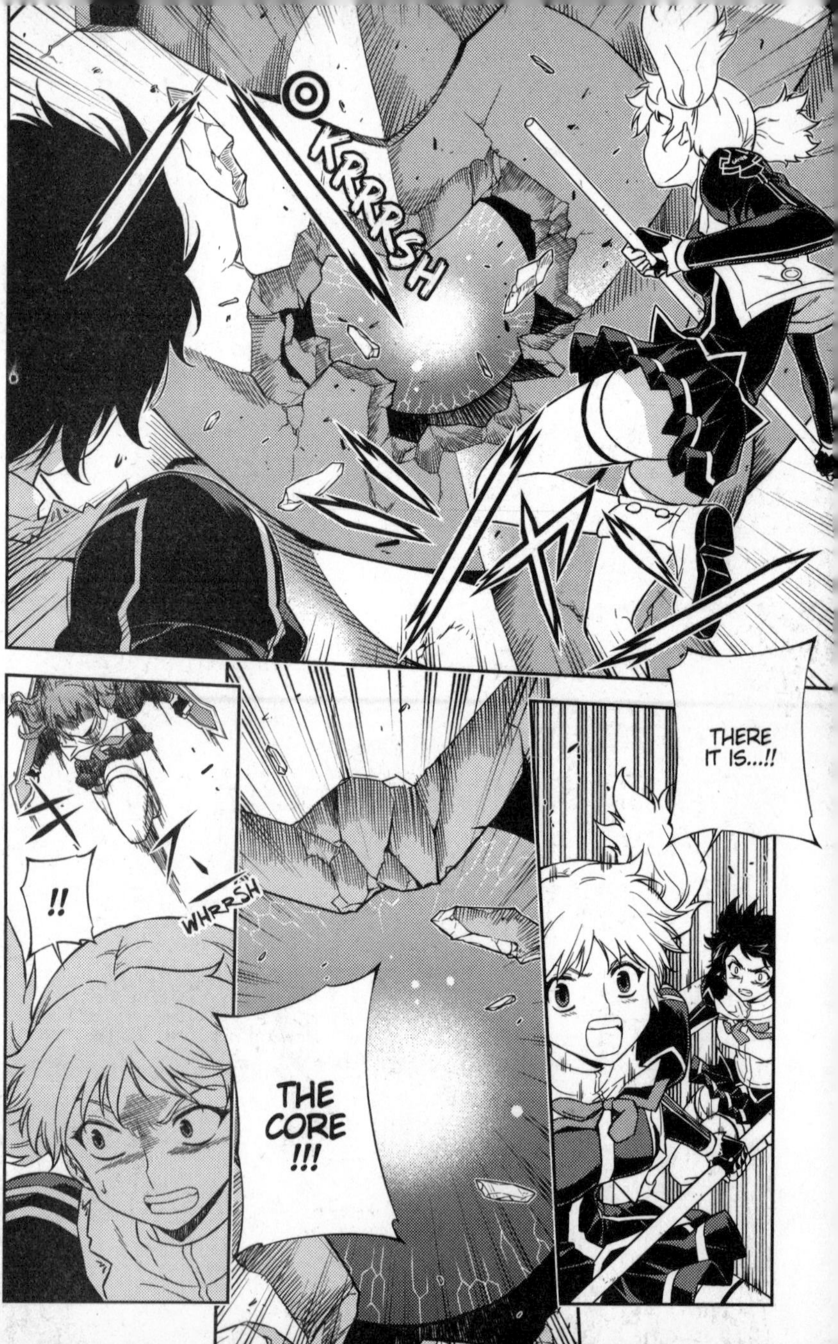
KRRRSH
THERE IT IS...!!
THE CORE !!!
!!
WHRRSH

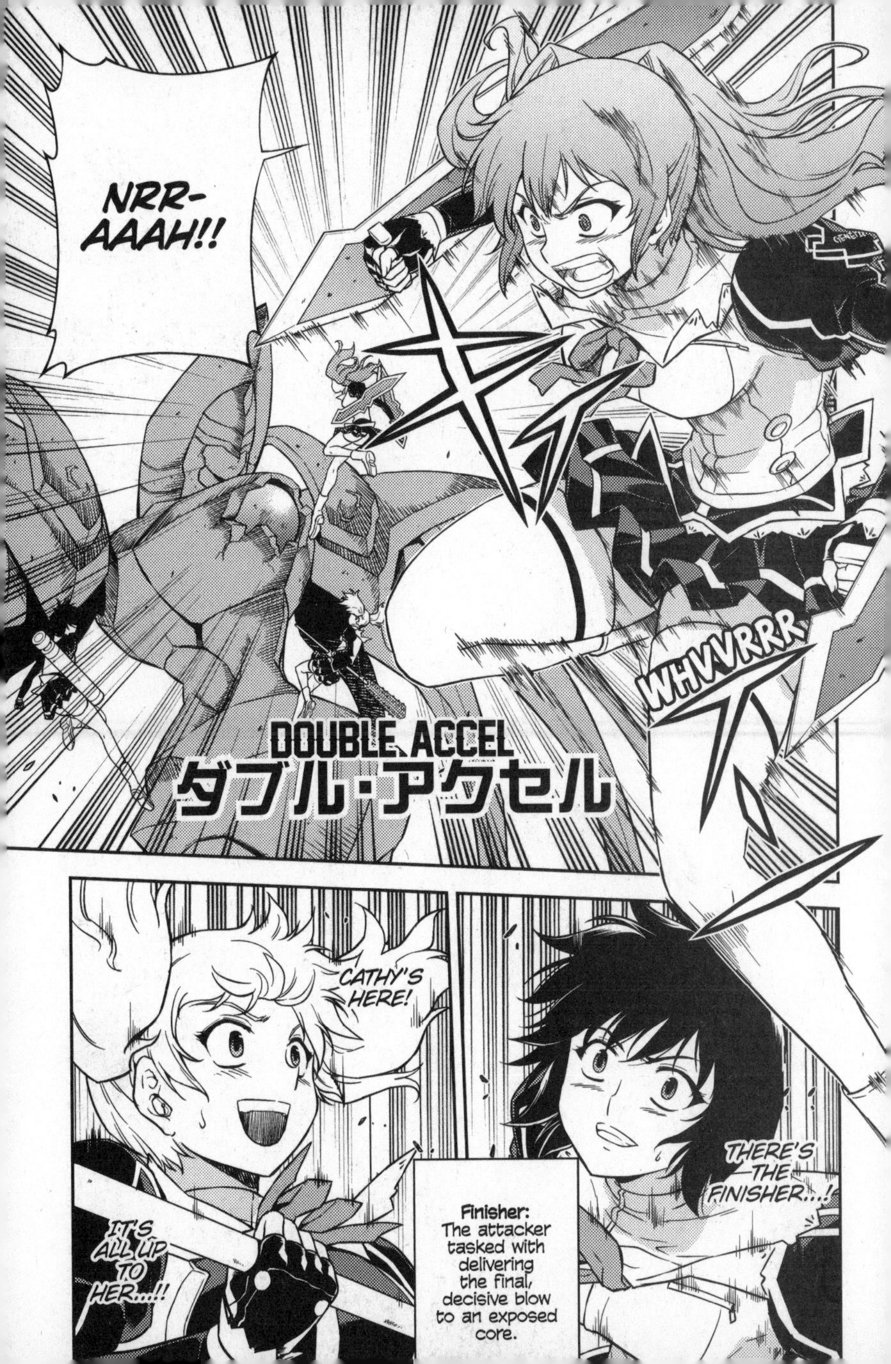
NRR-AAAH!!
WHVVRRR
DOUBLE ACCEL
ダブル・アクセル
THERE'S THE FINISHER...!
Finisher: The attacker tasked with delivering the final, decisive blow to an exposed core.
CATHY'S HERE!
IT'S ALL UP TO HER...!!

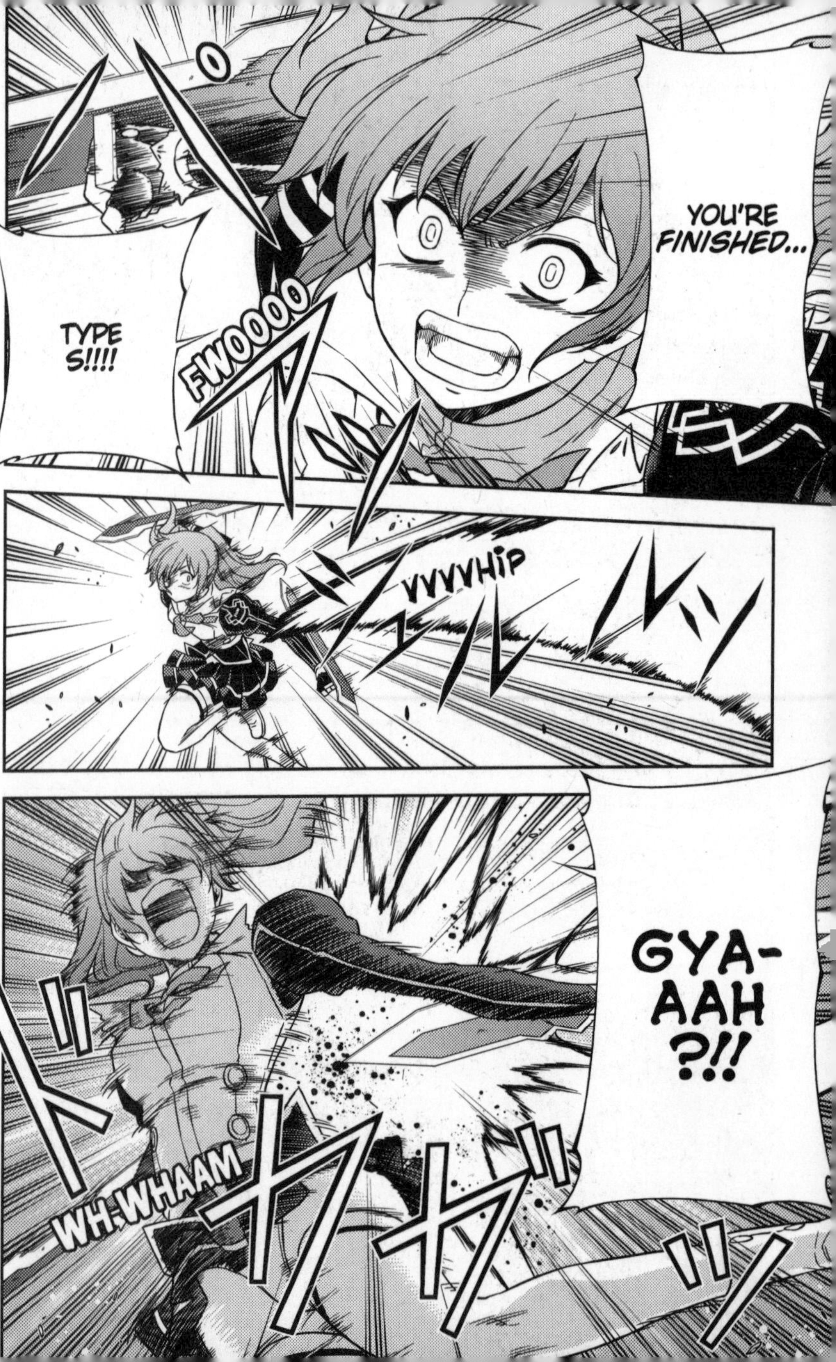
YOU'RE FINISHED...
FWOOOO
TYPE S!!!!
VVVVHIP
GYA-AAH ?!!
WH-WHAAM

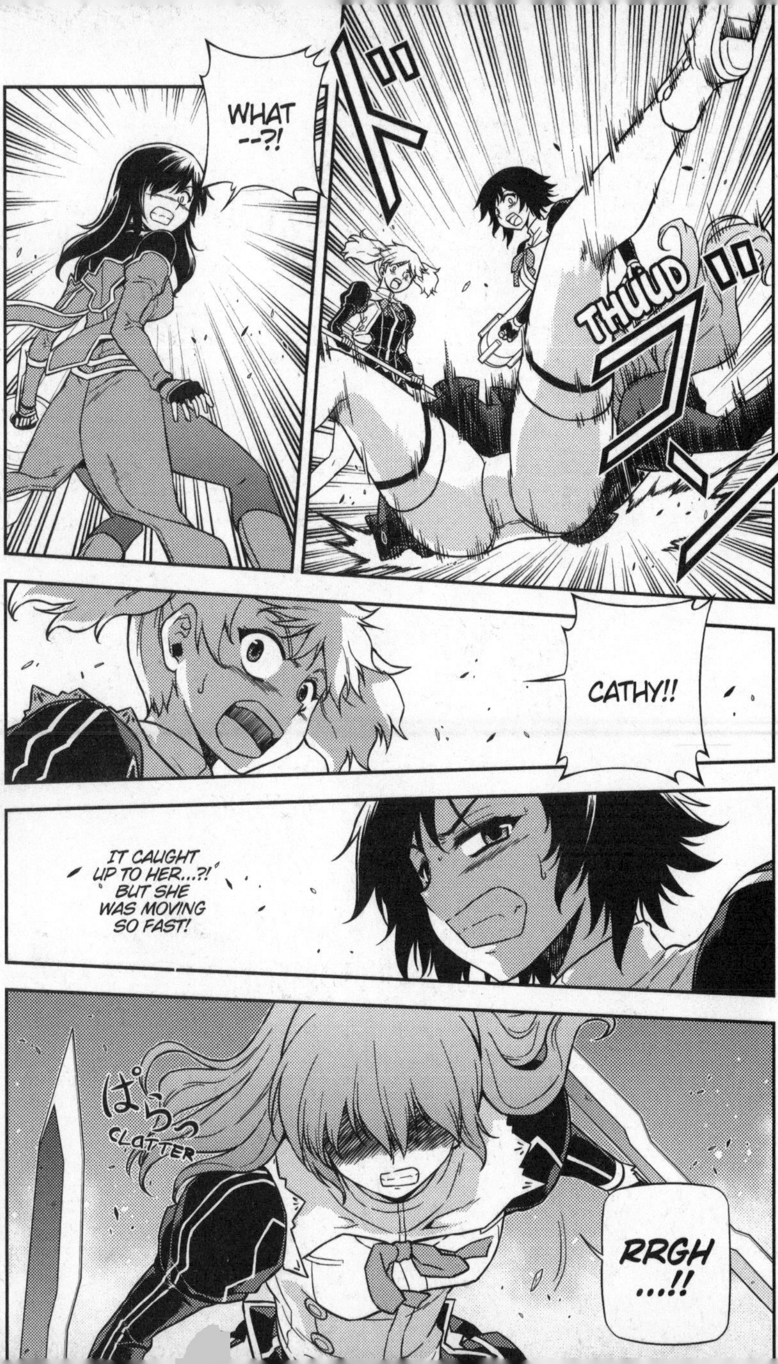
THUUD
WHAT --?!
CATHY!!
IT CAUGHT UP TO HER...?! BUT SHE WAS MOVING SO FAST!
ぱらっ
CLATTER
RRGH ...!!

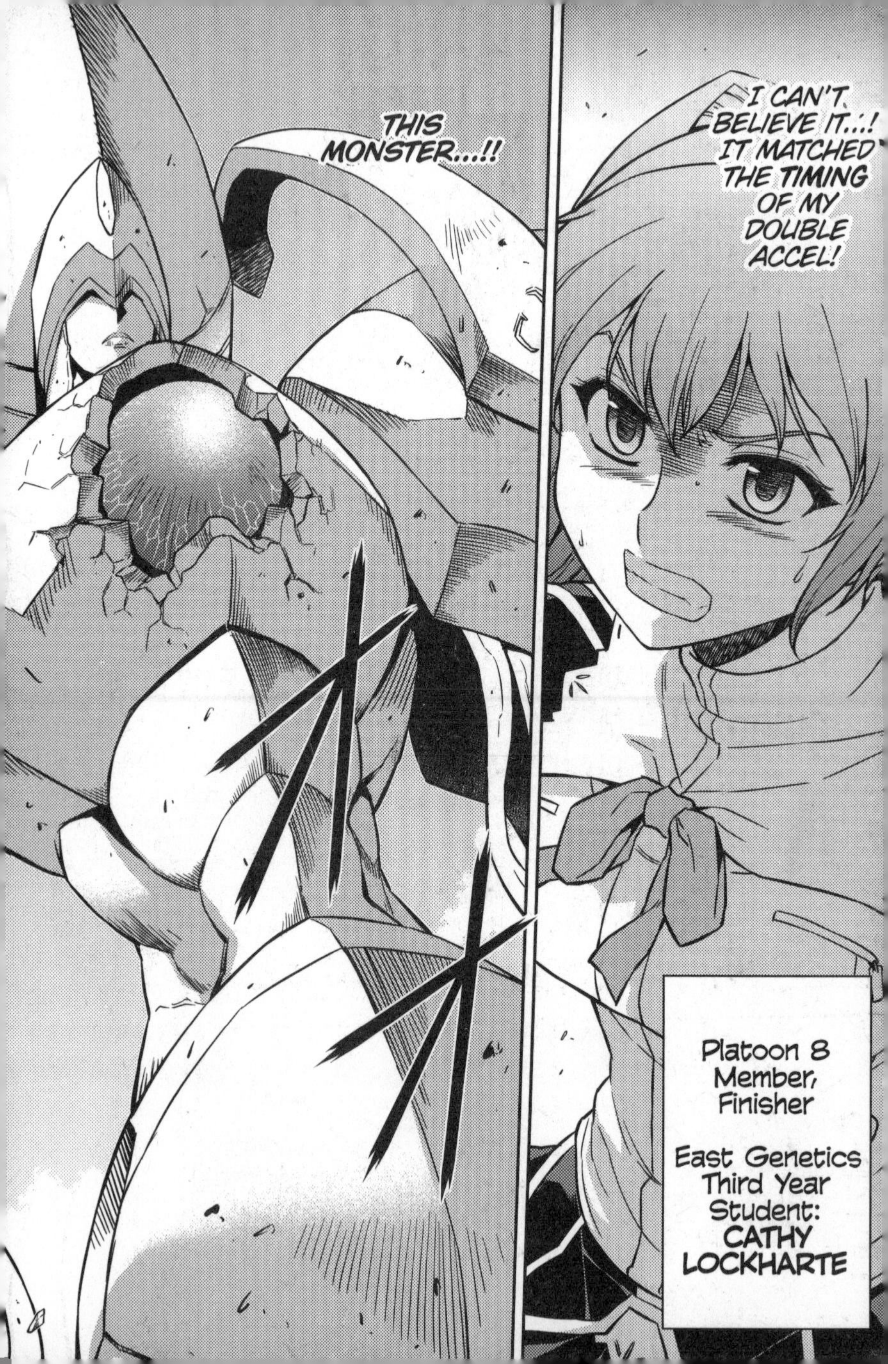
I CAN'T BELIEVE IT...! IT MATCHED THE TIMING OF MY DOUBLE ACCEL!
Platoon 8 Member, Finisher
East Genetics Third Year Student: CATHY LOCKHARTE
THIS MONSTER...!!

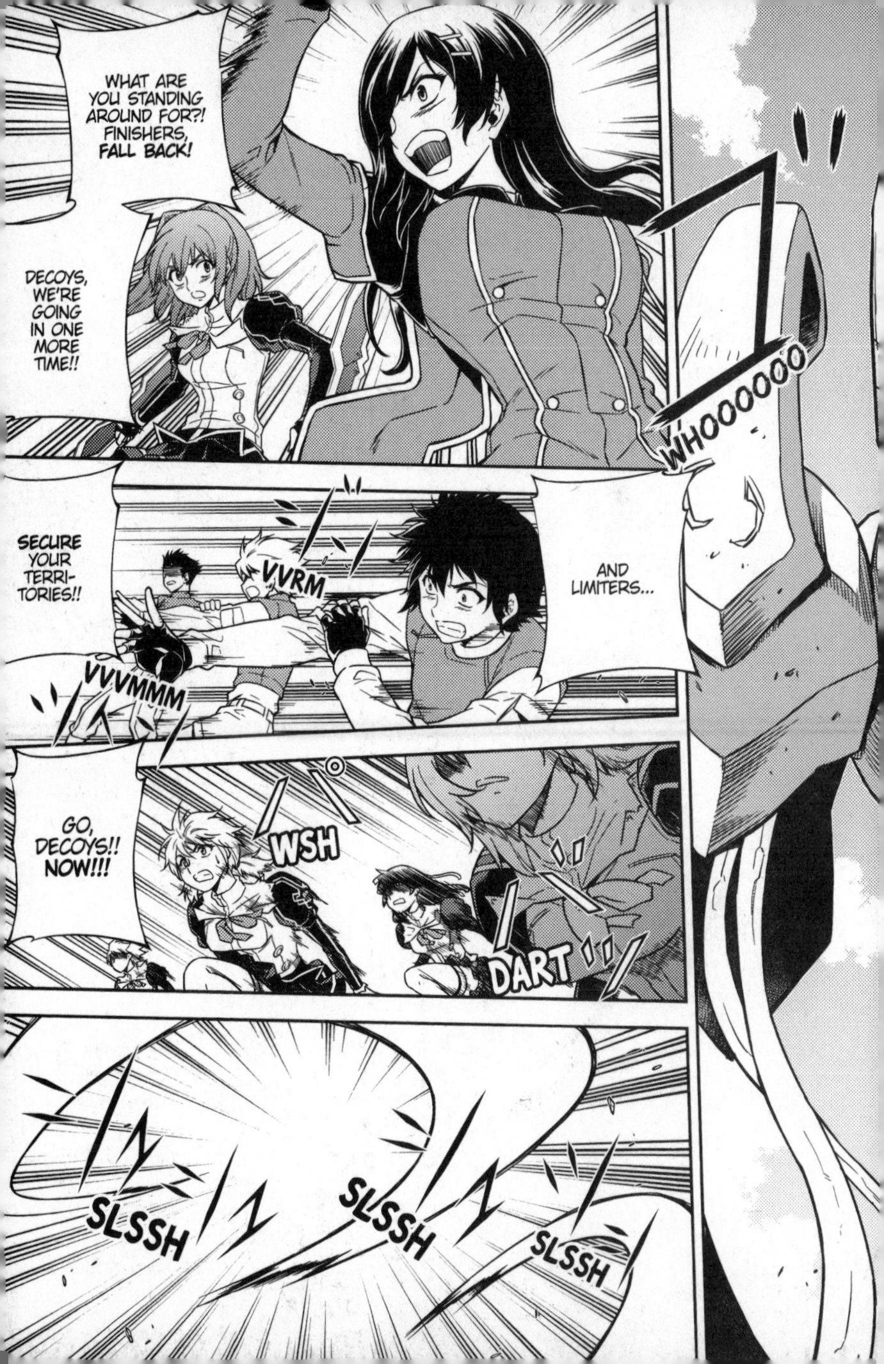
WHOOOOOO
WHAT ARE YOU STANDING AROUND FOR?! FINISHERS, FALL BACK!
DECOYS, WE'RE GOING IN ONE MORE TIME!!
AND LIMITERS...
VVRM
SECURE YOUR TERRI-TORIES!!
VVVMMM
DART
WSH
GO, DECOYS!! NOW!!!
SLSSH
SLSSH
SLSSH

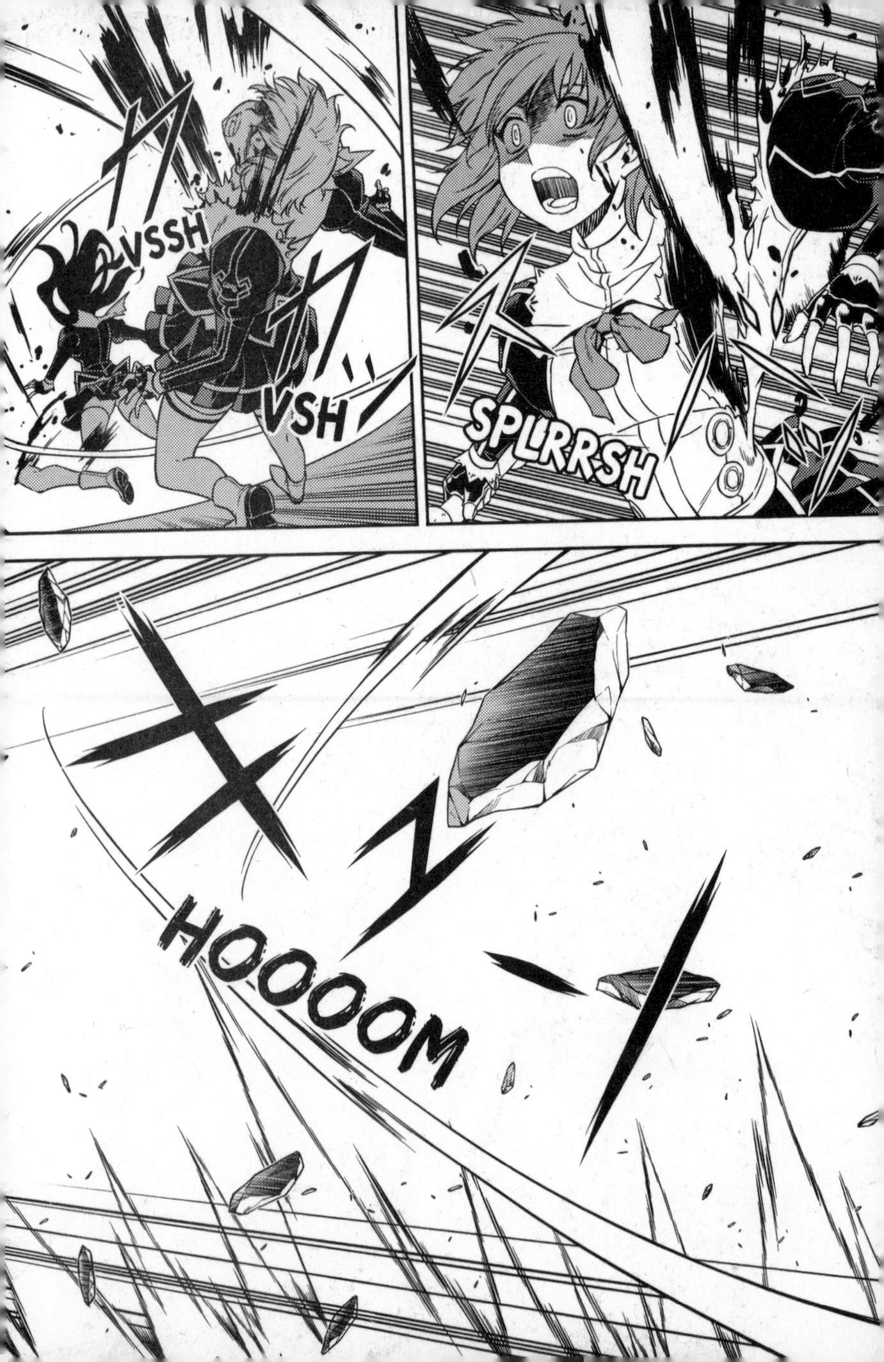
SPLRRRSH
VSSH
VSH
HOOOOOM

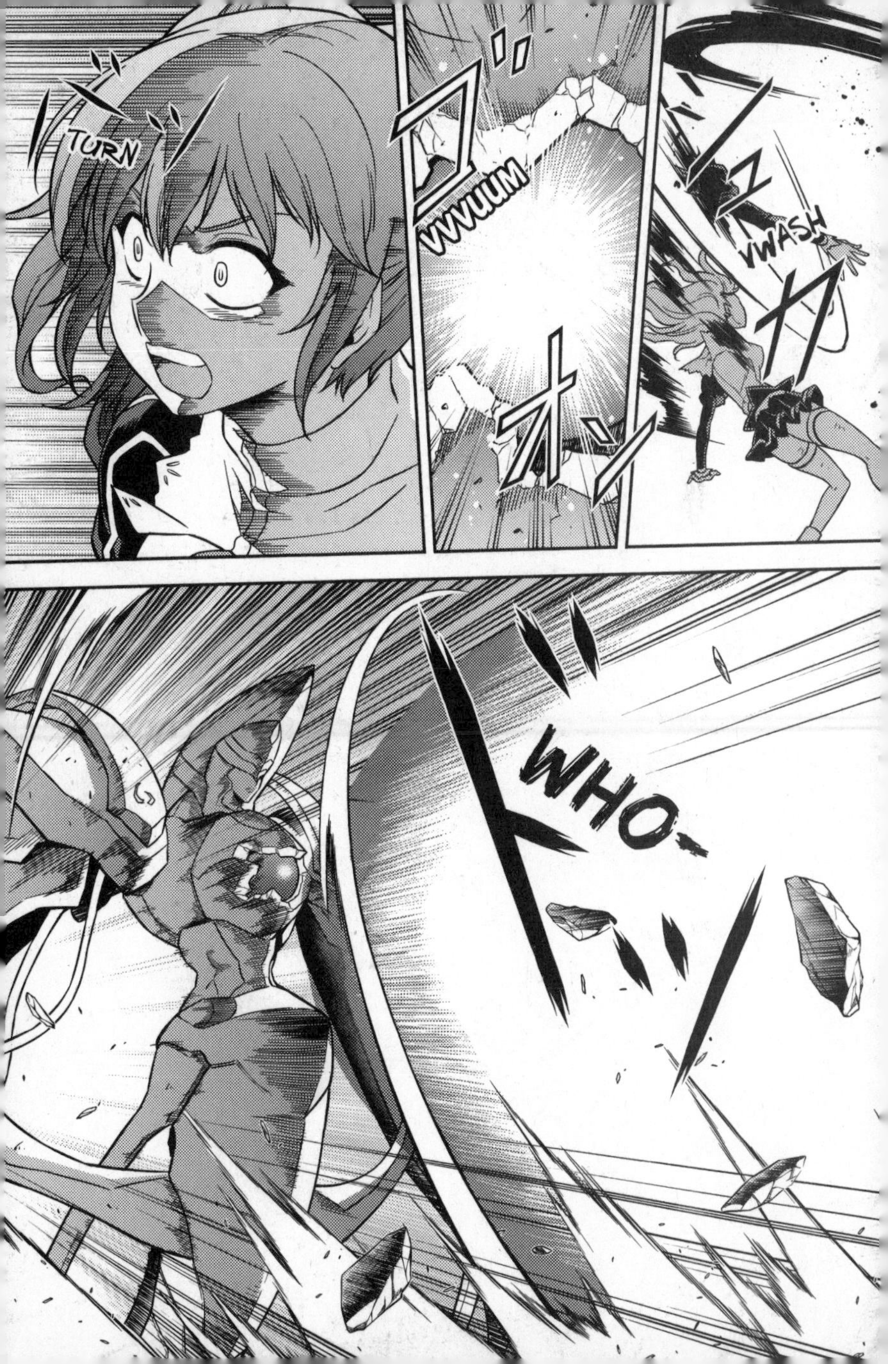
VWASH
VVUUM
TURN
WHO-

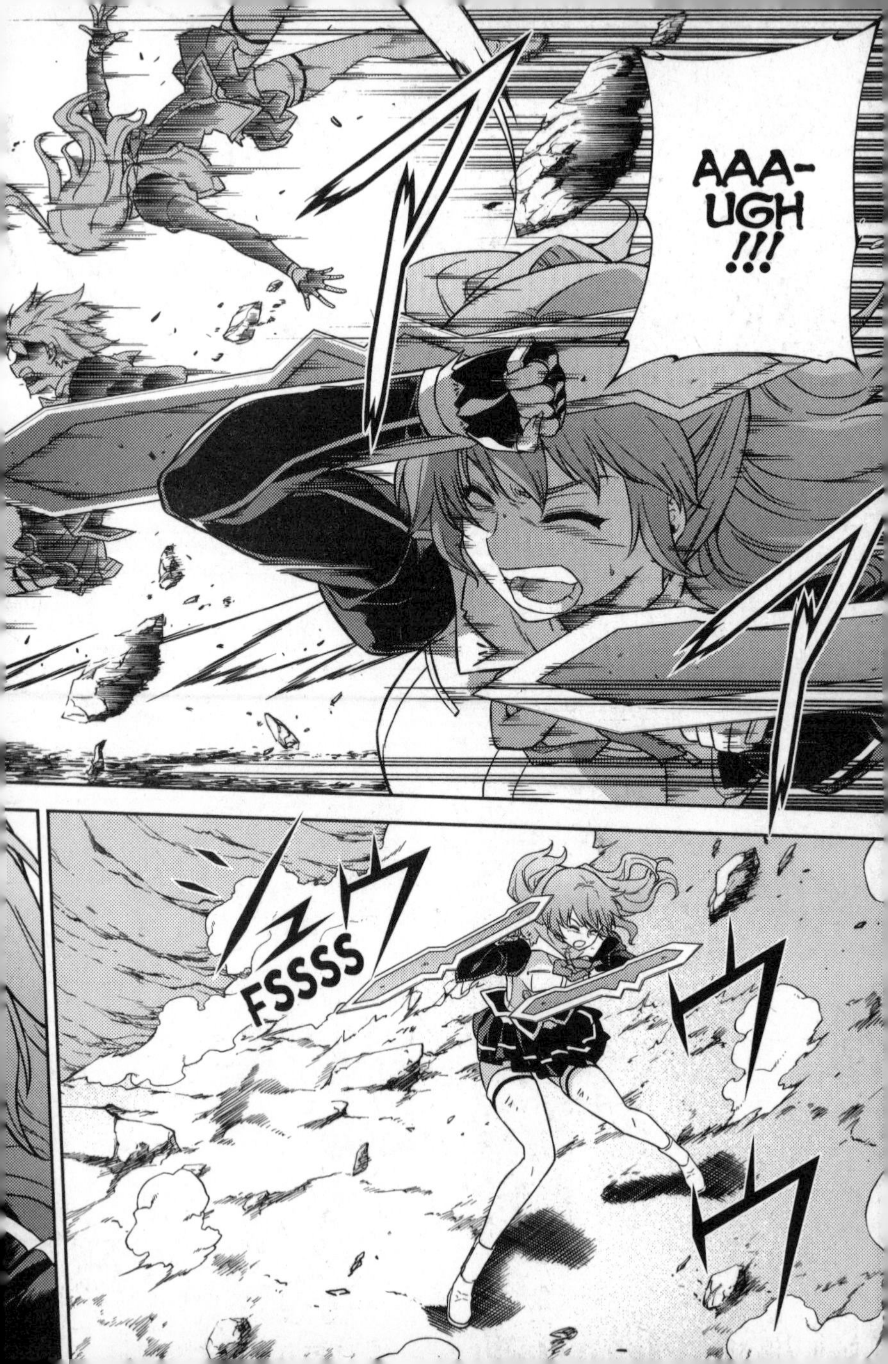
AAA-
UGH
!!!
FSSSS

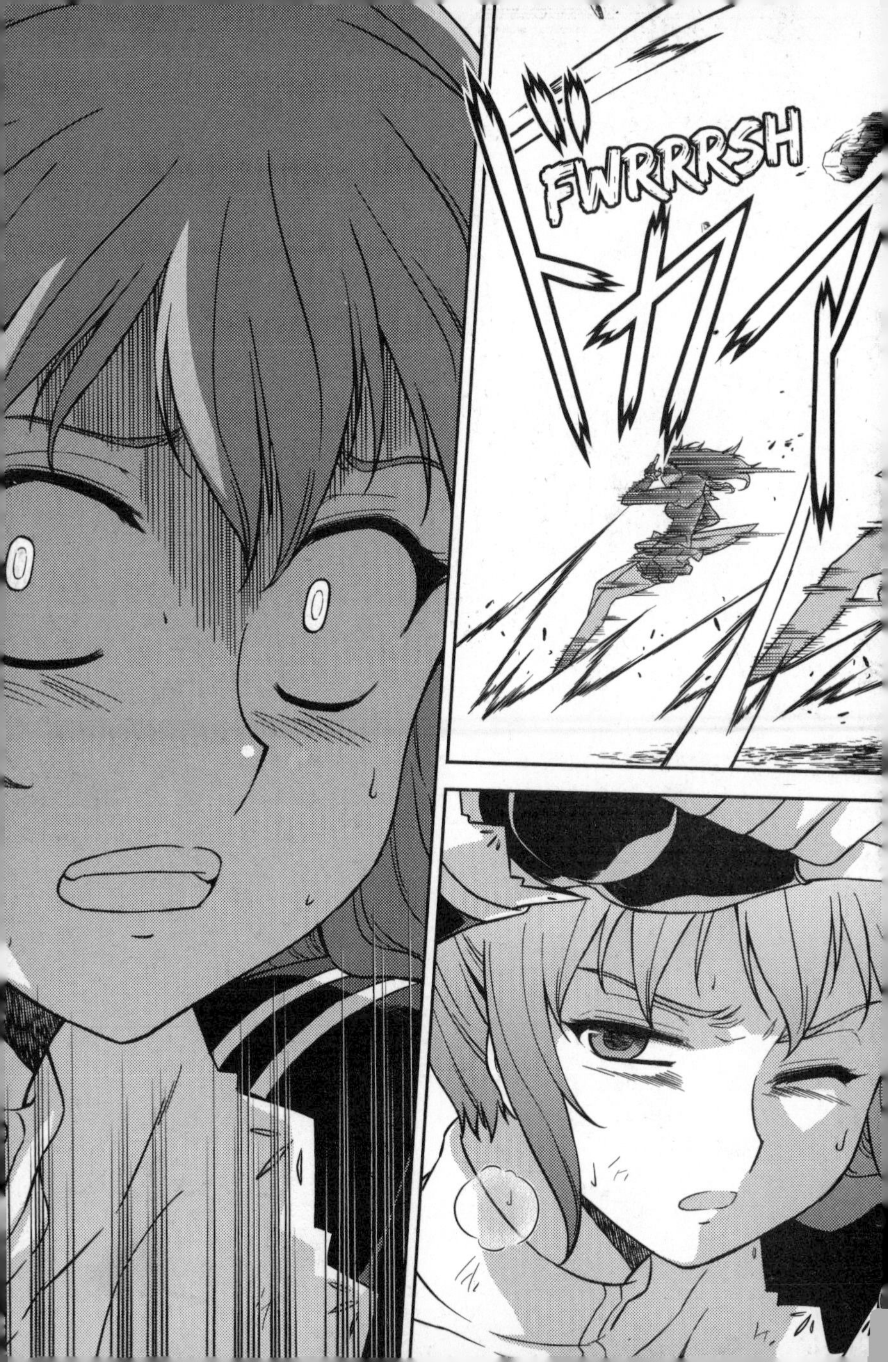
FWRRRSH

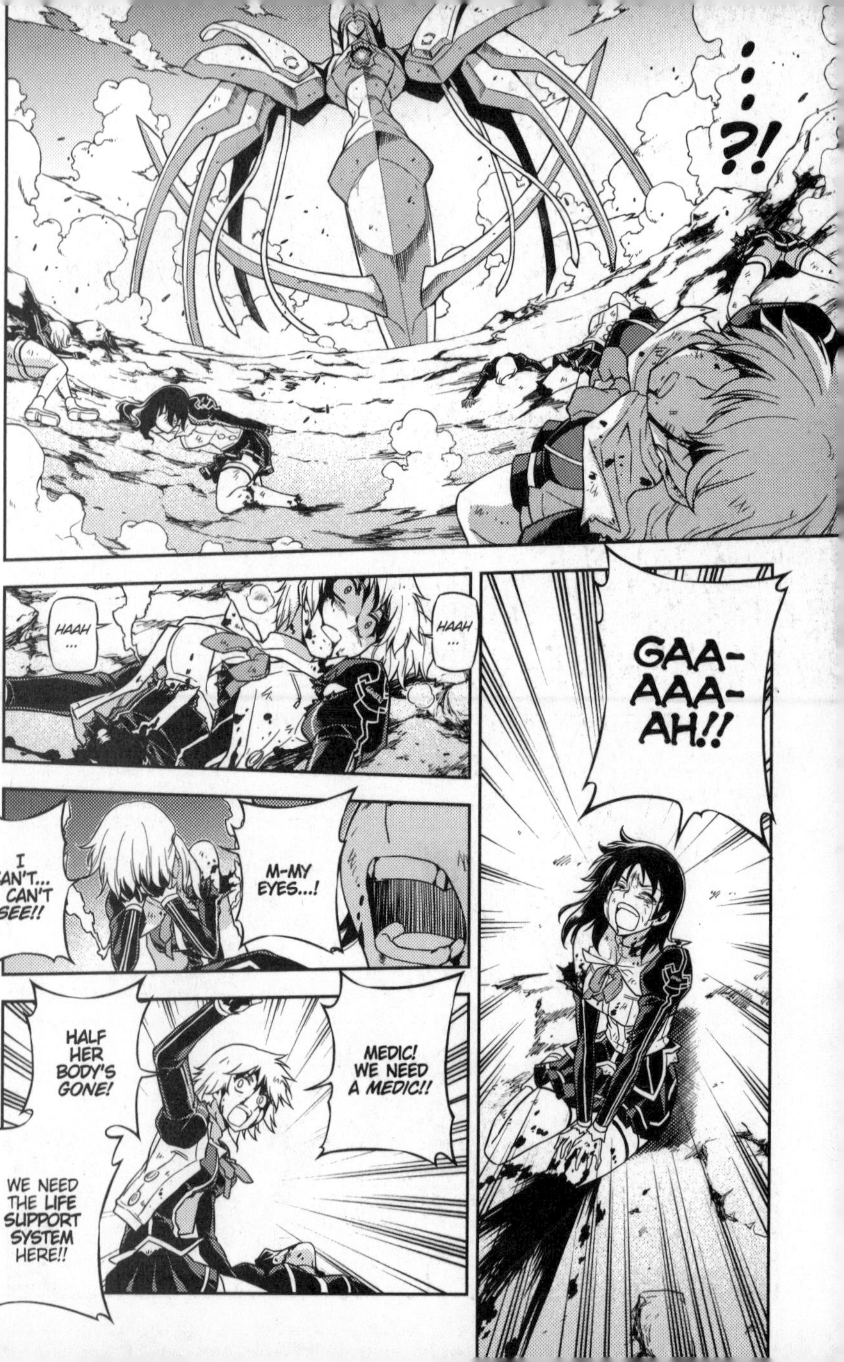
...?!
GAA-AAA-AH!!
HAAH ...
HAAH ...
M-MY EYES...!
I CAN'T... I CAN'T SEE!!
MEDIC! WE NEED A MEDIC!!
HALF HER BODY'S GONE!
WE NEED THE LIFE SUPPORT SYSTEM HERE!!

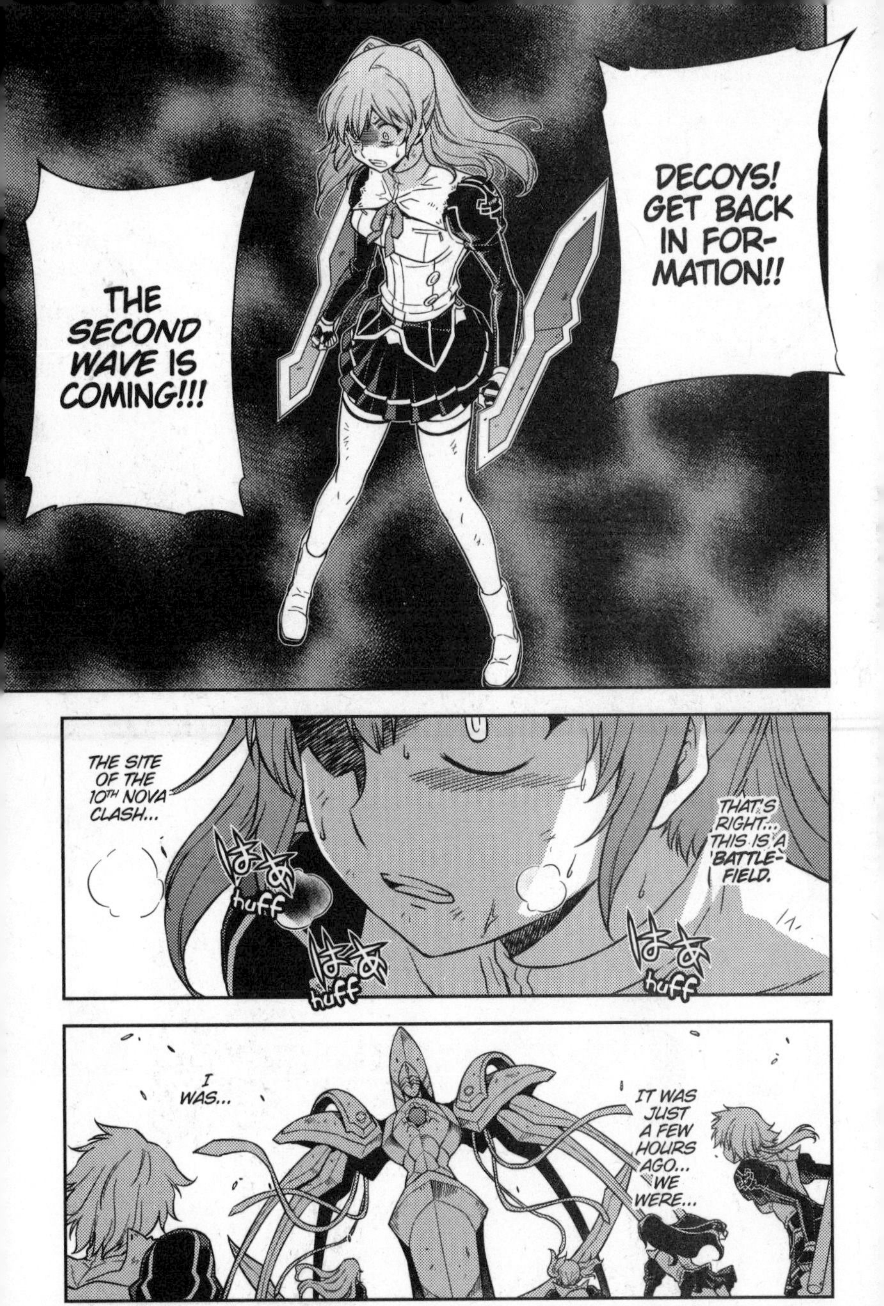
DECOYS! GET BACK IN FOR-MATION!!
THE SECOND WAVE IS COMING!!!
THAT'S RIGHT... THIS IS A BATTLE-FIELD.
はぁ huff
はぁ huff
はぁ huff
THE SITE OF THE 10TH NOVA CLASH...
IT WAS JUST A FEW HOURS AGO... WE WERE...
I WAS...

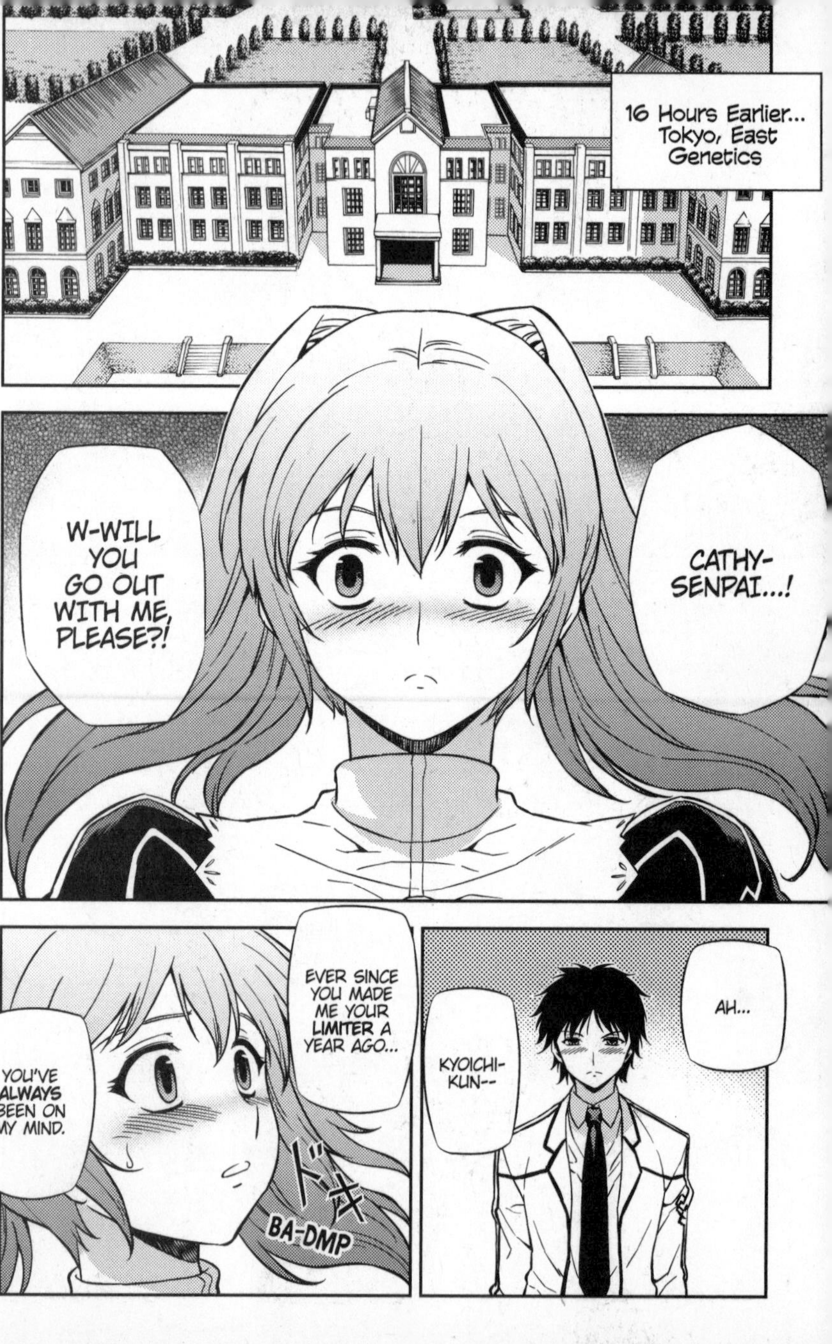
16 Hours Earlier... Tokyo, East Genetics
CATHY-SENPAI...!
W-WILL YOU GO OUT WITH ME, PLEASE?!
AH...
KYOICHI-KUN--
EVER SINCE YOU MADE ME YOUR LIMITER A YEAR AGO...
YOU'VE ALWAYS BEEN ON MY MIND.
ドキ
BA-DMP

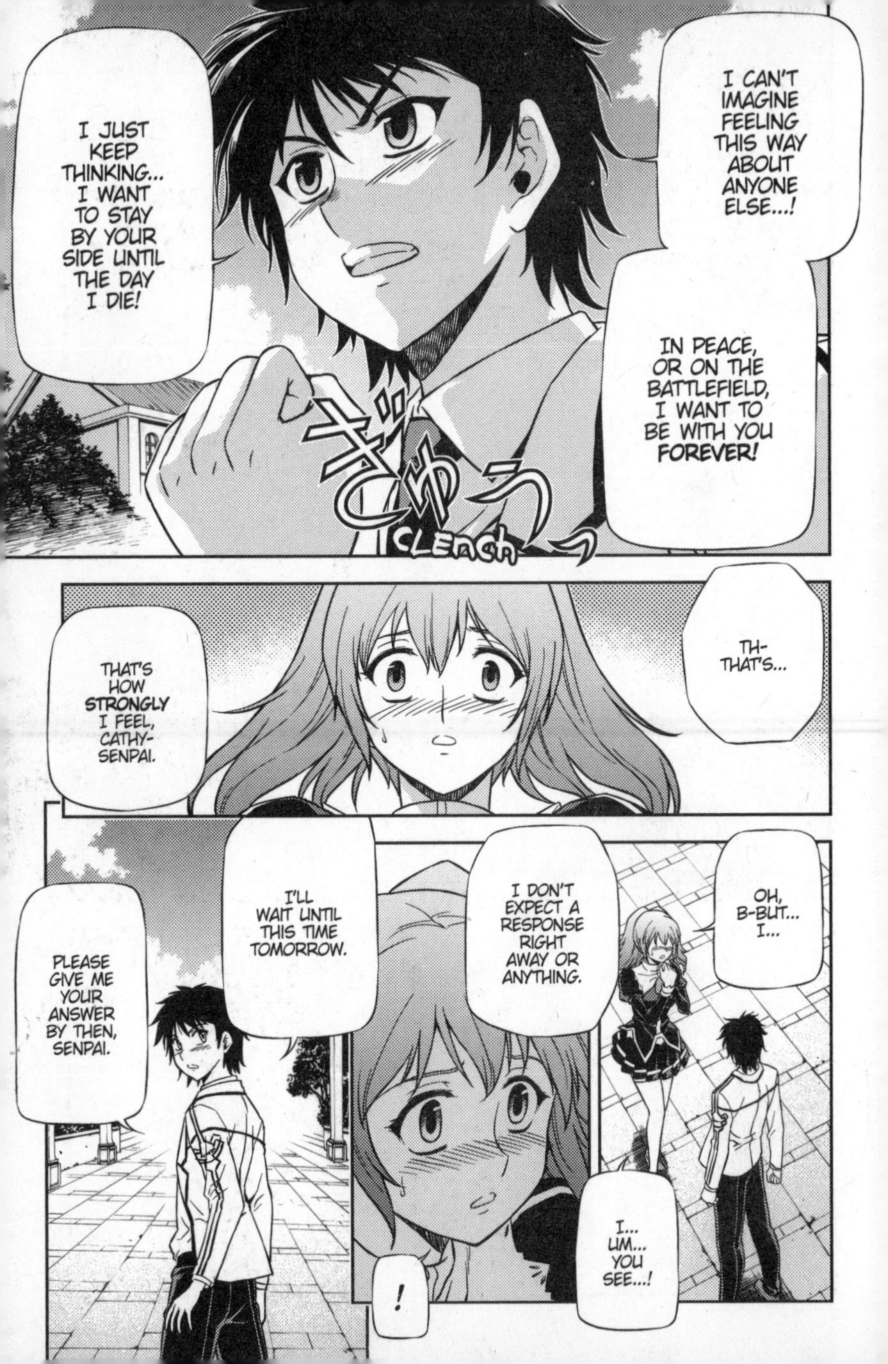
I CAN'T IMAGINE FEELING THIS WAY ABOUT ANYONE ELSE...!
I JUST KEEP THINKING... I WANT TO STAY BY YOUR SIDE UNTIL THE DAY I DIE!
IN PEACE, OR ON THE BATTLEFIELD, I WANT TO BE WITH YOU **FOREVER!**
ぎゅっ
CLENCH
TH- THAT'S...
THAT'S HOW **STRONGLY** I FEEL, CATHY-SENPAI.
OH, B-BUT... I...
I DON'T EXPECT A RESPONSE RIGHT AWAY OR ANYTHING.
I... UM... YOU SEE...!
!
I'LL WAIT UNTIL THIS TIME TOMORROW.
PLEASE GIVE ME YOUR ANSWER BY THEN, SENPAI.

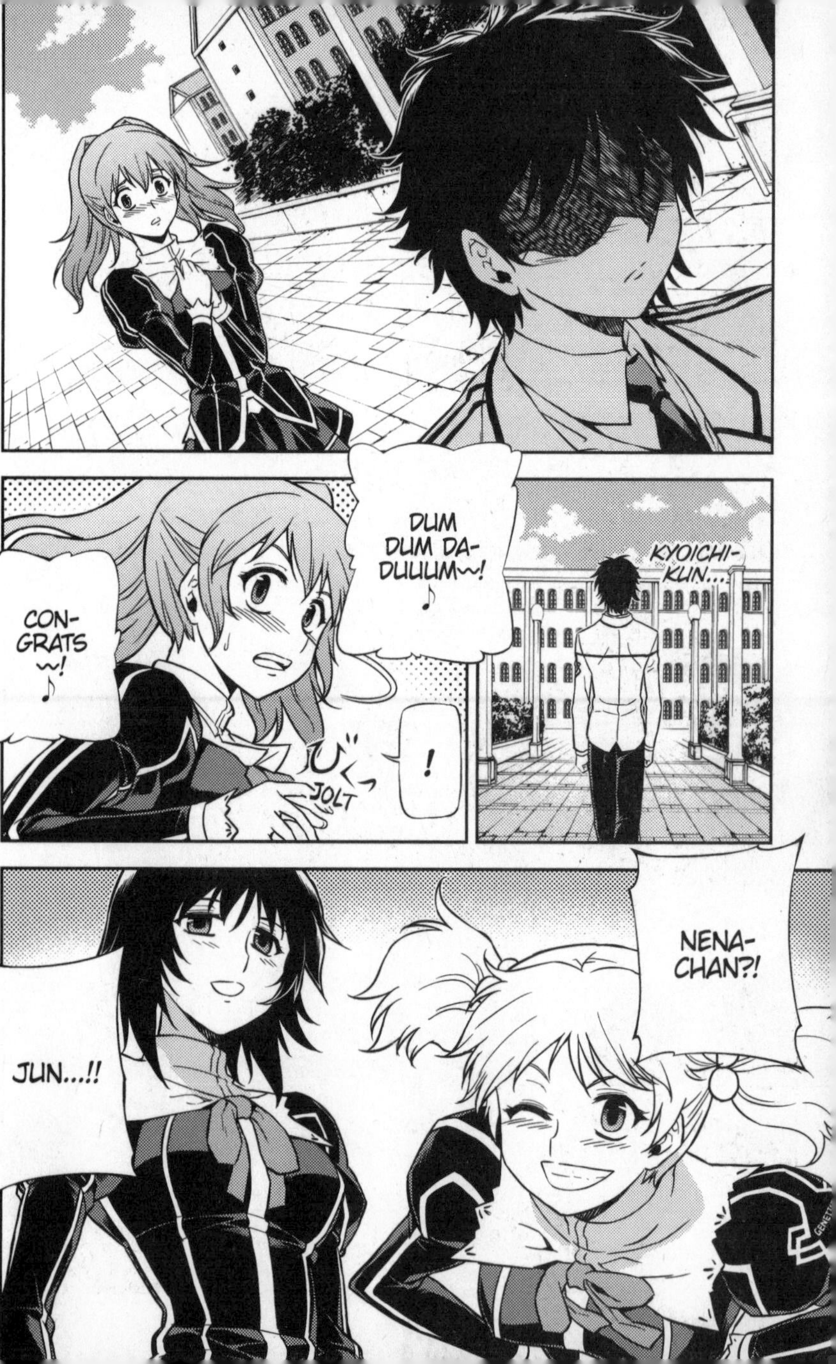
KYOICHI-KUN...
DUM DUM DA-DUULUM~! ♪
CON-GRATS ~! ♪
JOLT
!
NENA-CHAN?!
JUN...!!

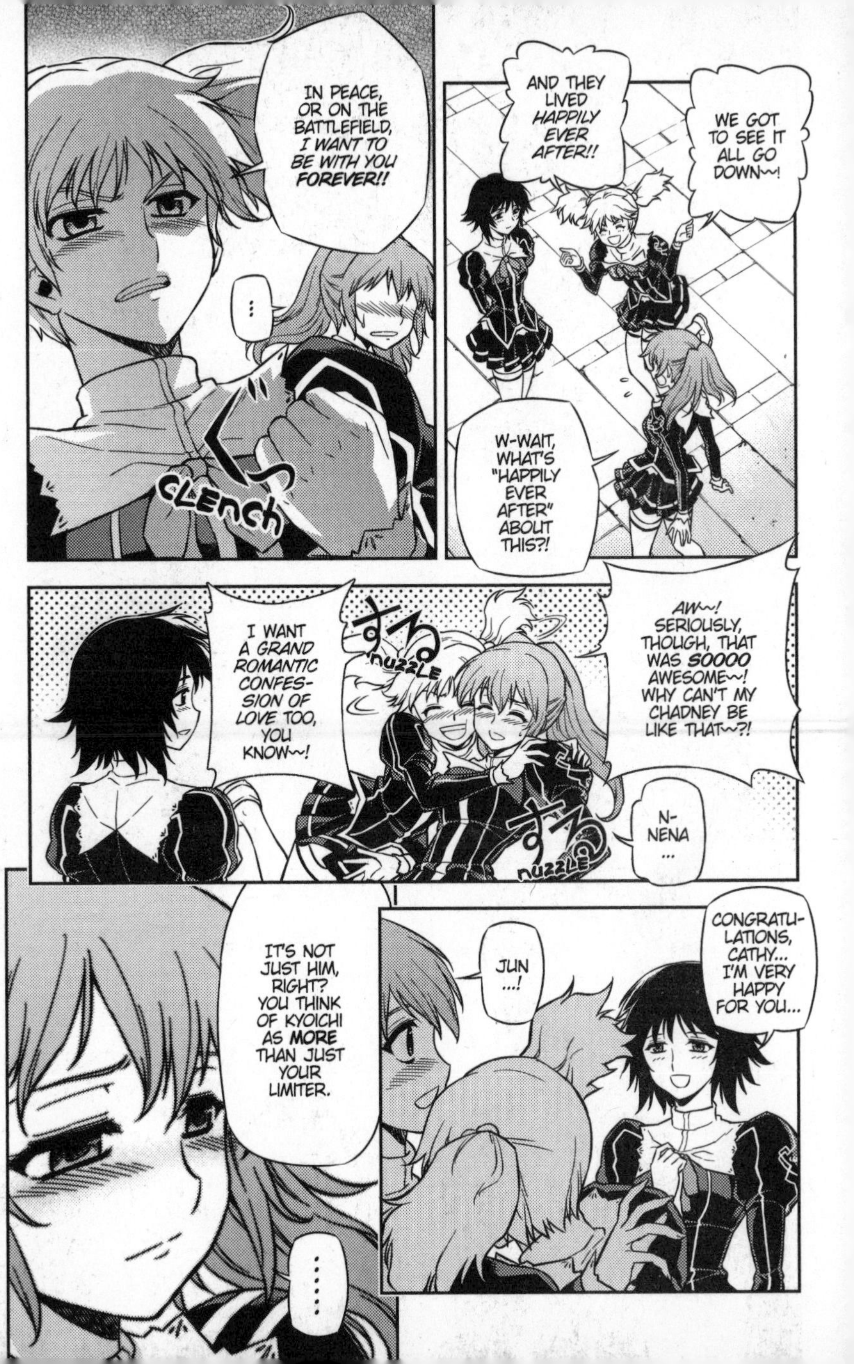
WE GOT TO SEE IT ALL GO DOWN~!
AND THEY LIVED HAPPILY EVER AFTER!!
W-WAIT, WHAT'S "HAPPILY EVER AFTER" ABOUT THIS?!
IN PEACE, OR ON THE BATTLEFIELD, I WANT TO BE WITH YOU FOREVER!!
...
CLENCH
AW~! SERIOUSLY, THOUGH, THAT WAS SOOOO AWESOME~! WHY CAN'T MY CHADNEY BE LIKE THAT~?!
I WANT A GRAND ROMANTIC CONFES-SION OF LOVE TOO, YOU KNOW~!
すり NUZZLE
すり NUZZLE
N-NENA ...
CONGRATU-LATIONS, CATHY... I'M VERY HAPPY FOR YOU...
JUN ...!
IT'S NOT JUST HIM, RIGHT? YOU THINK OF KYOICHI AS MORE THAN JUST YOUR LIMITER.
......

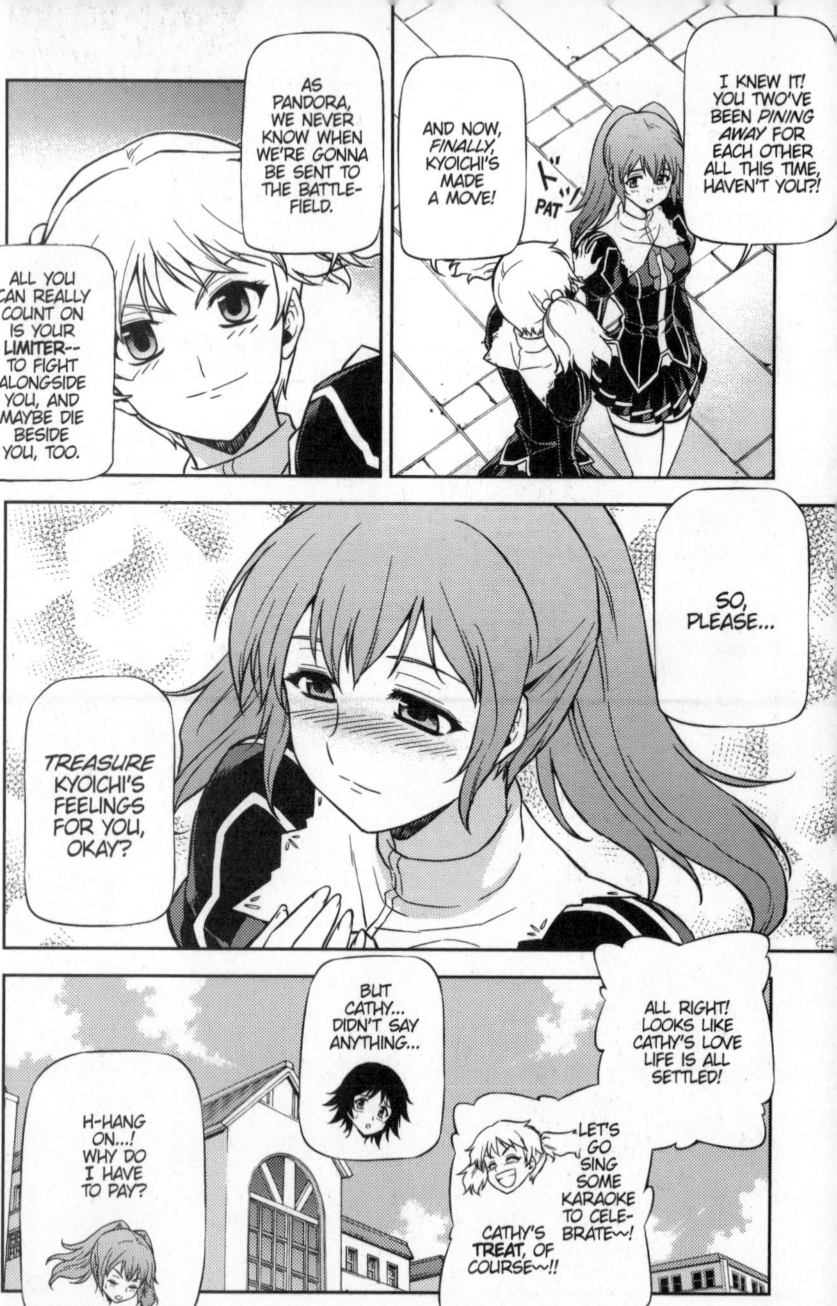
I KNEW IT! YOU TWO'VE BEEN *PINING AWAY* FOR EACH OTHER ALL THIS TIME, HAVEN'T YOU?!
AND NOW, *FINALLY*, KYOICHI'S MADE A MOVE!
PAT
AS PANDORA, WE NEVER KNOW WHEN WE'RE GONNA BE SENT TO THE BATTLE-FIELD.
ALL YOU CAN REALLY COUNT ON IS YOUR **LIMITER**-- TO FIGHT ALONGSIDE YOU, AND MAYBE DIE BESIDE YOU, TOO.
SO, PLEASE...
TREASURE KYOICHI'S FEELINGS FOR YOU, OKAY?
ALL RIGHT! LOOKS LIKE CATHY'S LOVE LIFE IS ALL SETTLED!
LET'S GO SING SOME KARAOKE TO CELE-BRATE~!
CATHY'S **TREAT**, OF COURSE~!!
BUT CATHY... DIDN'T SAY ANYTHING...
H-HANG ON...! WHY DO I HAVE TO PAY?

"I WANT TO BE WITH YOU FOREVER!"

"IN PEACE, OR ON THE BATTLE-FIELD...

!

KNOCK
コン
KNOCK
コン

KYOICHI-KUN!..

ぎゅっ
CLASP

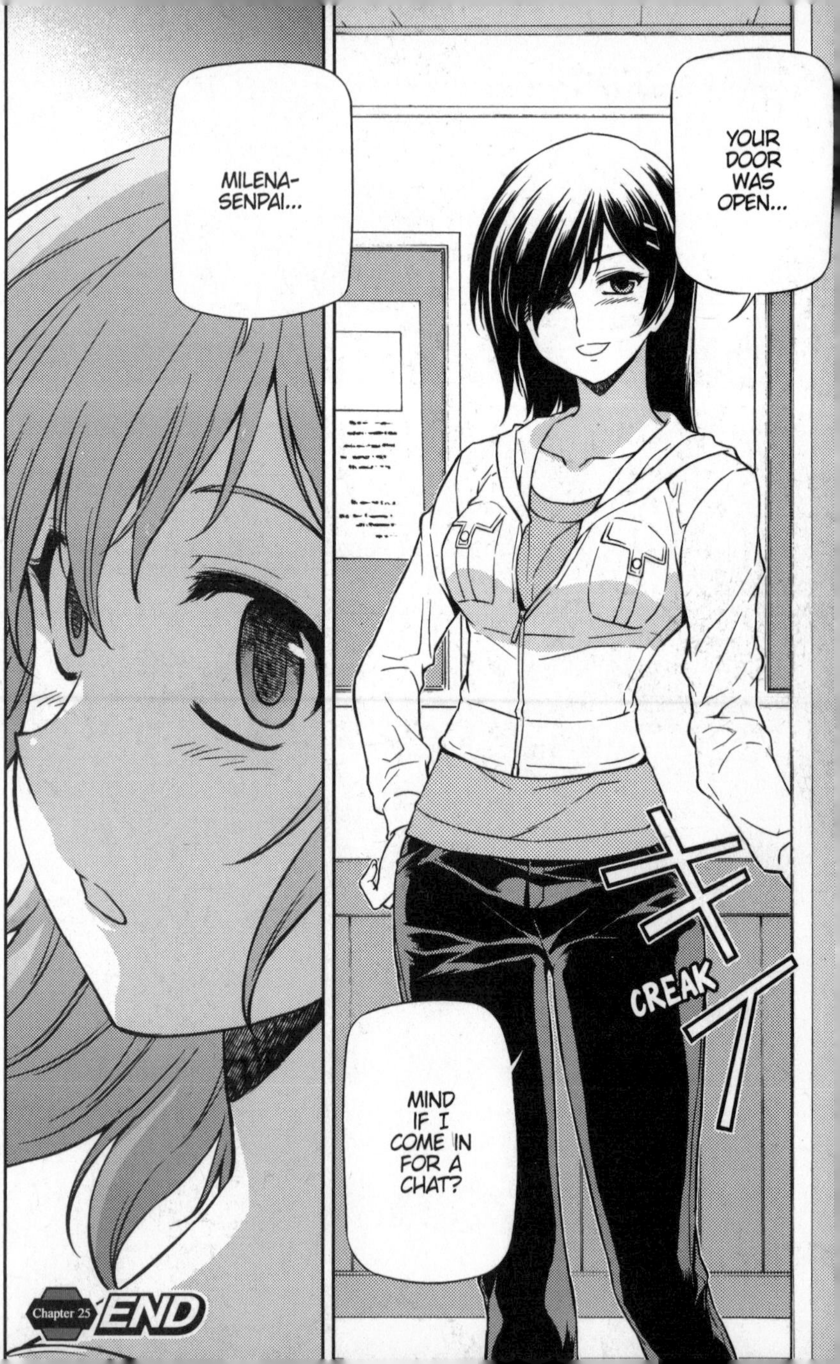
YOUR DOOR WAS OPEN...
CREAK
MIND IF I COME IN FOR A CHAT?
MILENA-SENPAI...
Chapter 25 END

Chapter 26 Cathy Lockharte

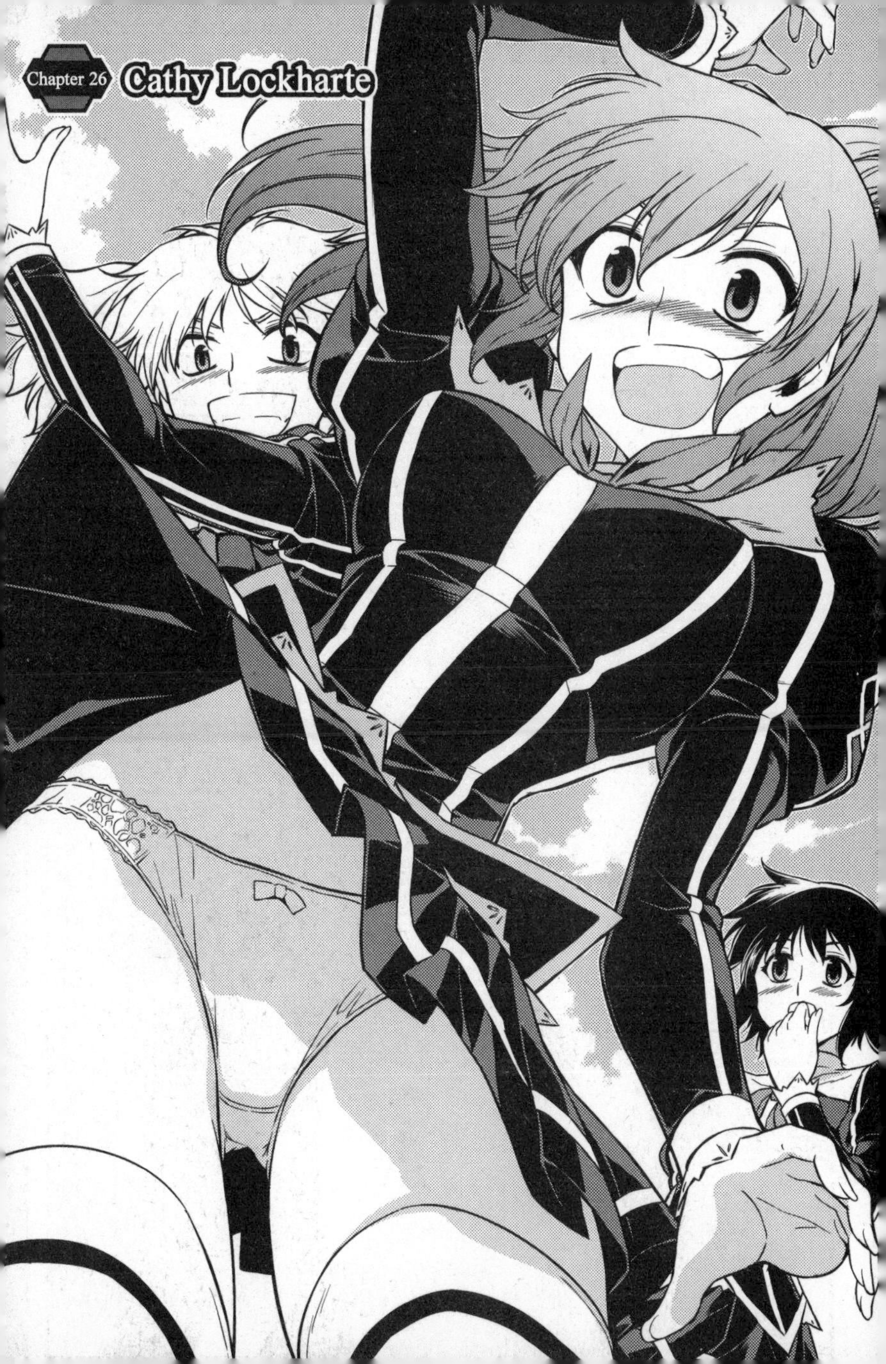

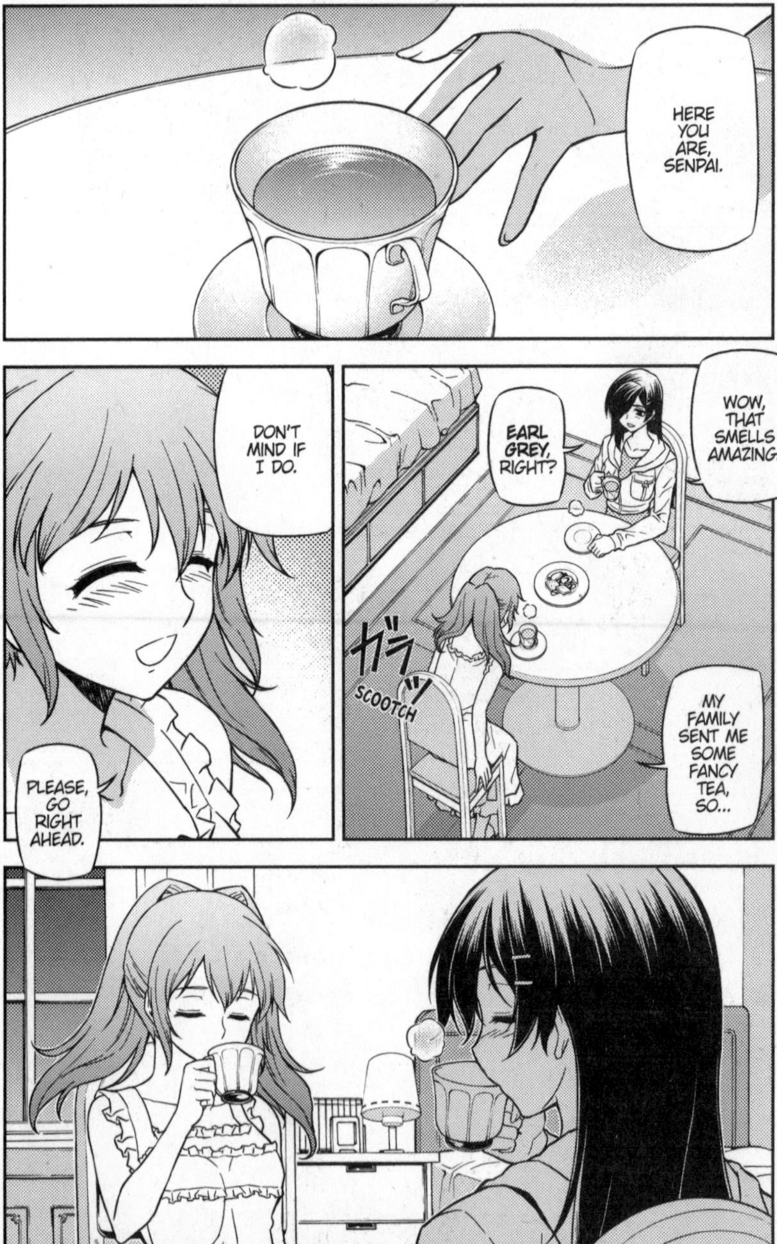
HERE YOU ARE, SENPAI.
WOW, THAT SMELLS AMAZING.
EARL GREY, RIGHT?
MY FAMILY SENT ME SOME FANCY TEA, SO...
ガラッ
SCOOTCH
DON'T MIND IF I DO.
PLEASE, GO RIGHT AHEAD.

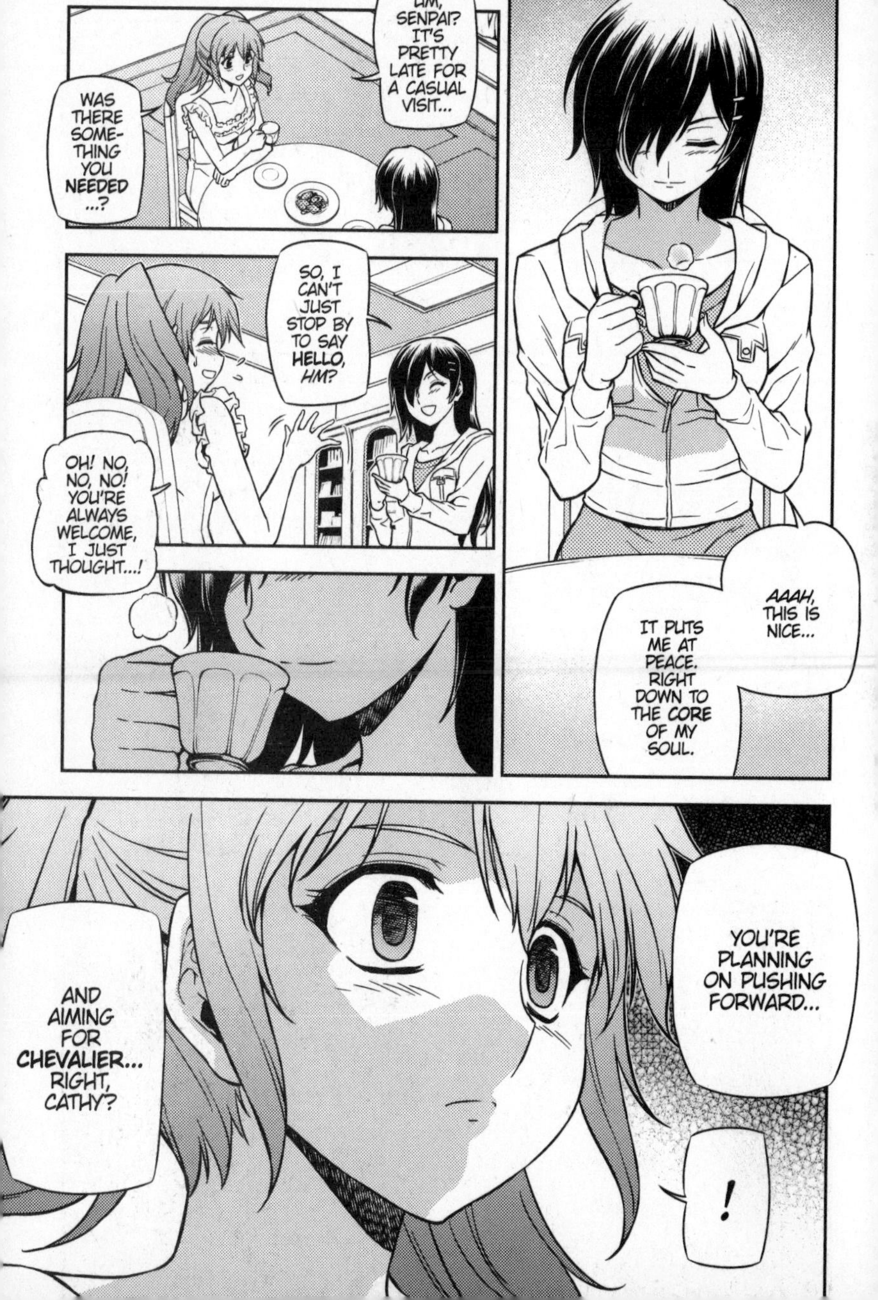
AAAH, THIS IS NICE...
IT PUTS ME AT PEACE. RIGHT DOWN TO THE CORE OF MY SOUL.
UM, SENPAI? IT'S PRETTY LATE FOR A CASUAL VISIT...
WAS THERE SOME-THING YOU NEEDED ...?
SO, I CAN'T JUST STOP BY TO SAY **HELLO**, *HM?*
OH! NO, NO, NO! YOU'RE ALWAYS WELCOME, I JUST THOUGHT...!
YOU'RE PLANNING ON PUSHING FORWARD...
AND AIMING FOR **CHEVALIER...** RIGHT, CATHY?
!

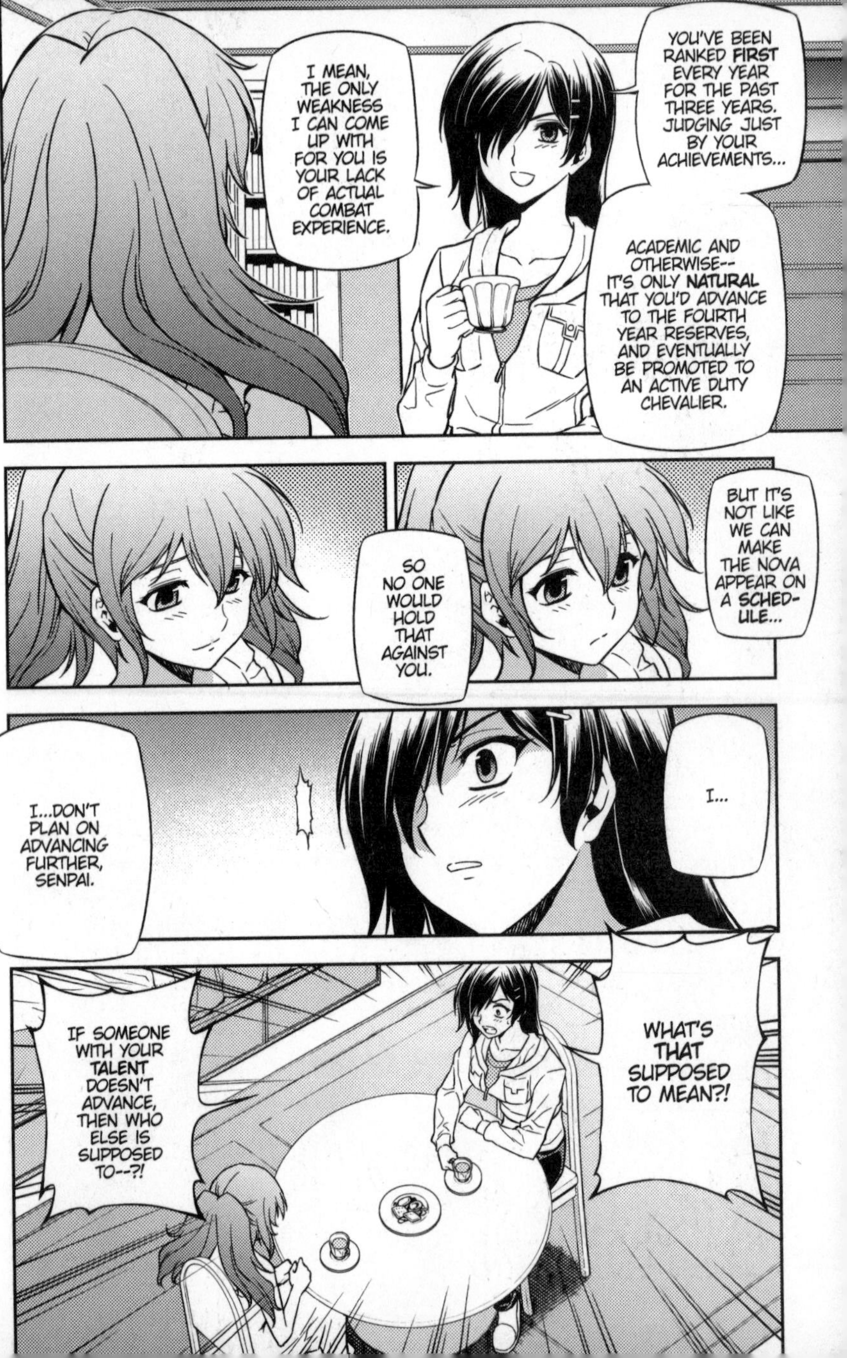
YOU'VE BEEN RANKED FIRST EVERY YEAR FOR THE PAST THREE YEARS. JUDGING JUST BY YOUR ACHIEVEMENTS...
ACADEMIC AND OTHERWISE-- IT'S ONLY NATURAL THAT YOU'D ADVANCE TO THE FOURTH YEAR RESERVES, AND EVENTUALLY BE PROMOTED TO AN ACTIVE DUTY CHEVALIER.
I MEAN, THE ONLY WEAKNESS I CAN COME UP WITH FOR YOU IS YOUR LACK OF ACTUAL COMBAT EXPERIENCE.
BUT IT'S NOT LIKE WE CAN MAKE THE NOVA APPEAR ON A SCHED-ULE...
SO NO ONE WOULD HOLD THAT AGAINST YOU.
I...
!
I...DON'T PLAN ON ADVANCING FURTHER, SENPAI.
WHAT'S THAT SUPPOSED TO MEAN?!
IF SOMEONE WITH YOUR TALENT DOESN'T ADVANCE, THEN WHO ELSE IS SUPPOSED TO--?!

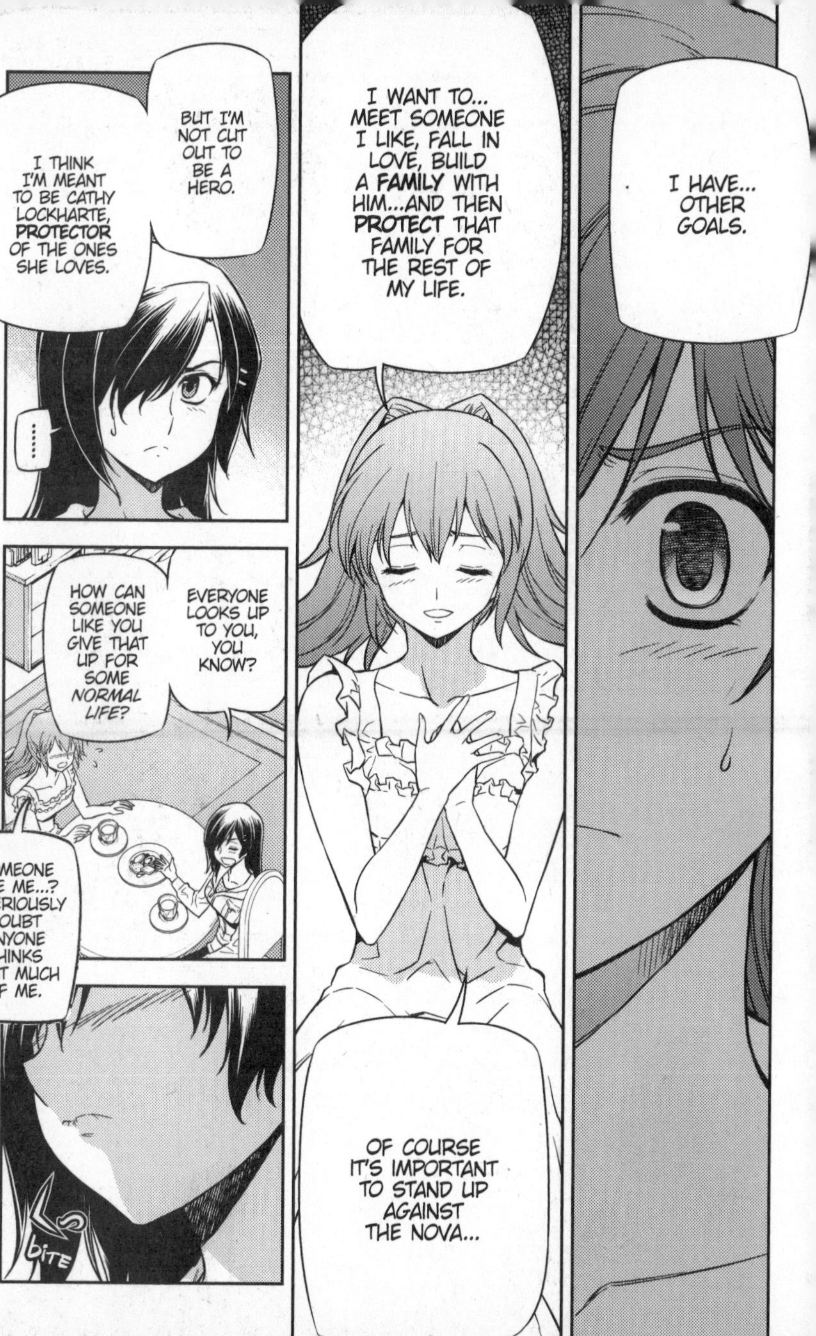
I HAVE... OTHER GOALS.
I WANT TO... MEET SOMEONE I LIKE, FALL IN LOVE, BUILD A **FAMILY** WITH HIM...AND THEN **PROTECT** THAT FAMILY FOR THE REST OF MY LIFE.
OF COURSE IT'S IMPORTANT TO STAND UP AGAINST THE NOVA...
BUT I'M NOT CUT OUT TO BE A HERO.
I THINK I'M MEANT TO BE CATHY LOCKHARTE, **PROTECTOR** OF THE ONES SHE LOVES.
......
EVERYONE LOOKS UP TO YOU, YOU KNOW?
HOW CAN SOMEONE LIKE YOU GIVE THAT UP FOR SOME *NORMAL LIFE*?
SOMEONE LIKE ME...? I SERIOUSLY DOUBT ANYONE THINKS THAT MUCH OF ME.
bite

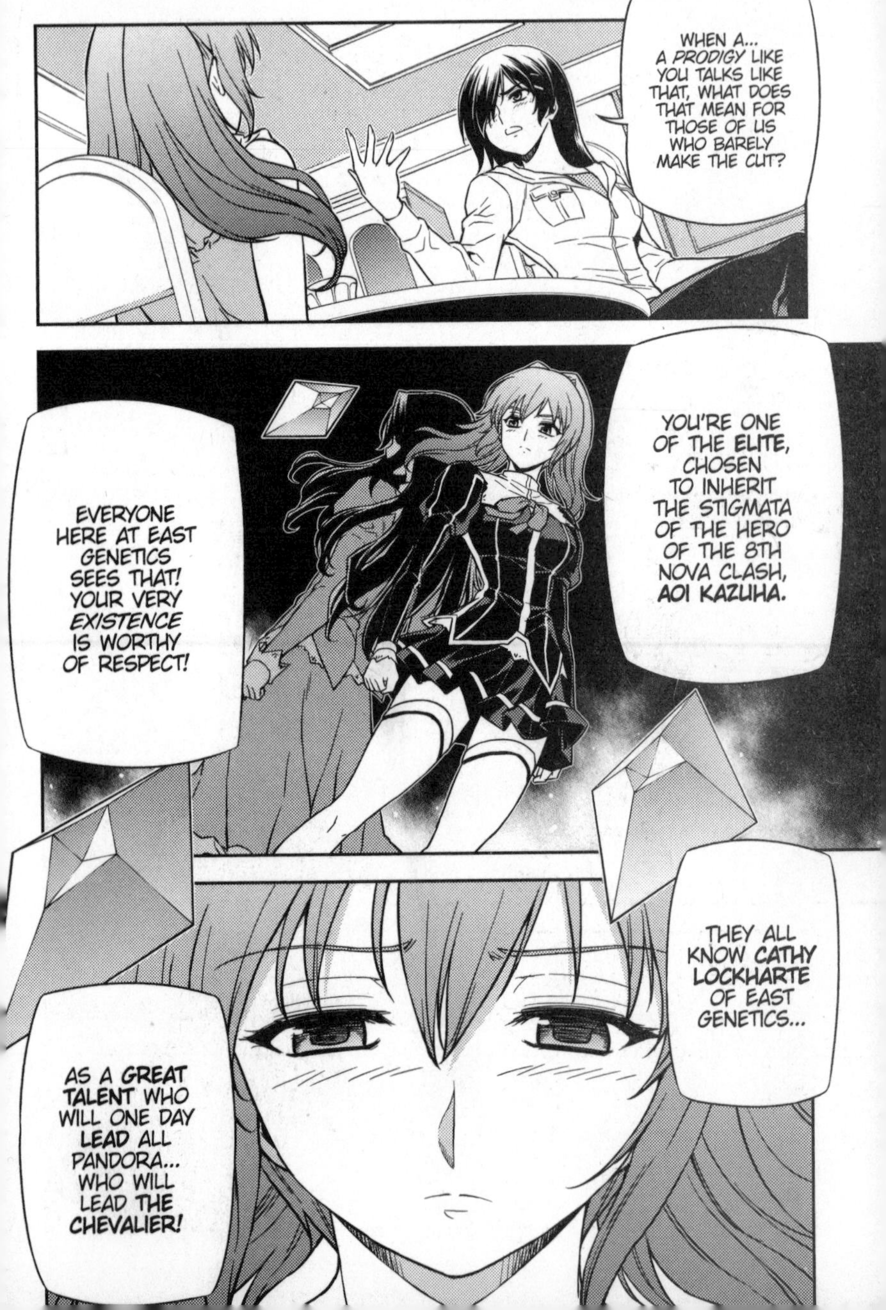
WHEN A... A *PRODIGY* LIKE YOU TALKS LIKE THAT, WHAT DOES THAT MEAN FOR THOSE OF US WHO BARELY MAKE THE CUT?
YOU'RE ONE OF THE **ELITE**, CHOSEN TO INHERIT THE STIGMATA OF THE HERO OF THE 8TH NOVA CLASH, **AOI KAZUHA.**
EVERYONE HERE AT EAST GENETICS SEES THAT! YOUR VERY *EXISTENCE* IS WORTHY OF RESPECT!
THEY ALL KNOW **CATHY LOCKHARTE** OF EAST GENETICS...
AS A **GREAT TALENT** WHO WILL ONE DAY **LEAD** ALL PANDORA... WHO WILL LEAD THE **CHEVALIER!**

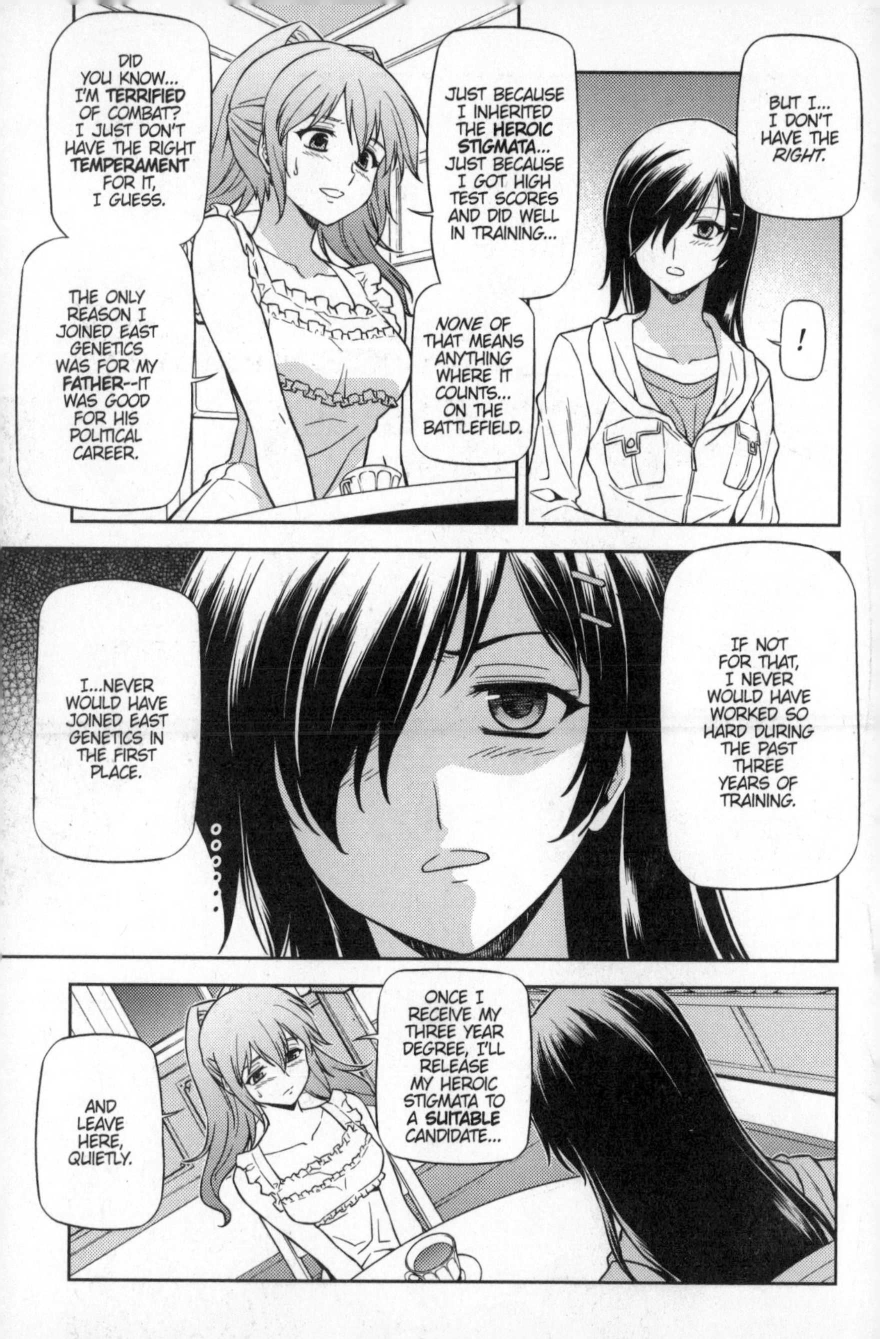
BUT I... I DON'T HAVE THE *RIGHT.*
!
DID YOU KNOW... I'M **TERRIFIED** OF COMBAT? I JUST DON'T HAVE THE RIGHT **TEMPERAMENT** FOR IT, I GUESS.
JUST BECAUSE I INHERITED THE **HEROIC STIGMATA**... JUST BECAUSE I GOT HIGH TEST SCORES AND DID WELL IN TRAINING...
NONE OF THAT MEANS ANYTHING WHERE IT COUNTS... ON THE BATTLEFIELD.
THE ONLY REASON I JOINED EAST GENETICS WAS FOR MY **FATHER**--IT WAS GOOD FOR HIS POLITICAL CAREER.
IF NOT FOR THAT, I NEVER WOULD HAVE WORKED SO HARD DURING THE PAST THREE YEARS OF TRAINING.
I...NEVER WOULD HAVE JOINED EAST GENETICS IN THE FIRST PLACE.
ONCE I RECEIVE MY THREE YEAR DEGREE, I'LL RELEASE MY HEROIC STIGMATA TO A **SUITABLE** CANDIDATE...
AND LEAVE HERE, QUIETLY.

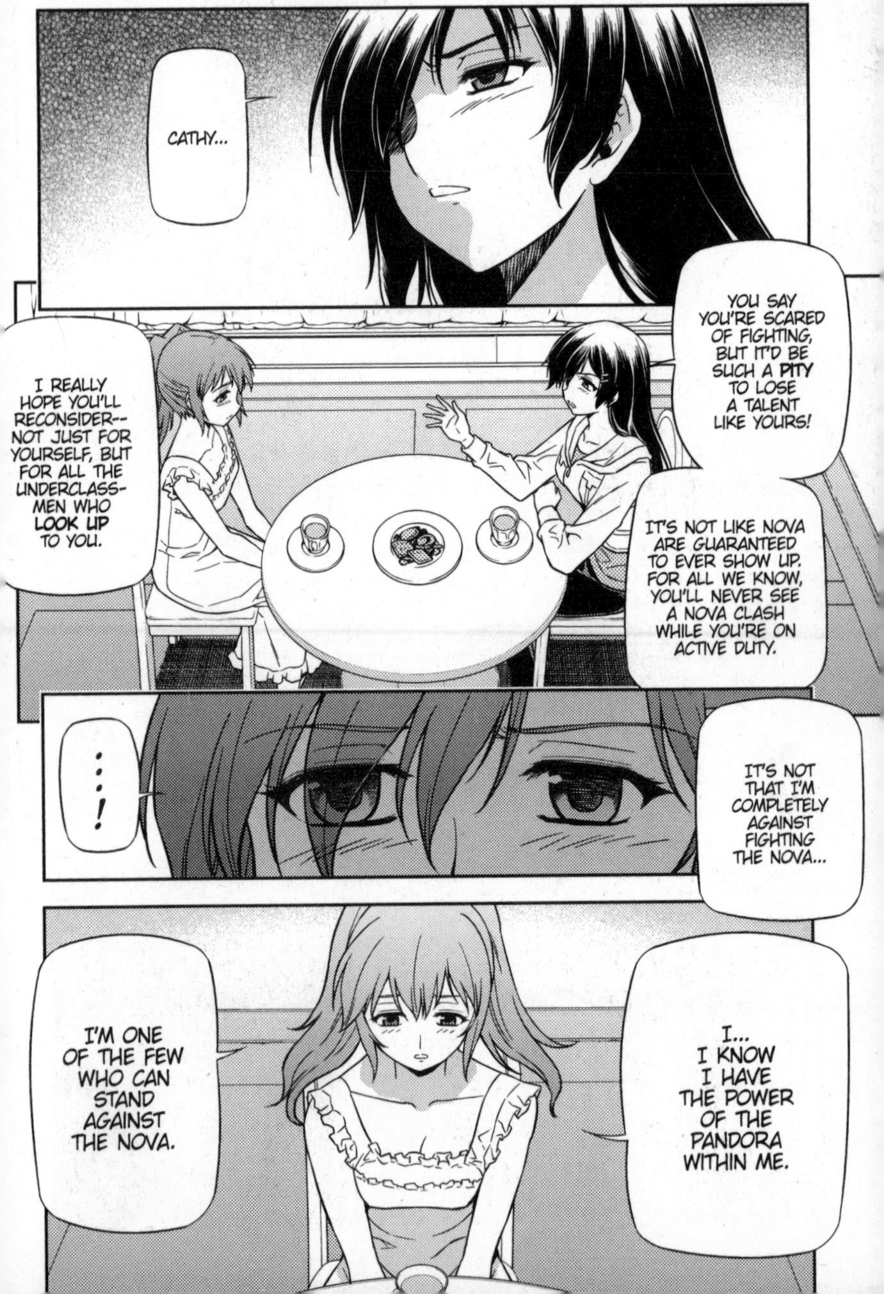
CATHY...
YOU SAY YOU'RE SCARED OF FIGHTING, BUT IT'D BE SUCH A PITY TO LOSE A TALENT LIKE YOURS!
IT'S NOT LIKE NOVA ARE GUARANTEED TO EVER SHOW UP. FOR ALL WE KNOW, YOU'LL NEVER SEE A NOVA CLASH WHILE YOU'RE ON ACTIVE DUTY.
I REALLY HOPE YOU'LL RECONSIDER--NOT JUST FOR YOURSELF, BUT FOR ALL THE UNDERCLASSMEN WHO LOOK UP TO YOU.
IT'S NOT THAT I'M COMPLETELY AGAINST FIGHTING THE NOVA...
...!
I... I KNOW I HAVE THE POWER OF THE PANDORA WITHIN ME.
I'M ONE OF THE FEW WHO CAN STAND AGAINST THE NOVA.

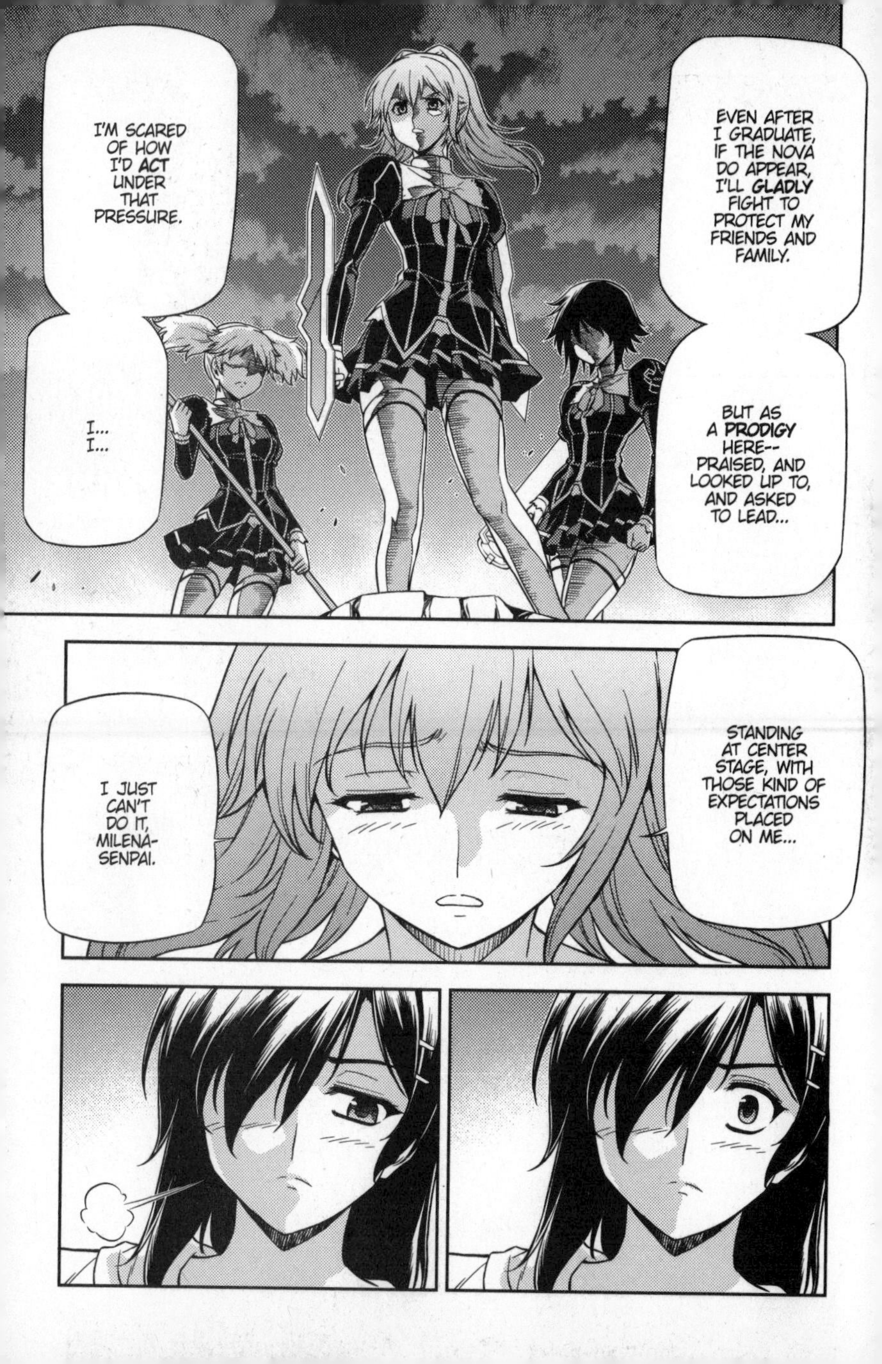
EVEN AFTER I GRADUATE, IF THE NOVA DO APPEAR, I'LL **GLADLY** FIGHT TO PROTECT MY FRIENDS AND FAMILY.
BUT AS A **PRODIGY** HERE-- PRAISED, AND LOOKED UP TO, AND ASKED TO LEAD...
I'M SCARED OF HOW I'D **ACT** UNDER THAT PRESSURE.
I... I...
STANDING AT CENTER STAGE, WITH THOSE KIND OF EXPECTATIONS PLACED ON ME...
I JUST CAN'T DO IT, MILENA-SENPAI.

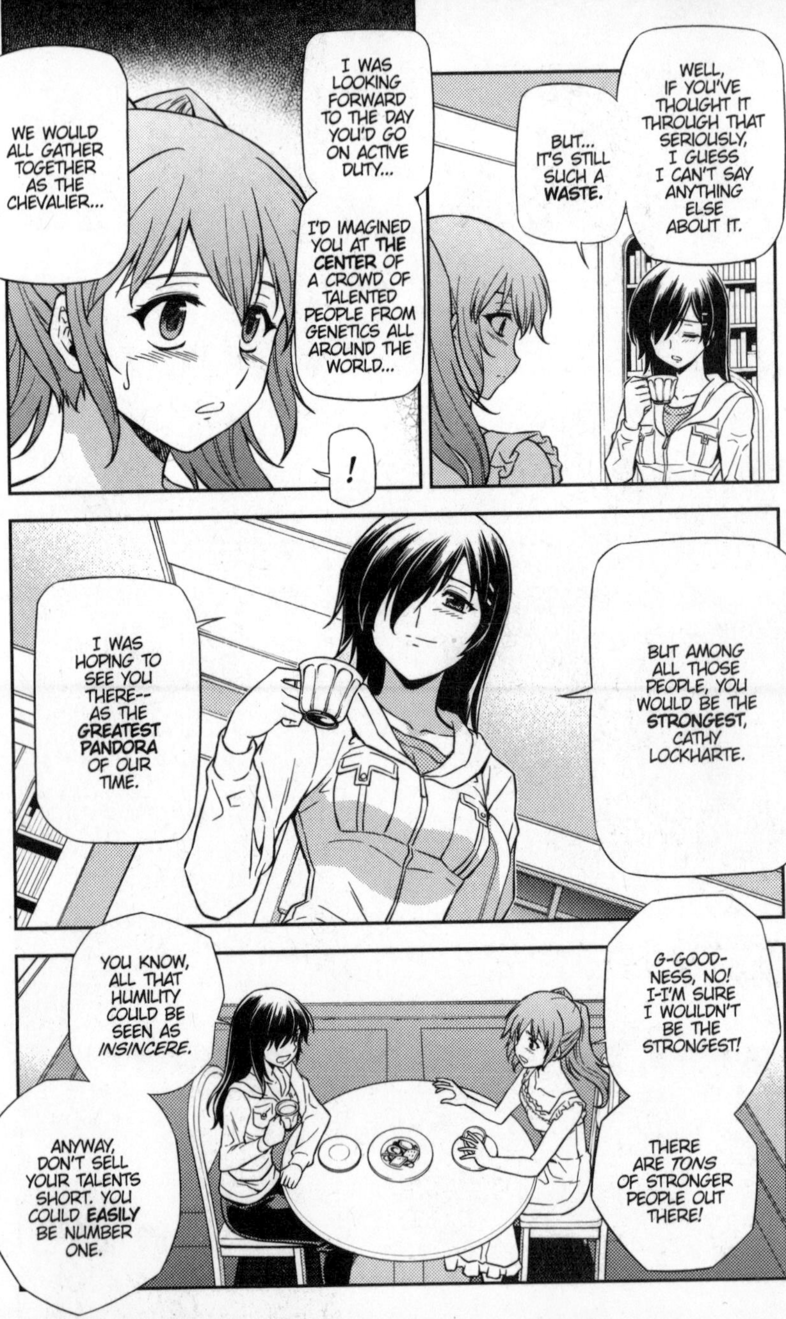
WELL, IF YOU'VE THOUGHT IT THROUGH THAT SERIOUSLY, I GUESS I CAN'T SAY ANYTHING ELSE ABOUT IT.
BUT... IT'S STILL SUCH A **WASTE.**
I WAS LOOKING FORWARD TO THE DAY YOU'D GO ON ACTIVE DUTY...
WE WOULD ALL GATHER TOGETHER AS THE CHEVALIER...
I'D IMAGINED YOU AT **THE CENTER** OF A CROWD OF TALENTED PEOPLE FROM GENETICS ALL AROUND THE WORLD...
!
BUT AMONG ALL THOSE PEOPLE, YOU WOULD BE THE **STRONGEST,** CATHY LOCKHARTE.
I WAS HOPING TO SEE YOU THERE-- AS THE **GREATEST PANDORA** OF OUR TIME.
G-GOOD-NESS, NO! I-I'M SURE I WOULDN'T BE THE STRONGEST!
YOU KNOW, ALL THAT HUMILITY COULD BE SEEN AS *INSINCERE.*
THERE ARE *TONS* OF STRONGER PEOPLE OUT THERE!
ANYWAY, DON'T SELL YOUR TALENTS SHORT. YOU COULD **EASILY** BE NUMBER ONE.

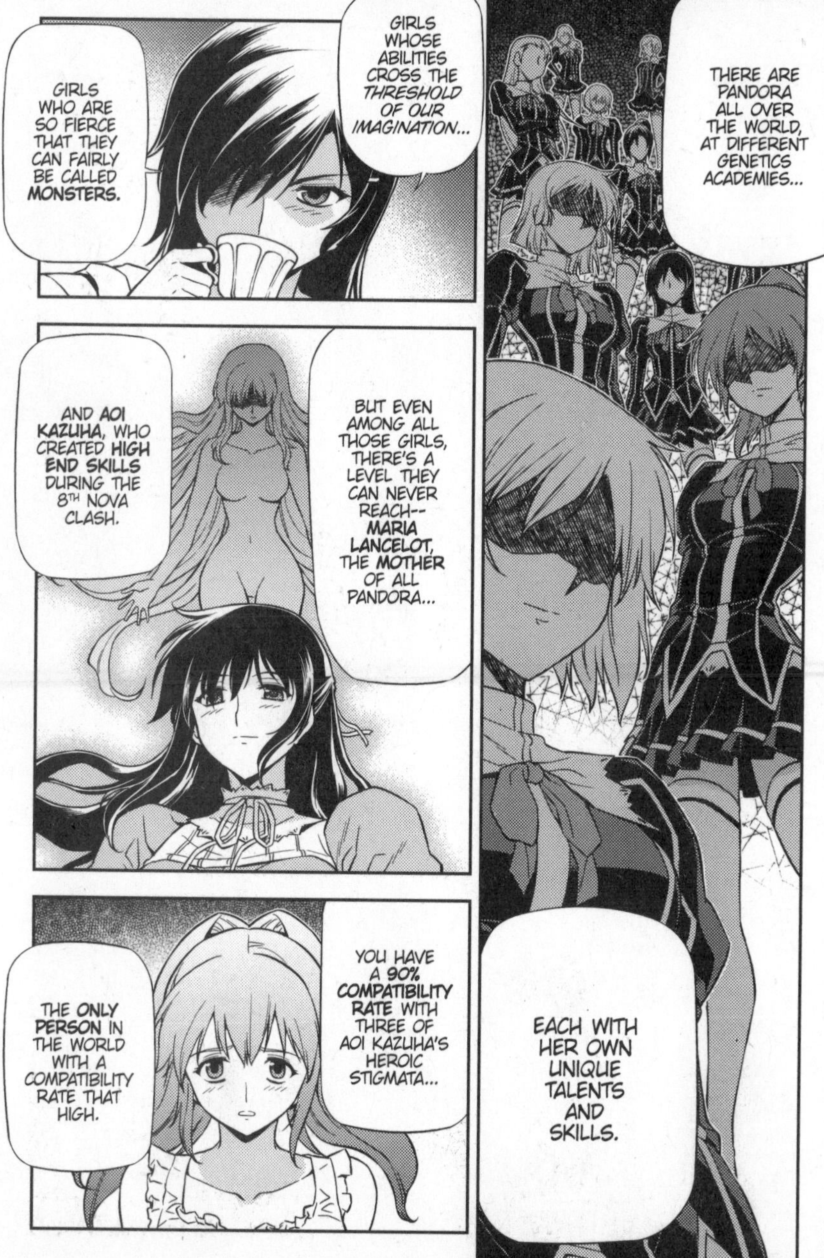
THERE ARE PANDORA ALL OVER THE WORLD, AT DIFFERENT GENETICS ACADEMIES...
EACH WITH HER OWN UNIQUE TALENTS AND SKILLS.
GIRLS WHOSE ABILITIES CROSS THE THRESHOLD OF OUR IMAGINATION...
GIRLS WHO ARE SO FIERCE THAT THEY CAN FAIRLY BE CALLED MONSTERS.
BUT EVEN AMONG ALL THOSE GIRLS, THERE'S A LEVEL THEY CAN NEVER REACH-- MARIA LANCELOT, THE MOTHER OF ALL PANDORA...
AND AOI KAZUHA, WHO CREATED HIGH END SKILLS DURING THE 8TH NOVA CLASH.
YOU HAVE A 90% COMPATIBILITY RATE WITH THREE OF AOI KAZUHA'S HEROIC STIGMATA...
THE ONLY PERSON IN THE WORLD WITH A COMPATIBILITY RATE THAT HIGH.

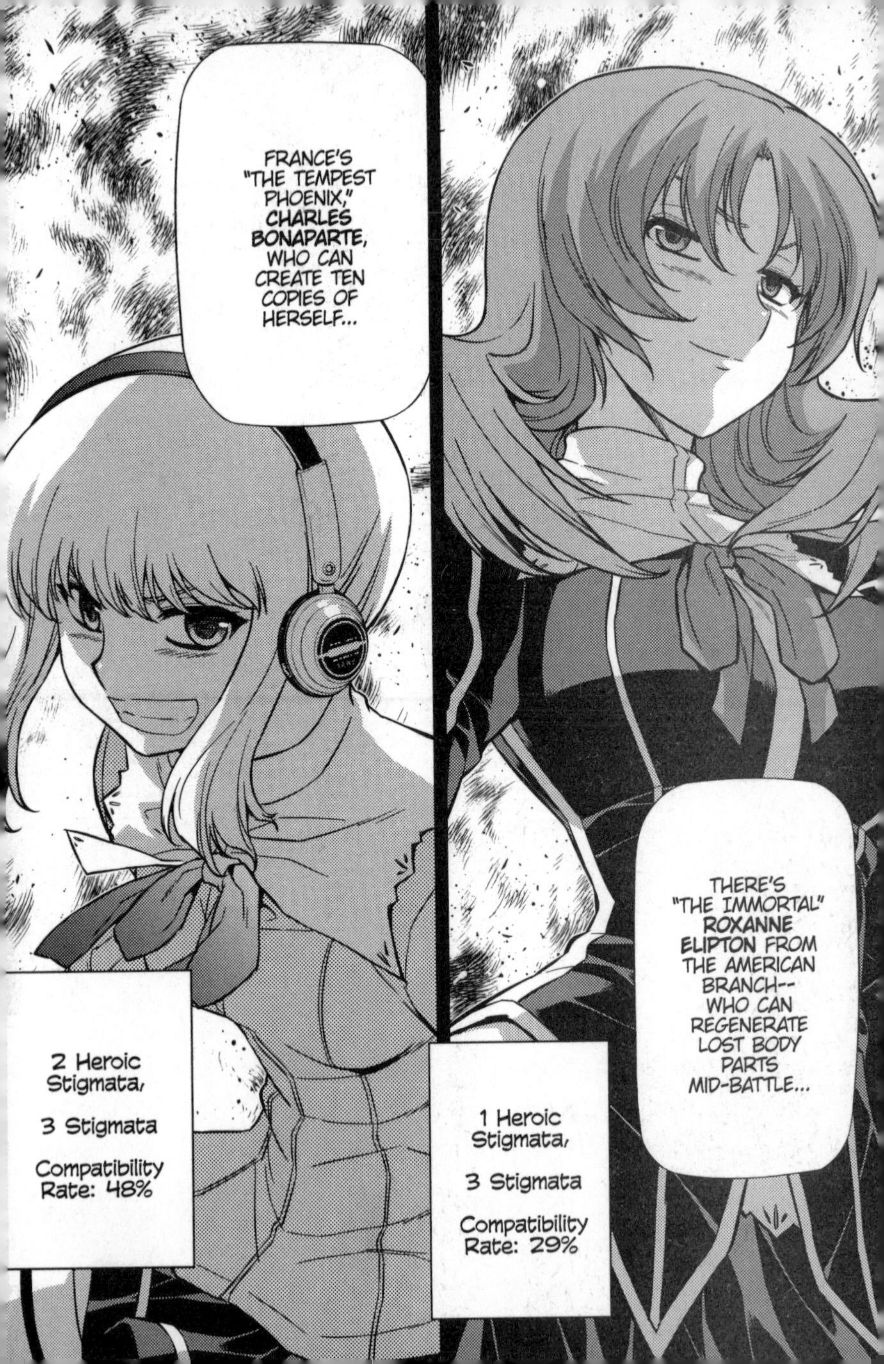
THERE'S "THE IMMORTAL" ROXANNE ELIPTON FROM THE AMERICAN BRANCH-- WHO CAN REGENERATE LOST BODY PARTS MID-BATTLE...
1 Heroic Stigmata, 3 Stigmata Compatibility Rate: 29%
FRANCE'S "THE TEMPEST PHOENIX," CHARLES BONAPARTE, WHO CAN CREATE TEN COPIES OF HERSELF...
2 Heroic Stigmata, 3 Stigmata Compatibility Rate: 48%

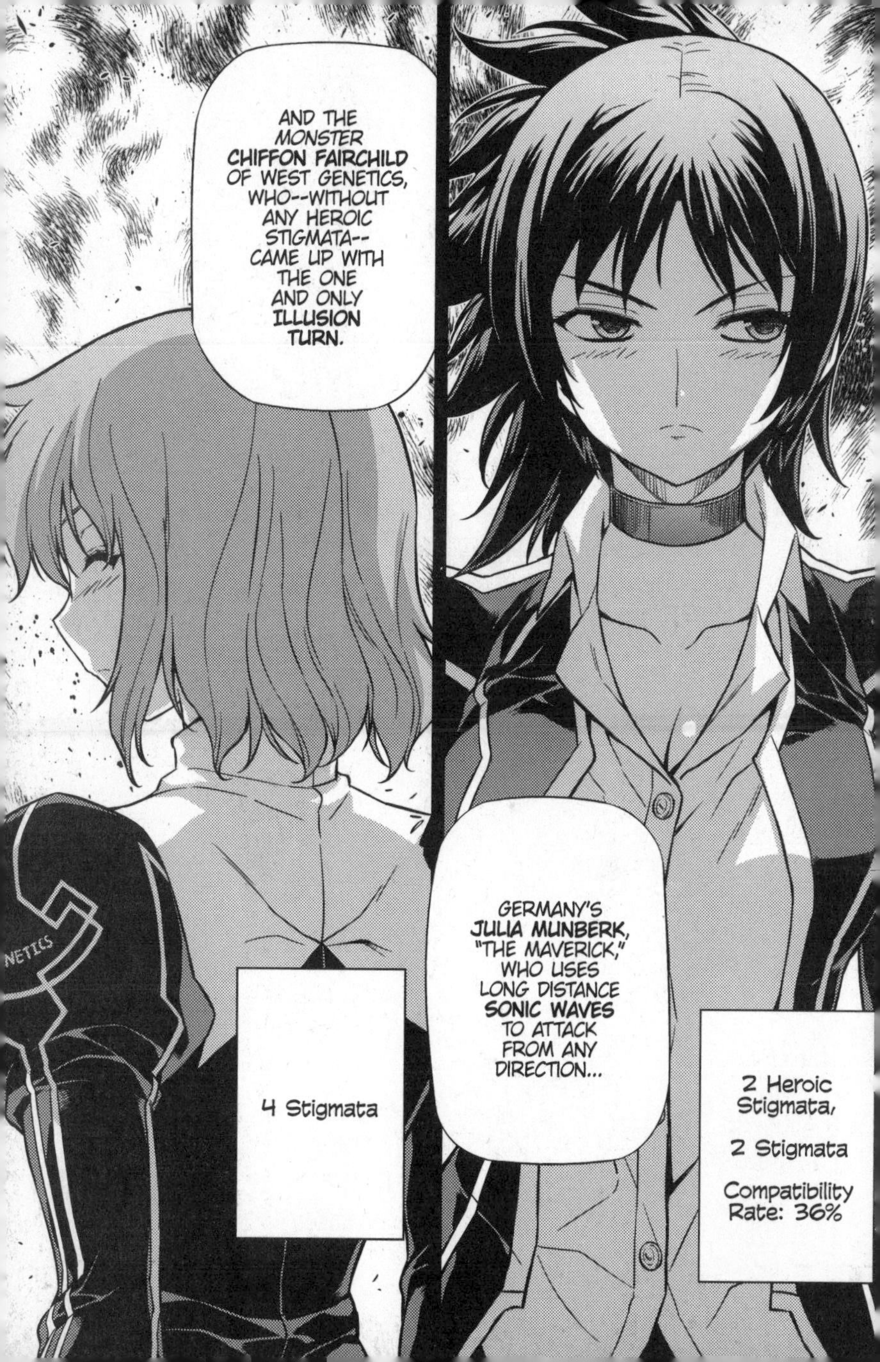
GERMANY'S **JULIA MUNBERK**, "THE MAVERICK," WHO USES LONG DISTANCE **SONIC WAVES** TO ATTACK FROM ANY DIRECTION...
2 Heroic Stigmata,
2 Stigmata
Compatibility Rate: 36%
AND THE MONSTER **CHIFFON FAIRCHILD** OF WEST GENETICS, WHO--WITHOUT ANY HEROIC STIGMATA--CAME UP WITH THE ONE AND ONLY **ILLUSION TURN**.
4 Stigmata
NETICS

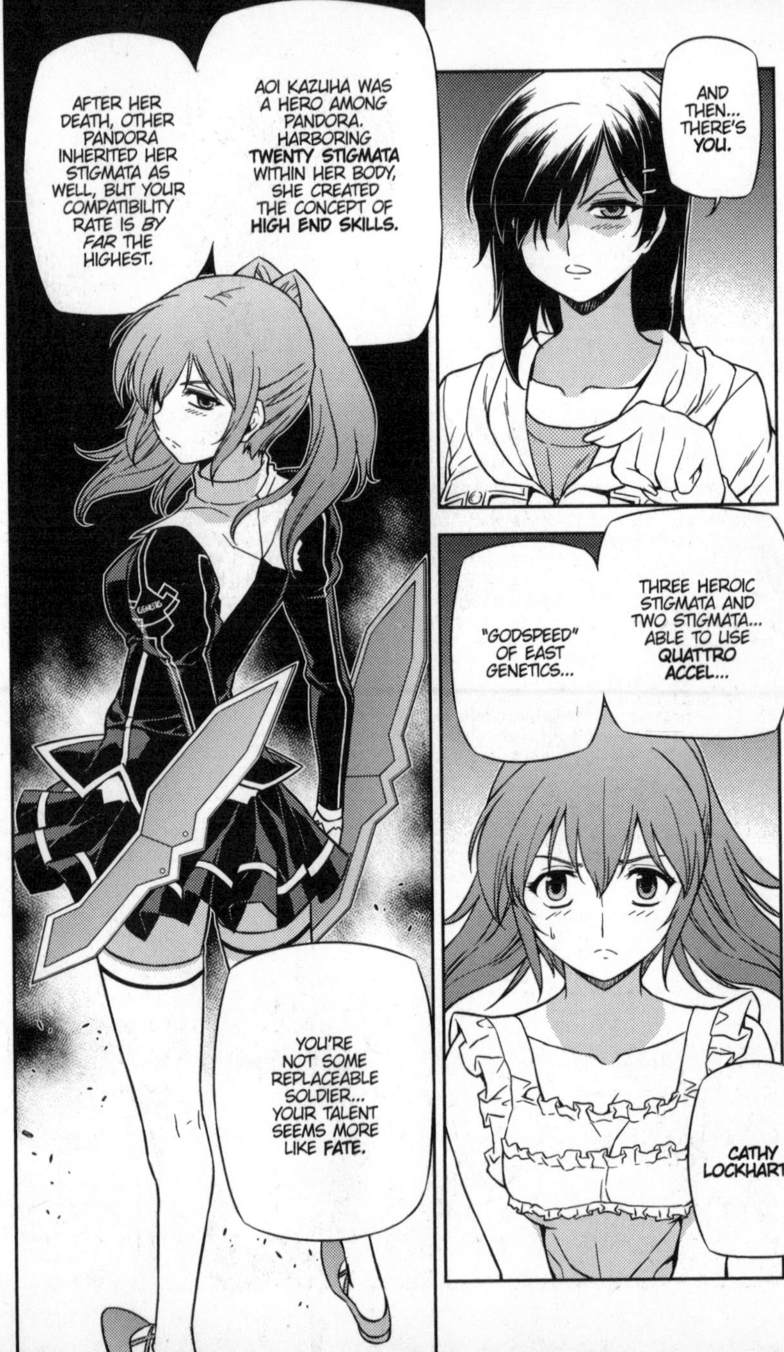
AND THEN... THERE'S YOU.
THREE HEROIC STIGMATA AND TWO STIGMATA... ABLE TO USE QUATTRO ACCEL...
"GODSPEED" OF EAST GENETICS...
CATHY LOCKHARTE!
AOI KAZUHA WAS A HERO AMONG PANDORA. HARBORING TWENTY STIGMATA WITHIN HER BODY, SHE CREATED THE CONCEPT OF HIGH END SKILLS.
AFTER HER DEATH, OTHER PANDORA INHERITED HER STIGMATA AS WELL, BUT YOUR COMPATIBILITY RATE IS BY FAR THE HIGHEST.
YOU'RE NOT SOME REPLACEABLE SOLDIER... YOUR TALENT SEEMS MORE LIKE FATE.

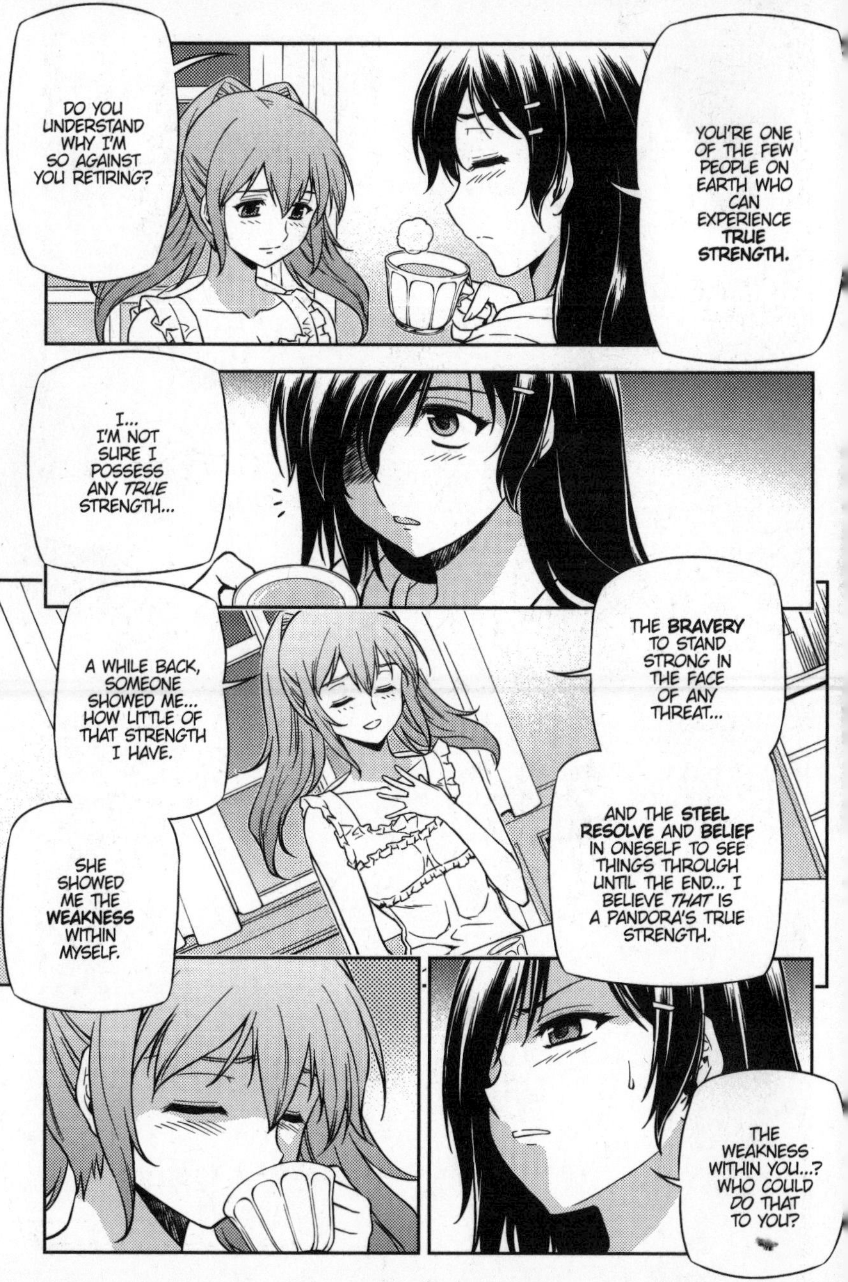
DO YOU UNDERSTAND WHY I'M SO AGAINST YOU RETIRING?
YOU'RE ONE OF THE FEW PEOPLE ON EARTH WHO CAN EXPERIENCE **TRUE STRENGTH.**
I... I'M NOT SURE I POSSESS ANY *TRUE* STRENGTH...
THE **BRAVERY** TO STAND STRONG IN THE FACE OF ANY THREAT...
AND THE **STEEL RESOLVE** AND **BELIEF** IN ONESELF TO SEE THINGS THROUGH UNTIL THE END... I BELIEVE *THAT* IS A PANDORA'S TRUE STRENGTH.
A WHILE BACK, SOMEONE SHOWED ME... HOW LITTLE OF THAT STRENGTH I HAVE.
SHE SHOWED ME THE **WEAKNESS** WITHIN MYSELF.
THE WEAKNESS WITHIN YOU...? WHO COULD *DO* THAT TO YOU?

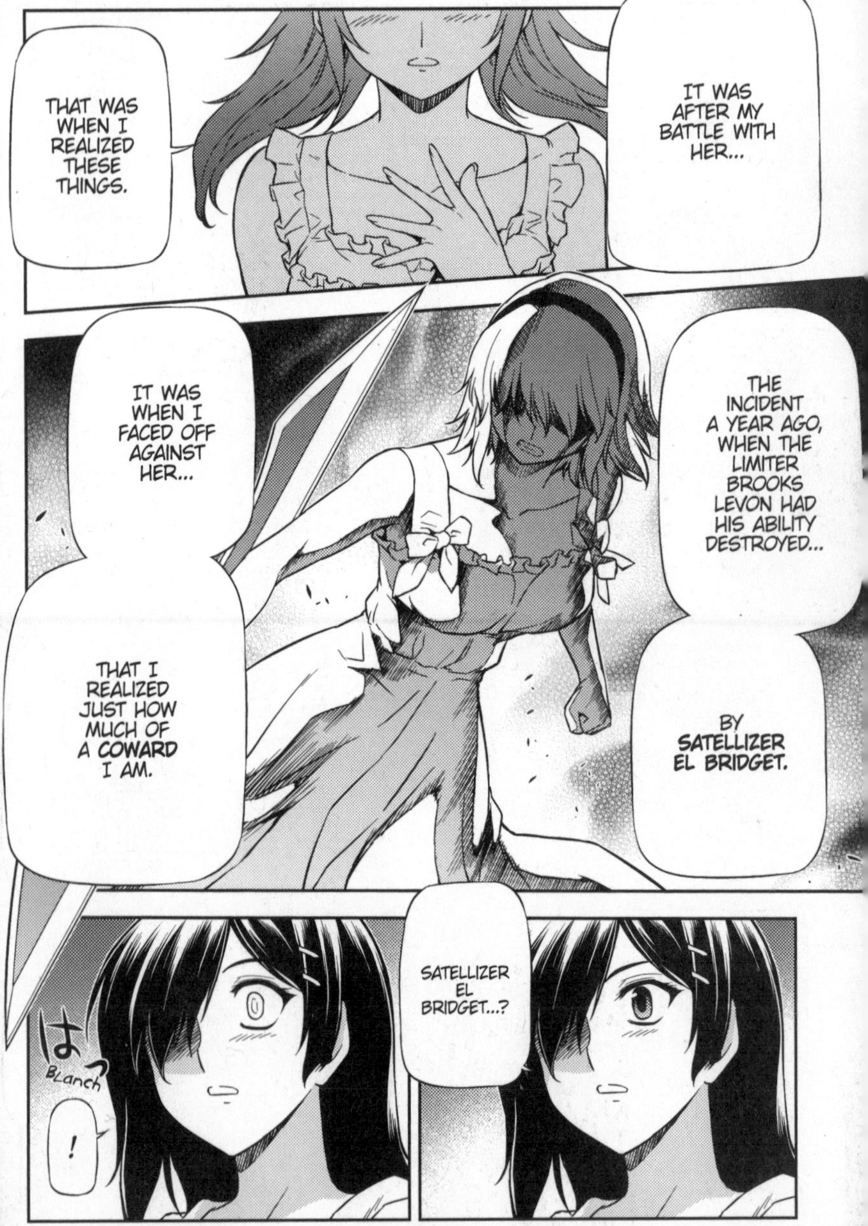
IT WAS AFTER MY BATTLE WITH HER...
THAT WAS WHEN I REALIZED THESE THINGS.
THE INCIDENT A YEAR AGO, WHEN THE LIMITER BROOKS LEVON HAD HIS ABILITY DESTROYED...
BY SATELLIZER EL BRIDGET.
IT WAS WHEN I FACED OFF AGAINST HER...
THAT I REALIZED JUST HOW MUCH OF A **COWARD** I AM.
SATELLIZER EL BRIDGET...?
はっ
BLanch
!

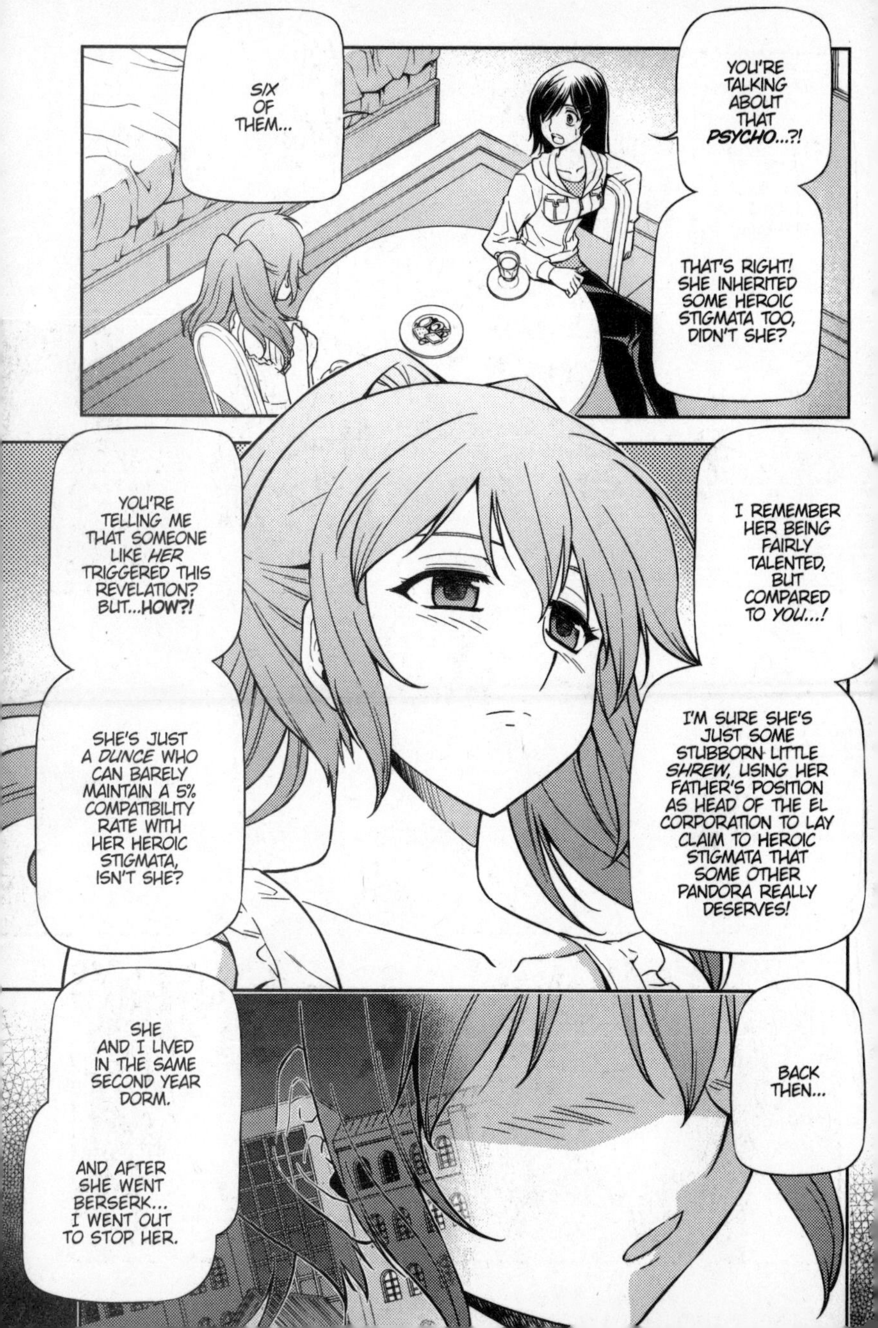
YOU'RE TALKING ABOUT THAT *PSYCHO*...?!
THAT'S RIGHT! SHE INHERITED SOME HEROIC STIGMATA TOO, DIDN'T SHE?
SIX OF THEM...
I REMEMBER HER BEING FAIRLY TALENTED, BUT COMPARED TO *YOU*...!
I'M SURE SHE'S JUST SOME STUBBORN LITTLE *SHREW*, USING HER FATHER'S POSITION AS HEAD OF THE EL CORPORATION TO LAY CLAIM TO HEROIC STIGMATA THAT SOME OTHER PANDORA REALLY DESERVES!
YOU'RE TELLING ME THAT SOMEONE LIKE *HER* TRIGGERED THIS REVELATION? BUT...**HOW?!**
SHE'S JUST A *DUNCE* WHO CAN BARELY MAINTAIN A 5% COMPATIBILITY RATE WITH HER HEROIC STIGMATA, ISN'T SHE?
BACK THEN...
SHE AND I LIVED IN THE SAME SECOND YEAR DORM.
AND AFTER SHE WENT BERSERK... I WENT OUT TO STOP HER.

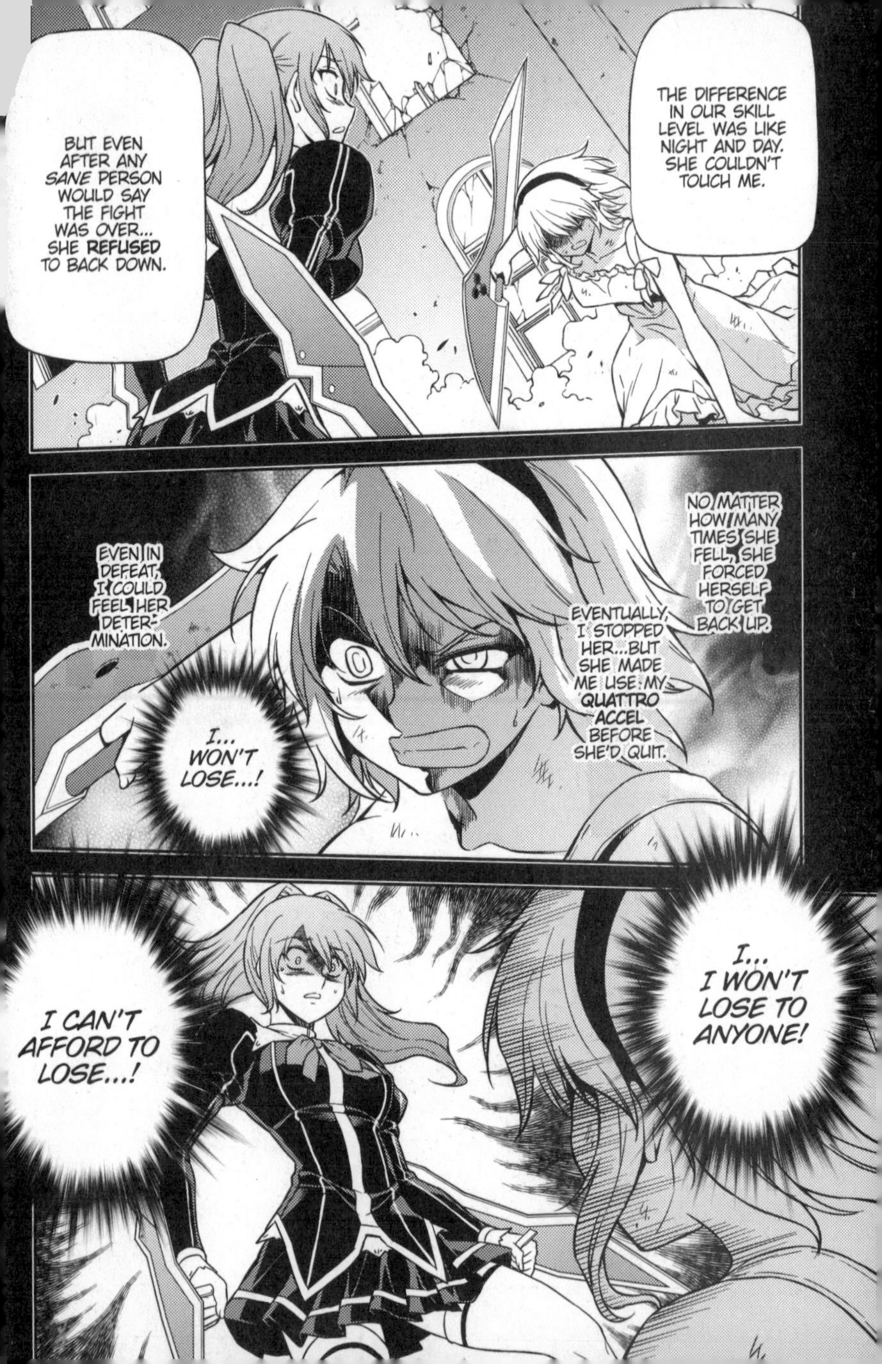
THE DIFFERENCE IN OUR SKILL LEVEL WAS LIKE NIGHT AND DAY. SHE COULDN'T TOUCH ME.
BUT EVEN AFTER ANY SANE PERSON WOULD SAY THE FIGHT WAS OVER... SHE **REFUSED** TO BACK DOWN.
NO MATTER HOW MANY TIMES SHE FELL, SHE FORCED HERSELF TO GET BACK UP.
EVENTUALLY, I STOPPED HER...BUT SHE MADE ME USE MY **QUATTRO ACCEL** BEFORE SHE'D QUIT.
EVEN IN DEFEAT, I COULD FEEL HER DETER-MINATION.
I... WON'T LOSE...!
I... I WON'T LOSE TO ANYONE!
I CAN'T AFFORD TO LOSE...!

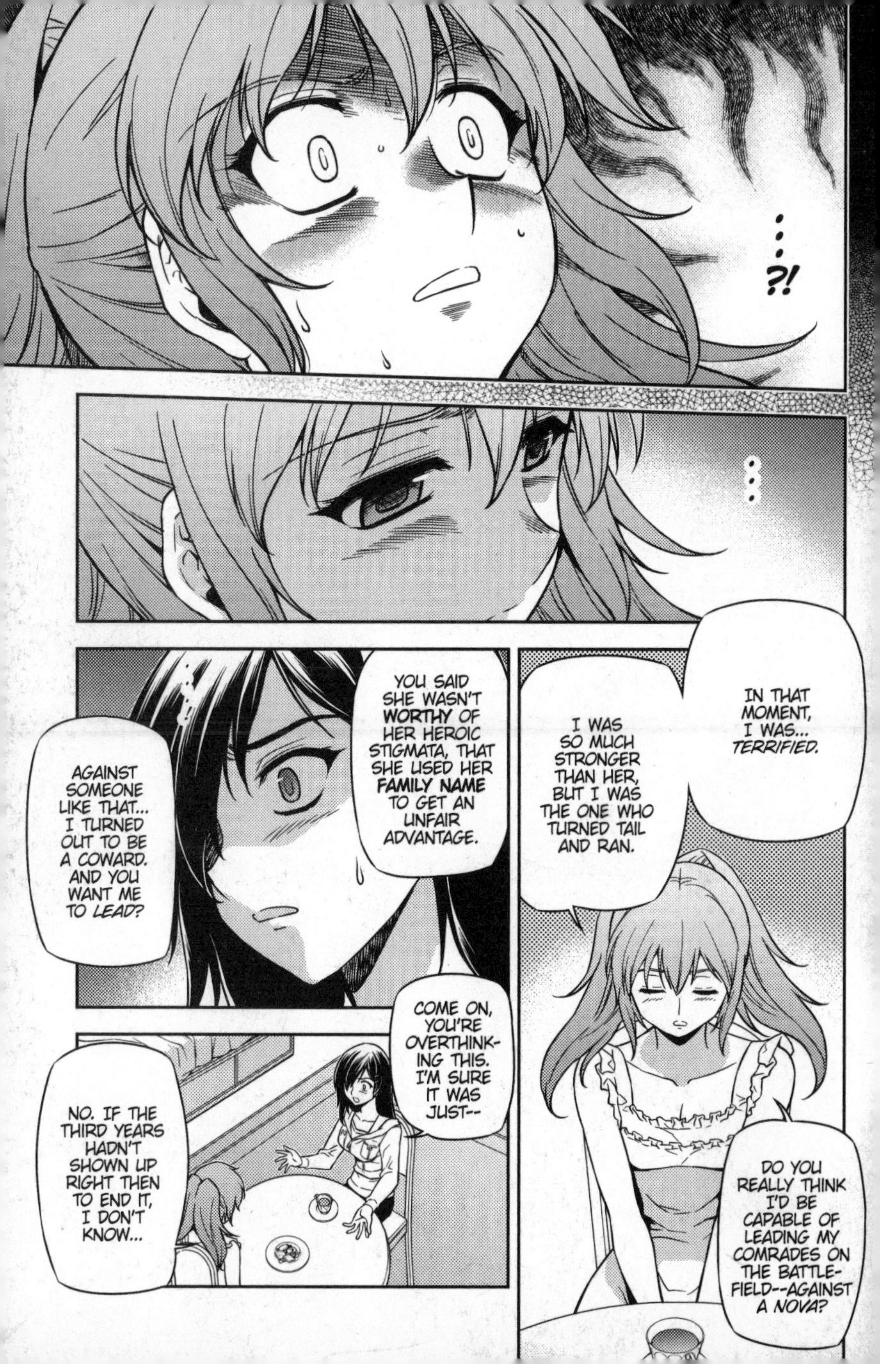

...?!
...
IN THAT MOMENT, I WAS... *TERRIFIED.*
I WAS SO MUCH STRONGER THAN HER, BUT I WAS THE ONE WHO TURNED TAIL AND RAN.
DO YOU REALLY THINK I'D BE CAPABLE OF LEADING MY COMRADES ON THE BATTLE-FIELD--AGAINST A *NOVA?*
YOU SAID SHE WASN'T **WORTHY** OF HER HEROIC STIGMATA, THAT SHE USED HER **FAMILY NAME** TO GET AN UNFAIR ADVANTAGE.
AGAINST SOMEONE LIKE THAT... I TURNED OUT TO BE A COWARD. AND YOU WANT ME TO *LEAD?*
COME ON, YOU'RE OVERTHINK-ING THIS. I'M SURE IT WAS JUST--
NO. IF THE THIRD YEARS HADN'T SHOWN UP RIGHT THEN TO END IT, I DON'T KNOW...

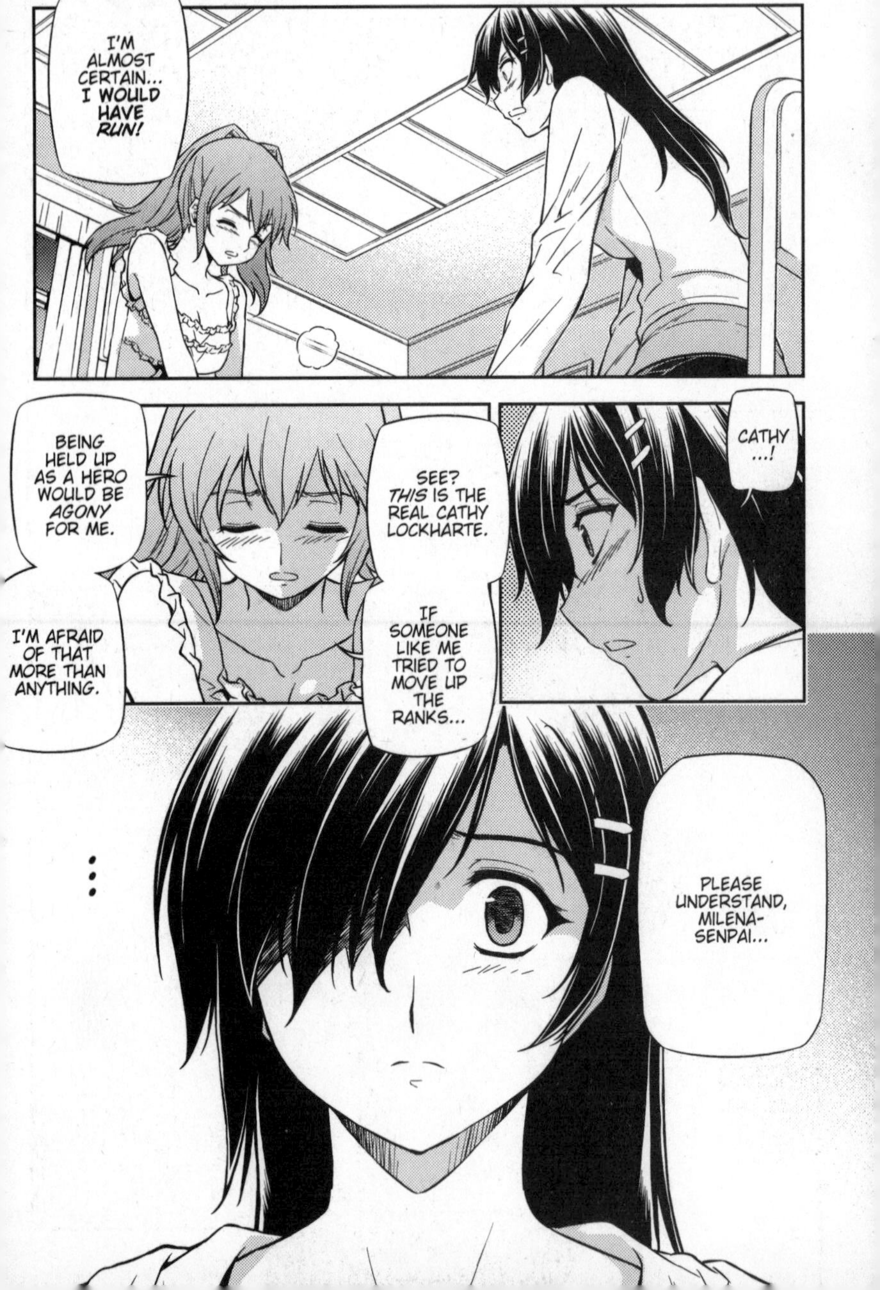
I'M ALMOST CERTAIN... I WOULD HAVE *RUN!*
CATHY ...!
SEE? *THIS* IS THE REAL CATHY LOCKHARTE.
IF SOMEONE LIKE ME TRIED TO MOVE UP THE RANKS...
BEING HELD UP AS A HERO WOULD BE *AGONY* FOR ME.
I'M AFRAID OF THAT MORE THAN ANYTHING.
PLEASE UNDERSTAND, MILENA-SENPAI...
• • •

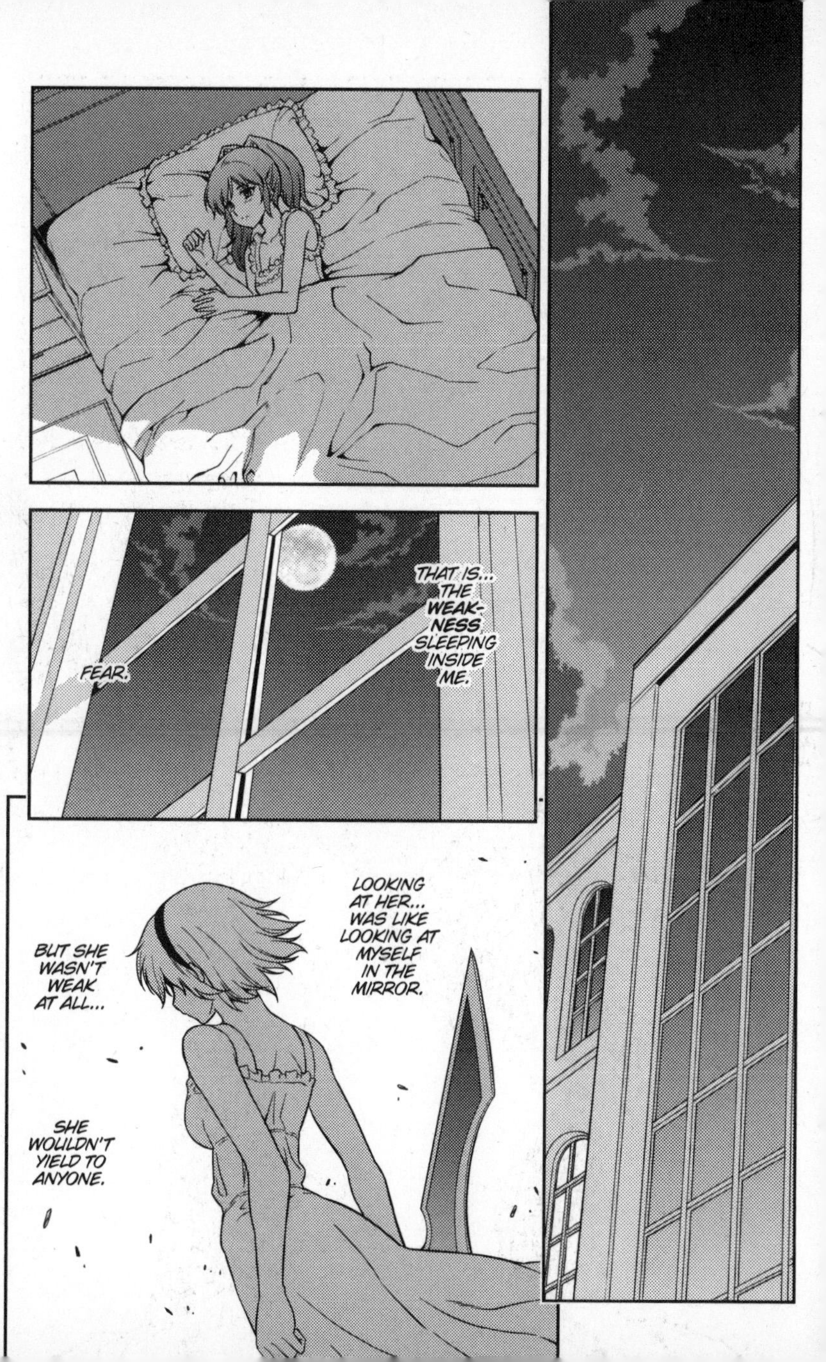
THAT IS... THE WEAK-NESS SLEEPING INSIDE ME.
FEAR.
LOOKING AT HER... WAS LIKE LOOKING AT MYSELF IN THE MIRROR.
BUT SHE WASN'T WEAK AT ALL...
SHE WOULDN'T YIELD TO ANYONE.

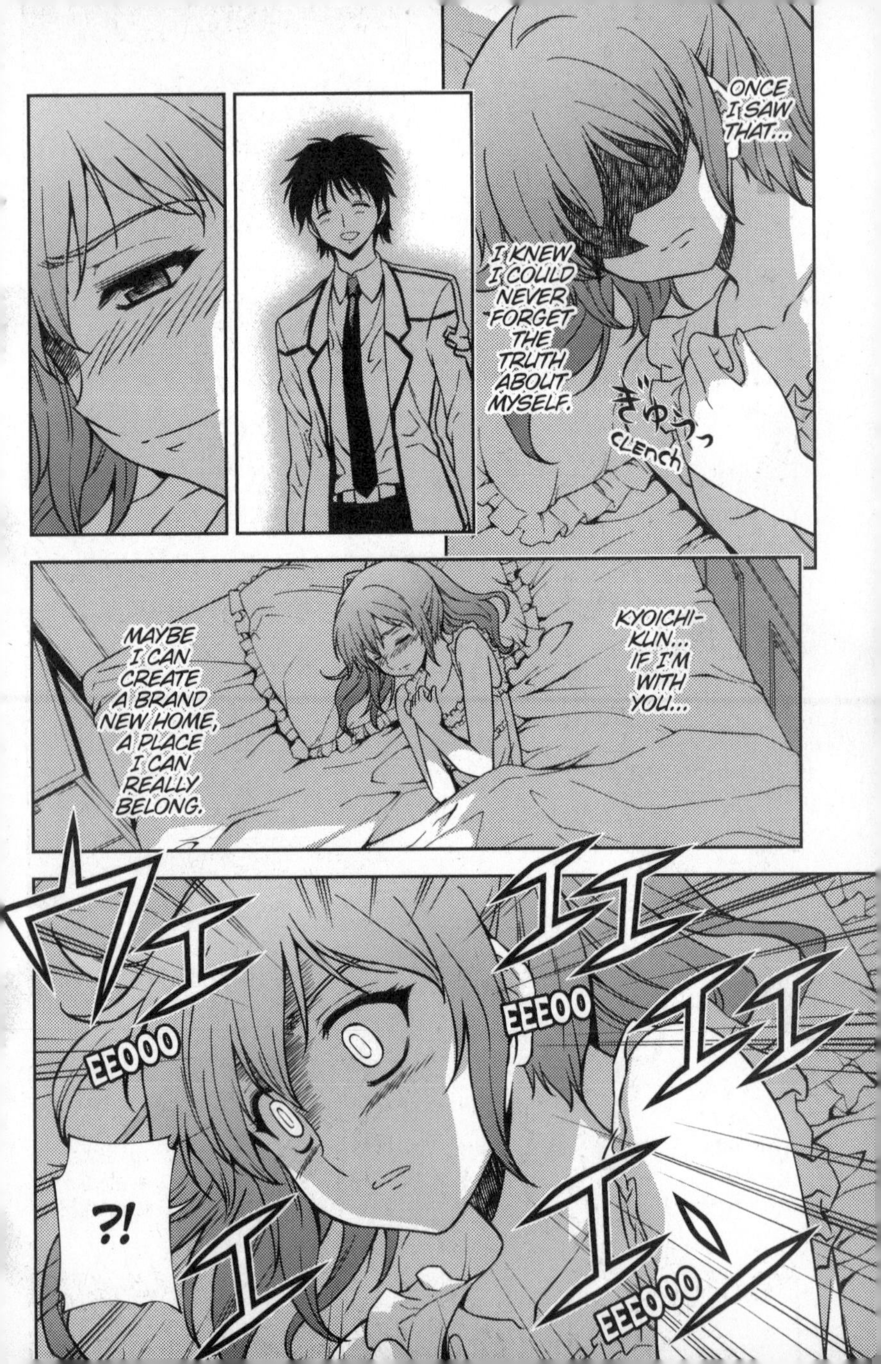
ONCE I SAW THAT...
I KNEW I COULD NEVER FORGET THE TRUTH ABOUT MYSELF.
CLENCH
KYOICHI-KUN... IF I'M WITH YOU...
MAYBE I CAN CREATE A BRAND NEW HOME, A PLACE I CAN REALLY BELONG.
EEEOO
EEOOO
?!
EEEOOO

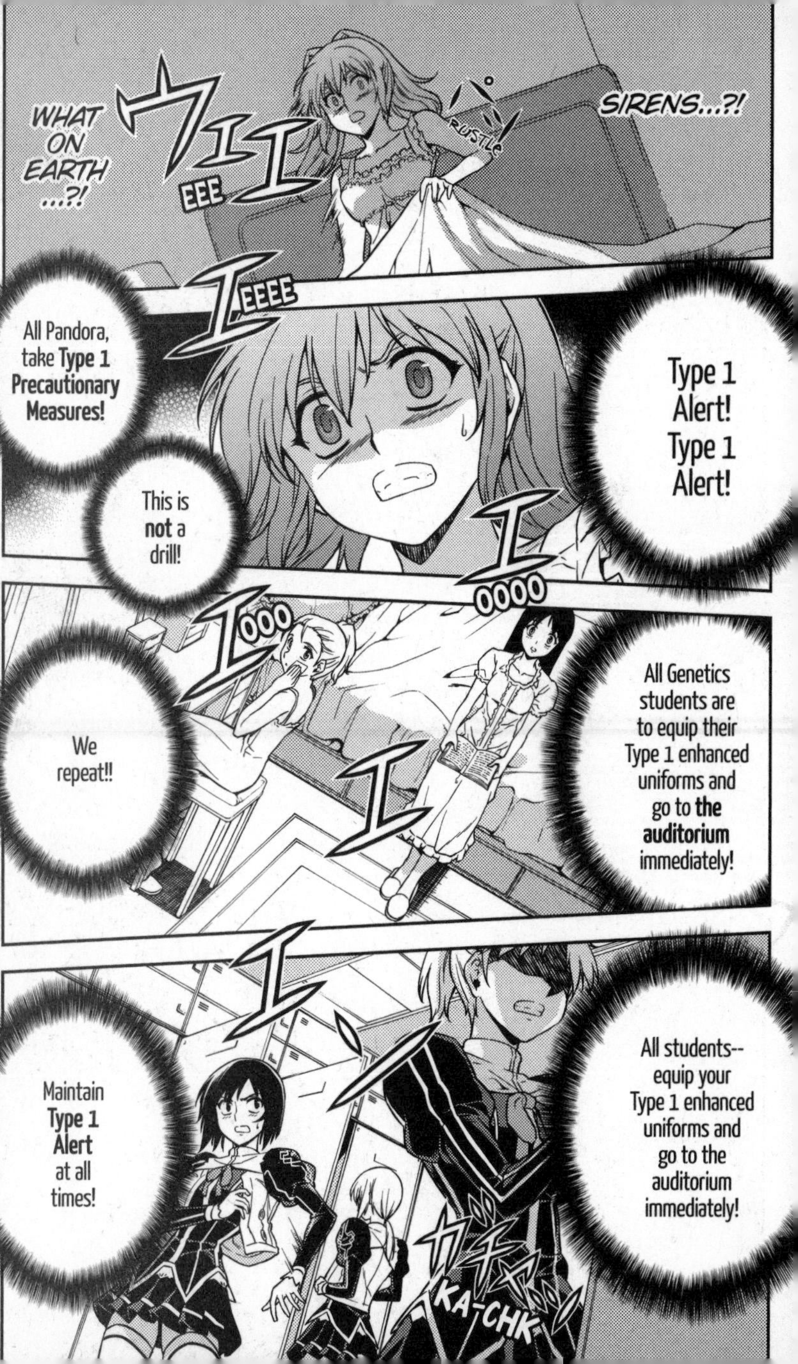
SIRENS...?!
RUSTLE
WHAT ON EARTH ...?!
EEE
EEEE
Type 1 Alert! Type 1 Alert!
All Pandora, take **Type 1 Precautionary Measures!**
This is **not** a drill!
OOOO
OOO
All Genetics students are to equip their Type 1 enhanced uniforms and go to **the auditorium** immediately!
We repeat!!
All students-- equip your Type 1 enhanced uniforms and go to the auditorium immediately!
Maintain **Type 1 Alert** at all times!
KA-CHK

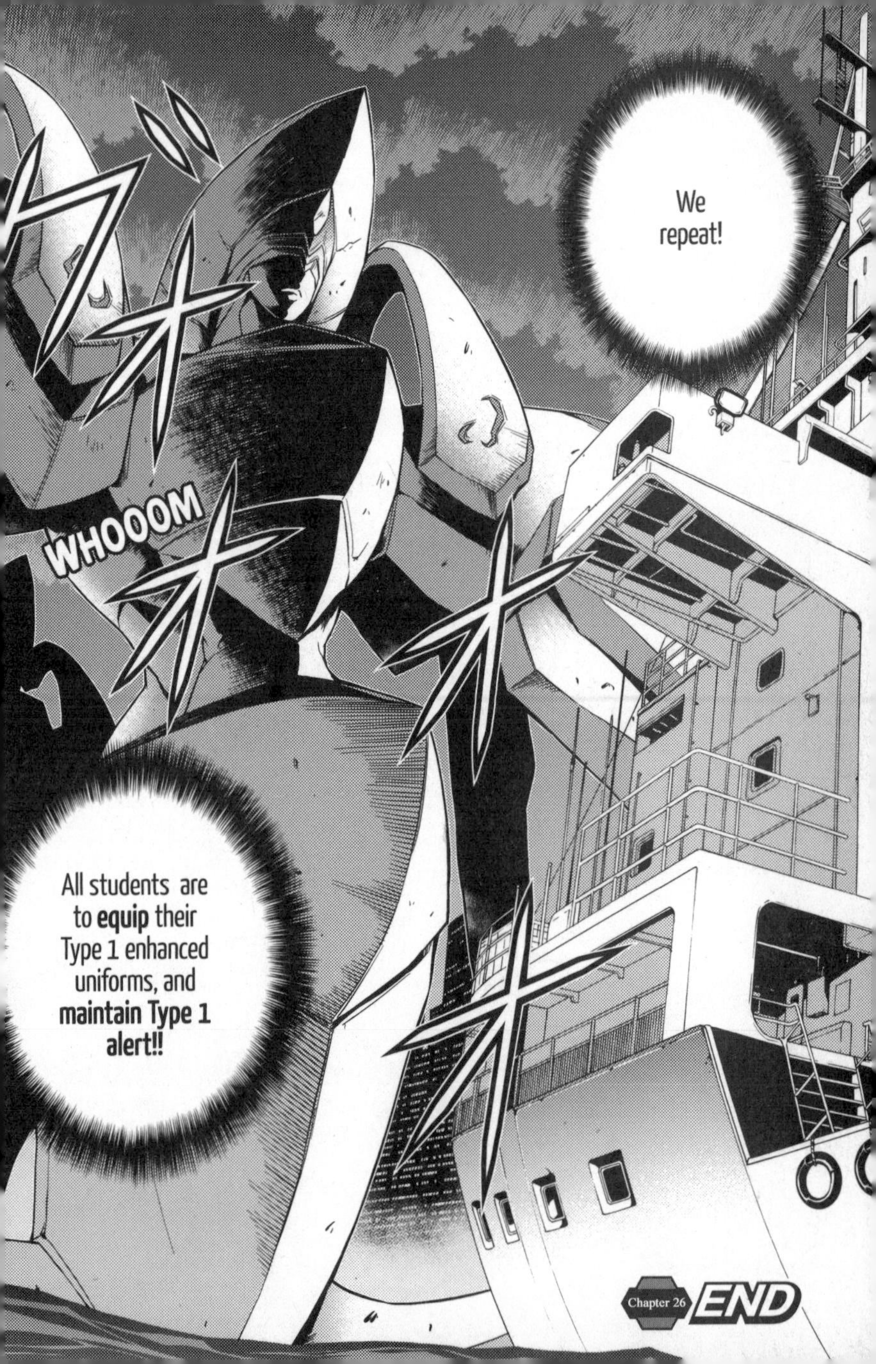
We repeat!
WHOOOM
All students are to **equip** their Type 1 enhanced uniforms, and **maintain Type 1** alert!!
Chapter 26 END

FREEZING VOLUME.5
HIGHLIGHT SCENE

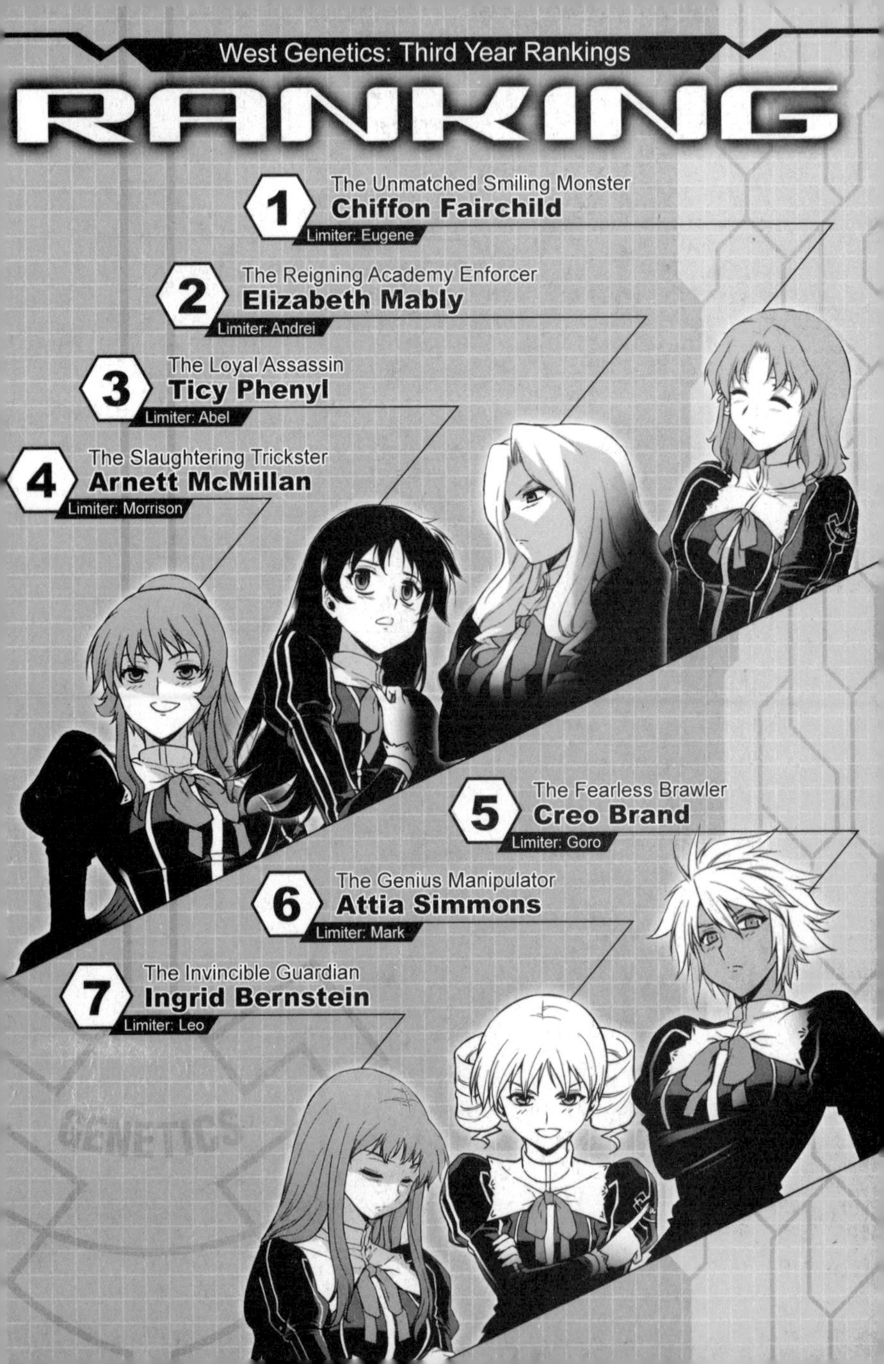
West Genetics: Third Year Rankings
RANKING
1
The Unmatched Smiling Monster
Chiffon Fairchild
Limiter: Eugene
2
The Reigning Academy Enforcer
Elizabeth Mably
Limiter: Andrei
3
The Loyal Assassin
Ticy Phenyl
Limiter: Abel
4
The Slaughtering Trickster
Arnett McMillan
Limiter: Morrison
5
The Fearless Brawler
Creo Brand
Limiter: Goro
6
The Genius Manipulator
Attia Simmons
Limiter: Mark
7
The Invincible Guardian
Ingrid Bernstein
Limiter: Leo
GENETICS

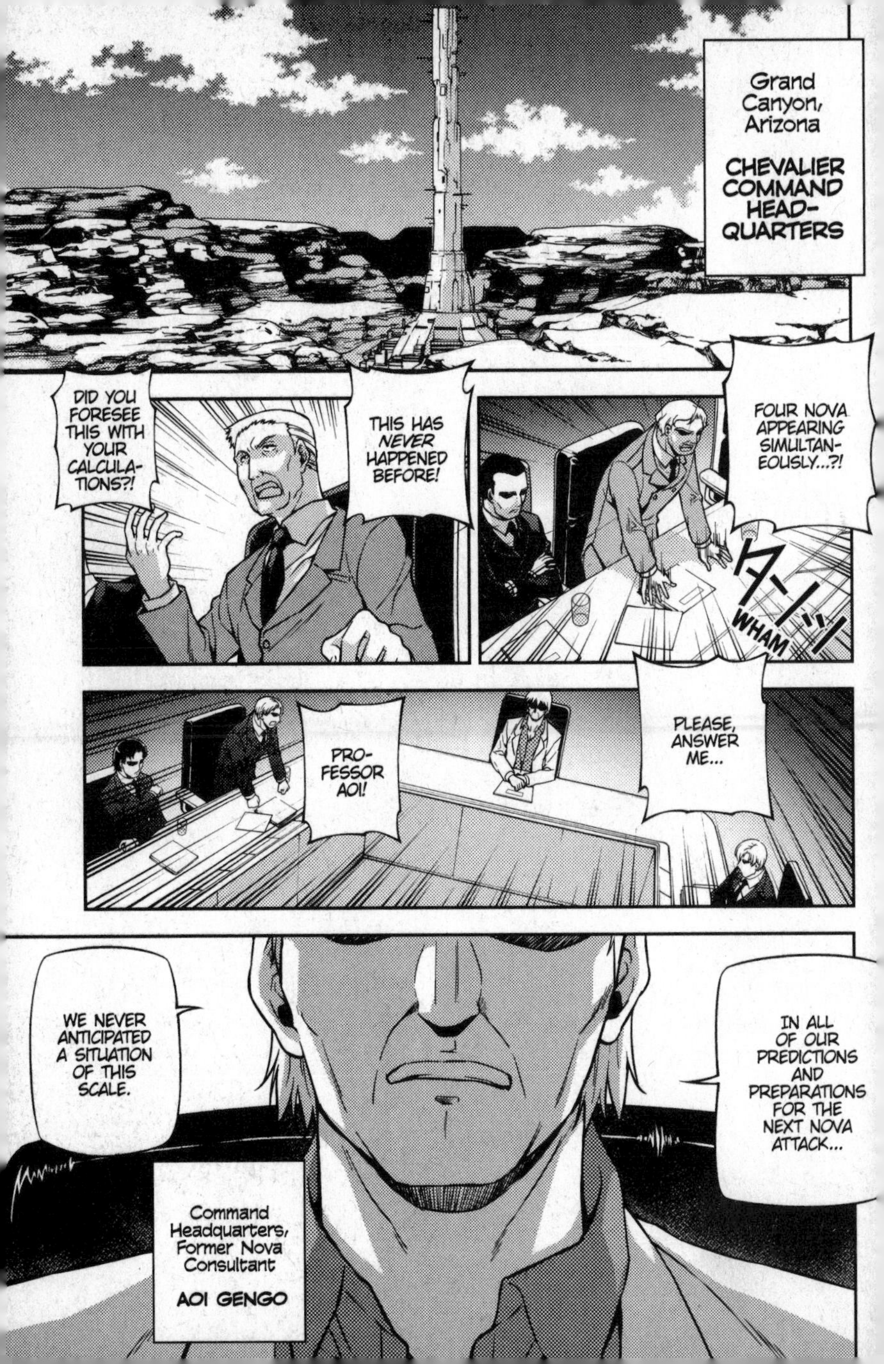
Grand Canyon, Arizona
CHEVALIER COMMAND HEADQUARTERS
FOUR NOVA APPEARING SIMULTANEOUSLY...?!
WHAM
THIS HAS *NEVER* HAPPENED BEFORE!
DID YOU FORESEE THIS WITH YOUR CALCULATIONS?!
PLEASE, ANSWER ME...
PROFESSOR AOI!
IN ALL OF OUR PREDICTIONS AND PREPARATIONS FOR THE NEXT NOVA ATTACK...
WE NEVER ANTICIPATED A SITUATION OF THIS SCALE.
Command Headquarters, Former Nova Consultant
AOI GENGO

Chapter 27 Corrosion

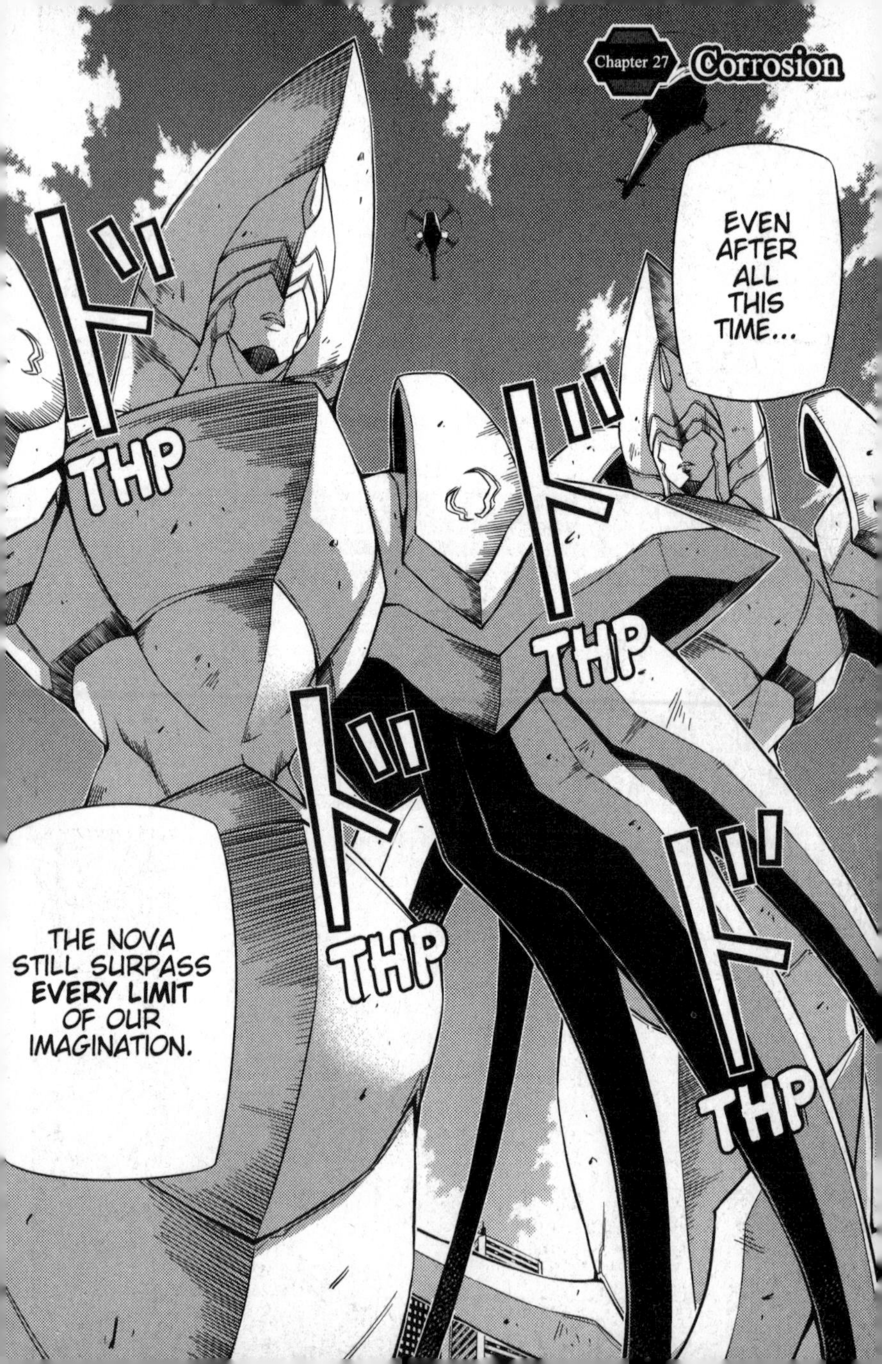
EVEN AFTER ALL THIS TIME...
ド THP
ド THP
ド THP
ド THP
THE NOVA STILL SURPASS EVERY LIMIT OF OUR IMAGINATION.

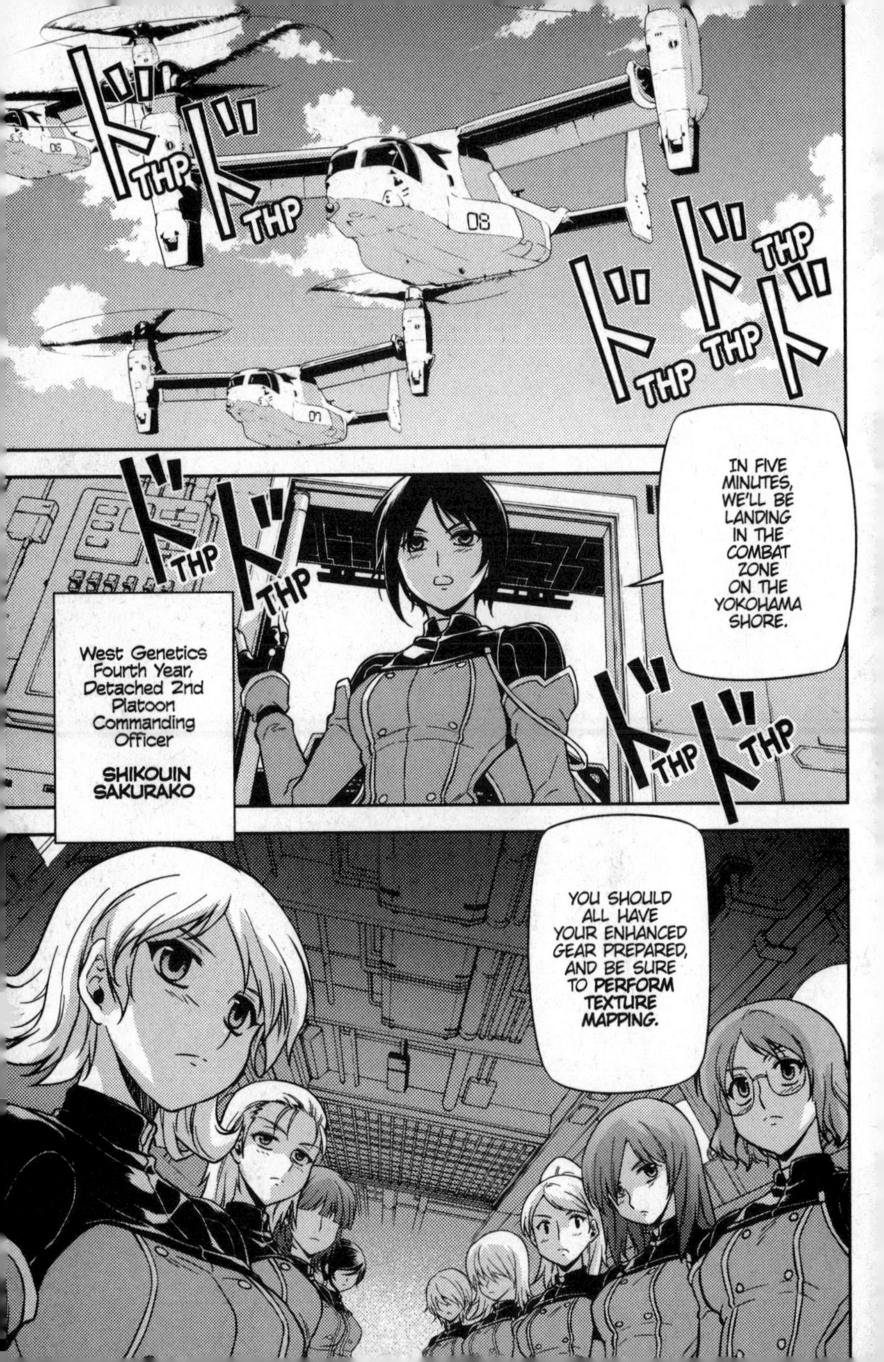

ドド THP THP
ドド THP THP
ドド THP THP
IN FIVE MINUTES, WE'LL BE LANDING IN THE COMBAT ZONE ON THE YOKOHAMA SHORE.
ドド THP THP
ドド THP THP
West Genetics Fourth Year, Detached 2nd Platoon Commanding Officer
SHIKOUIN SAKURAKO
YOU SHOULD ALL HAVE YOUR ENHANCED GEAR PREPARED, AND BE SURE TO PERFORM TEXTURE MAPPING.

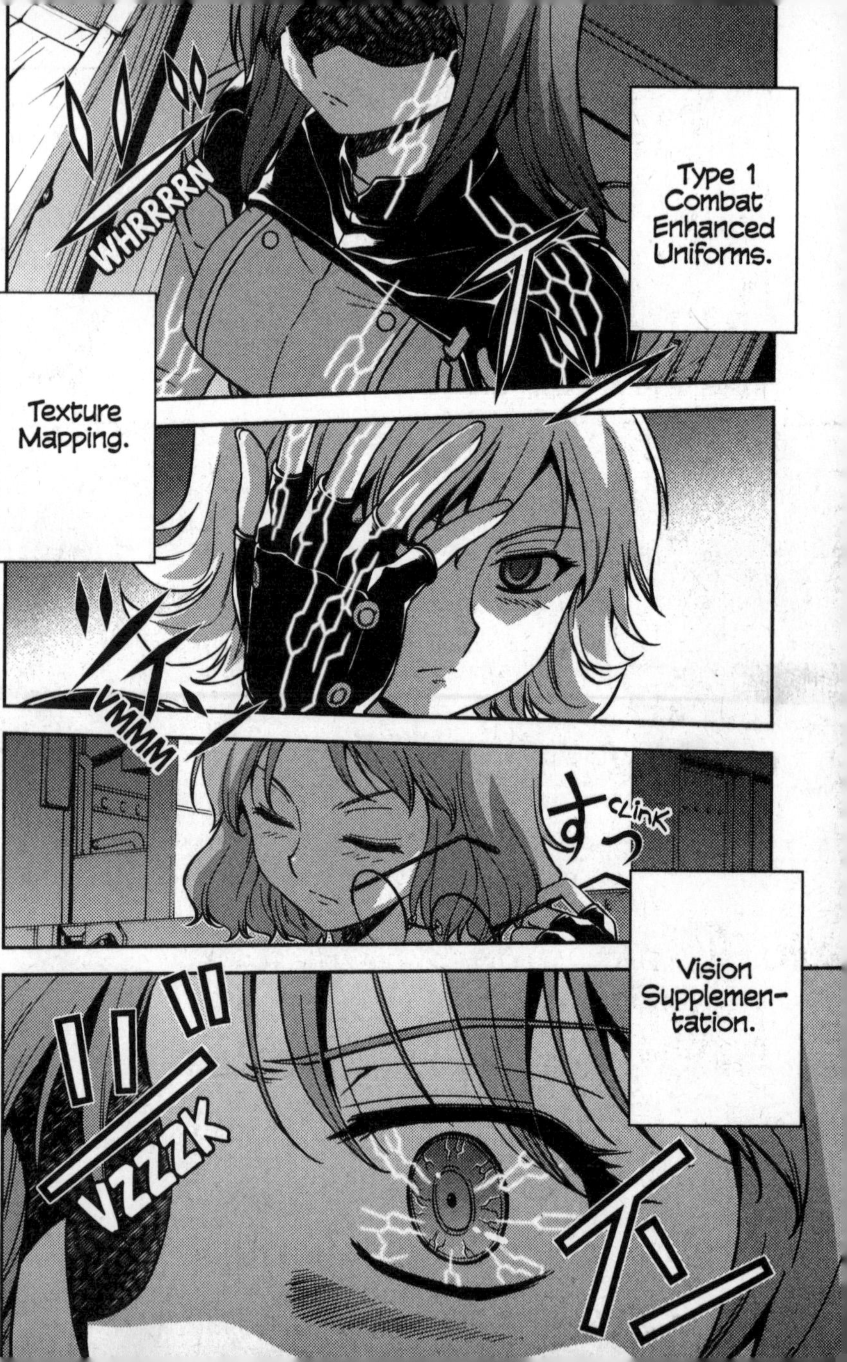
Type 1 Combat Enhanced Uniforms.
WHRRRRN
Texture Mapping.
VMMMM
すっ
CLINK
Vision Supplemen-tation.
VZZZK

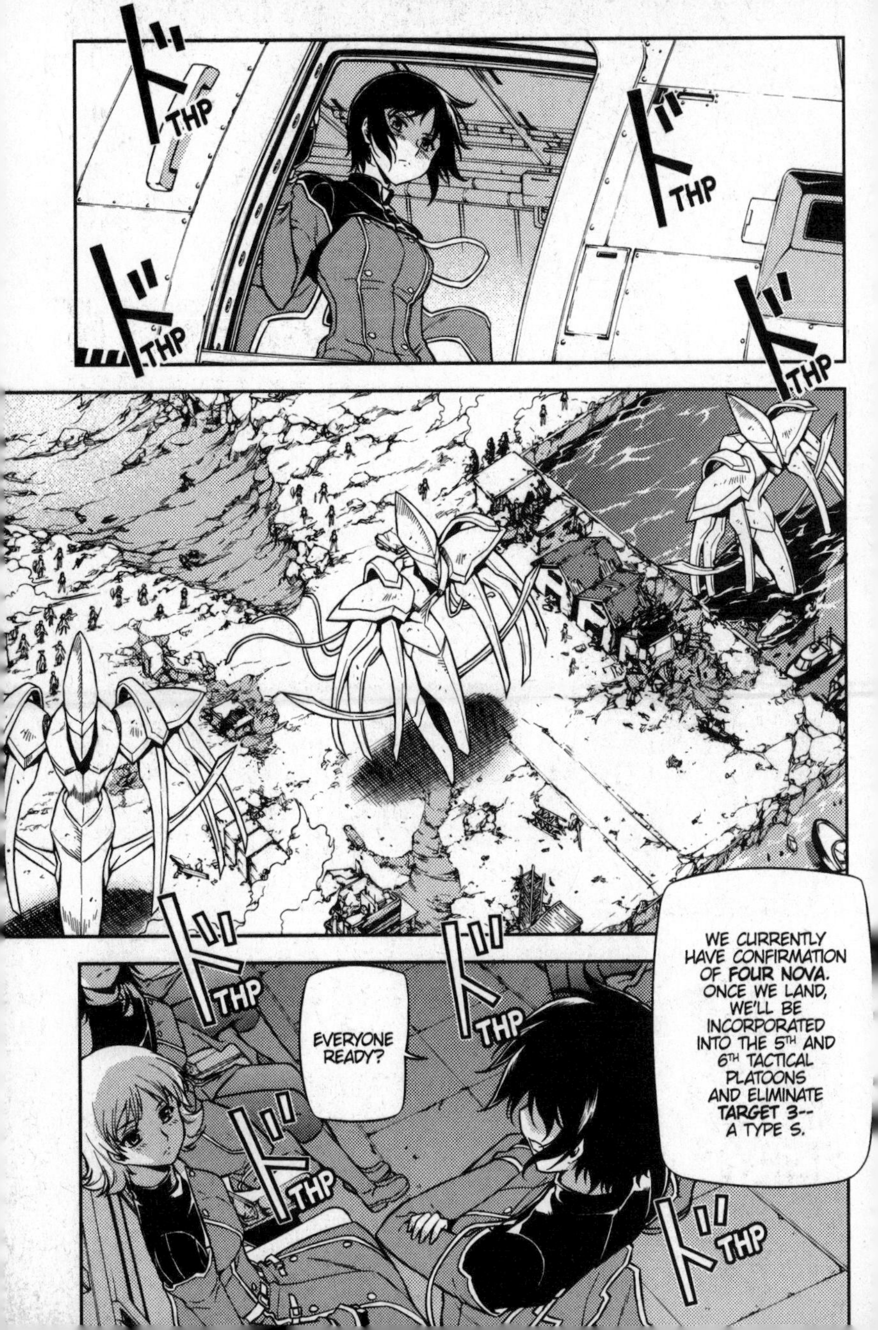

ド THP
ド THP
ド THP
ド THP
ド THP
WE CURRENTLY HAVE CONFIRMATION OF FOUR NOVA. ONCE WE LAND, WE'LL BE INCORPORATED INTO THE 5TH AND 6TH TACTICAL PLATOONS AND ELIMINATE TARGET 3-- A TYPE S.
ド THP
EVERYONE READY?
ド THP
ド THP
ド THP

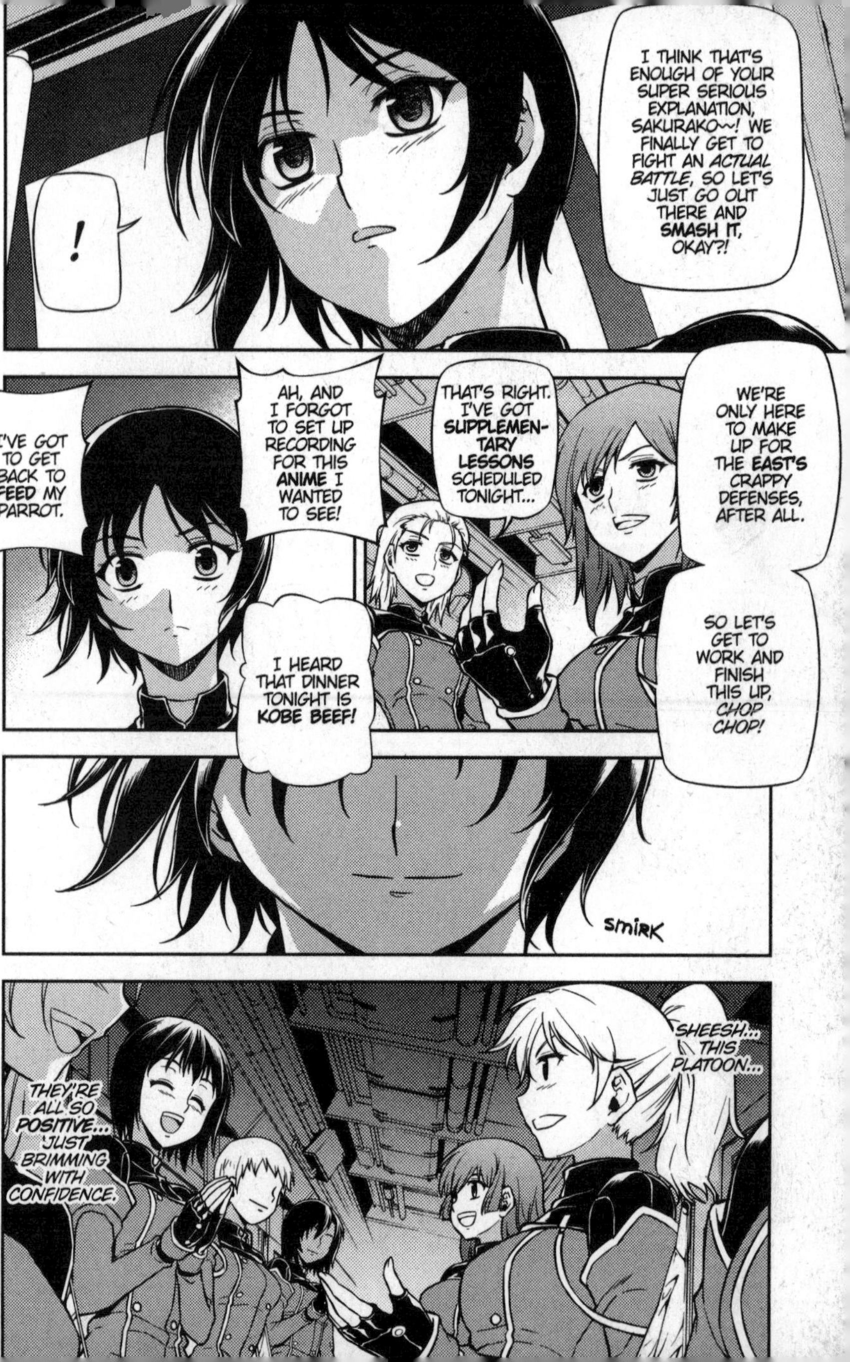
I THINK THAT'S ENOUGH OF YOUR SUPER SERIOUS EXPLANATION, SAKURAKO~! WE FINALLY GET TO FIGHT AN *ACTUAL BATTLE*, SO LET'S JUST GO OUT THERE AND **SMASH IT**, OKAY?!
!
WE'RE ONLY HERE TO MAKE UP FOR THE **EAST'S** CRAPPY DEFENSES, AFTER ALL.
THAT'S RIGHT. I'VE GOT **SUPPLEMENTARY LESSONS** SCHEDULED TONIGHT...
AH, AND I FORGOT TO SET UP RECORDING FOR THIS **ANIME** I WANTED TO SEE!
I'VE GOT TO GET BACK TO **FEED** MY PARROT.
I HEARD THAT DINNER TONIGHT IS **KOBE BEEF!**
SO LET'S GET TO WORK AND FINISH THIS UP, *CHOP CHOP!*
SMIRK
SHEESH... THIS PLATOON...
THEY'RE ALL SO *POSITIVE*... JUST BRIMMING WITH CONFIDENCE.

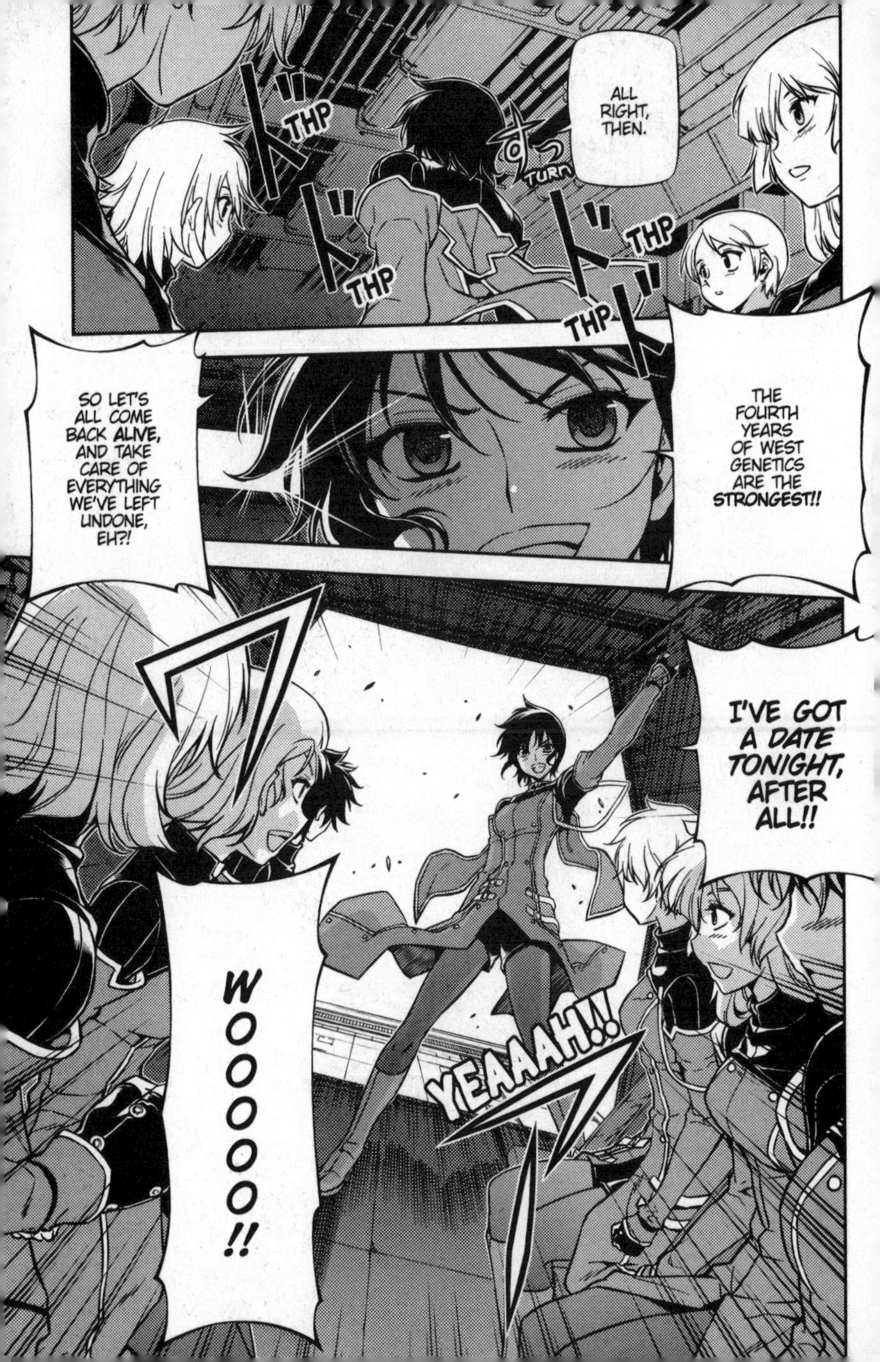
ALL RIGHT, THEN.
TURN
THP
THP
THP
THP
THE FOURTH YEARS OF WEST GENETICS ARE THE STRONGEST!!
SO LET'S ALL COME BACK ALIVE, AND TAKE CARE OF EVERYTHING WE'VE LEFT UNDONE, EH?!
I'VE GOT A DATE TONIGHT, AFTER ALL!!
YEAAAH!!
WOOOOOOO!!

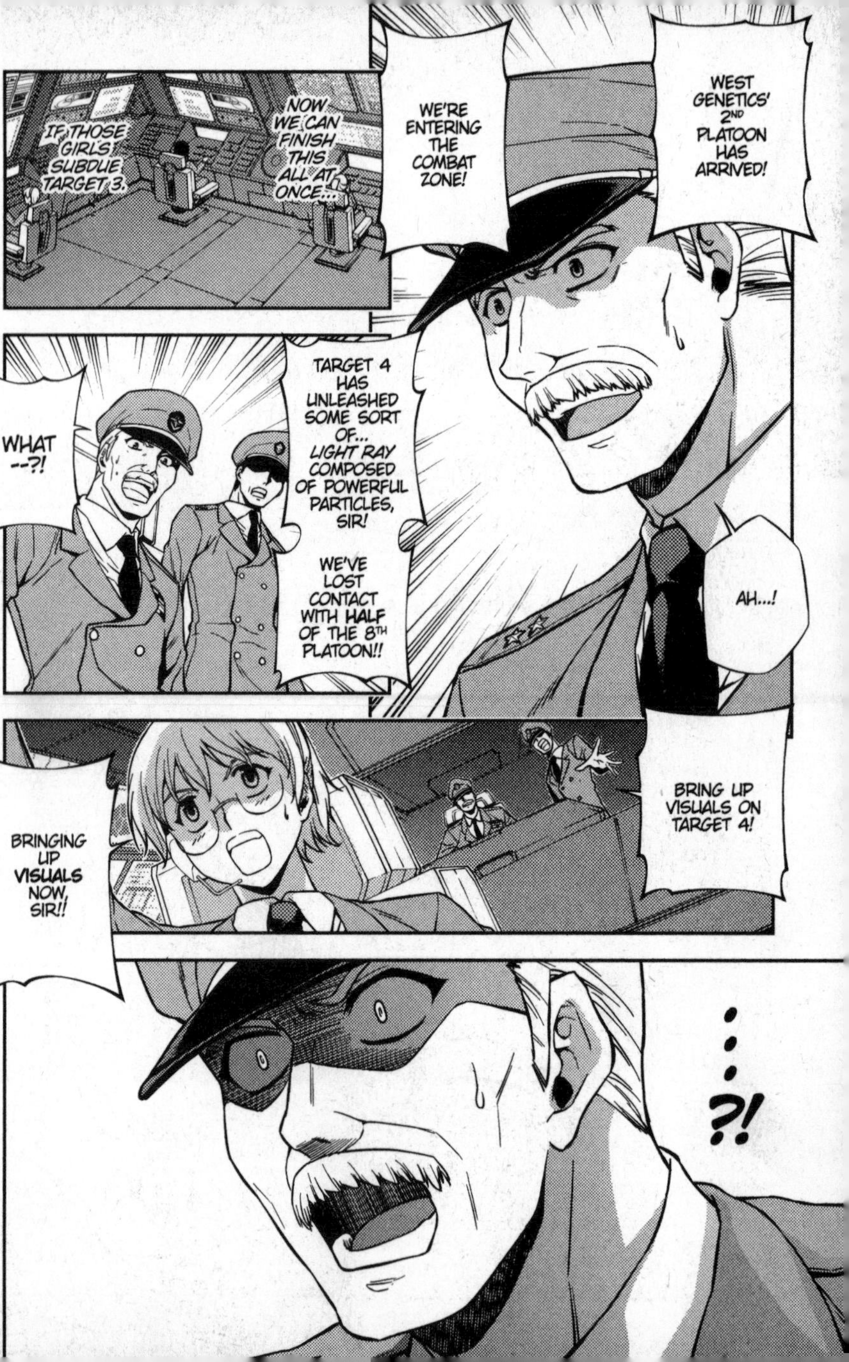
WEST GENETICS' 2ND PLATOON HAS ARRIVED!
WE'RE ENTERING THE COMBAT ZONE!
AH...!
NOW WE CAN FINISH THIS ALL AT ONCE...
IF THOSE GIRLS SUBDUE TARGET 3.
TARGET 4 HAS UNLEASHED SOME SORT OF... *LIGHT RAY COMPOSED OF POWERFUL PARTICLES*, SIR!
WE'VE LOST CONTACT WITH **HALF** OF THE 8TH PLATOON!!
WHAT --?!
BRING UP VISUALS ON TARGET 4!
BRINGING UP **VISUALS** NOW, SIR!!
...?!

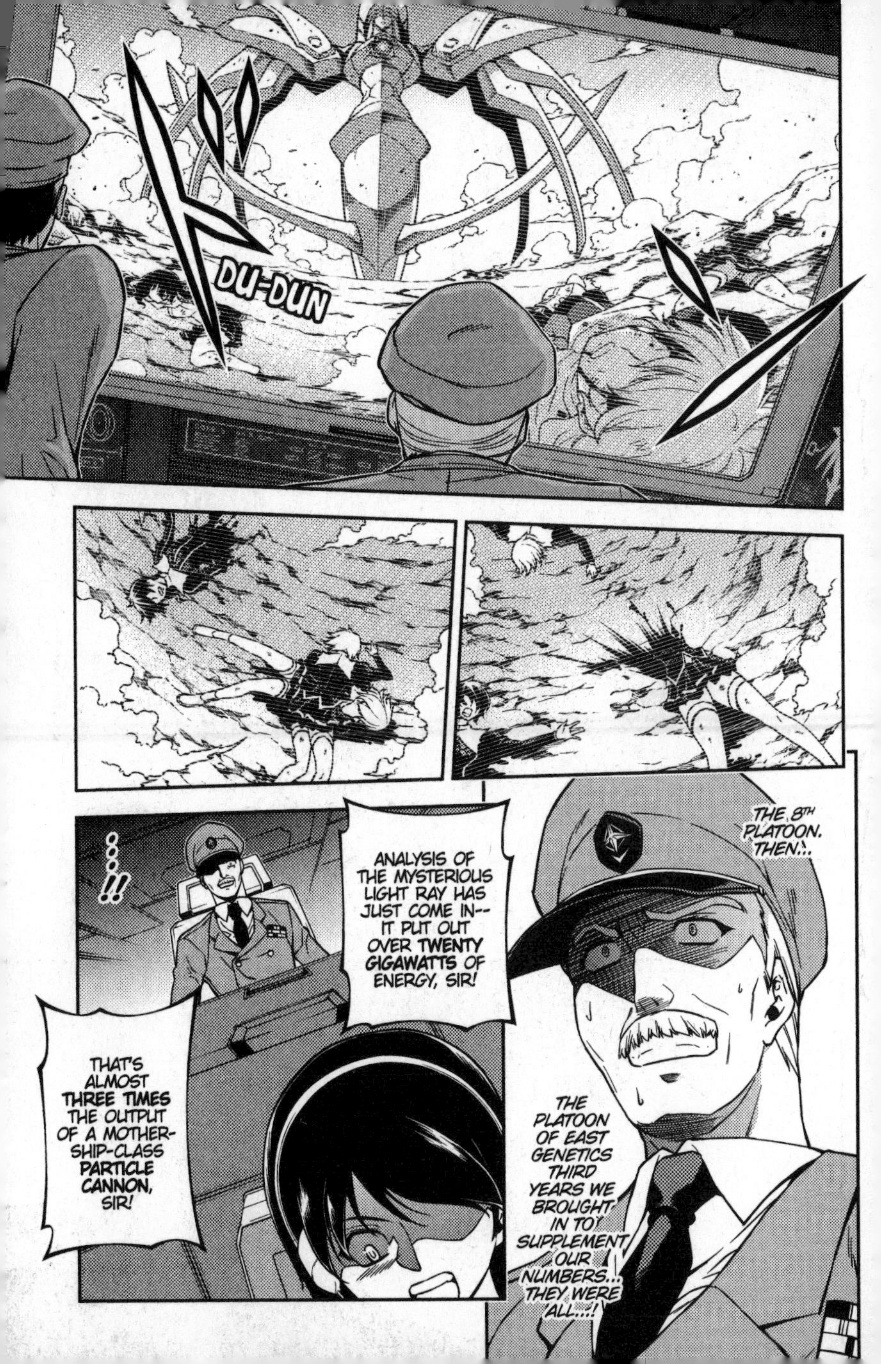
DU-DUN
THE 8TH PLATOON. THEN...
THE PLATOON OF EAST GENETICS THIRD YEARS WE BROUGHT IN TO SUPPLEMENT OUR NUMBERS... THEY WERE ALL...!
ANALYSIS OF THE MYSTERIOUS LIGHT RAY HAS JUST COME IN-- IT PUT OUT OVER TWENTY GIGAWATTS OF ENERGY, SIR!
...!!
THAT'S ALMOST THREE TIMES THE OUTPUT OF A MOTHER-SHIP-CLASS PARTICLE CANNON, SIR!

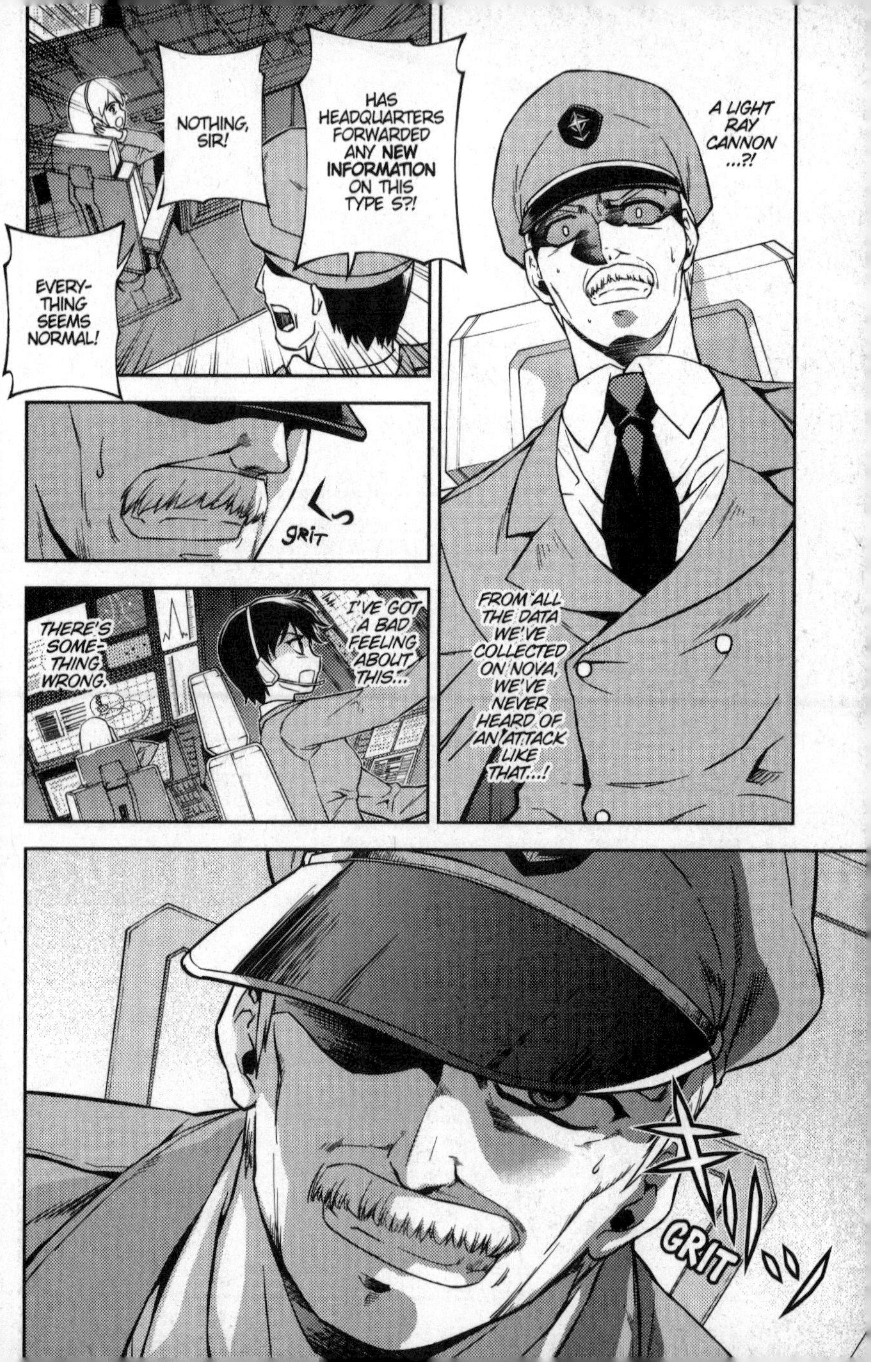
A LIGHT RAY CANNON ...?!
FROM ALL THE DATA WE'VE COLLECTED ON NOVA, WE'VE NEVER HEARD OF AN ATTACK LIKE THAT...!
HAS HEADQUARTERS FORWARDED ANY NEW INFORMATION ON THIS TYPE S?!
NOTHING, SIR!
EVERY-THING SEEMS NORMAL!
GRIT
I'VE GOT A BAD FEELING ABOUT THIS...
THERE'S SOME-THING WRONG.
GRIT

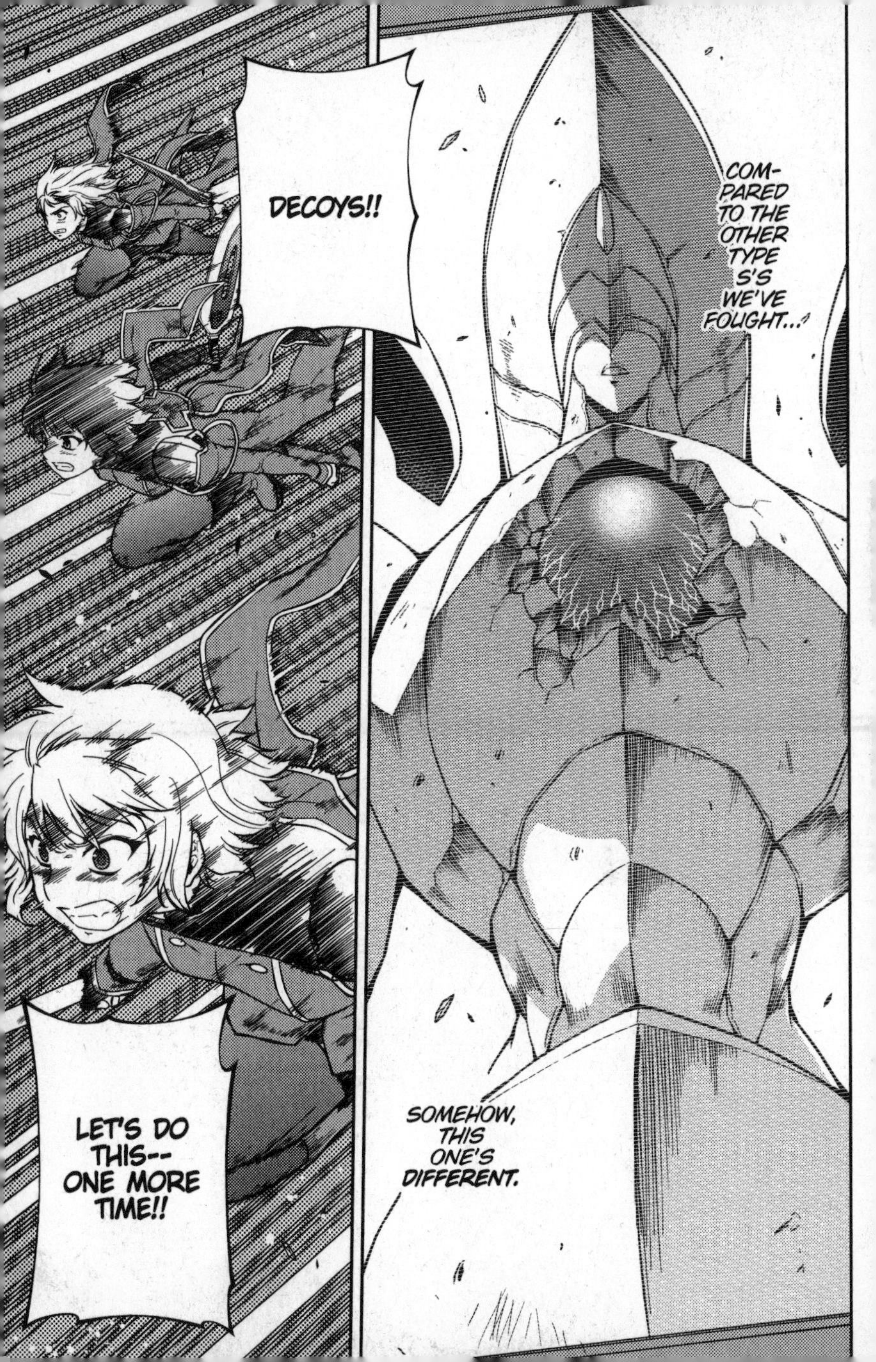
COM-PARED TO THE OTHER TYPE S'S WE'VE FOUGHT...
SOMEHOW, THIS ONE'S DIFFERENT.
DECOYS!!
LET'S DO THIS-- ONE MORE TIME!!

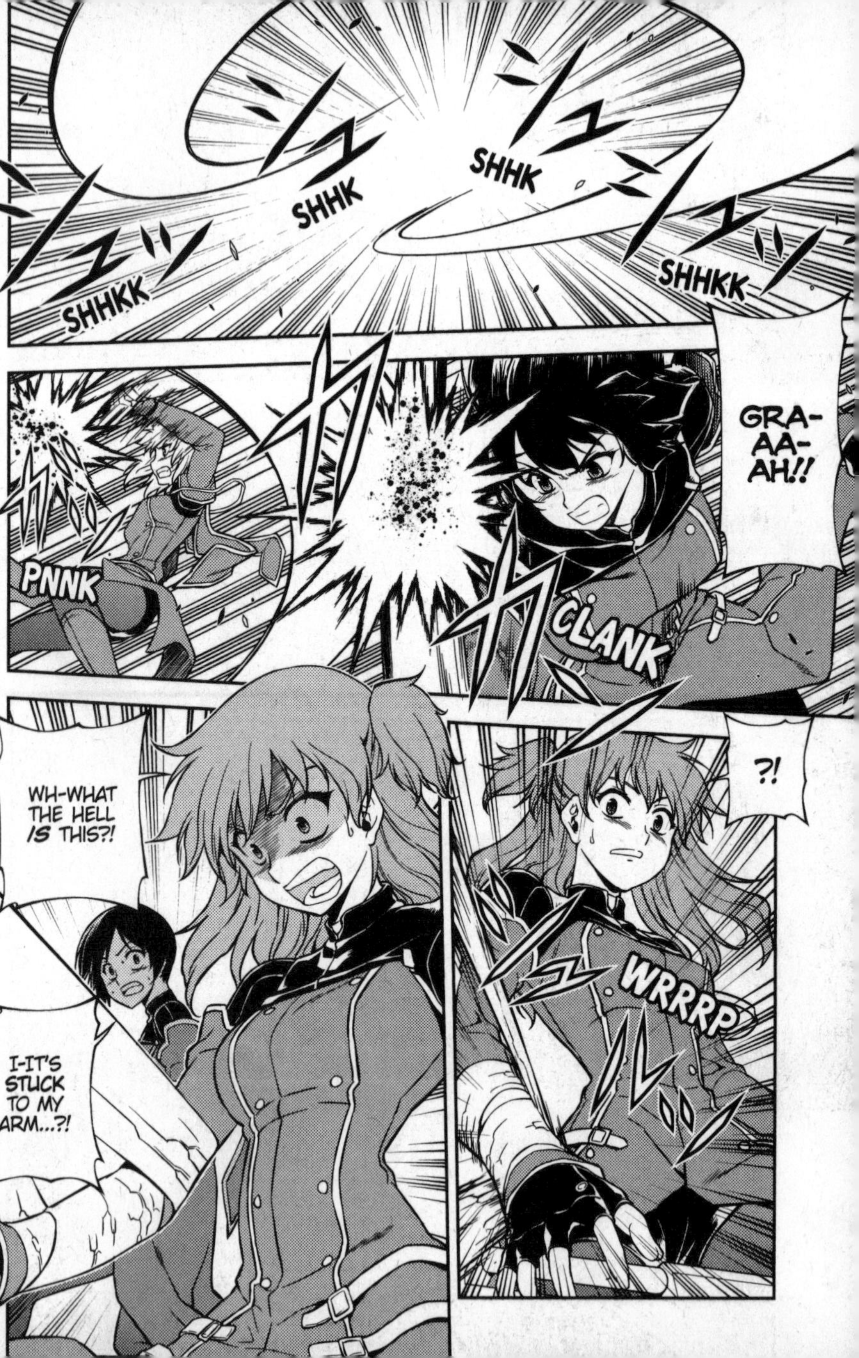
SHHKK
SHHK
SHHK
SHHKK
GRA-AA-AH!!
CLANK
PNNK
?!
WRRRP
WH-WHAT THE HELL *IS* THIS?!
I-IT'S STUCK TO MY ARM...?!

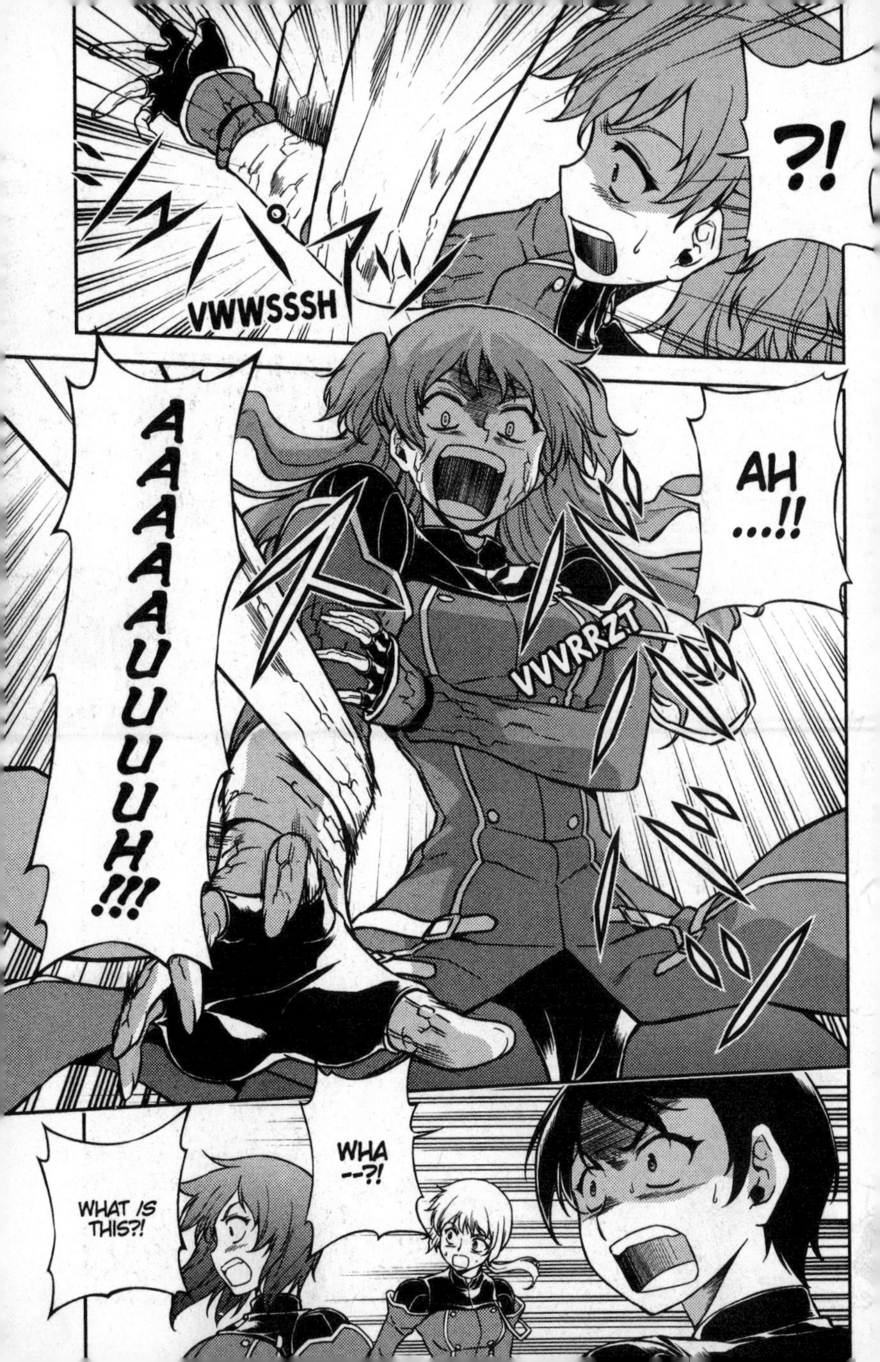
?!
VWWSSSH
AH ...!!
VVVRRZT
AAAAAUUUUUH!!!
WHA--?!
WHAT IS THIS?!

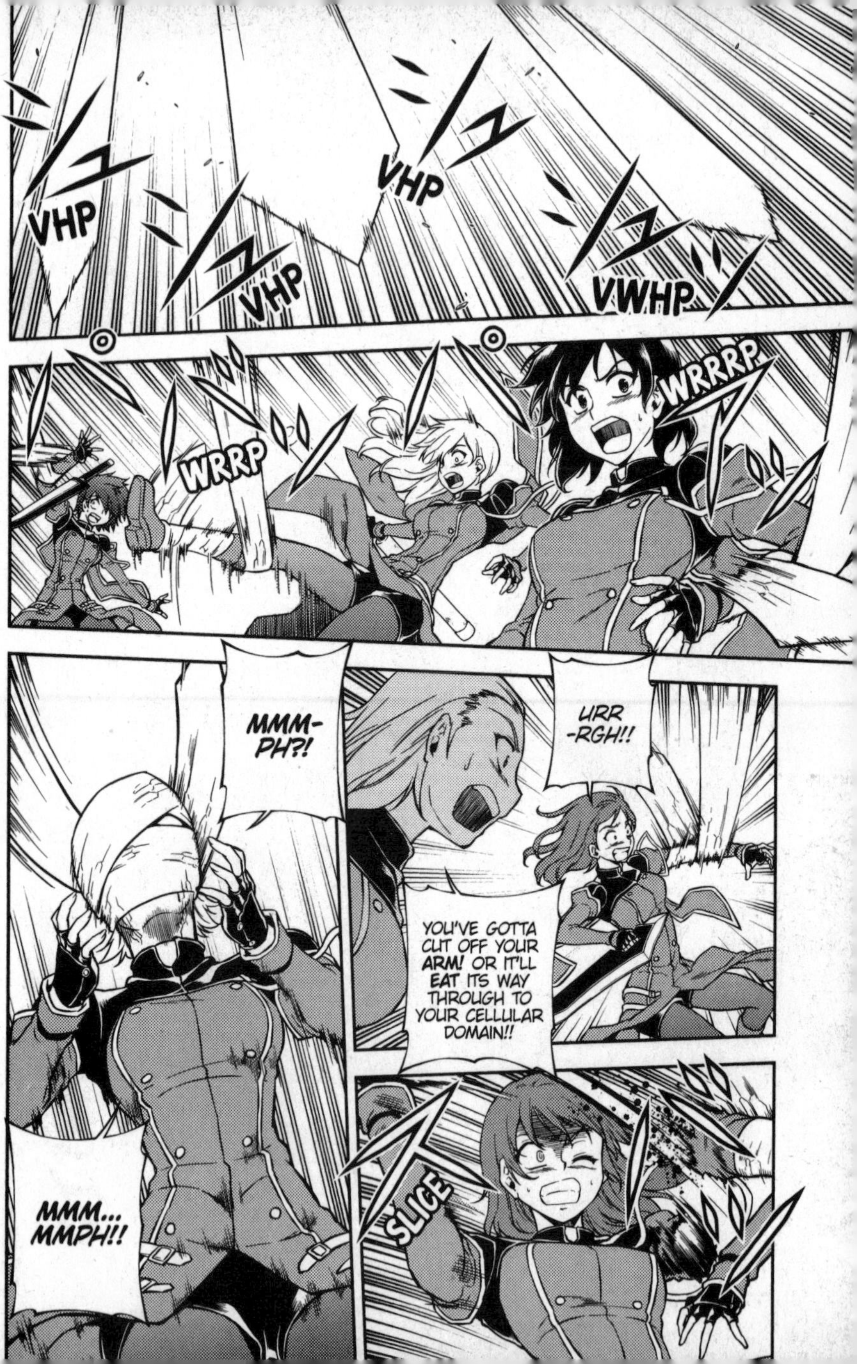
VWHP
VHP
VHP
VHP
WRRRP
WRRP
URR -RGH!!
YOU'VE GOTTA CUT OFF YOUR ARM! OR IT'LL EAT ITS WAY THROUGH TO YOUR CELLULAR DOMAIN!!
SLICE
MMM-PH?!
MMM... MMPH!!

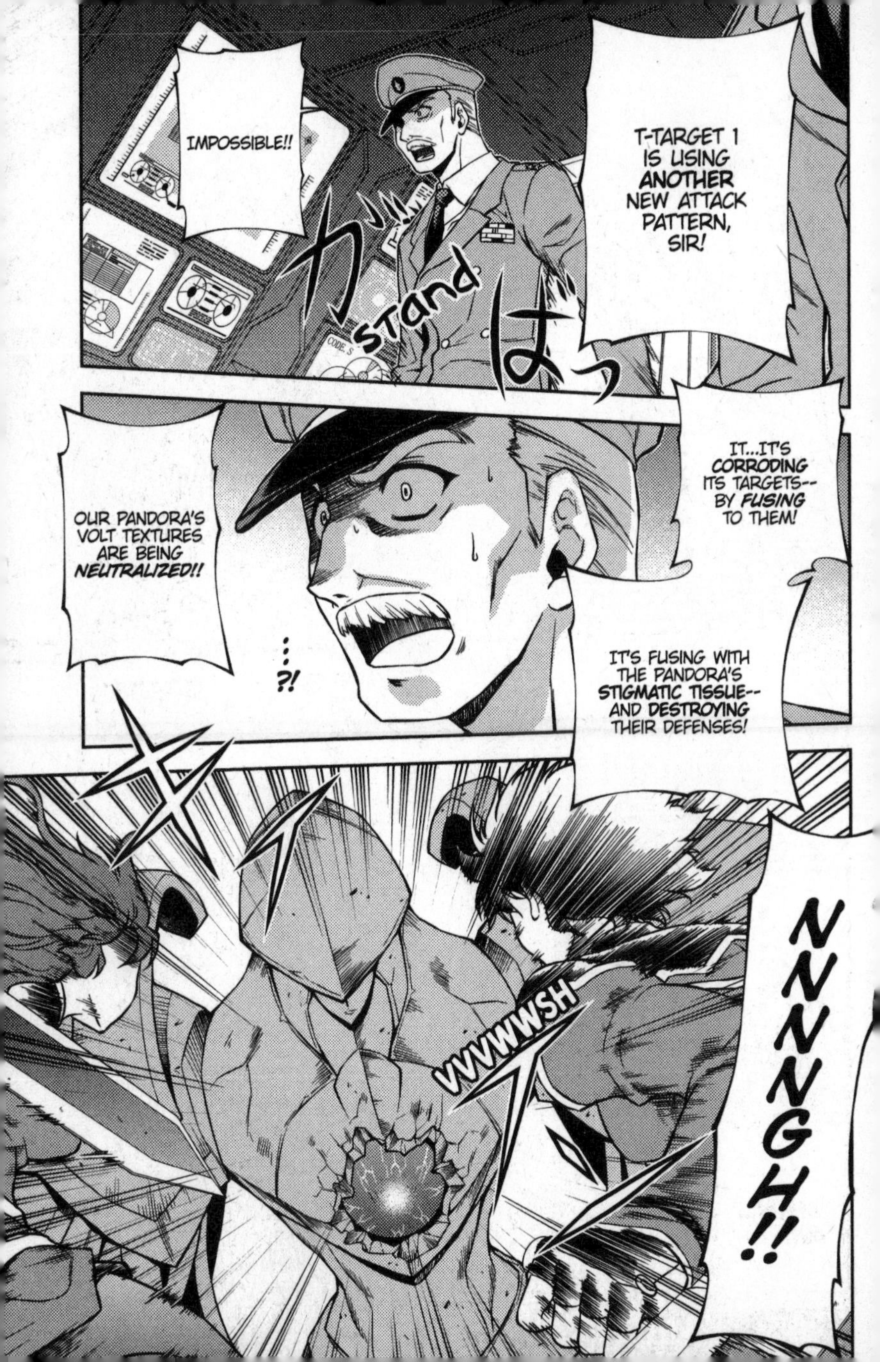
T-TARGET 1 IS USING ANOTHER NEW ATTACK PATTERN, SIR!
IMPOSSIBLE!!
stand
IT...IT'S CORRODING ITS TARGETS-- BY FUSING TO THEM!
IT'S FUSING WITH THE PANDORA'S STIGMATIC TISSUE-- AND DESTROYING THEIR DEFENSES!
OUR PANDORA'S VOLT TEXTURES ARE BEING NEUTRALIZED!!
...?!
NNNNGH!!
VVVWWSH

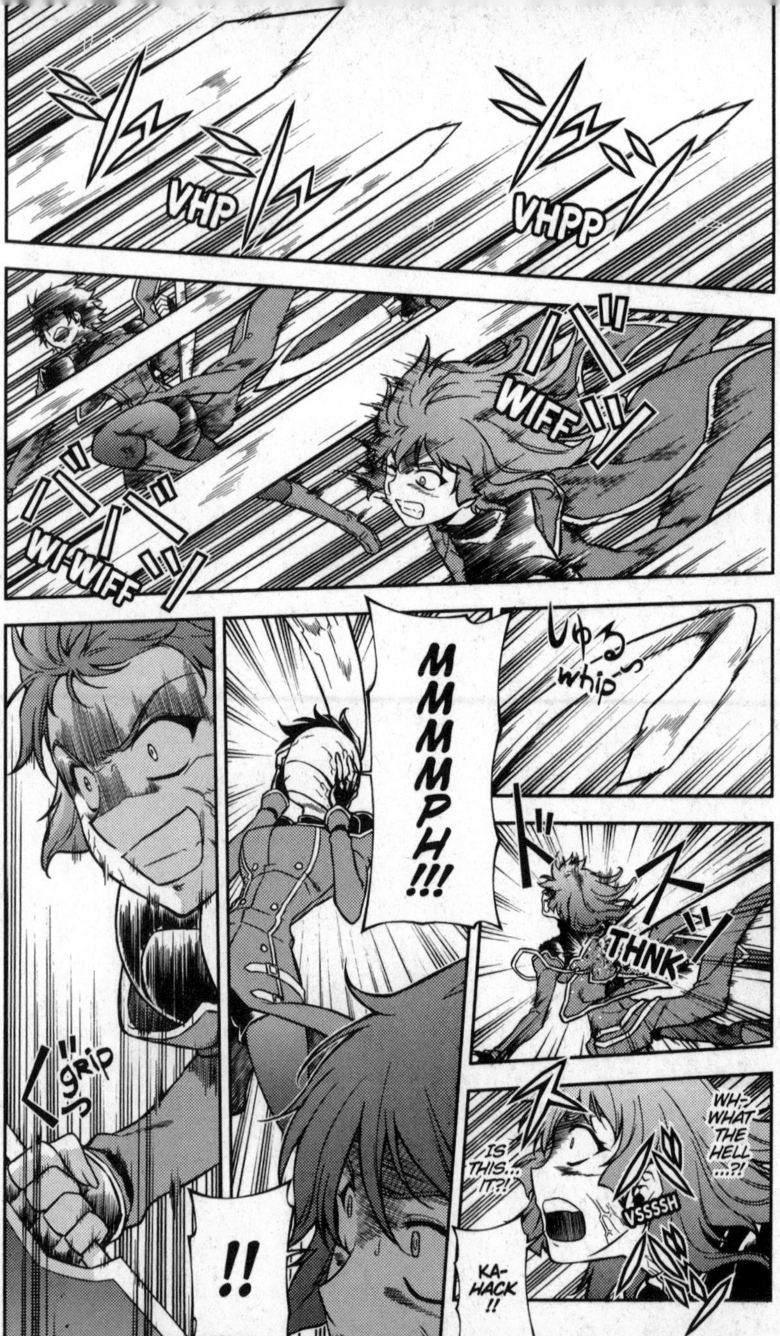
VHPP
VHP
WIFF
WI-WIFF
しゅる whip
THNK
WH- WHAT THE HELL...?!
IS THIS... IT?!
VSSSSH
KA-HACK!!
MMMMMPH!!!
grip
!!

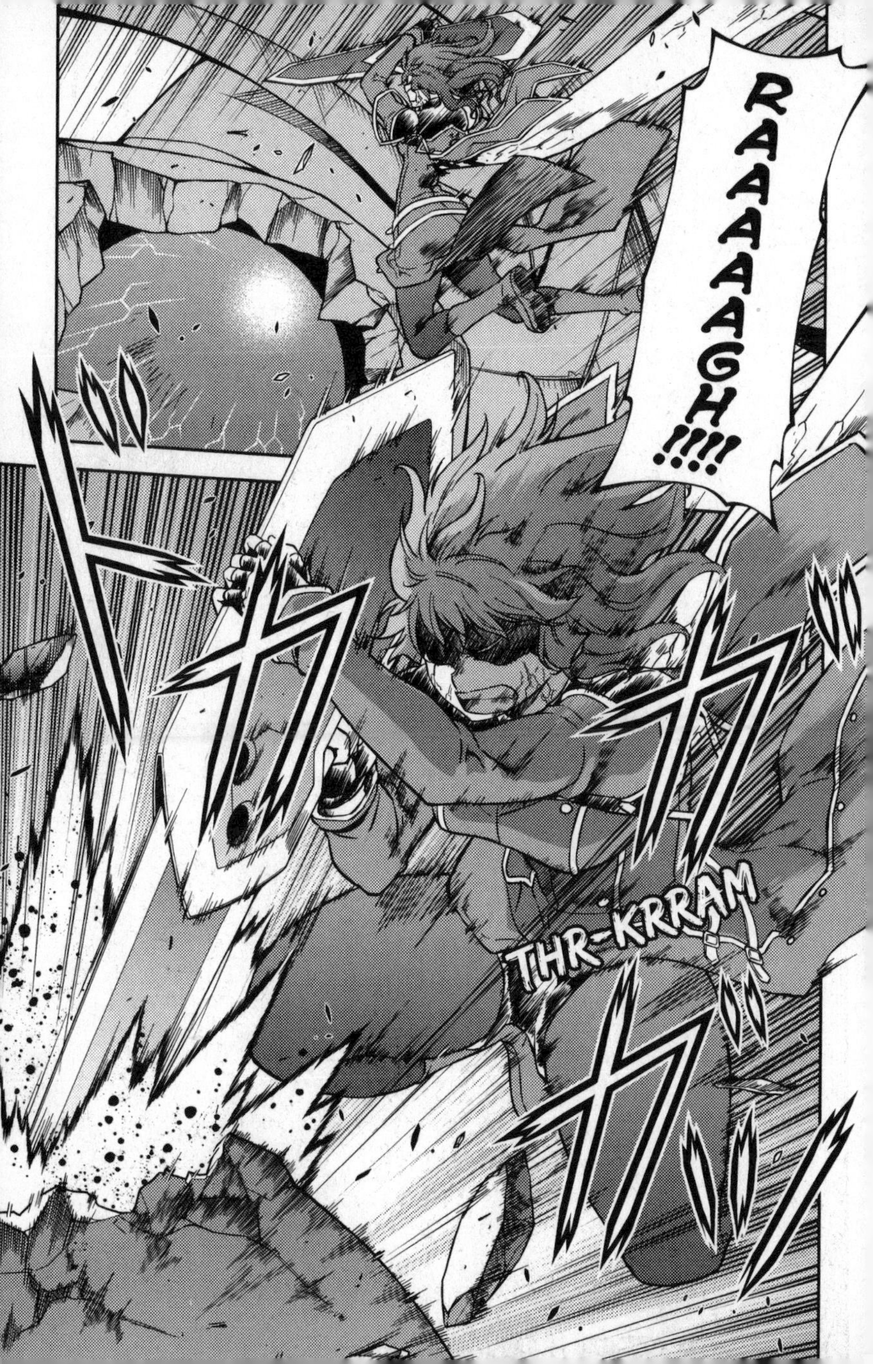
RAAAAAGH!!!!
THR-KRRAM

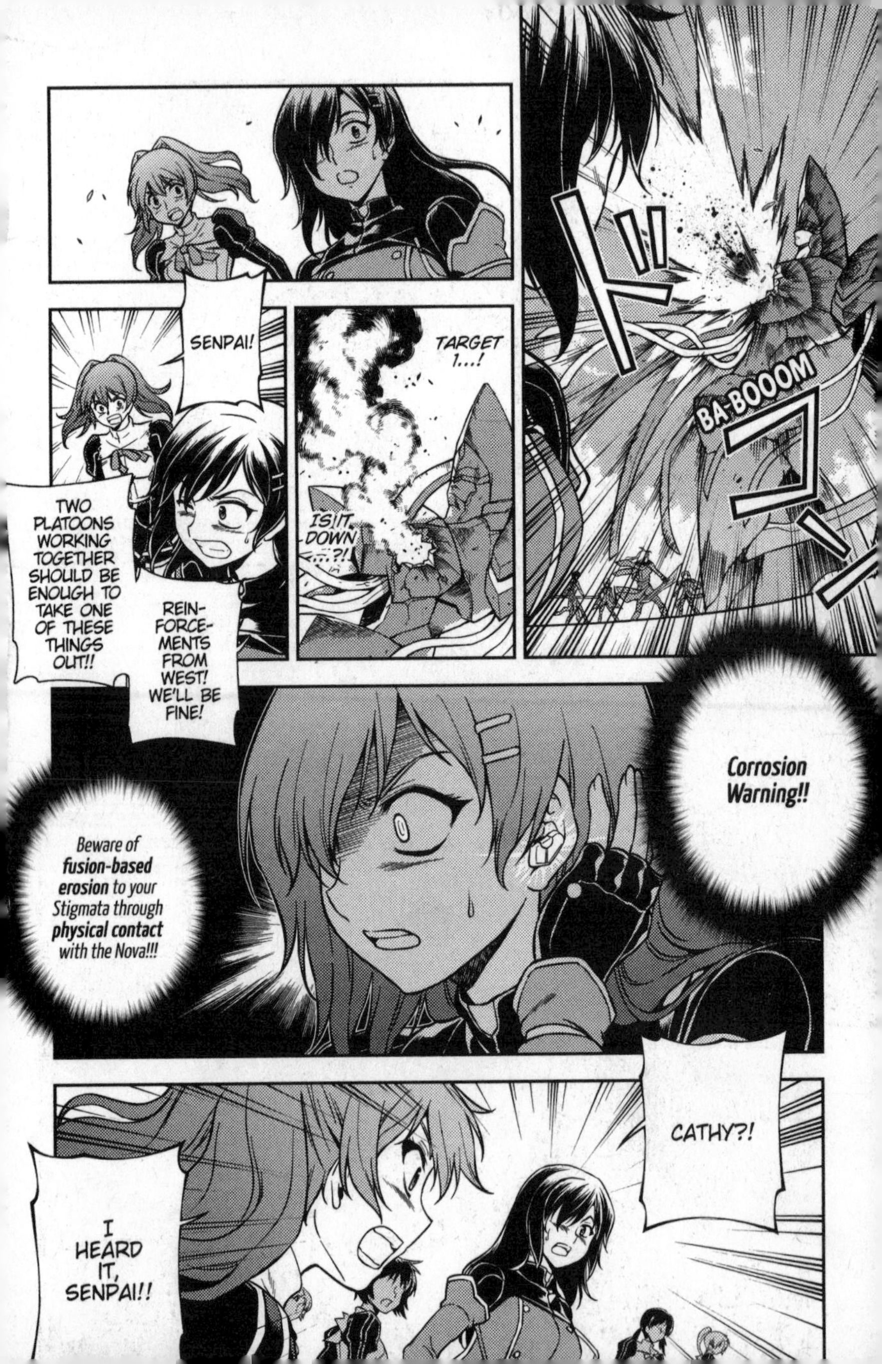
BA-BOOOM
TARGET 1...!
IS IT DOWN ...?!
SENPAI!
REIN-FORCE-MENTS FROM WEST! WE'LL BE FINE!
TWO PLATOONS WORKING TOGETHER SHOULD BE ENOUGH TO TAKE ONE OF THESE THINGS OUT!!
Corrosion Warning!!
Beware of fusion-based erosion to your Stigmata through physical contact with the Nova!!!
CATHY?!
I HEARD IT, SENPAI!!

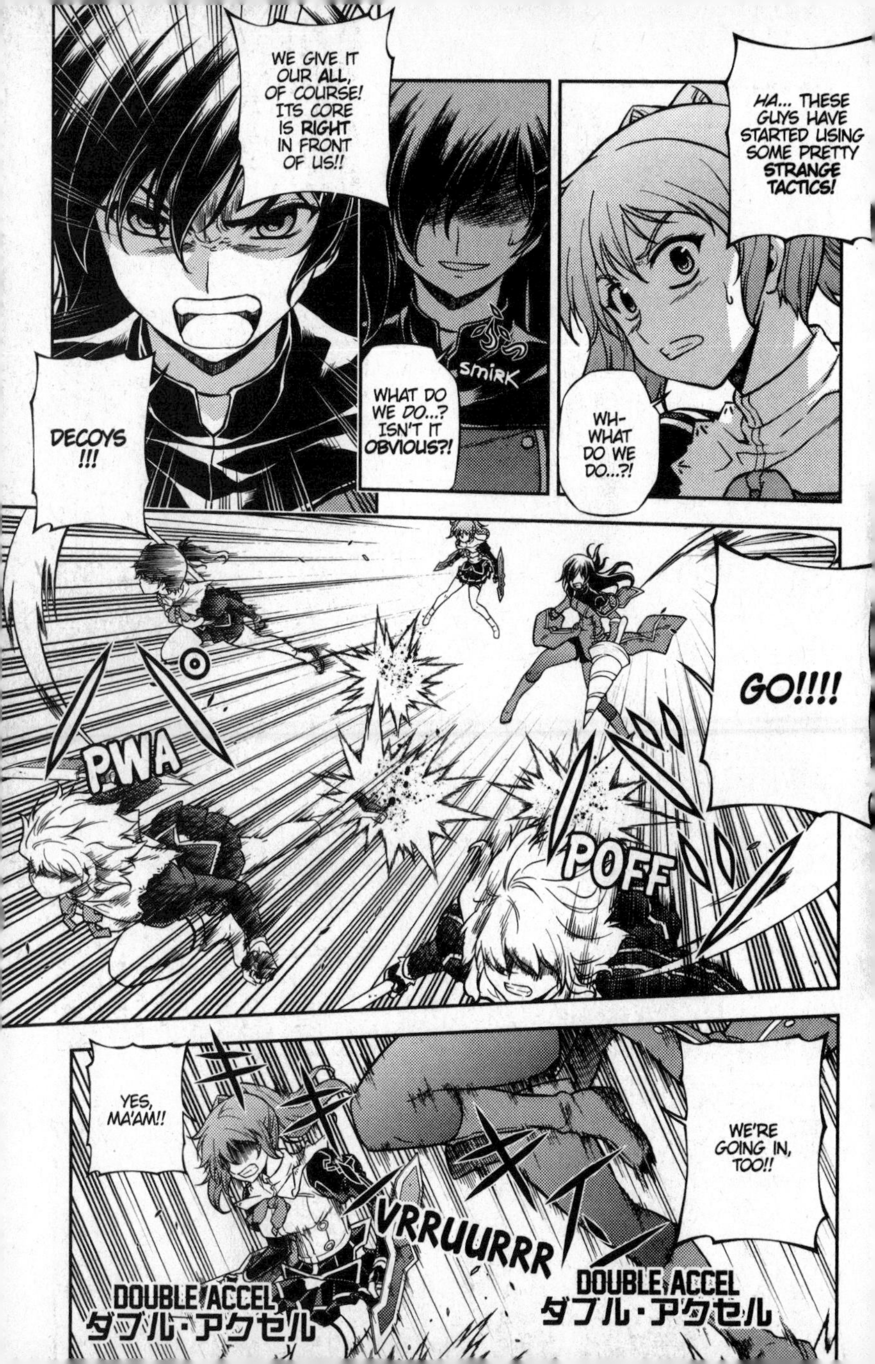
HA... THESE GUYS HAVE STARTED USING SOME PRETTY STRANGE TACTICS!
WH-WHAT DO WE DO...?!
WHAT DO WE DO...? ISN'T IT OBVIOUS?!
smirk
WE GIVE IT OUR ALL, OF COURSE! ITS CORE IS RIGHT IN FRONT OF US!!
DECOYS !!!
GO!!!!
POFF
PWA
WE'RE GOING IN, TOO!!
DOUBLE ACCEL
ダブル・アクセル
VRRUURRR
YES, MA'AM!!
DOUBLE ACCEL
ダブル・アクセル

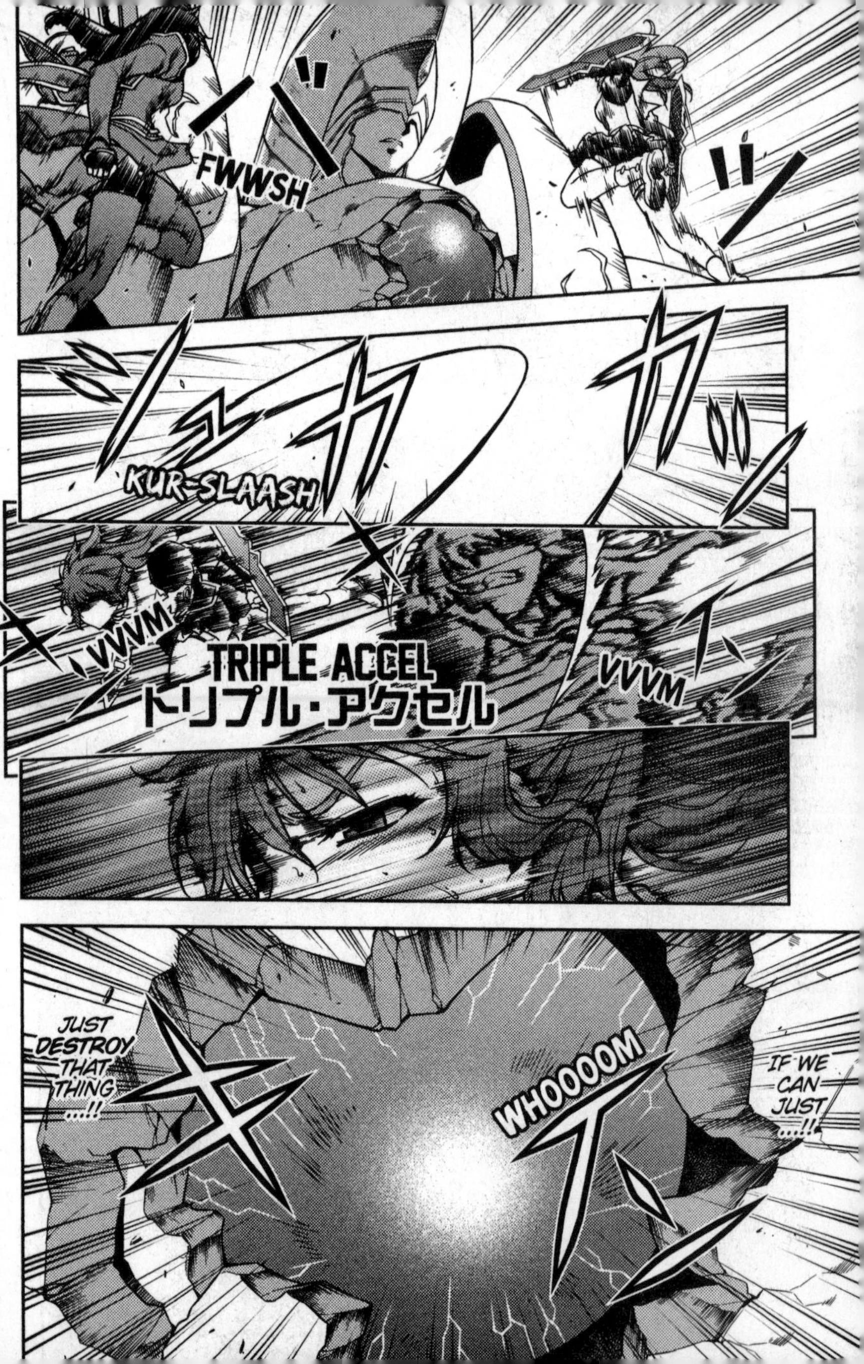
FWWSH
KUR-SLAASH
VVVM
TRIPLE ACCEL
トリプル・アクセル
VVVM
IF WE CAN JUST ...!!
WHOOOOM
JUST DESTROY THAT THING ...!!

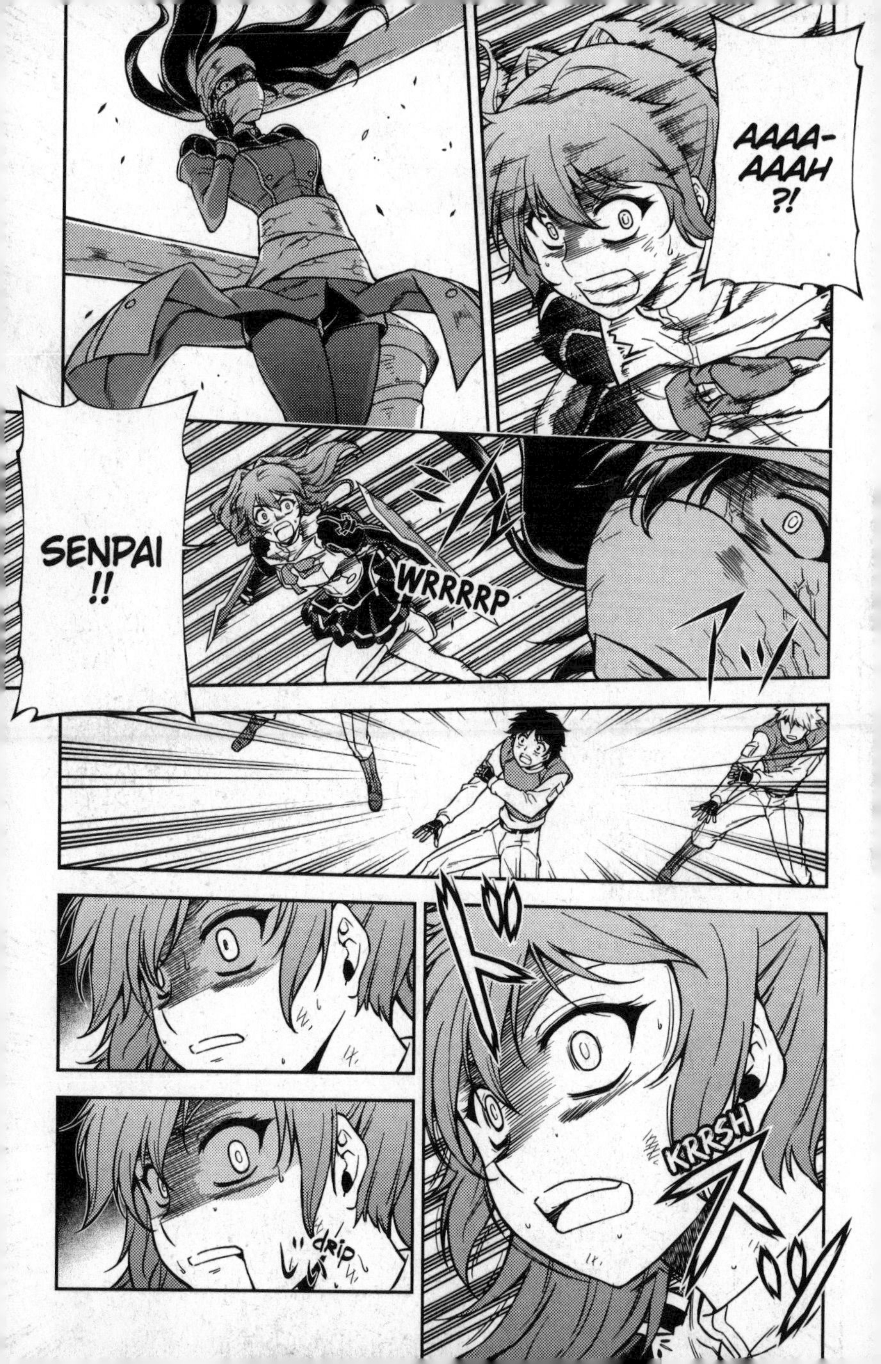
AAAA-AAAH ?!
WRRRRP
SENPAI !!
KRRSH
drip

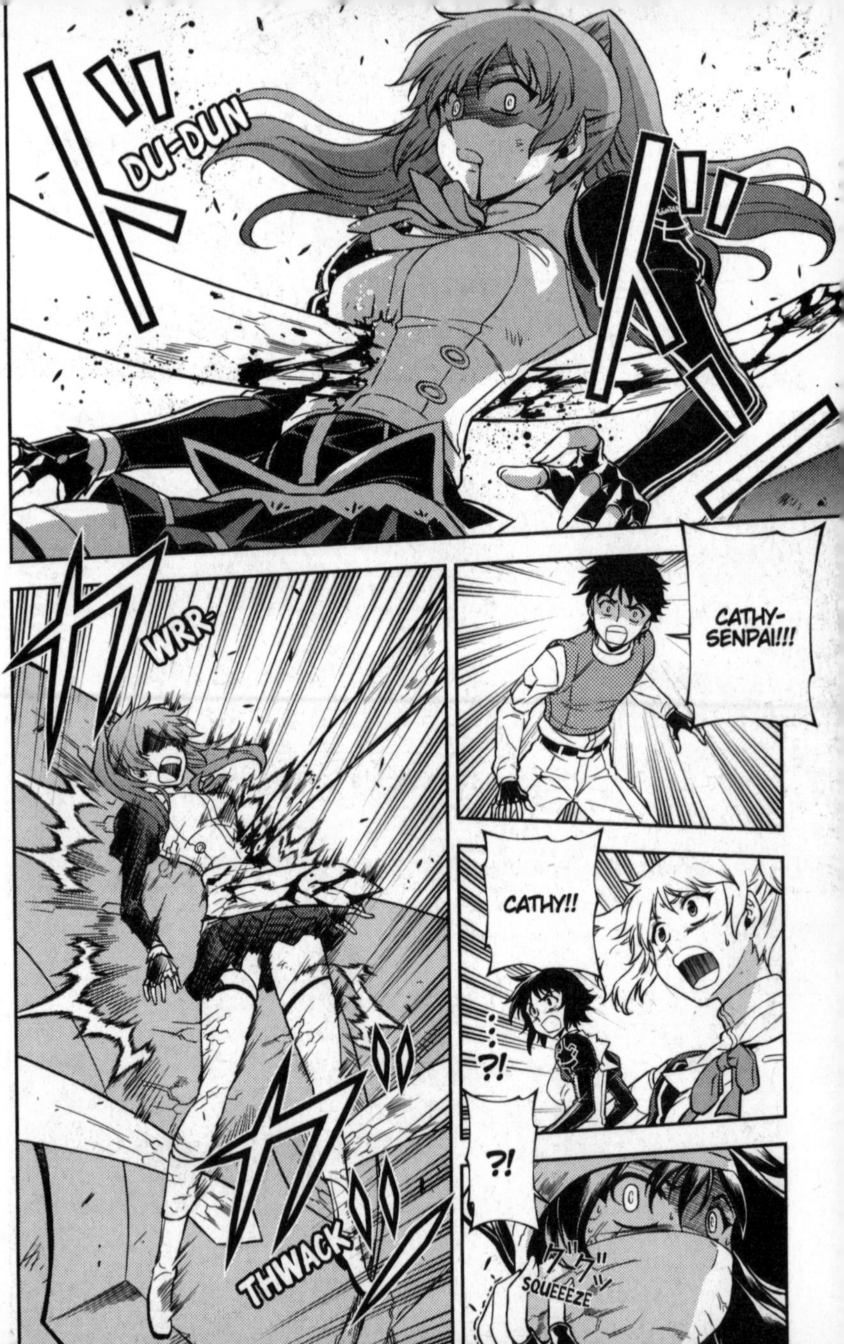
DU-DUN
CATHY-SENPAI!!!
CATHY!!
...?!
?!
SQUEEEZE
WRR
THWACK

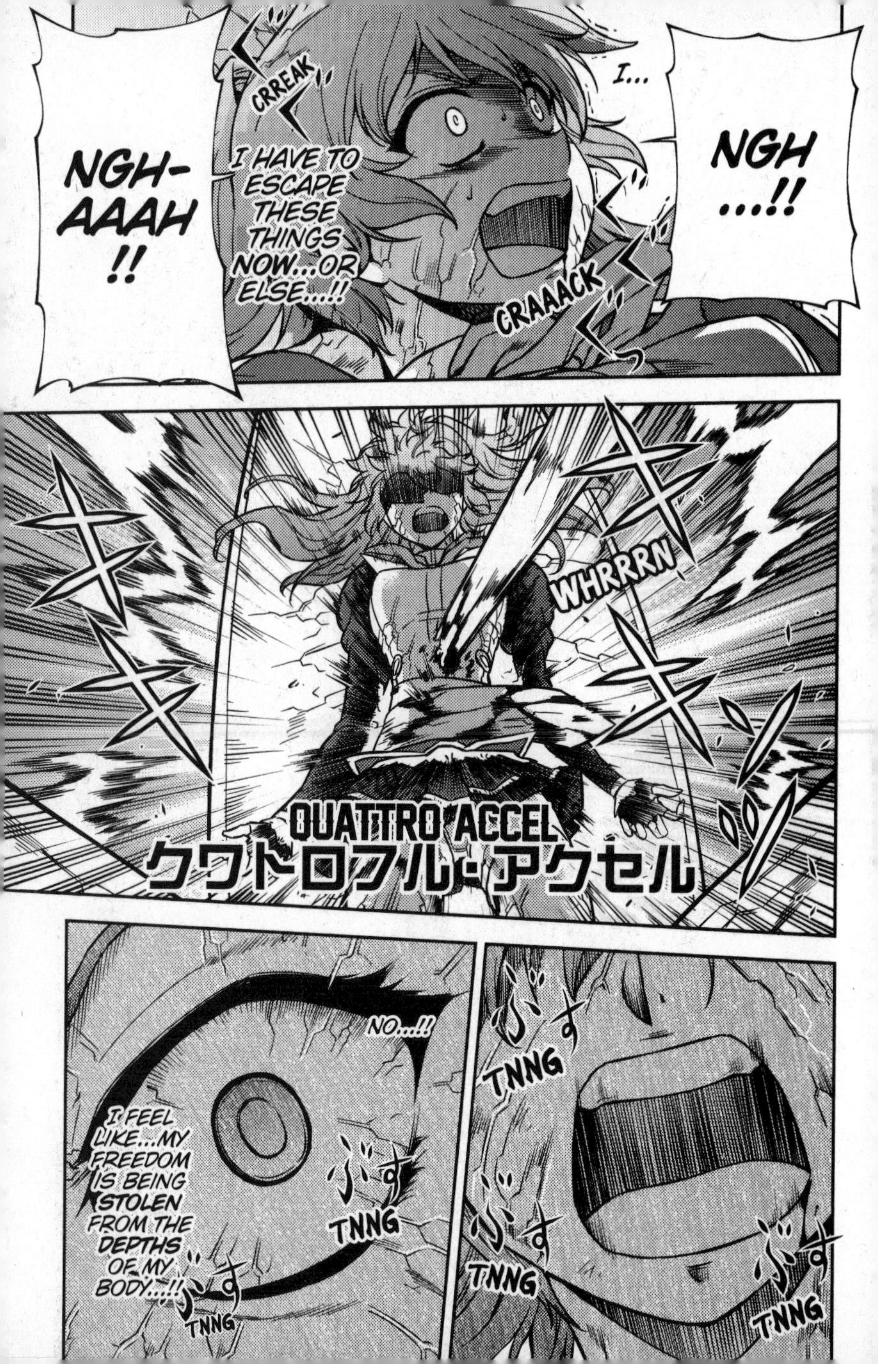
I...
NGH ...!!
CRREAK
I HAVE TO ESCAPE THESE THINGS NOW...OR ELSE...!!
CRAAACK
NGH-AAAH !!
WHRRRN
QUATTRO ACCEL
クワトロフル・アクセル
ぶす
TNNG
ぶす
TNNG
ぶす
TNNG
NO...!!
I FEEL LIKE...MY FREEDOM IS BEING STOLEN FROM THE DEPTHS OF MY BODY...!!
ぶす
TNNG
ぶす
TNNG

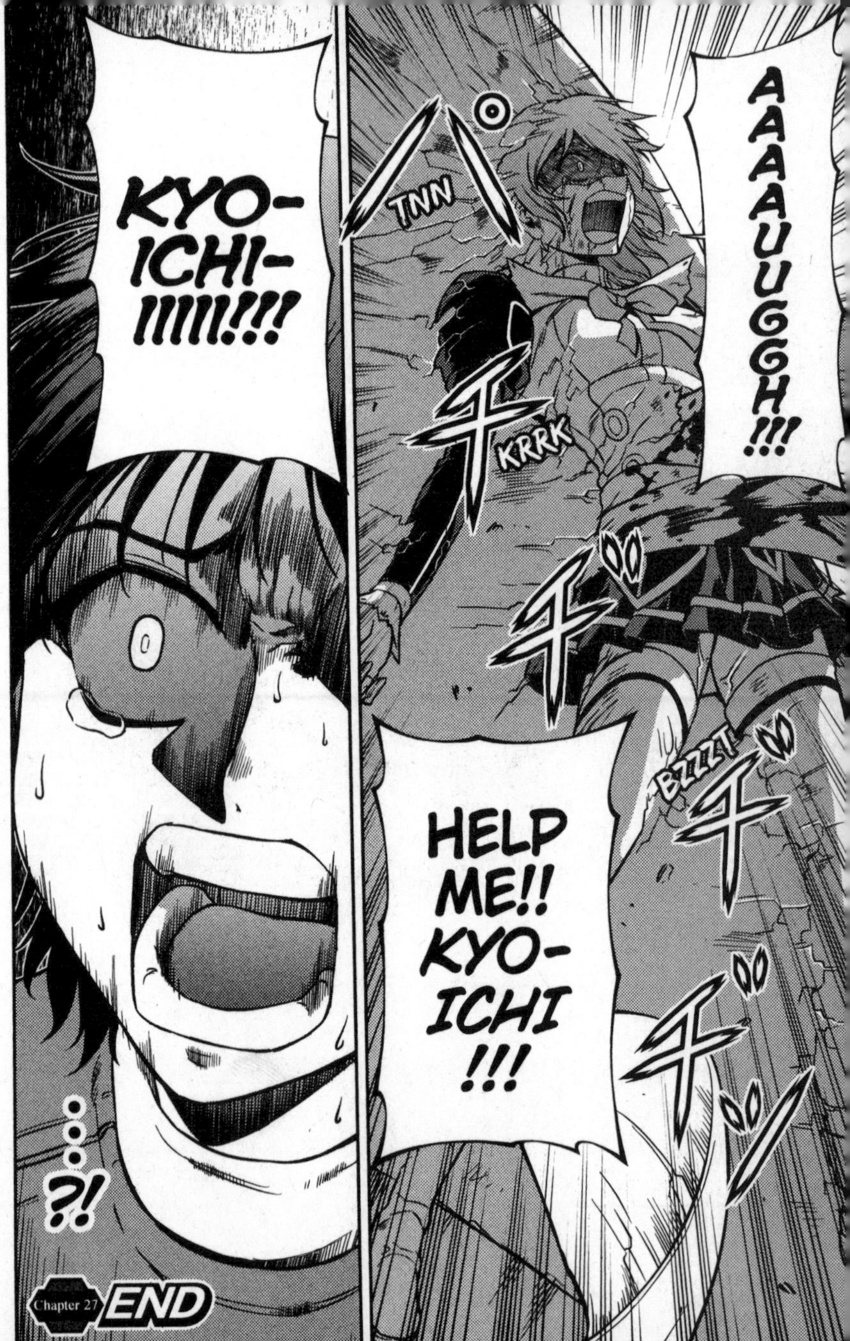
AAAAUUGGGH!!!
TNN
KRRK
BZZZT
HELP ME!! KYO-ICHI!!!
KYO-ICHI-!!!!!!!!!
.....?!

Chapter 27 END

FREEZING VOLUME.5
HIGHLIGHT SCENE

FREEZING Vol.5

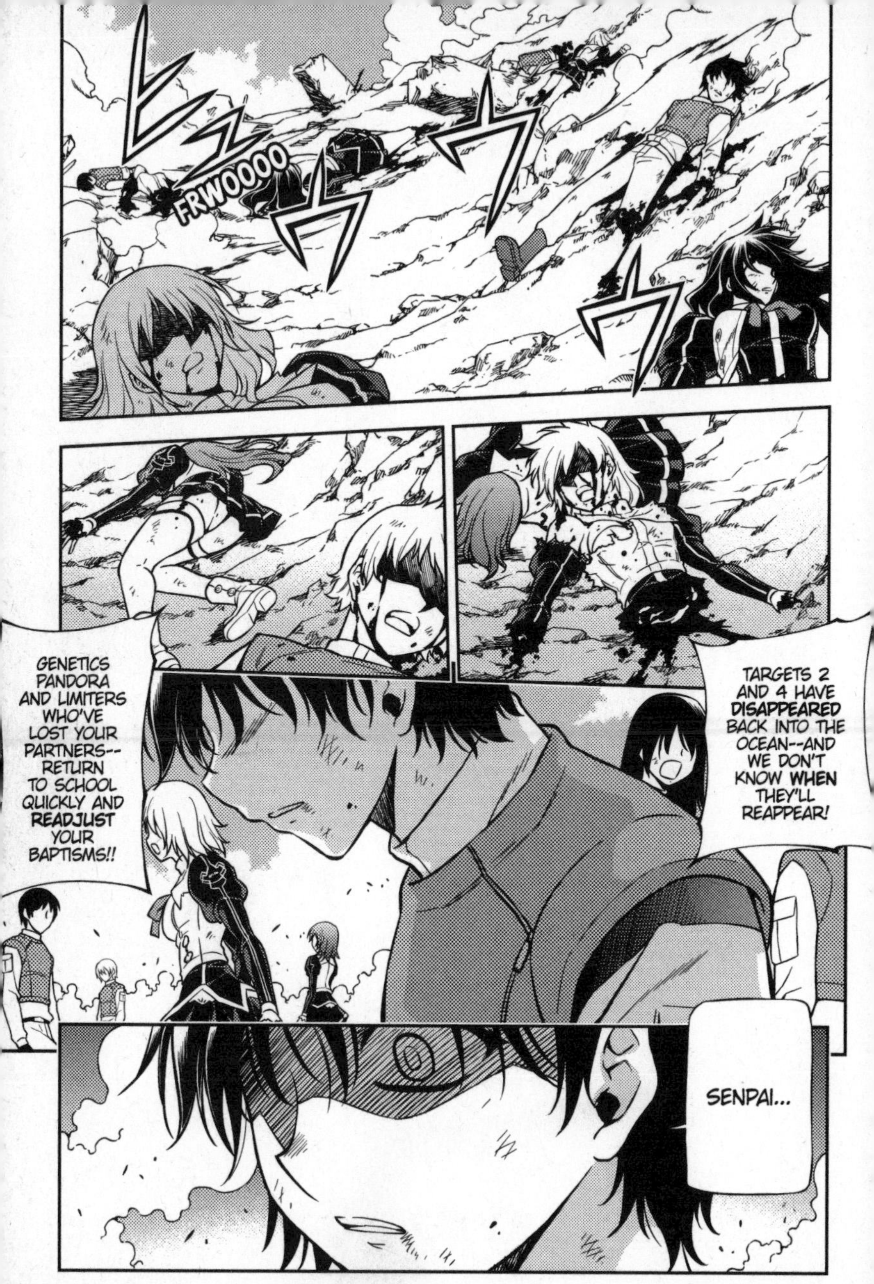
FRWOOOO
TARGETS 2 AND 4 HAVE DISAPPEARED BACK INTO THE OCEAN--AND WE DON'T KNOW WHEN THEY'LL REAPPEAR!
GENETICS PANDORA AND LIMITERS WHO'VE LOST YOUR PARTNERS--RETURN TO SCHOOL QUICKLY AND READJUST YOUR BAPTISMS!!
SENPAI...

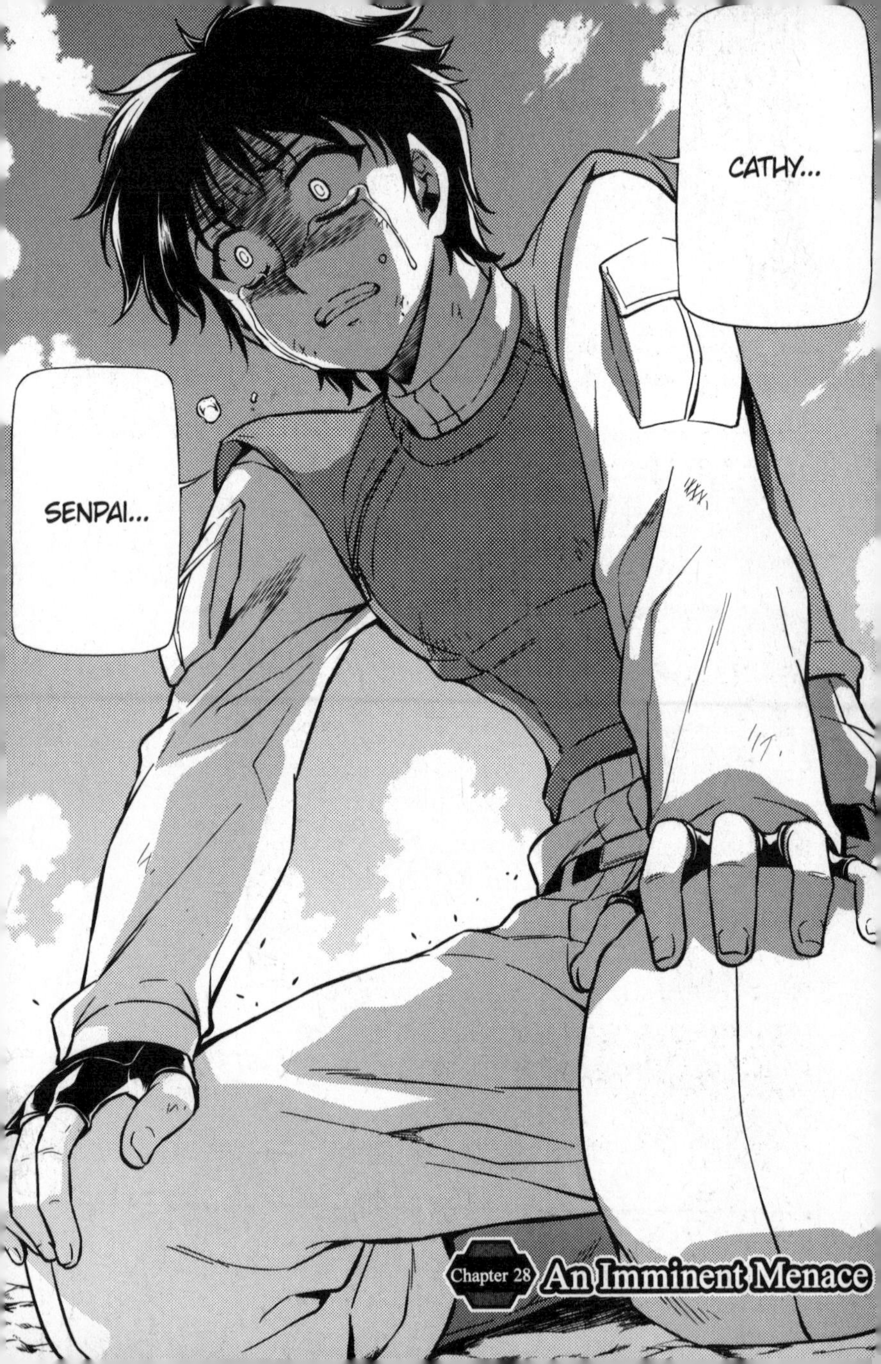
CATHY...
SENPAI...

Chapter 28 An Imminent Menace

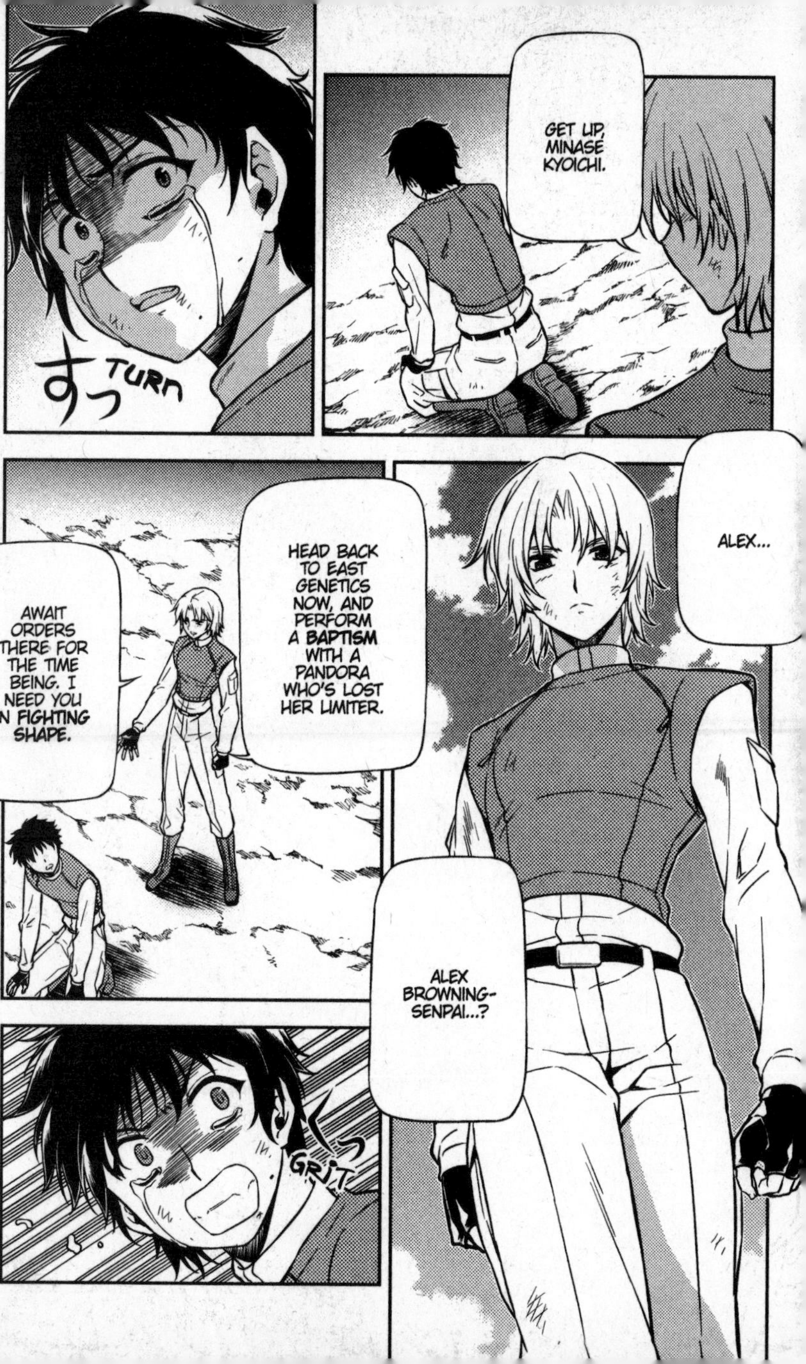
GET UP, MINASE KYOICHI.
すっ TURN
ALEX...
ALEX BROWNING-SENPAI...?
HEAD BACK TO EAST GENETICS NOW, AND PERFORM A **BAPTISM** WITH A PANDORA WHO'S LOST HER LIMITER.
AWAIT ORDERS THERE FOR THE TIME BEING. I NEED YOU IN **FIGHTING SHAPE.**
GRIT

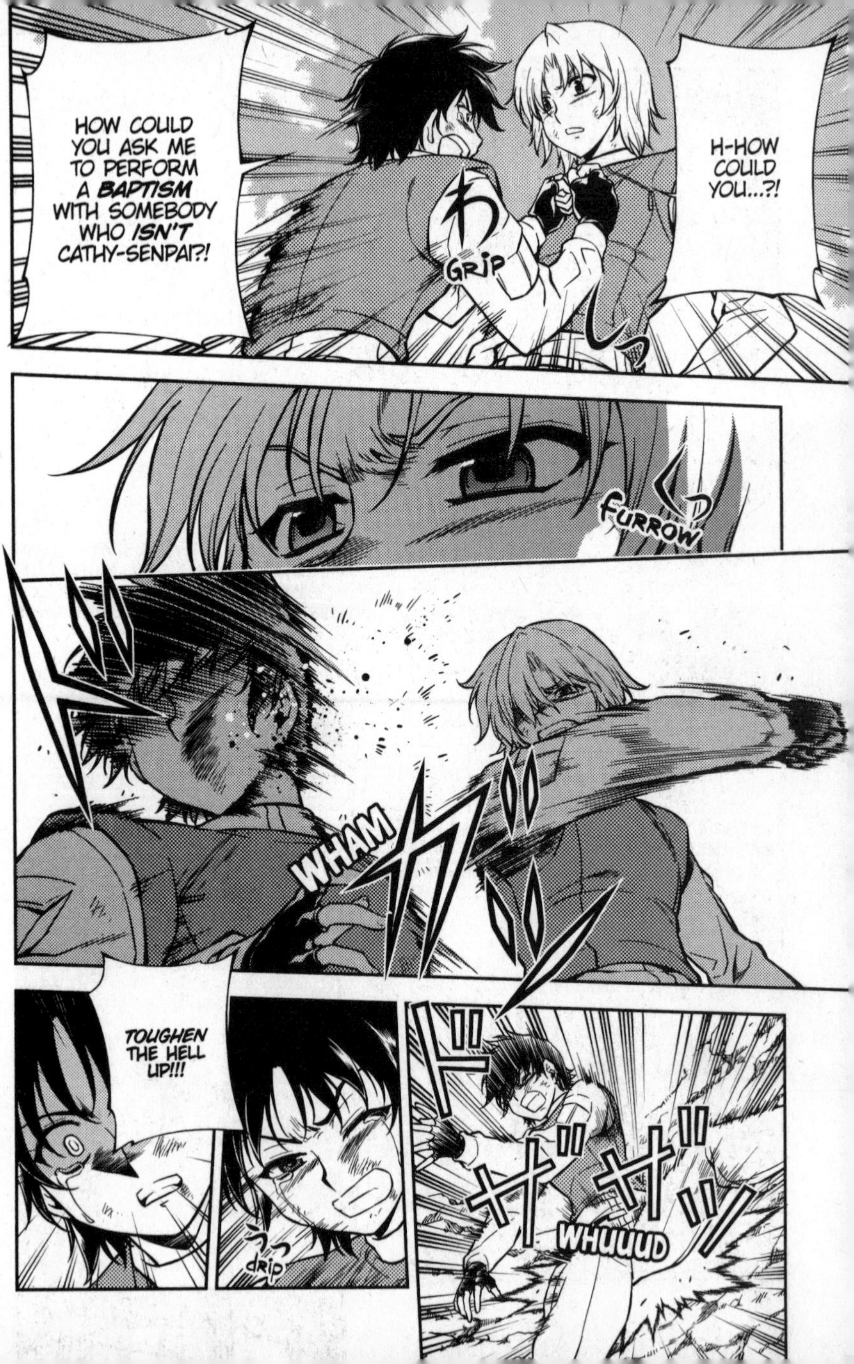
H-HOW COULD YOU...?!
HOW COULD YOU ASK ME TO PERFORM A *BAPTISM* WITH SOMEBODY WHO *ISN'T* CATHY-SENPAI?!
GRIP
FURROW
WHAM
WHUUUD
drip
TOUGHEN THE HELL UP!!!

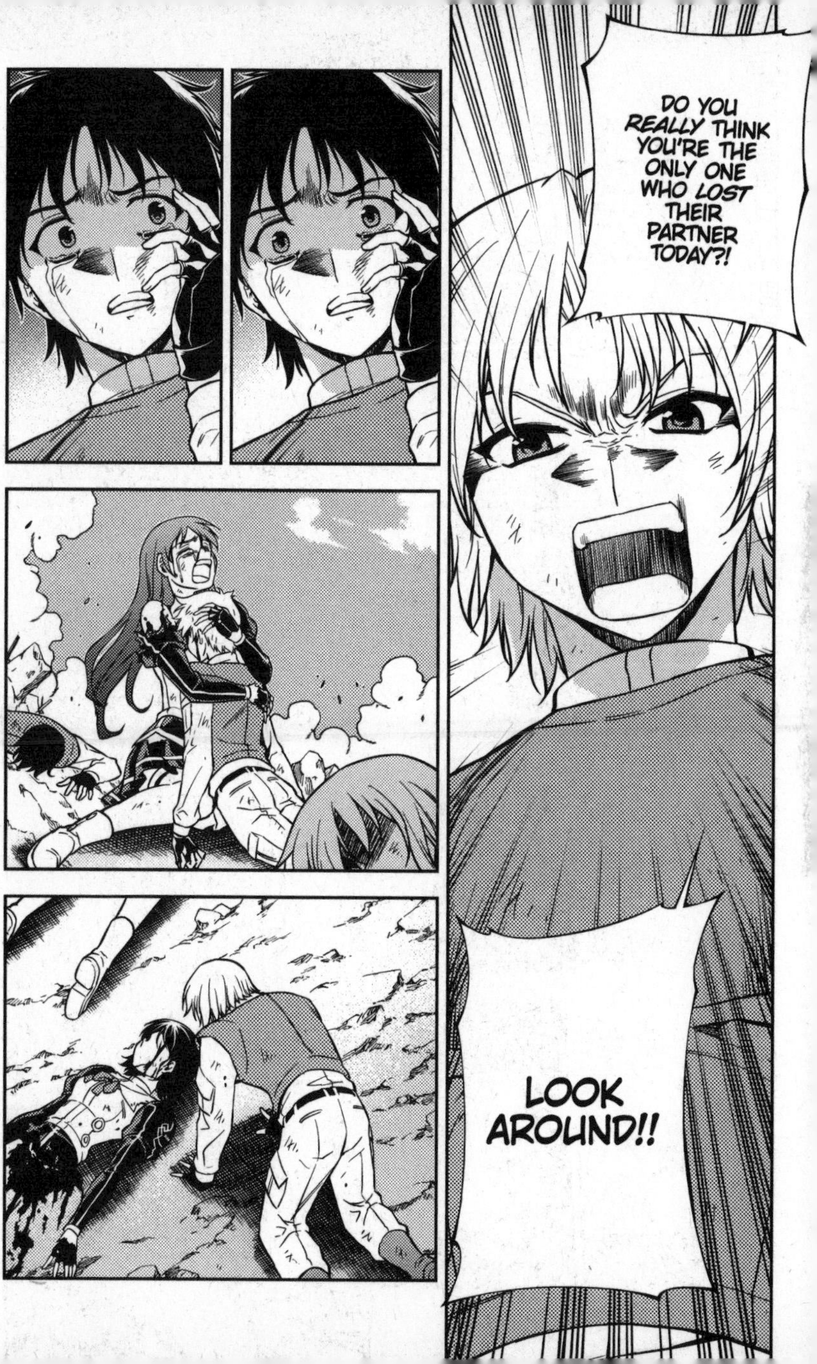
DO YOU REALLY THINK YOU'RE THE ONLY ONE WHO LOST THEIR PARTNER TODAY?!
LOOK AROUND!!

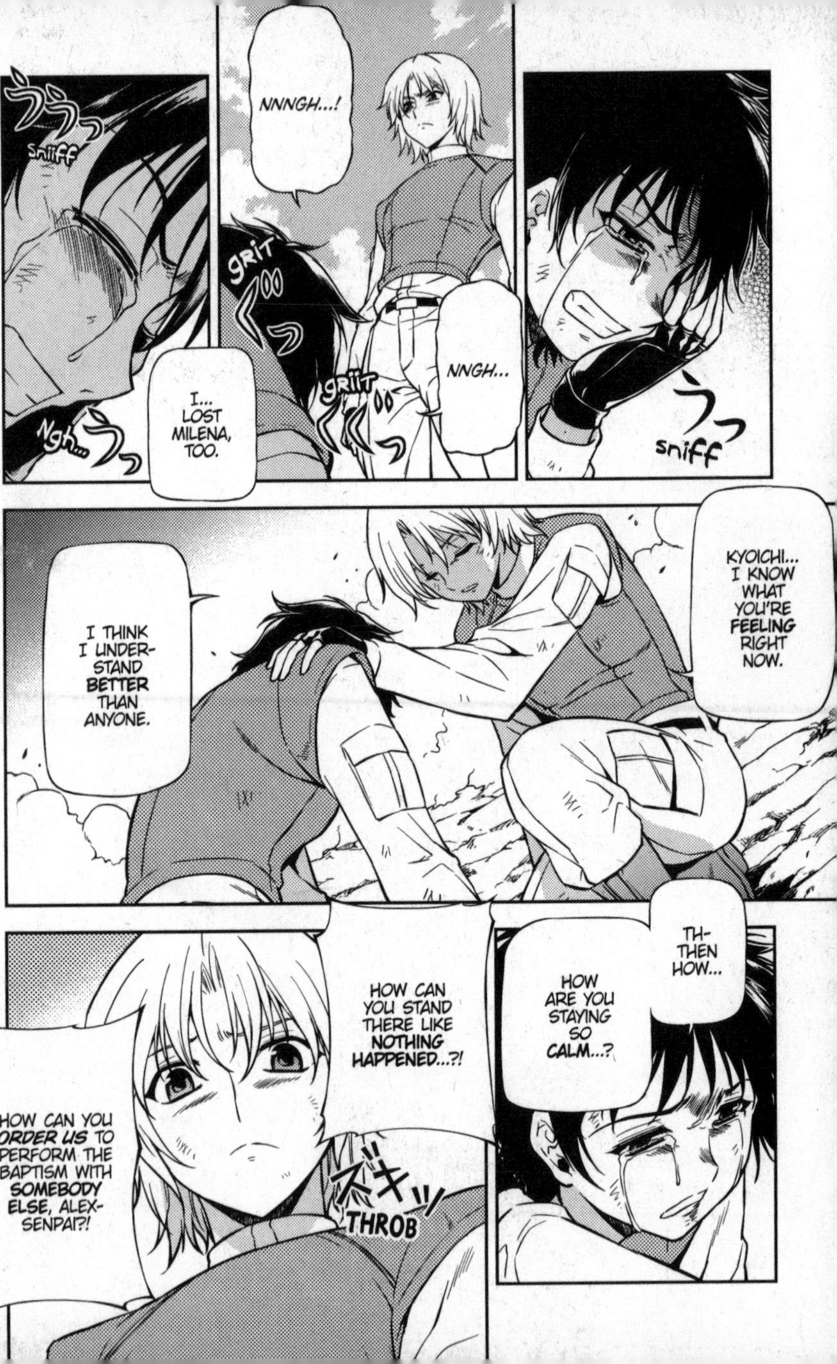
うっ
sniff
NNNGH...!
grit
くっ
NNGH...
griit
くっ
I... LOST MILENA, TOO.
ううっ
sniff
Ngh... うっ
KYOICHI... I KNOW WHAT YOU'RE FEELING RIGHT NOW.
I THINK I UNDERSTAND BETTER THAN ANYONE.
TH-THEN HOW...
HOW ARE YOU STAYING SO CALM...?
HOW CAN YOU STAND THERE LIKE NOTHING HAPPENED...?!
ズキッ
THROB
HOW CAN YOU ORDER US TO PERFORM THE BAPTISM WITH SOMEBODY ELSE, ALEX-SENPAI?!

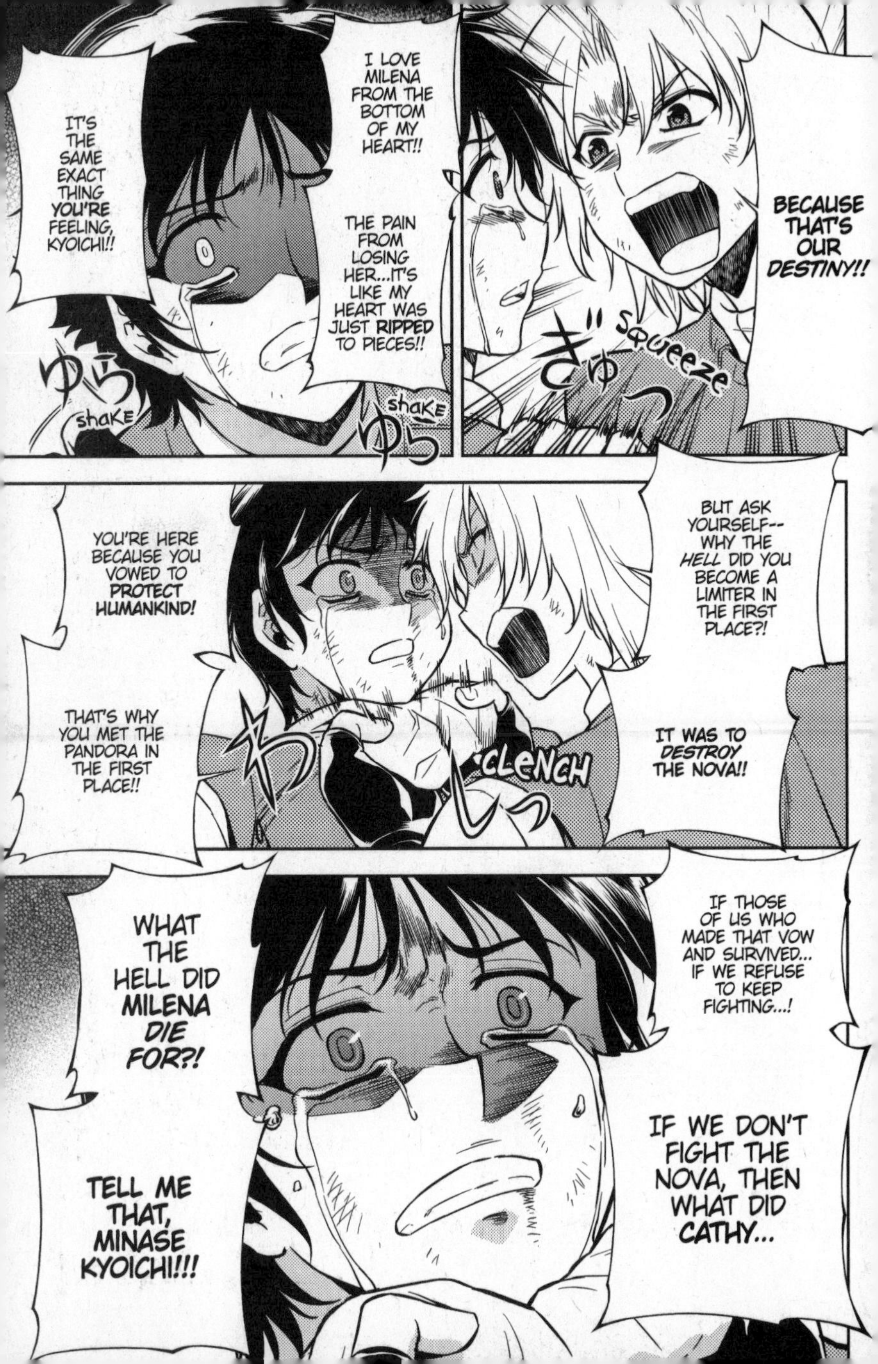
BECAUSE THAT'S OUR DESTINY!!
ぎゅっ squeeze
I LOVE MILENA FROM THE BOTTOM OF MY HEART!!
THE PAIN FROM LOSING HER...IT'S LIKE MY HEART WAS JUST RIPPED TO PIECES!!
shake
IT'S THE SAME EXACT THING YOU'RE FEELING, KYOICHI!!
shake
BUT ASK YOURSELF-- WHY THE HELL DID YOU BECOME A LIMITER IN THE FIRST PLACE?!
IT WAS TO DESTROY THE NOVA!!
YOU'RE HERE BECAUSE YOU VOWED TO PROTECT HUMANKIND!
CLENCH
THAT'S WHY YOU MET THE PANDORA IN THE FIRST PLACE!!
IF THOSE OF US WHO MADE THAT VOW AND SURVIVED... IF WE REFUSE TO KEEP FIGHTING...!
IF WE DON'T FIGHT THE NOVA, THEN WHAT DID CATHY...
WHAT THE HELL DID MILENA DIE FOR?!
TELL ME THAT, MINASE KYOICHI!!!

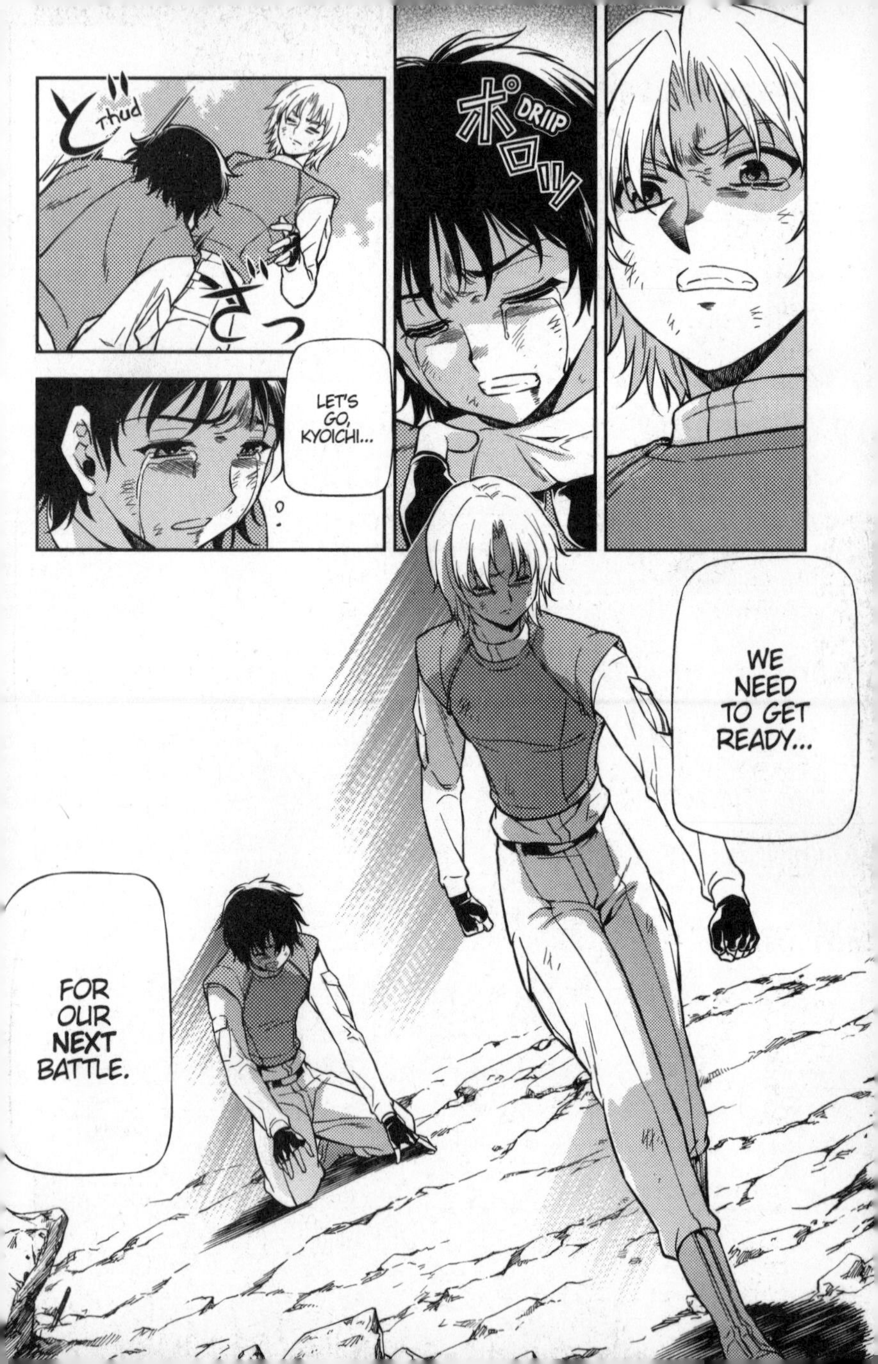
DRIIP
ポロッ
thud
LET'S GO, KYOICHI...
WE NEED TO GET READY...
FOR OUR NEXT BATTLE.

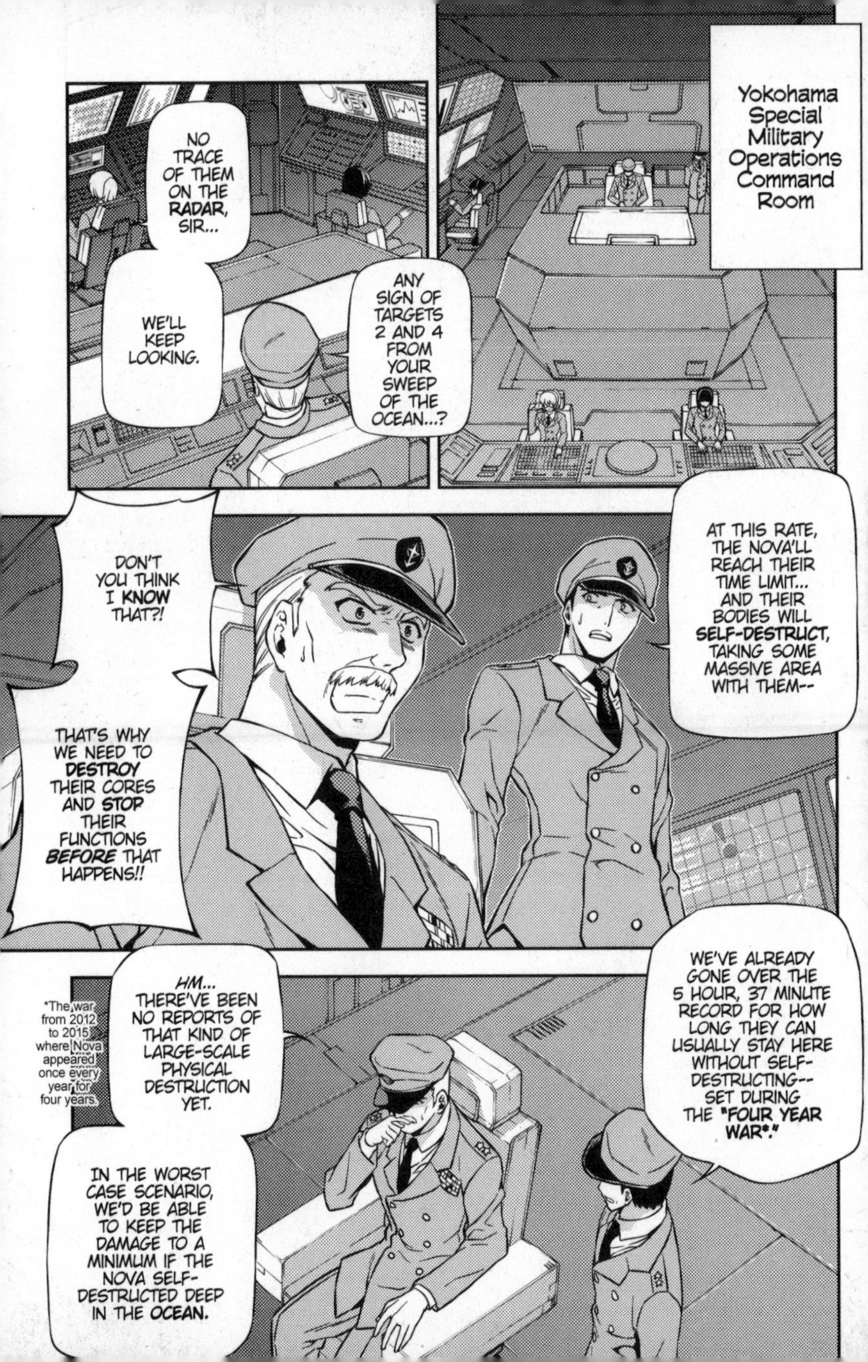
Yokohama Special Military Operations Command Room
ANY SIGN OF TARGETS 2 AND 4 FROM YOUR SWEEP OF THE OCEAN...?
NO TRACE OF THEM ON THE RADAR, SIR...
WE'LL KEEP LOOKING.
AT THIS RATE, THE NOVA'LL REACH THEIR TIME LIMIT... AND THEIR BODIES WILL SELF-DESTRUCT, TAKING SOME MASSIVE AREA WITH THEM--
DON'T YOU THINK I KNOW THAT?!
THAT'S WHY WE NEED TO DESTROY THEIR CORES AND STOP THEIR FUNCTIONS BEFORE THAT HAPPENS!!
WE'VE ALREADY GONE OVER THE 5 HOUR, 37 MINUTE RECORD FOR HOW LONG THEY CAN USUALLY STAY HERE WITHOUT SELF-DESTRUCTING-- SET DURING THE "FOUR YEAR WAR*."
HM... THERE'VE BEEN NO REPORTS OF THAT KIND OF LARGE-SCALE PHYSICAL DESTRUCTION YET.
*The war from 2012 to 2015 where Nova appeared once every year for four years.
IN THE WORST CASE SCENARIO, WE'D BE ABLE TO KEEP THE DAMAGE TO A MINIMUM IF THE NOVA SELF-DESTRUCTED DEEP IN THE OCEAN.

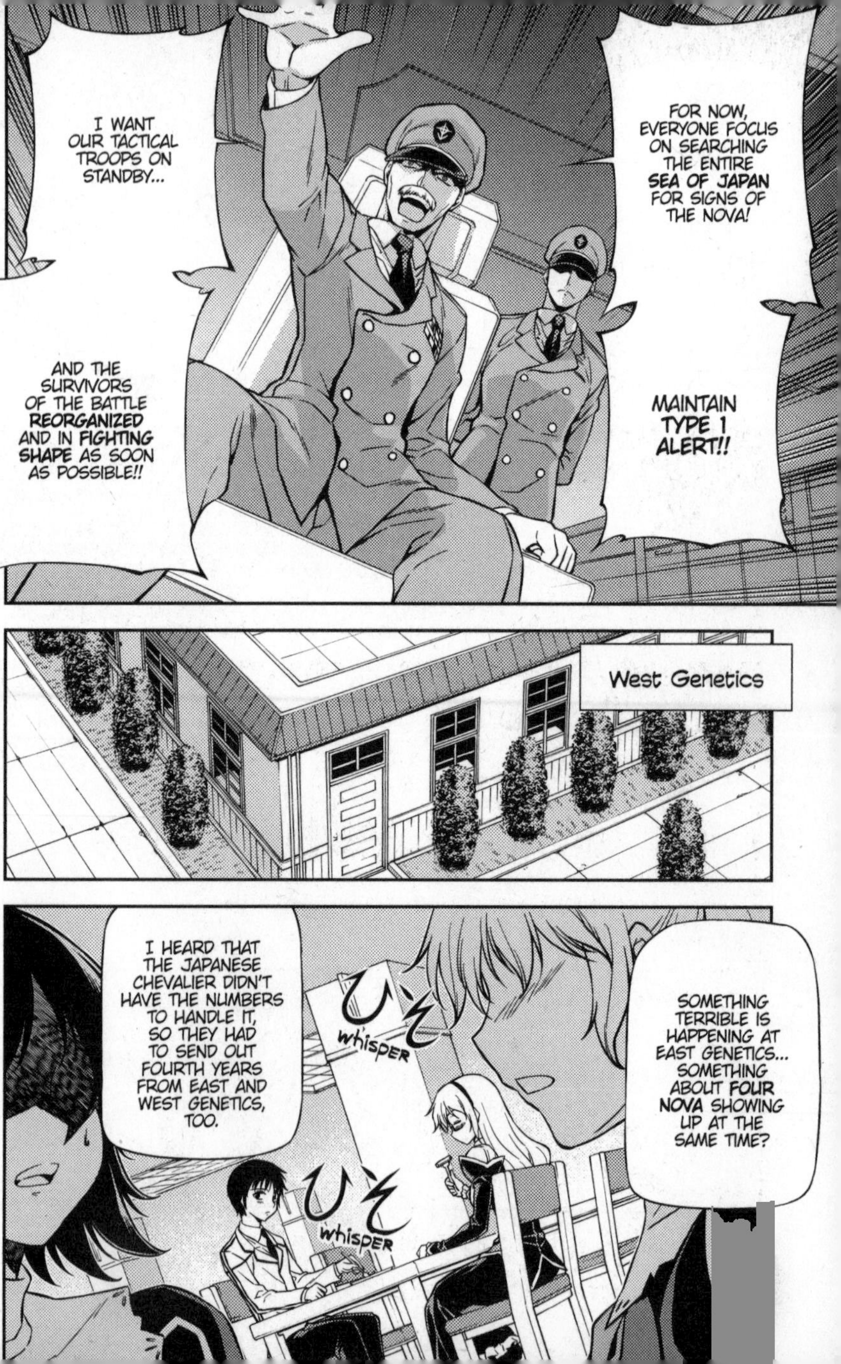
FOR NOW, EVERYONE FOCUS ON SEARCHING THE ENTIRE SEA OF JAPAN FOR SIGNS OF THE NOVA!
I WANT OUR TACTICAL TROOPS ON STANDBY...
AND THE SURVIVORS OF THE BATTLE REORGANIZED AND IN FIGHTING SHAPE AS SOON AS POSSIBLE!!
MAINTAIN TYPE 1 ALERT!!
West Genetics
SOMETHING TERRIBLE IS HAPPENING AT EAST GENETICS... SOMETHING ABOUT FOUR NOVA SHOWING UP AT THE SAME TIME?
whisper
I HEARD THAT THE JAPANESE CHEVALIER DIDN'T HAVE THE NUMBERS TO HANDLE IT, SO THEY HAD TO SEND OUT FOURTH YEARS FROM EAST AND WEST GENETICS, TOO.
whisper

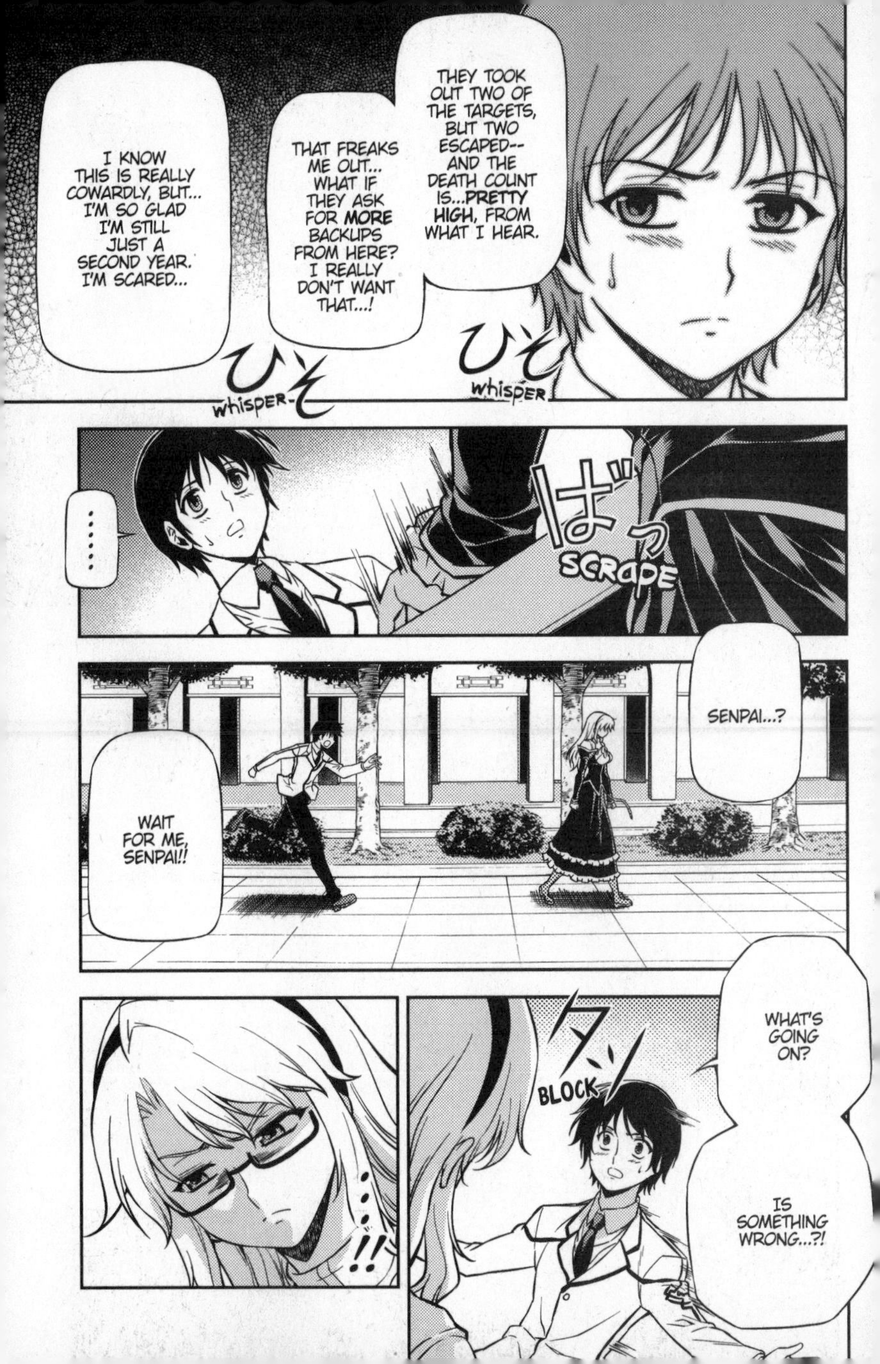
THEY TOOK OUT TWO OF THE TARGETS, BUT TWO ESCAPED-- AND THE DEATH COUNT IS...**PRETTY HIGH**, FROM WHAT I HEAR.
THAT FREAKS ME OUT... WHAT IF THEY ASK FOR **MORE** BACKUPS FROM HERE? I REALLY DON'T WANT THAT...!
I KNOW THIS IS REALLY COWARDLY, BUT... I'M SO GLAD I'M STILL JUST A SECOND YEAR. I'M SCARED...
ひそ
whisper
ひそ
whisper-
ばっ
SCRAPE
......
SENPAI...?
WAIT FOR ME, SENPAI!!
WHAT'S GOING ON?
IS SOMETHING WRONG...?!
BLOCK
......!!

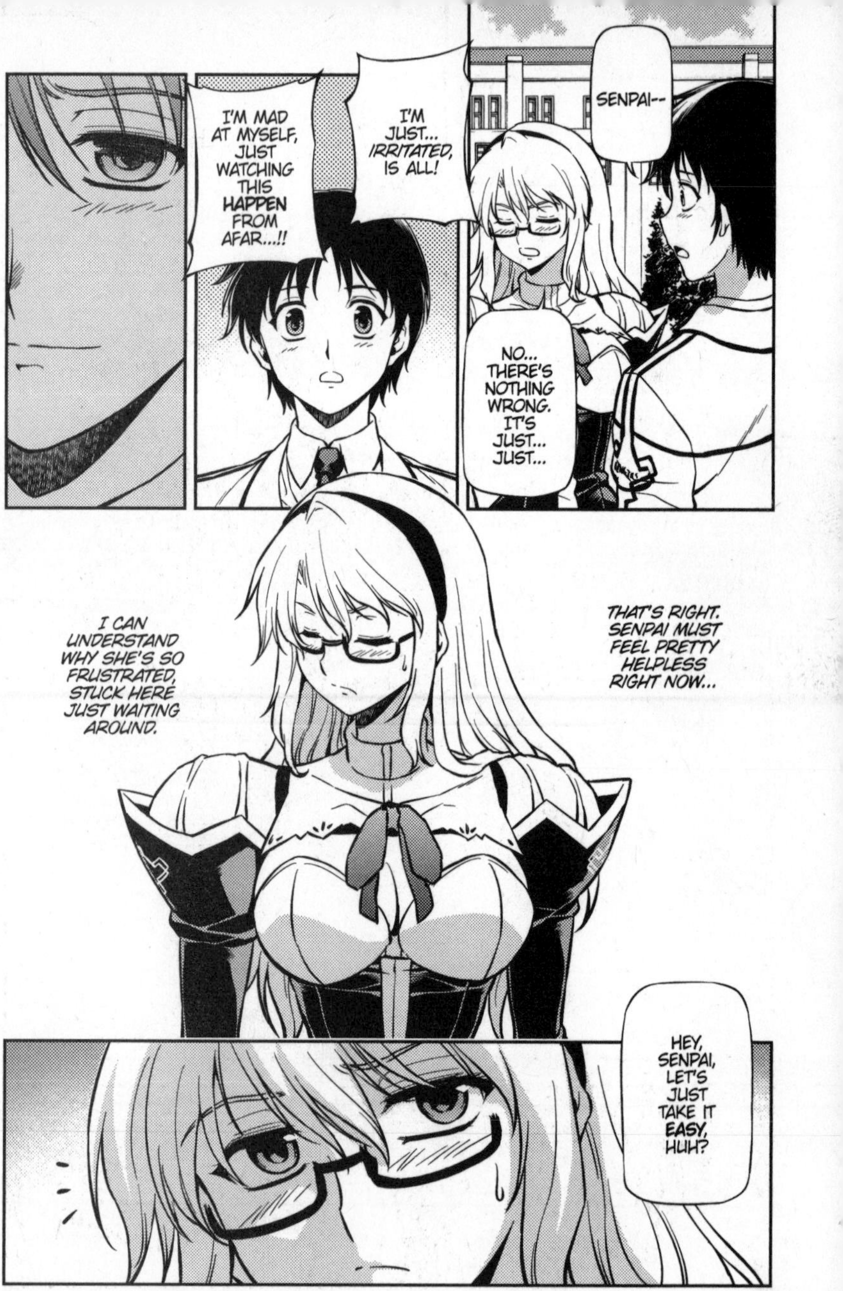
SENPAI--
NO... THERE'S NOTHING WRONG. IT'S JUST... JUST...
I'M JUST... IRRITATED, IS ALL!
I'M MAD AT MYSELF, JUST WATCHING THIS HAPPEN FROM AFAR...!!
THAT'S RIGHT. SENPAI MUST FEEL PRETTY HELPLESS RIGHT NOW...
I CAN UNDERSTAND WHY SHE'S SO FRUSTRATED, STUCK HERE JUST WAITING AROUND.
HEY, SENPAI, LET'S JUST TAKE IT EASY, HUH?

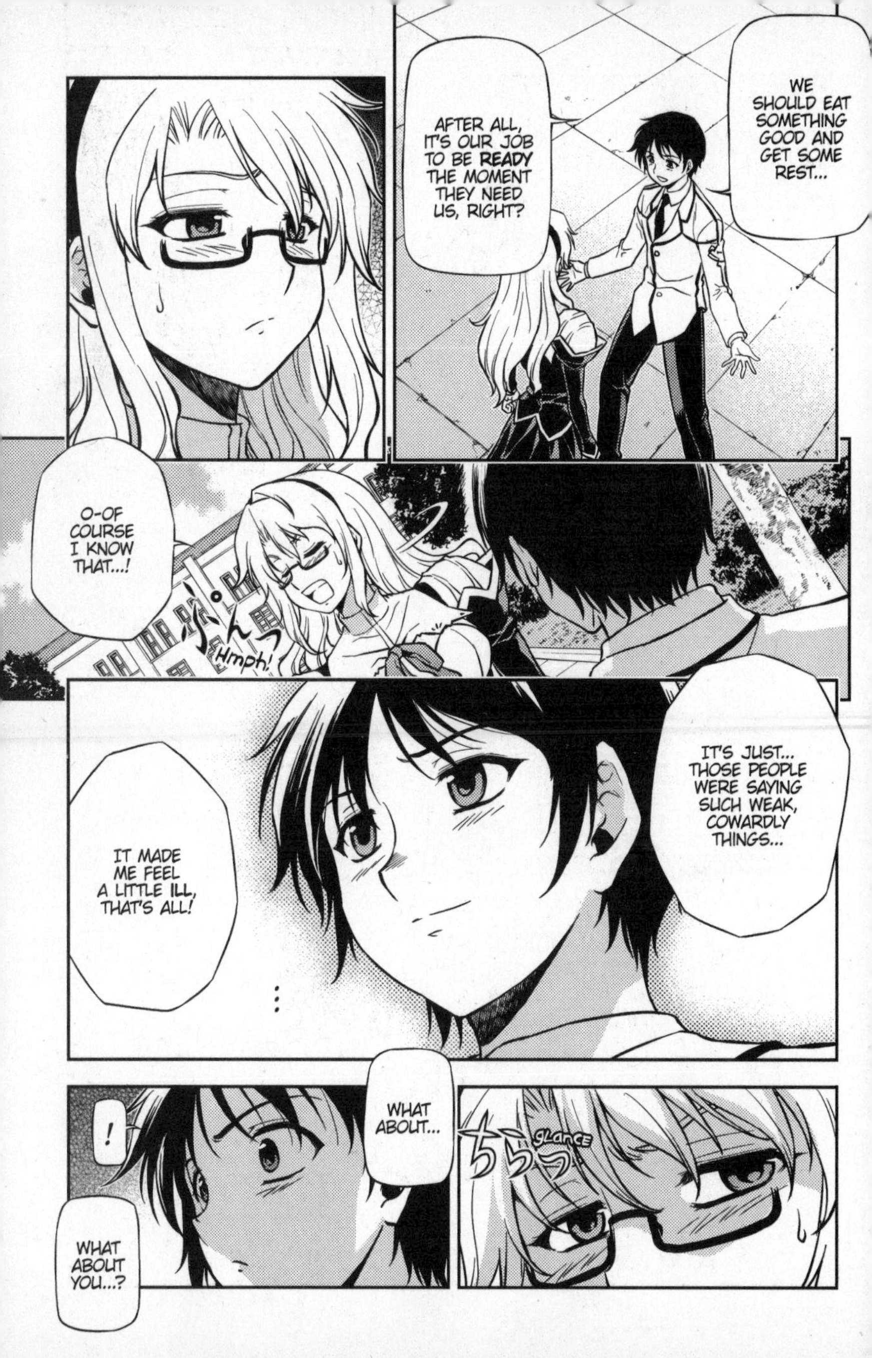
WE SHOULD EAT SOMETHING GOOD AND GET SOME REST...
AFTER ALL, IT'S OUR JOB TO BE **READY** THE MOMENT THEY NEED US, RIGHT?
O-OF COURSE I KNOW THAT...!
Hmph!
IT'S JUST... THOSE PEOPLE WERE SAYING SUCH WEAK, COWARDLY THINGS...
IT MADE ME FEEL A LITTLE ILL, THAT'S ALL!
...
WHAT ABOUT...
GLANCE
!
WHAT ABOUT YOU...?

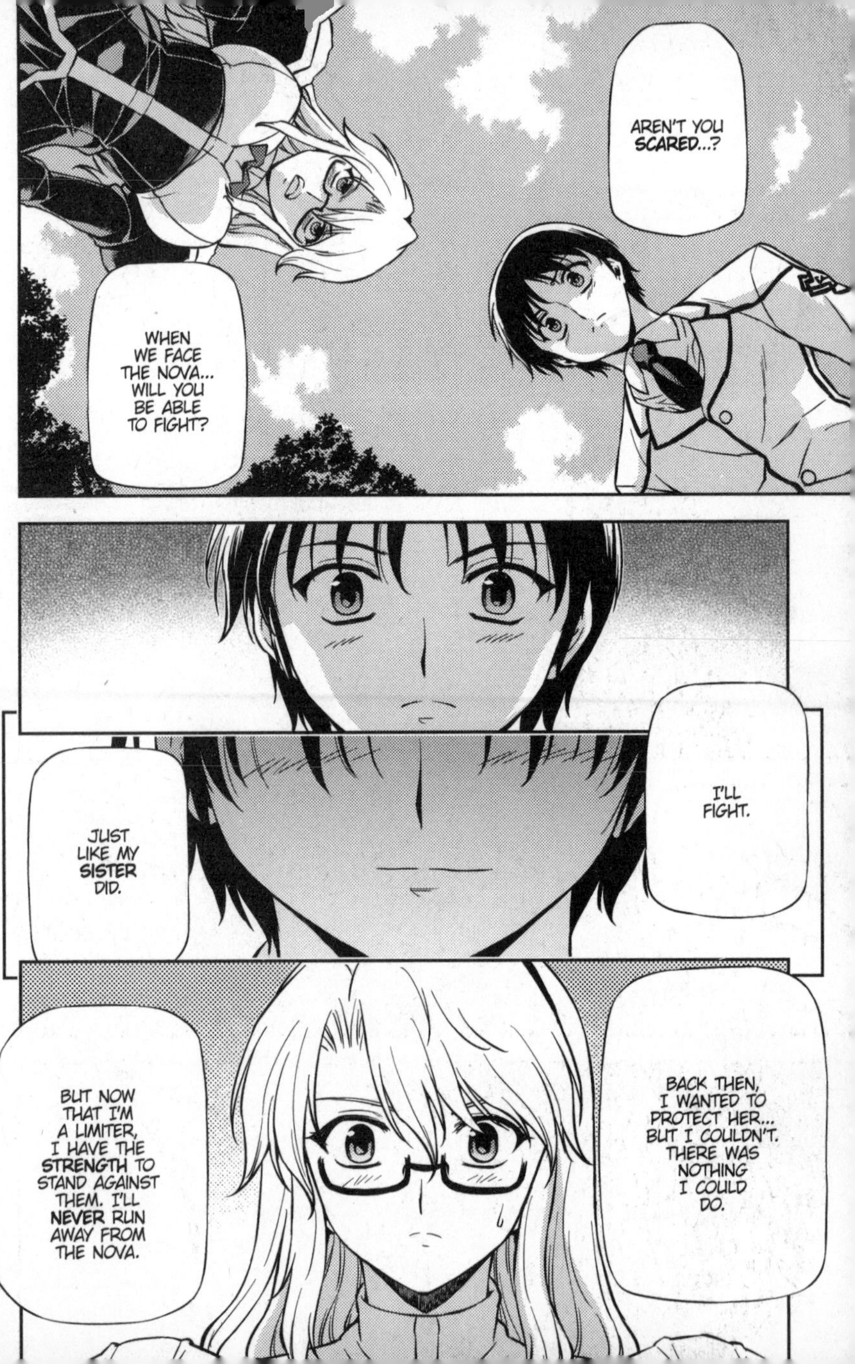
AREN'T YOU SCARED...?
WHEN WE FACE THE NOVA... WILL YOU BE ABLE TO FIGHT?
I'LL FIGHT.
JUST LIKE MY SISTER DID.
BACK THEN, I WANTED TO PROTECT HER... BUT I COULDN'T. THERE WAS NOTHING I COULD DO.
BUT NOW THAT I'M A LIMITER, I HAVE THE STRENGTH TO STAND AGAINST THEM. I'LL NEVER RUN AWAY FROM THE NOVA.

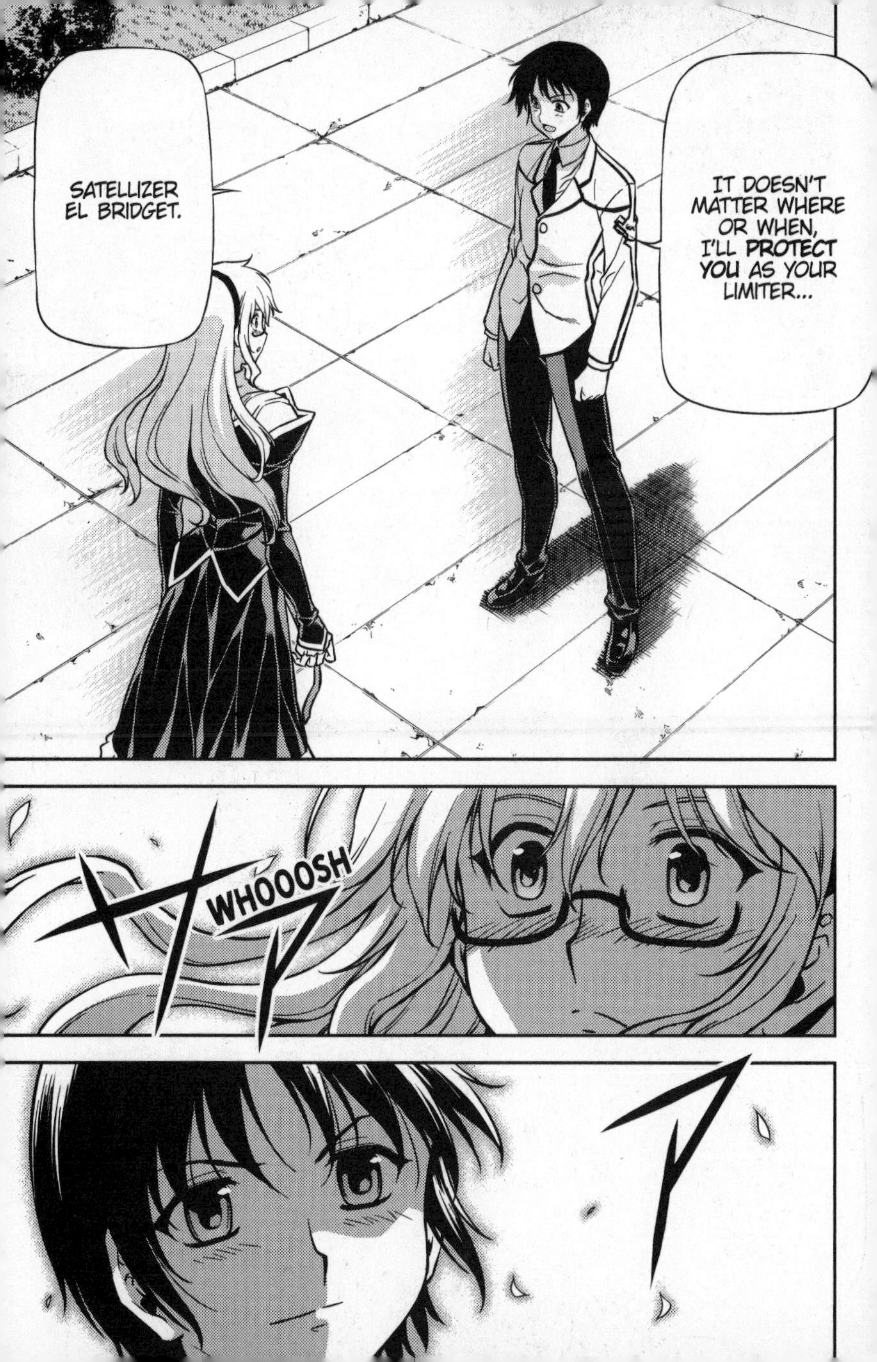
IT DOESN'T MATTER WHERE OR WHEN, I'LL PROTECT YOU AS YOUR LIMITER...
SATELLIZER EL BRIDGET.
WHOOOSH

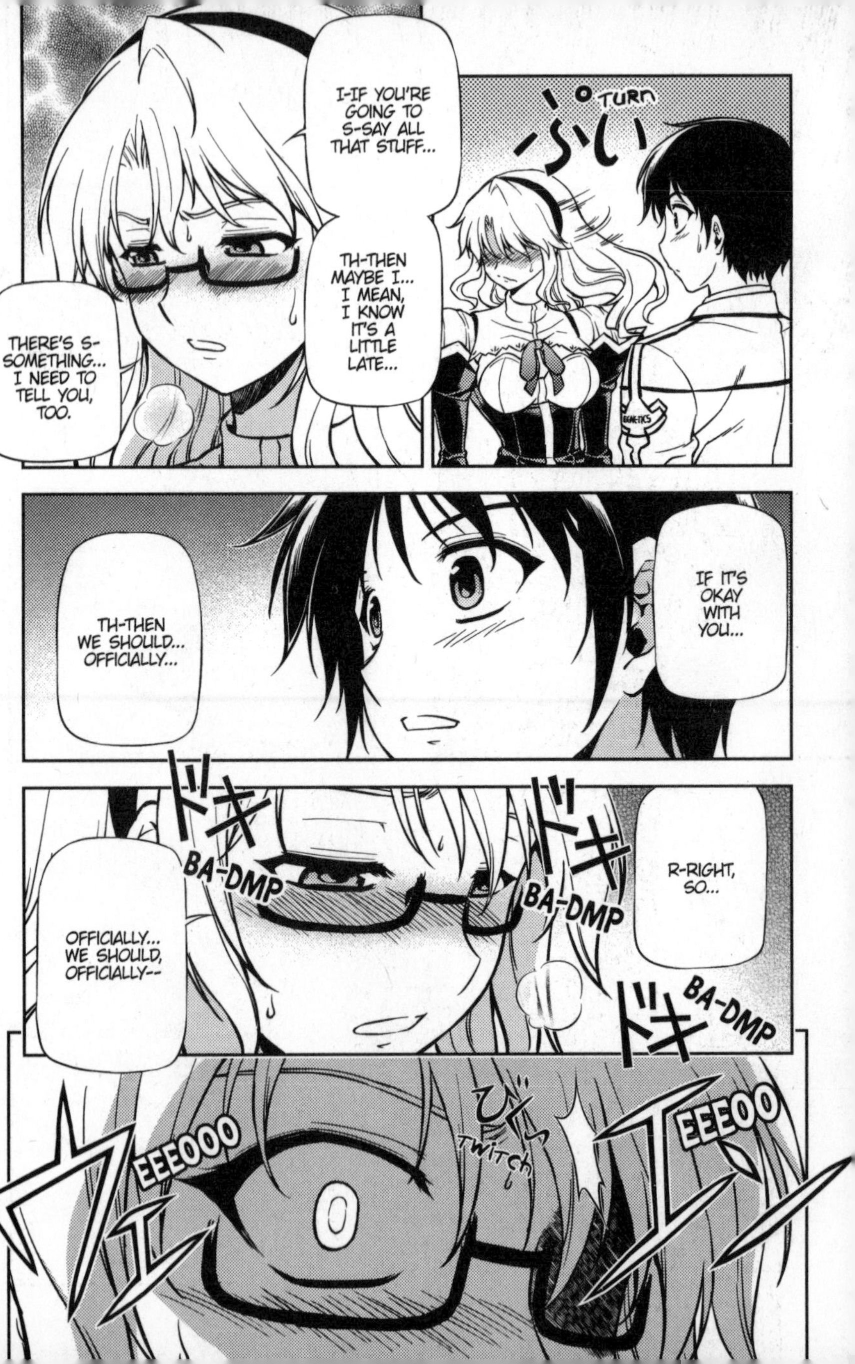

ふい
TURN
I-IF YOU'RE GOING TO S-SAY ALL THAT STUFF...
TH-THEN MAYBE I... I MEAN, I KNOW IT'S A LITTLE LATE...
THERE'S S-SOMETHING... I NEED TO TELL YOU, TOO.
IF IT'S OKAY WITH YOU...
TH-THEN WE SHOULD... OFFICIALLY...
R-RIGHT, SO...
ドキ
BA-DMP
ドキ
BA-DMP
OFFICIALLY... WE SHOULD, OFFICIALLY--
ドキ
BA-DMP
EEEOO
TWITCH
EEEOOO

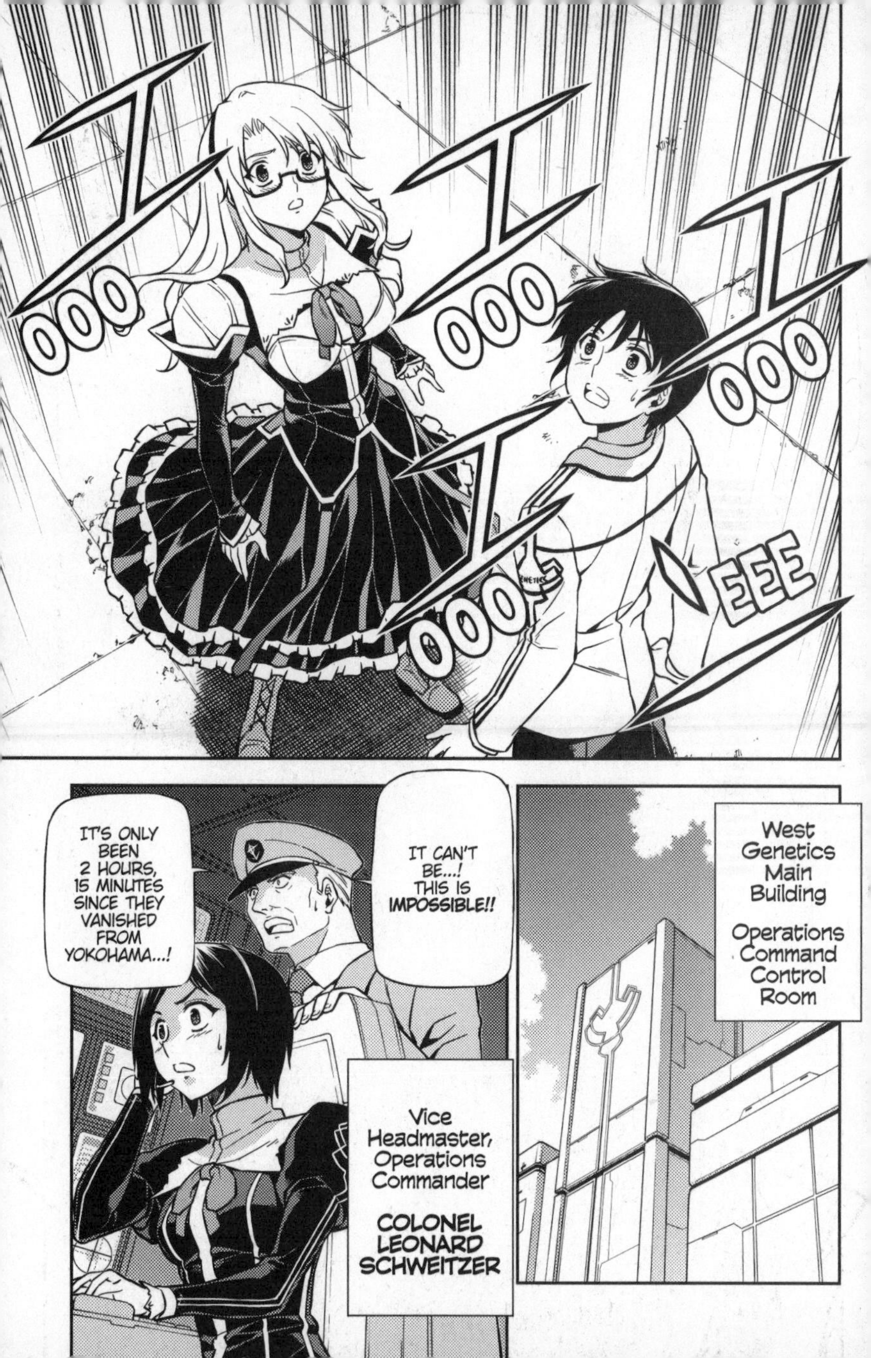
IOOO IOOO IOOO IOOO EEE
West Genetics Main Building
Operations Command Control Room
IT CAN'T BE...! THIS IS IMPOSSIBLE!!
IT'S ONLY BEEN 2 HOURS, 15 MINUTES SINCE THEY VANISHED FROM YOKOHAMA...!
Vice Headmaster, Operations Commander
COLONEL LEONARD SCHWEITZER

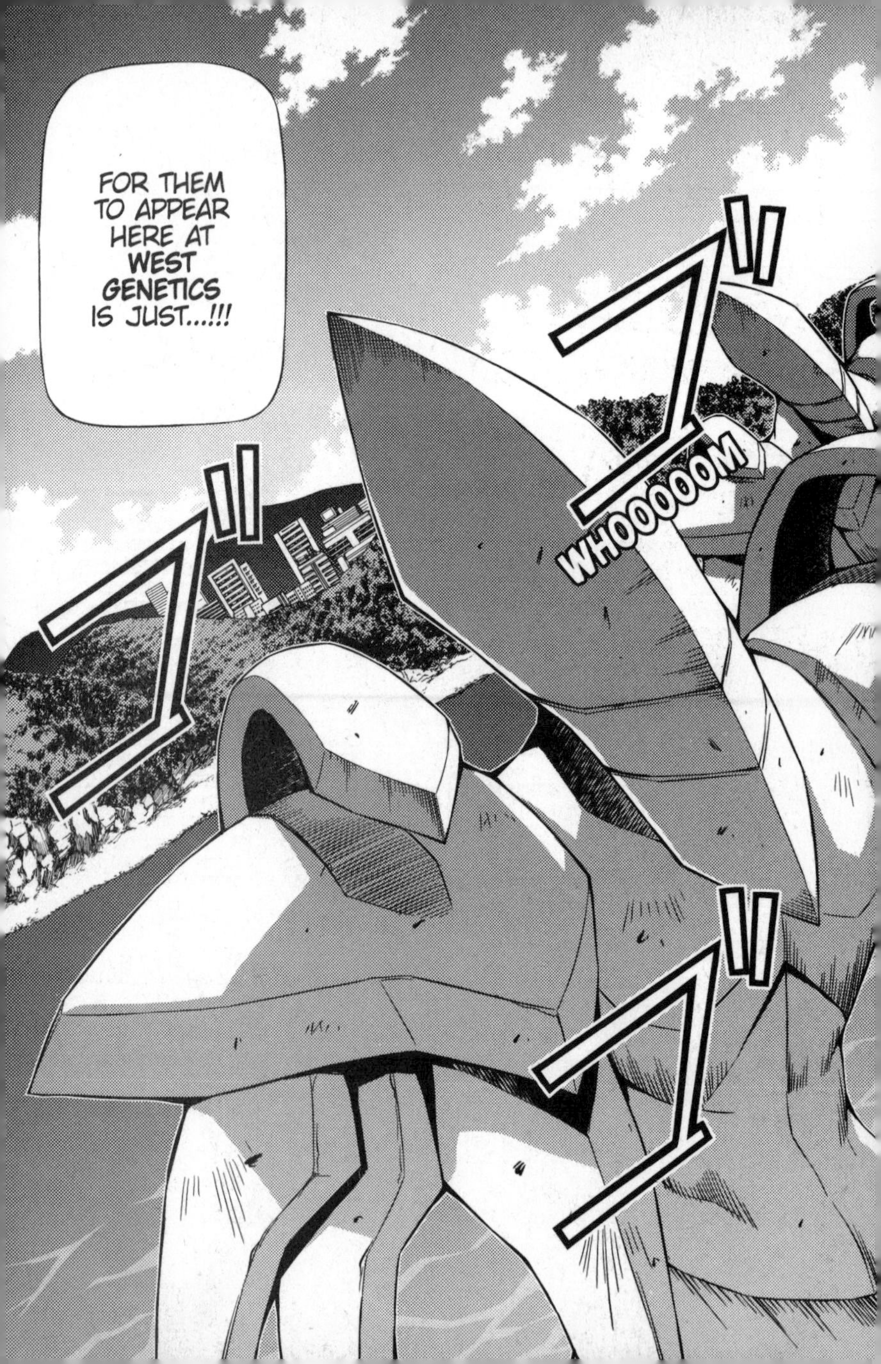
FOR THEM TO APPEAR HERE AT WEST GENETICS IS JUST...!!!
WHOOOOOM

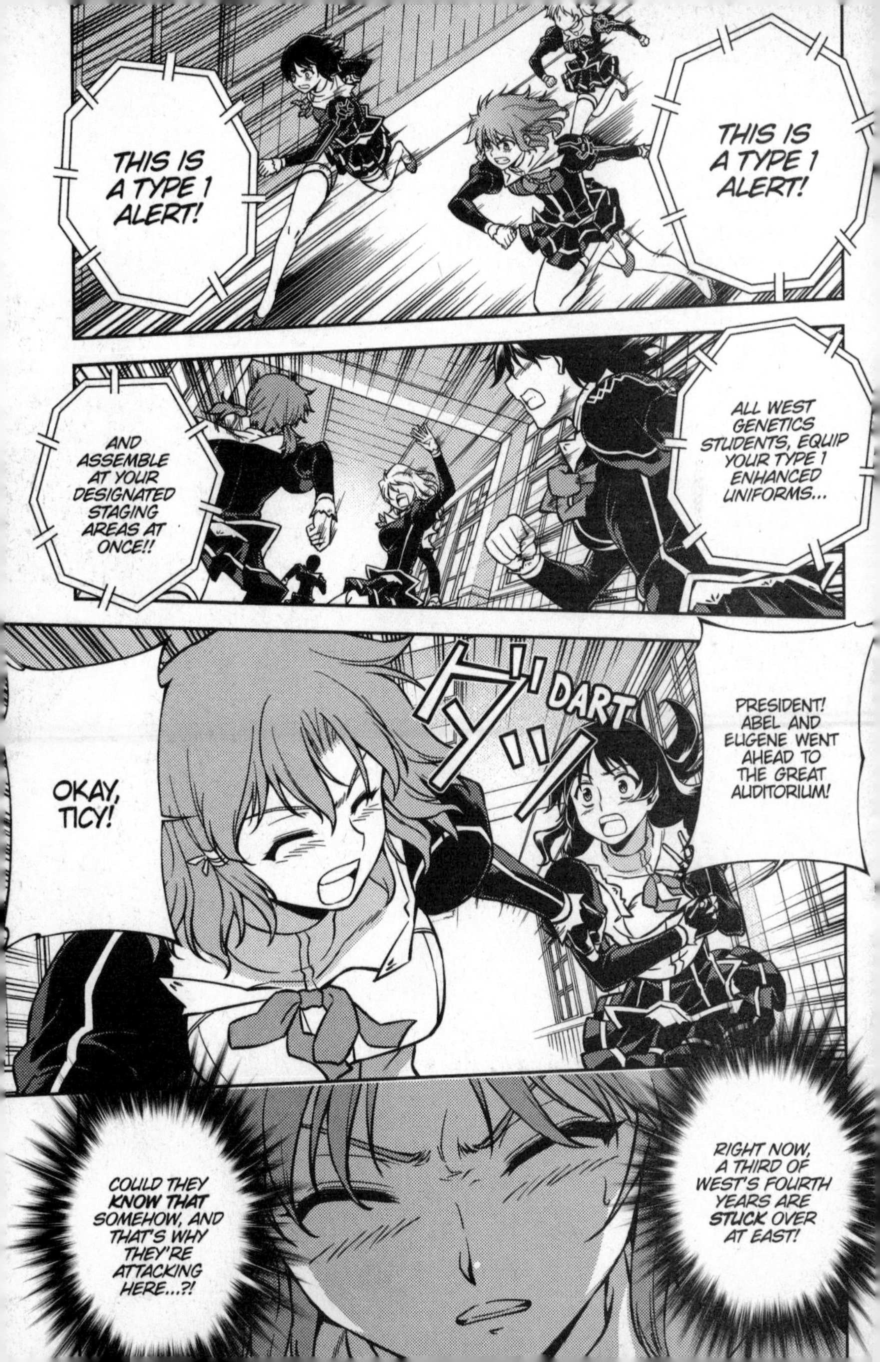
THIS IS A TYPE 1 ALERT!
THIS IS A TYPE 1 ALERT!
ALL WEST GENETICS STUDENTS, EQUIP YOUR TYPE 1 ENHANCED UNIFORMS...
AND ASSEMBLE AT YOUR DESIGNATED STAGING AREAS AT ONCE!!
PRESIDENT! ABEL AND EUGENE WENT AHEAD TO THE GREAT AUDITORIUM!
DART
OKAY, TICY!
RIGHT NOW, A THIRD OF WEST'S FOURTH YEARS ARE STUCK OVER AT EAST!
COULD THEY KNOW THAT SOMEHOW, AND THAT'S WHY THEY'RE ATTACKING HERE...?!

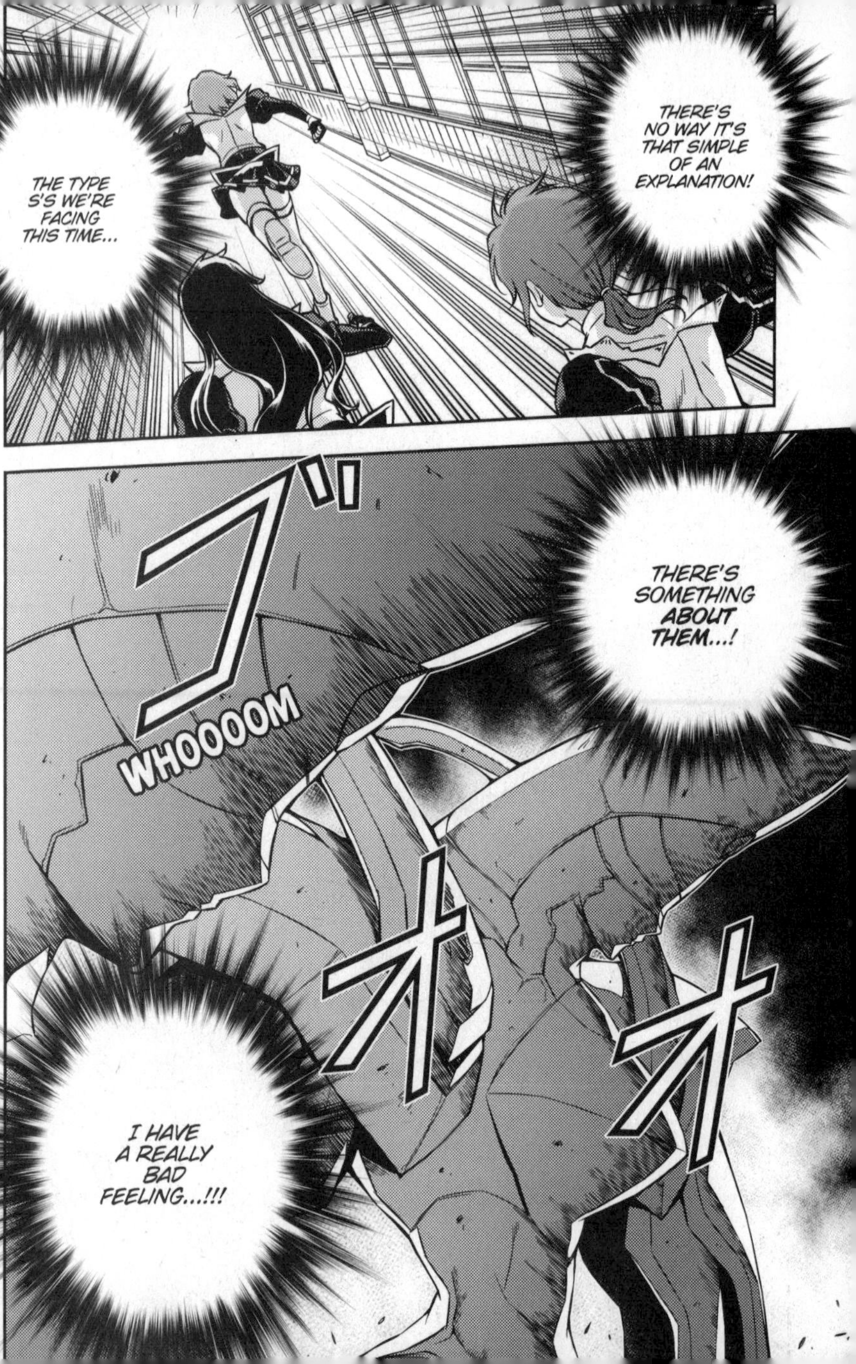
THERE'S NO WAY IT'S THAT SIMPLE OF AN EXPLANATION!
THE TYPE S'S WE'RE FACING THIS TIME...
THERE'S SOMETHING ABOUT THEM...!
ブオオ
WHOOOOM
I HAVE A REALLY BAD FEELING...!!!

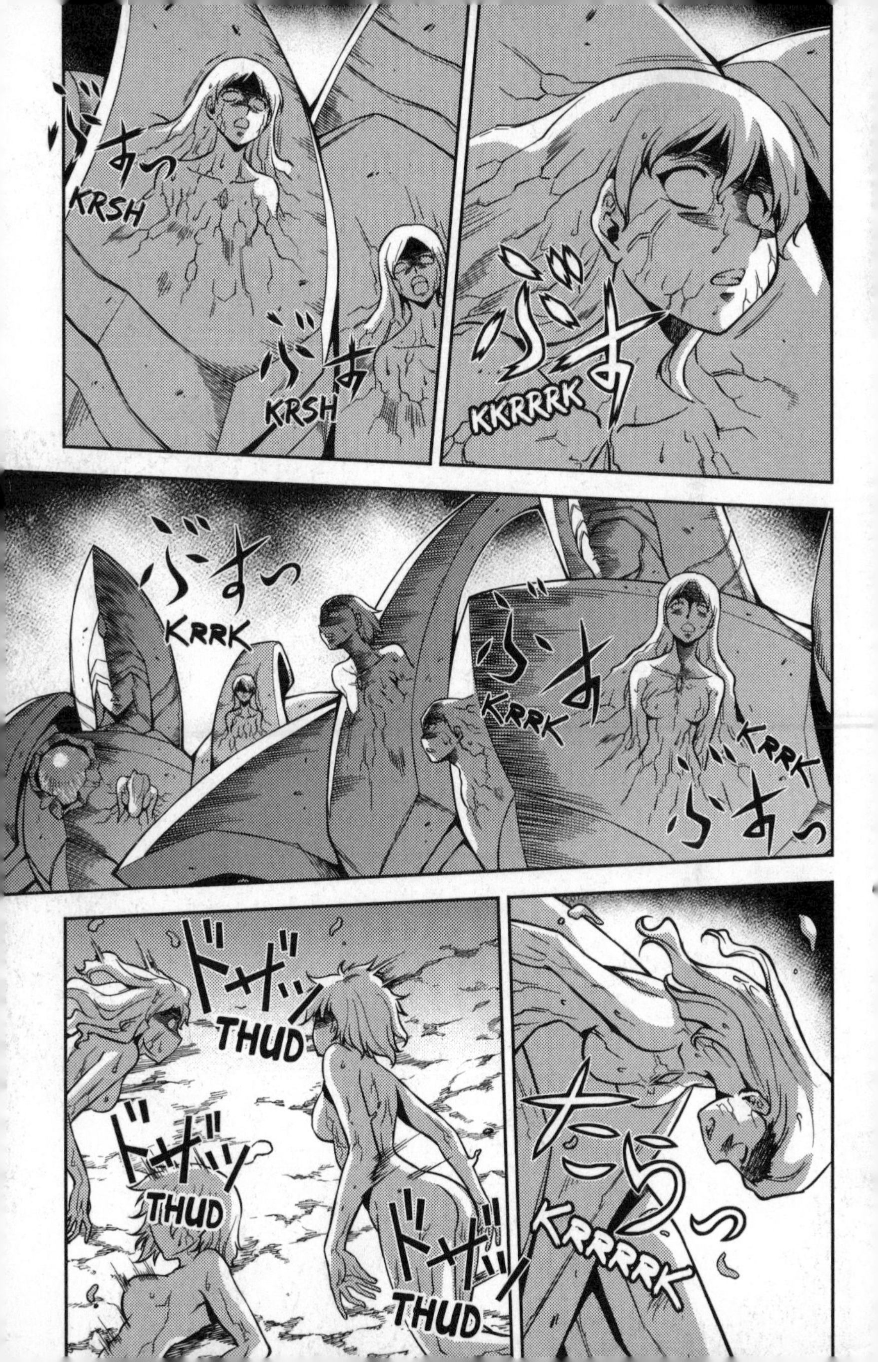
ぶぉ
KKRRRK
ぶぉ
KRSH
ぶぉっ
KRSH
ぶぉ
KRRK
ぶぉっ
KRRK
ぶすっ
KRRK
たらっ
KRRRRK
ドザッ
THUD
ドザッ
THUD
ドザッ
THUD

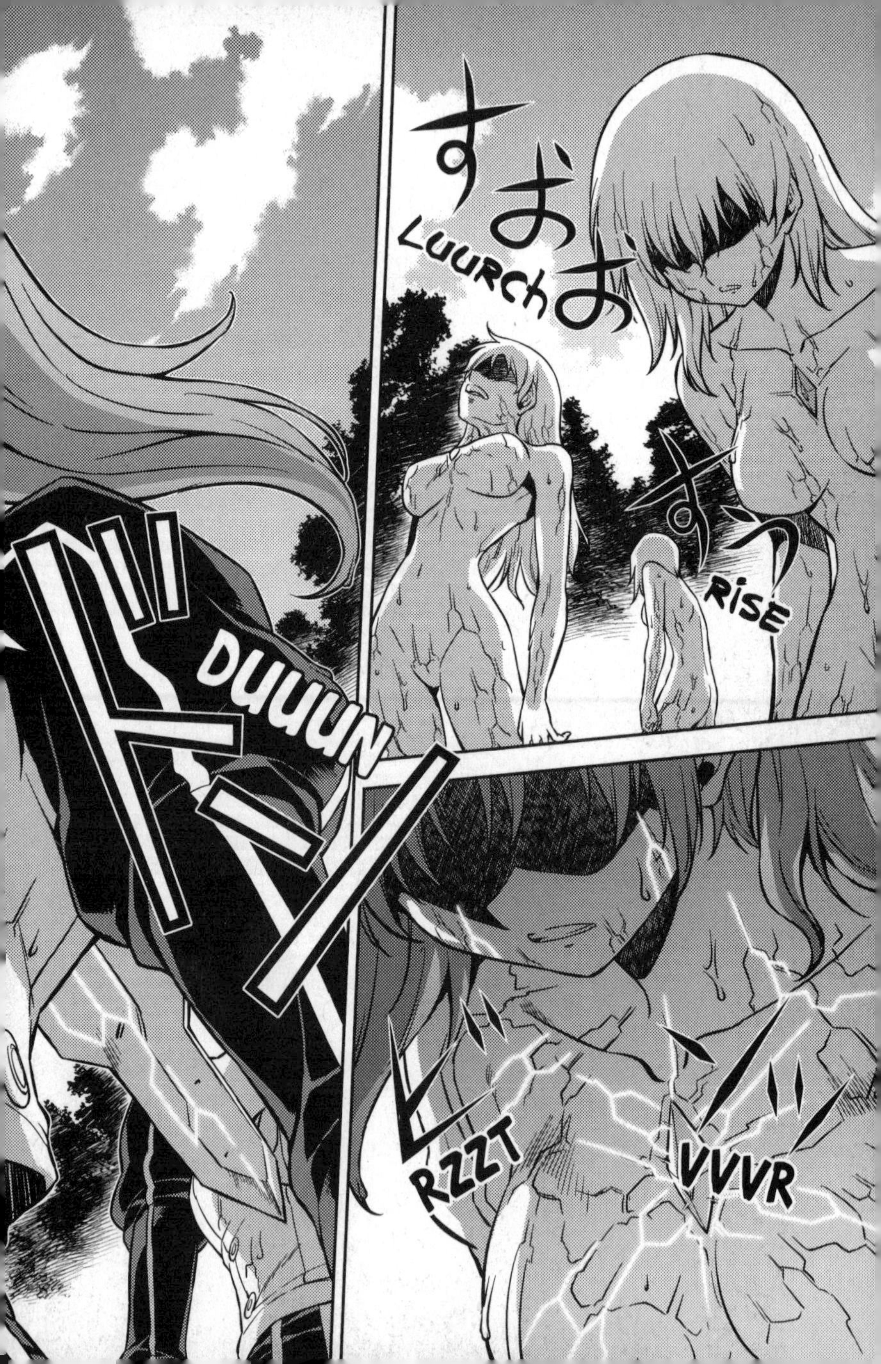
すおお
LUURCH
すっ
RISE
RZZT
VVVR
ドーン
DUUUN

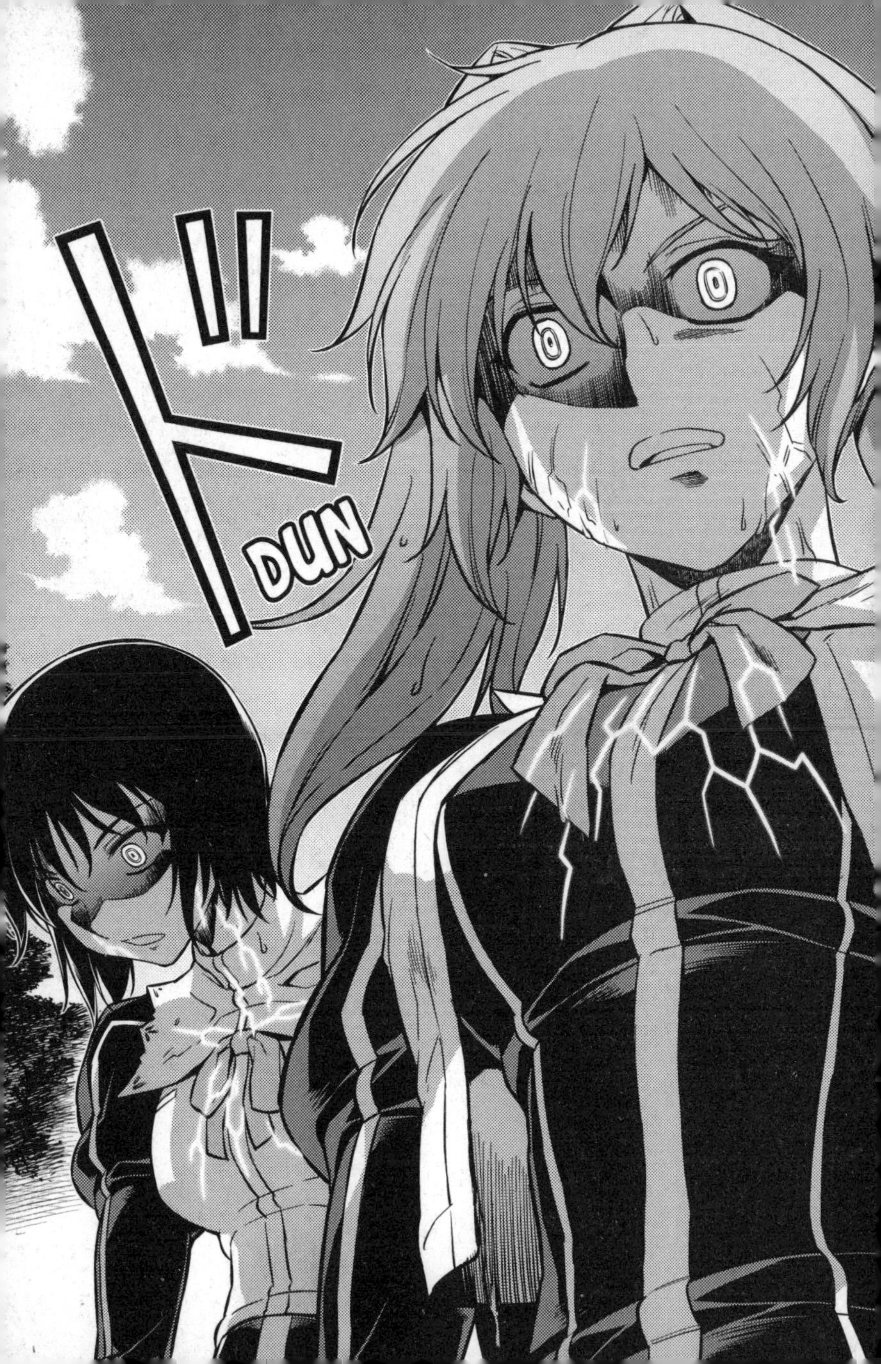
ド
DUN

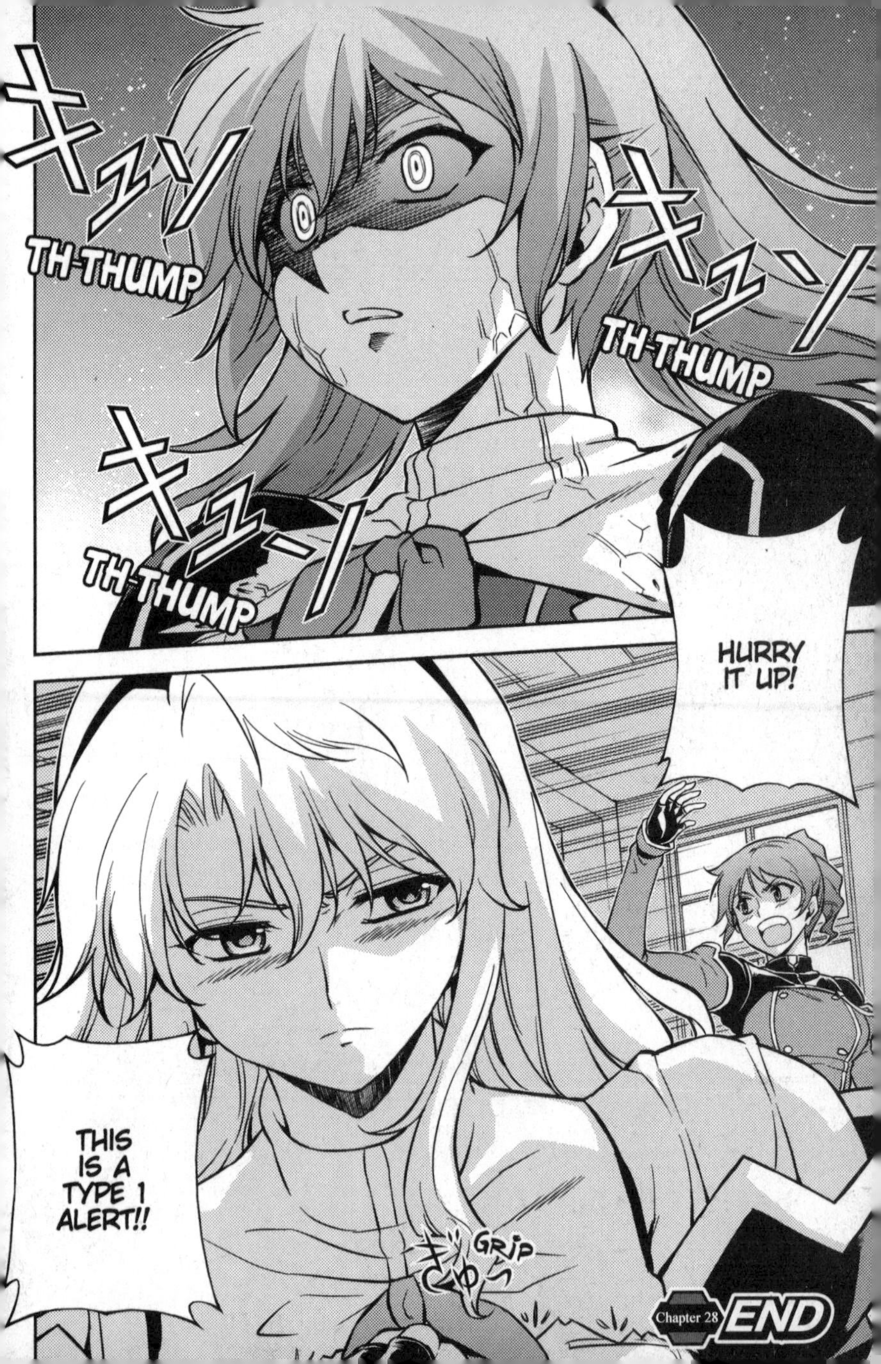

キューン
TH-THUMP
キュン
TH-THUMP
キューン
TH-THUMP
HURRY IT UP!
THIS IS A TYPE 1 ALERT!!
ぎゅっ
GRIP
Chapter 28 END

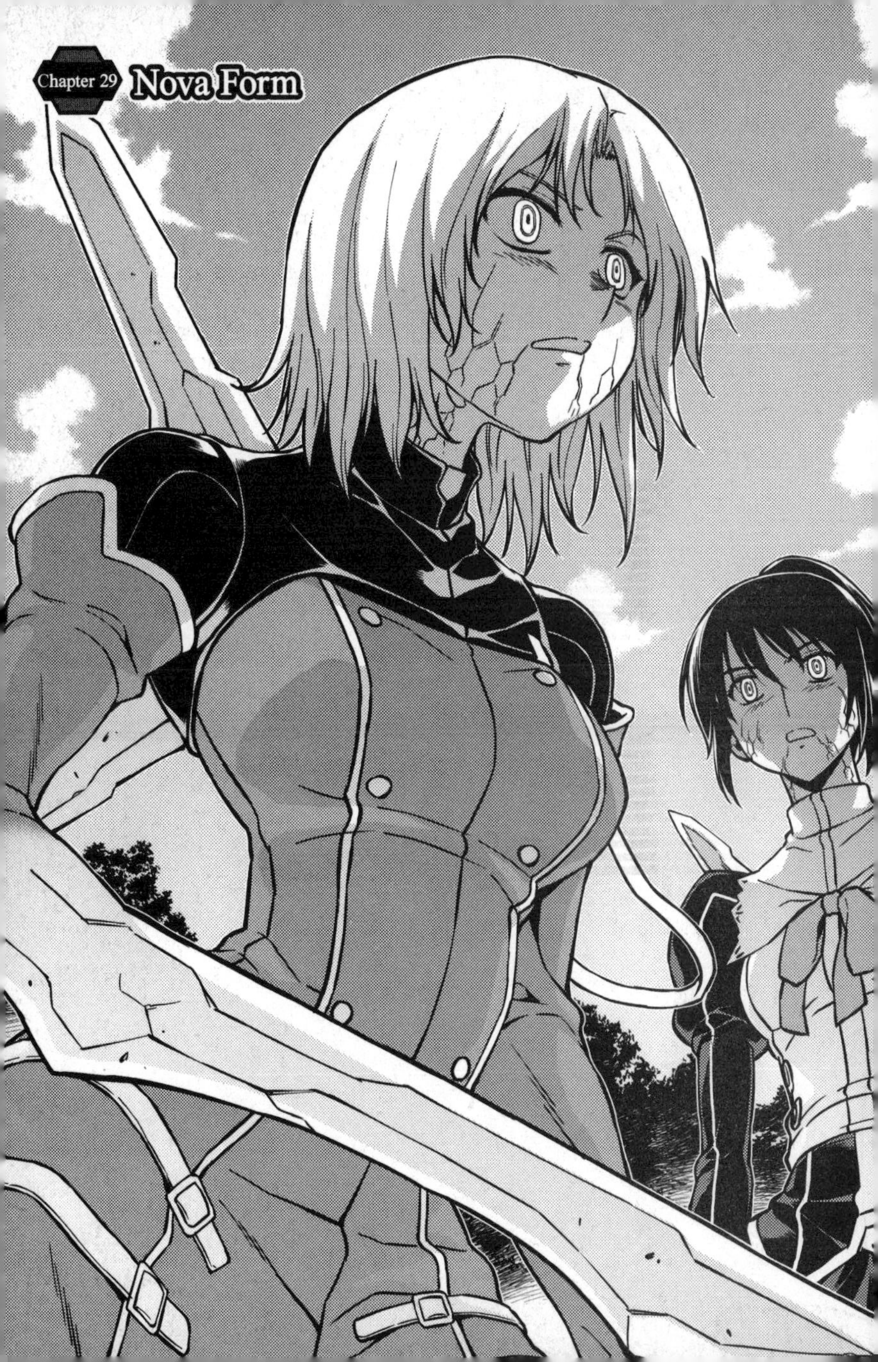
Chapter 29
Nova Form

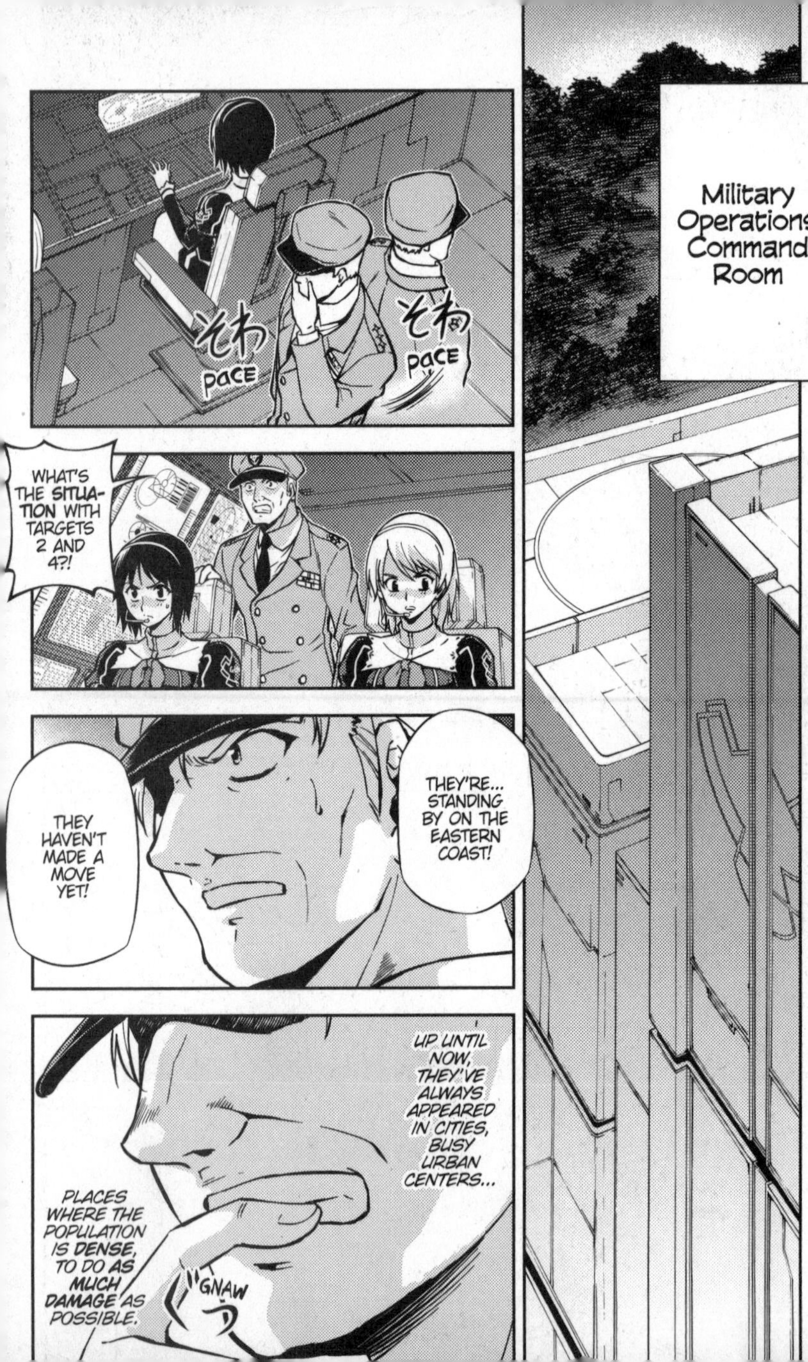
Military Operations Command Room
そわ
pace
そわ
pace
WHAT'S THE SITUATION WITH TARGETS 2 AND 4?!
THEY'RE... STANDING BY ON THE EASTERN COAST!
THEY HAVEN'T MADE A MOVE YET!
UP UNTIL NOW, THEY'VE ALWAYS APPEARED IN CITIES, BUSY URBAN CENTERS...
PLACES WHERE THE POPULATION IS DENSE, TO DO AS MUCH DAMAGE AS POSSIBLE.
GNAW
っ

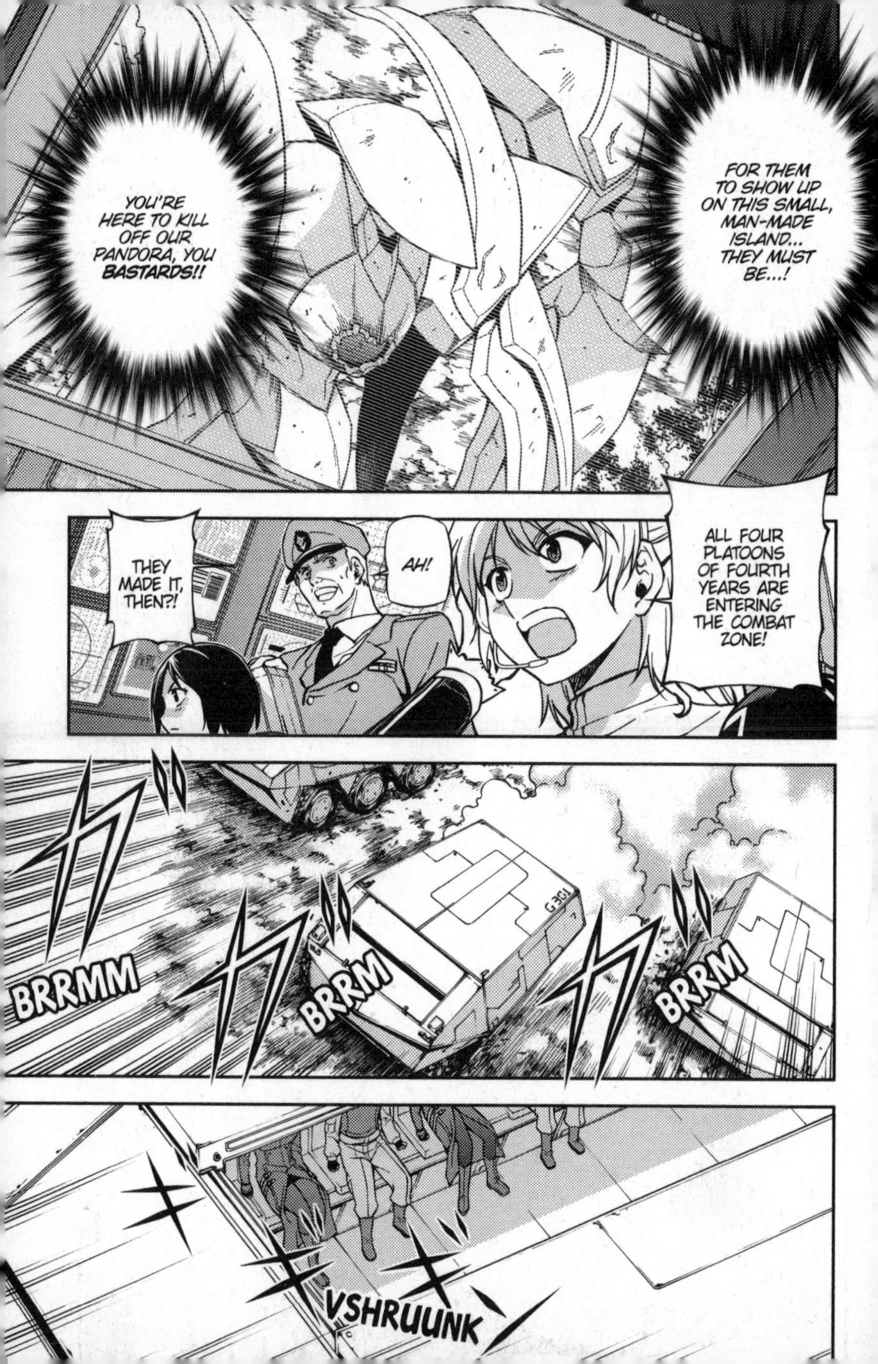
FOR THEM TO SHOW UP ON THIS SMALL, MAN-MADE ISLAND... THEY MUST BE...!
YOU'RE HERE TO KILL OFF OUR PANDORA, YOU BASTARDS!!
ALL FOUR PLATOONS OF FOURTH YEARS ARE ENTERING THE COMBAT ZONE!
AH!
THEY MADE IT, THEN?!
BRRM
BRRM
BRRMM
VSHRUUNK

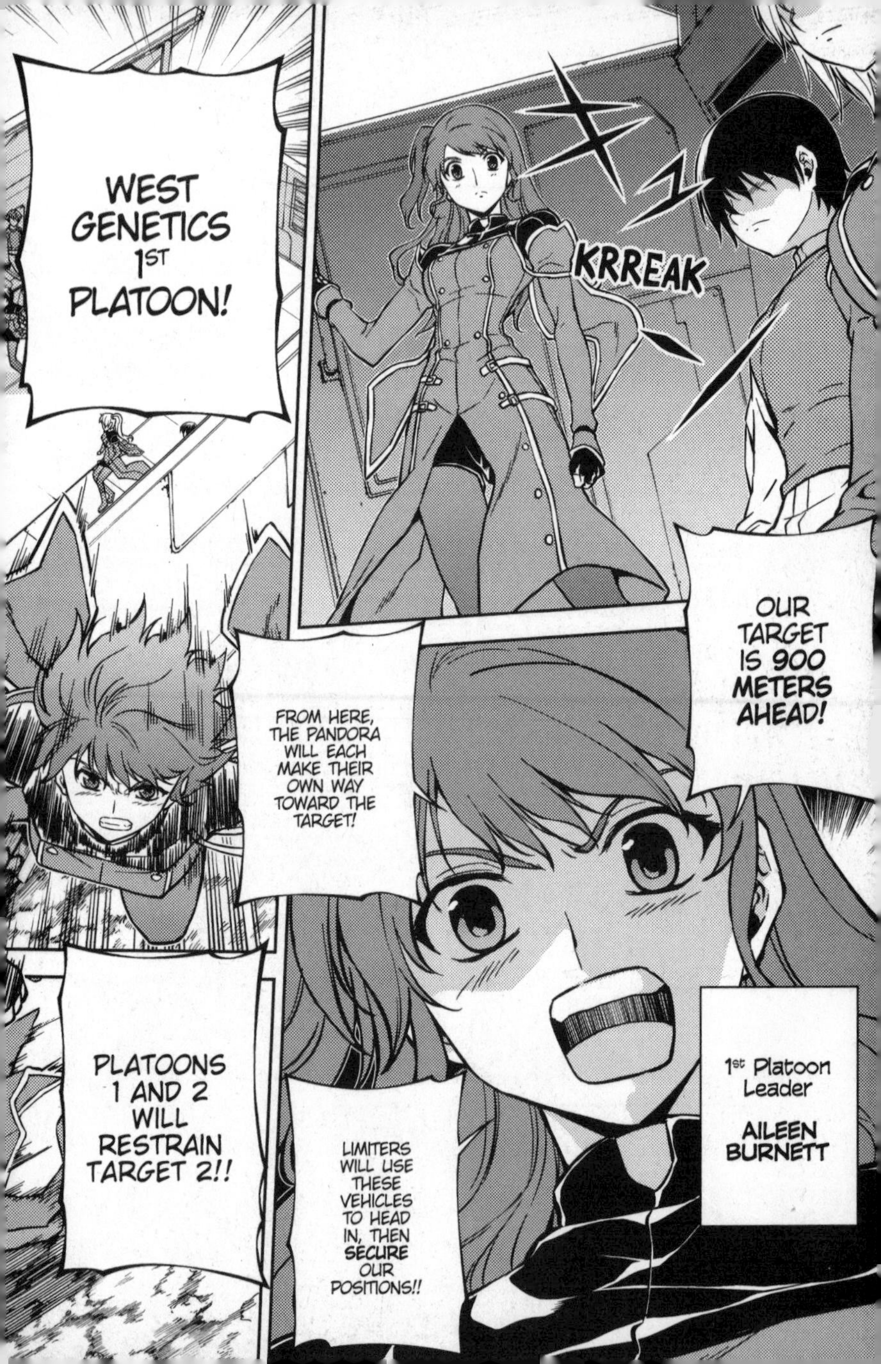
KRREAK
WEST GENETICS 1ST PLATOON!
OUR TARGET IS 900 METERS AHEAD!
FROM HERE, THE PANDORA WILL EACH MAKE THEIR OWN WAY TOWARD THE TARGET!
1st Platoon Leader
AILEEN BURNETT
LIMITERS WILL USE THESE VEHICLES TO HEAD IN, THEN SECURE OUR POSITIONS!!
PLATOONS 1 AND 2 WILL RESTRAIN TARGET 2!!

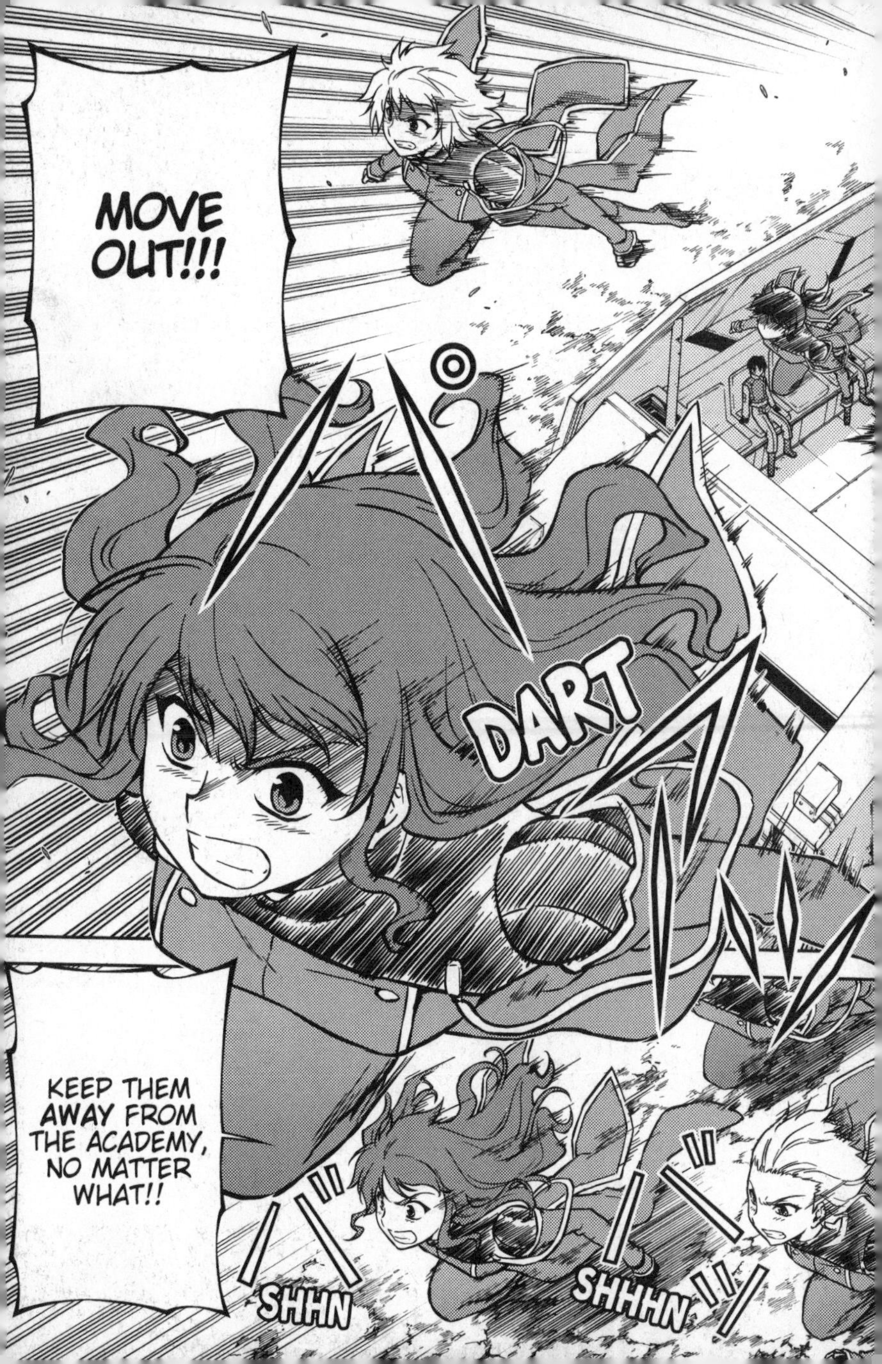
MOVE OUT!!!
DART
KEEP THEM AWAY FROM THE ACADEMY, NO MATTER WHAT!!
SHHHN
SHHN

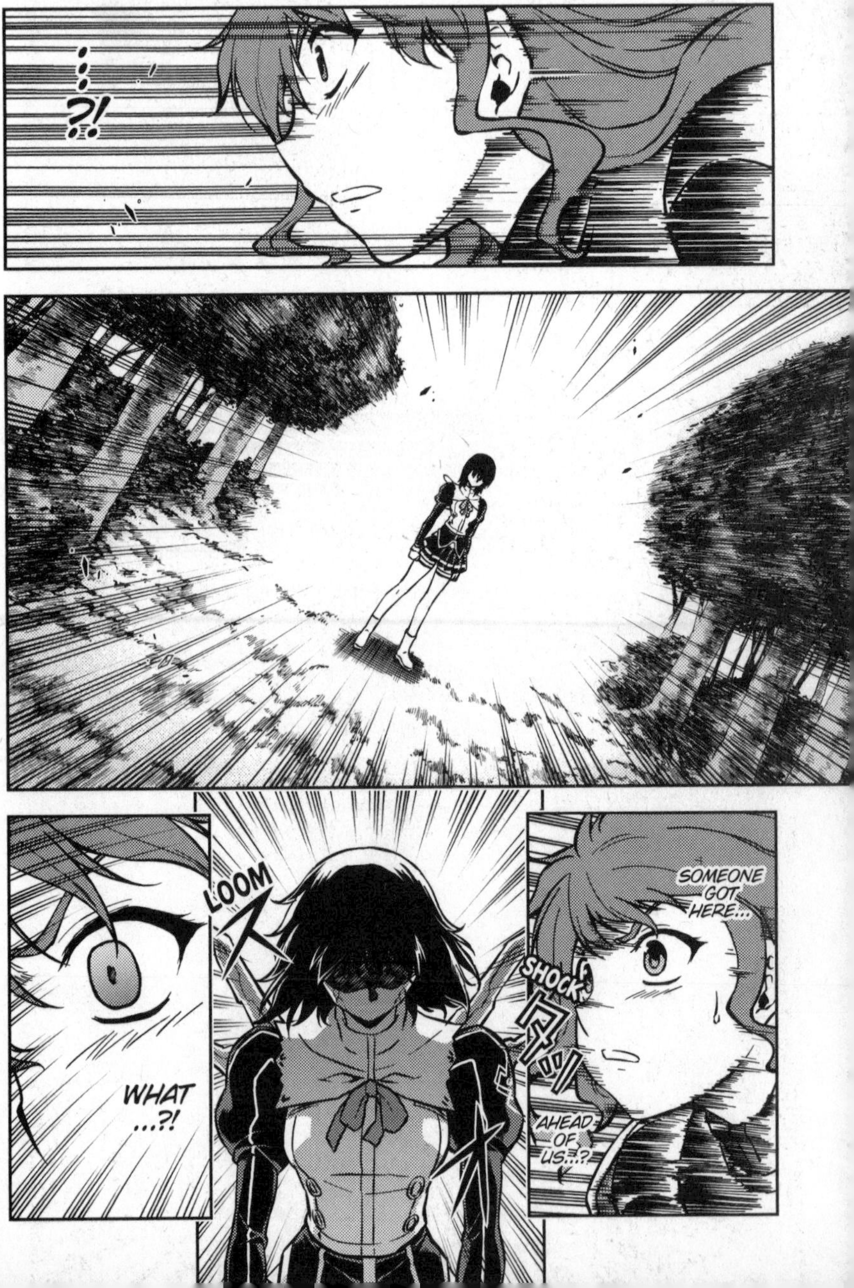
...?!
SOMEONE GOT HERE...
SHOCK
AHEAD OF US...?
LOOM
WHAT ...?!

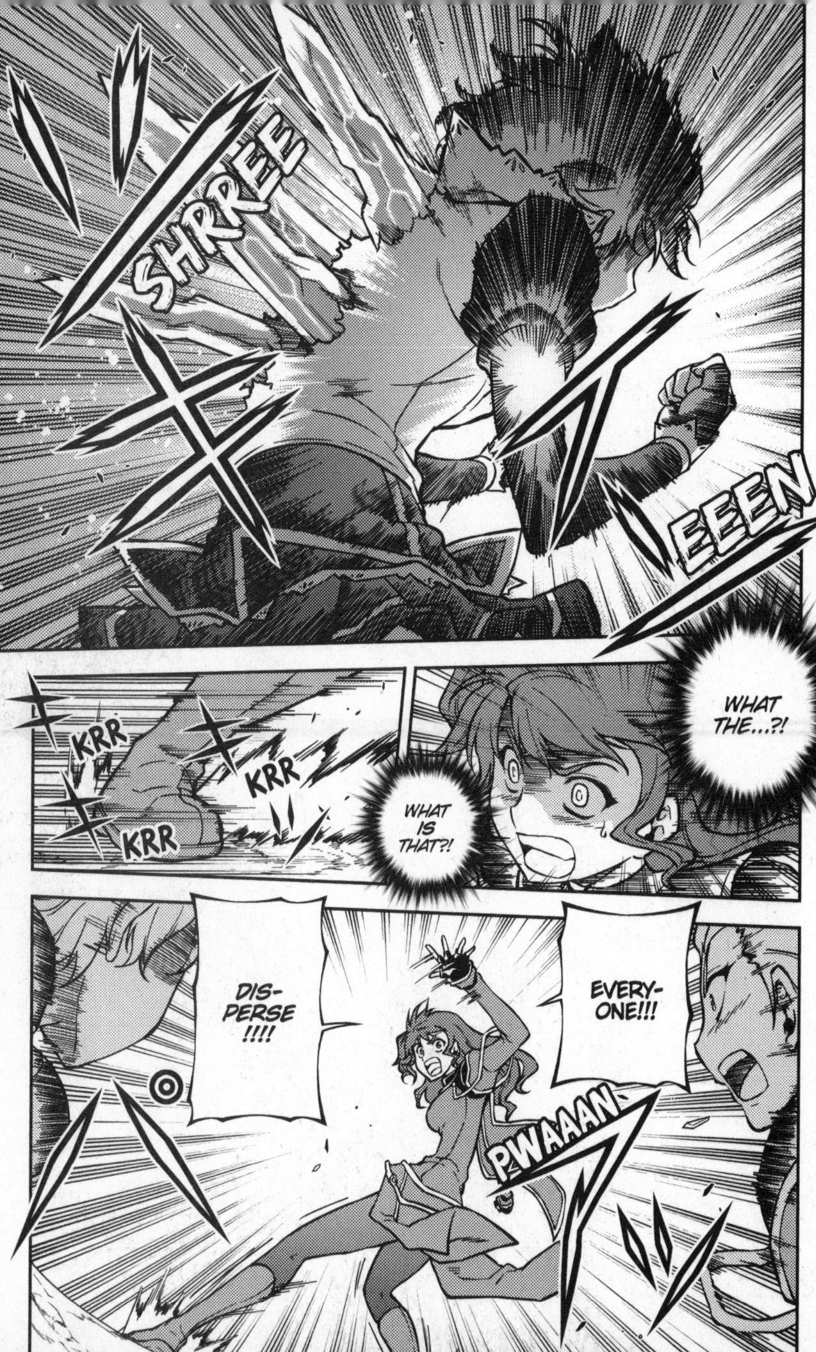
SHREE
EEEN
WHAT THE...?!
WHAT IS THAT?!
KRR
KRR
KRR
EVERY-ONE!!!
DIS-PERSE!!!!
PWAAAN

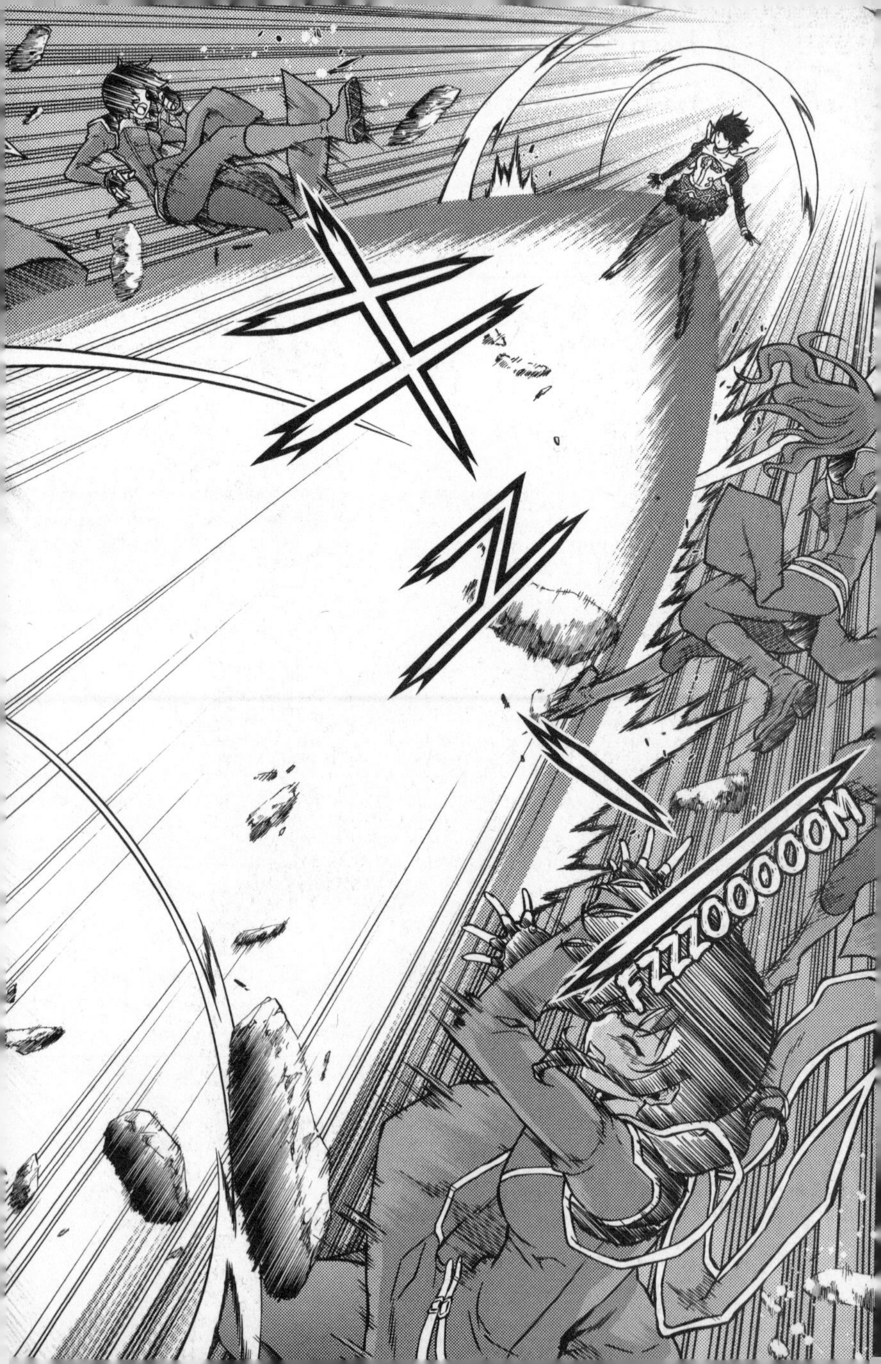
FZZZOOOOOOM

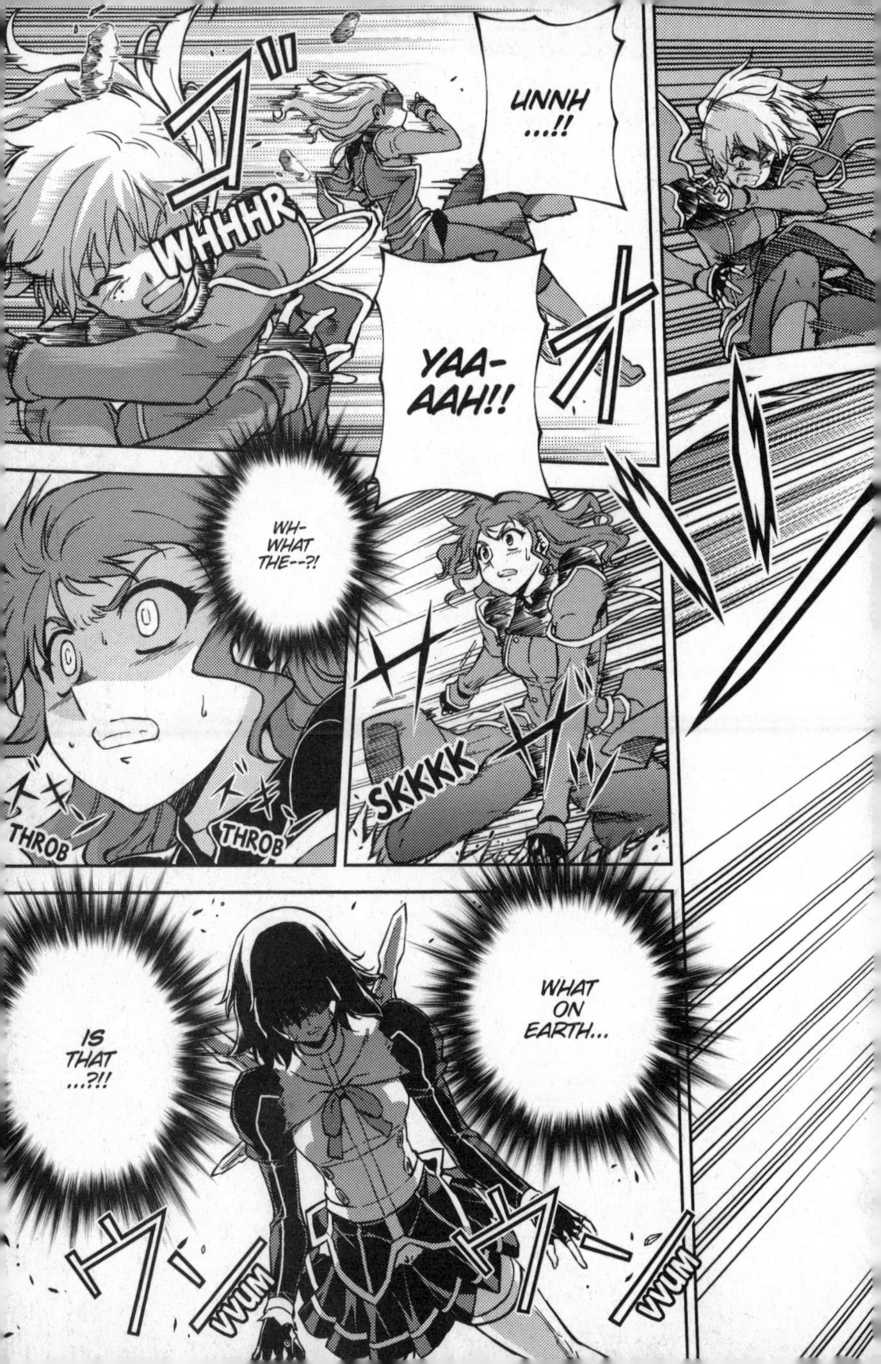
UNNH ...!!
WHHHR
YAA-AAH!!
SKKKK
WH-WHAT THE--?!
THROB
THROB
WHAT ON EARTH...
IS THAT ...?!!
VVUM
VVUM

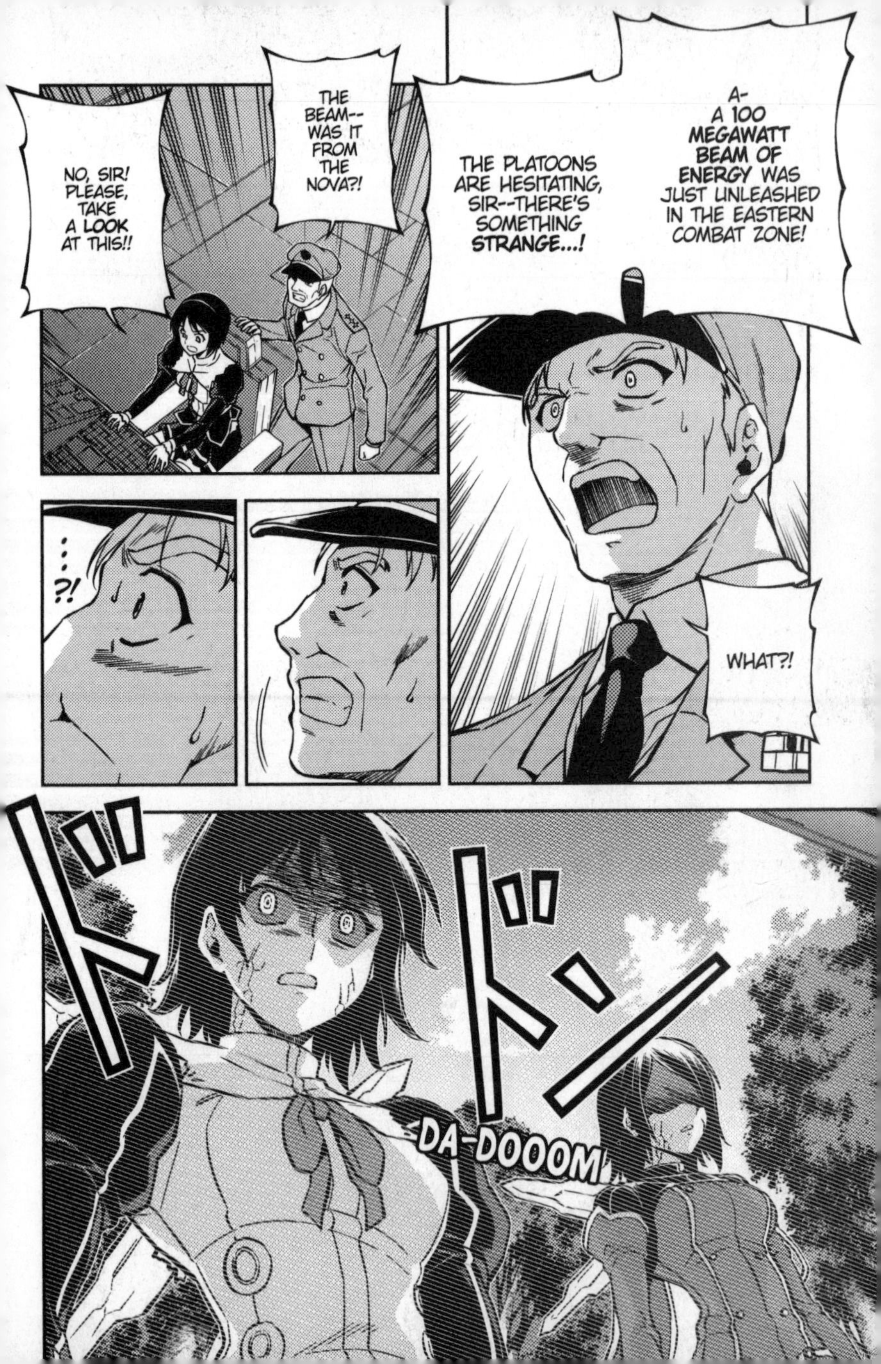
A- A 100 MEGAWATT BEAM OF ENERGY WAS JUST UNLEASHED IN THE EASTERN COMBAT ZONE!
THE PLATOONS ARE HESITATING, SIR--THERE'S SOMETHING STRANGE...!
WHAT?!
THE BEAM--WAS IT FROM THE NOVA?!
NO, SIR! PLEASE, TAKE A LOOK AT THIS!!
...?!
DA-DOOOM

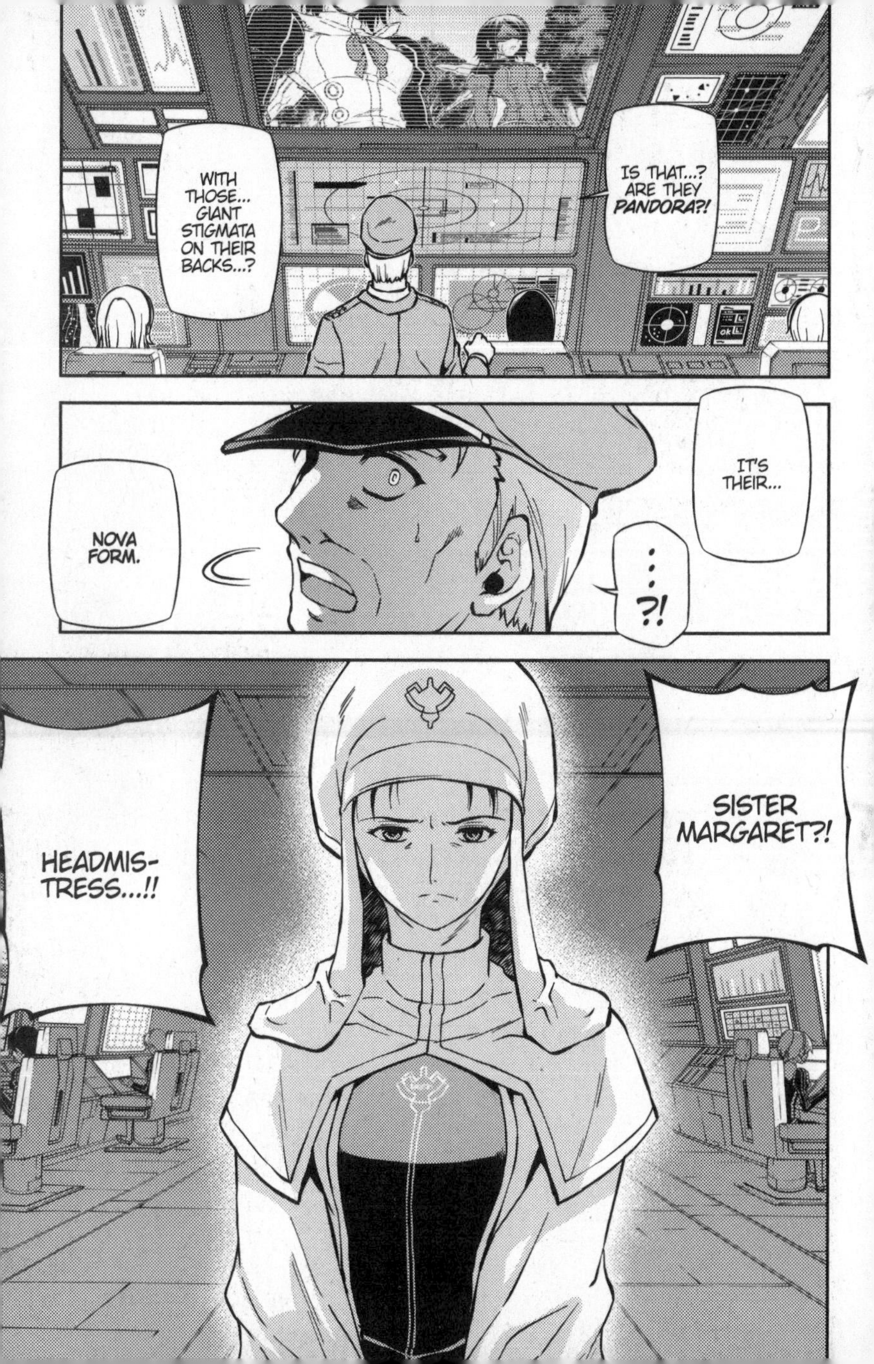
IS THAT...? ARE THEY *PANDORA*?!
WITH THOSE... GIANT STIGMATA ON THEIR BACKS...?
IT'S THEIR...
...?!
NOVA FORM.
SISTER MARGARET?!
HEADMIS-TRESS...!!

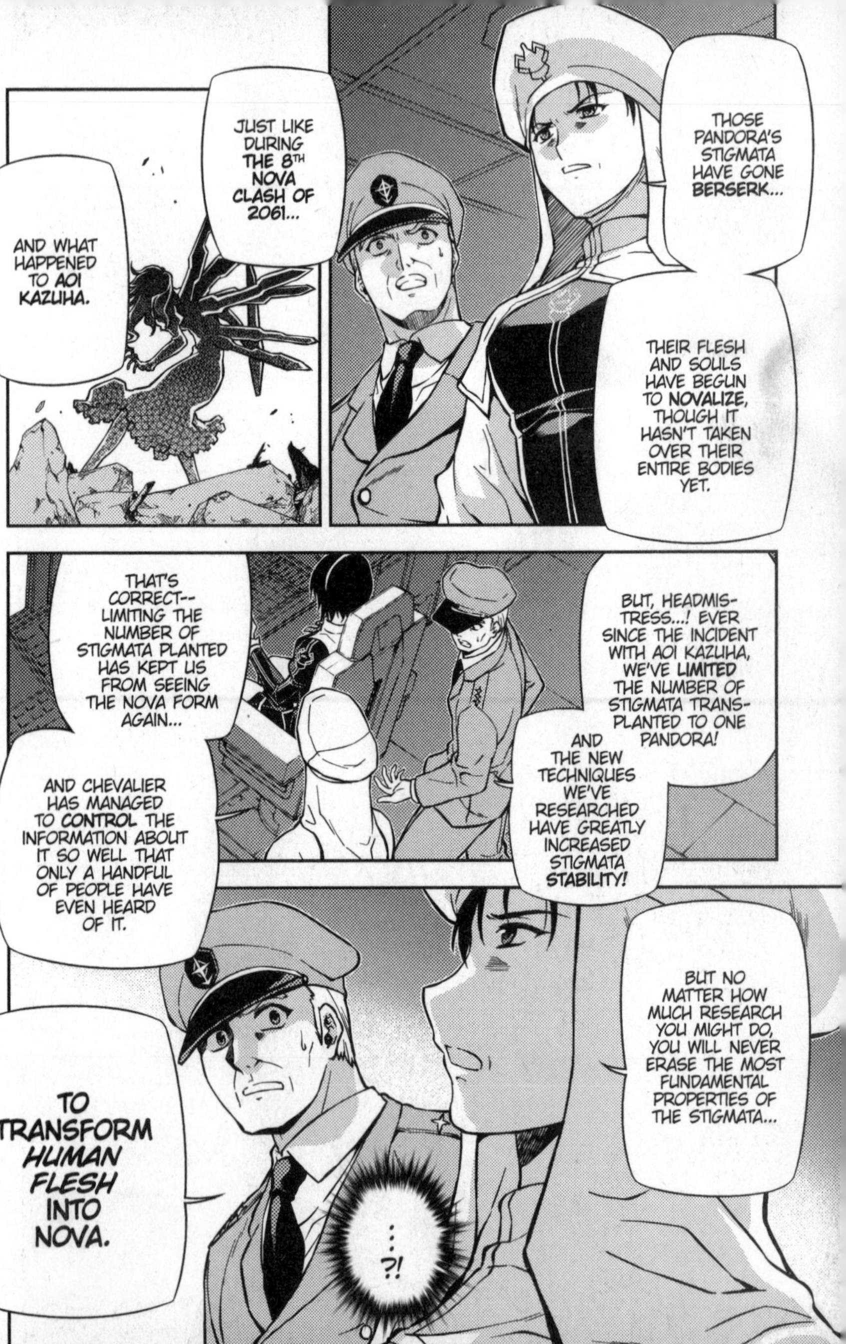
THOSE PANDORA'S STIGMATA HAVE GONE BERSERK...
THEIR FLESH AND SOULS HAVE BEGUN TO NOVALIZE, THOUGH IT HASN'T TAKEN OVER THEIR ENTIRE BODIES YET.
JUST LIKE DURING THE 8TH NOVA CLASH OF 2061...
AND WHAT HAPPENED TO AOI KAZUHA.
BUT, HEADMISTRESS...! EVER SINCE THE INCIDENT WITH AOI KAZUHA, WE'VE LIMITED THE NUMBER OF STIGMATA TRANSPLANTED TO ONE PANDORA!
AND THE NEW TECHNIQUES WE'VE RESEARCHED HAVE GREATLY INCREASED STIGMATA STABILITY!
THAT'S CORRECT--LIMITING THE NUMBER OF STIGMATA PLANTED HAS KEPT US FROM SEEING THE NOVA FORM AGAIN...
AND CHEVALIER HAS MANAGED TO CONTROL THE INFORMATION ABOUT IT SO WELL THAT ONLY A HANDFUL OF PEOPLE HAVE EVEN HEARD OF IT.
BUT NO MATTER HOW MUCH RESEARCH YOU MIGHT DO, YOU WILL NEVER ERASE THE MOST FUNDAMENTAL PROPERTIES OF THE STIGMATA...
TO TRANSFORM HUMAN FLESH INTO NOVA.
...?!

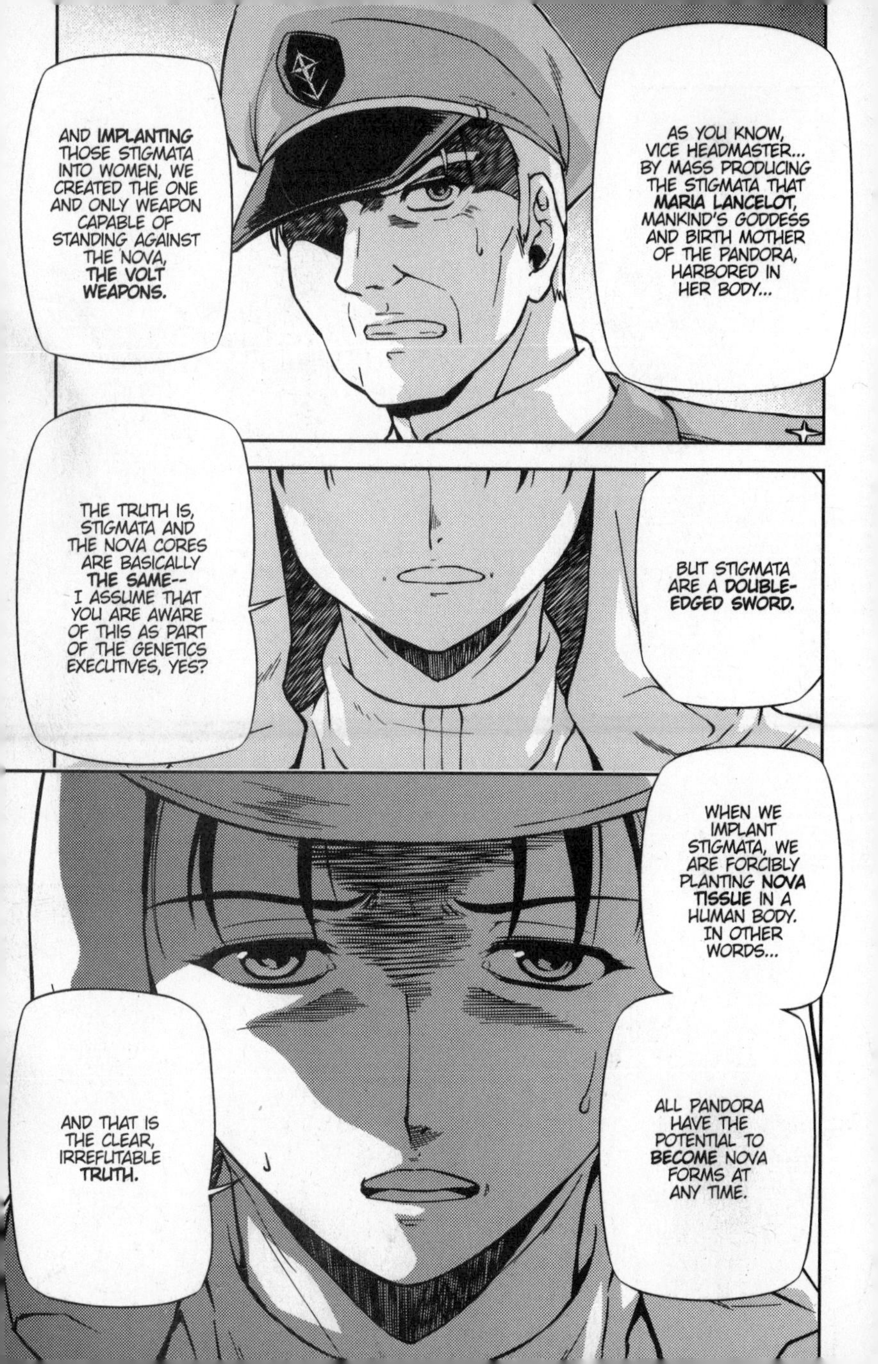
AS YOU KNOW, VICE HEADMASTER... BY MASS PRODUCING THE STIGMATA THAT MARIA LANCELOT, MANKIND'S GODDESS AND BIRTH MOTHER OF THE PANDORA, HARBORED IN HER BODY...
AND IMPLANTING THOSE STIGMATA INTO WOMEN, WE CREATED THE ONE AND ONLY WEAPON CAPABLE OF STANDING AGAINST THE NOVA, THE VOLT WEAPONS.
THE TRUTH IS, STIGMATA AND THE NOVA CORES ARE BASICALLY THE SAME-- I ASSUME THAT YOU ARE AWARE OF THIS AS PART OF THE GENETICS EXECUTIVES, YES?
BUT STIGMATA ARE A DOUBLE-EDGED SWORD.
WHEN WE IMPLANT STIGMATA, WE ARE FORCIBLY PLANTING NOVA TISSUE IN A HUMAN BODY. IN OTHER WORDS...
ALL PANDORA HAVE THE POTENTIAL TO BECOME NOVA FORMS AT ANY TIME.
AND THAT IS THE CLEAR, IRREFUTABLE TRUTH.

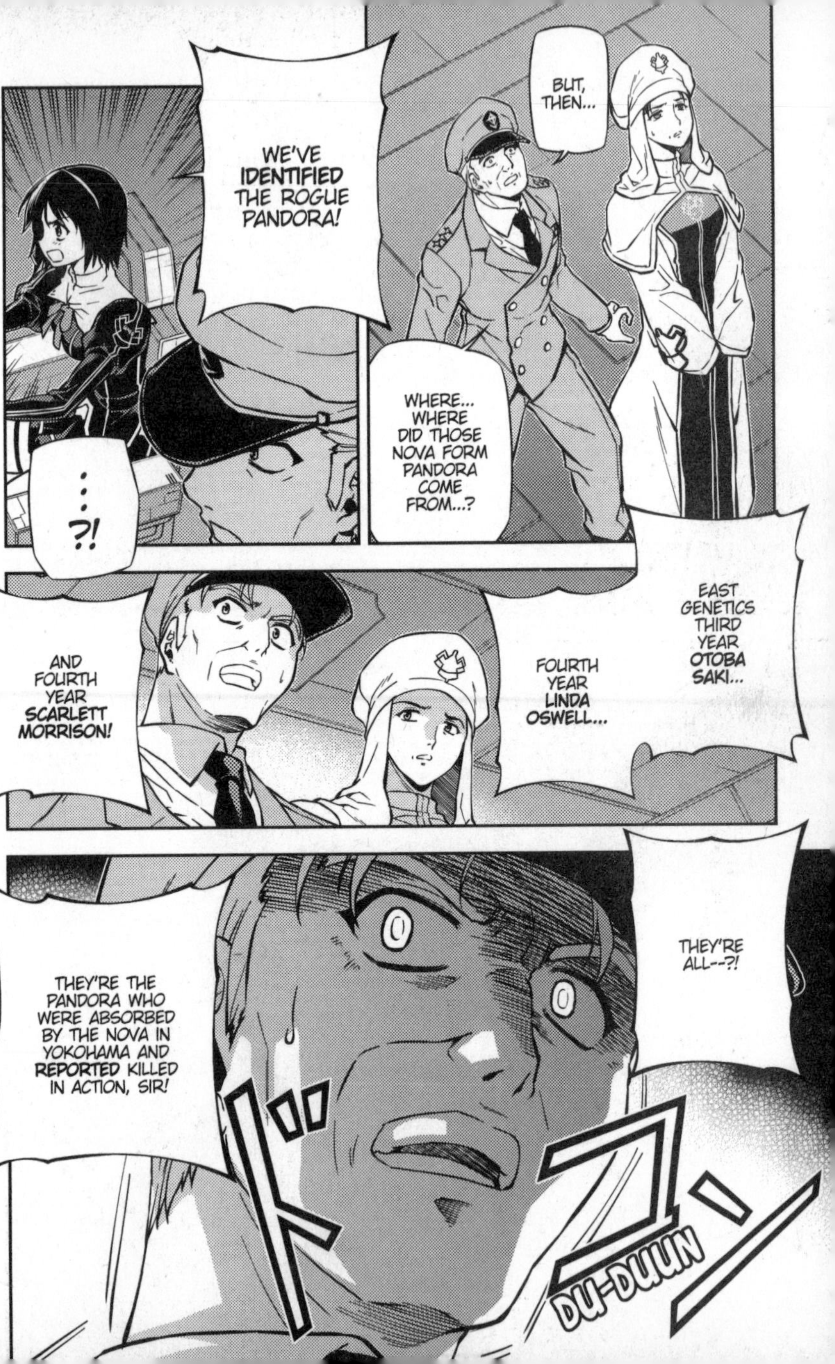
BUT, THEN...
WHERE... WHERE DID THOSE NOVA FORM PANDORA COME FROM...?
WE'VE **IDENTIFIED** THE ROGUE PANDORA!
...?!
EAST GENETICS THIRD YEAR **OTOBA SAKI**...
FOURTH YEAR **LINDA OSWELL**...
AND FOURTH YEAR **SCARLETT MORRISON!**
THEY'RE ALL--?!
THEY'RE THE PANDORA WHO WERE ABSORBED BY THE NOVA IN YOKOHAMA AND **REPORTED** KILLED IN ACTION, SIR!
DU-DUUN

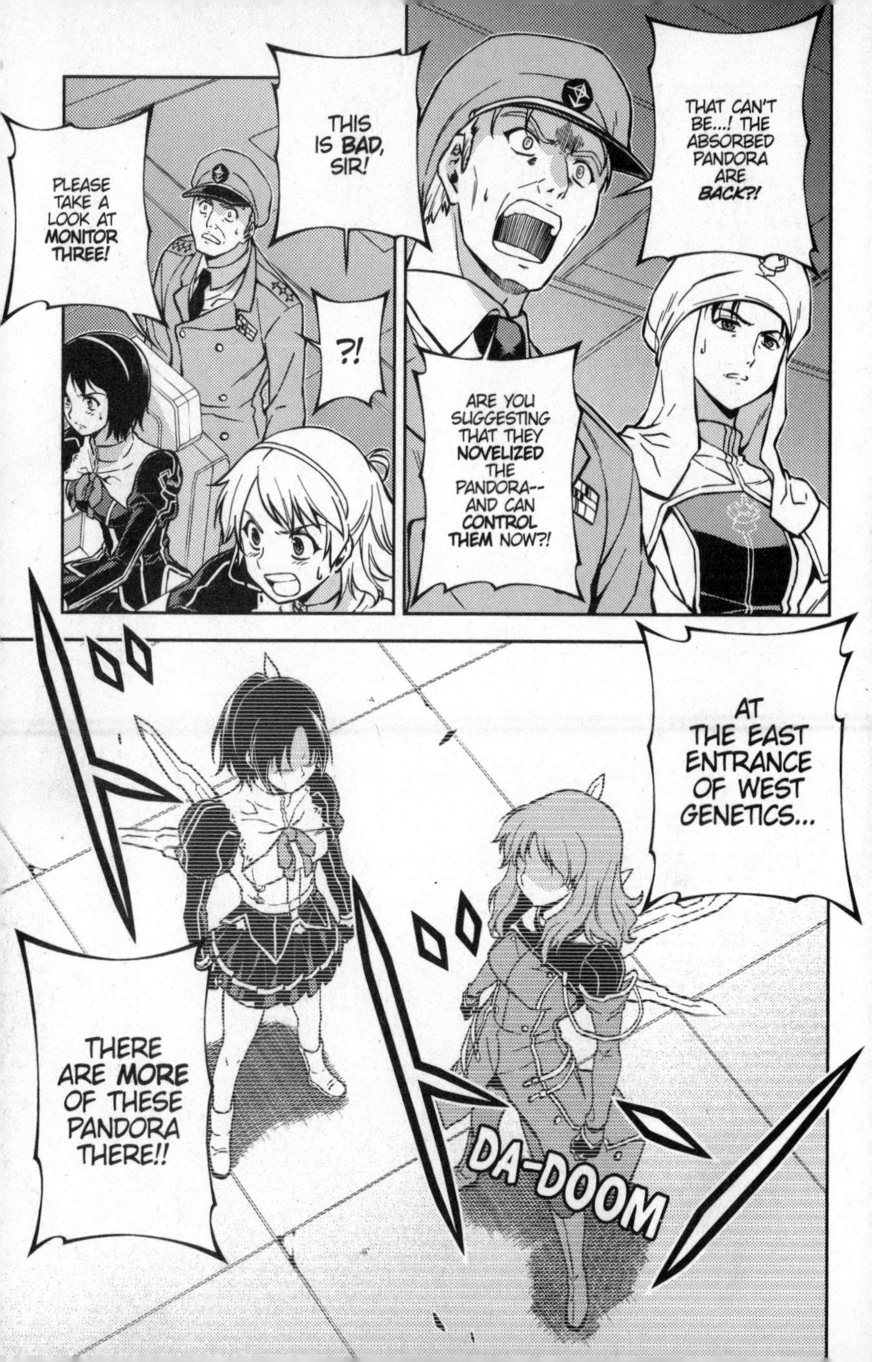
THAT CAN'T BE...! THE ABSORBED PANDORA ARE BACK?!
ARE YOU SUGGESTING THAT THEY NOVELIZED THE PANDORA-- AND CAN CONTROL THEM NOW?!
THIS IS BAD, SIR!
PLEASE TAKE A LOOK AT MONITOR THREE!
?!
AT THE EAST ENTRANCE OF WEST GENETICS...
THERE ARE MORE OF THESE PANDORA THERE!!
DA-DOOM

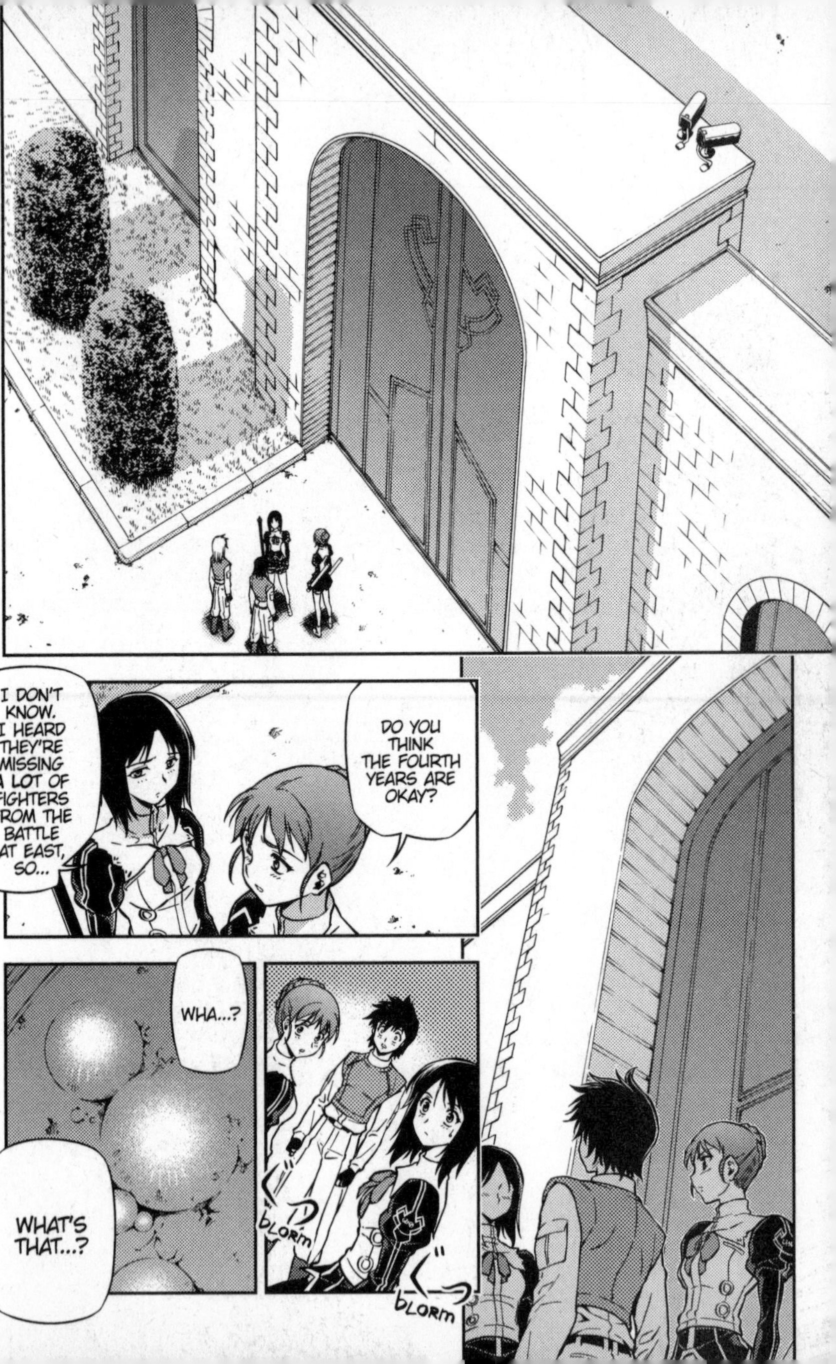
blorm
DO YOU THINK THE FOURTH YEARS ARE OKAY?
I DON'T KNOW. I HEARD THEY'RE MISSING A LOT OF FIGHTERS FROM THE BATTLE AT EAST, SO...
WHA...?
blorm
WHAT'S THAT...?

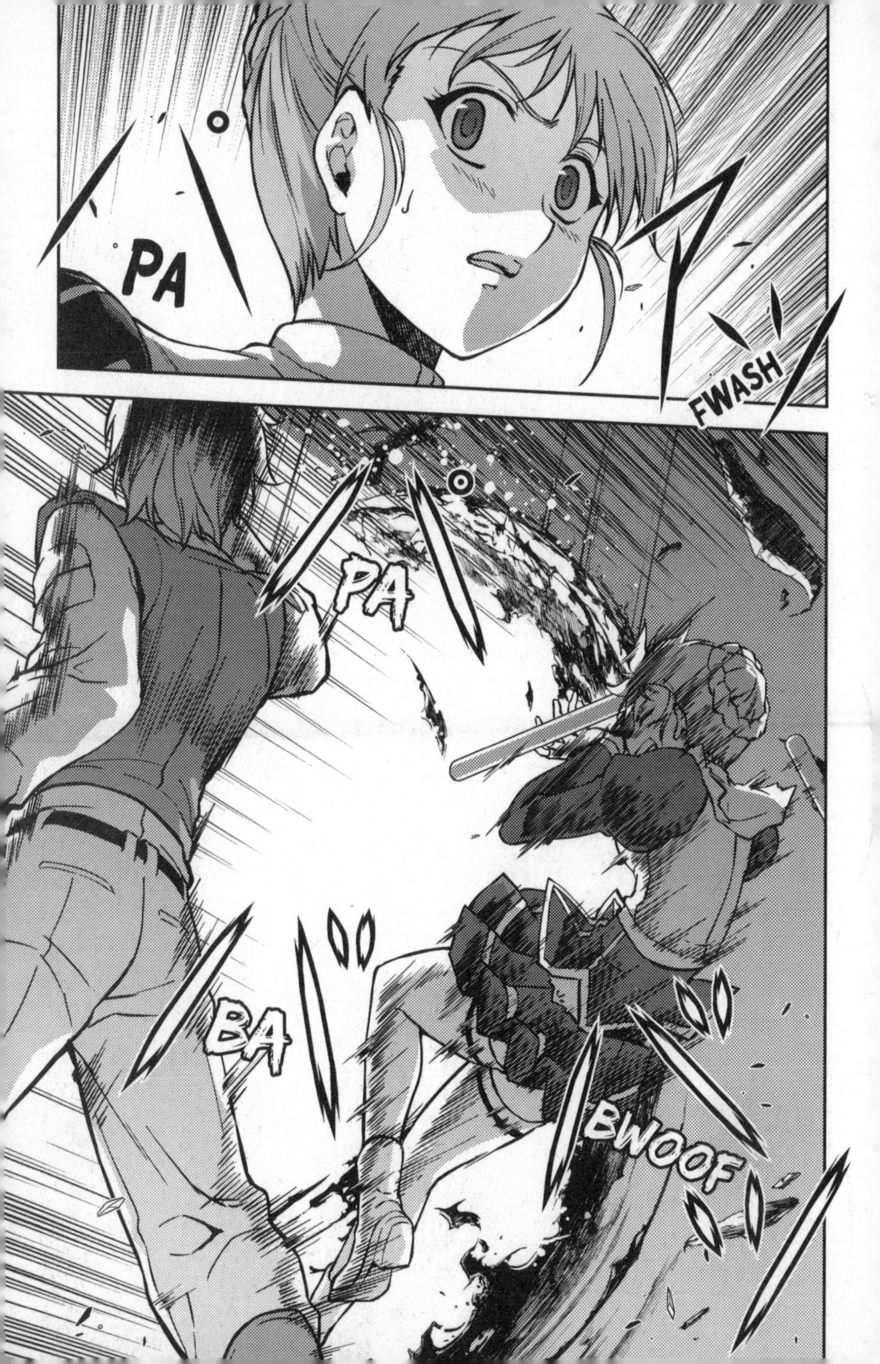
FWASH
PA
PA
BA
BWOOF

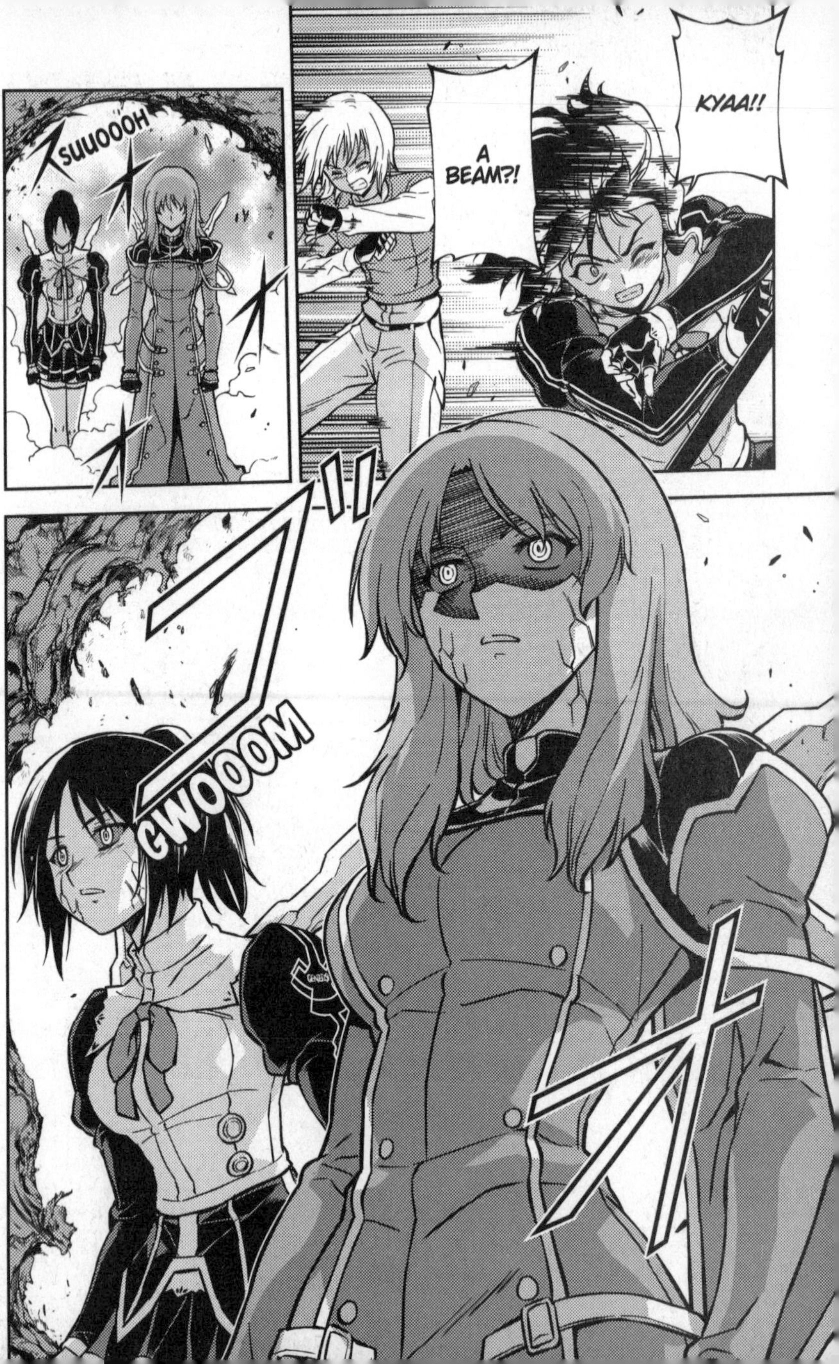
KYAA!!
A BEAM?!
SUUOOOH
GWOOOM

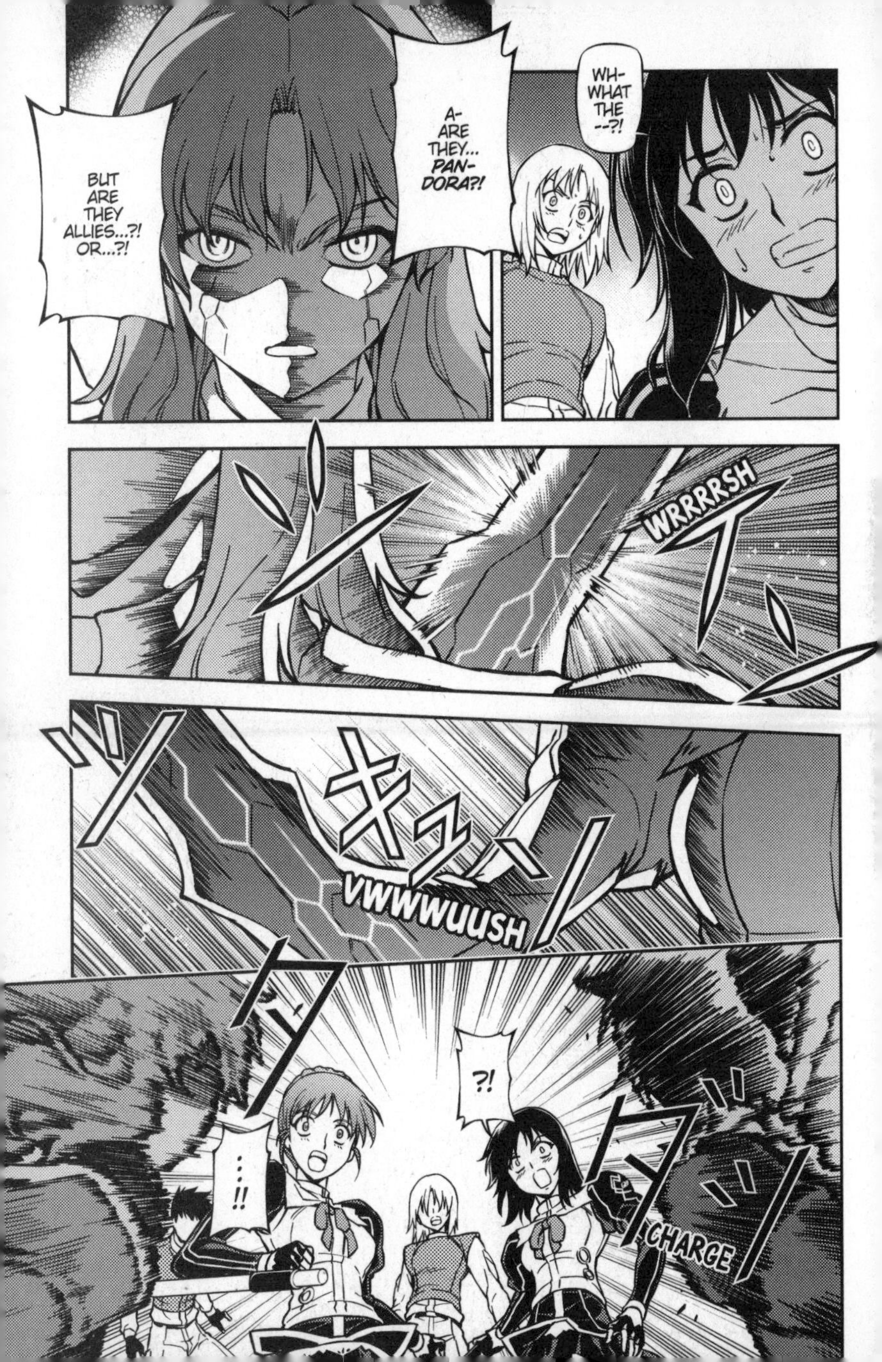
WH-WHAT THE --?!
A-ARE THEY... PANDORA?!
BUT ARE THEY ALLIES...?! OR...?!
WRRRRSH
VWWWUUSH
?!
...!!
CHARGE

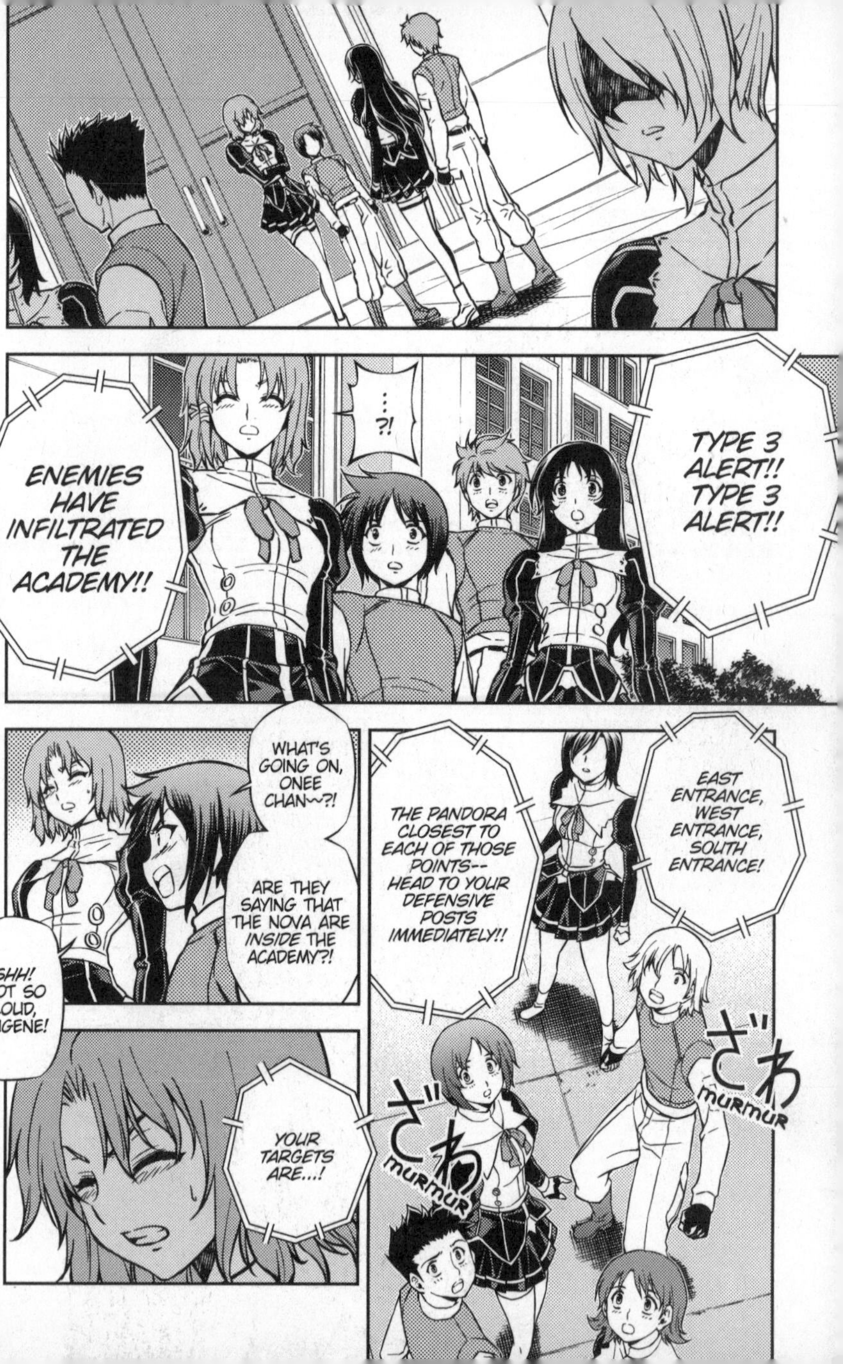

TYPE 3 ALERT!! TYPE 3 ALERT!!
...?!
ENEMIES HAVE INFILTRATED THE ACADEMY!!
EAST ENTRANCE, WEST ENTRANCE, SOUTH ENTRANCE!
THE PANDORA CLOSEST TO EACH OF THOSE POINTS-- HEAD TO YOUR DEFENSIVE POSTS IMMEDIATELY!!
ざわ MURMUR
ざわ MURMUR
WHAT'S GOING ON, ONEE CHAN~?!
ARE THEY SAYING THAT THE NOVA ARE *INSIDE* THE ACADEMY?!
SHH! NOT SO LOUD, EUGENE!
YOUR TARGETS ARE...!

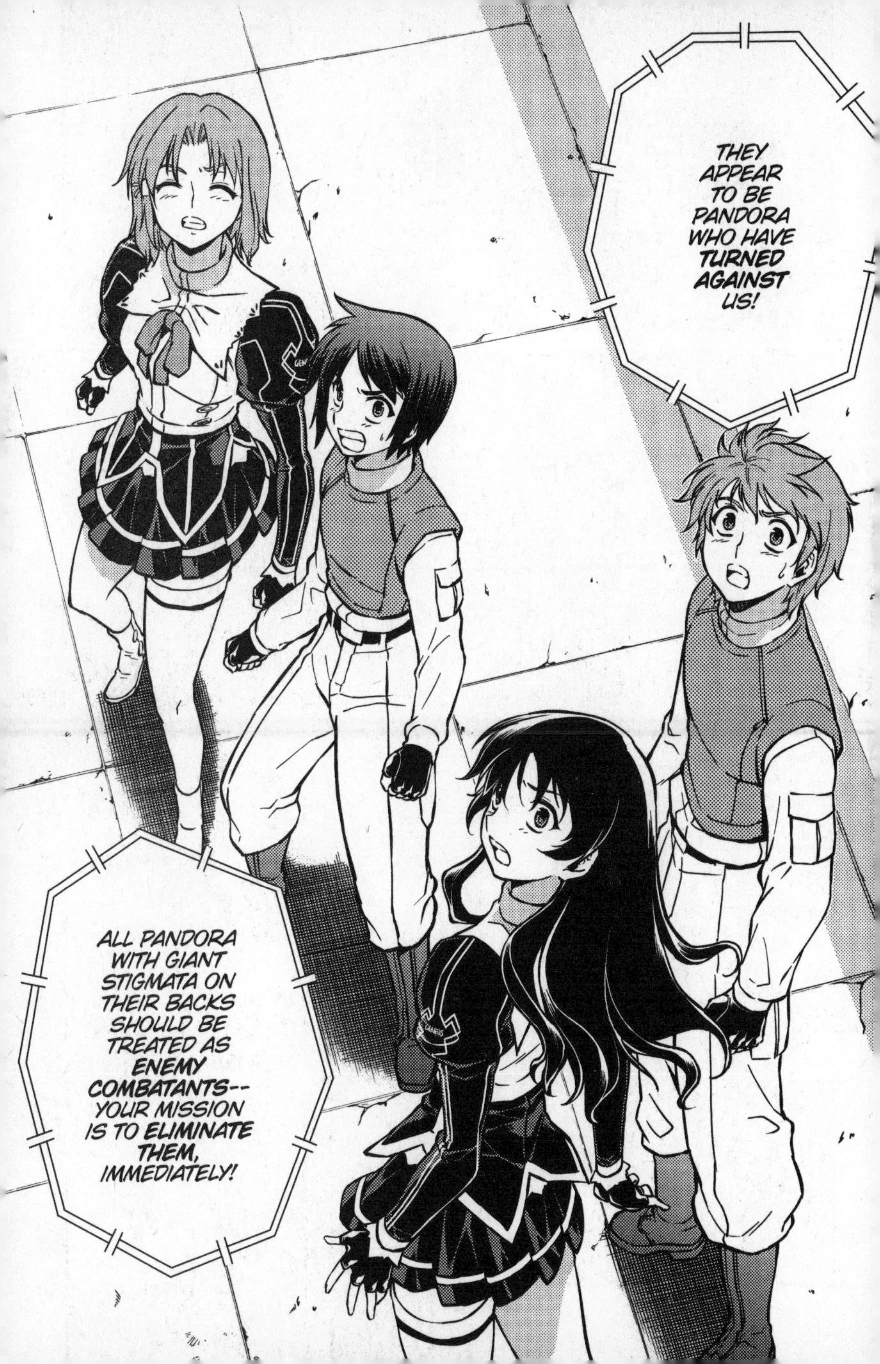
THEY APPEAR TO BE PANDORA WHO HAVE TURNED AGAINST US!
ALL PANDORA WITH GIANT STIGMATA ON THEIR BACKS SHOULD BE TREATED AS ENEMY COMBATANTS-- YOUR MISSION IS TO ELIMINATE THEM, IMMEDIATELY!

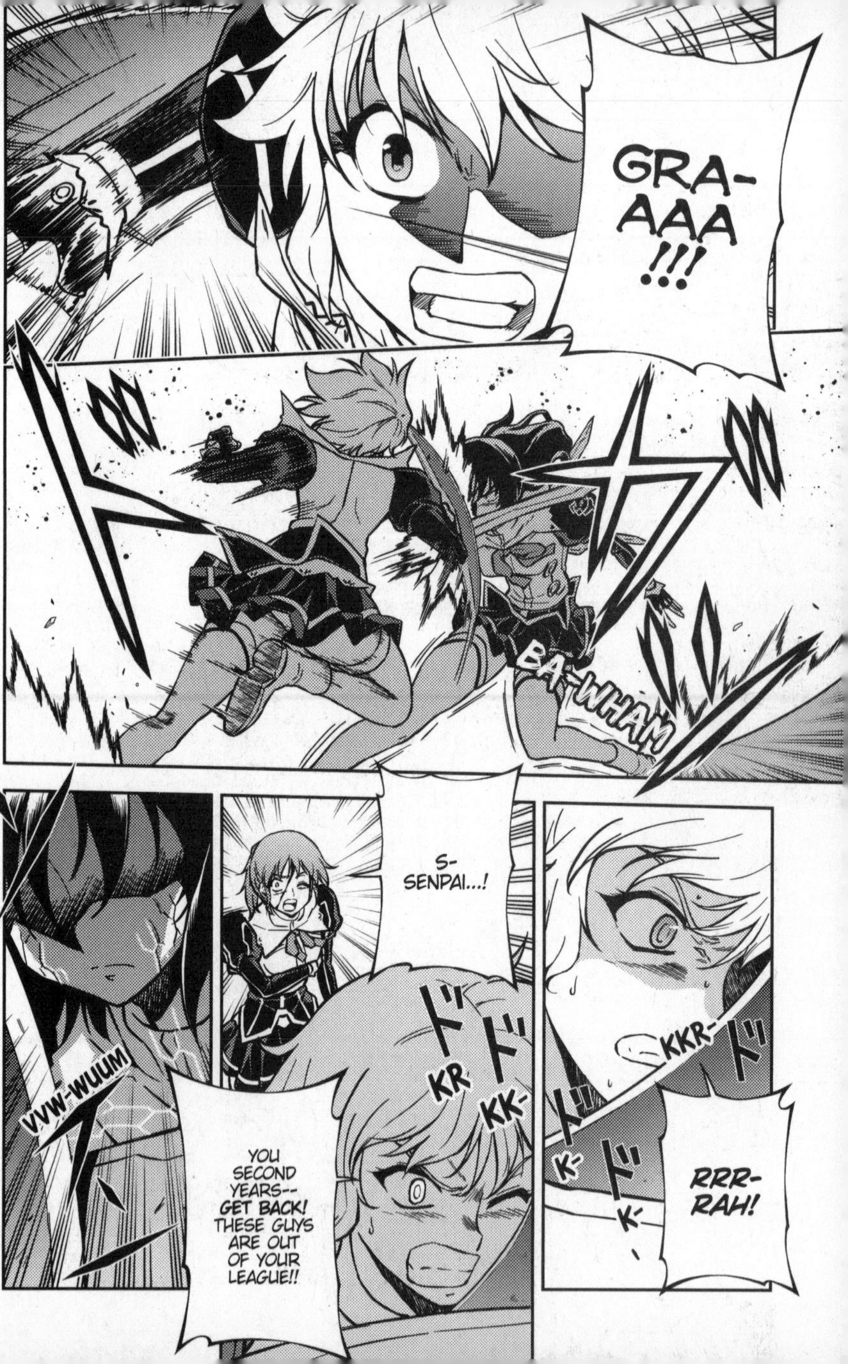
GRA-AAA!!!
BA-WHAM
KKR-
RRR-RAH!
S-SENPAI...!
KR
KK-
YOU SECOND YEARS-- GET BACK! THESE GUYS ARE OUT OF YOUR LEAGUE!!
VVW-WUUM

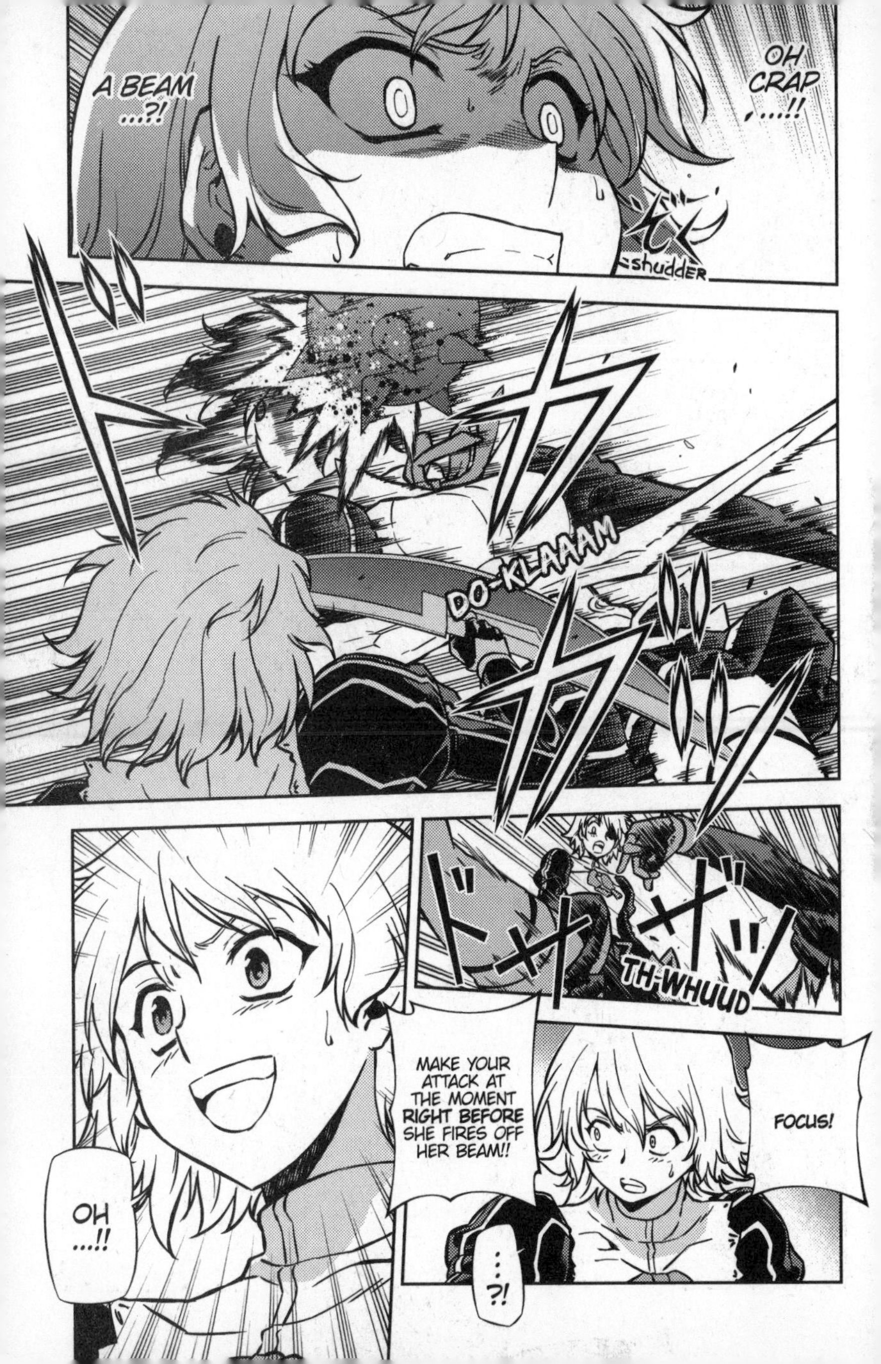
OH CRAP ...!!
A BEAM ...?!
shudder
DO-KLAAAM
TH-WHUUD
FOCUS!
MAKE YOUR ATTACK AT THE MOMENT **RIGHT BEFORE** SHE FIRES OFF HER BEAM!!
...?!
OH ...!!

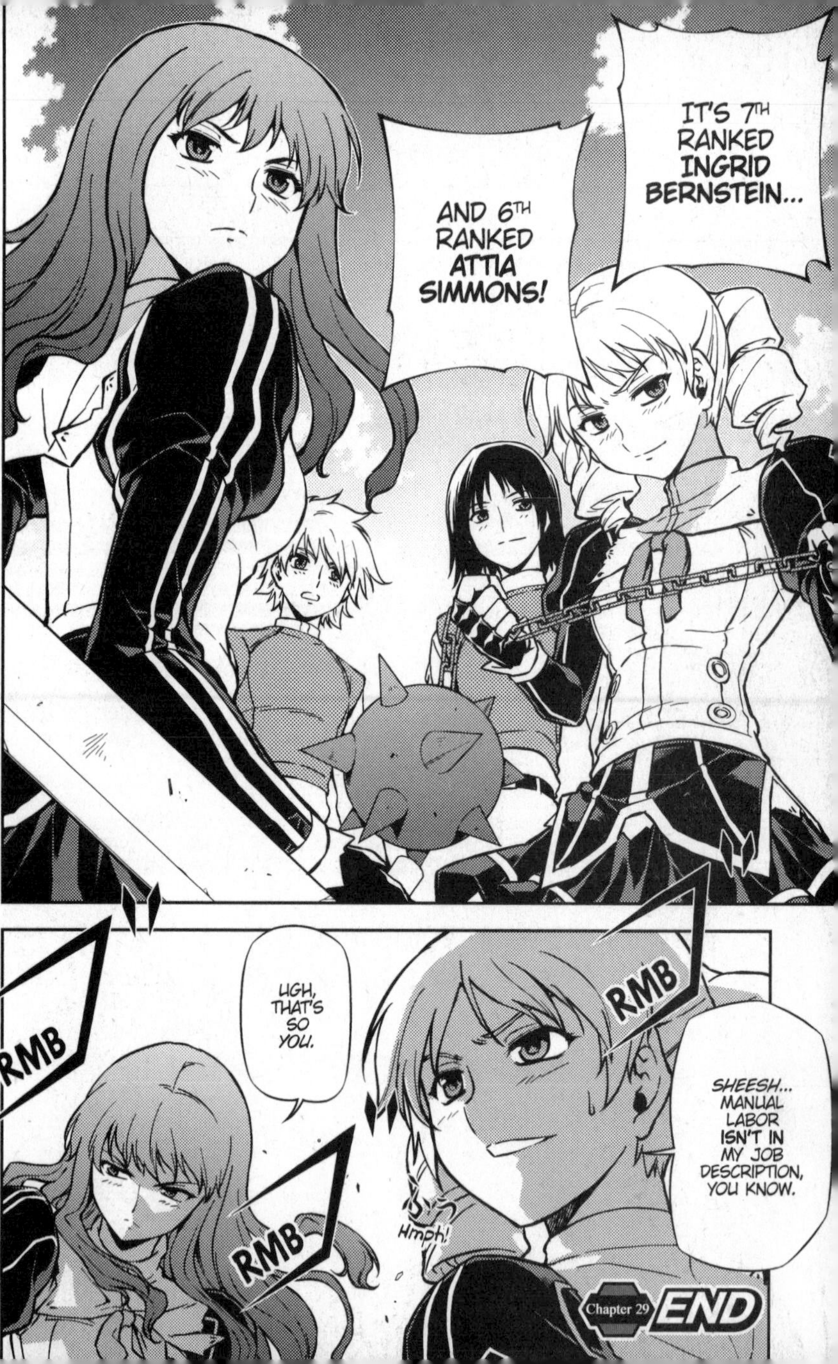
IT'S 7TH RANKED INGRID BERNSTEIN...
AND 6TH RANKED ATTIA SIMMONS!
RMB
SHEESH... MANUAL LABOR ISN'T IN MY JOB DESCRIPTION, YOU KNOW.
UGH, THAT'S SO YOU.
RMB
Hmph!
RMB
Chapter 29 END

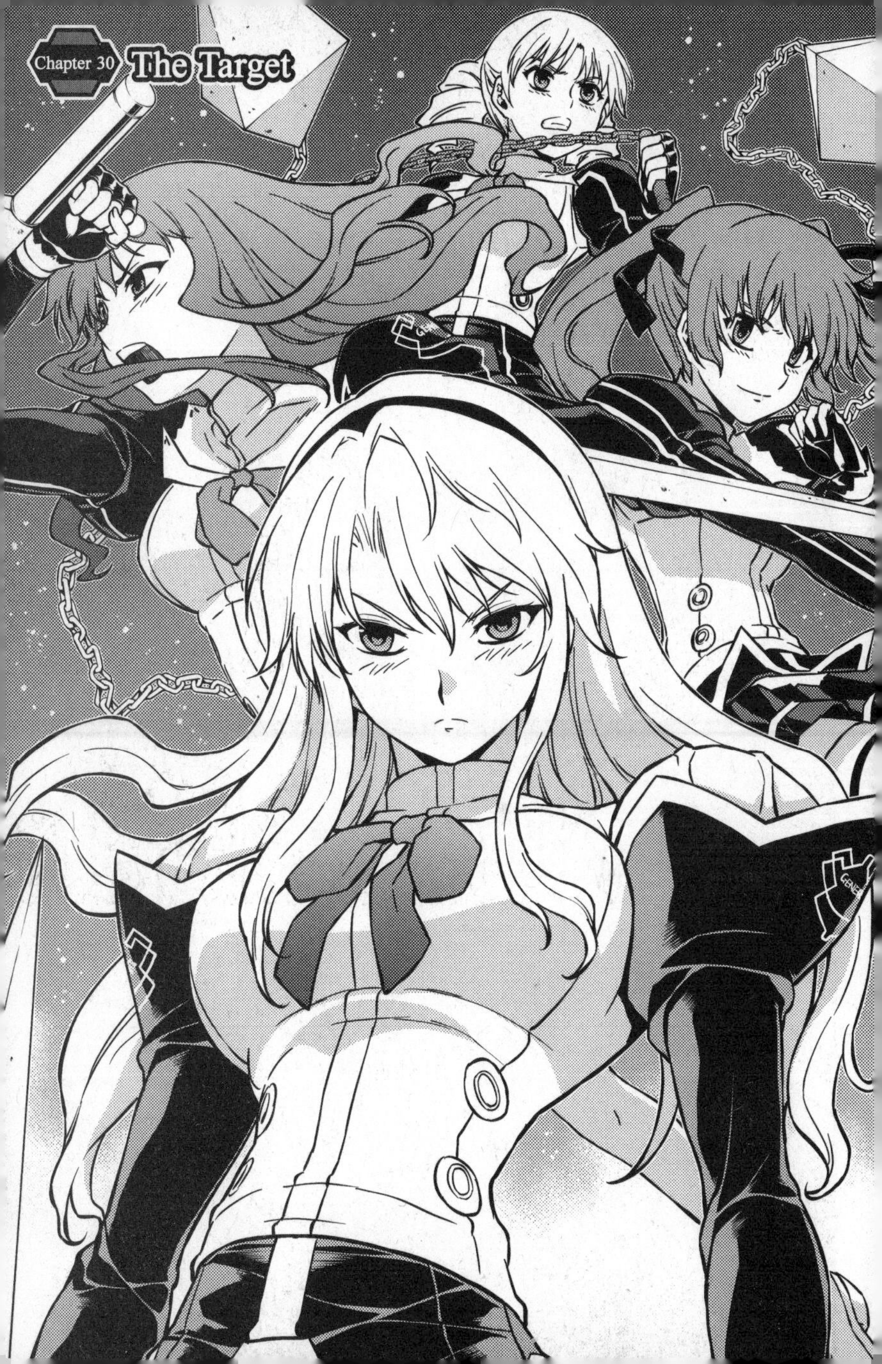
Chapter 30
The Target

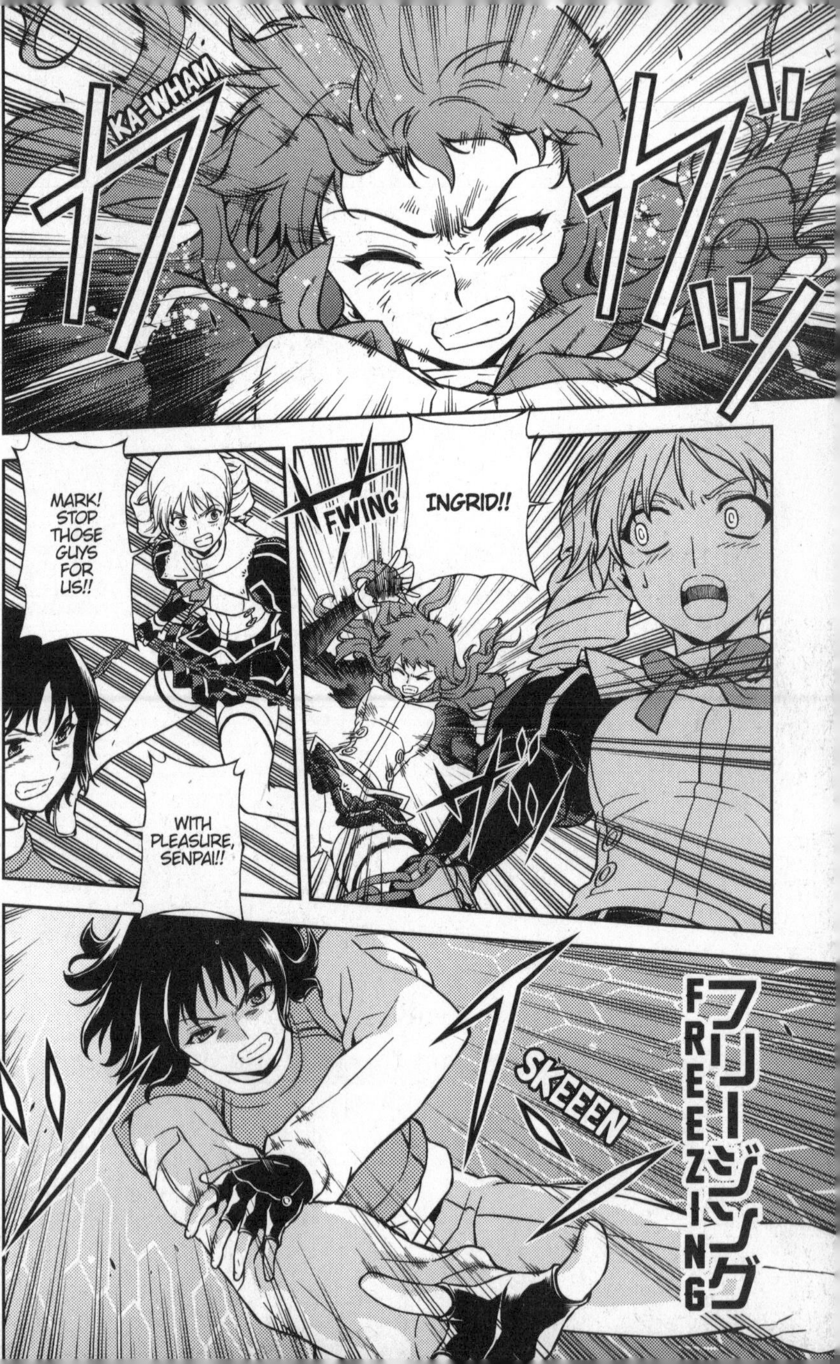
KA-WHAM
INGRID!!
FWING
MARK! STOP THOSE GUYS FOR US!!
WITH PLEASURE, SENPAI!!
フリージング
FREEZING
SKEEEN

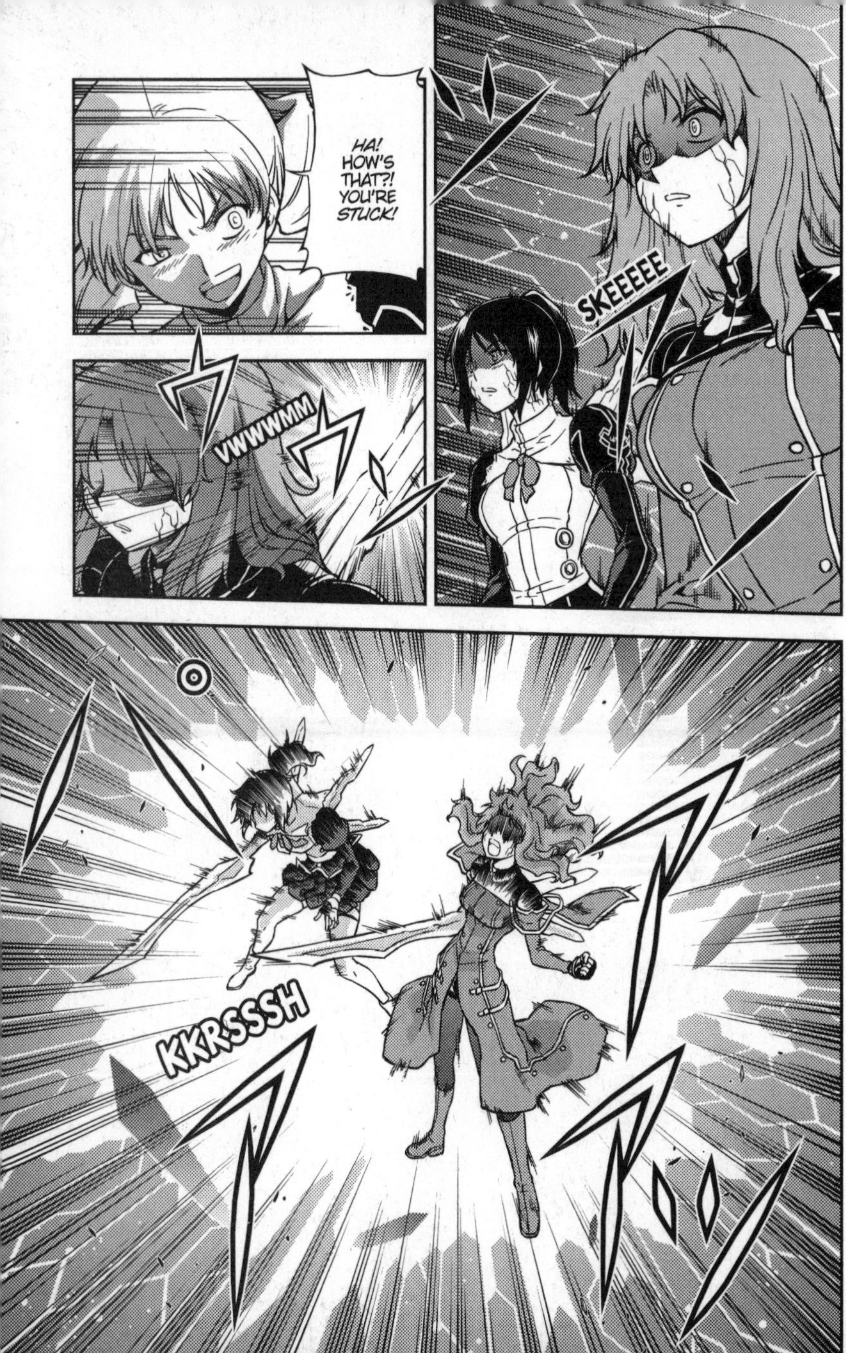
SKEEEEE
HA! HOW'S THAT?! YOU'RE STUCK!
VWWWMM
KKRSSSH

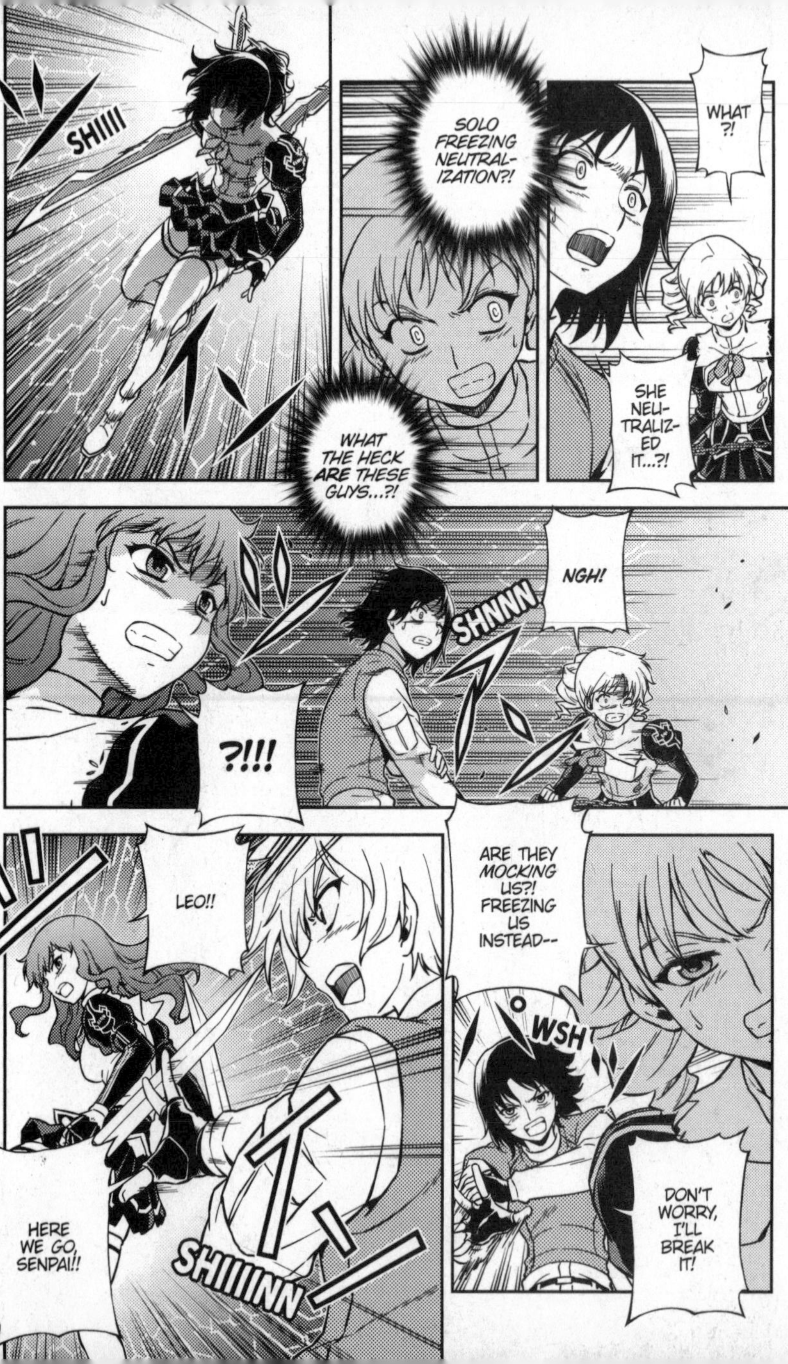
WHAT ?!
SHE NEUTRALIZED IT...?!
SOLO FREEZING NEUTRALIZATION?!
WHAT THE HECK ARE THESE GUYS...?!
SHIIII
NGH!
SHNNN
?!!!
ARE THEY MOCKING US?! FREEZING US INSTEAD--
WSH
DON'T WORRY, I'LL BREAK IT!
LEO!!
HERE WE GO, SENPAI!!
SHIIIINN

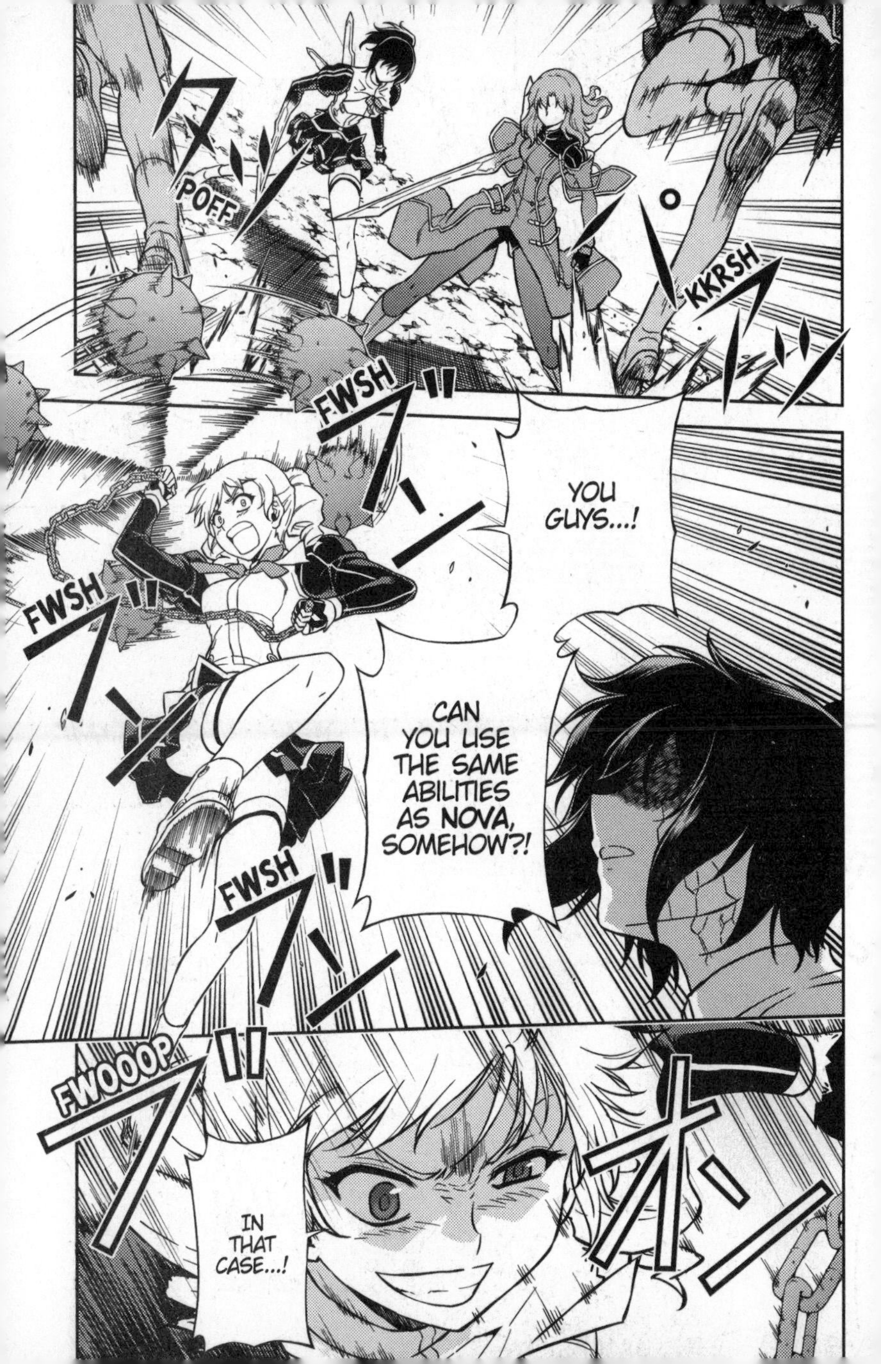
KKRSH
POFF
FWSH
YOU GUYS...!
CAN YOU USE THE SAME ABILITIES AS NOVA, SOMEHOW?!
FWSH
FWSH
FWOOOP
IN THAT CASE...!

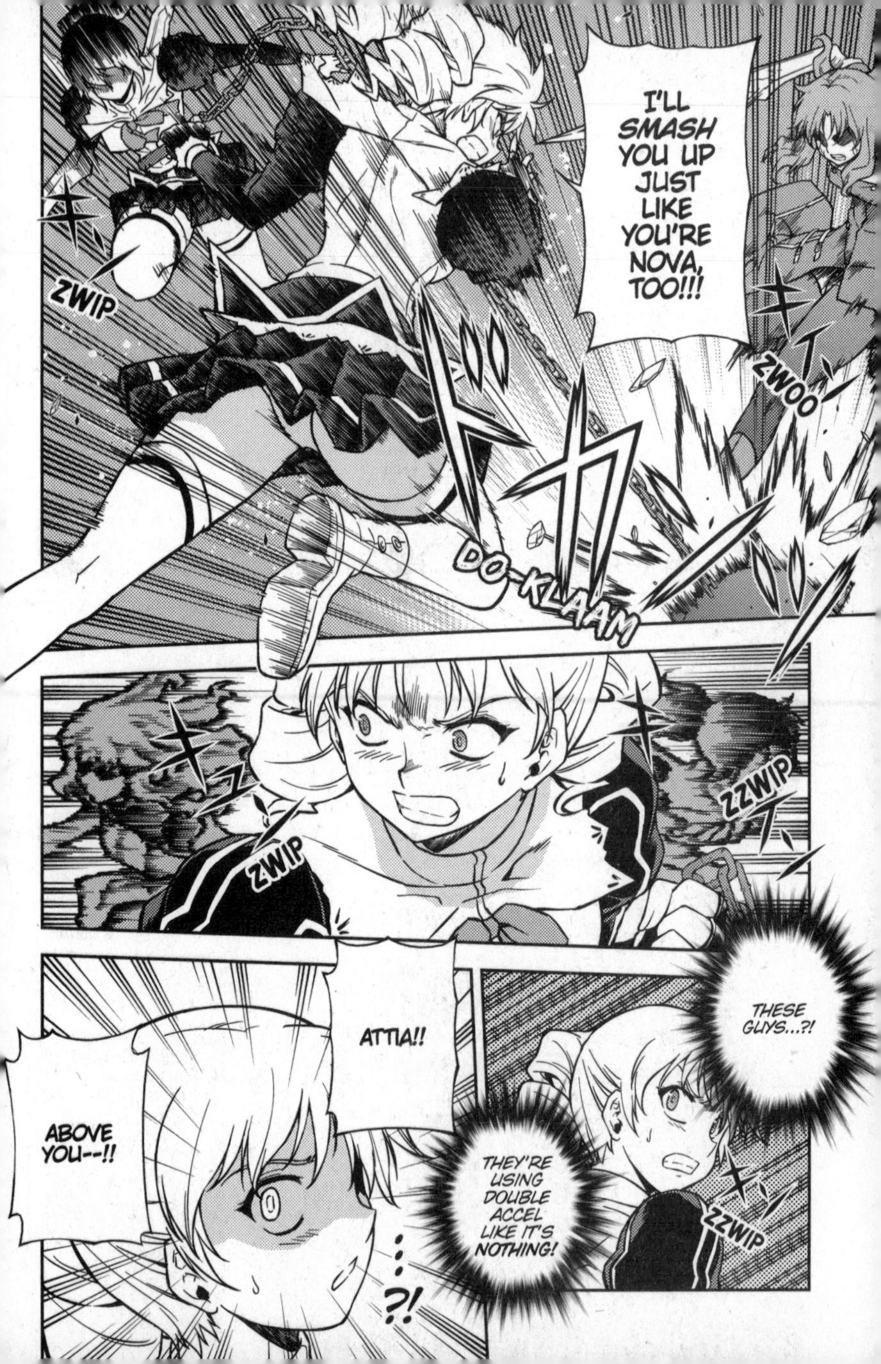
I'LL SMASH YOU UP JUST LIKE YOU'RE NOVA, TOO!!!
ZWOO
DO-KLAAM
ZWIP
ZZWIP
ZWIP
THESE GUYS...?!
THEY'RE USING DOUBLE ACCEL LIKE IT'S NOTHING!
ZZWIP
ATTIA!!
ABOVE YOU--!!
...?!

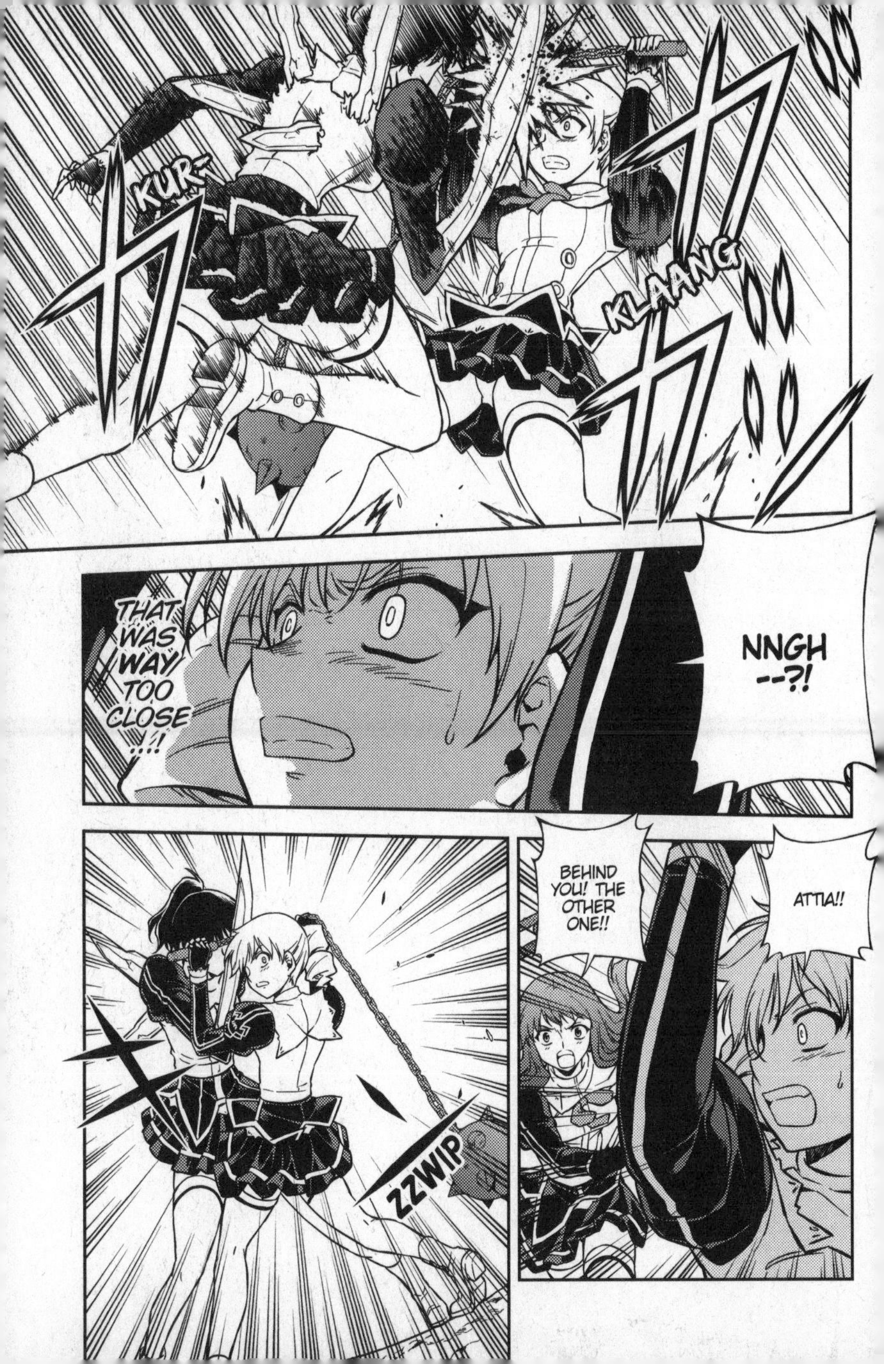
KLAANG
KUR-
NNGH --?!
THAT WAS WAY TOO CLOSE ...!
ATTIA!!
BEHIND YOU! THE OTHER ONE!!
ZZWIP

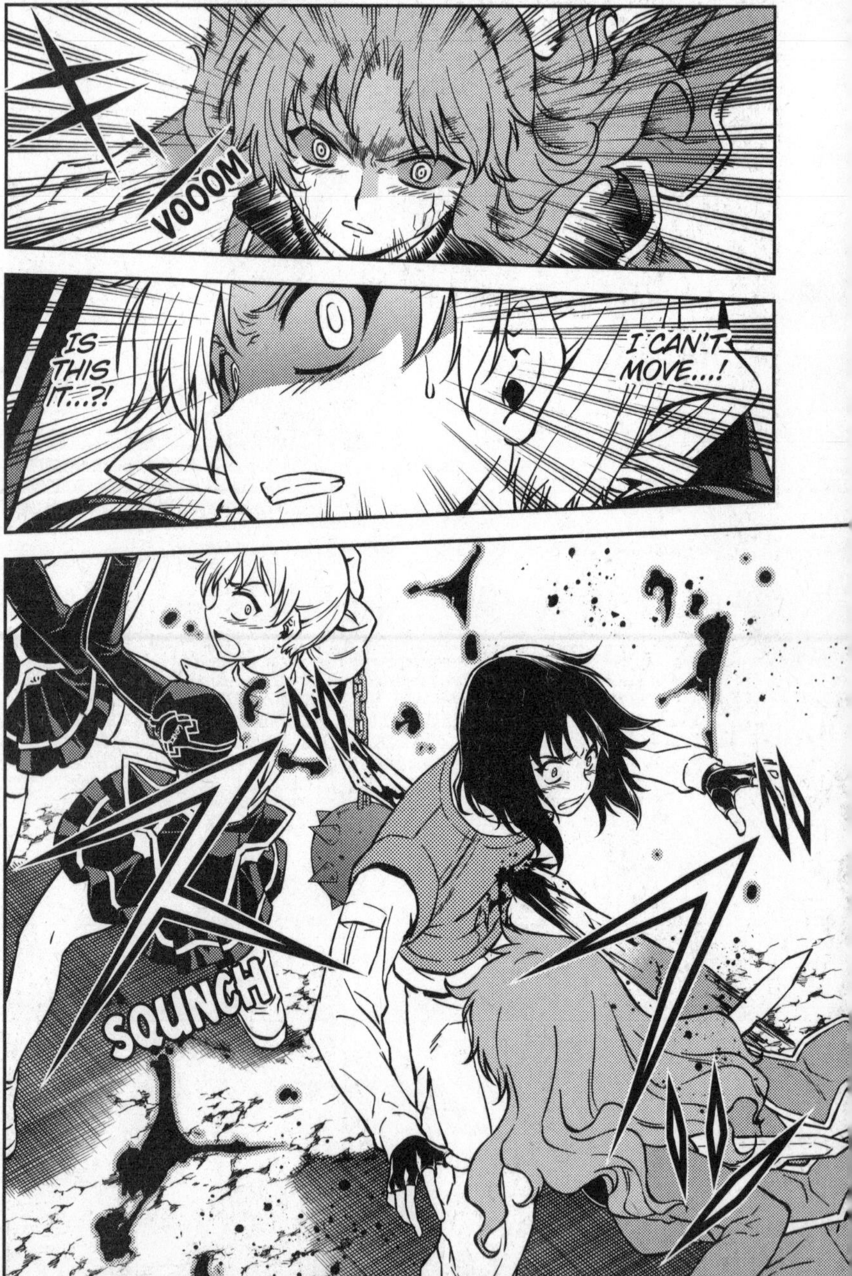
VOOOM
I CAN'T MOVE...!
IS THIS IT...?!
SQUNCH

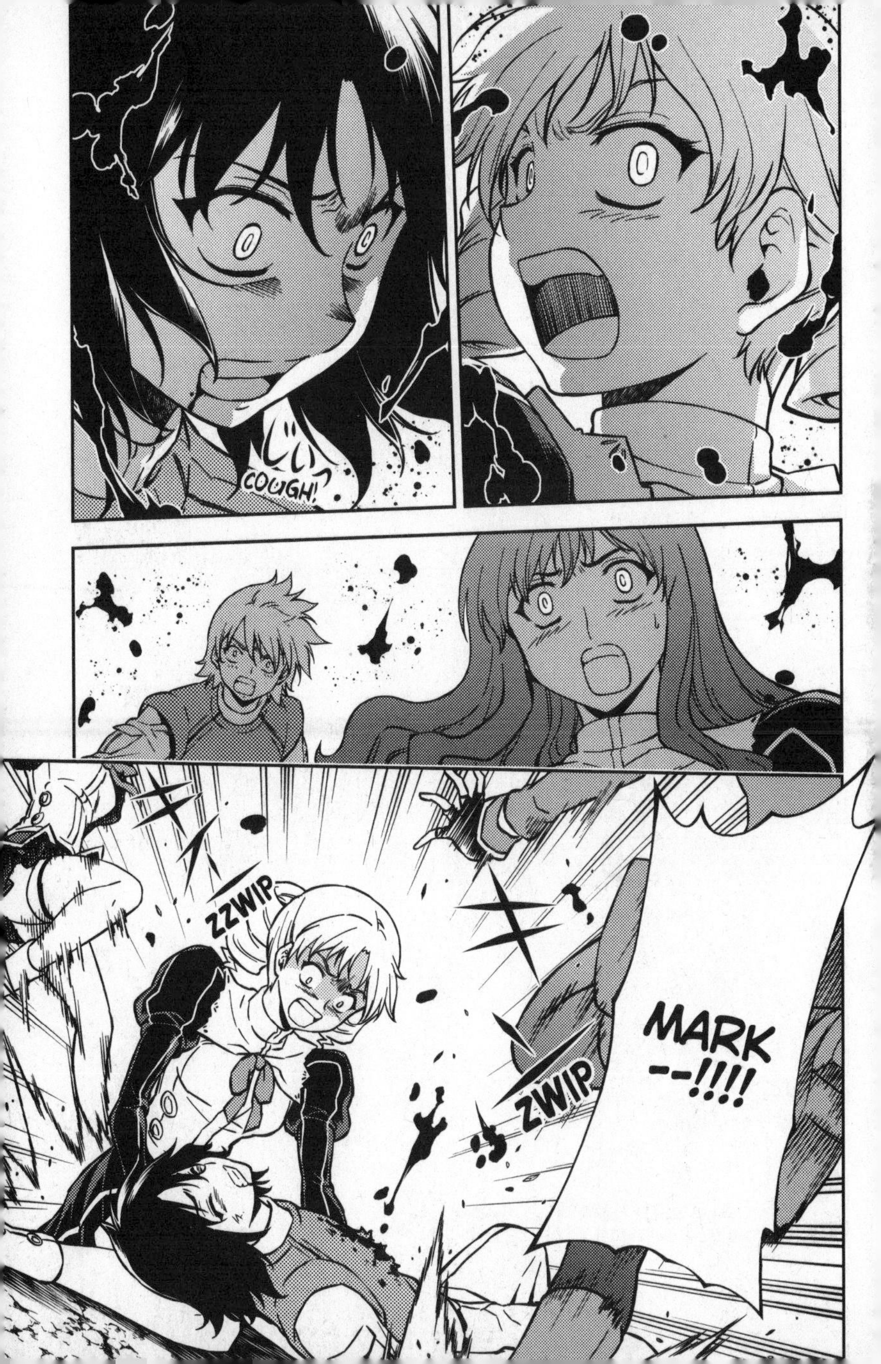
COUGH!
MARK
--!!!!
ZWIP
ZZWIP

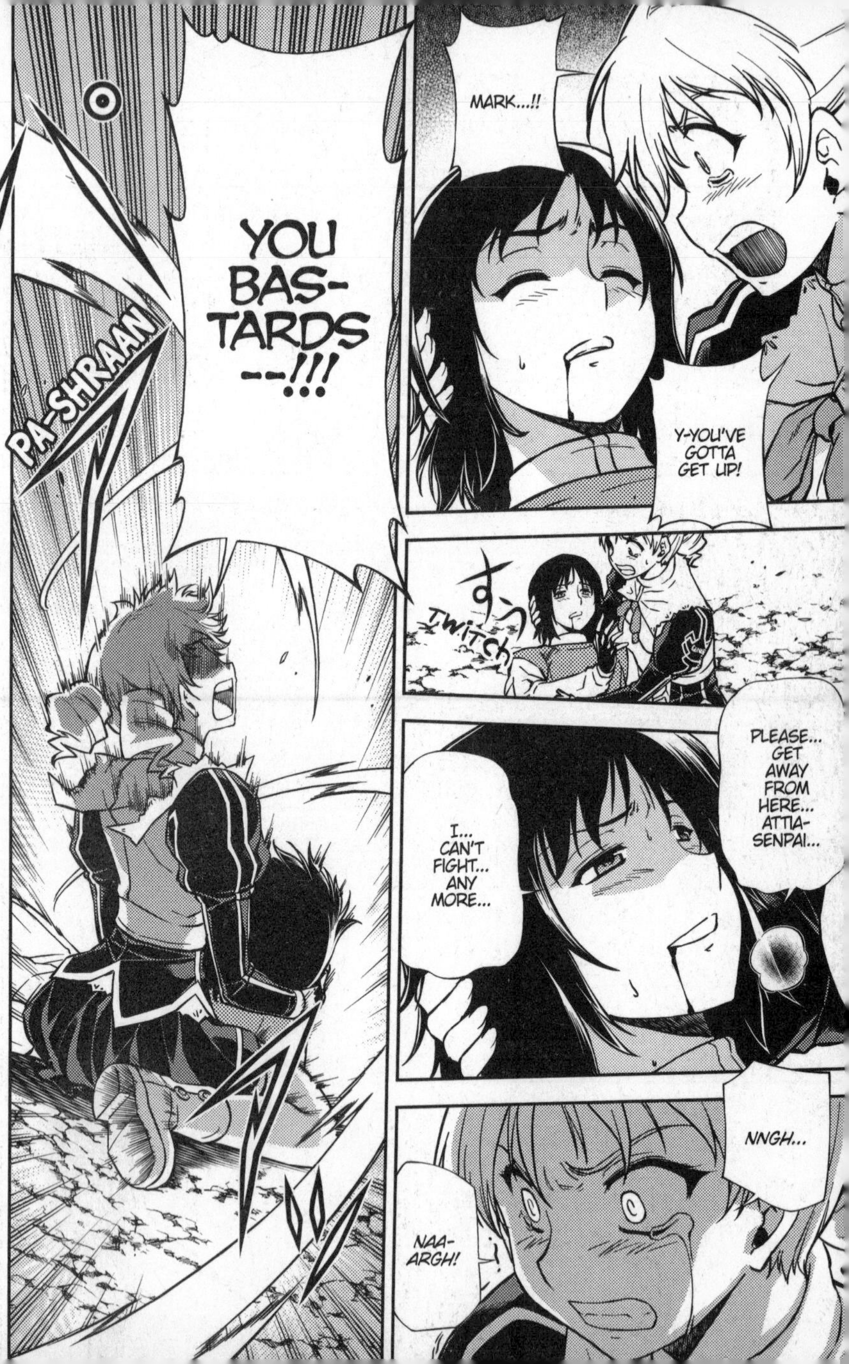
MARK...!!
Y-YOU'VE GOTTA GET UP!
すっ
TWITCH
PLEASE... GET AWAY FROM HERE... ATTIA-SENPAI...
I... CAN'T FIGHT... ANY MORE...
NNGH...
NAA-ARGH!
YOU BAS-TARDS --!!!
PA-SHRAAN

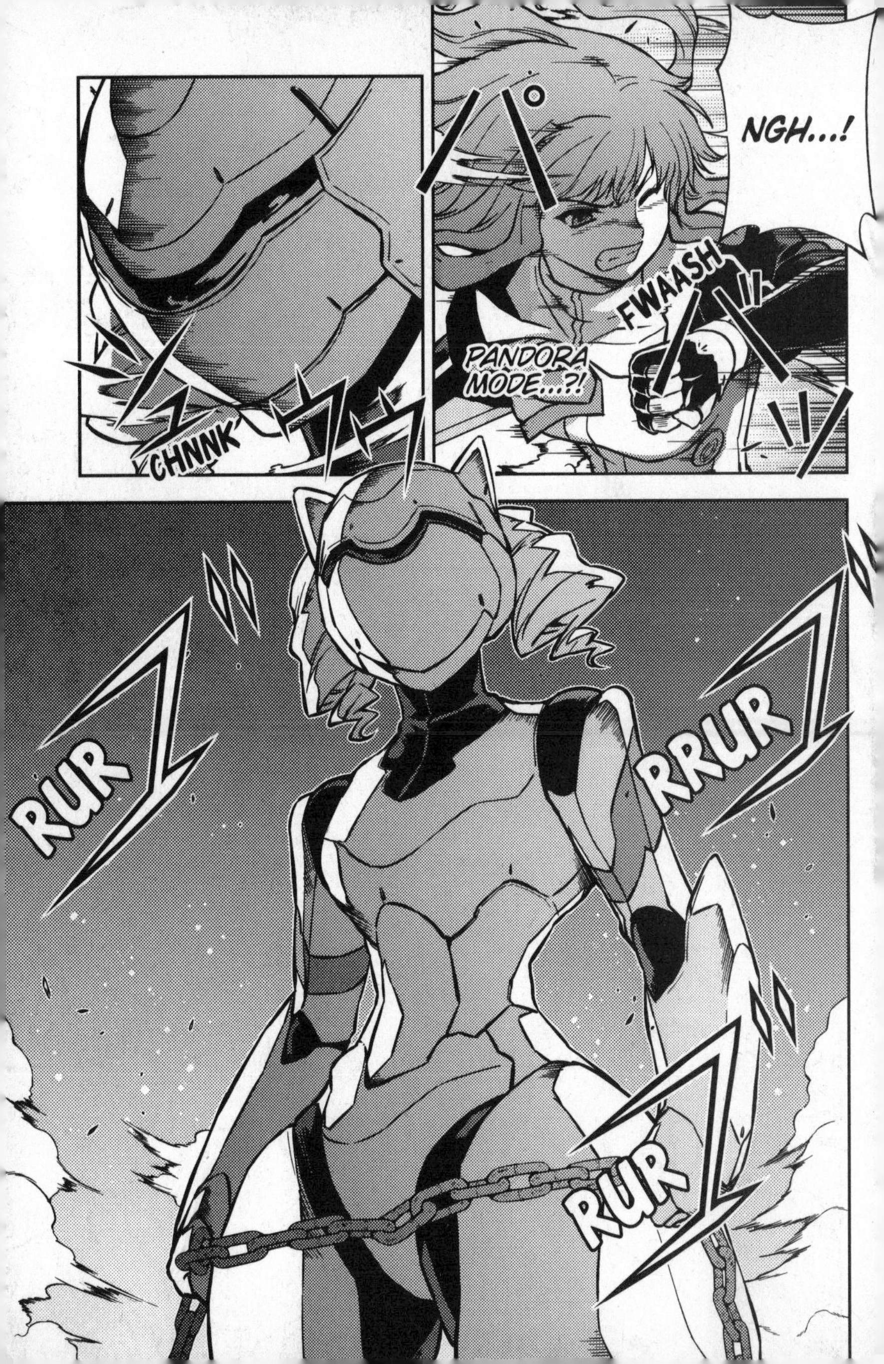
NGH...!
PANDORA MODE...?!
FWAASH
CHNNK
RRUR
RUR
RUR

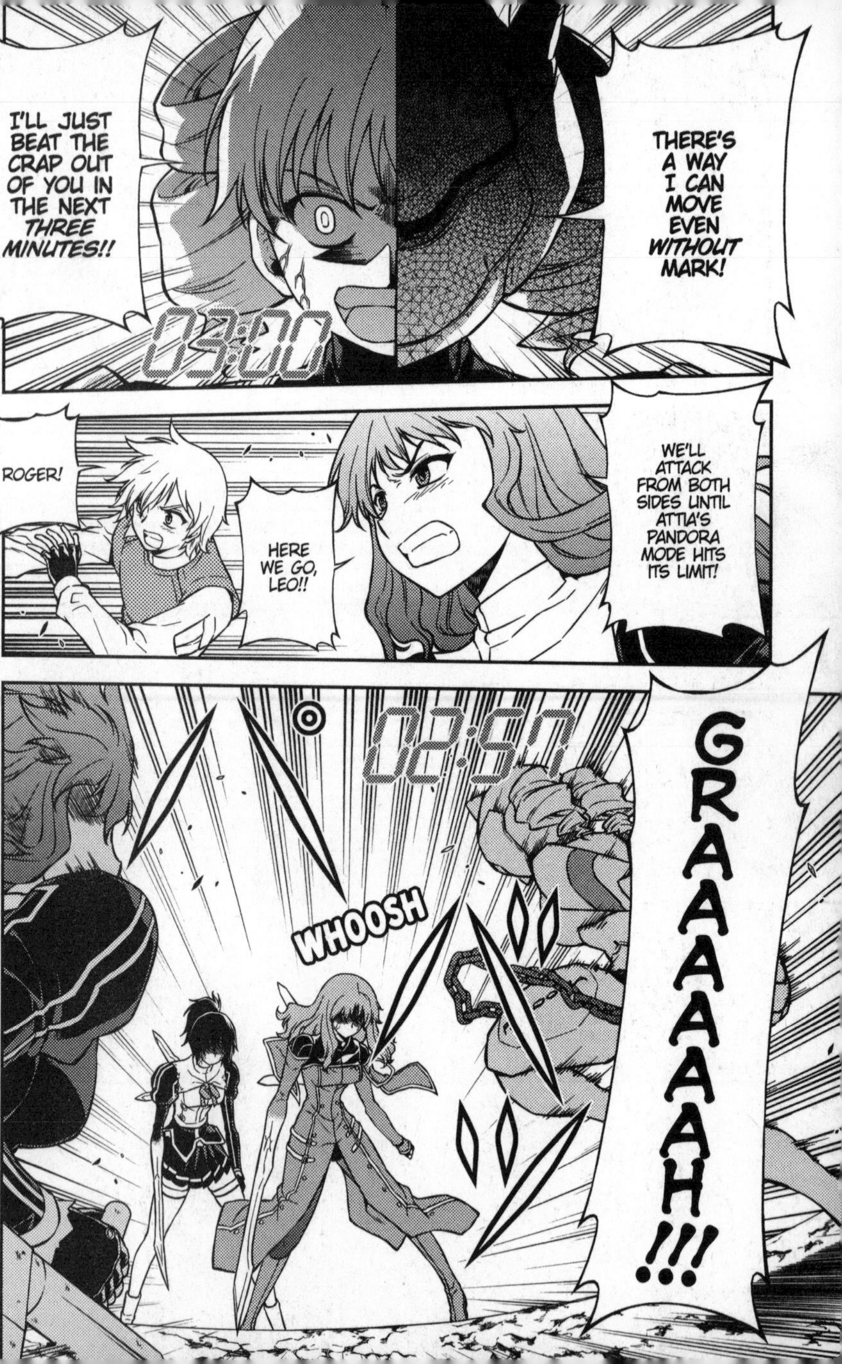
THERE'S A WAY I CAN MOVE EVEN *WITHOUT* MARK!
I'LL JUST BEAT THE CRAP OUT OF YOU IN THE NEXT *THREE MINUTES!!*
03:00
WE'LL ATTACK FROM BOTH SIDES UNTIL ATTIA'S PANDORA MODE HITS ITS LIMIT!
HERE WE GO, LEO!!
ROGER!
GRAAAAAAH!!!
02:57
WHOOSH

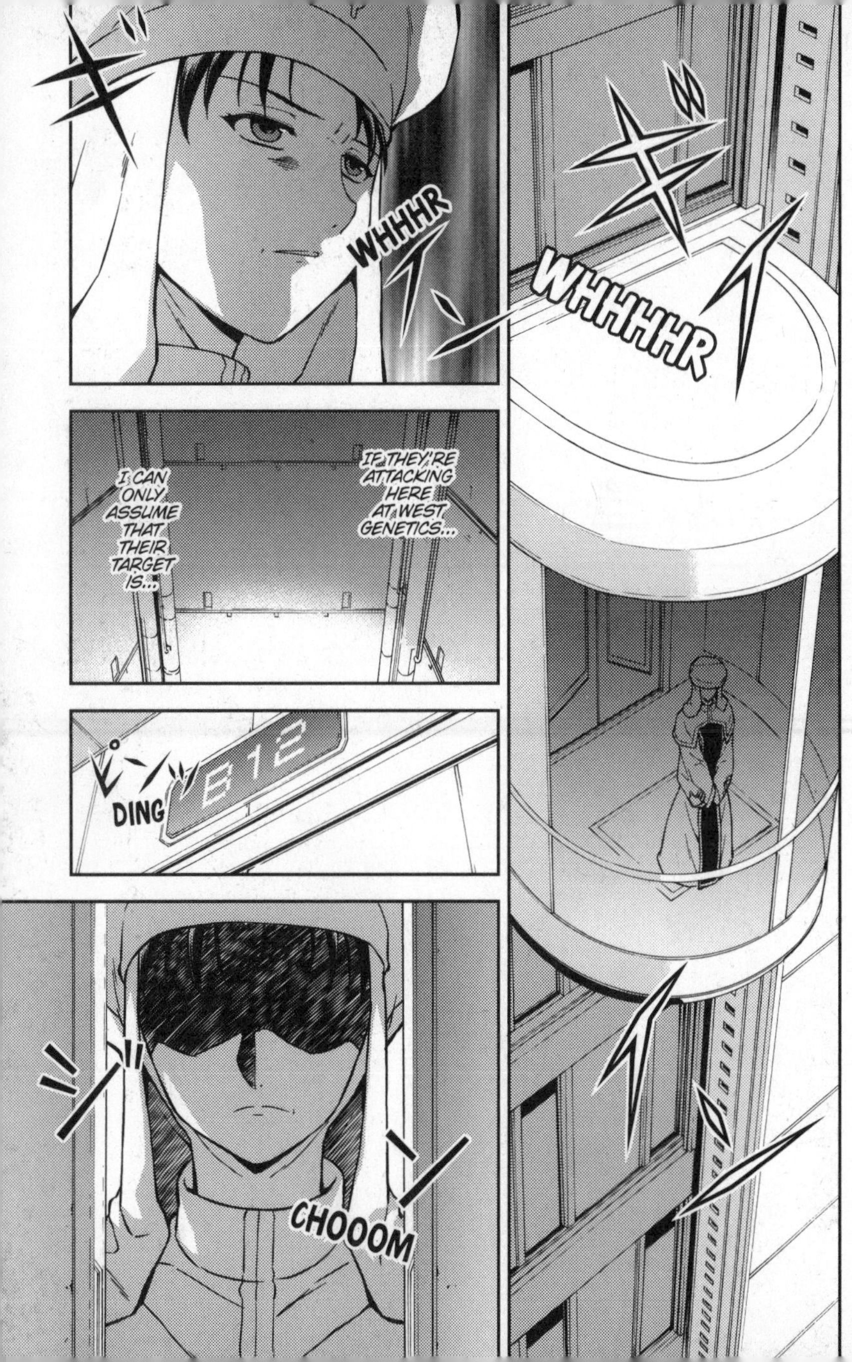
WHHHHR
WHHHR
IF THEY'RE ATTACKING HERE AT WEST GENETICS...
I CAN ONLY ASSUME THAT THEIR TARGET IS...
B12
DING
CHOOOM

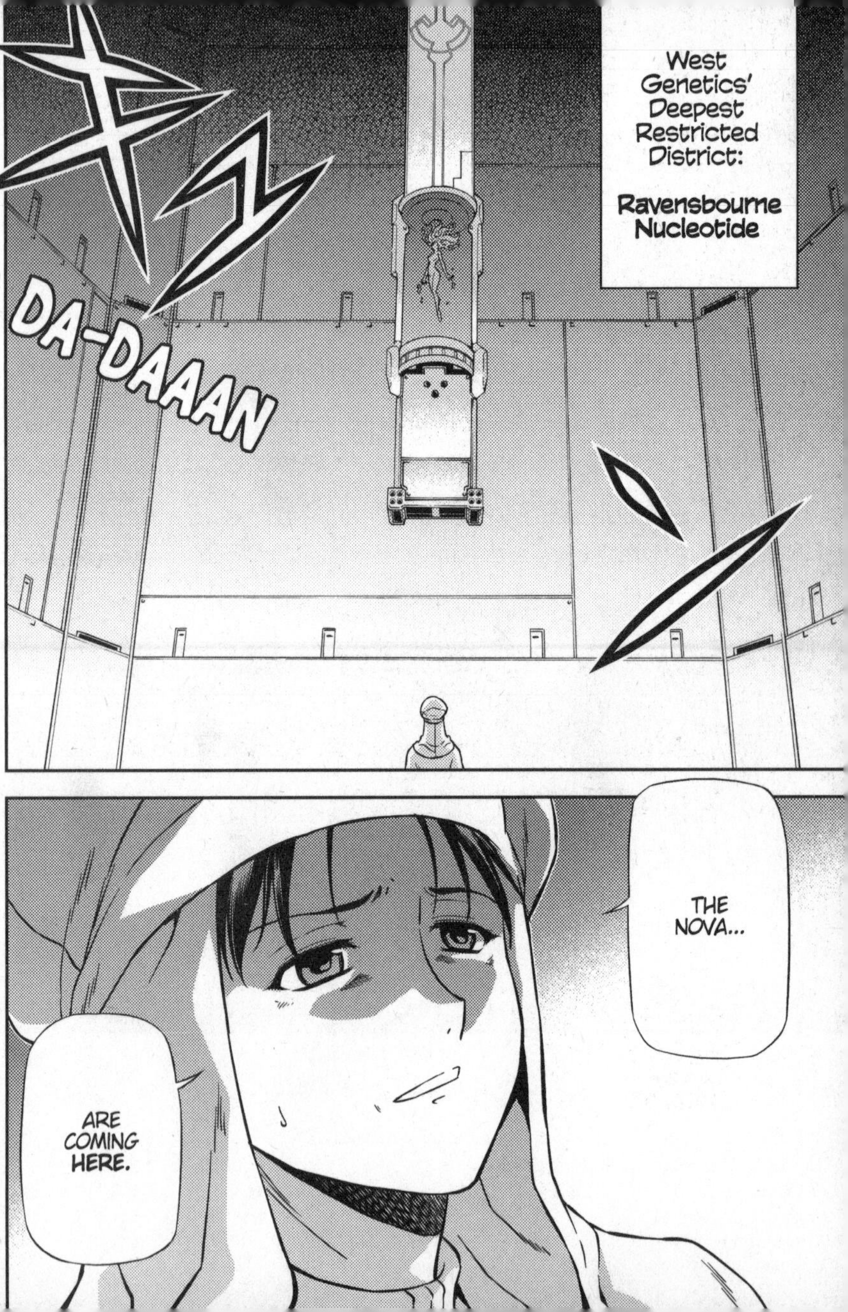
West Genetics' Deepest Restricted District:
Ravensbourne Nucleotide
DA-DAAAN
THE NOVA...
ARE COMING HERE.

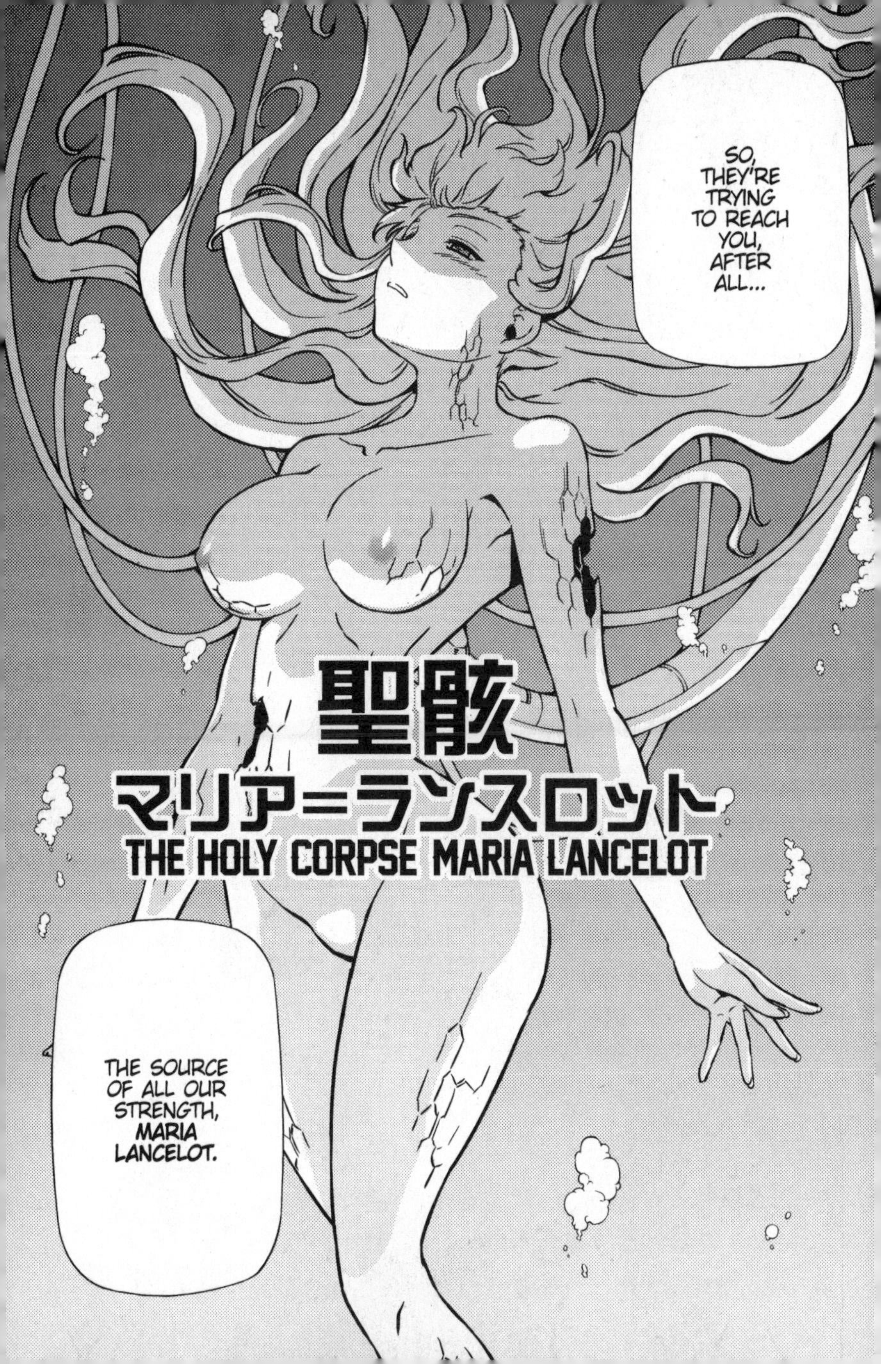
SO, THEY'RE TRYING TO REACH YOU, AFTER ALL...
聖骸
マリア=ランスロット
THE HOLY CORPSE MARIA LANCELOT
THE SOURCE OF ALL OUR STRENGTH, MARIA LANCELOT.

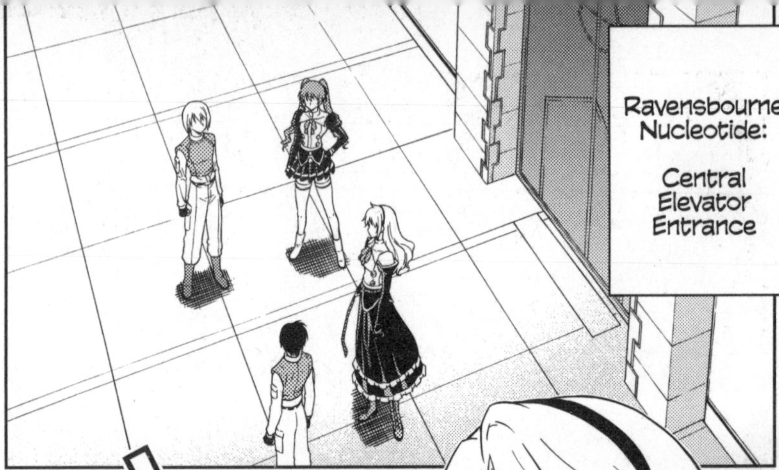
Ravensbourne Nucleotide:
Central Elevator Entrance
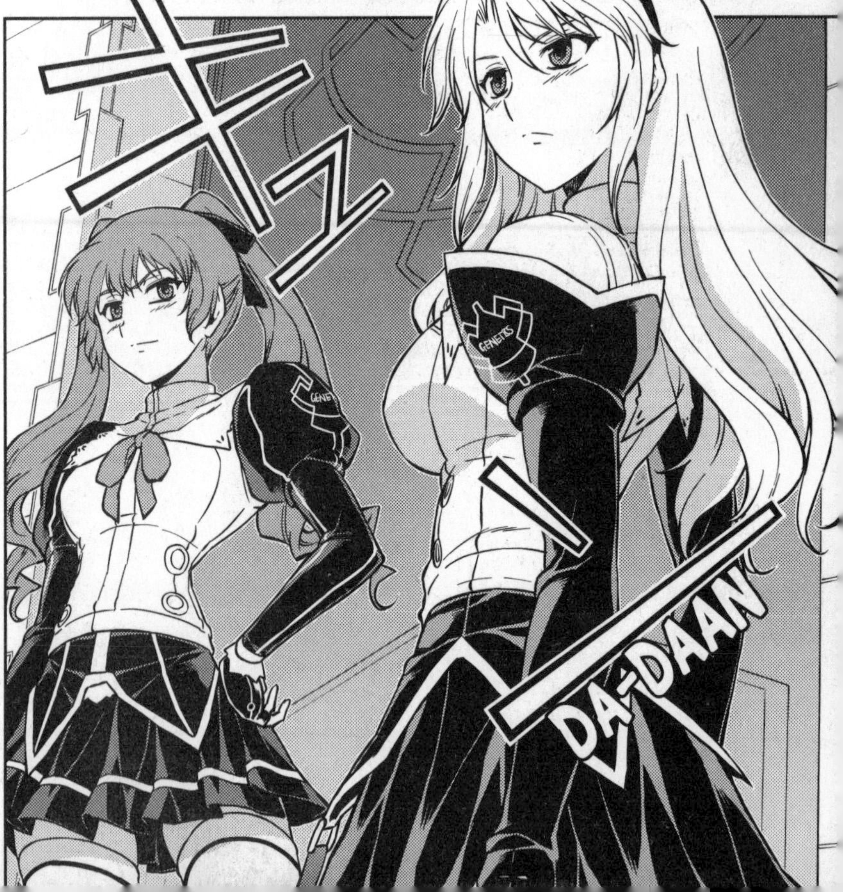
DA-DAAN

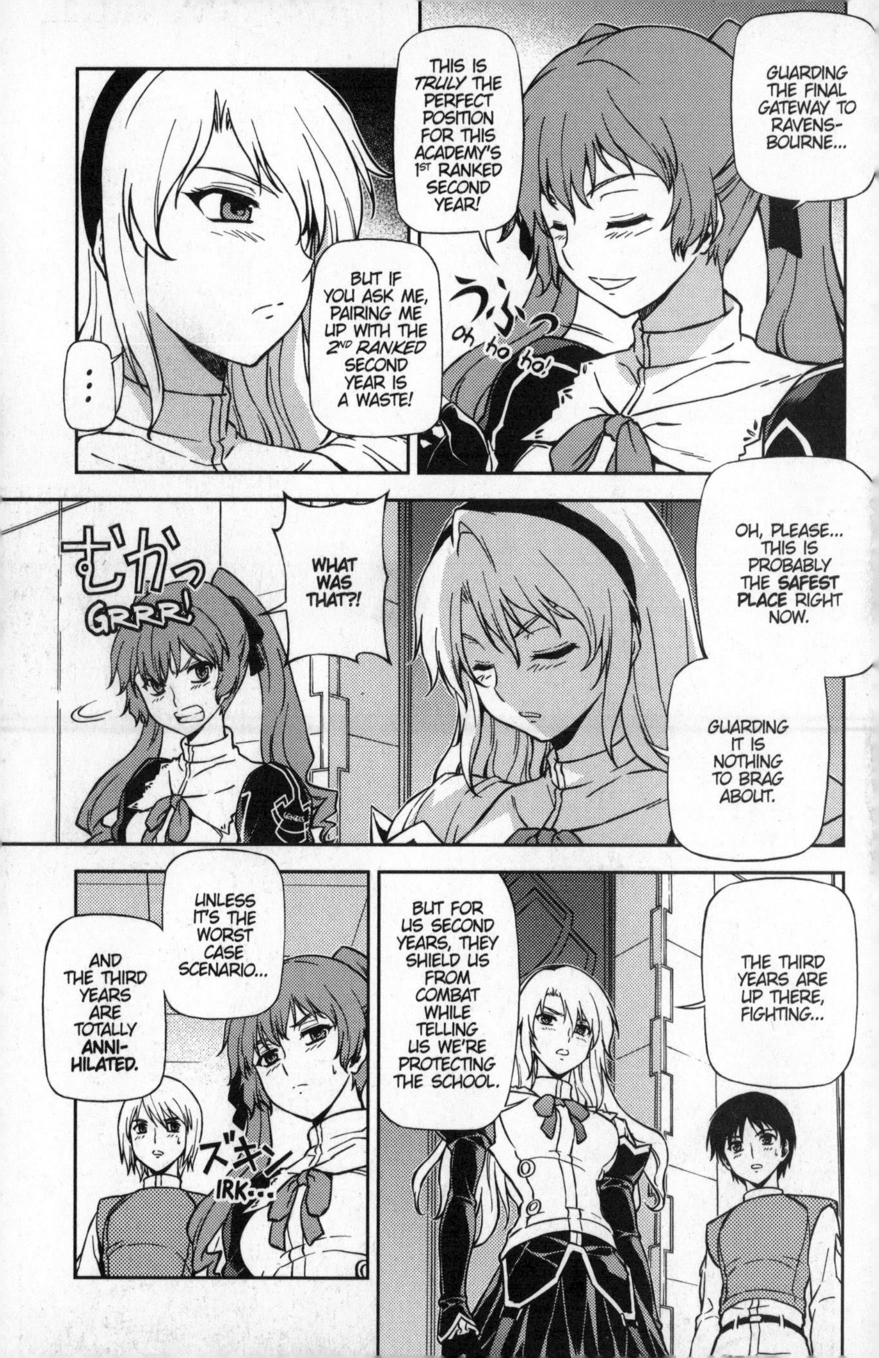

GUARDING THE FINAL GATEWAY TO RAVENS-BOURNE...
THIS IS TRULY THE PERFECT POSITION FOR THIS ACADEMY'S 1ST RANKED SECOND YEAR!
うふっ
OH HO HO!
BUT IF YOU ASK ME, PAIRING ME UP WITH THE 2ND RANKED SECOND YEAR IS A WASTE!
...
OH, PLEASE... THIS IS PROBABLY THE SAFEST PLACE RIGHT NOW.
GUARDING IT IS NOTHING TO BRAG ABOUT.
WHAT WAS THAT?!
むかっ
GRRR!
THE THIRD YEARS ARE UP THERE, FIGHTING...
BUT FOR US SECOND YEARS, THEY SHIELD US FROM COMBAT WHILE TELLING US WE'RE PROTECTING THE SCHOOL.
UNLESS IT'S THE WORST CASE SCENARIO...
AND THE THIRD YEARS ARE TOTALLY ANNI-HILATED.
ズキン
IRK...

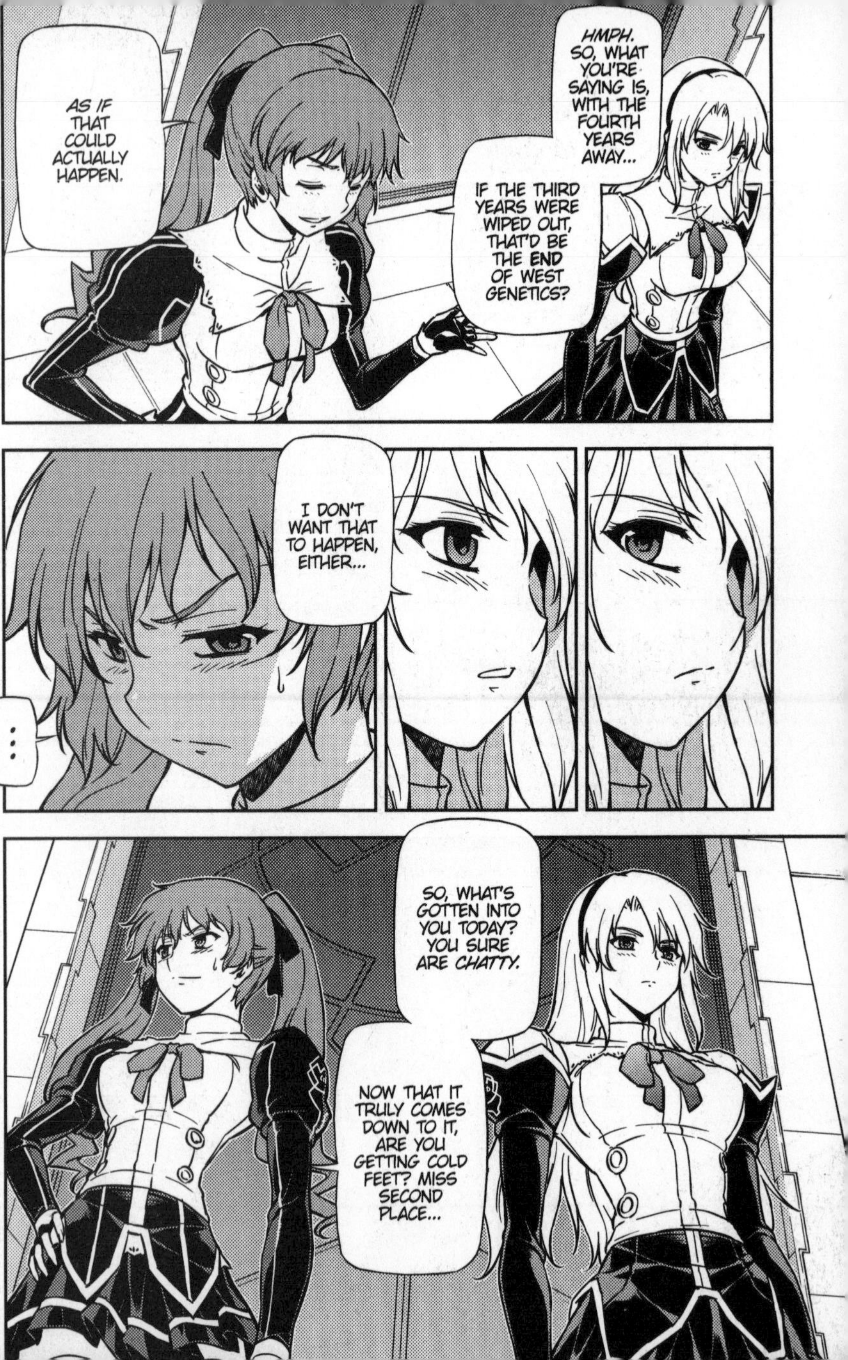
HMPH. SO, WHAT YOU'RE SAYING IS, WITH THE FOURTH YEARS AWAY...
IF THE THIRD YEARS WERE WIPED OUT, THAT'D BE THE END OF WEST GENETICS?
AS IF THAT COULD ACTUALLY HAPPEN.
I DON'T WANT THAT TO HAPPEN, EITHER...
...
SO, WHAT'S GOTTEN INTO YOU TODAY? YOU SURE ARE CHATTY.
NOW THAT IT TRULY COMES DOWN TO IT, ARE YOU GETTING COLD FEET? MISS SECOND PLACE...

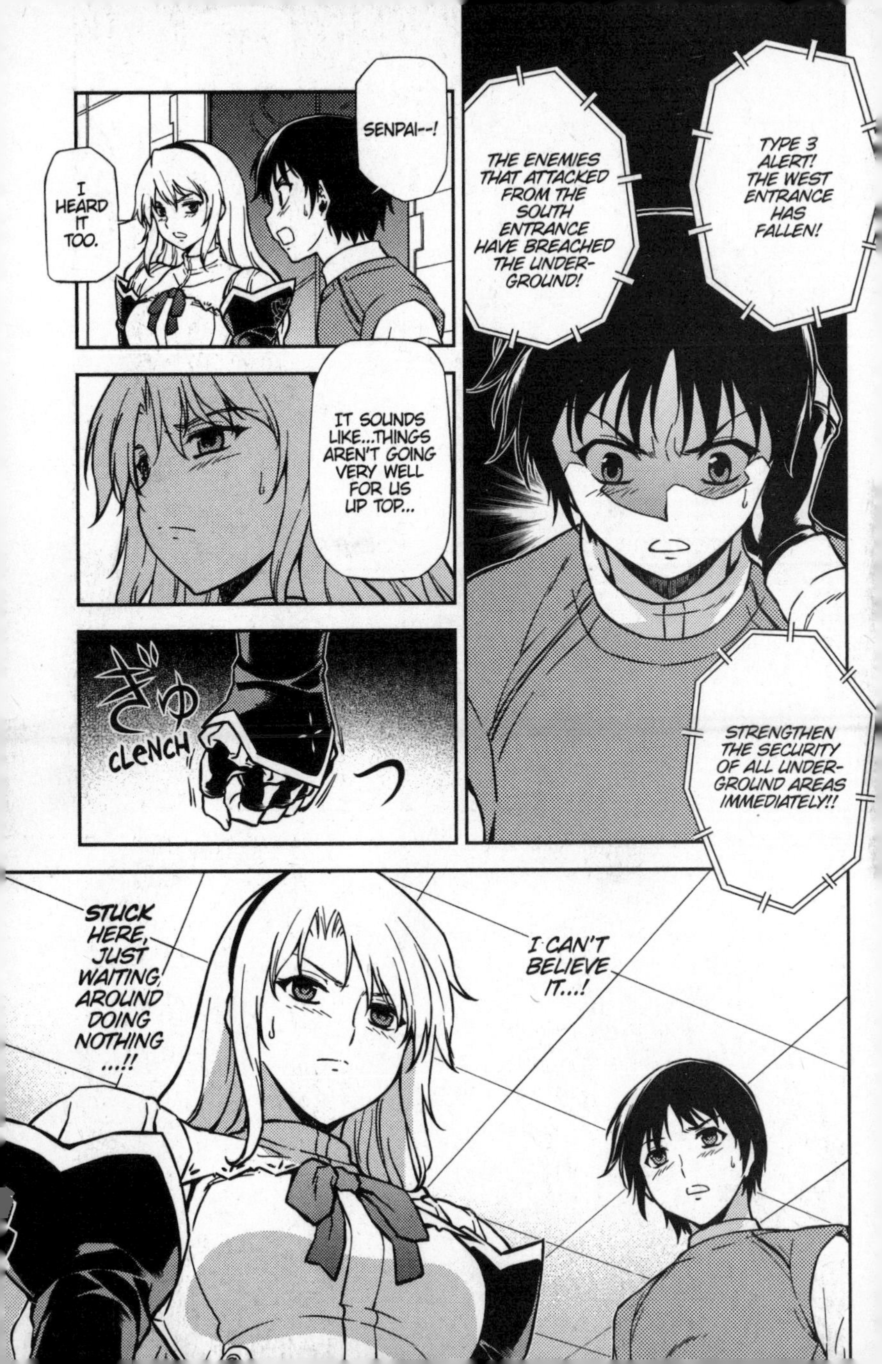
TYPE 3 ALERT! THE WEST ENTRANCE HAS FALLEN!
THE ENEMIES THAT ATTACKED FROM THE SOUTH ENTRANCE HAVE BREACHED THE UNDER-GROUND!
STRENGTHEN THE SECURITY OF ALL UNDER-GROUND AREAS IMMEDIATELY!!
SENPAI--!
I HEARD IT TOO.
IT SOUNDS LIKE...THINGS AREN'T GOING VERY WELL FOR US UP TOP...
ぎゅ
CLENCH
I CAN'T BELIEVE IT...!
STUCK HERE, JUST WAITING, AROUND DOING NOTHING ...!!

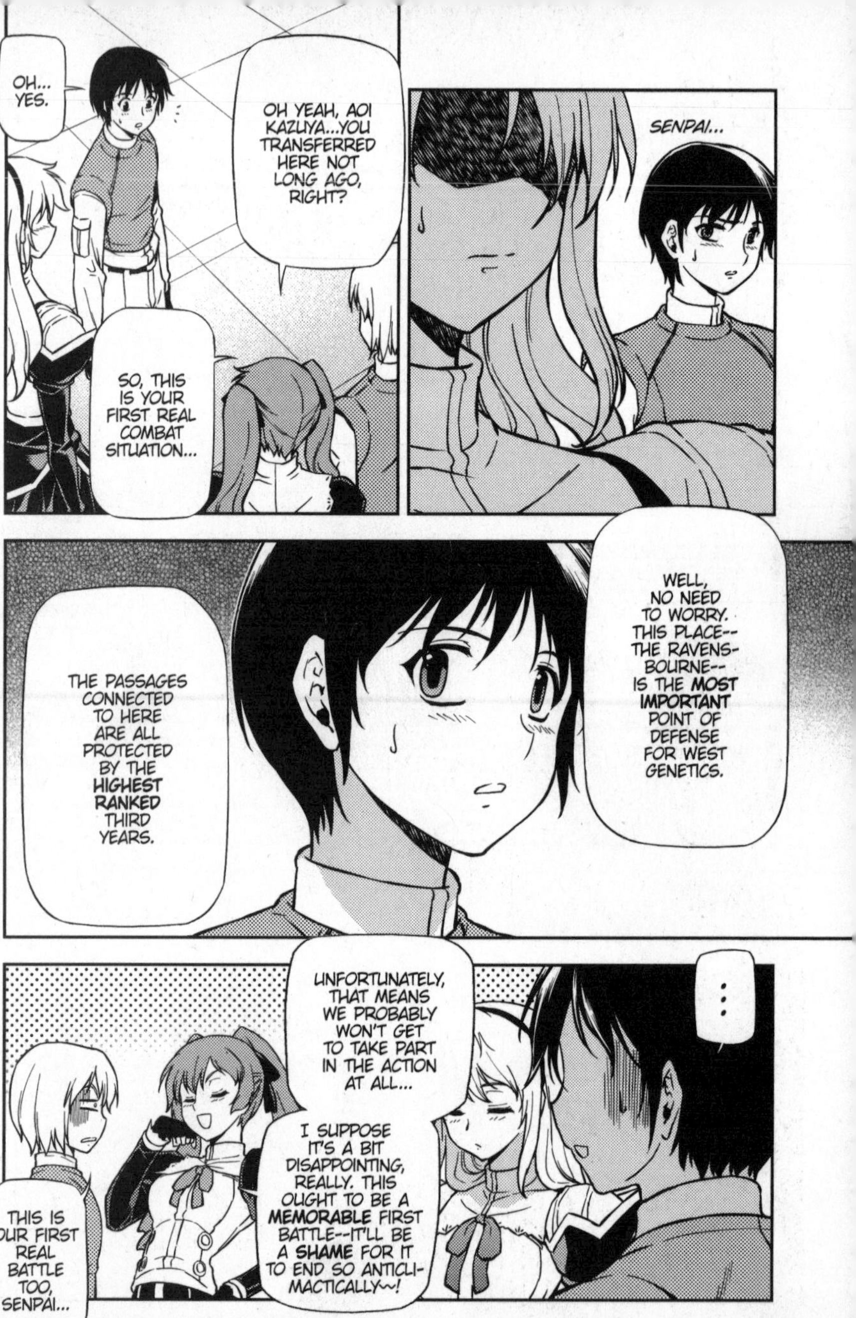
SENPAI...
OH YEAH, AOI KAZUYA...YOU TRANSFERRED HERE NOT LONG AGO, RIGHT?
OH... YES.
SO, THIS IS YOUR FIRST REAL COMBAT SITUATION...
WELL, NO NEED TO WORRY. THIS PLACE--THE RAVENS-BOURNE--IS THE **MOST IMPORTANT** POINT OF DEFENSE FOR WEST GENETICS.
THE PASSAGES CONNECTED TO HERE ARE ALL PROTECTED BY THE **HIGHEST RANKED** THIRD YEARS.
...
UNFORTUNATELY, THAT MEANS WE PROBABLY WON'T GET TO TAKE PART IN THE ACTION AT ALL...
I SUPPOSE IT'S A BIT DISAPPOINTING, REALLY. THIS OUGHT TO BE A **MEMORABLE** FIRST BATTLE--IT'LL BE A **SHAME** FOR IT TO END SO ANTICLI-MACTICALLY~!
THIS IS OUR FIRST REAL BATTLE TOO, SENPAI...

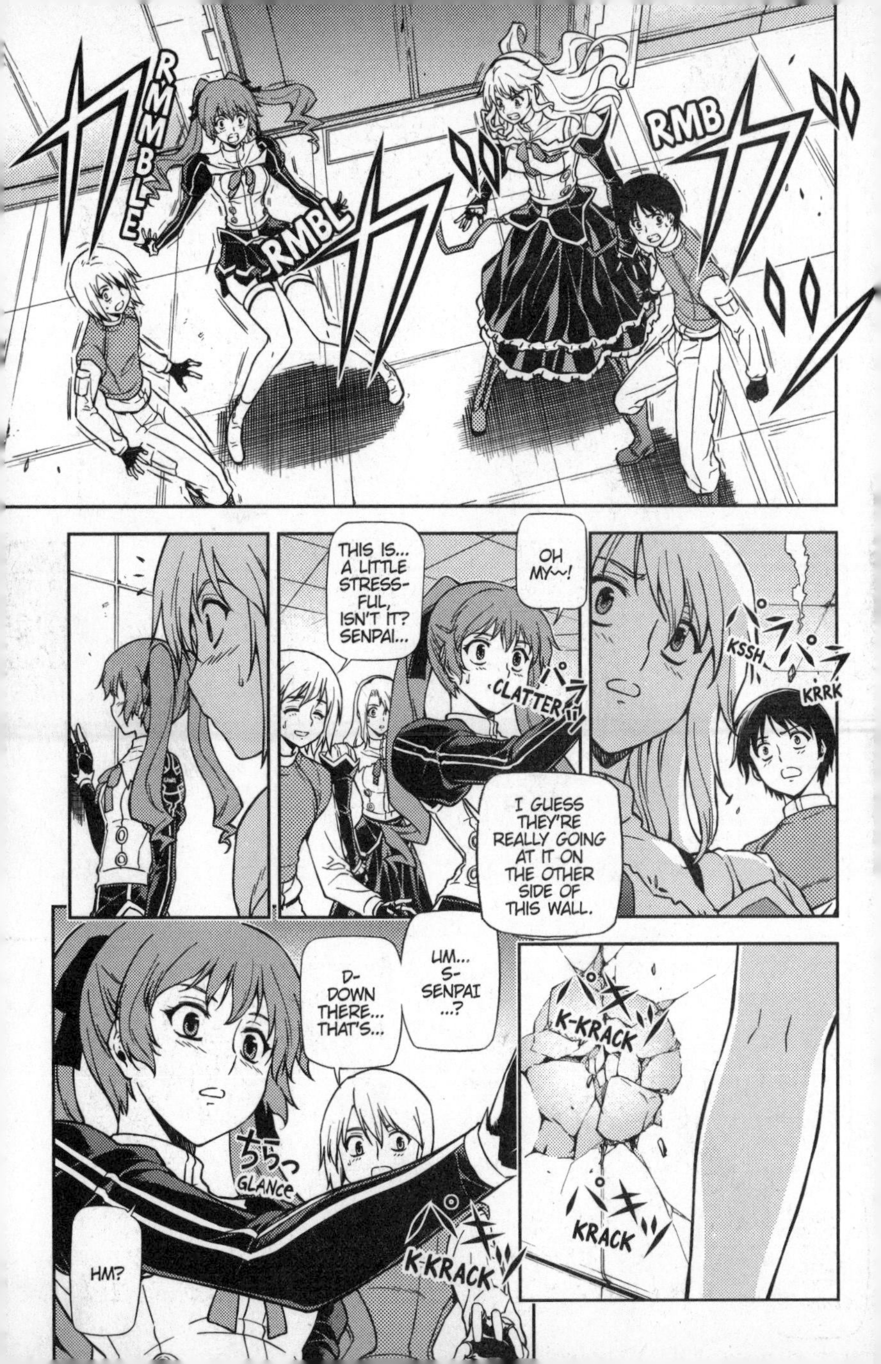
RMB
RMBL
RMMBLE
KSSH
KRRK
OH MY~~!
THIS IS... A LITTLE STRESS-FUL, ISN'T IT? SENPAI...
CLATTER
I GUESS THEY'RE REALLY GOING AT IT ON THE OTHER SIDE OF THIS WALL.
K-KRACK
KRACK
UM... S-SENPAI ...?
D-DOWN THERE... THAT'S...
ちらっ
GLANCE
K-KRACK
HM?

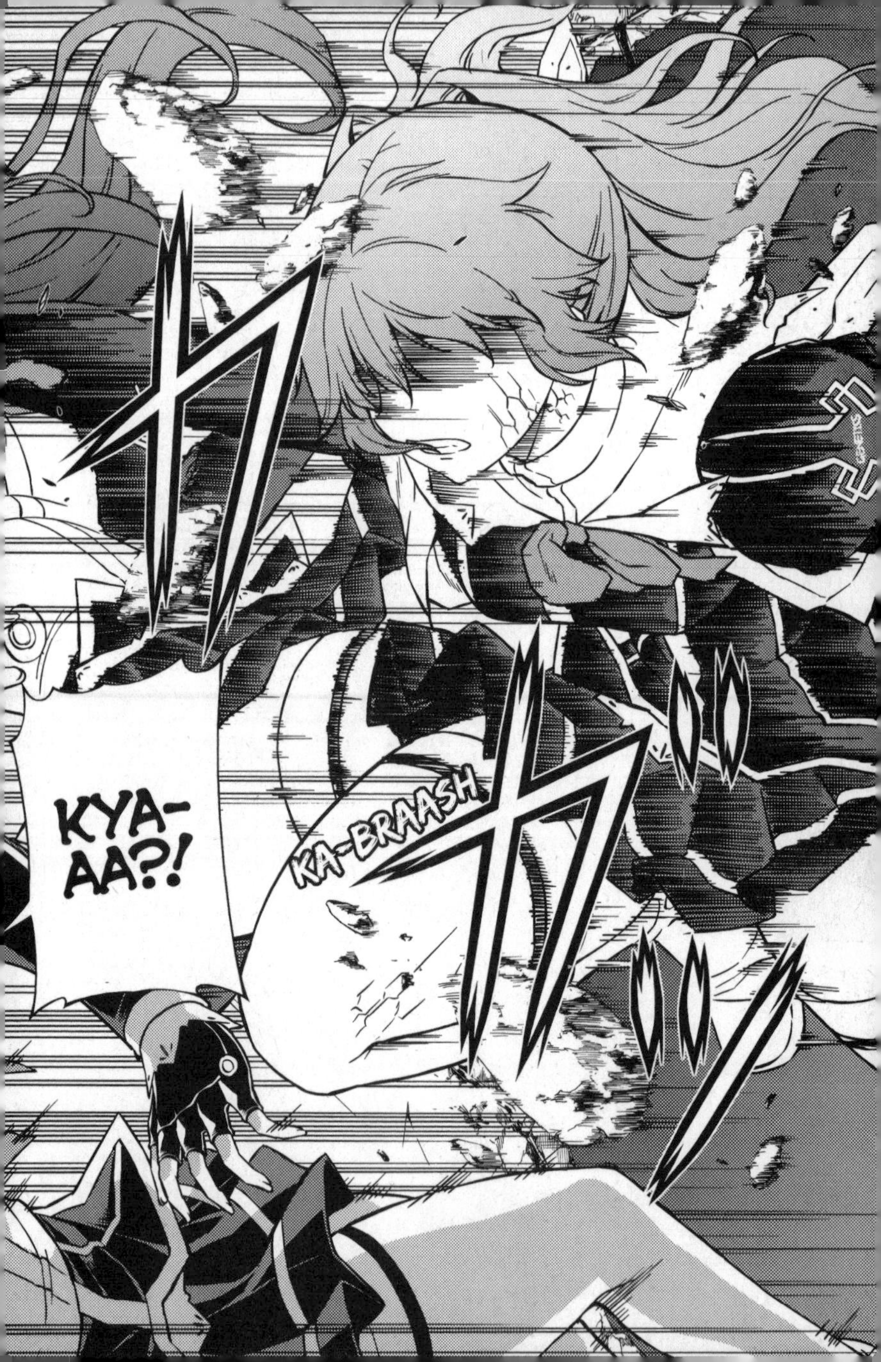

KYA-AA?!
KA-BRAASH

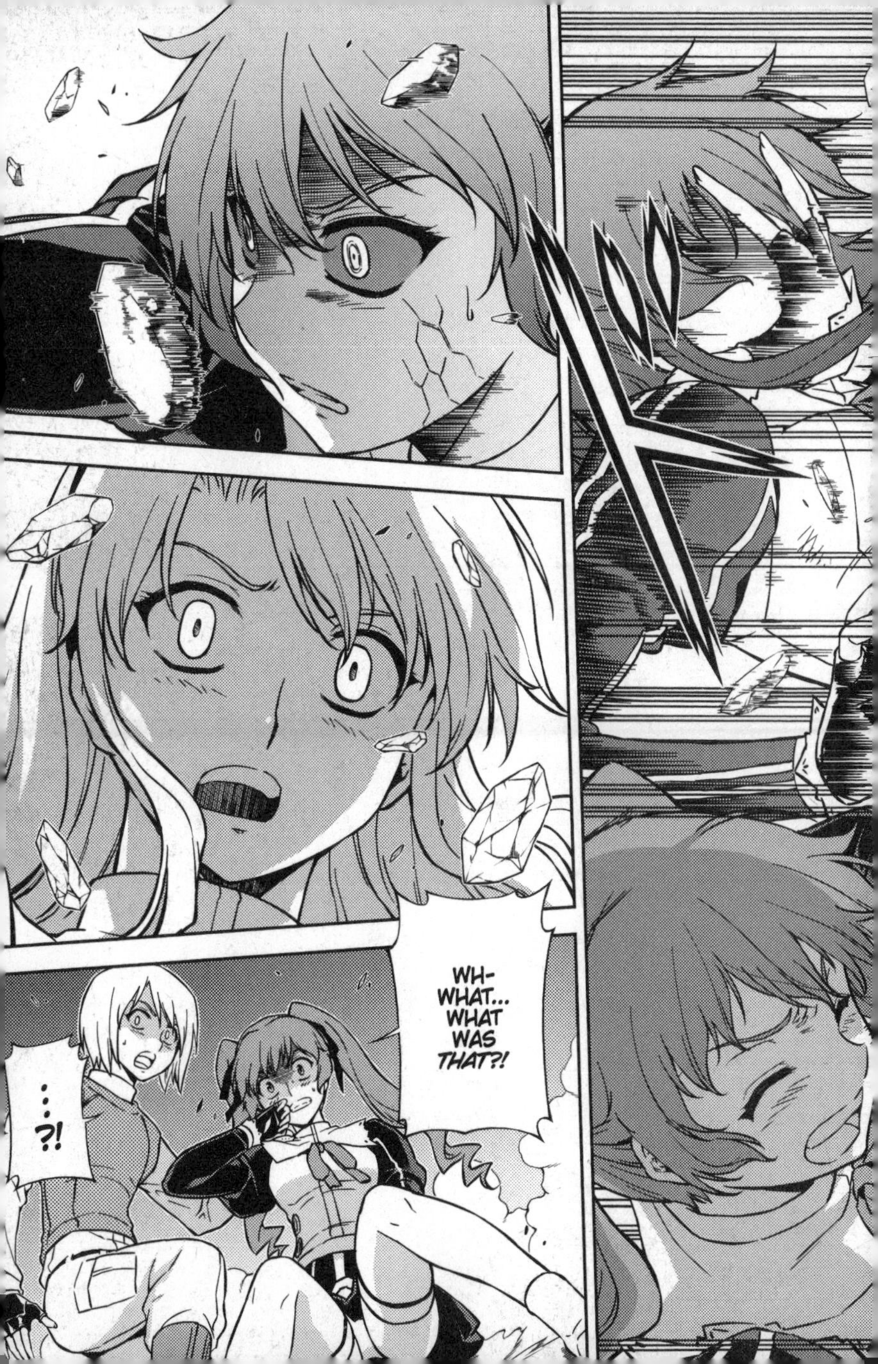
WH-WHAT... WHAT WAS THAT?!
...?!

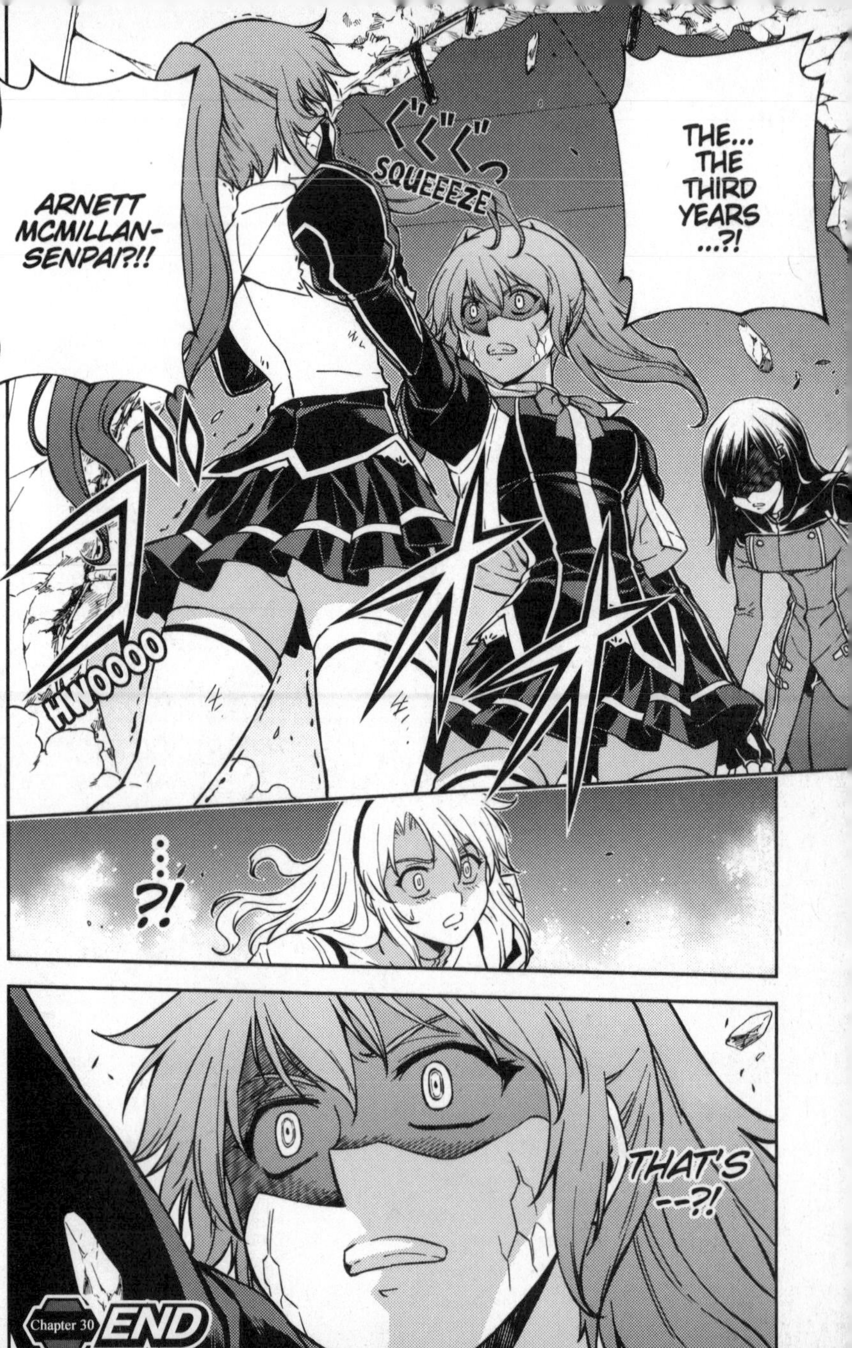
THE... THE THIRD YEARS ...?!
ぐぐぐっ
SQUEEEZE
ARNETT MCMILLAN-SENPAI?!!
HWOOOO
...?!
THAT'S --?!
Chapter 30 END

FREEZING VOLUME.5
HIGHLIGHT SCENE

FREEZING Vol.5

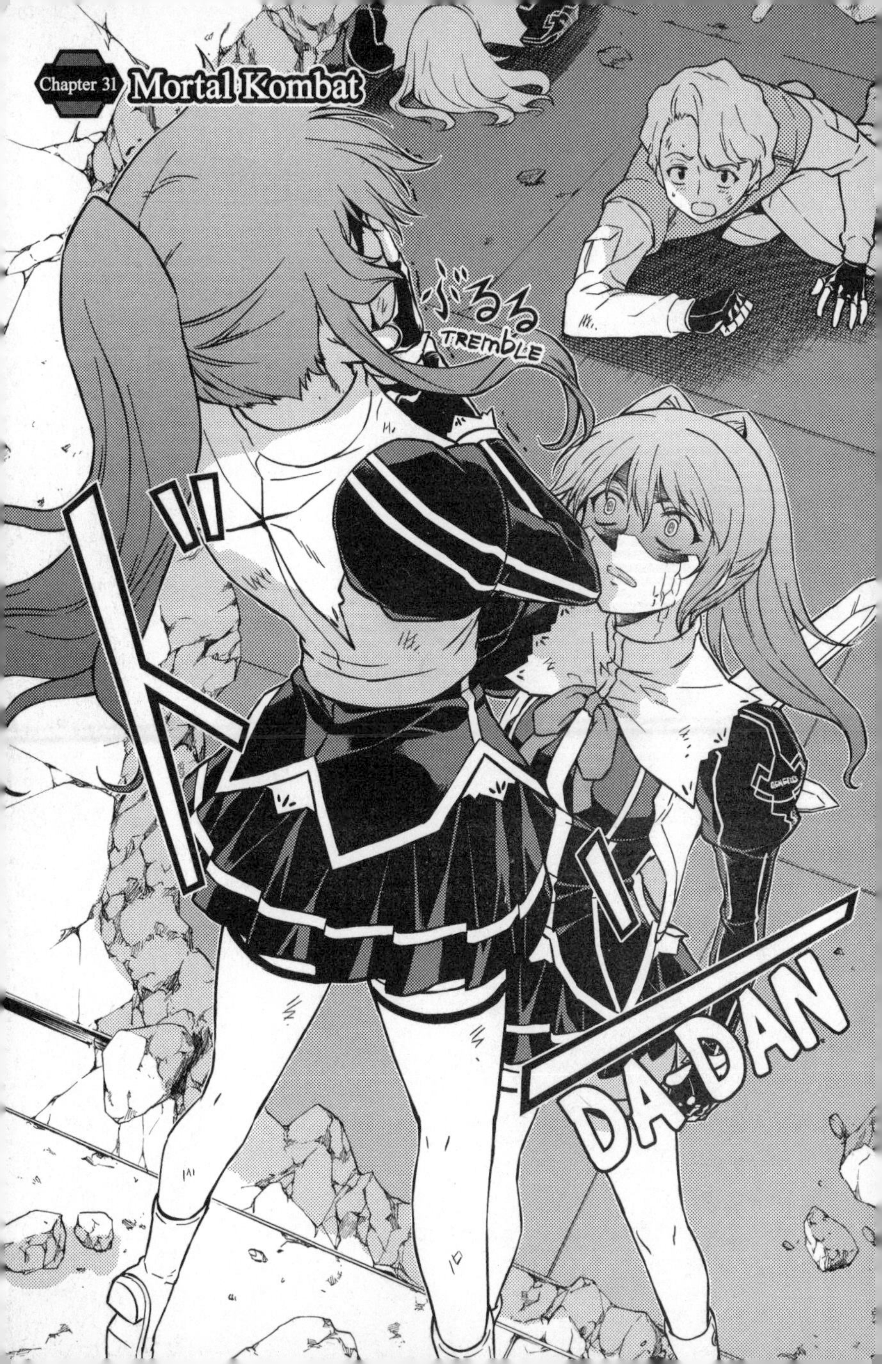
Chapter 31
Mortal Kombat
ぷるる
TREMBLE
DA-DAN

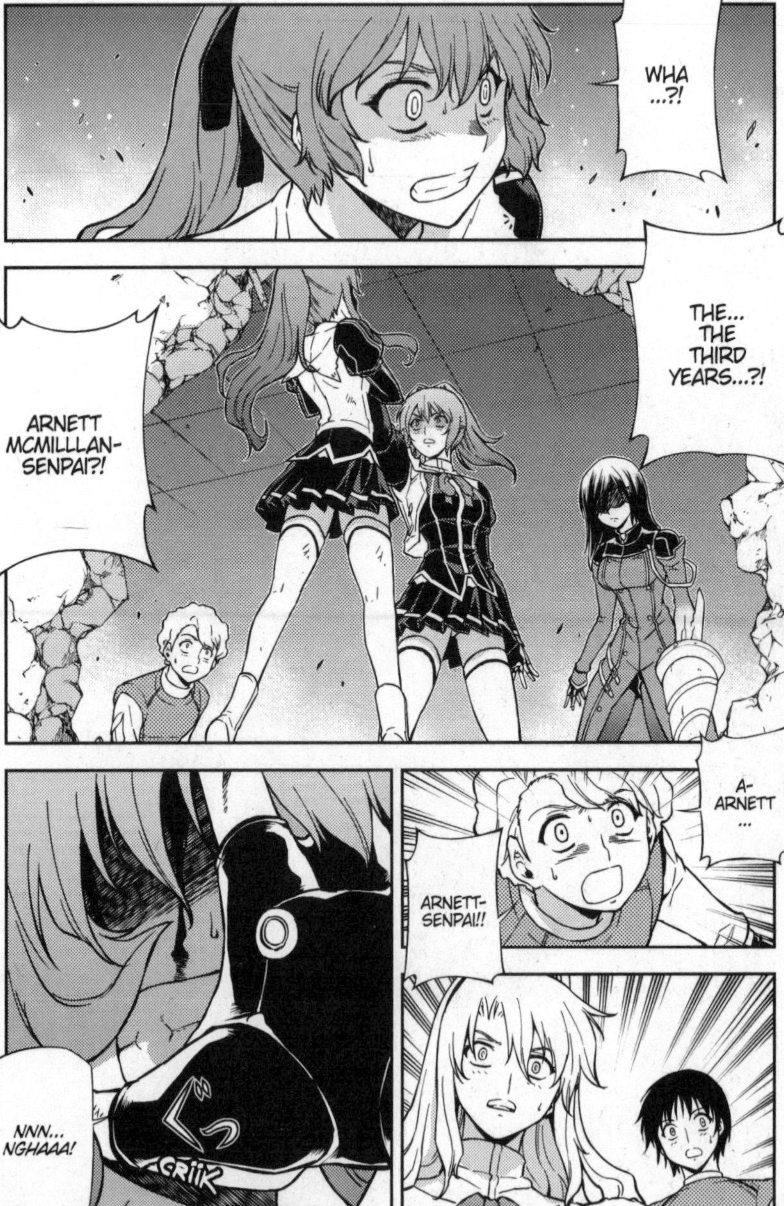

WHA ...?!
THE... THE THIRD YEARS...?!
ARNETT MCMILLLAN-SENPAI?!
A- ARNETT ...
ARNETT-SENPAI!!
NNN... NGHAAA!
GRIIK

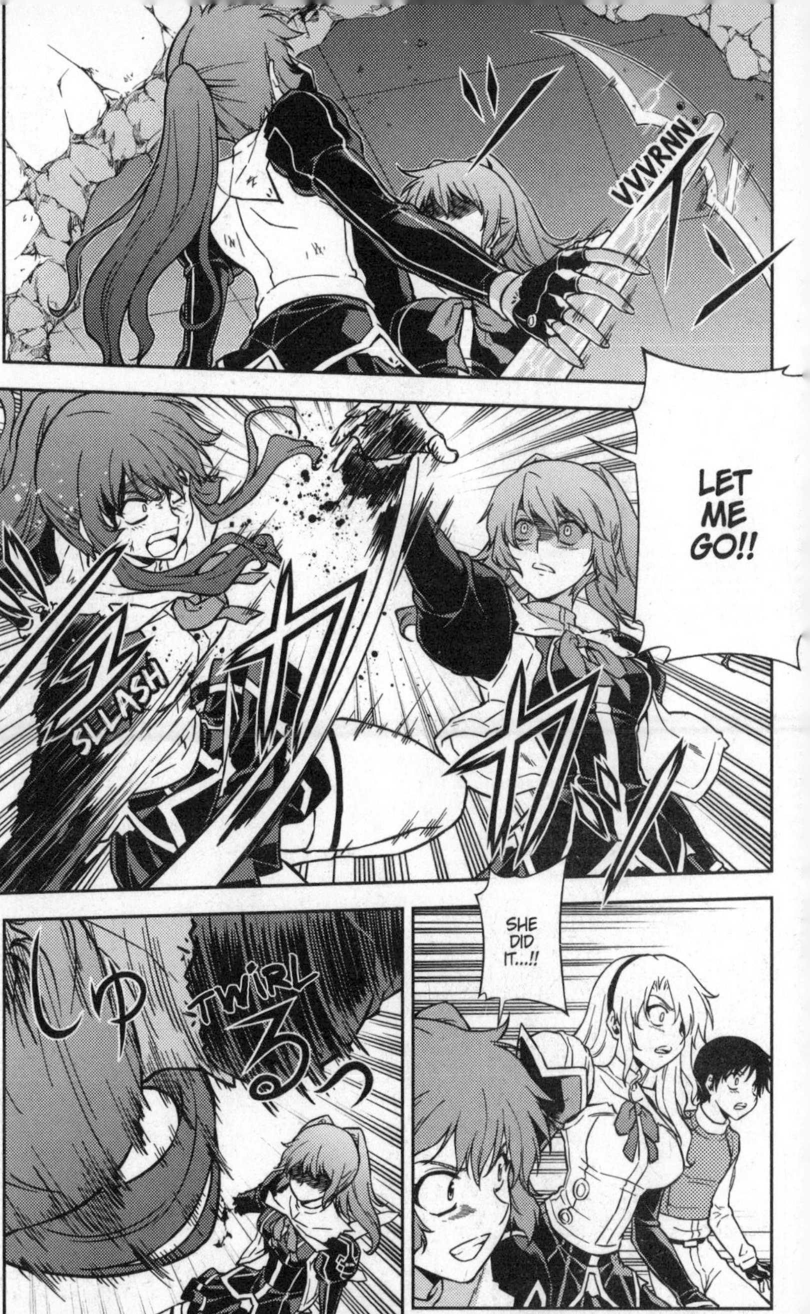
VVVRNN
LET ME GO!!
SLLASH
SHE DID IT...!!
TWIRL

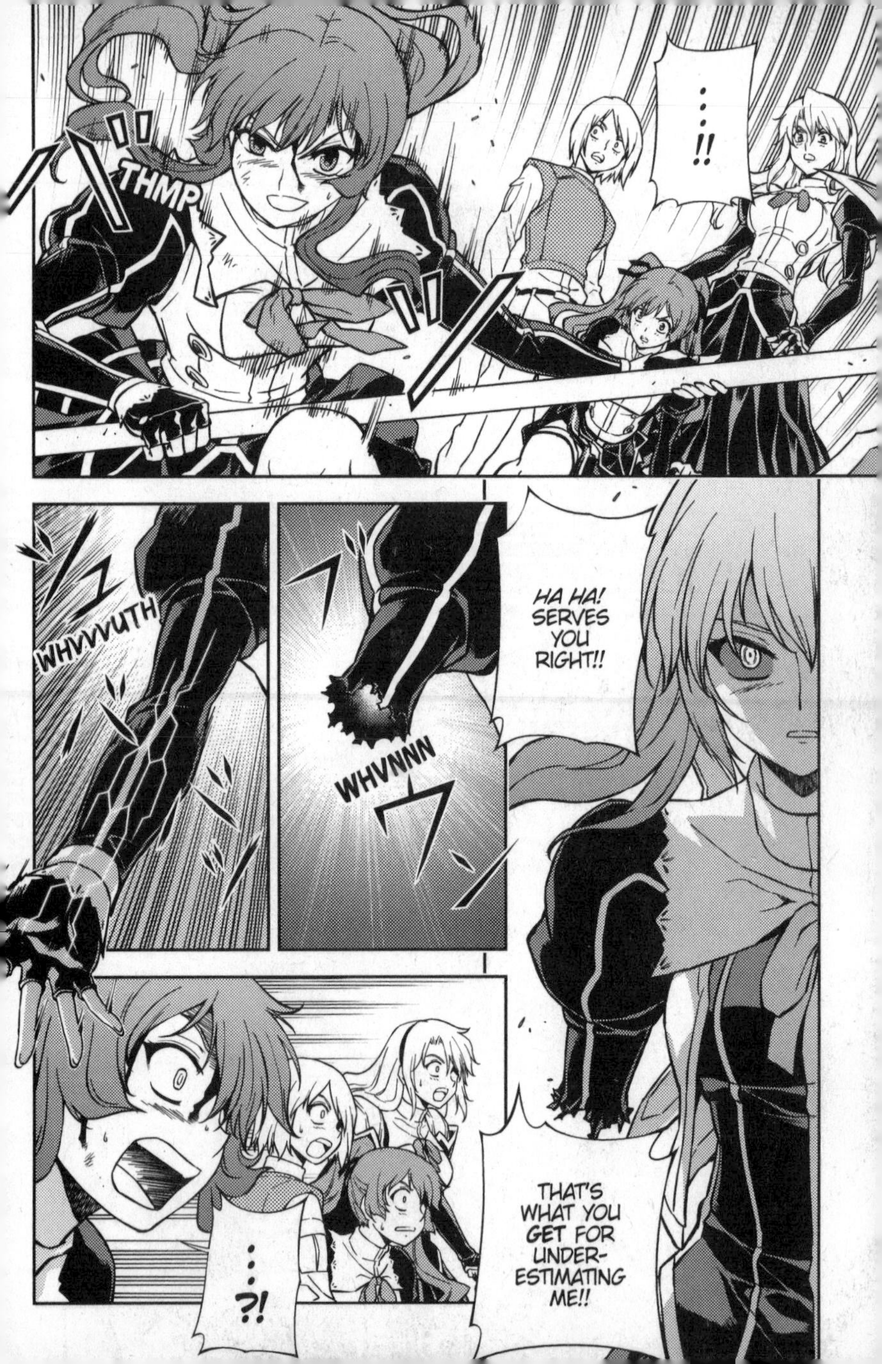

. . . !!
THMP
HA HA! SERVES YOU RIGHT!!
THAT'S WHAT YOU GET FOR UNDER-ESTIMATING ME!!
WHVNNN
WHVVVUTH
. . . ?!

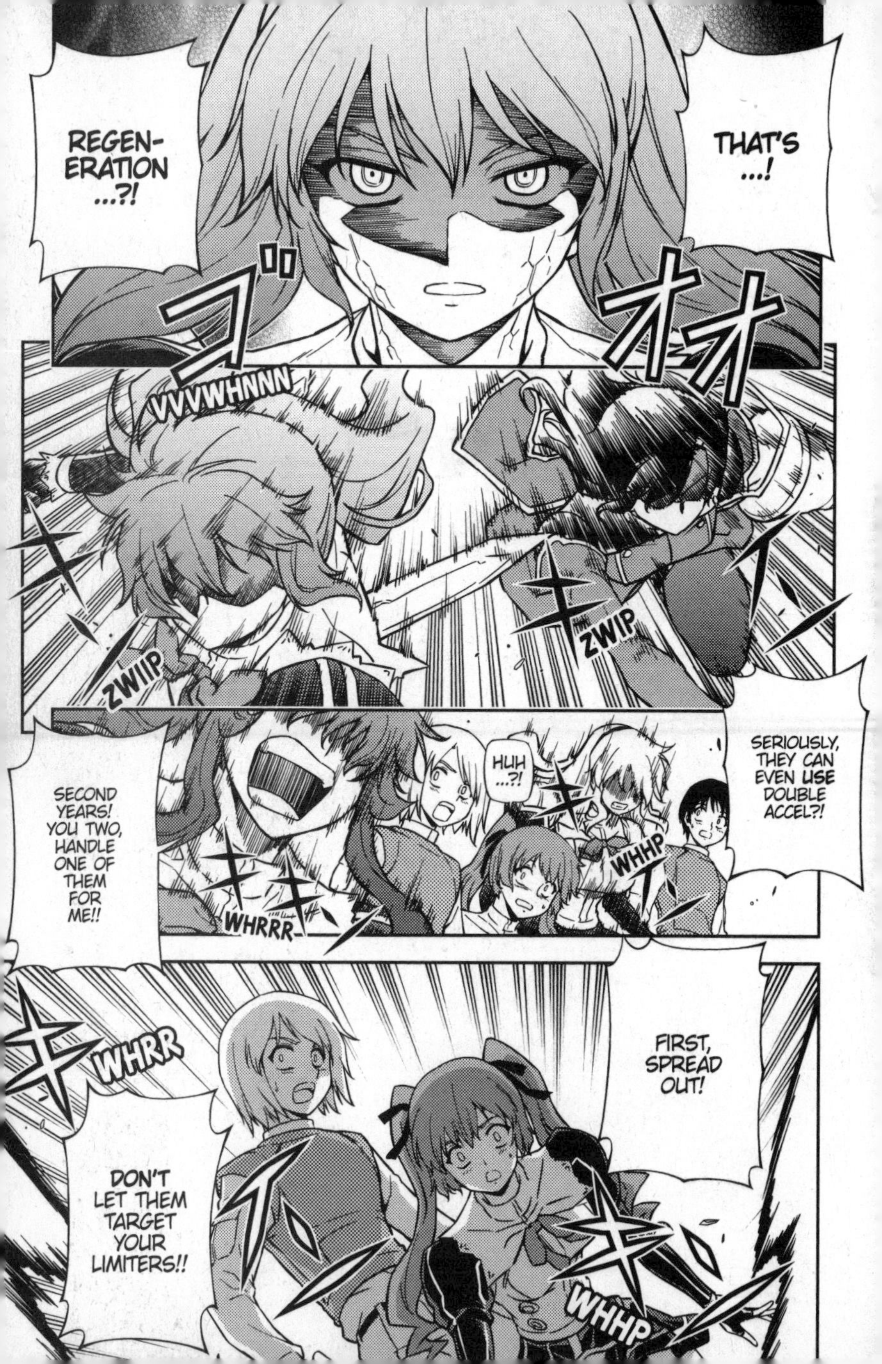
THAT'S ...!
REGEN-ERATION ...?!
ゴオオ
VVVWHNNN
ZWIP
ZWIIP
SERIOUSLY, THEY CAN EVEN USE DOUBLE ACCEL?!
WHHP
HUH ...?!
SECOND YEARS! YOU TWO, HANDLE ONE OF THEM FOR ME!!
WHRRR
FIRST, SPREAD OUT!
WHRR
DON'T LET THEM TARGET YOUR LIMITERS!!
WHHP

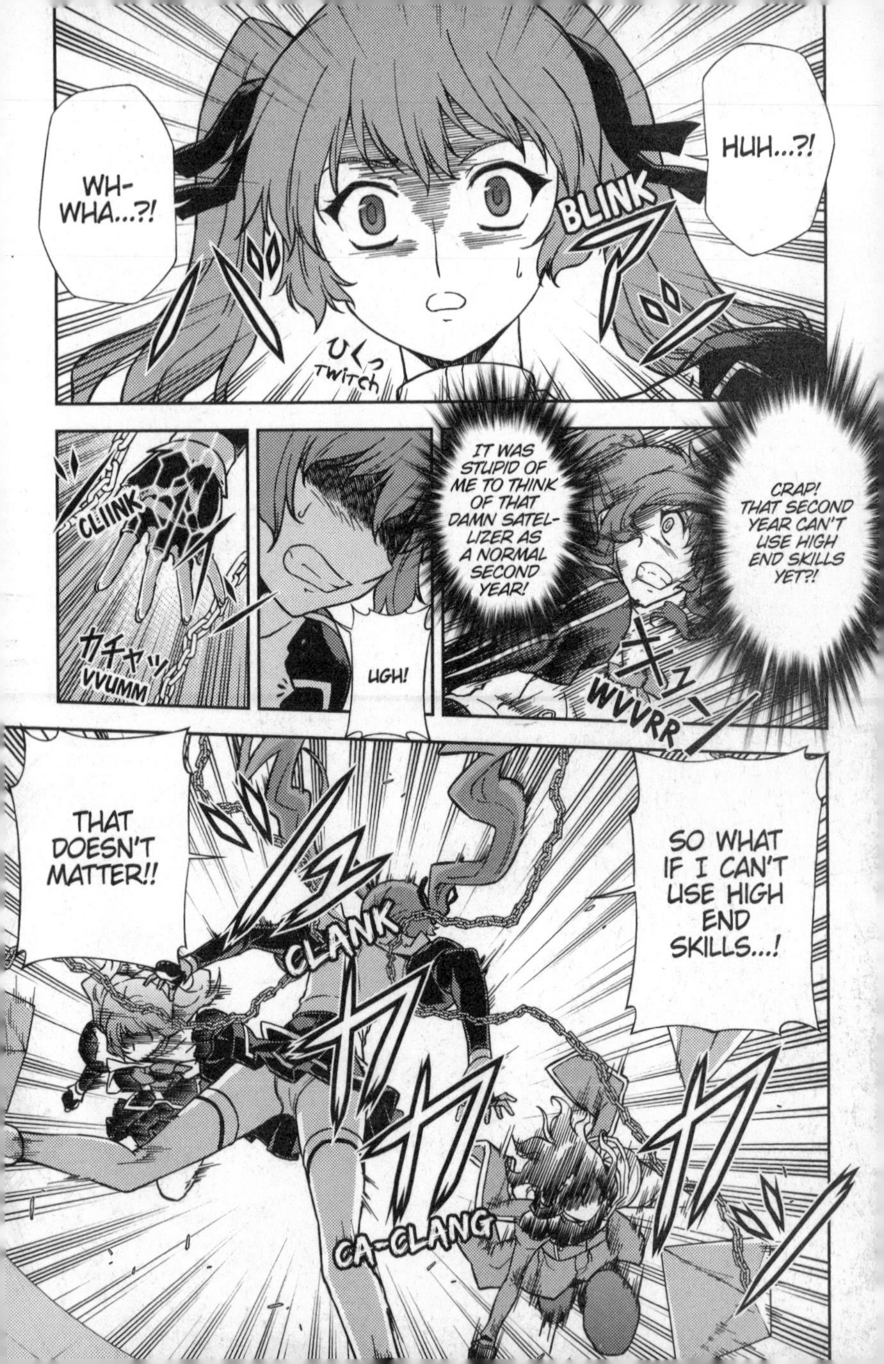
HUH...?!
BLINK
WH- WHA...?!
ひくっ TWITCH
CRAP! THAT SECOND YEAR CAN'T USE HIGH END SKILLS YET?!
IT WAS STUPID OF ME TO THINK OF THAT DAMN SATELLIZER AS A NORMAL SECOND YEAR!
WVVRR
UGH!
CLIINK
カチャッ VVUMM
SO WHAT IF I CAN'T USE HIGH END SKILLS...!
THAT DOESN'T MATTER!!
CLANK
CA-CLANG

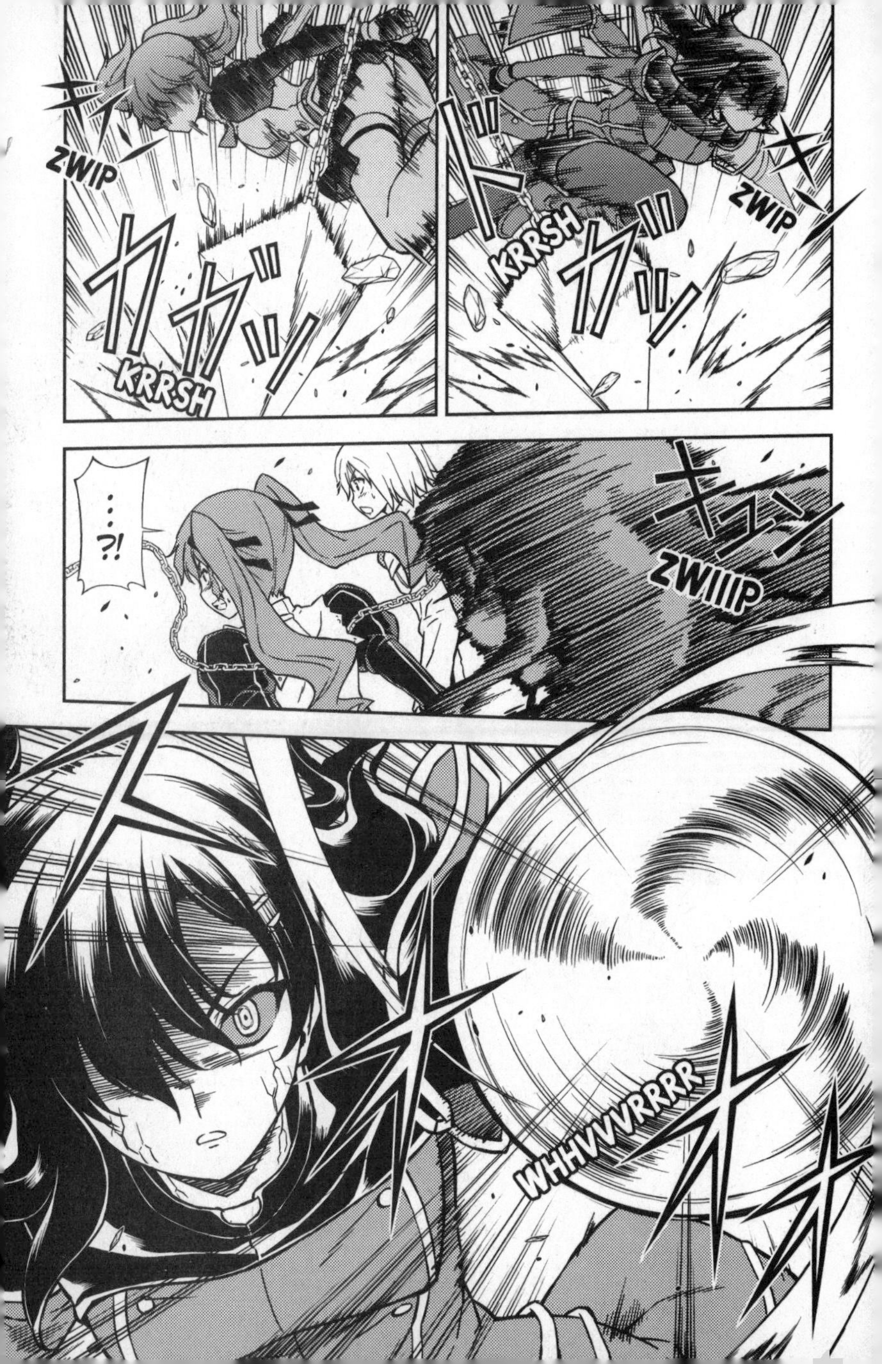
ZWIP
KRRSH
ガッ
ZWIP
カガッ
KRRSH
...?!
キュン
ZWIIIP
WHHVVVRRRR

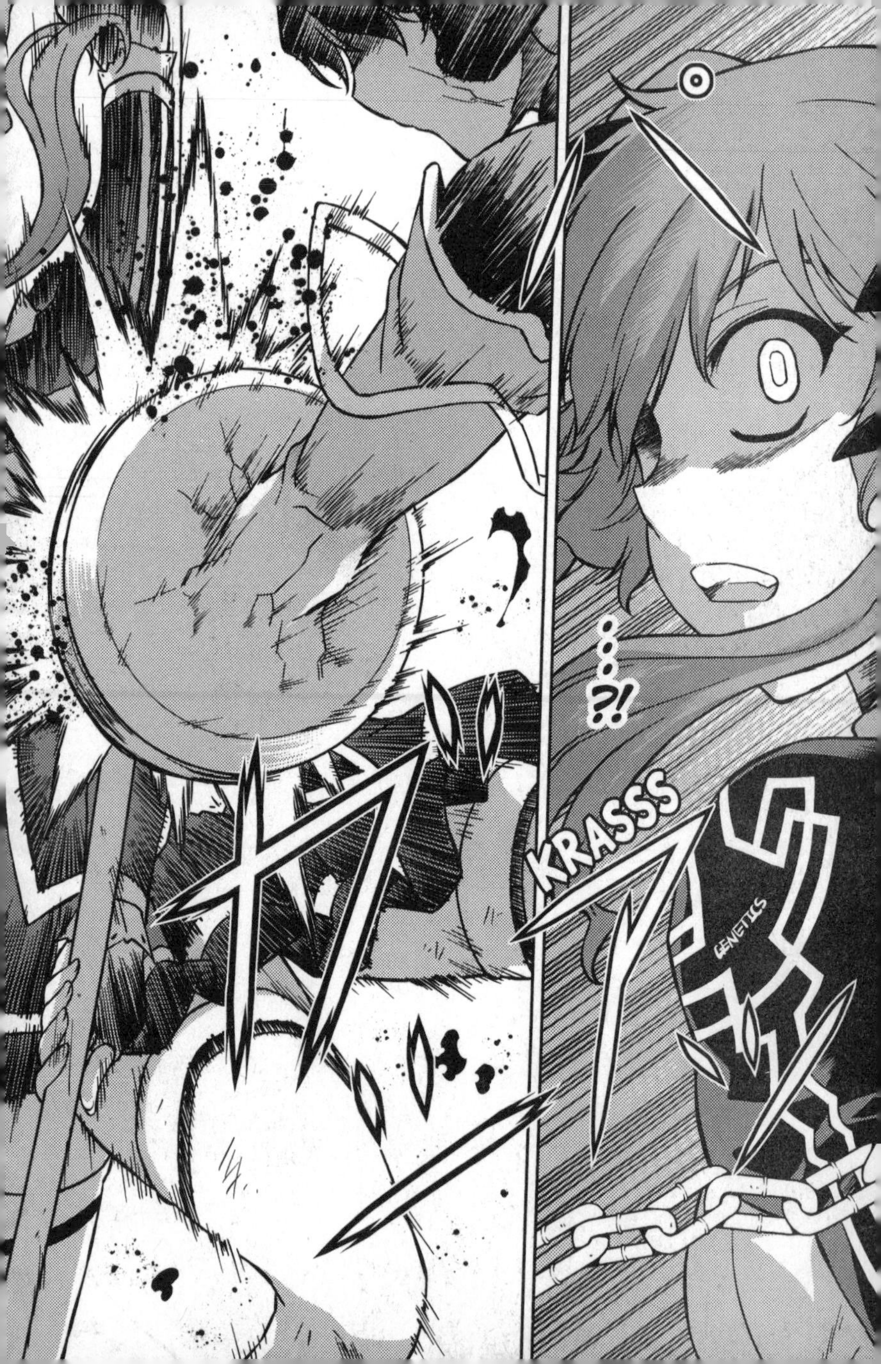
...?!
KRASSS
GENETICS

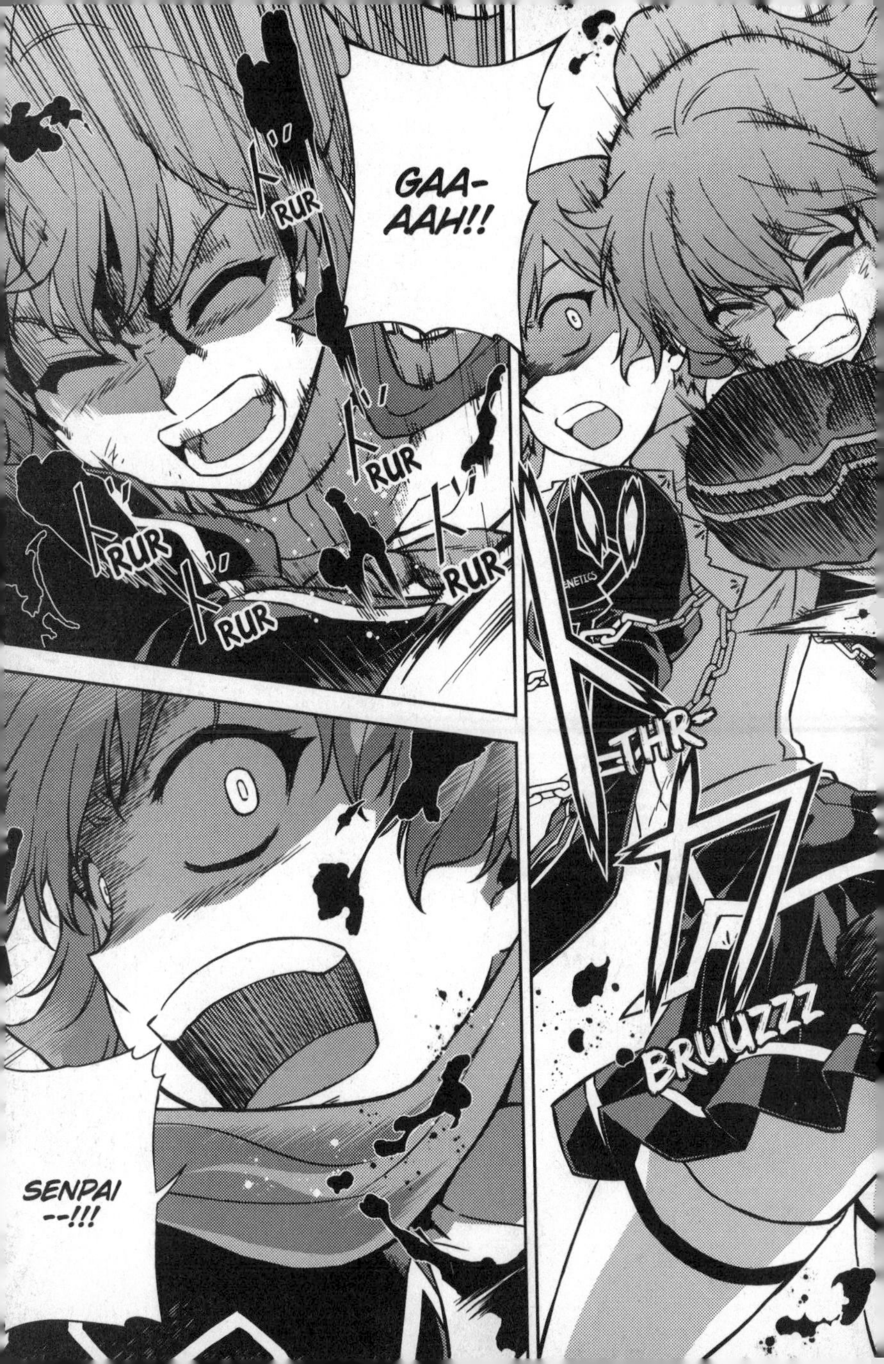
THR
BRUUZZZ
GAA-
AAH!!
RUR
RUR
RUR
RUR
RUR
SENPAI
--!!!

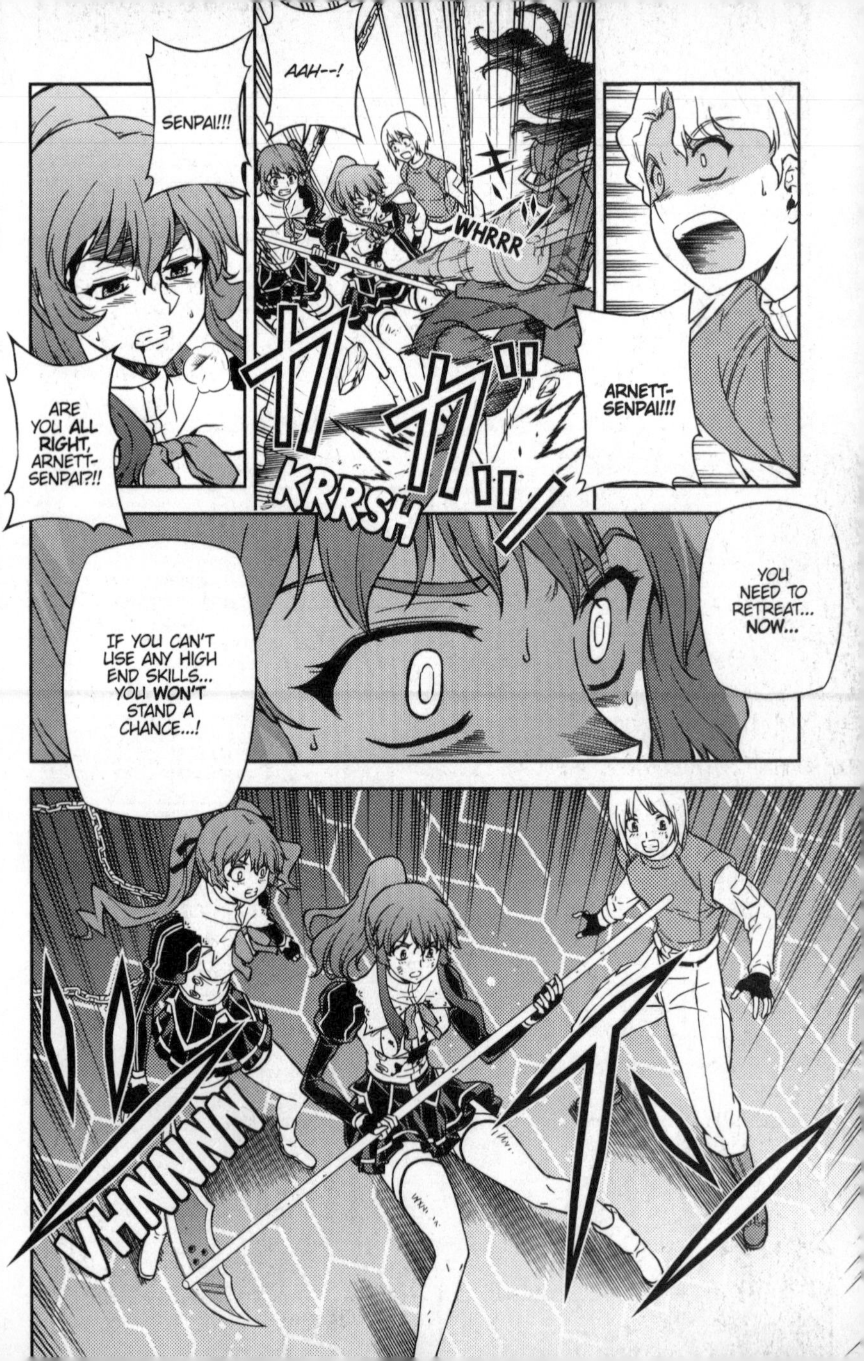
ARNETT-SENPAI!!!
AAH--!
WHRRR
カガッ
KRRSH
SENPAI!!!
ARE YOU ALL RIGHT, ARNETT-SENPAI?!!
YOU NEED TO RETREAT... NOW...
IF YOU CAN'T USE ANY HIGH END SKILLS... YOU WON'T STAND A CHANCE...!
VHNNNNN

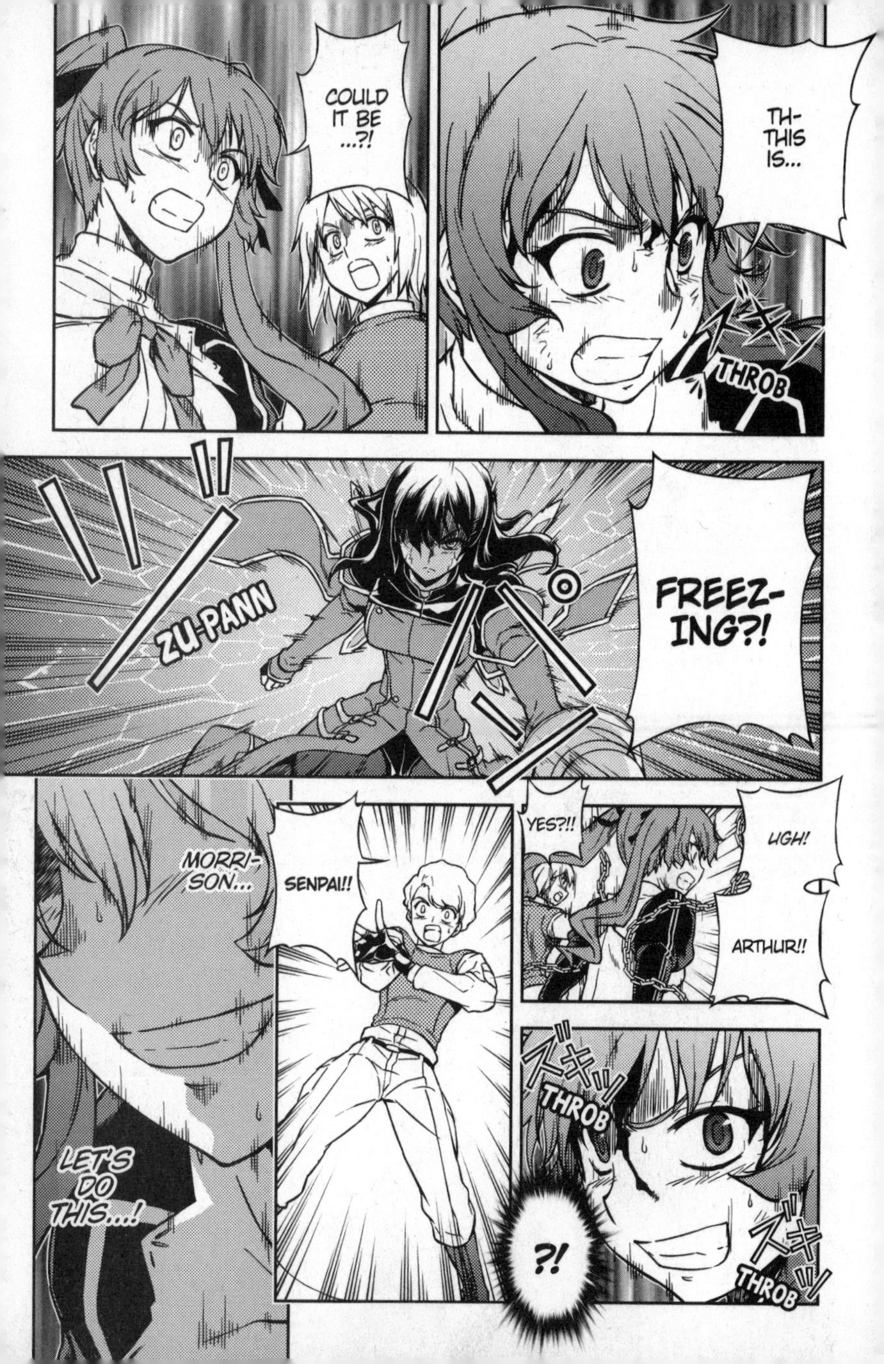
TH- THIS IS...
THROB
COULD IT BE ...?!
FREEZ- ING?!
ZU-PANN
UGH!
ARTHUR!!
YES?!!
THROB
THROB
?!
SENPAI!!
MORRI- SON...
LET'S DO THIS...!

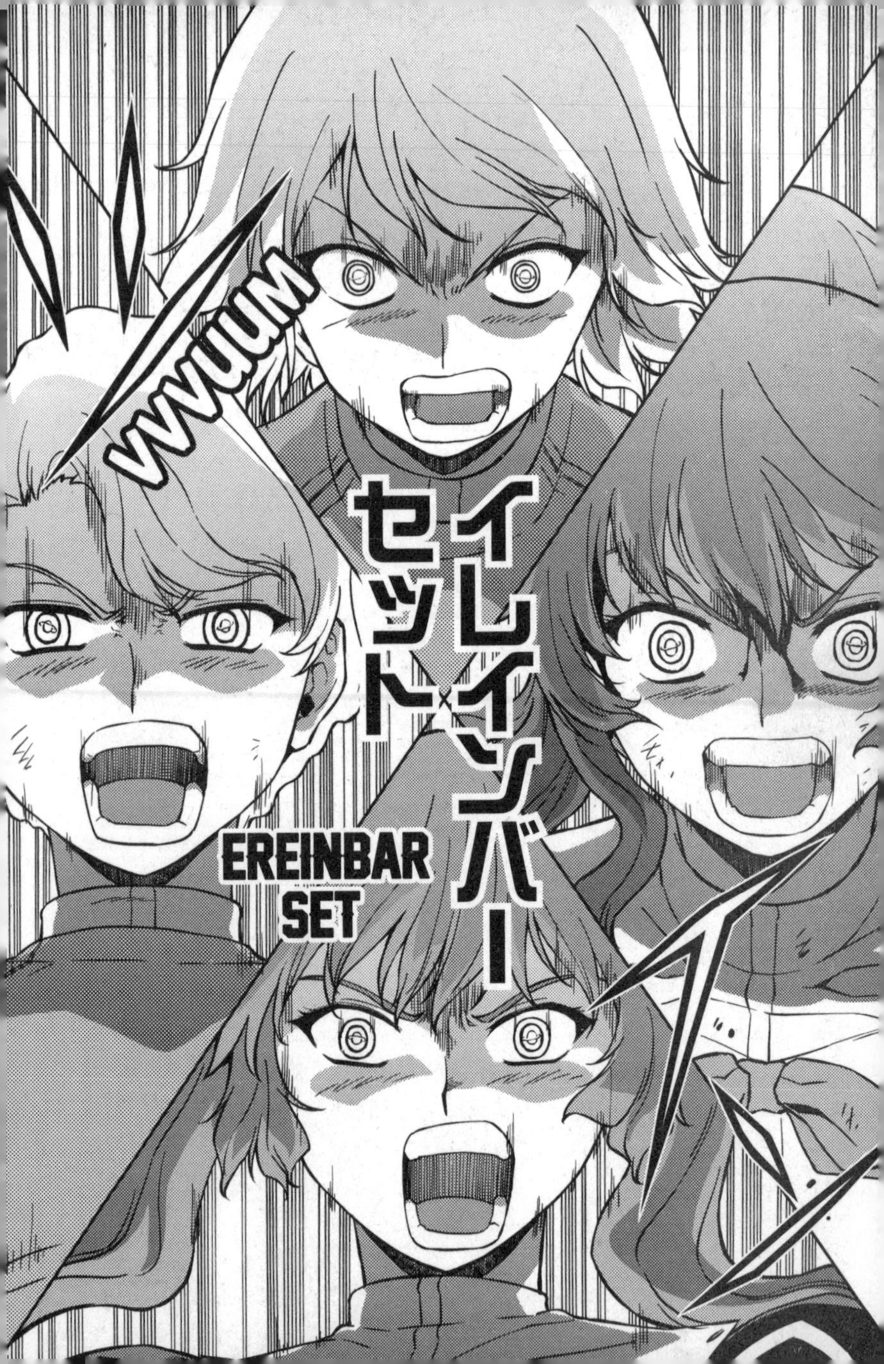
VVVUUM
イレインバー
セット
EREINBAR SET

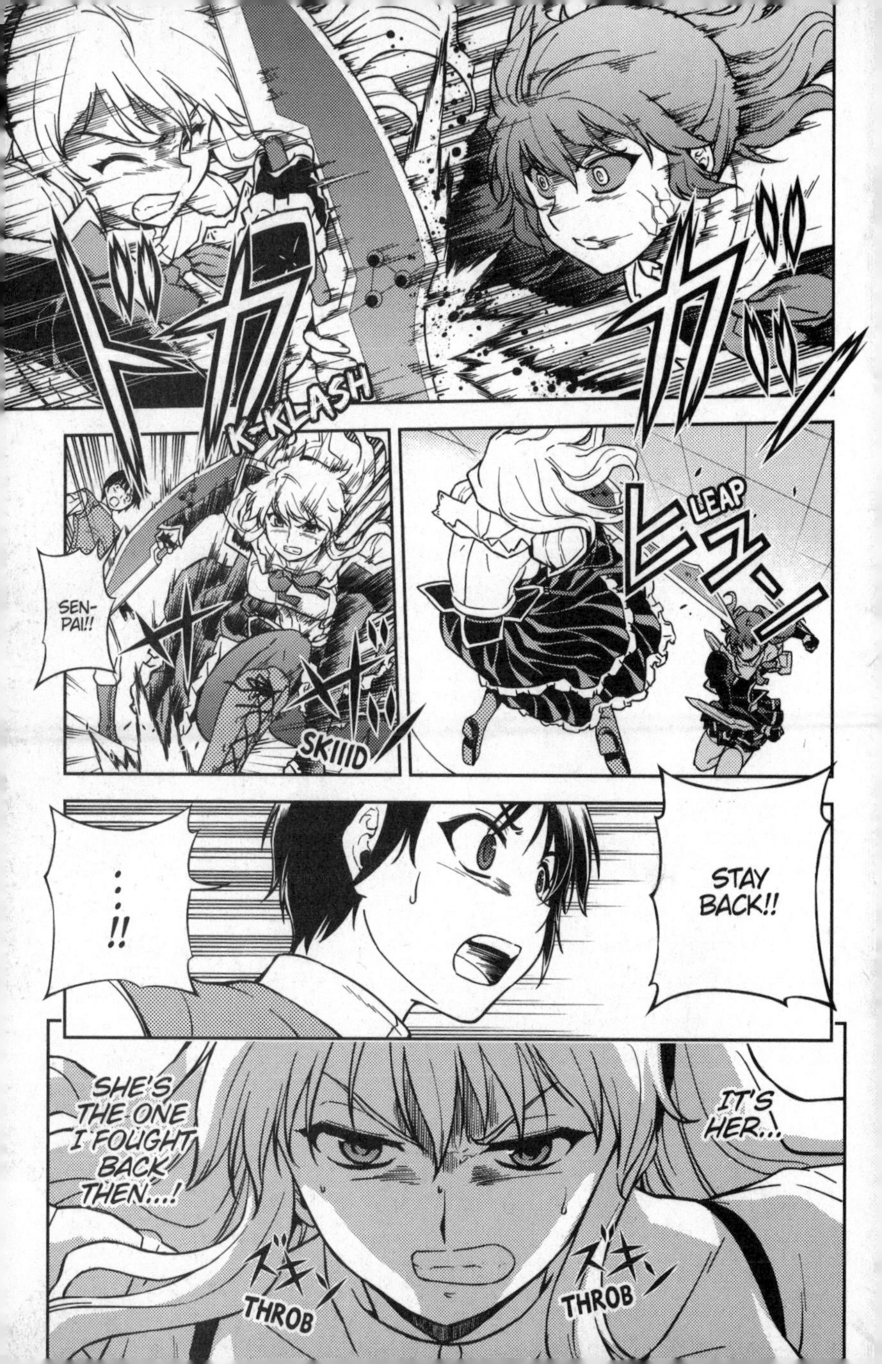
K-KLASH
LEAP
SEN-PAI!!
SKIIID
STAY BACK!!
...!!
IT'S HER...
SHE'S THE ONE I FOUGHT BACK THEN...!
THROB
THROB

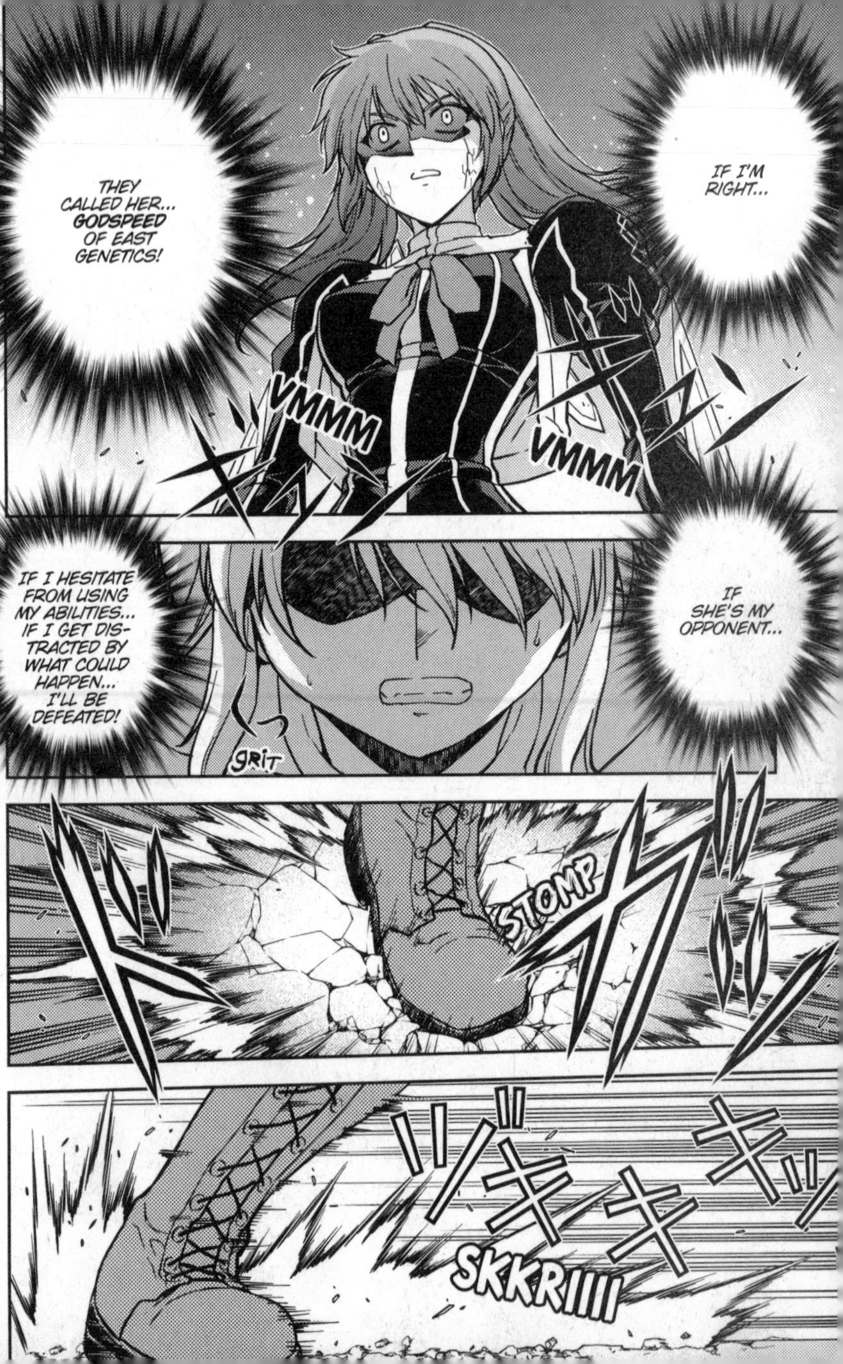
IF I'M RIGHT...
THEY CALLED HER... GODSPEED OF EAST GENETICS!
VMMM
VMMM
IF SHE'S MY OPPONENT...
IF I HESITATE FROM USING MY ABILITIES... IF I GET DIS-TRACTED BY WHAT COULD HAPPEN... I'LL BE DEFEATED!
grit
STOMP
SKKRIIII

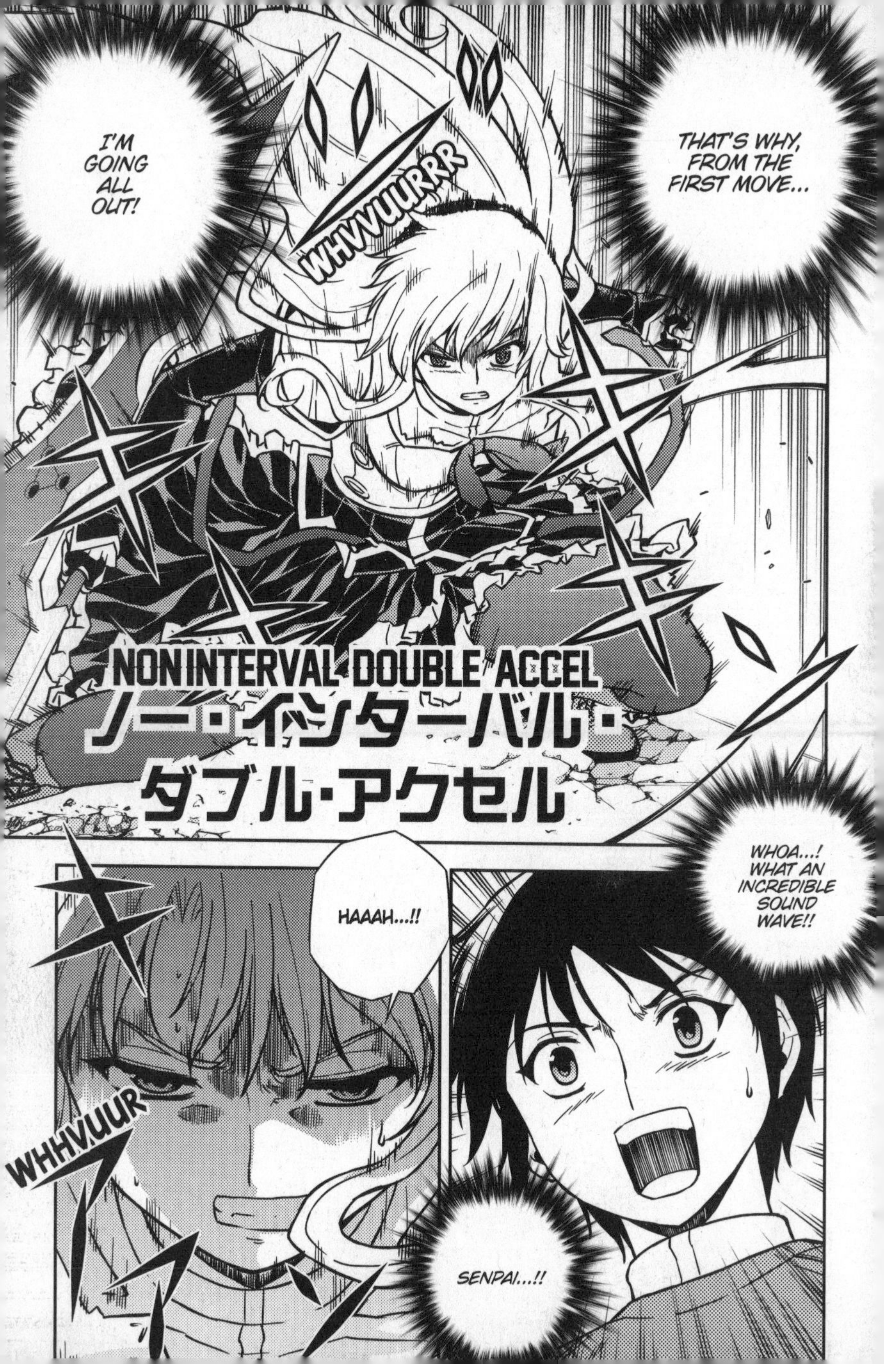
THAT'S WHY, FROM THE FIRST MOVE...
I'M GOING ALL OUT!
WHVVUURRR
NONINTERVAL DOUBLE ACCEL
ノー・インターバル・ダブル・アクセル
WHOA...! WHAT AN INCREDIBLE SOUND WAVE!!
SENPAI...!!
HAAAH...!!
WHHVUUR

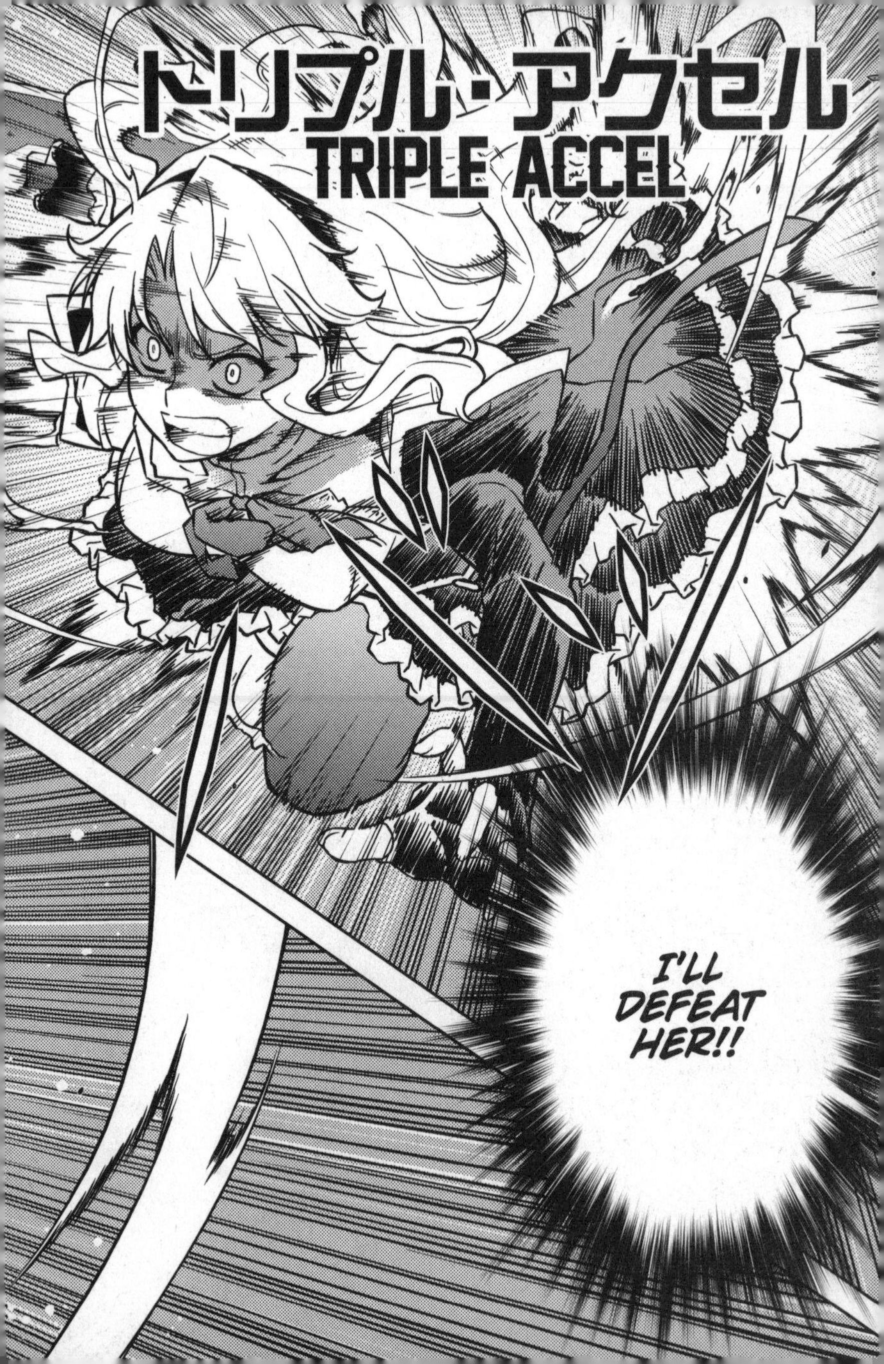
トリプル・アクセル
TRIPLE ACCEL
I'LL DEFEAT HER!!

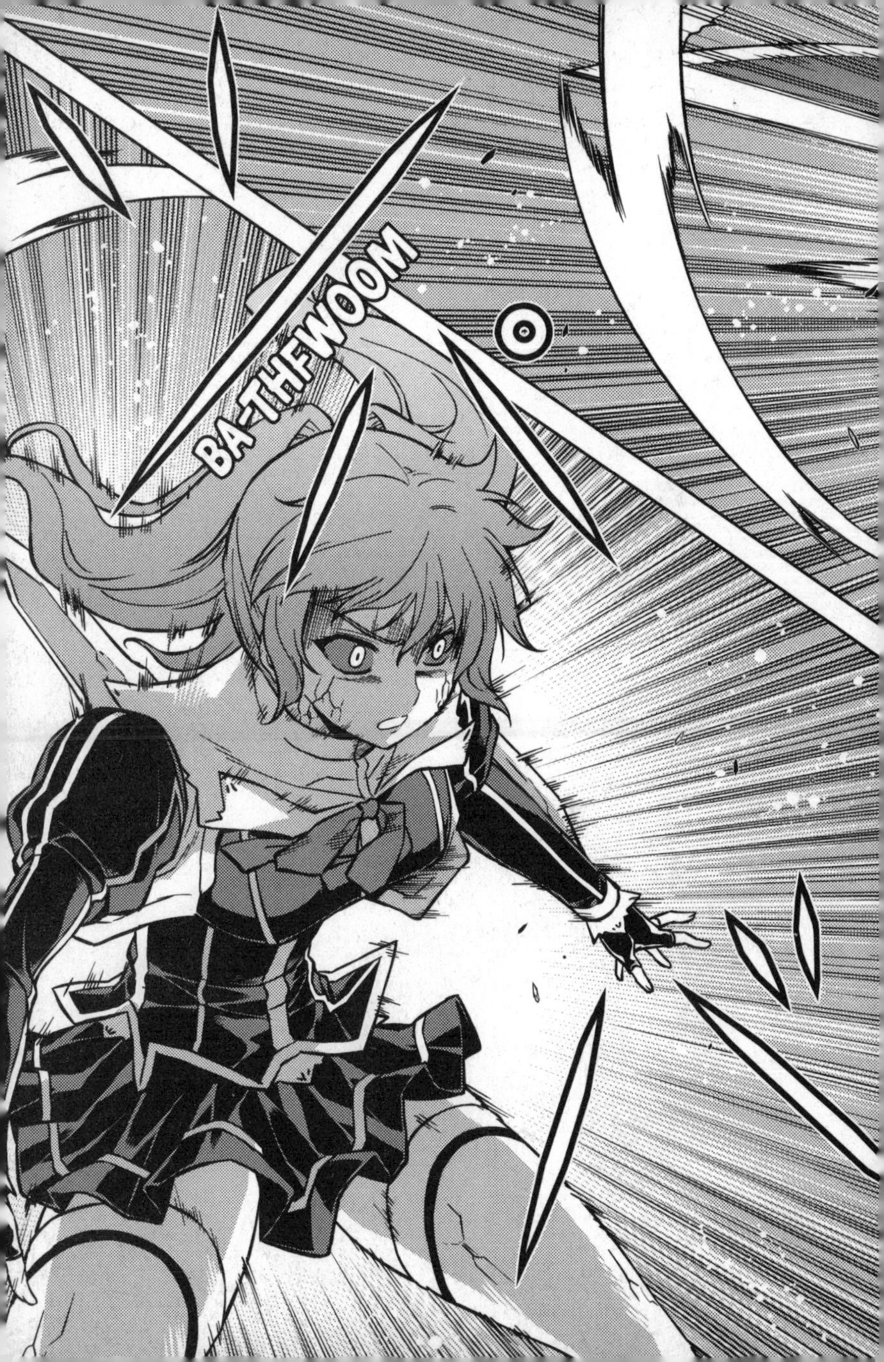
BA-THFWOOM

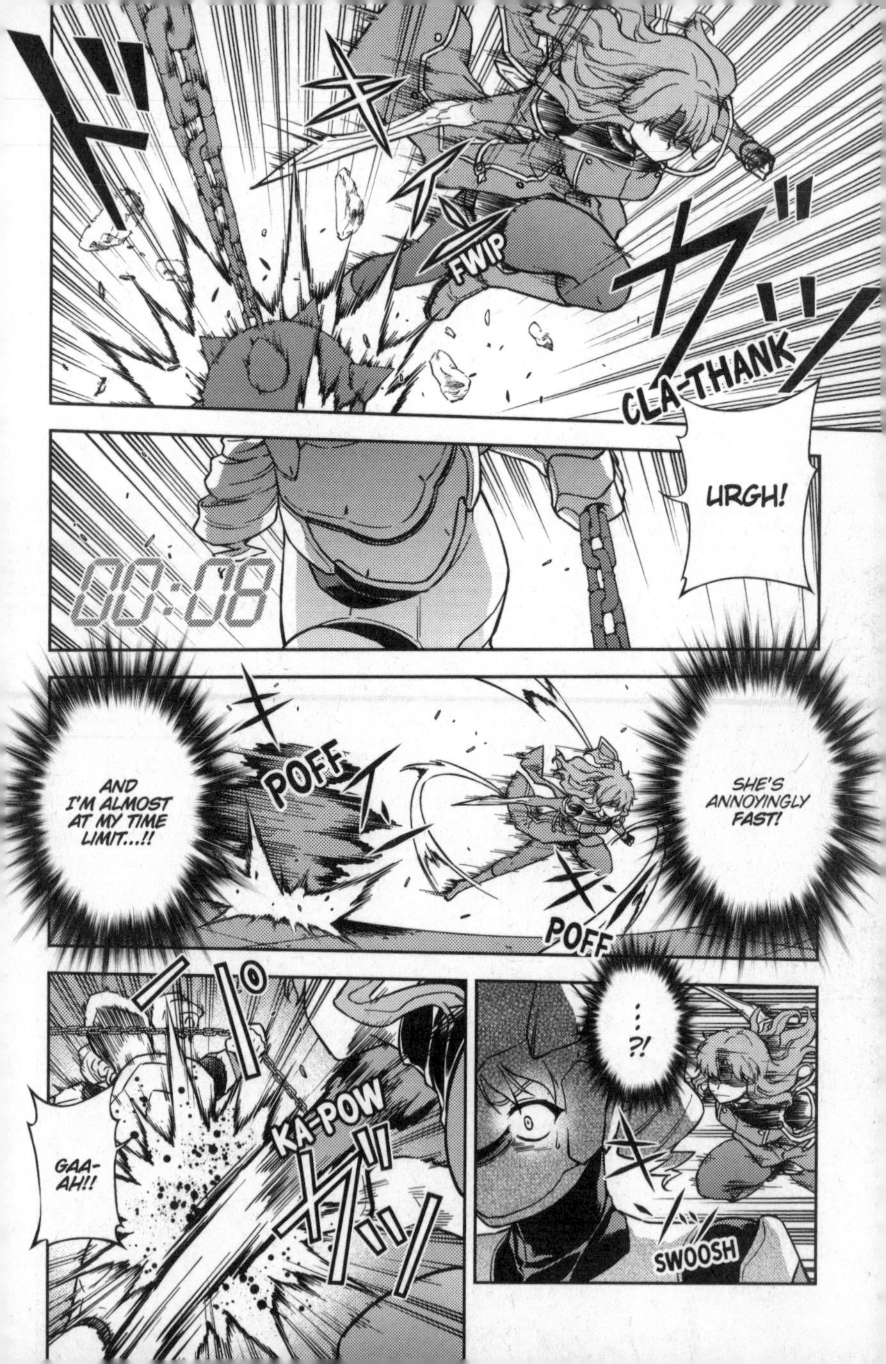

FWIP
CLA-THANK
URGH!
00:08
SHE'S ANNOYINGLY FAST!
POFF
AND I'M ALMOST AT MY TIME LIMIT...!!
POFF
...?!
SWOOSH
KA-POW
GAA-AH!!

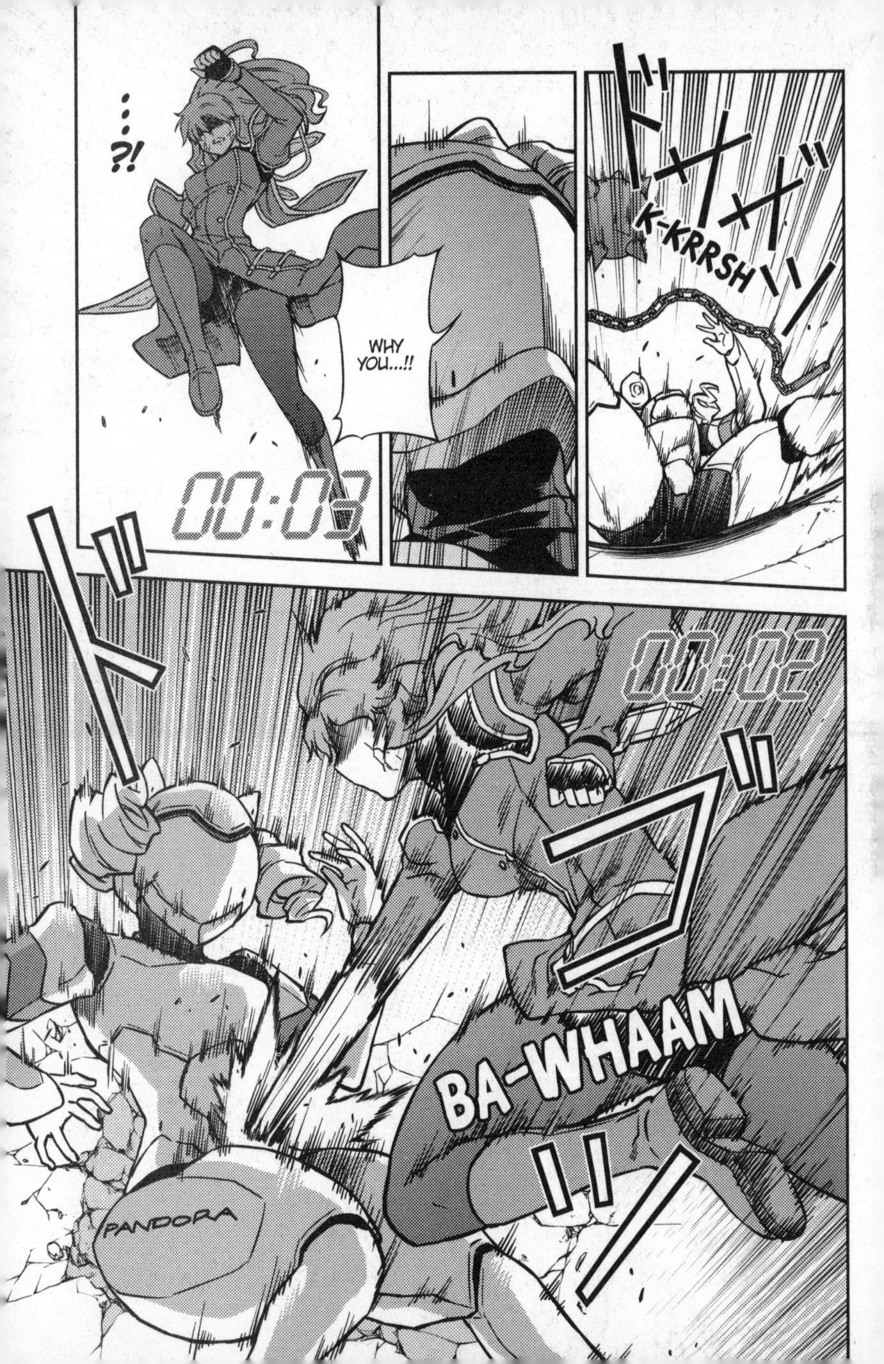
K-KRRSH
WHY YOU...!!
...
?!
00:03
00:02
BA-WHAAM
PANDORA

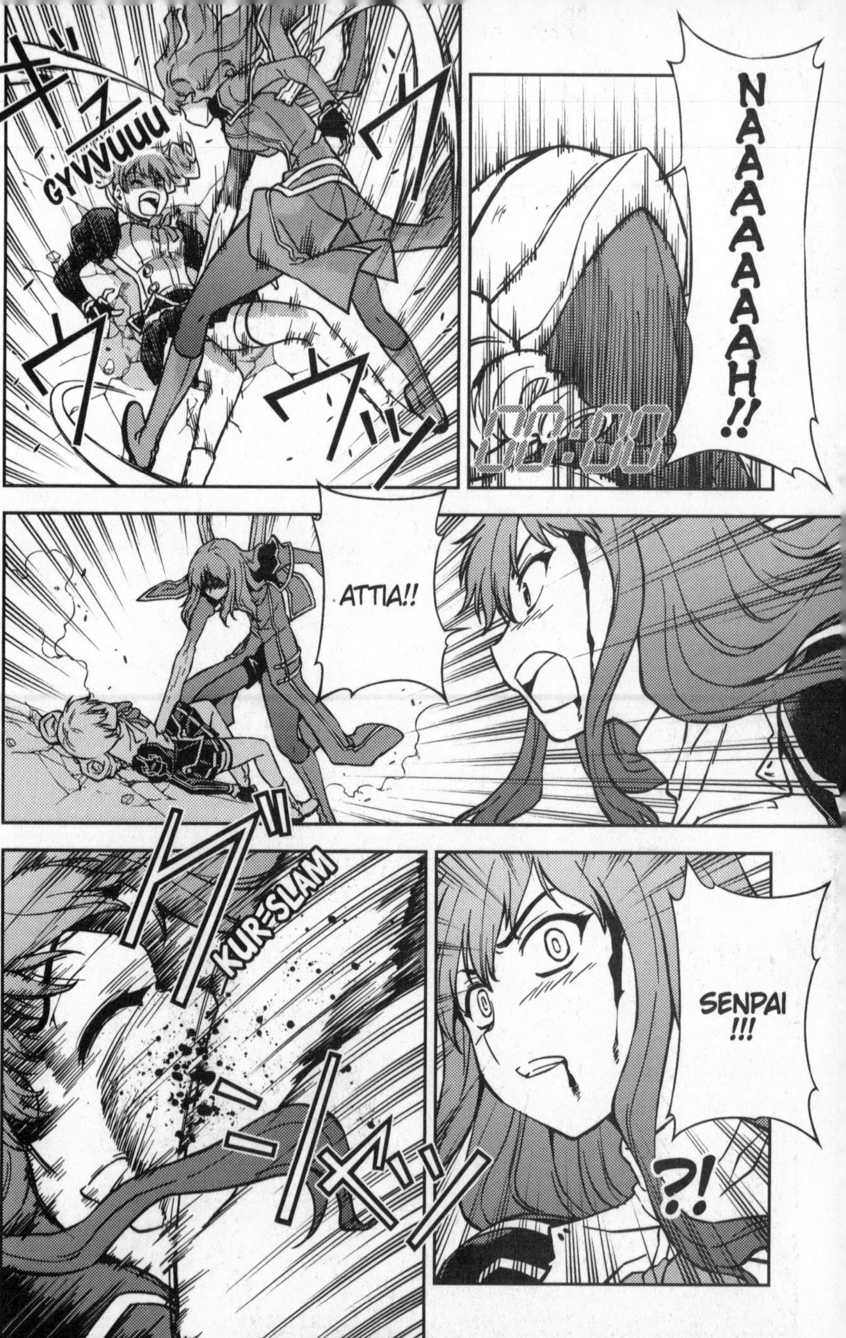
NAAAAAAAH!!
00:00
GYVVUUU
ATTIA!!
SENPAI !!!
?!
KUR-SLAM

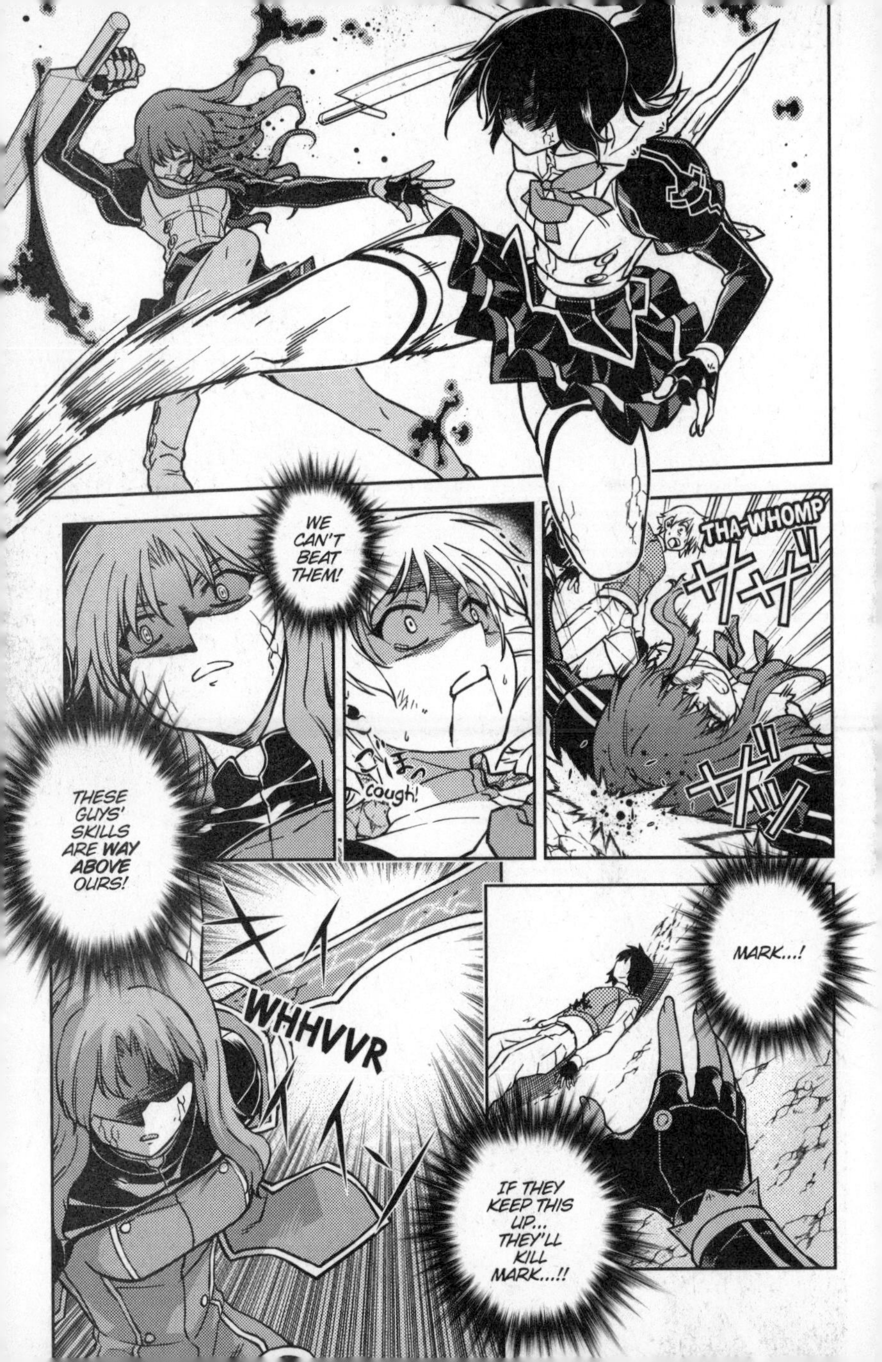
THA-WHOMP
cough!
WE CAN'T BEAT THEM!
THESE GUYS' SKILLS ARE WAY ABOVE OURS!
MARK...!
IF THEY KEEP THIS UP... THEY'LL KILL MARK...!!
WHHVVR

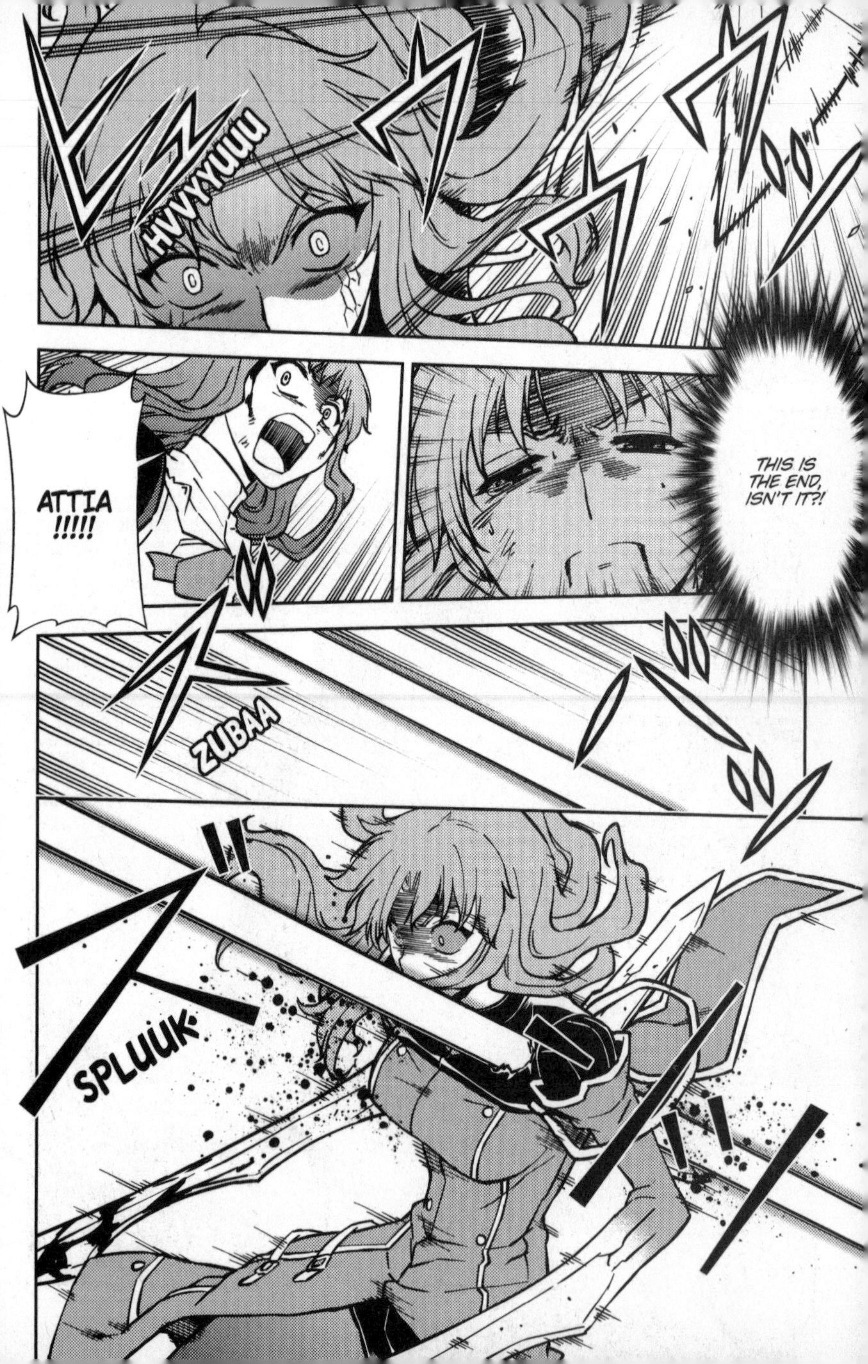
HVVYYUUU
THIS IS THE END, ISN'T IT?!
ATTIA !!!!!
ZUBAA
SPLUUK

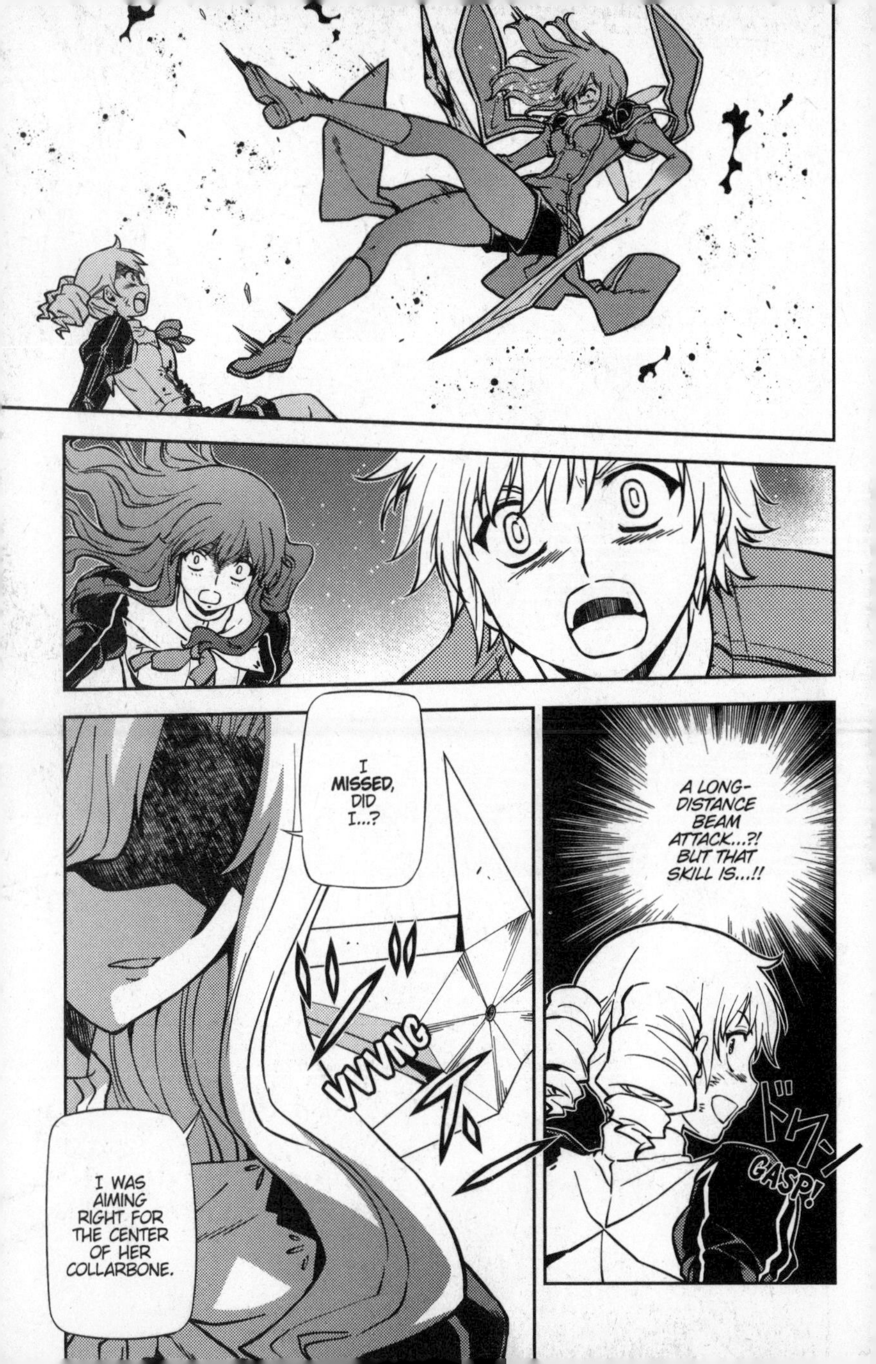
A LONG-DISTANCE BEAM ATTACK...?! BUT THAT SKILL IS...!!
GASP!
I MISSED, DID I...?
VVVNG
I WAS AIMING RIGHT FOR THE CENTER OF HER COLLARBONE.

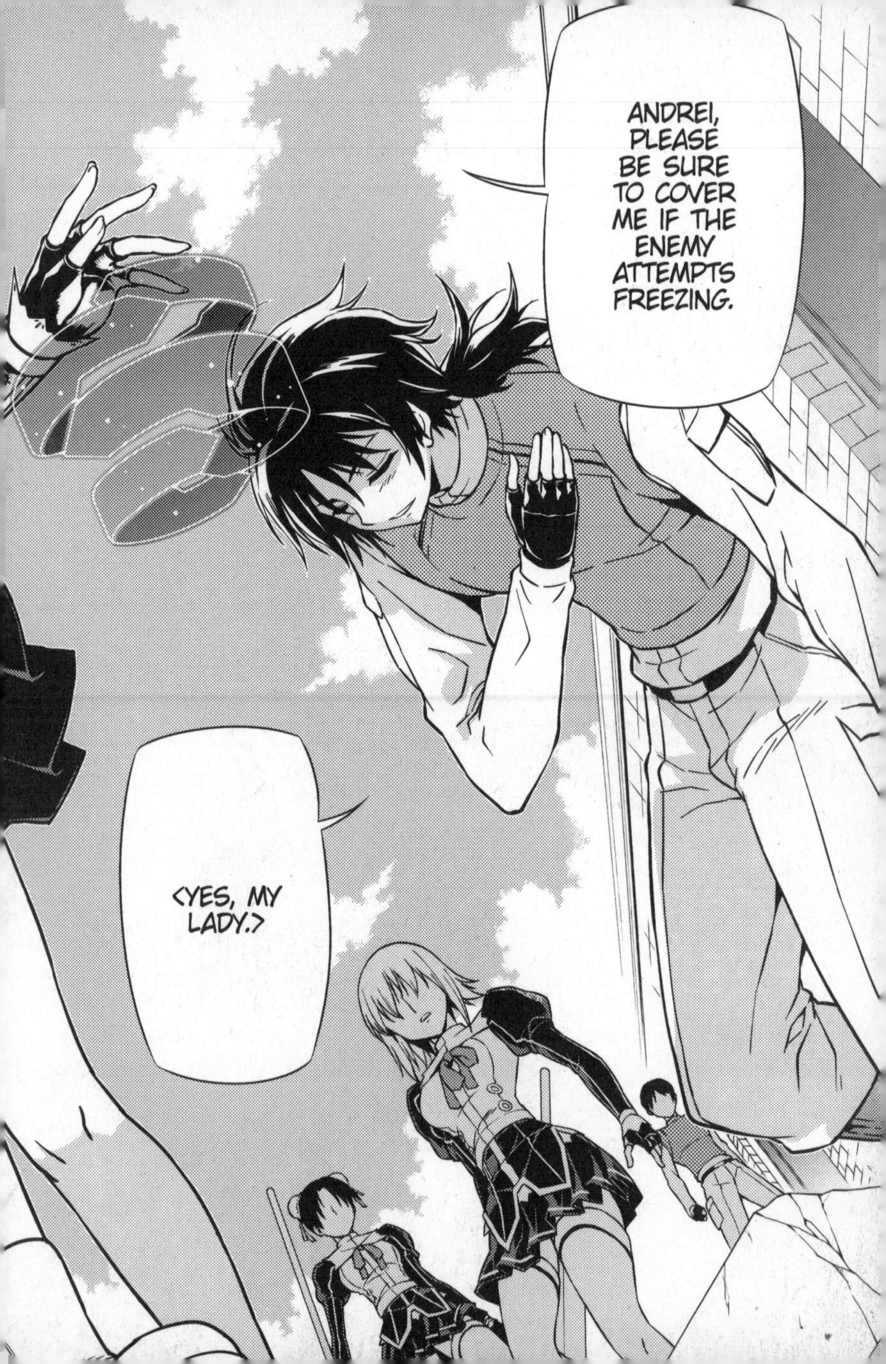
ANDREI, PLEASE BE SURE TO COVER ME IF THE ENEMY ATTEMPTS FREEZING.
<YES, MY LADY.>

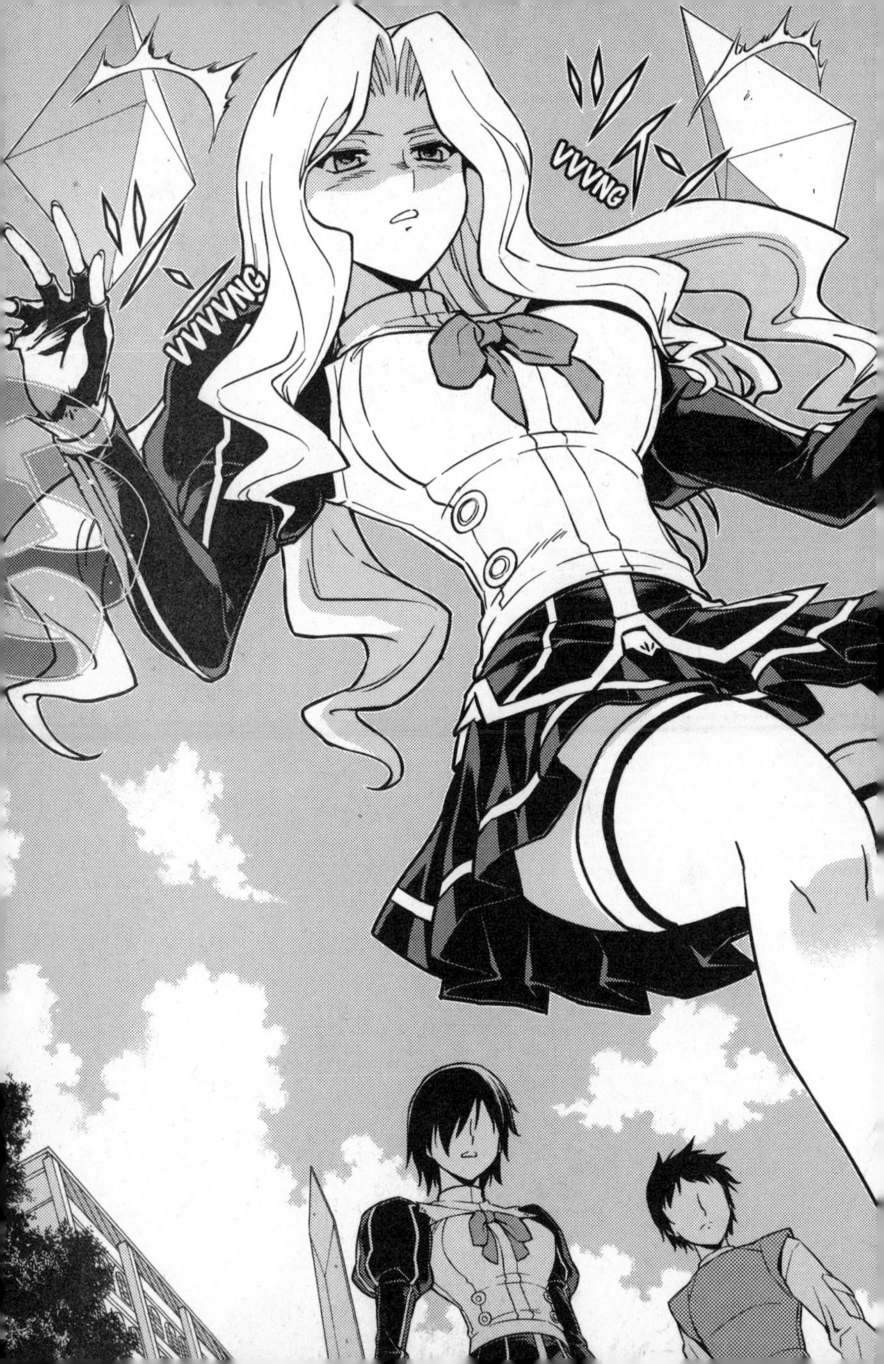
VVVNG
VVVVNG

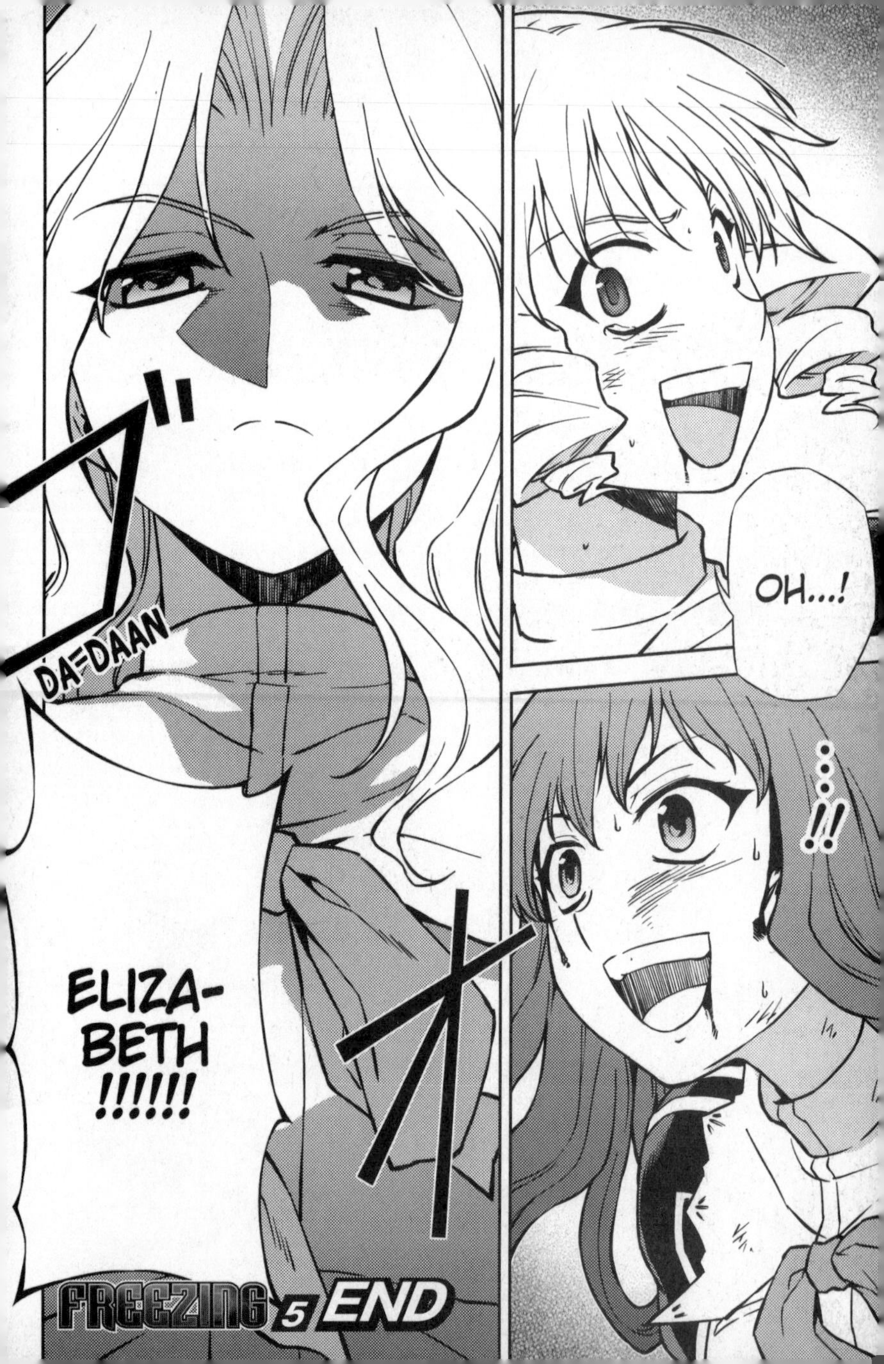
OH...!
...!!
DA=DAAN
ELIZA-
BETH
!!!!!!
FREEZING 5 END

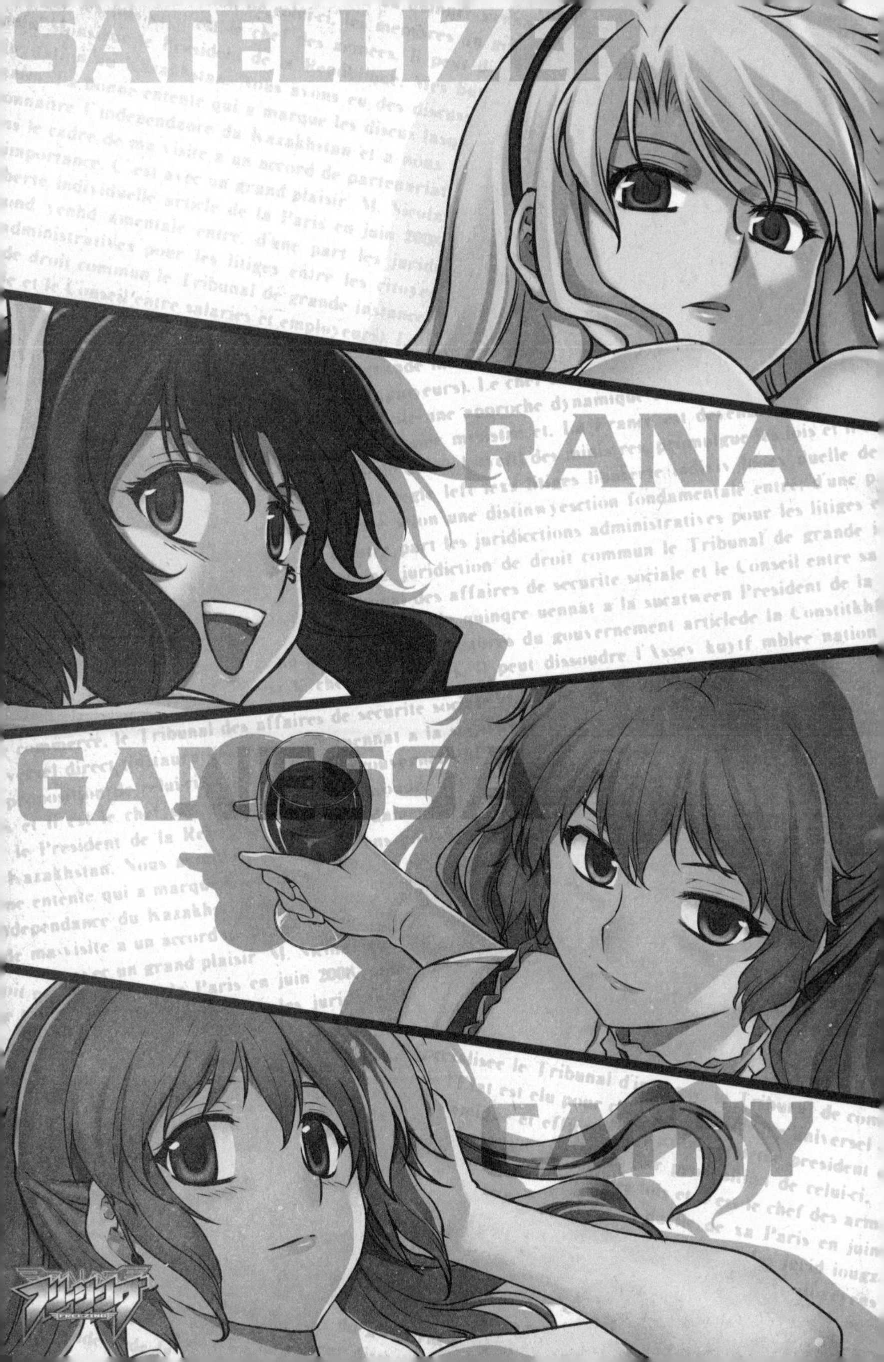
SATELLIZER
RANA

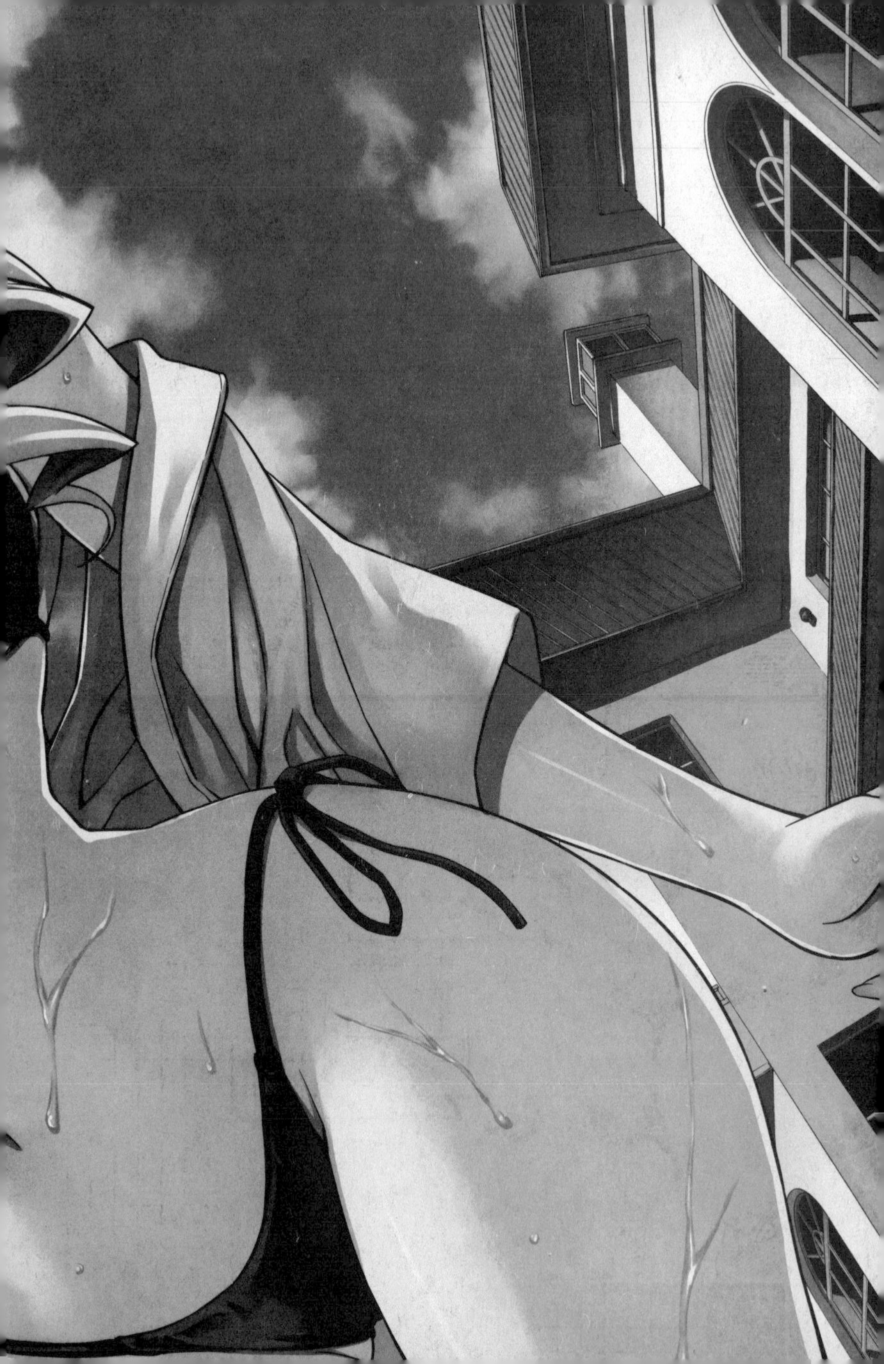

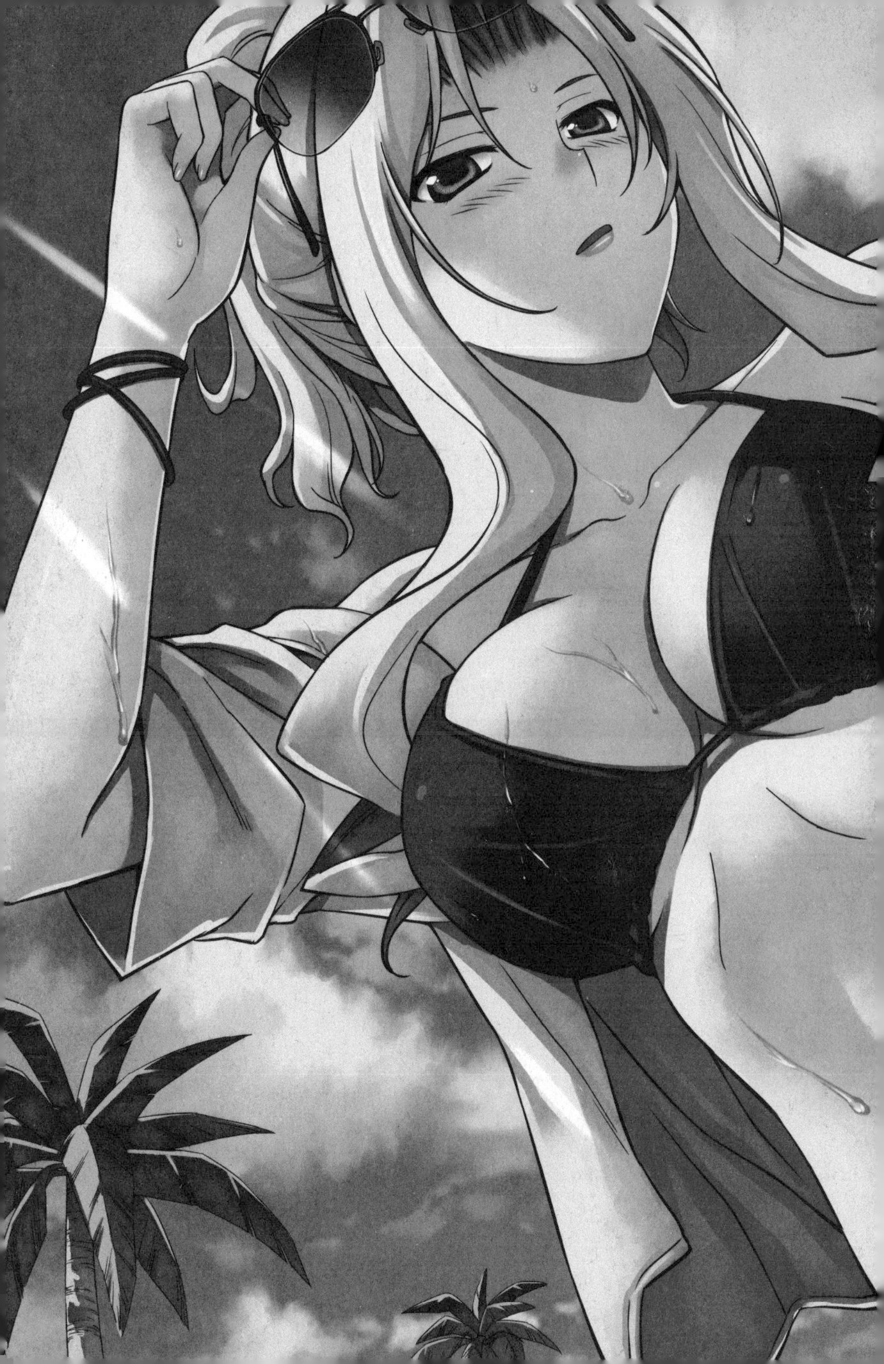

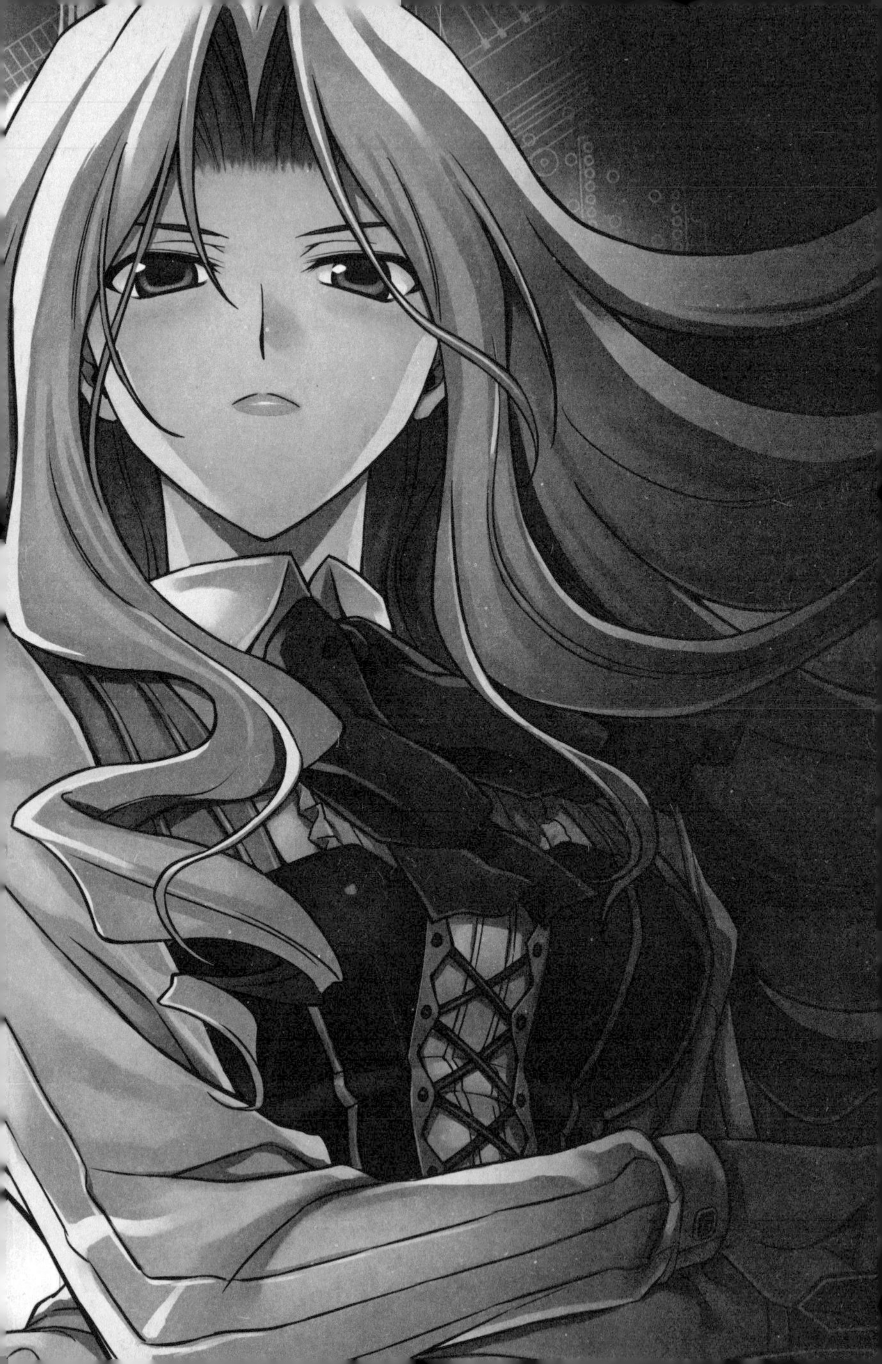

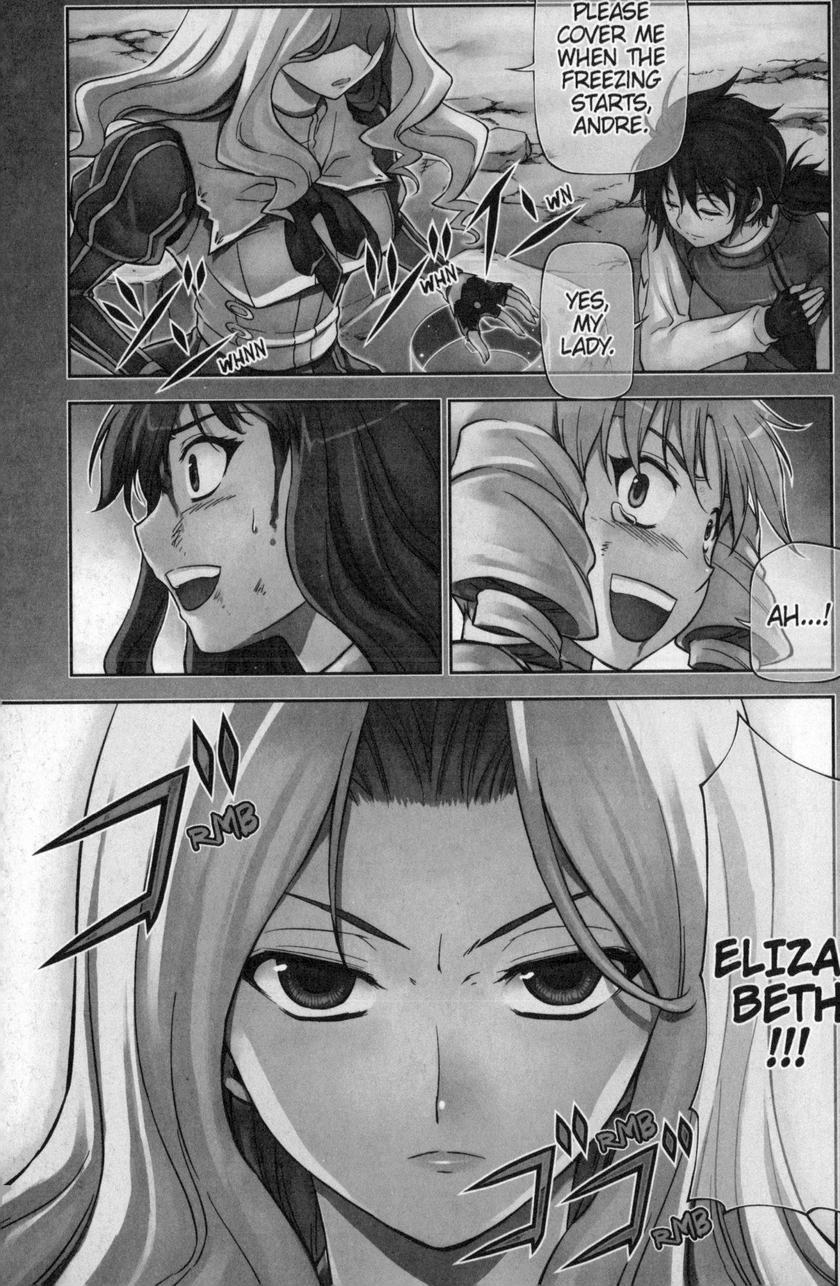
PLEASE COVER ME WHEN THE FREEZING STARTS, ANDRE.
WN
YES, MY LADY.
WHN
WHNN
AH...!
ELIZA-BETH!!!
RMB
RMB
RMB

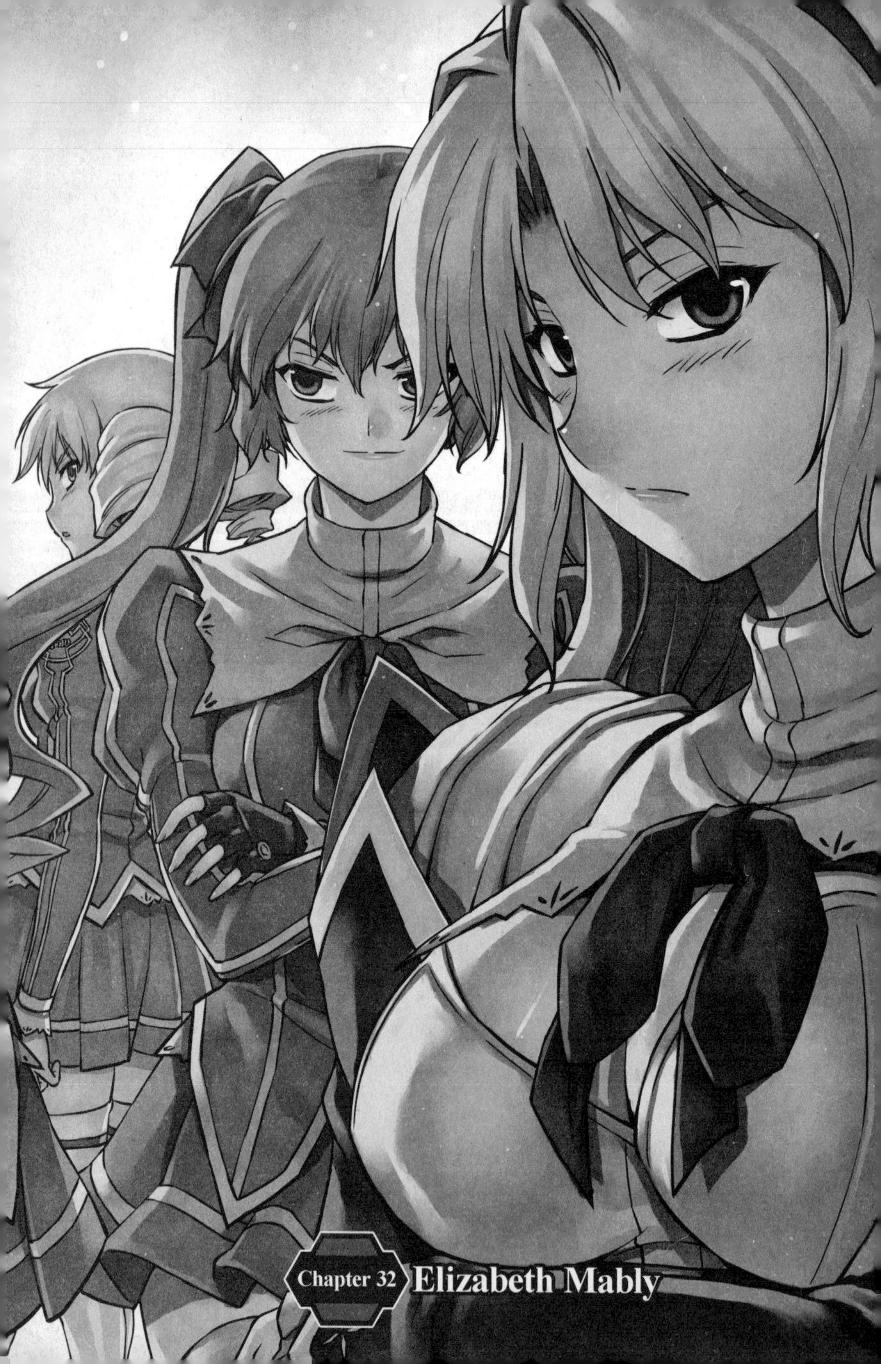

Chapter 32 Elizabeth Mably

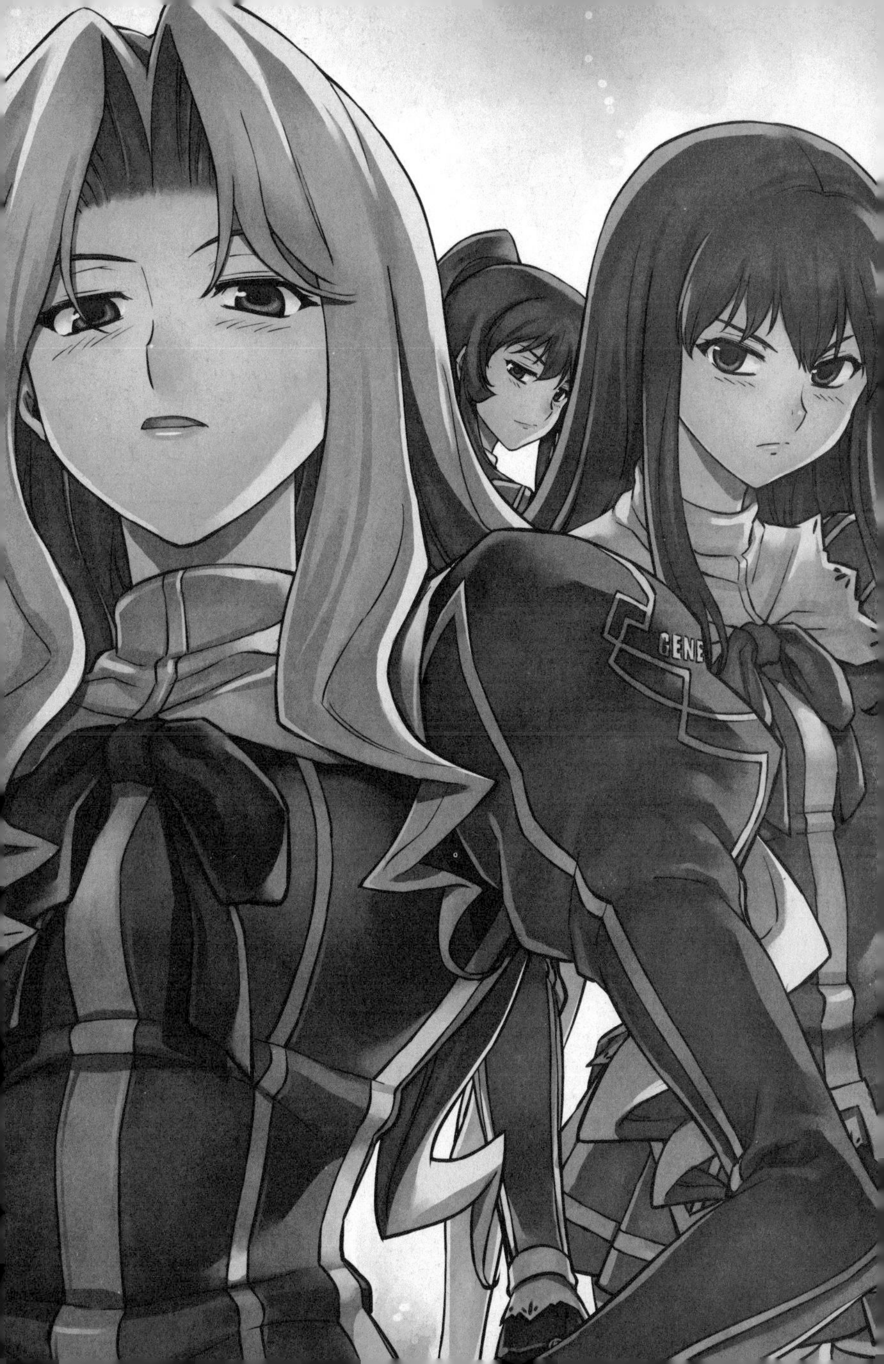
GENE

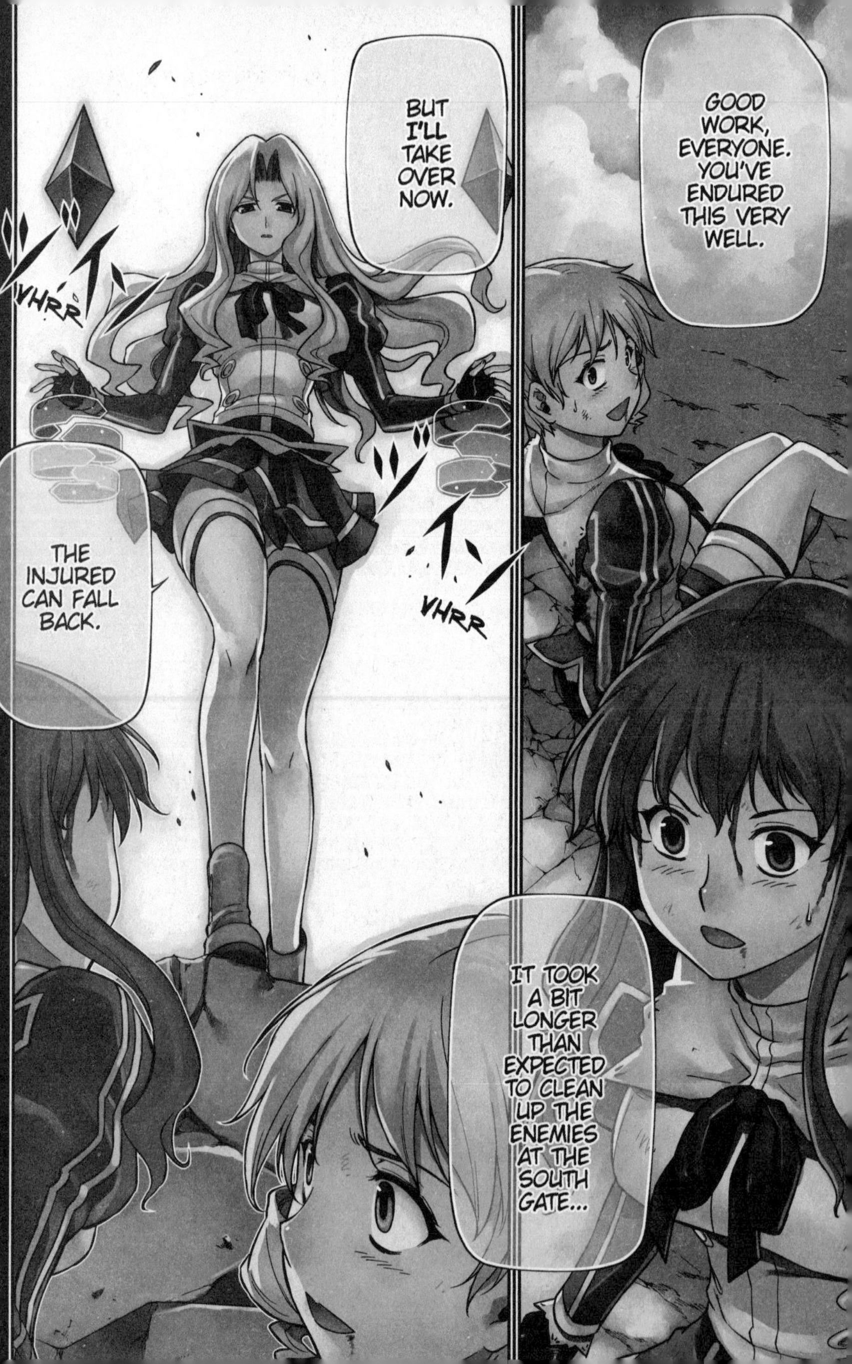
GOOD WORK, EVERYONE. YOU'VE ENDURED THIS VERY WELL.
IT TOOK A BIT LONGER THAN EXPECTED TO CLEAN UP THE ENEMIES AT THE SOUTH GATE...
BUT I'LL TAKE OVER NOW.
VHRR
THE INJURED CAN FALL BACK.
VHRR

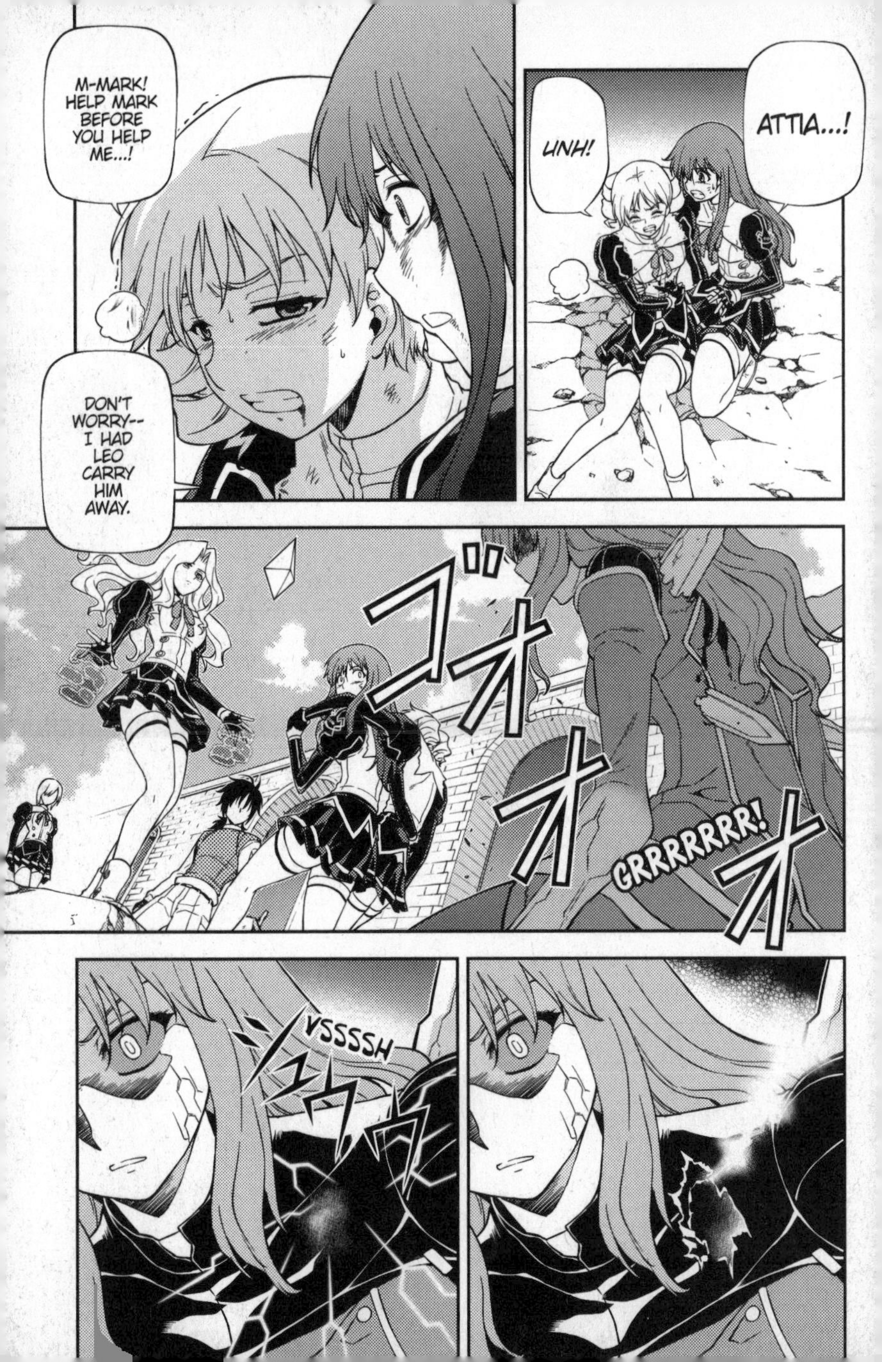
ATTIA...!
UNH!
M-MARK! HELP MARK BEFORE YOU HELP ME...!
DON'T WORRY-- I HAD LEO CARRY HIM AWAY.
GRRRRRRR!
VSSSSH

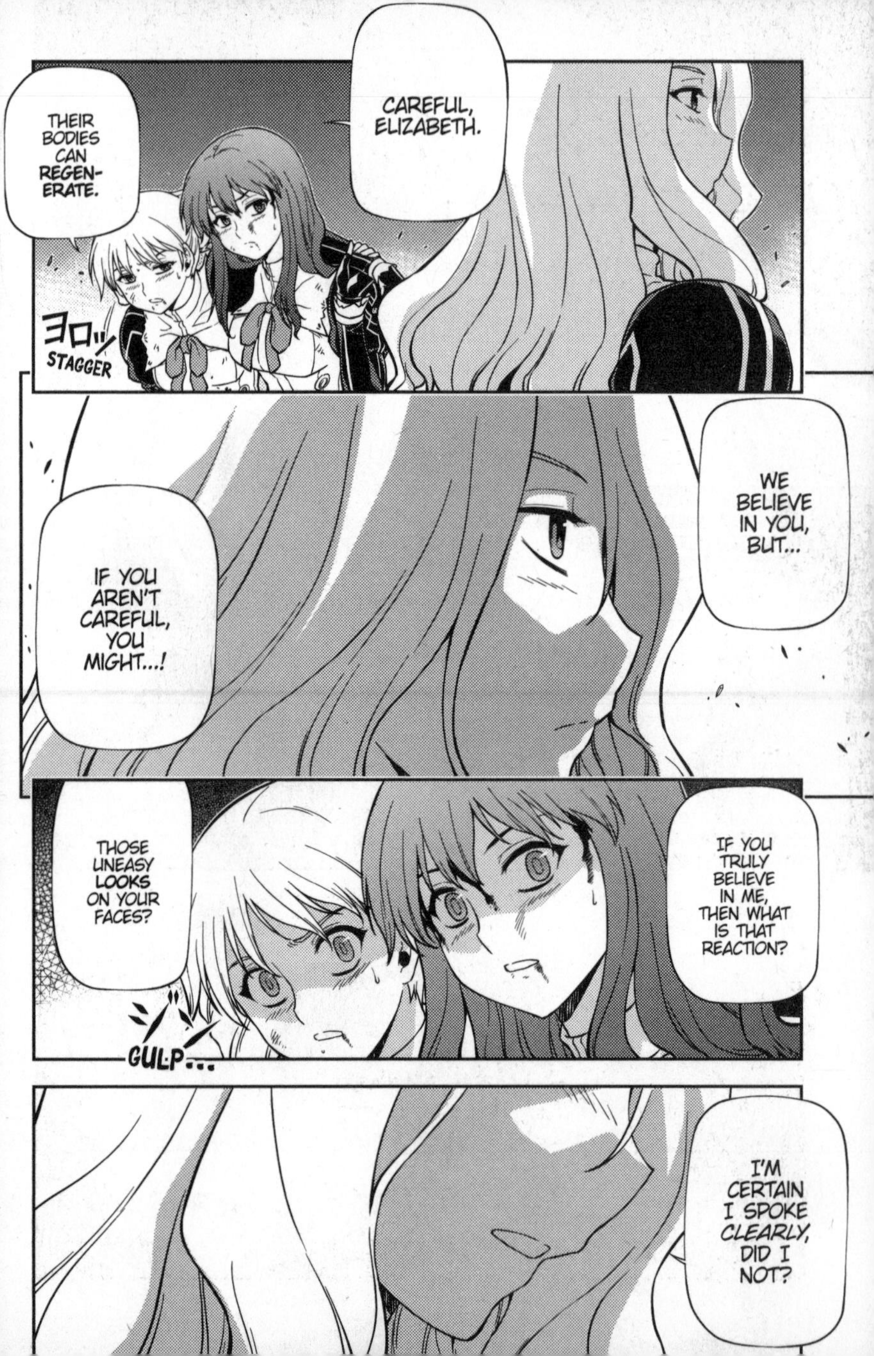
CAREFUL, ELIZABETH.
THEIR BODIES CAN REGEN-ERATE.
ヨロッ
STAGGER
WE BELIEVE IN YOU, BUT...
IF YOU AREN'T CAREFUL, YOU MIGHT...!
IF YOU TRULY BELIEVE IN ME, THEN WHAT IS THAT REACTION?
THOSE UNEASY LOOKS ON YOUR FACES?
GULP...
I'M CERTAIN I SPOKE *CLEARLY*, DID I NOT?

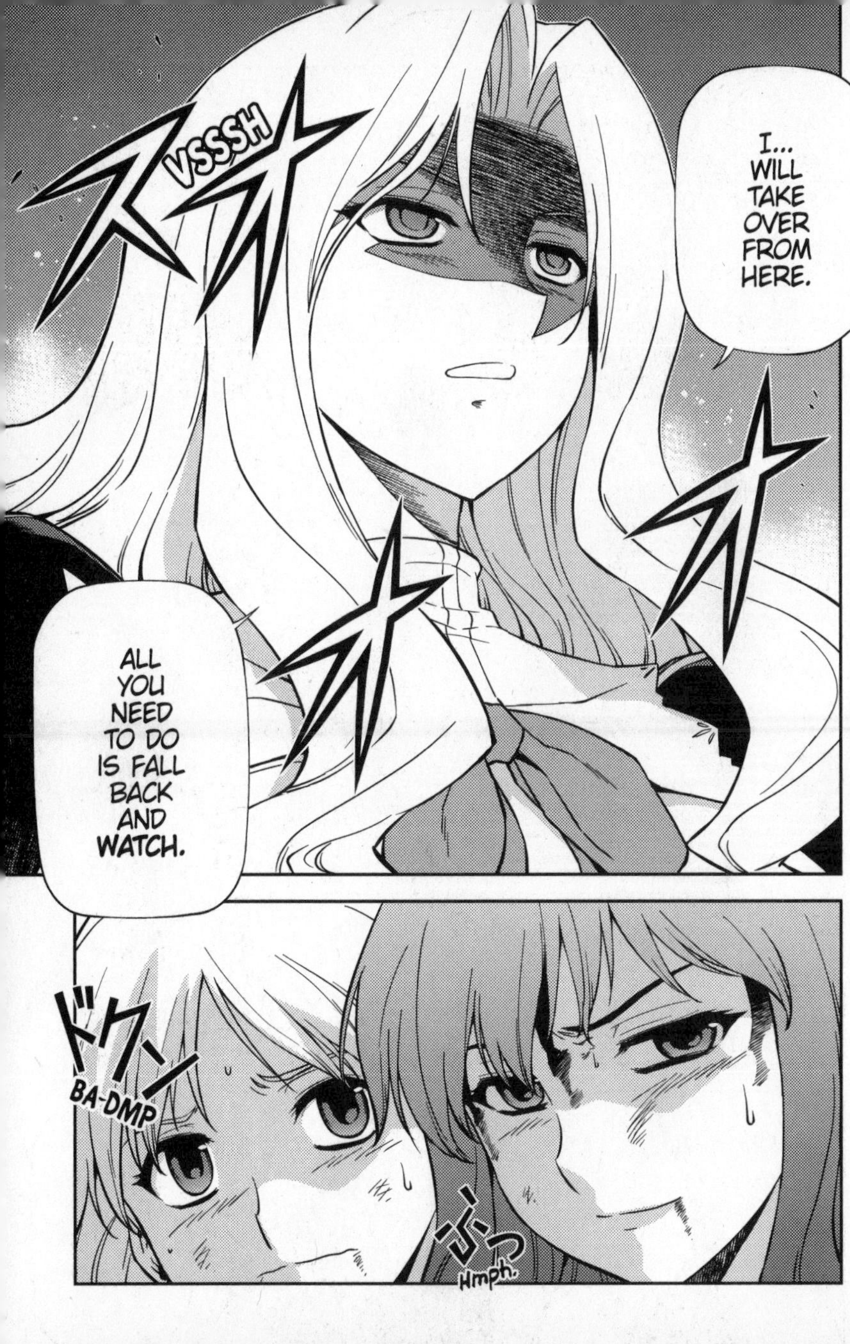
I... WILL TAKE OVER FROM HERE.
VSSSH
ALL YOU NEED TO DO IS FALL BACK AND WATCH.
ドクン
BA-DMP
ふっ
Hmph.

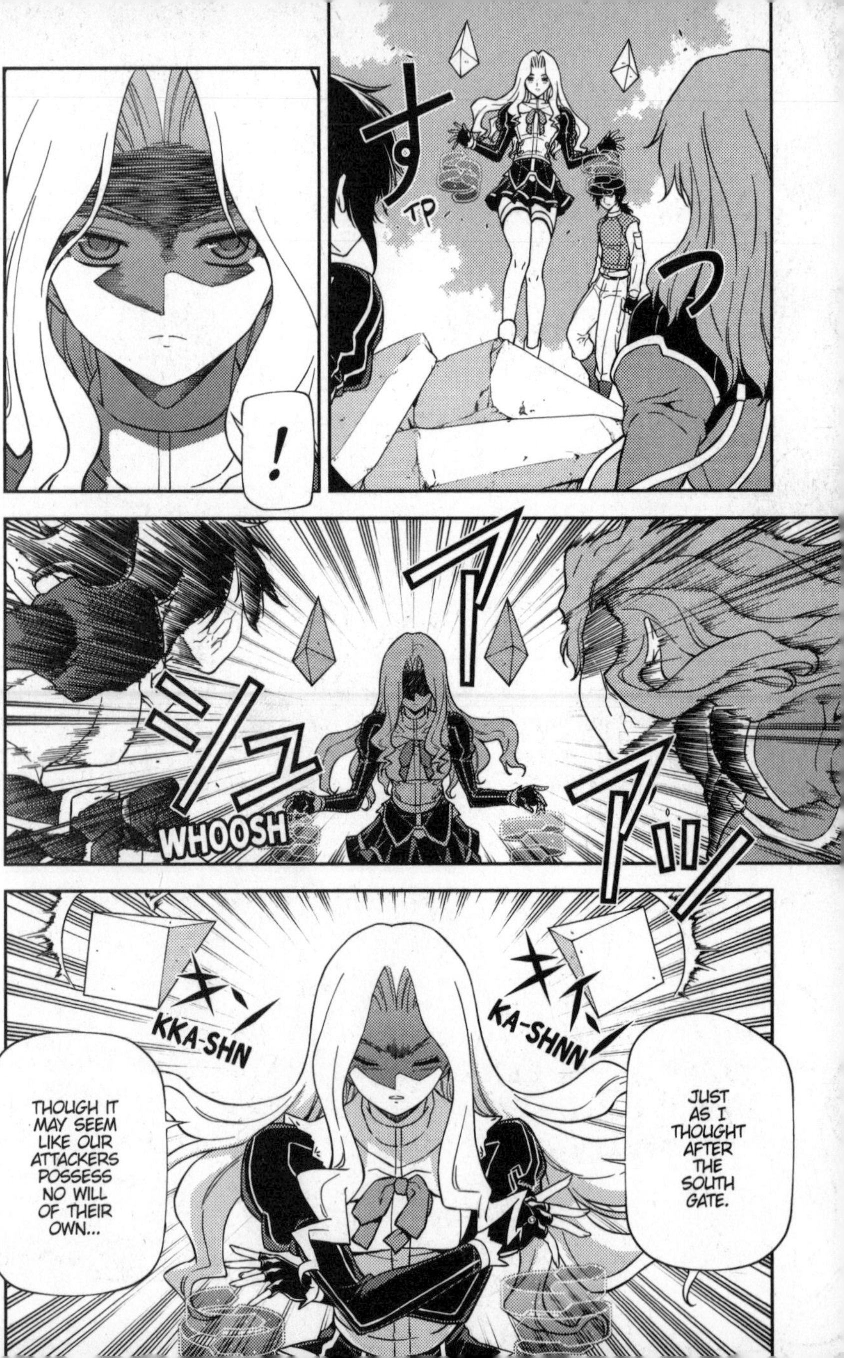
TP
!
WHOOSH
KA-SHNN
KKA-SHN
JUST AS I THOUGHT AFTER THE SOUTH GATE.
THOUGH IT MAY SEEM LIKE OUR ATTACKERS POSSESS NO WILL OF THEIR OWN...

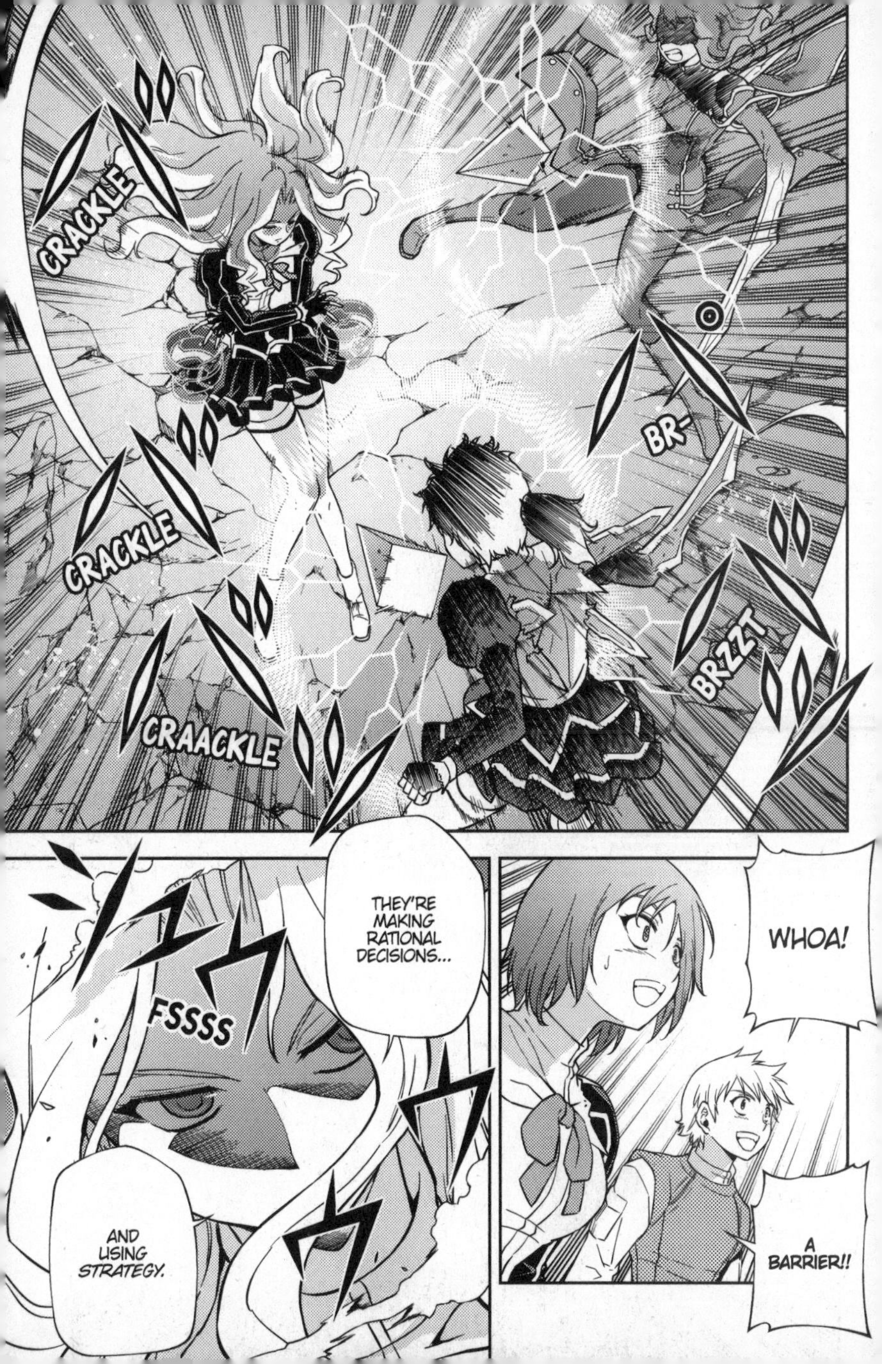
BR-
BRZZT
CRACKLE
CRACKLE
CRAACKLE
WHOA!
A BARRIER!!
THEY'RE MAKING RATIONAL DECISIONS...
FSSSS
AND USING STRATEGY.

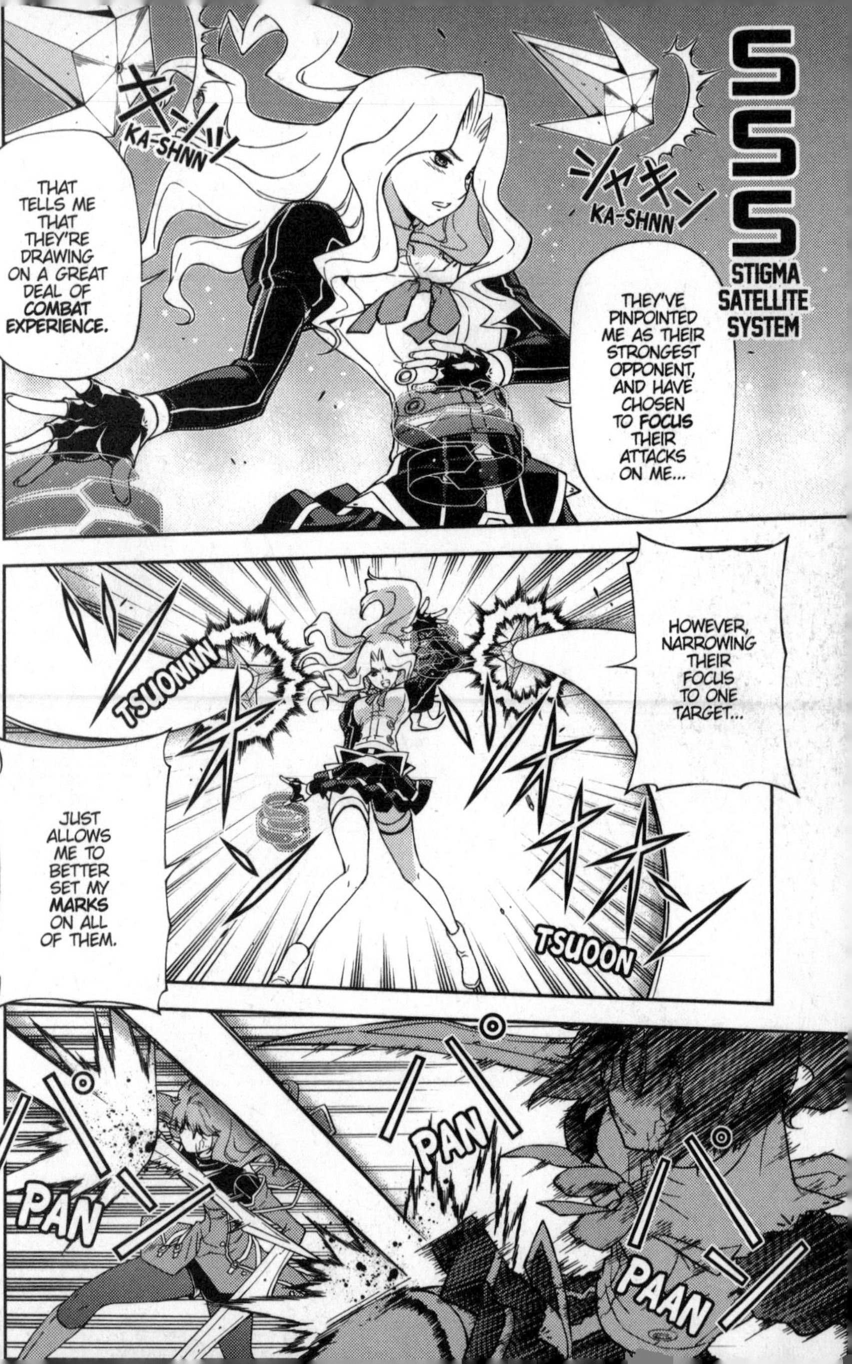
SSS
STIGMA SATELLITE SYSTEM
シャキン
KA-SHNN
THEY'VE PINPOINTED ME AS THEIR STRONGEST OPPONENT, AND HAVE CHOSEN TO FOCUS THEIR ATTACKS ON ME...
キーン
KA-SHNN
THAT TELLS ME THAT THEY'RE DRAWING ON A GREAT DEAL OF COMBAT EXPERIENCE.
HOWEVER, NARROWING THEIR FOCUS TO ONE TARGET...
TSUONNN
TSUOON
JUST ALLOWS ME TO BETTER SET MY MARKS ON ALL OF THEM.
PAN
PAAN
PAN

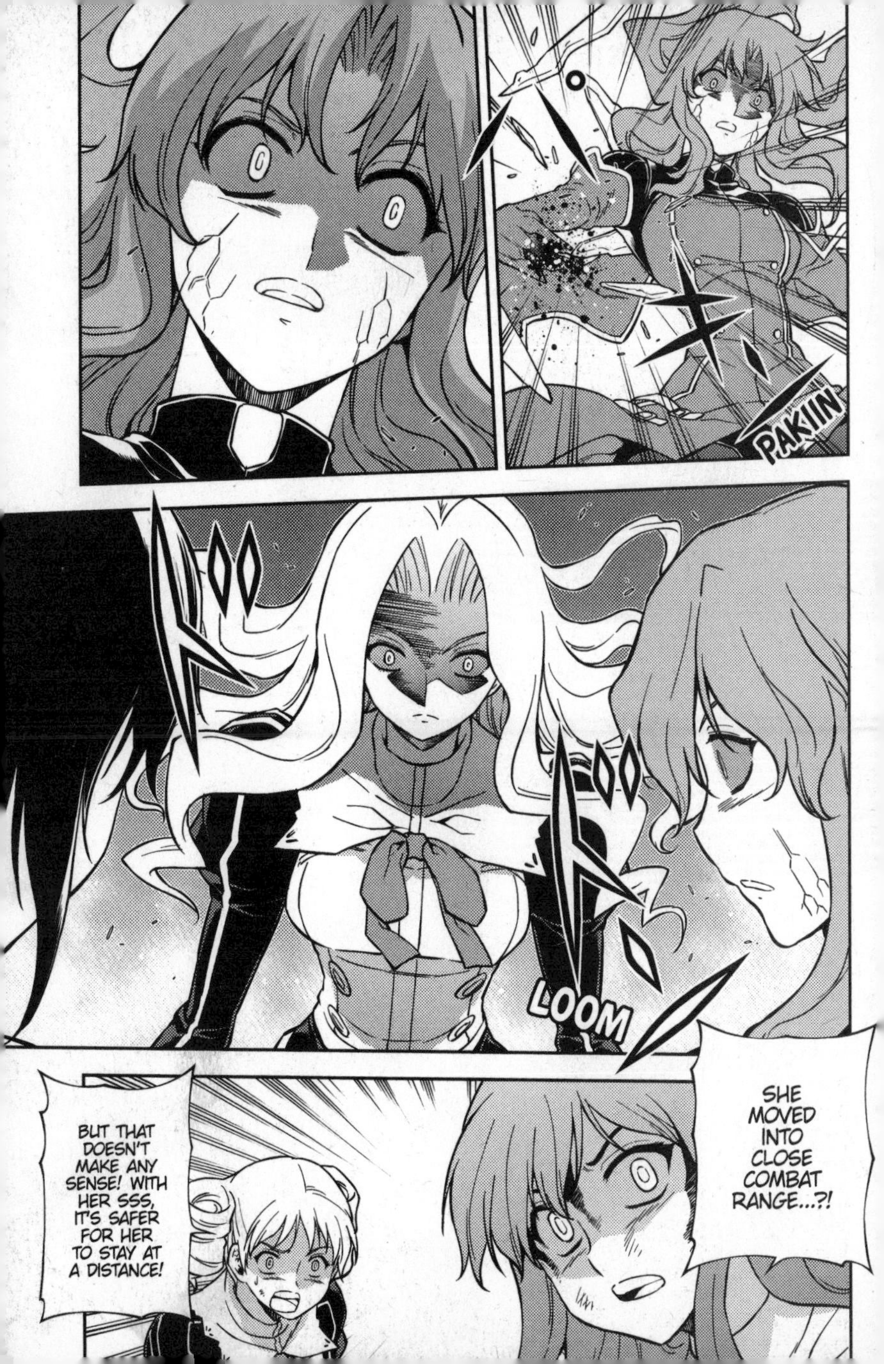
PAKIIN
LOOM
SHE MOVED INTO CLOSE COMBAT RANGE...?!
BUT THAT DOESN'T MAKE ANY SENSE! WITH HER SSS, IT'S SAFER FOR HER TO STAY AT A DISTANCE!

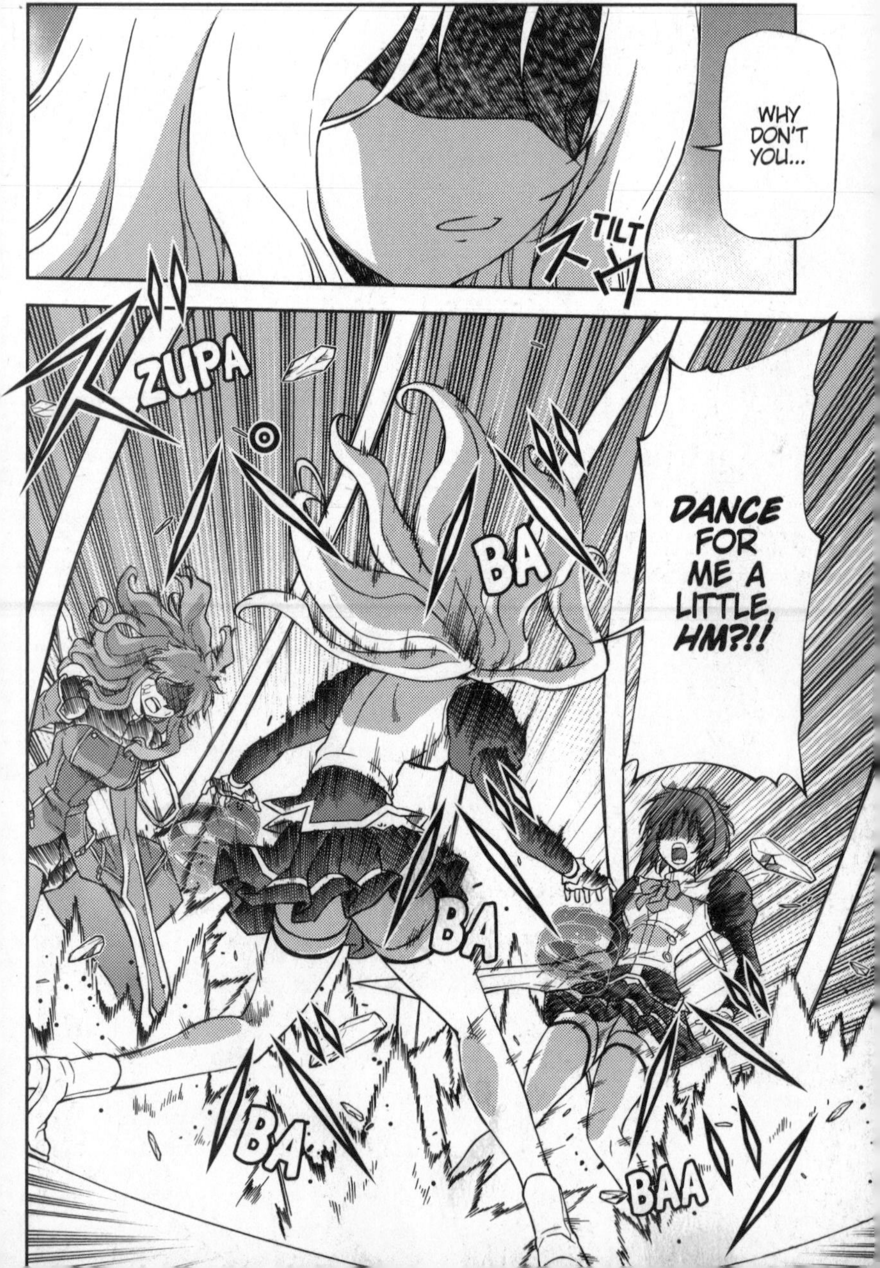
WHY DON'T YOU...
TILT
ZUPA
BA
DANCE FOR ME A LITTLE, HM?!!
BA
BA
BAA

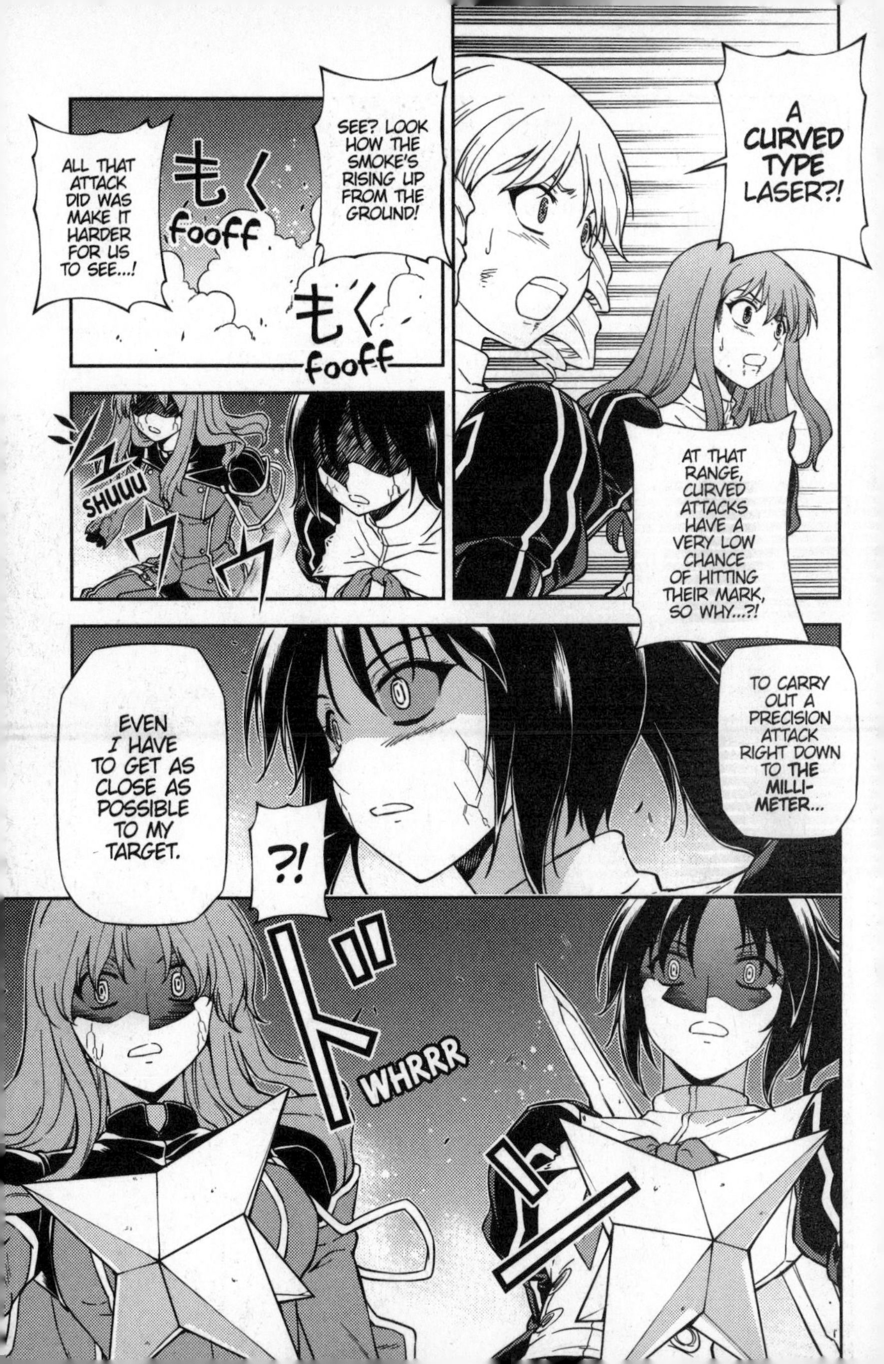
A CURVED TYPE LASER?!
AT THAT RANGE, CURVED ATTACKS HAVE A VERY LOW CHANCE OF HITTING THEIR MARK, SO WHY...?!
SEE? LOOK HOW THE SMOKE'S RISING UP FROM THE GROUND!
もく fooff
もく fooff
ALL THAT ATTACK DID WAS MAKE IT HARDER FOR US TO SEE...!
SHUUU
TO CARRY OUT A PRECISION ATTACK RIGHT DOWN TO THE MILLI-METER...
EVEN I HAVE TO GET AS CLOSE AS POSSIBLE TO MY TARGET.
?!
WHRRR

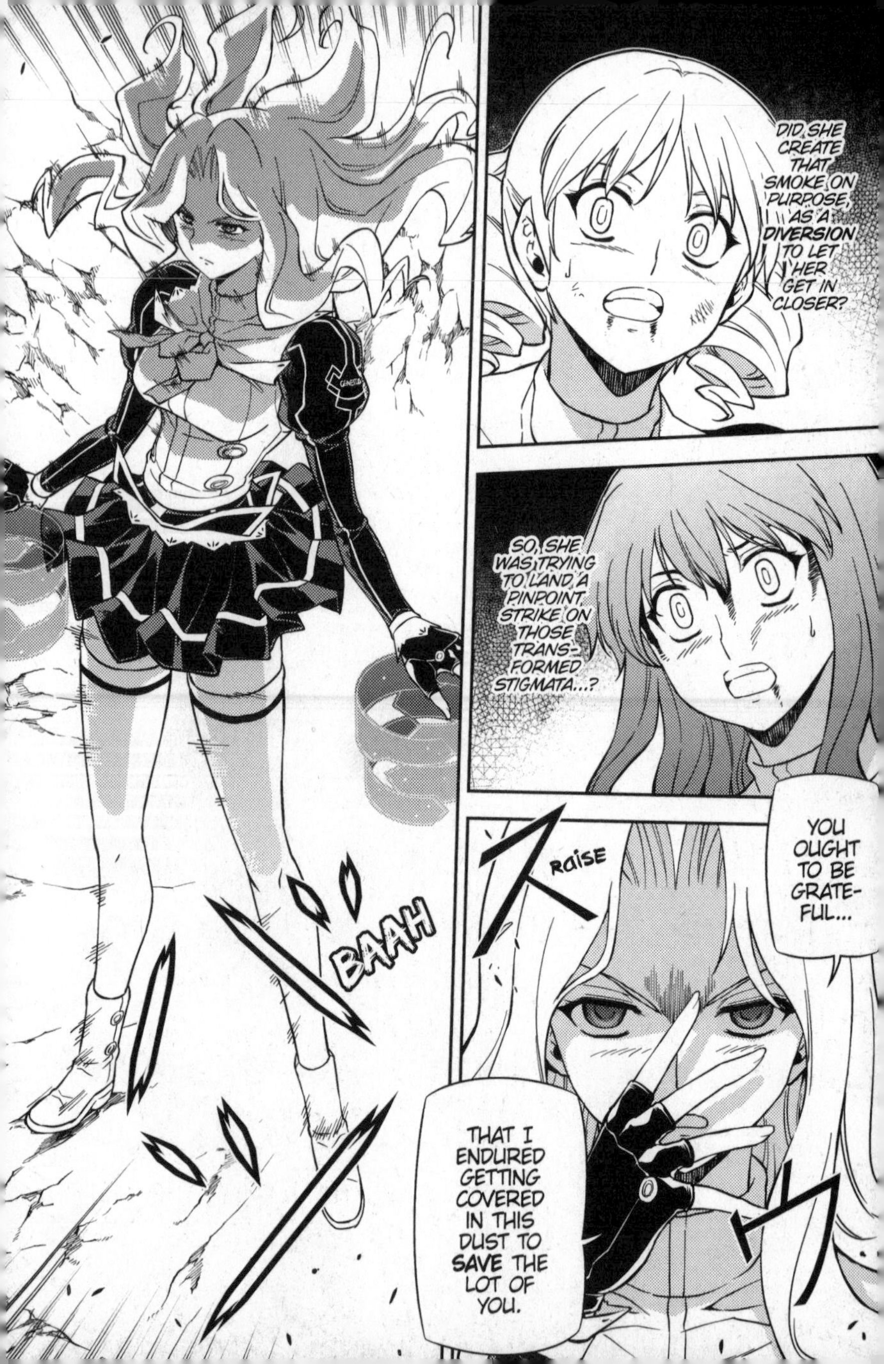
DID SHE CREATE THAT SMOKE ON PURPOSE, AS A DIVERSION TO LET HER GET IN CLOSER?
SO, SHE WAS TRYING TO LAND A PINPOINT STRIKE ON THOSE TRANS-FORMED STIGMATA...?
Raise
YOU OUGHT TO BE GRATE-FUL...
THAT I ENDURED GETTING COVERED IN THIS DUST TO SAVE THE LOT OF YOU.
BAAH

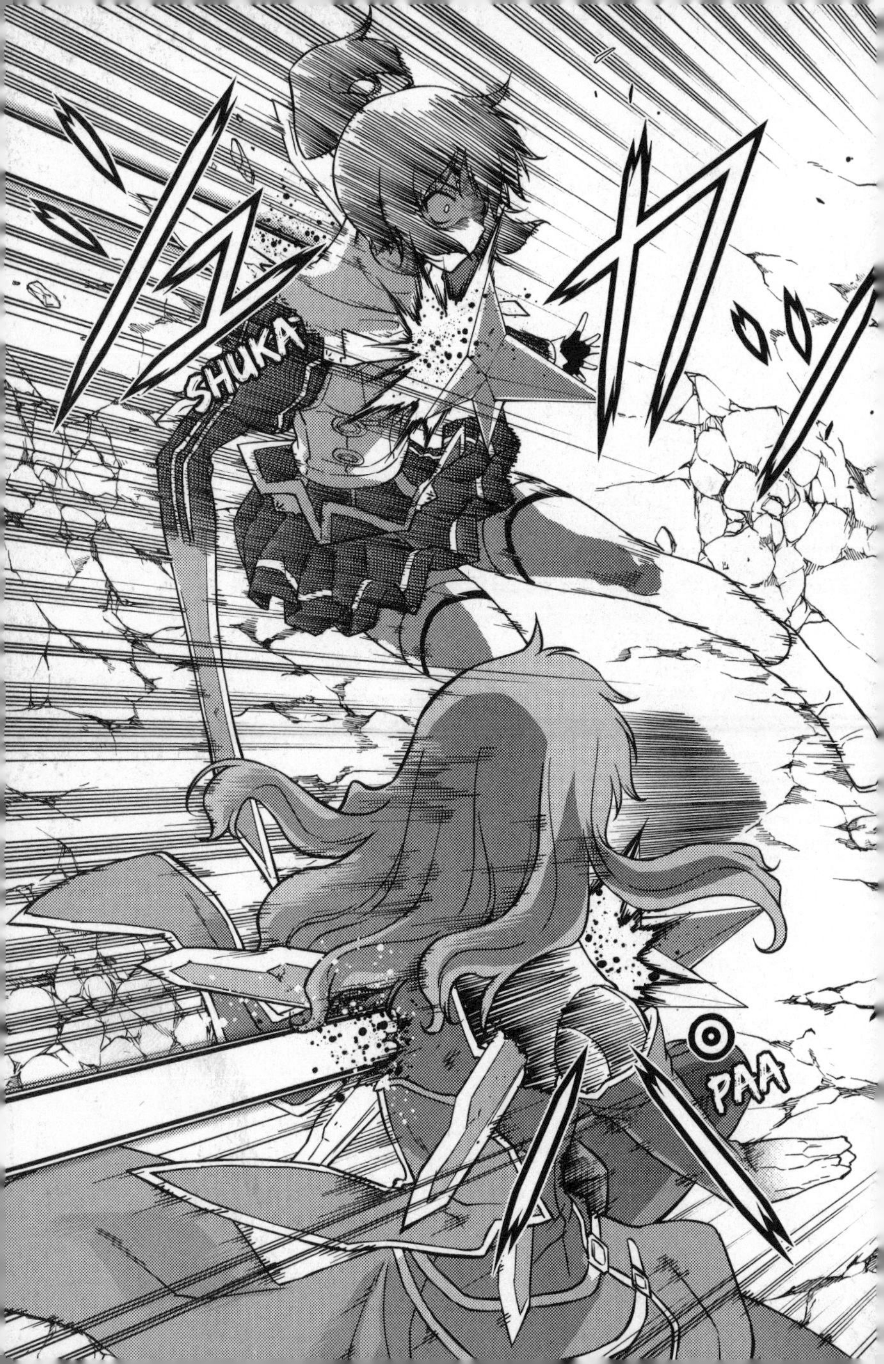
SHUKA
PAA

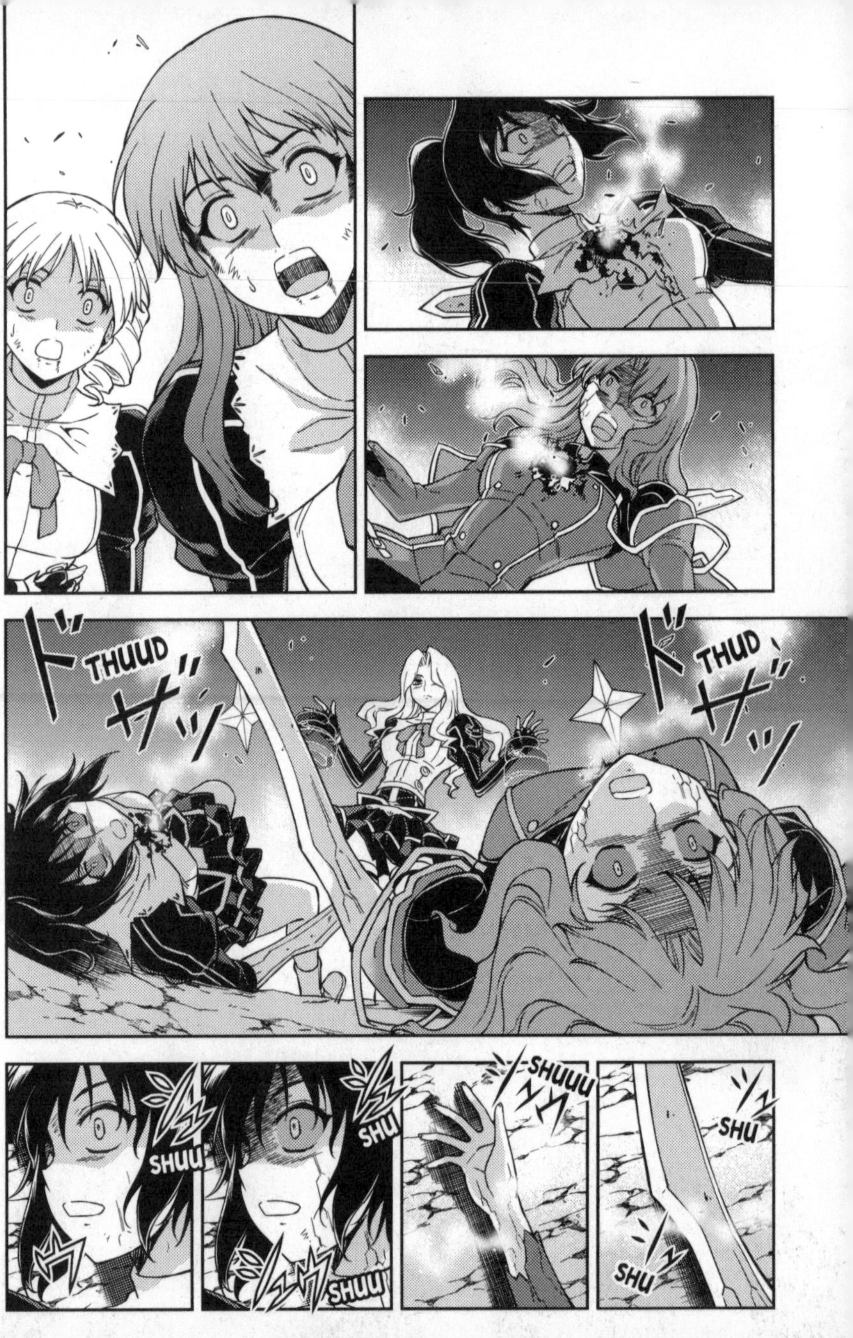
ド
THUD
ザッ
ド
THUUD
ザッ
SHU
SHU
SHUUU
SHU
SHUU
SHUU
SHUU

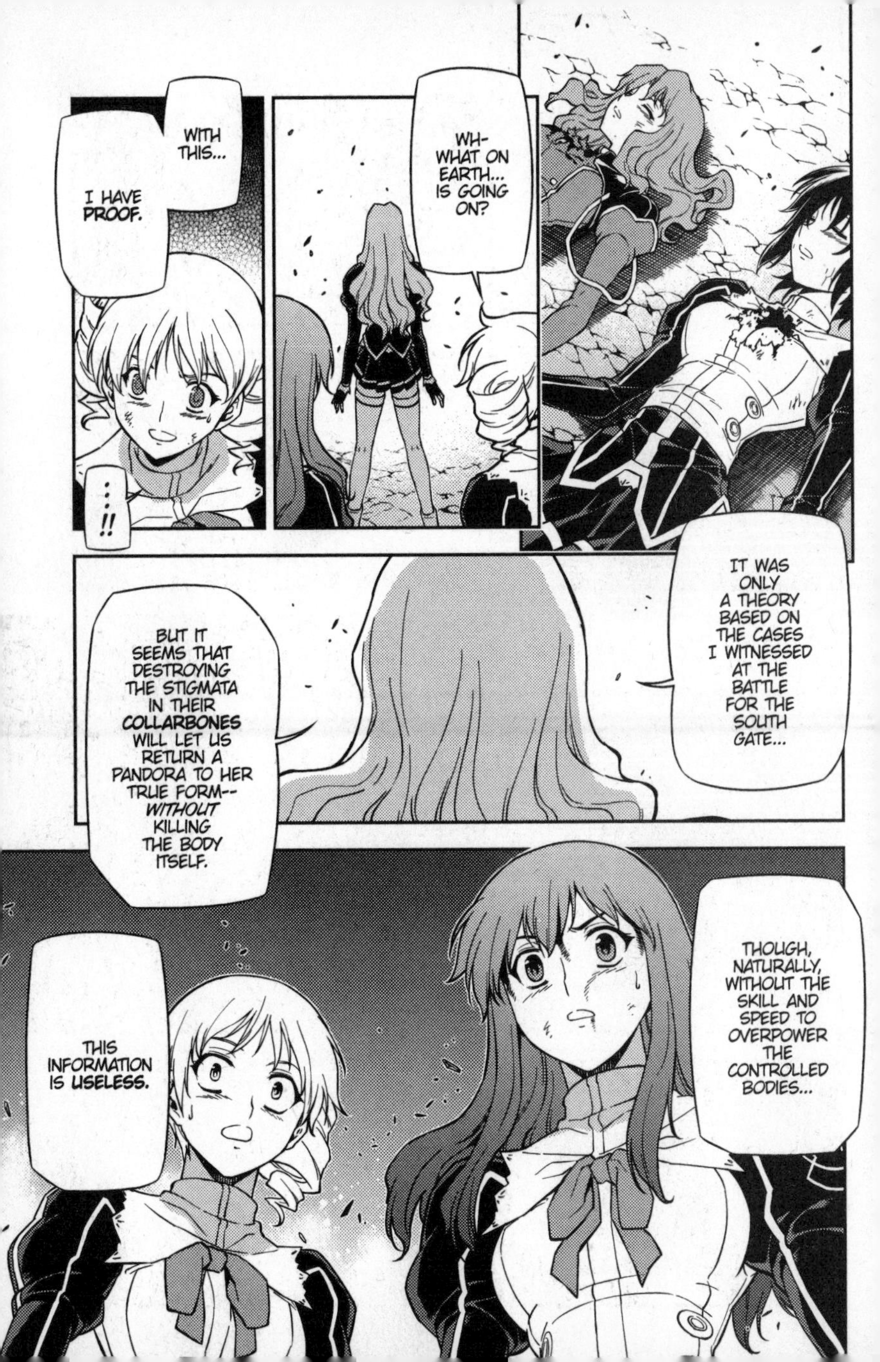
WH-WHAT ON EARTH... IS GOING ON?
WITH THIS...
I HAVE **PROOF**.
...!!
IT WAS ONLY A THEORY BASED ON THE CASES I WITNESSED AT THE BATTLE FOR THE SOUTH GATE...
BUT IT SEEMS THAT DESTROYING THE STIGMATA IN THEIR **COLLARBONES** WILL LET US RETURN A PANDORA TO HER TRUE FORM-- *WITHOUT* KILLING THE BODY ITSELF.
THOUGH, NATURALLY, WITHOUT THE SKILL AND SPEED TO OVERPOWER THE CONTROLLED BODIES...
THIS INFORMATION IS **USELESS**.

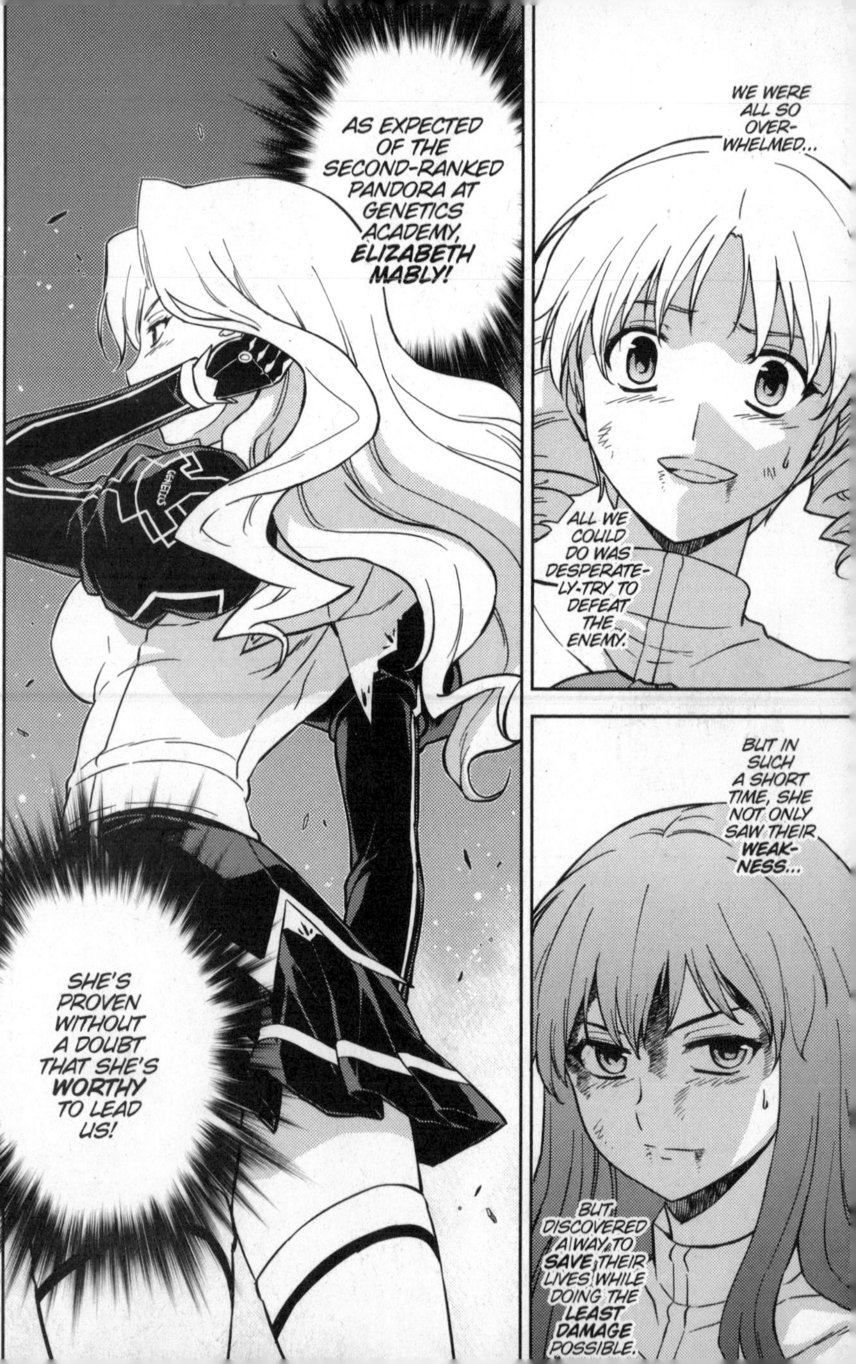
WE WERE ALL SO OVER-WHELMED...
ALL WE COULD DO WAS DESPERATE-LY-TRY TO DEFEAT THE ENEMY.
BUT IN SUCH A SHORT TIME, SHE NOT ONLY SAW THEIR WEAK-NESS...
BUT DISCOVERED A WAY TO SAVE THEIR LIVES WHILE DOING THE LEAST DAMAGE POSSIBLE.
AS EXPECTED OF THE SECOND-RANKED PANDORA AT GENETICS ACADEMY, ELIZABETH MABLY!
GENETICS
SHE'S PROVEN WITHOUT A DOUBT THAT SHE'S WORTHY TO LEAD US!

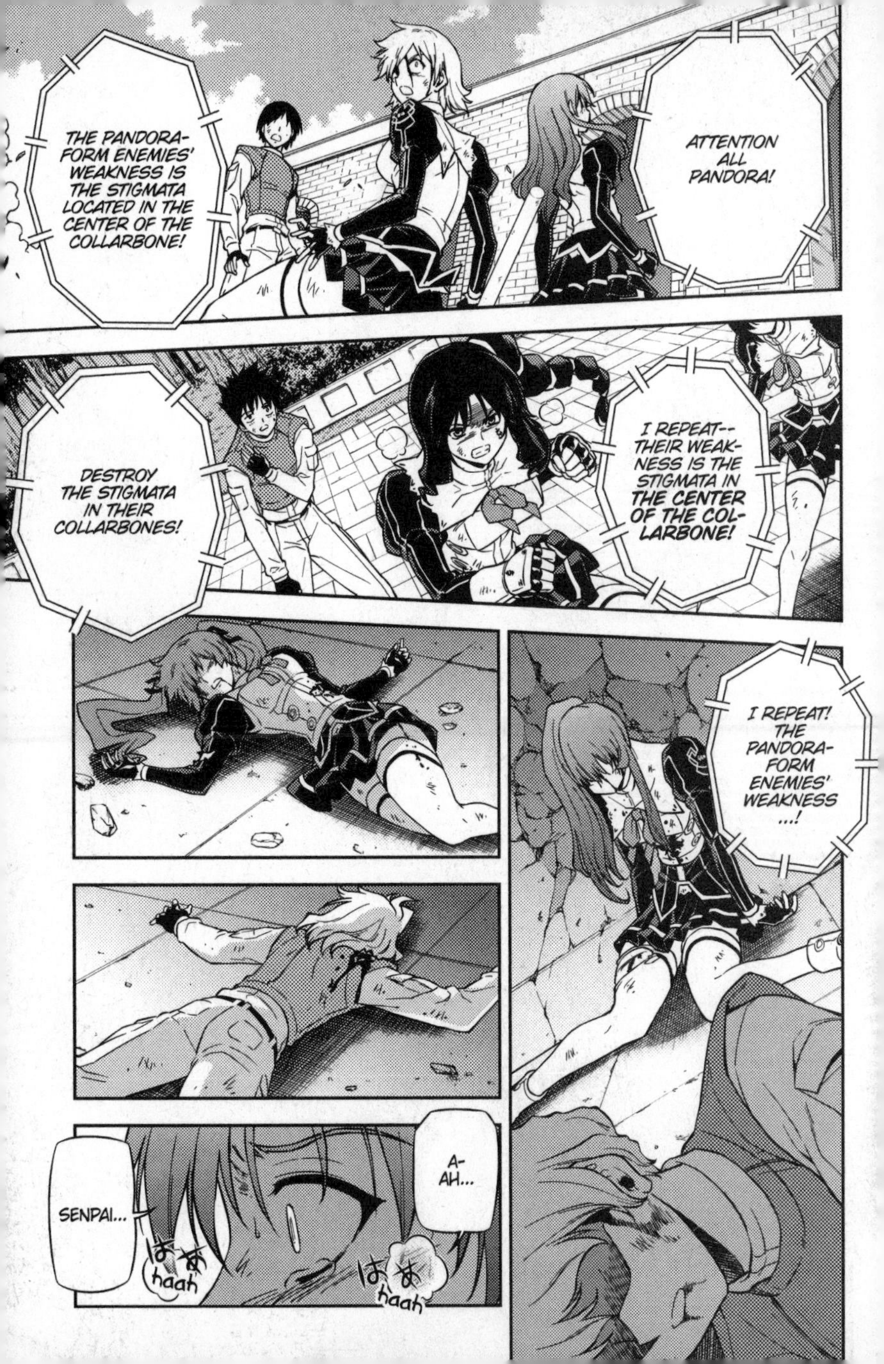
ATTENTION ALL PANDORA!
THE PANDORA-FORM ENEMIES' WEAKNESS IS THE STIGMATA LOCATED IN THE CENTER OF THE COLLARBONE!
I REPEAT-- THEIR WEAK-NESS IS THE STIGMATA IN THE CENTER OF THE COL-LARBONE!
DESTROY THE STIGMATA IN THEIR COLLARBONES!
I REPEAT! THE PANDORA-FORM ENEMIES' WEAKNESS ...!
A-AH...
SENPAI...
はぁ haah
はぁ haah

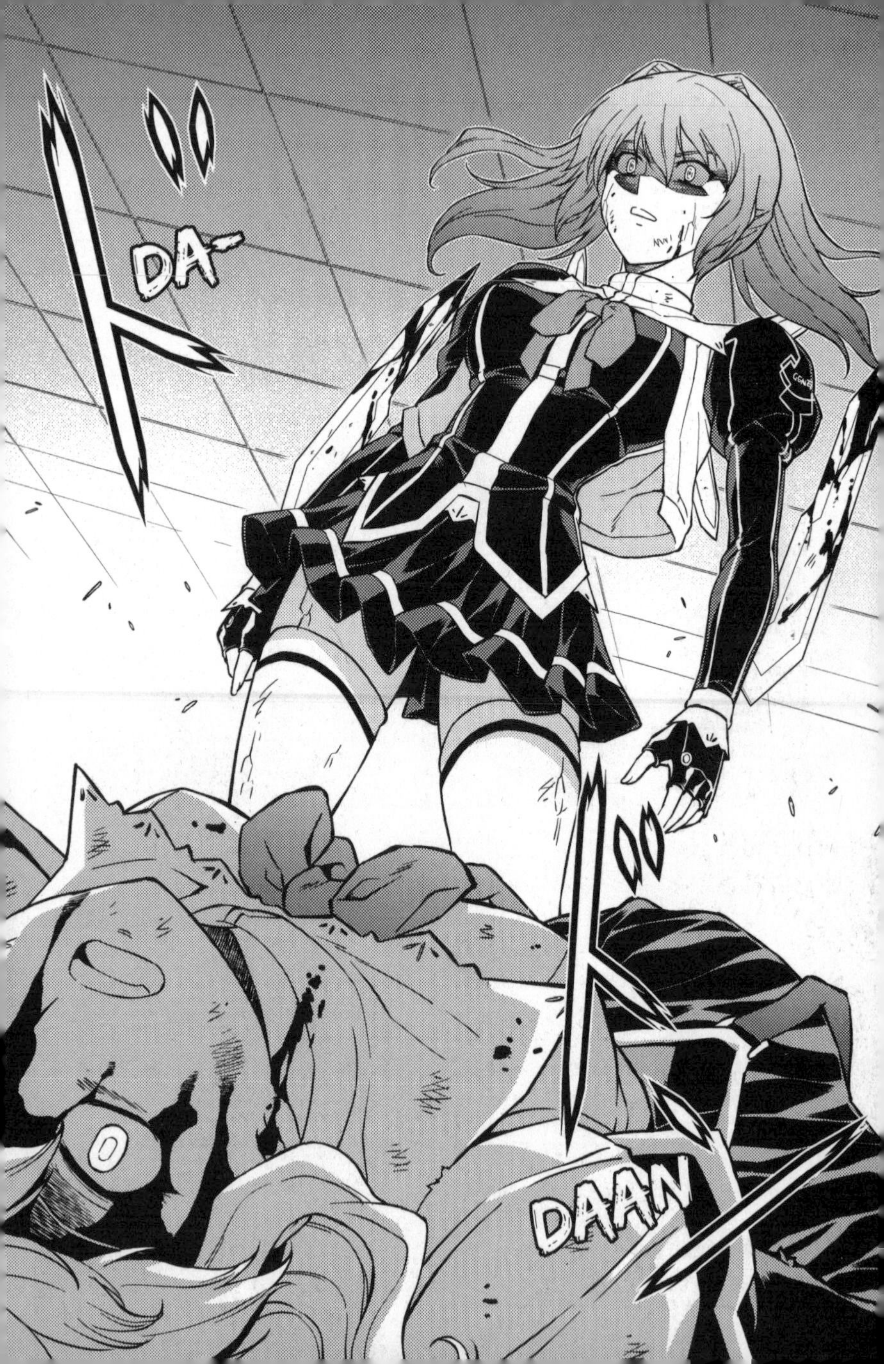
DA-
DAAN

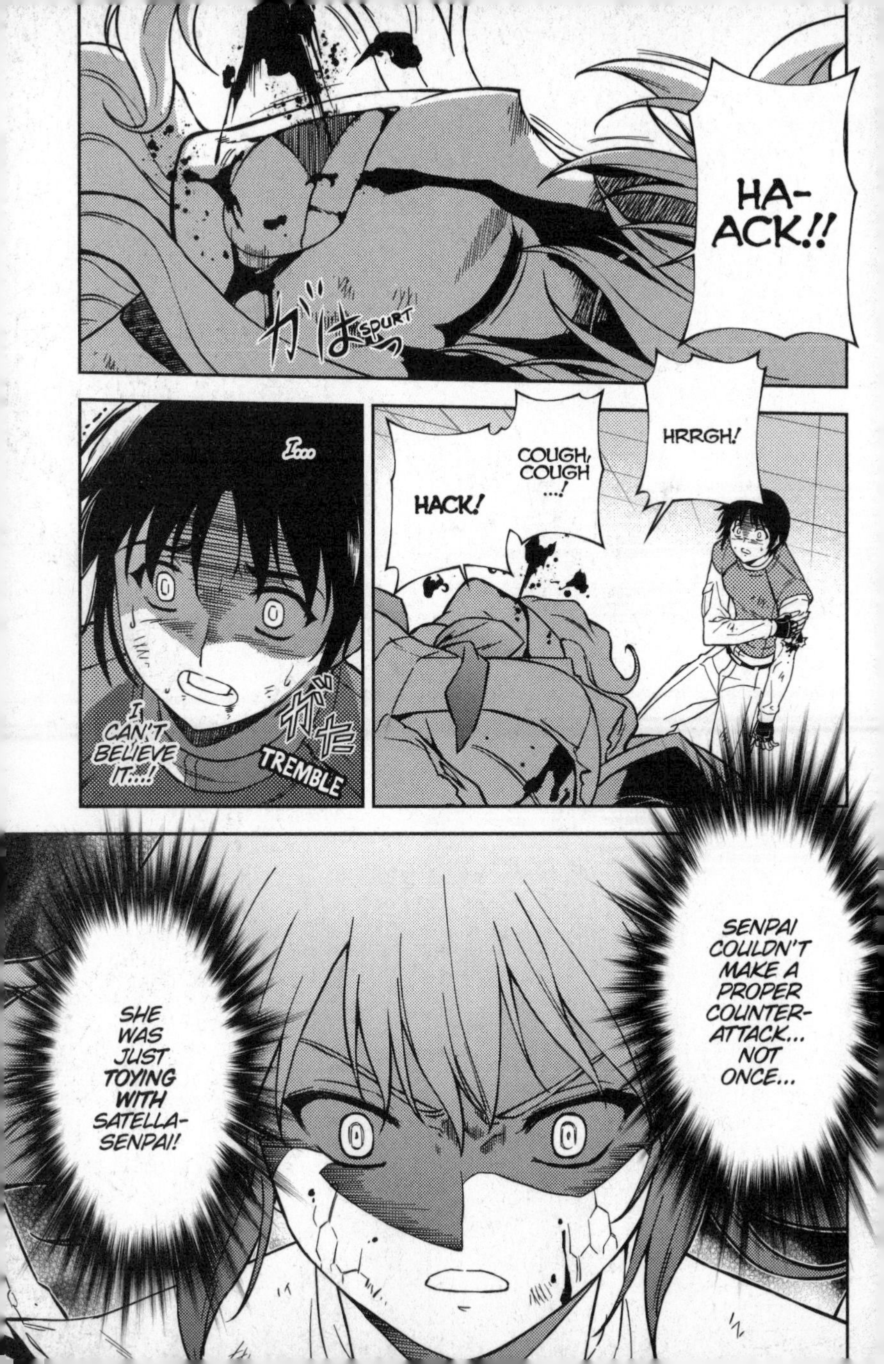
HA-ACK!!
がは SPURT
HRRGH!
COUGH, COUGH ...!
HACK!
I...
I CAN'T BELIEVE IT...!
がた TREMBLE
SENPAI COULDN'T MAKE A PROPER COUNTER-ATTACK... NOT ONCE...
SHE WAS JUST TOYING WITH SATELLA-SENPAI!

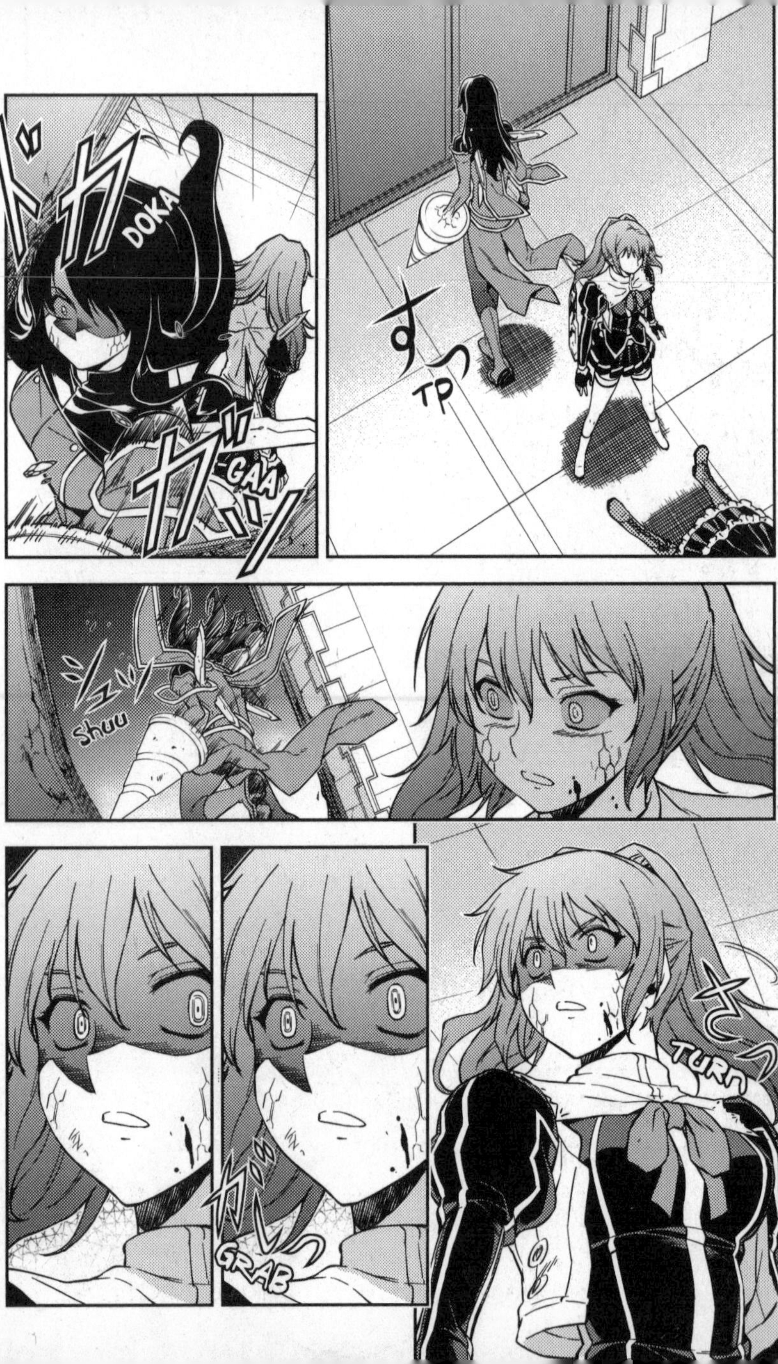
すっ
TP
ドカ
DOKA
GAA
Shuu
TURN
GRAB

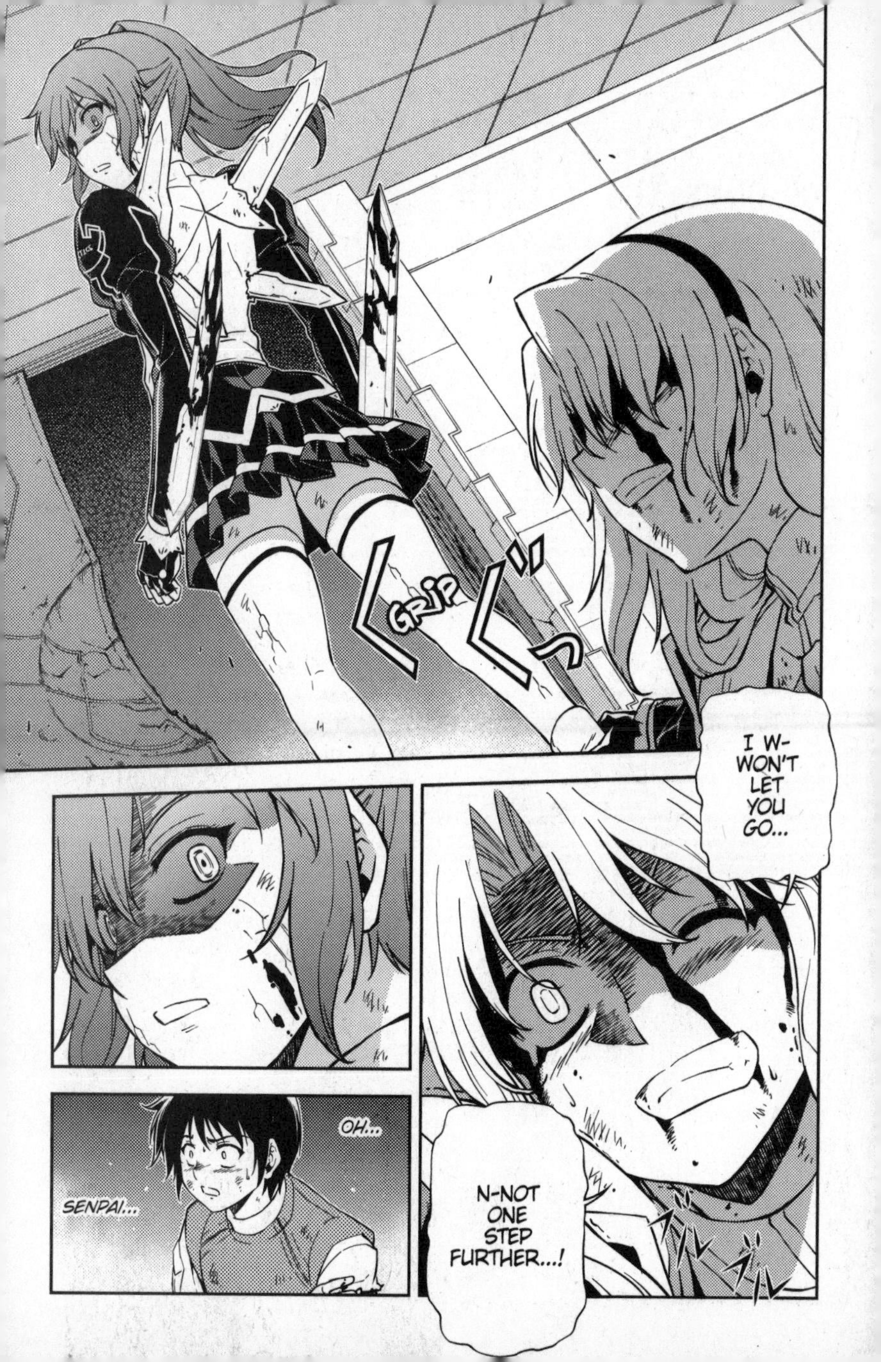
GRIP
I W-WON'T LET YOU GO...
N-NOT ONE STEP FURTHER...!
OH...
SENPAI...

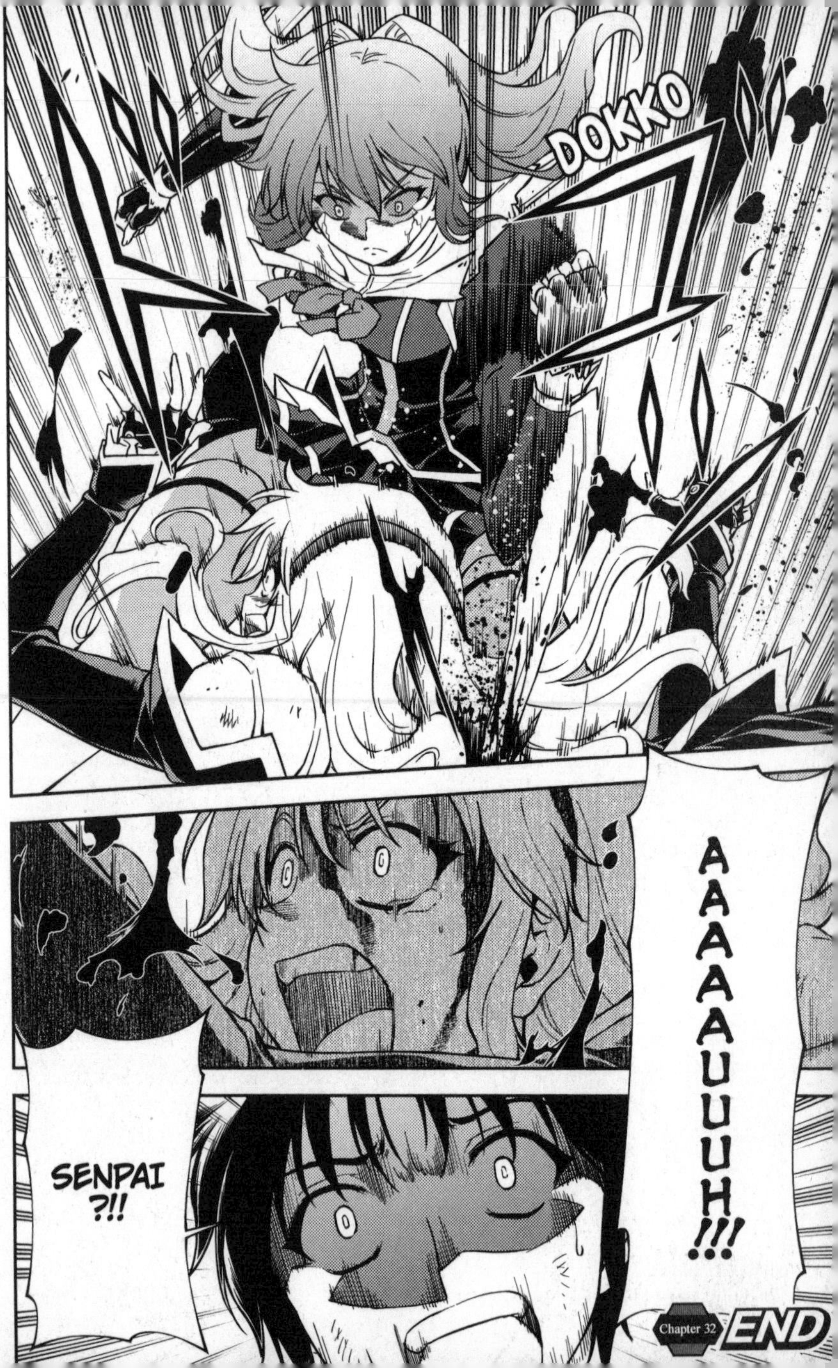
DOKKO
AAAAAUUUH!!!
SENPAI ?!!
Chapter 32 END

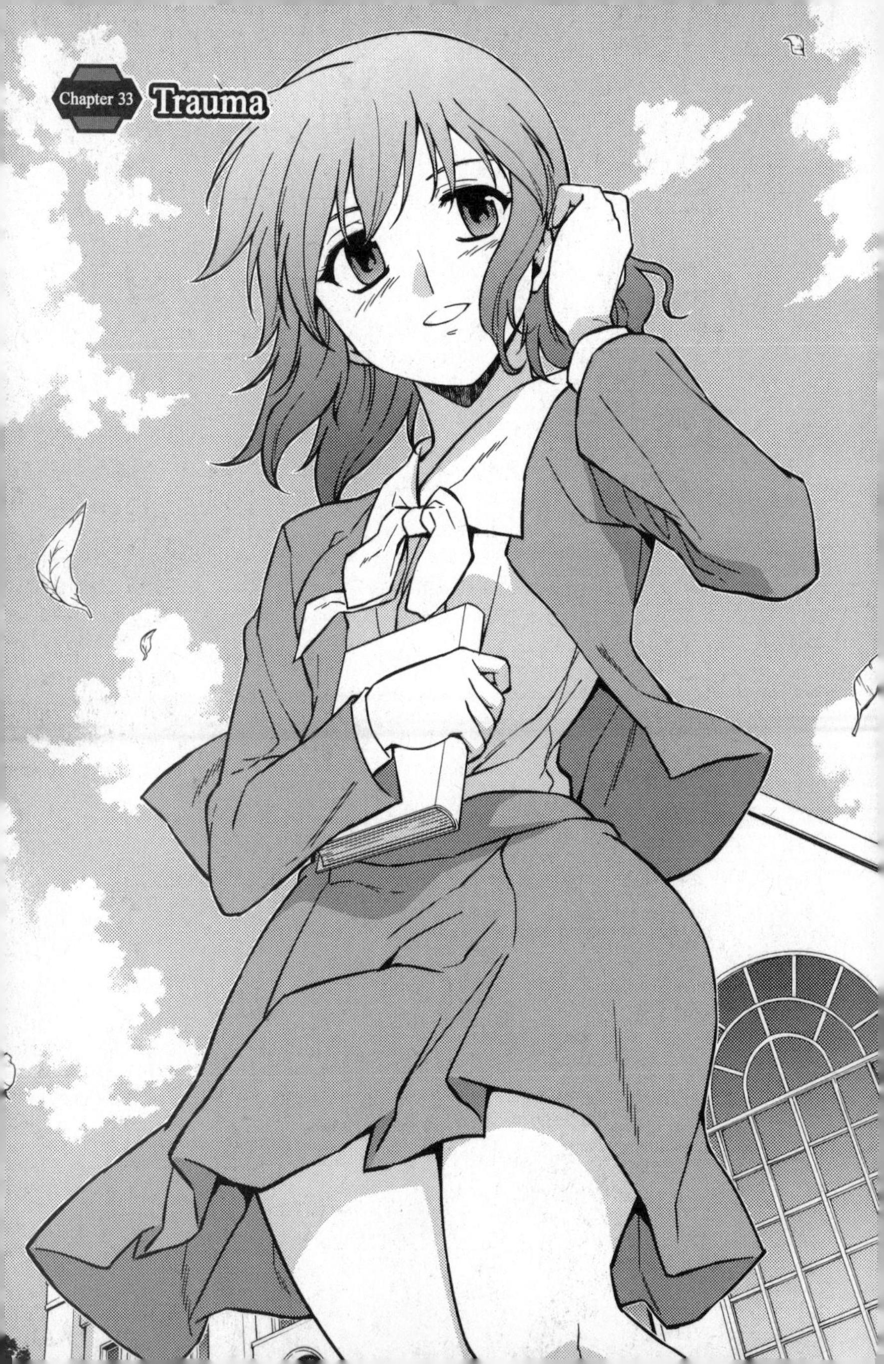
Chapter 33
Trauma

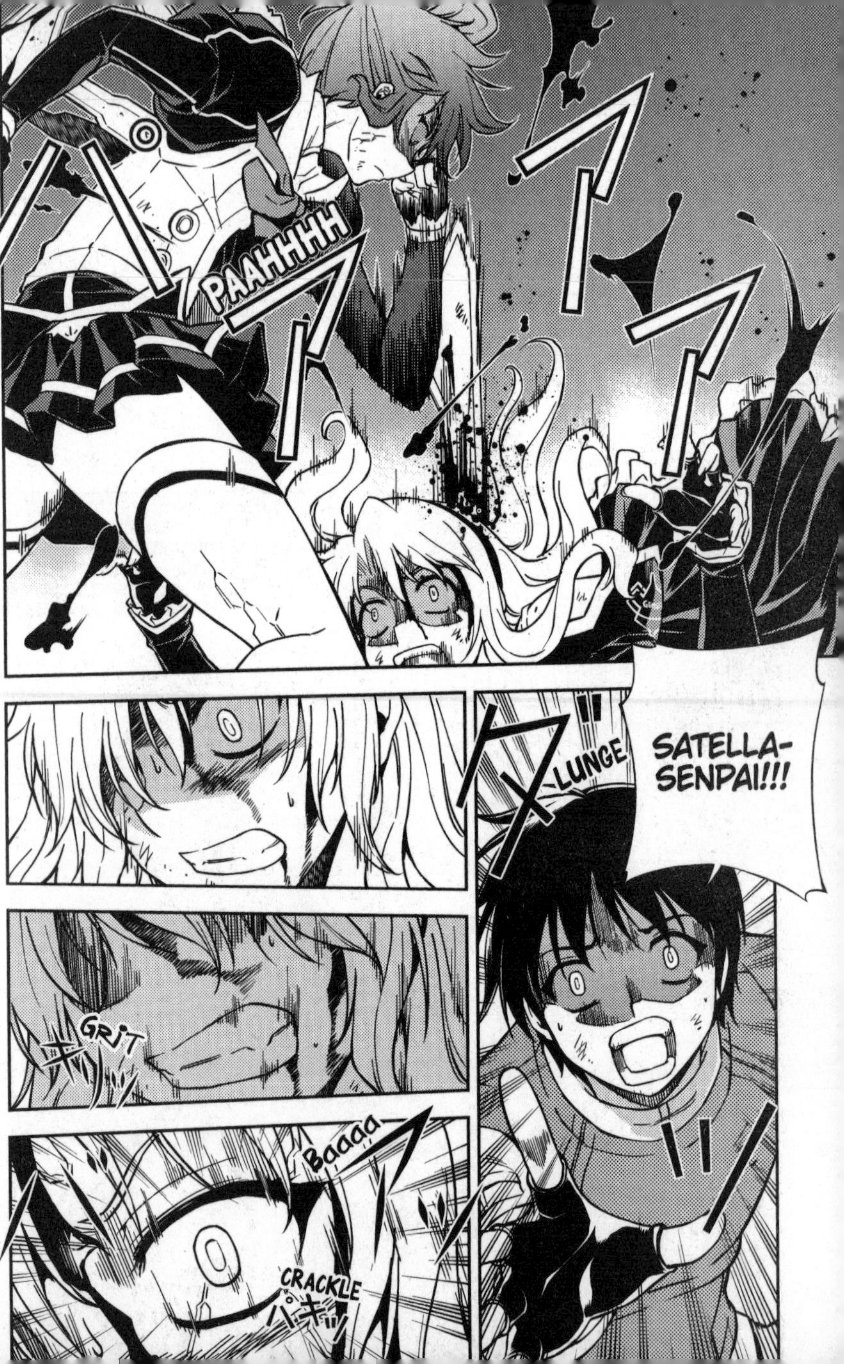
PAAHHHH
SATELLA-SENPAI!!!
LUNGE
GRIT
Baaaa
CRACKLE

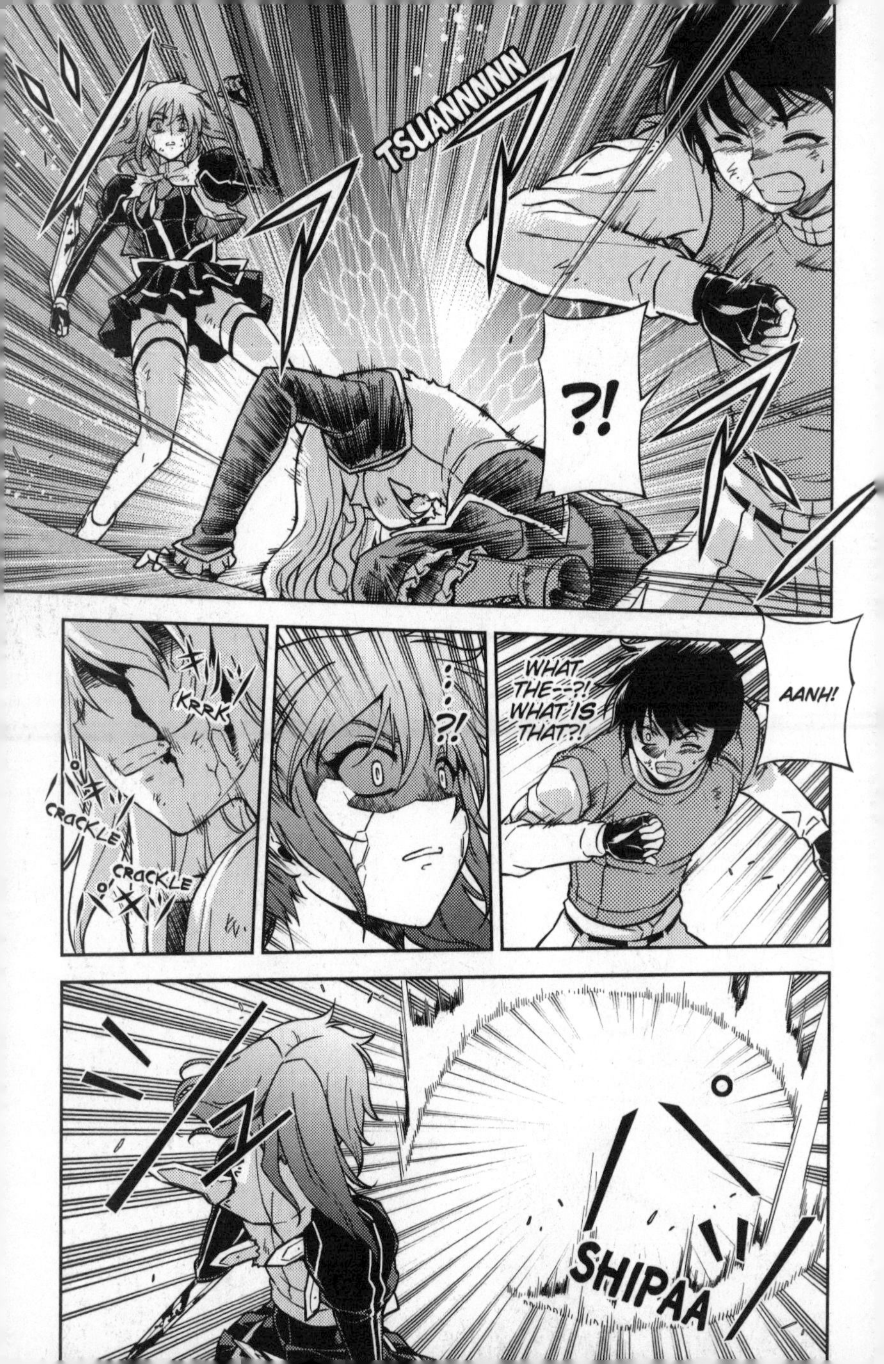
TSUANNNNN
?!
AANH!
WHAT THE--?! WHAT IS THAT?!
...?!
KRRK
CRACKLE
CRACKLE
SHIPAA

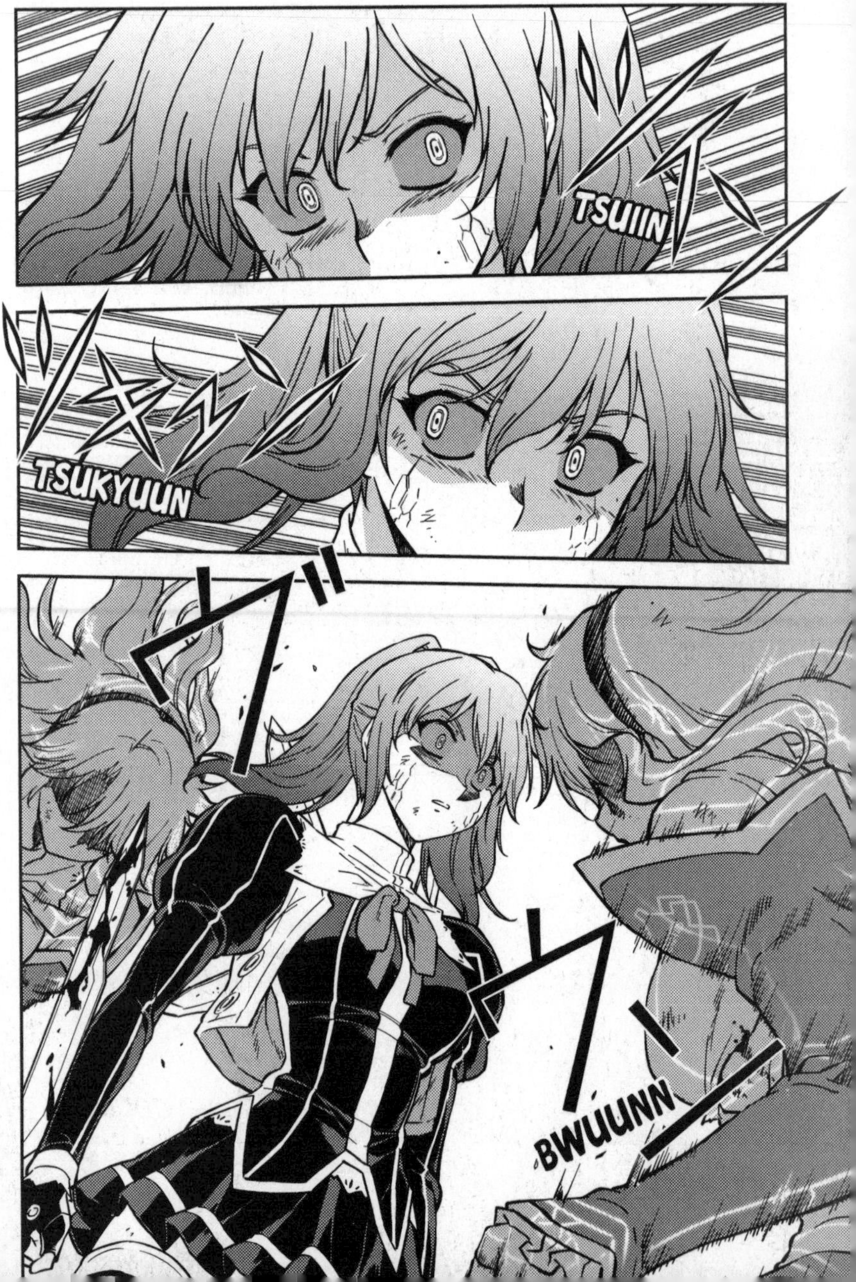
TSUIIN
TSUKYUUN
BWUUNN

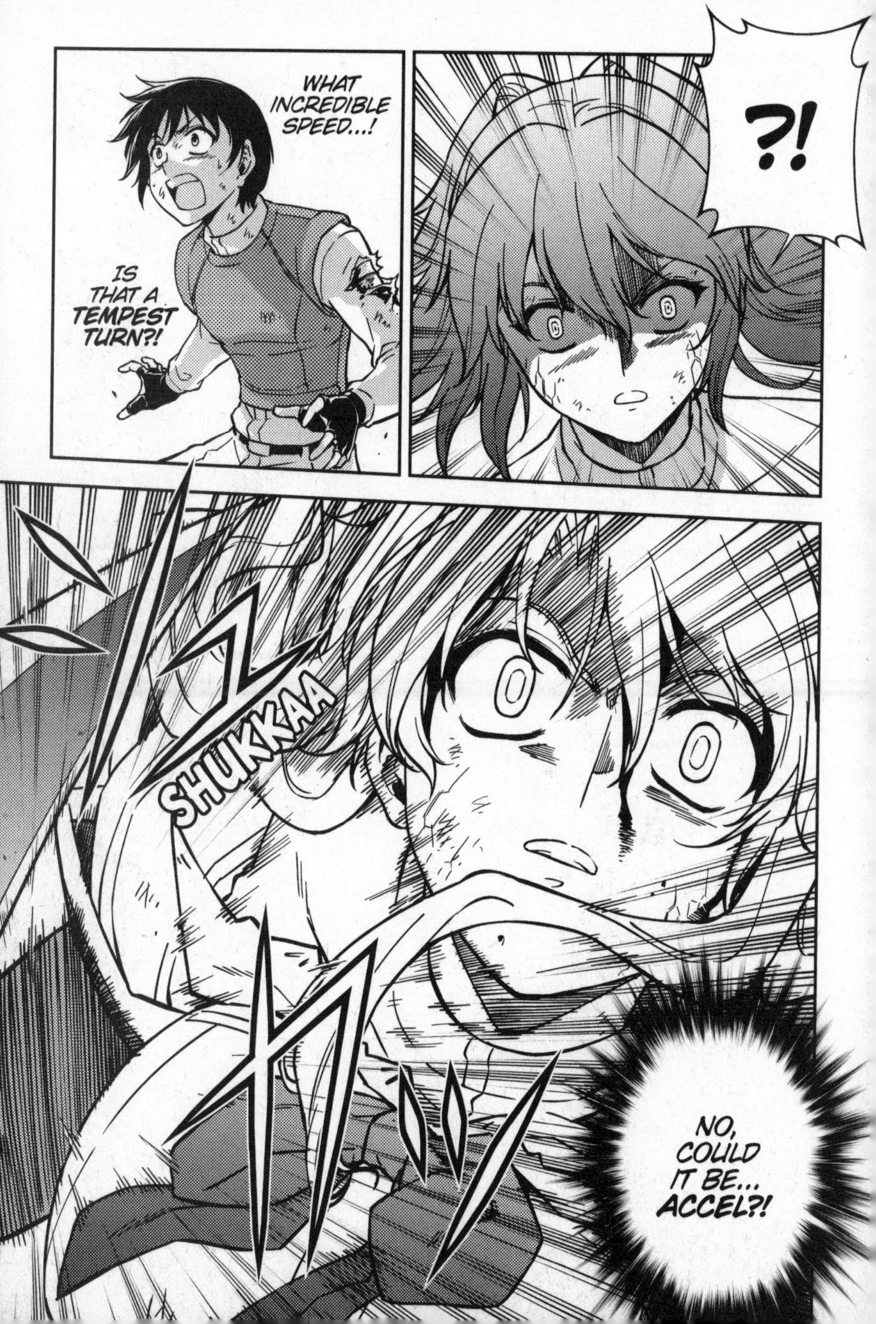
?!
WHAT INCREDIBLE SPEED...!
IS THAT A TEMPEST TURN?!
SHUKKAA
NO, COULD IT BE... ACCEL?!

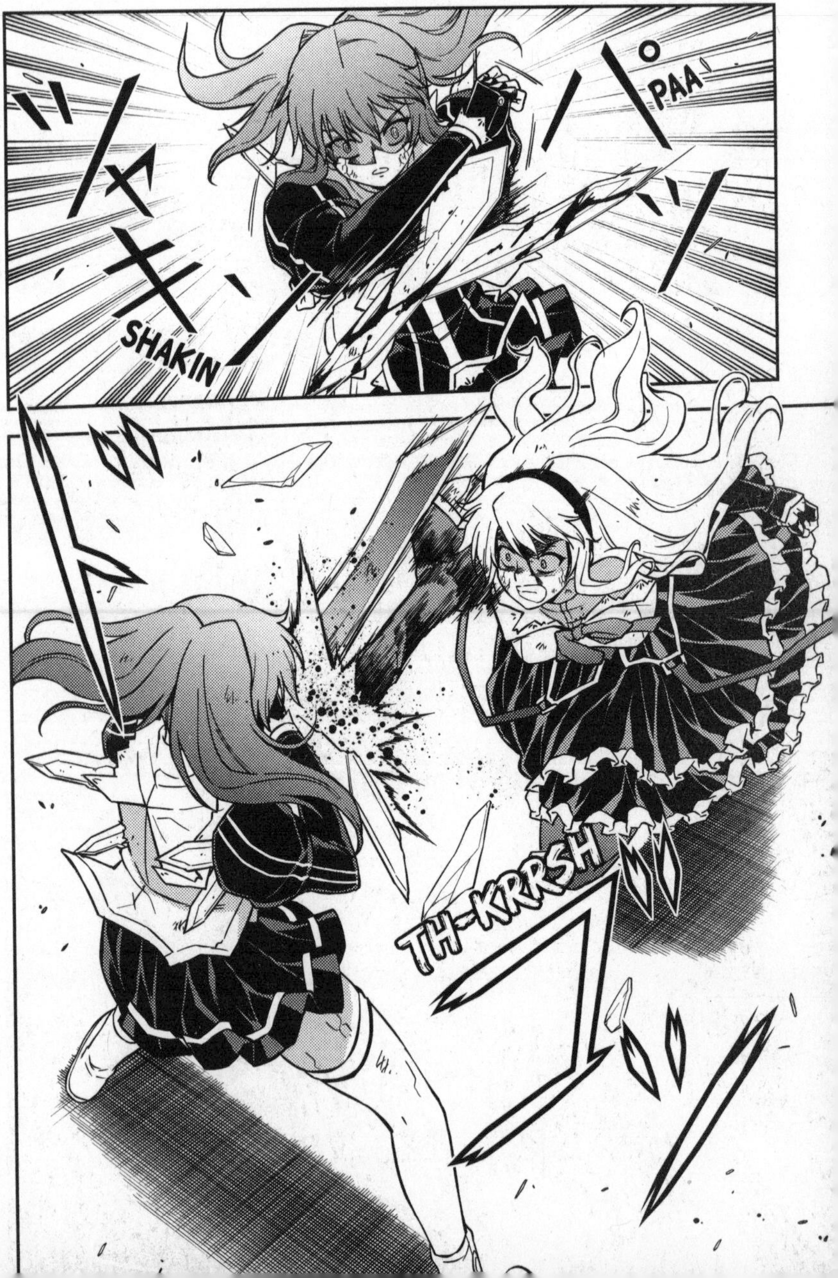
PAA
SHAKIN
TH-KRRSH

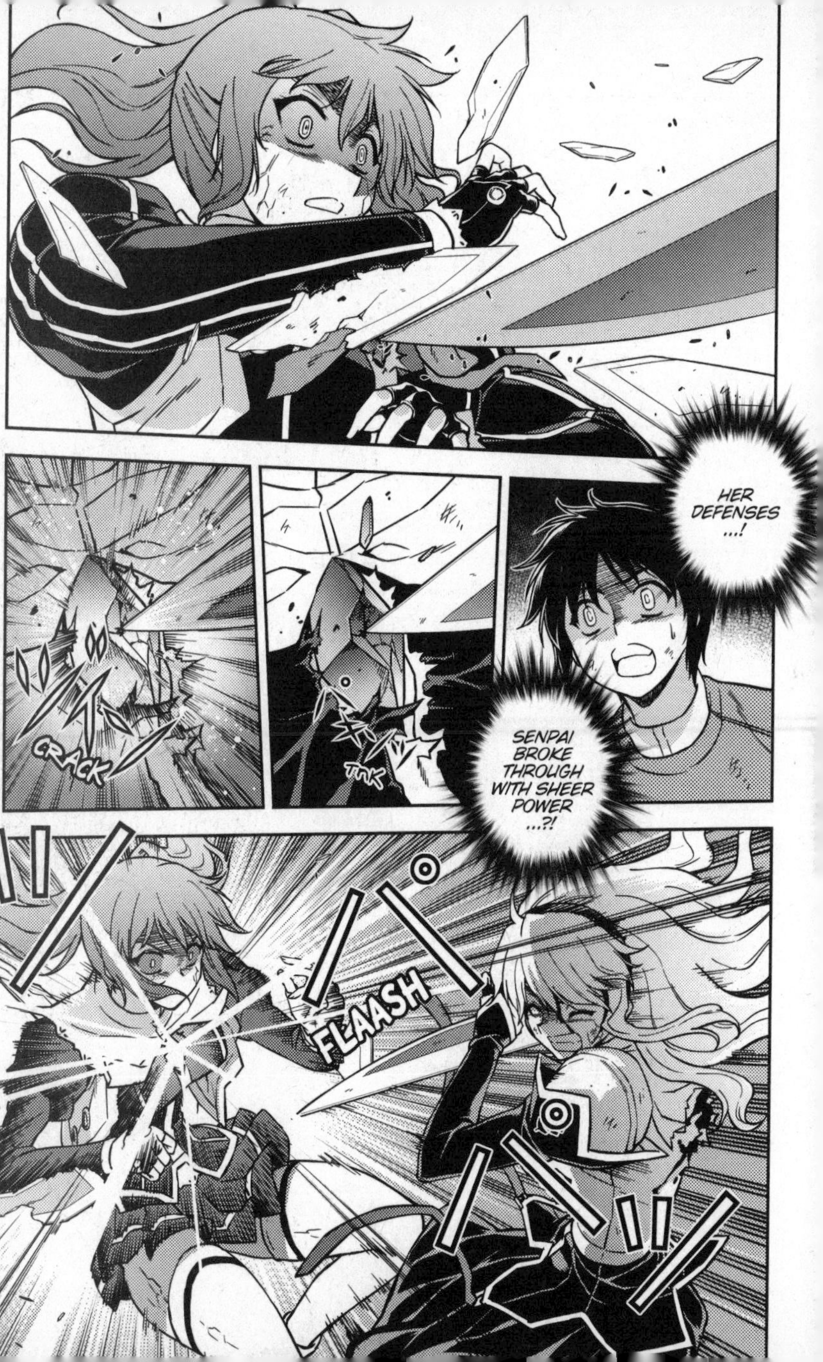
HER DEFENSES ...!
SENPAI BROKE THROUGH WITH SHEER POWER ...?!
TNK
CRACK
FLAASH

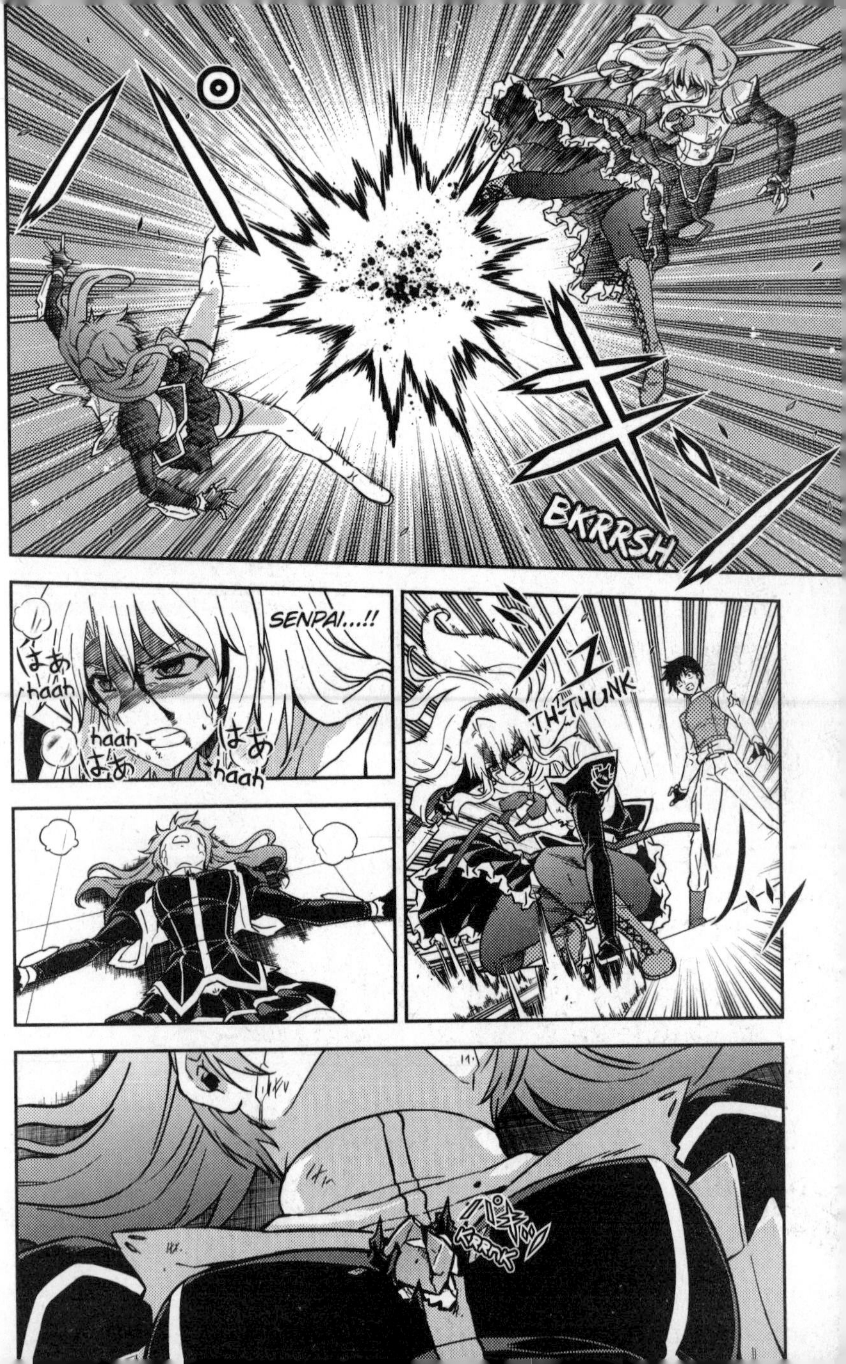
BKRRSH
TH-THUNK
SENPAI...!!
はあ haah
haah はあ
はあ haah
パキッ
KRRNK

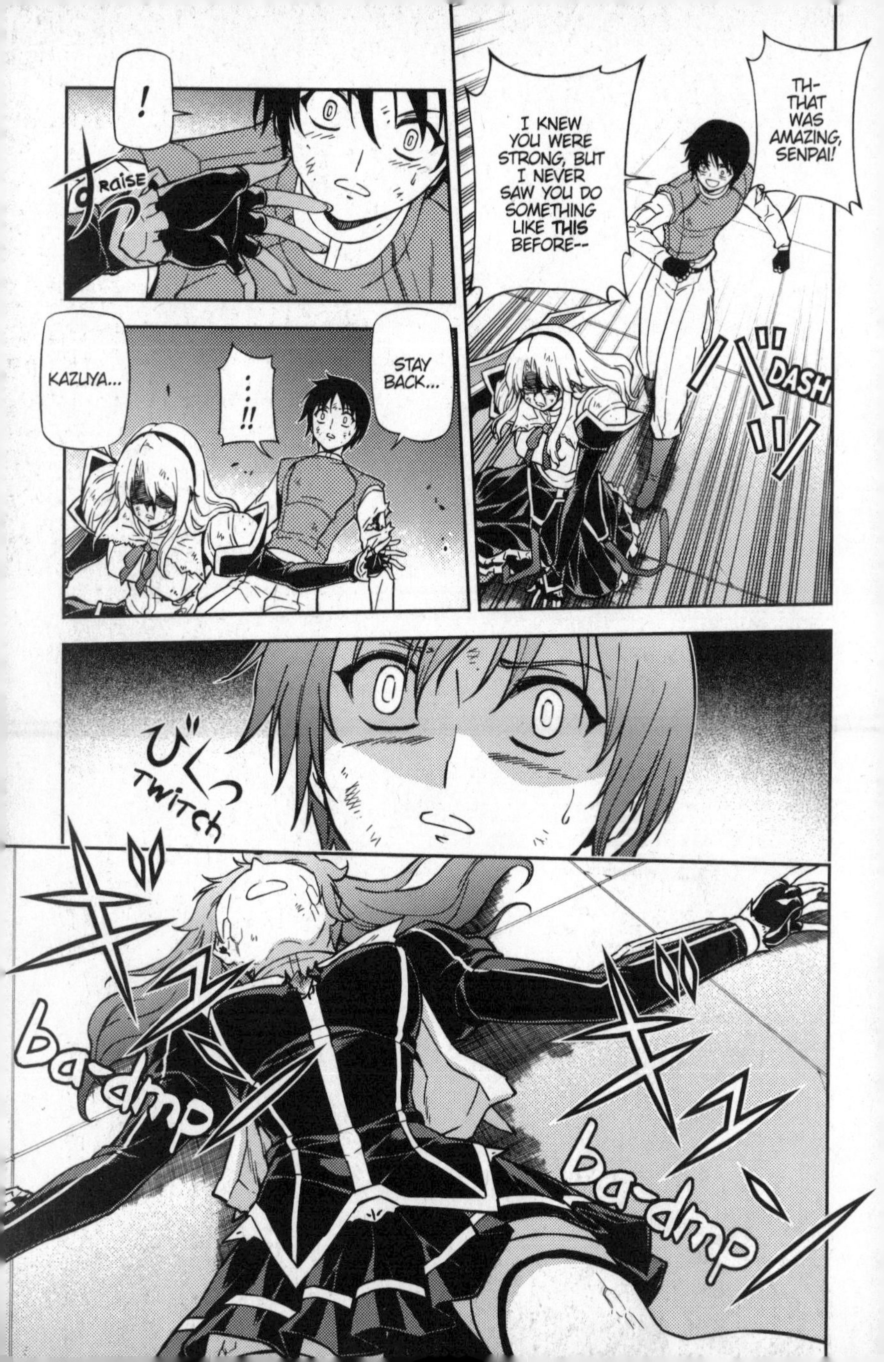

TH-THAT WAS AMAZING, SENPAI!
I KNEW YOU WERE STRONG, BUT I NEVER SAW YOU DO SOMETHING LIKE THIS BEFORE--
DASH
!
RAISE
STAY BACK...
...!!
KAZUYA...
TWITCH
ba-dmp
ba-dmp

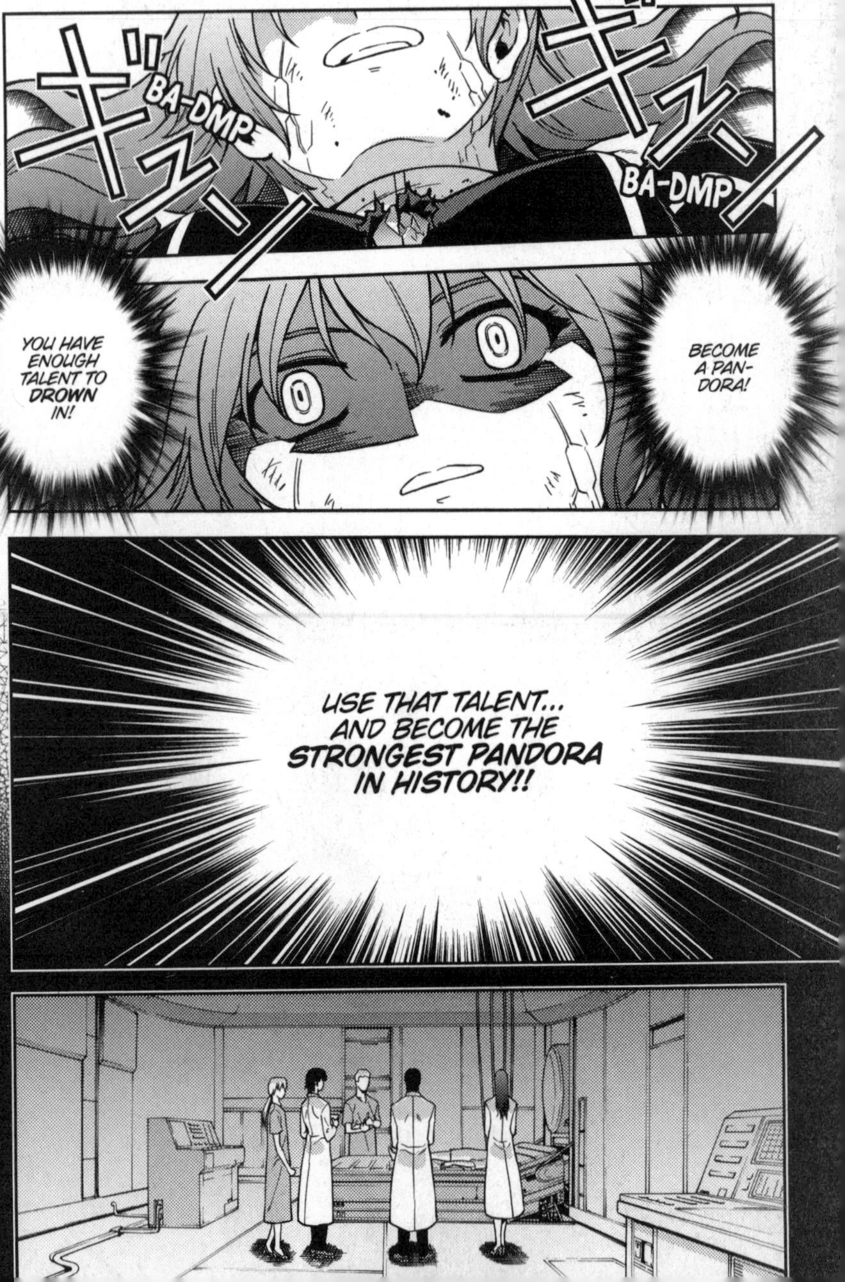

ギン
BA-DMP
ギン
BA-DMP
BECOME A PAN-DORA!
YOU HAVE ENOUGH TALENT TO DROWN IN!
USE THAT TALENT... AND BECOME THE STRONGEST PANDORA IN HISTORY!!

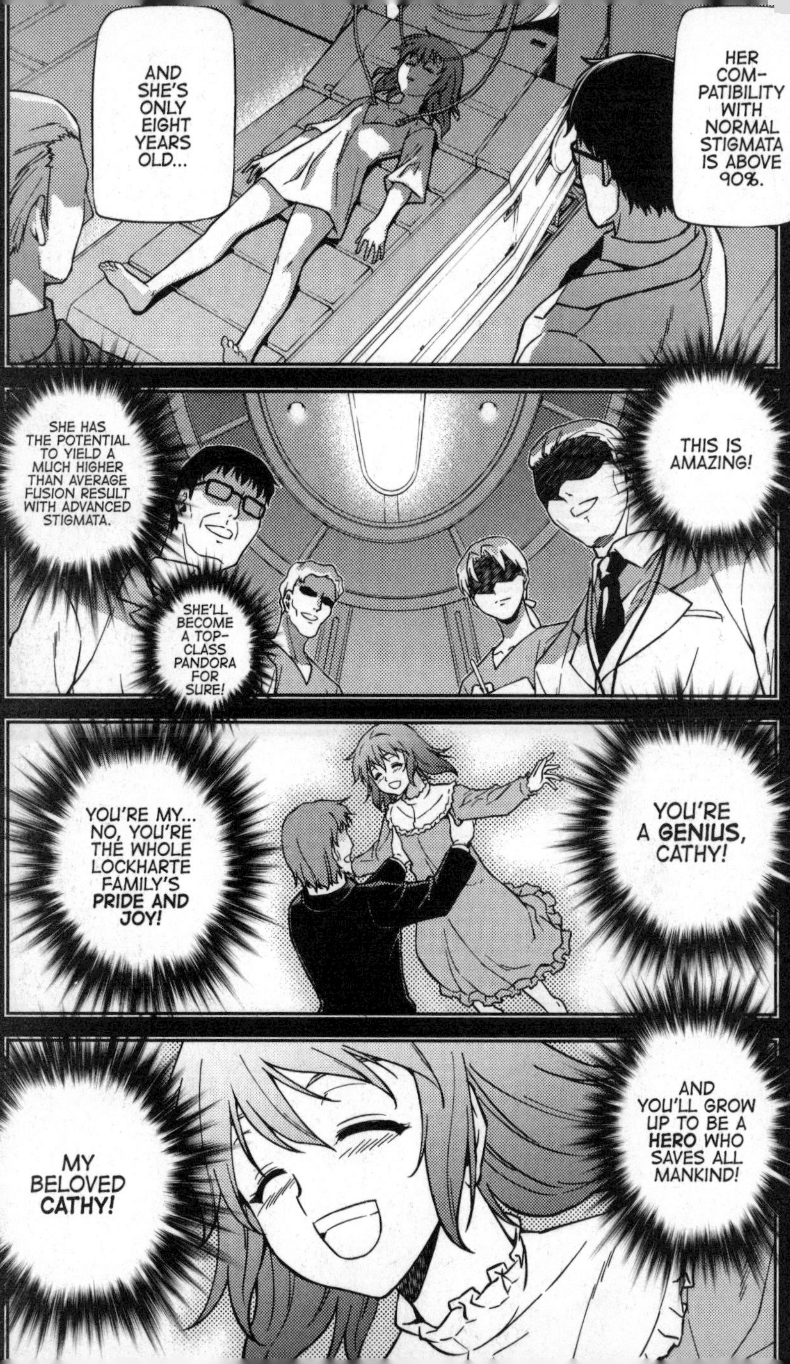
HER COMPATIBILITY WITH NORMAL STIGMATA IS ABOVE 90%.
AND SHE'S ONLY EIGHT YEARS OLD...
THIS IS AMAZING!
SHE HAS THE POTENTIAL TO YIELD A MUCH HIGHER THAN AVERAGE FUSION RESULT WITH ADVANCED STIGMATA.
SHE'LL BECOME A TOP-CLASS PANDORA FOR SURE!
YOU'RE A **GENIUS**, CATHY!
YOU'RE MY... NO, YOU'RE THE WHOLE LOCKHARTE FAMILY'S **PRIDE AND JOY!**
AND YOU'LL GROW UP TO BE A **HERO** WHO SAVES ALL MANKIND!
MY BELOVED **CATHY!**

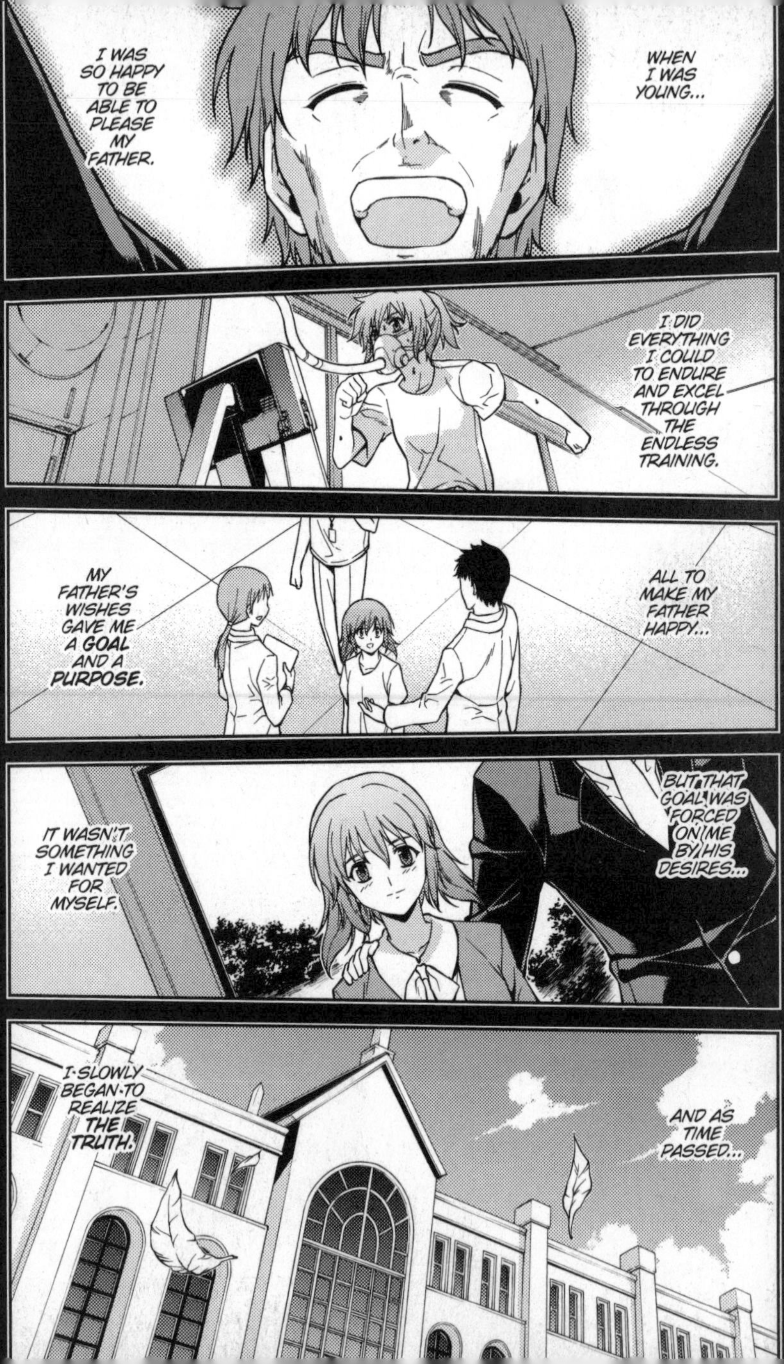
WHEN I WAS YOUNG...
I WAS SO HAPPY TO BE ABLE TO PLEASE MY FATHER.
I DID EVERYTHING I COULD TO ENDURE AND EXCEL THROUGH THE ENDLESS TRAINING.
ALL TO MAKE MY FATHER HAPPY...
MY FATHER'S WISHES GAVE ME A **GOAL** AND A **PURPOSE**.
BUT THAT GOAL WAS FORCED ON ME BY HIS DESIRES...
IT WASN'T SOMETHING I WANTED FOR MYSELF.
AND AS TIME PASSED...
I SLOWLY BEGAN TO REALIZE **THE TRUTH**.

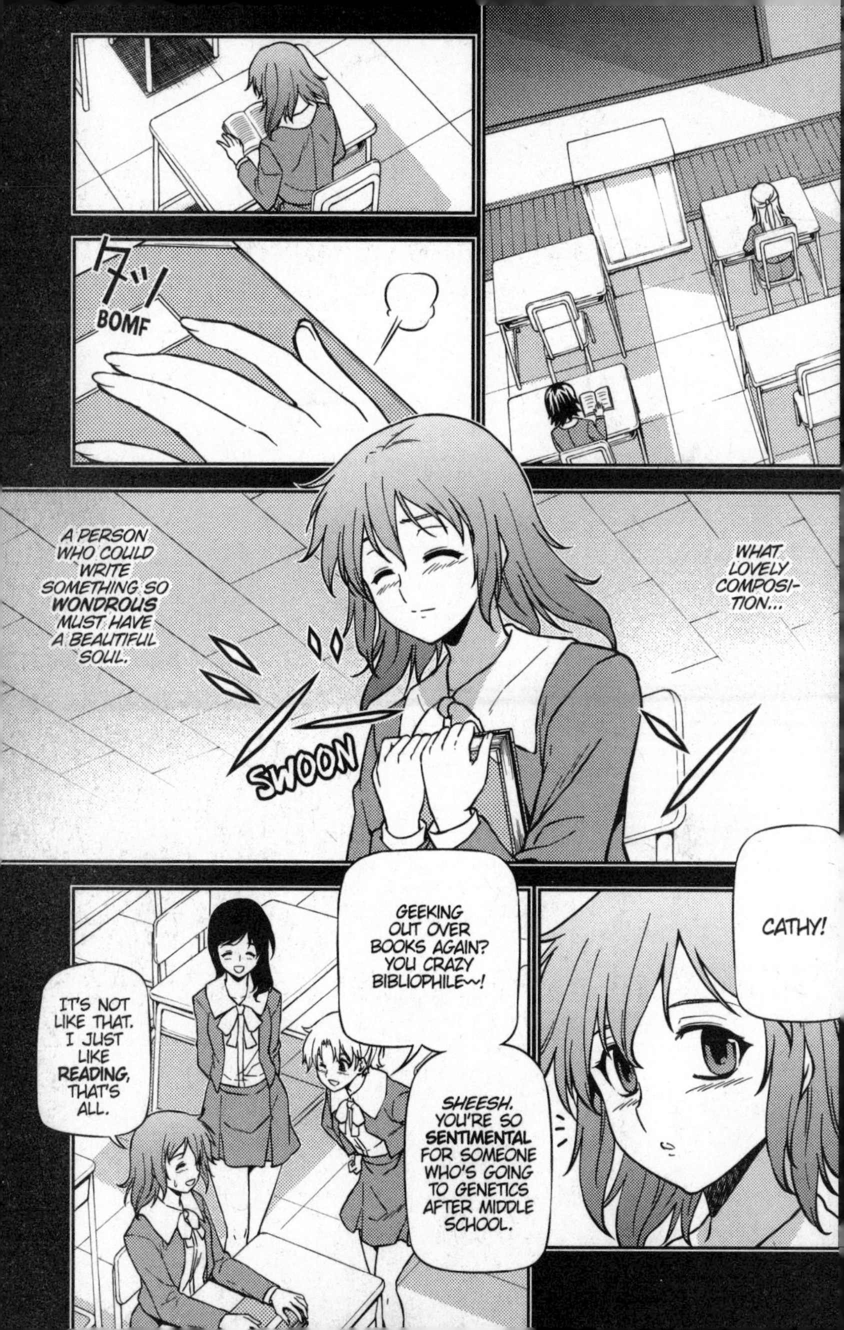
BOMF
WHAT LOVELY COMPOSITION...
A PERSON WHO COULD WRITE SOMETHING SO WONDROUS MUST HAVE A BEAUTIFUL SOUL.
SWOON
CATHY!
GEEKING OUT OVER BOOKS AGAIN? YOU CRAZY BIBLIOPHILE~~!
SHEESH. YOU'RE SO SENTIMENTAL FOR SOMEONE WHO'S GOING TO GENETICS AFTER MIDDLE SCHOOL.
IT'S NOT LIKE THAT. I JUST LIKE READING, THAT'S ALL.

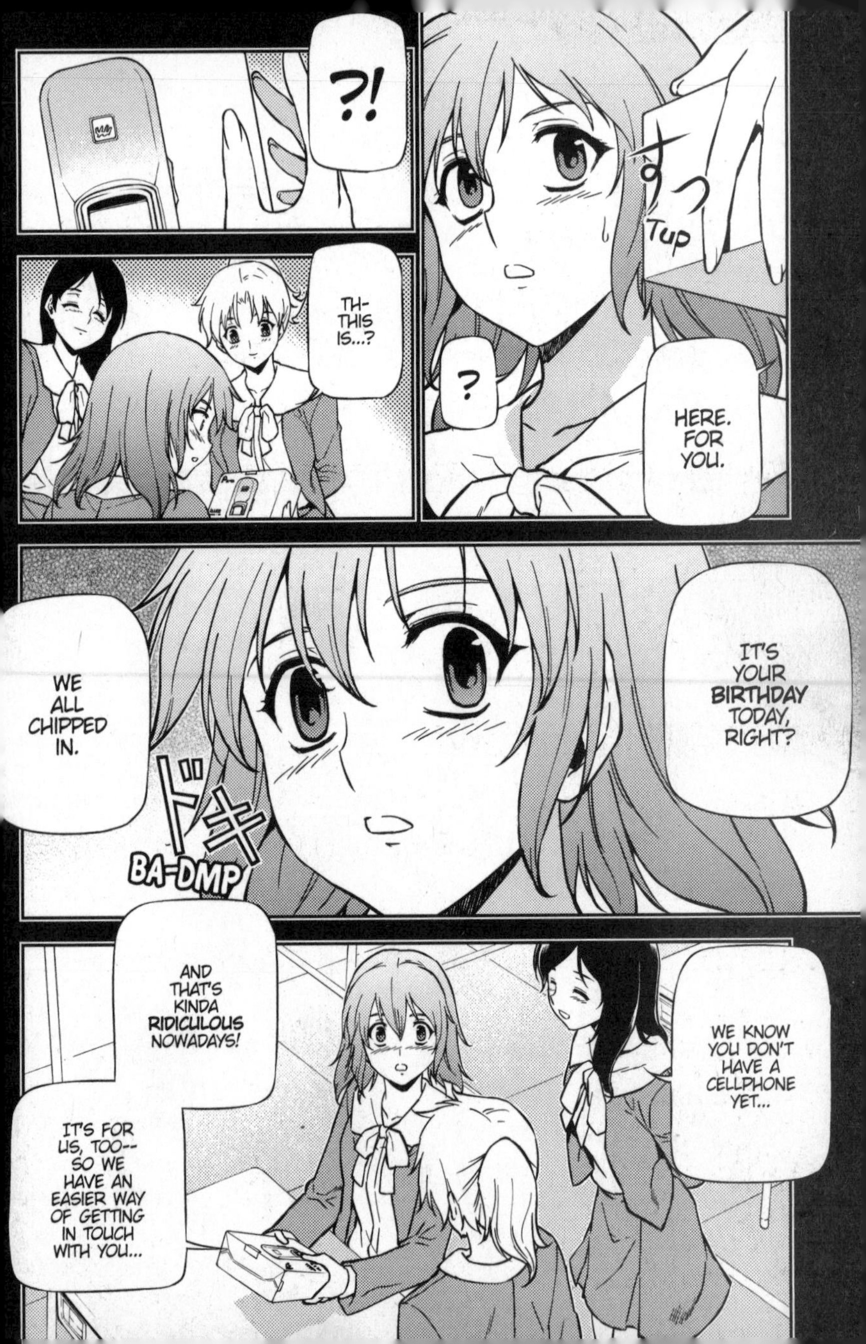
すっ
TUP
HERE. FOR YOU.
?
?!
TH-THIS IS...?
IT'S YOUR BIRTHDAY TODAY, RIGHT?
ドキ
BA-DMP
WE ALL CHIPPED IN.
WE KNOW YOU DON'T HAVE A CELLPHONE YET...
AND THAT'S KINDA RIDICULOUS NOWADAYS!
IT'S FOR US, TOO--SO WE HAVE AN EASIER WAY OF GETTING IN TOUCH WITH YOU...

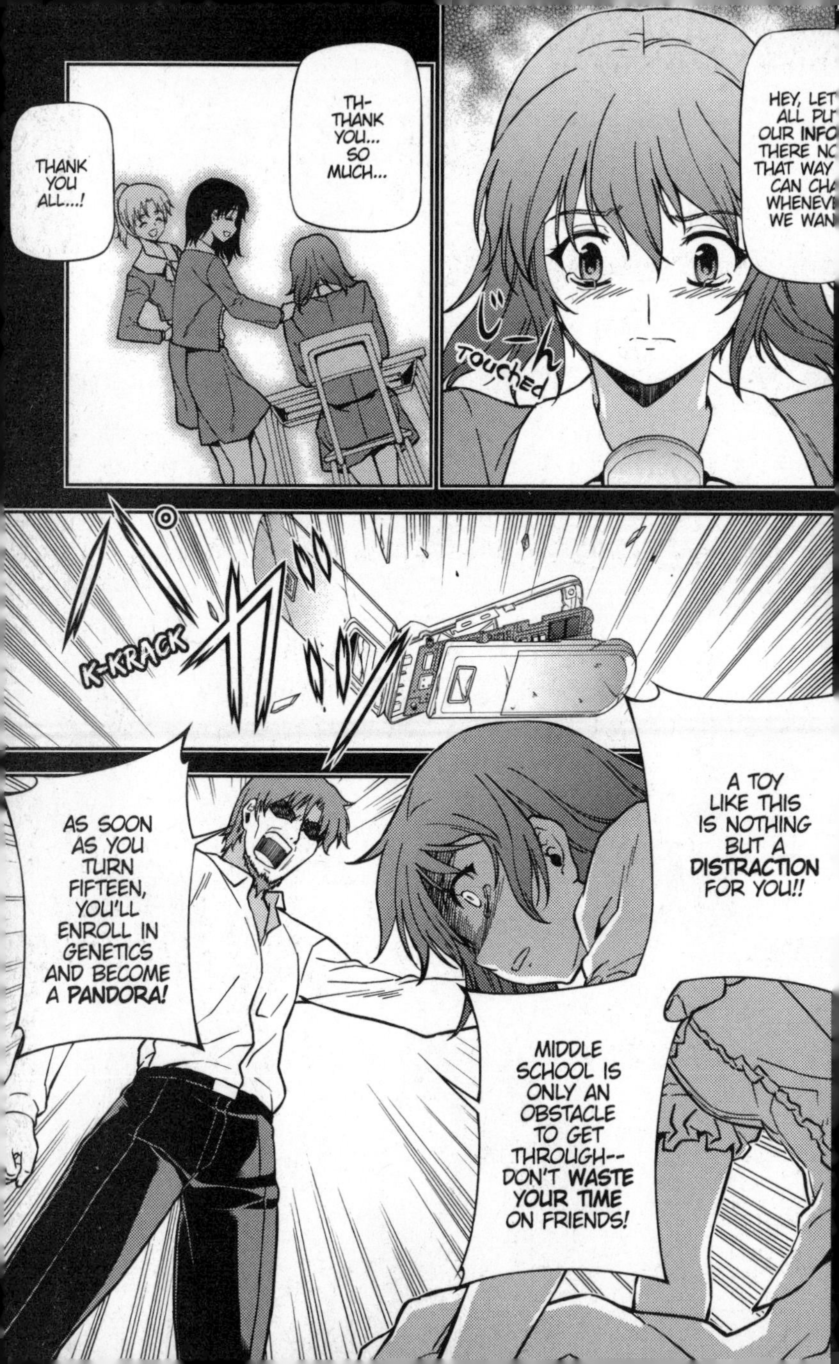
HEY, LET
ALL PU
OUR INFO
THERE NO
THAT WAY
CAN CHA
WHENEV
WE WAN
touched
TH- THANK YOU... SO MUCH...
THANK YOU ALL...!
K-KRACK
A TOY LIKE THIS IS NOTHING BUT A DISTRACTION FOR YOU!!
AS SOON AS YOU TURN FIFTEEN, YOU'LL ENROLL IN GENETICS AND BECOME A PANDORA!
MIDDLE SCHOOL IS ONLY AN OBSTACLE TO GET THROUGH-- DON'T WASTE YOUR TIME ON FRIENDS!

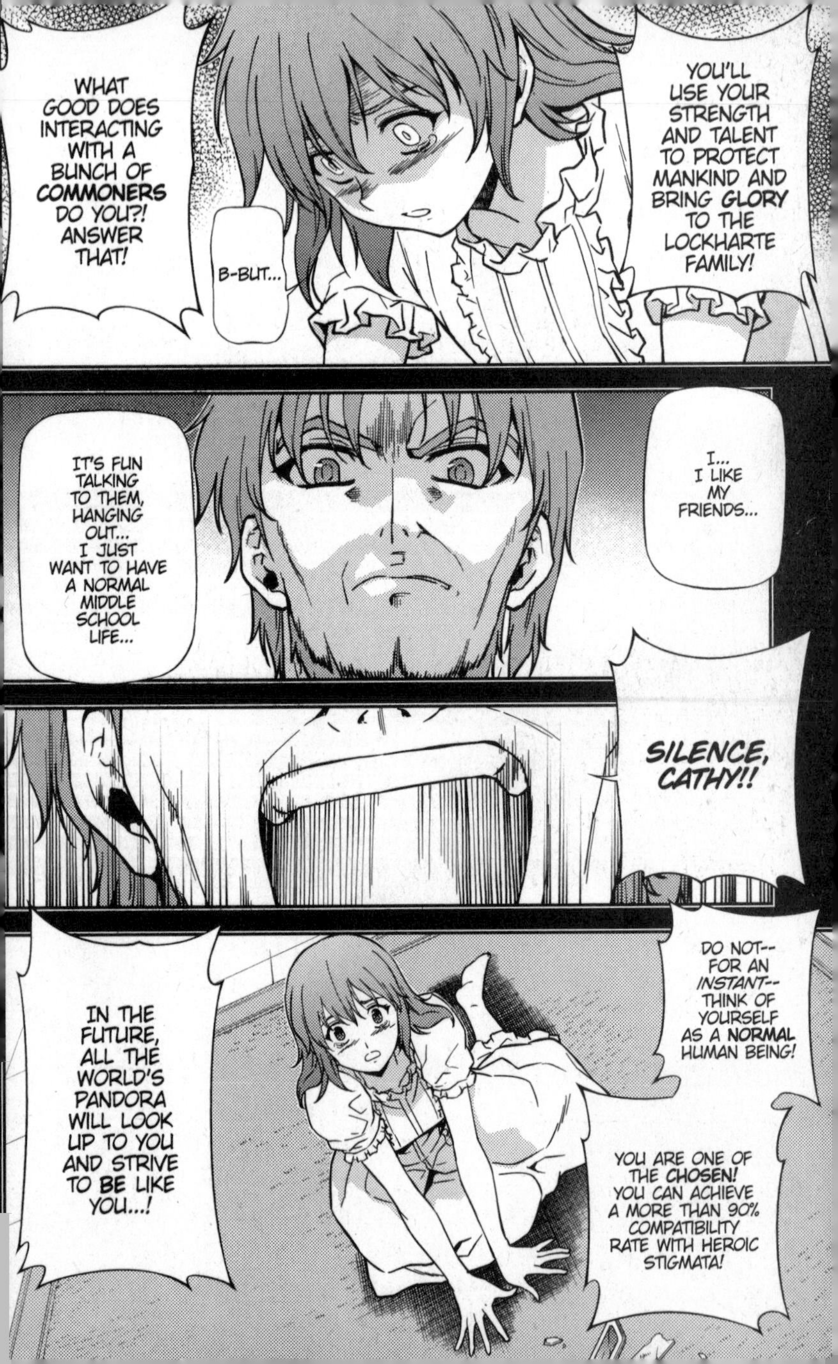
YOU'LL USE YOUR STRENGTH AND TALENT TO PROTECT MANKIND AND BRING **GLORY** TO THE LOCKHARTE FAMILY!
WHAT GOOD DOES INTERACTING WITH A BUNCH OF **COMMONERS** DO YOU?! ANSWER THAT!
B-BUT...
I... I LIKE MY FRIENDS...
IT'S FUN TALKING TO THEM, HANGING OUT... I JUST WANT TO HAVE A NORMAL MIDDLE SCHOOL LIFE...
SILENCE, CATHY!!
DO NOT-- FOR AN *INSTANT*-- THINK OF YOURSELF AS A **NORMAL** HUMAN BEING!
YOU ARE ONE OF THE **CHOSEN**! YOU CAN ACHIEVE A MORE THAN 90% COMPATIBILITY RATE WITH HEROIC STIGMATA!
IN THE FUTURE, ALL THE WORLD'S PANDORA WILL LOOK UP TO YOU AND STRIVE TO **BE** LIKE YOU...!

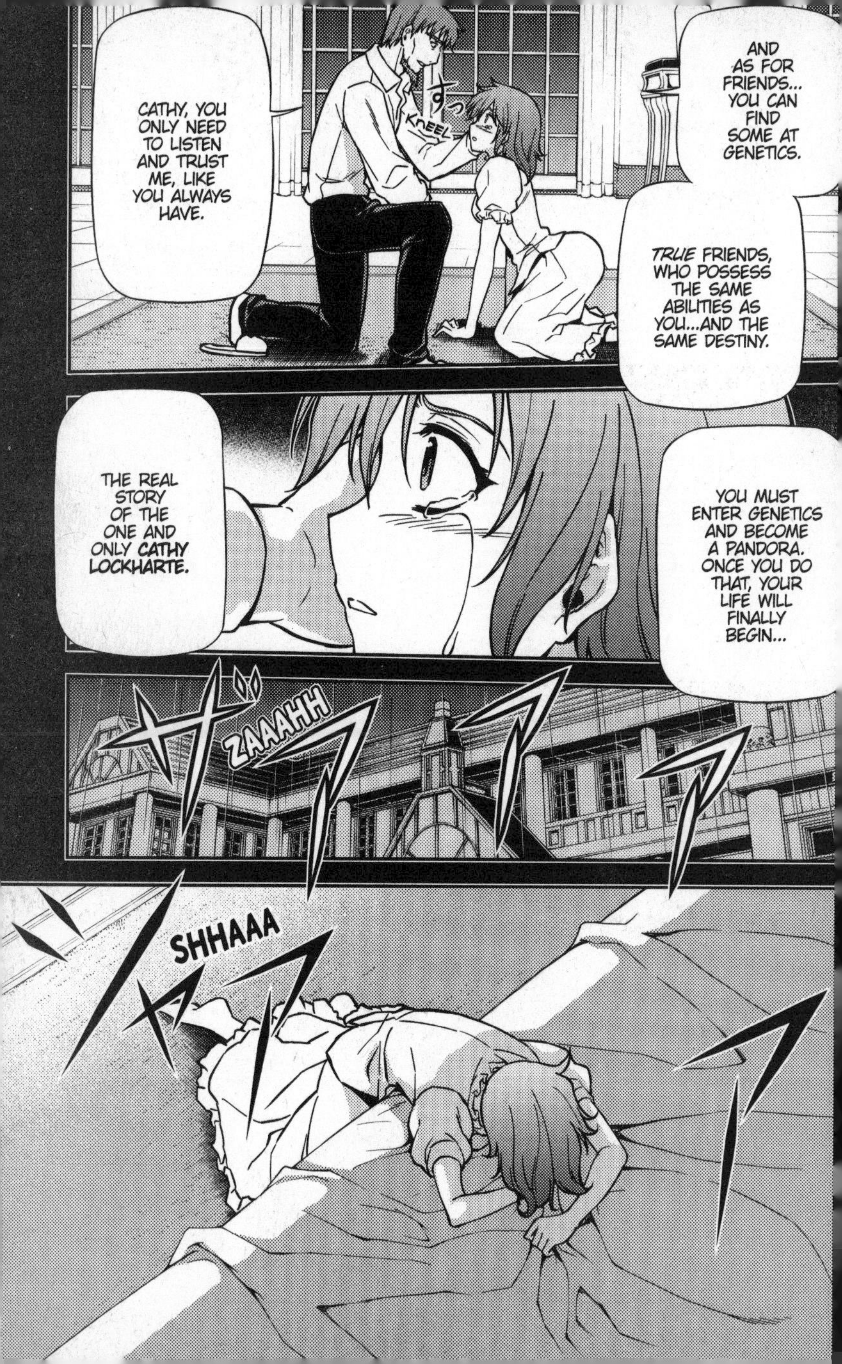
AND AS FOR FRIENDS... YOU CAN FIND SOME AT GENETICS.
TRUE FRIENDS, WHO POSSESS THE SAME ABILITIES AS YOU...AND THE SAME DESTINY.
KNEEL
CATHY, YOU ONLY NEED TO LISTEN AND TRUST ME, LIKE YOU ALWAYS HAVE.
YOU MUST ENTER GENETICS AND BECOME A PANDORA. ONCE YOU DO THAT, YOUR LIFE WILL FINALLY BEGIN...
THE REAL STORY OF THE ONE AND ONLY CATHY LOCKHARTE.
ZAAAHH
SHHAAA

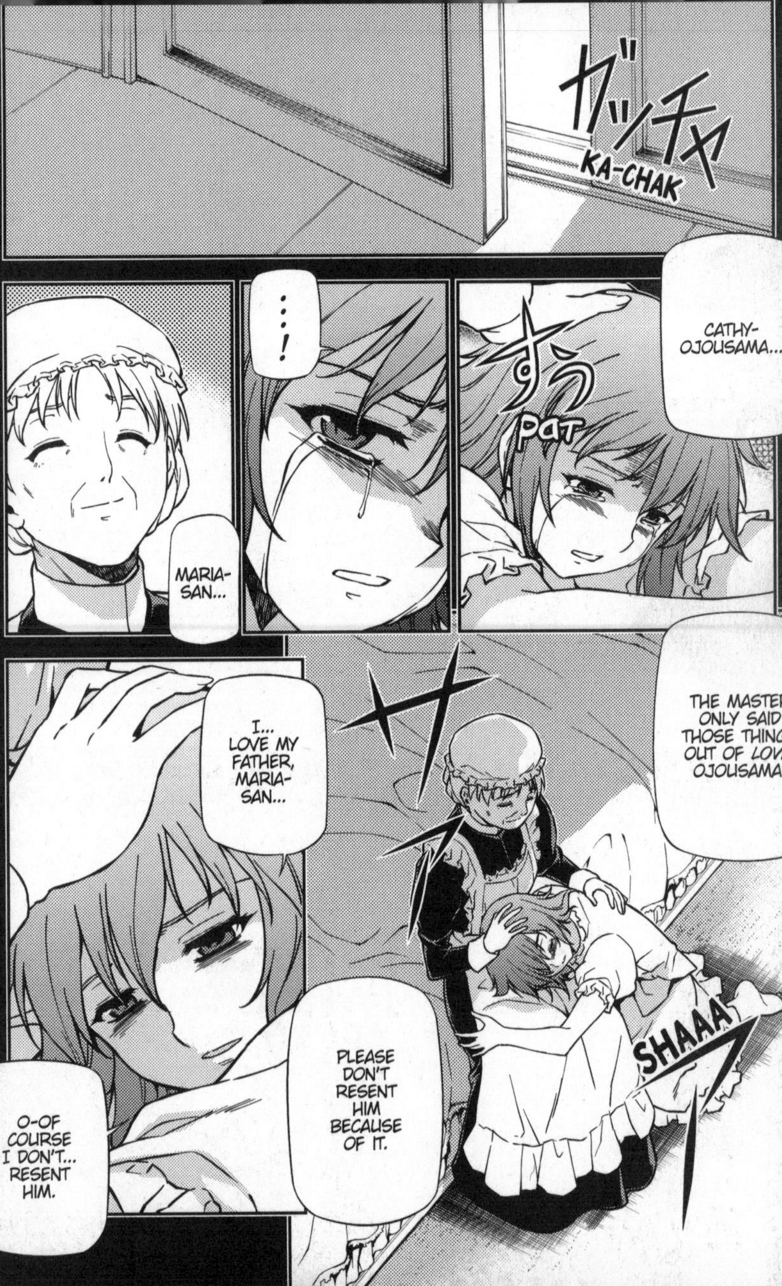
ガッチャ
KA-CHAK
CATHY-OJOUSAMA...
すう
PAT
...!
MARIA-SAN...
THE MASTER ONLY SAID THOSE THINGS OUT OF LOVE, OJOUSAMA.
SHAAA
PLEASE DON'T RESENT HIM BECAUSE OF IT.
I... LOVE MY FATHER, MARIA-SAN...
O-OF COURSE I DON'T... RESENT HIM.

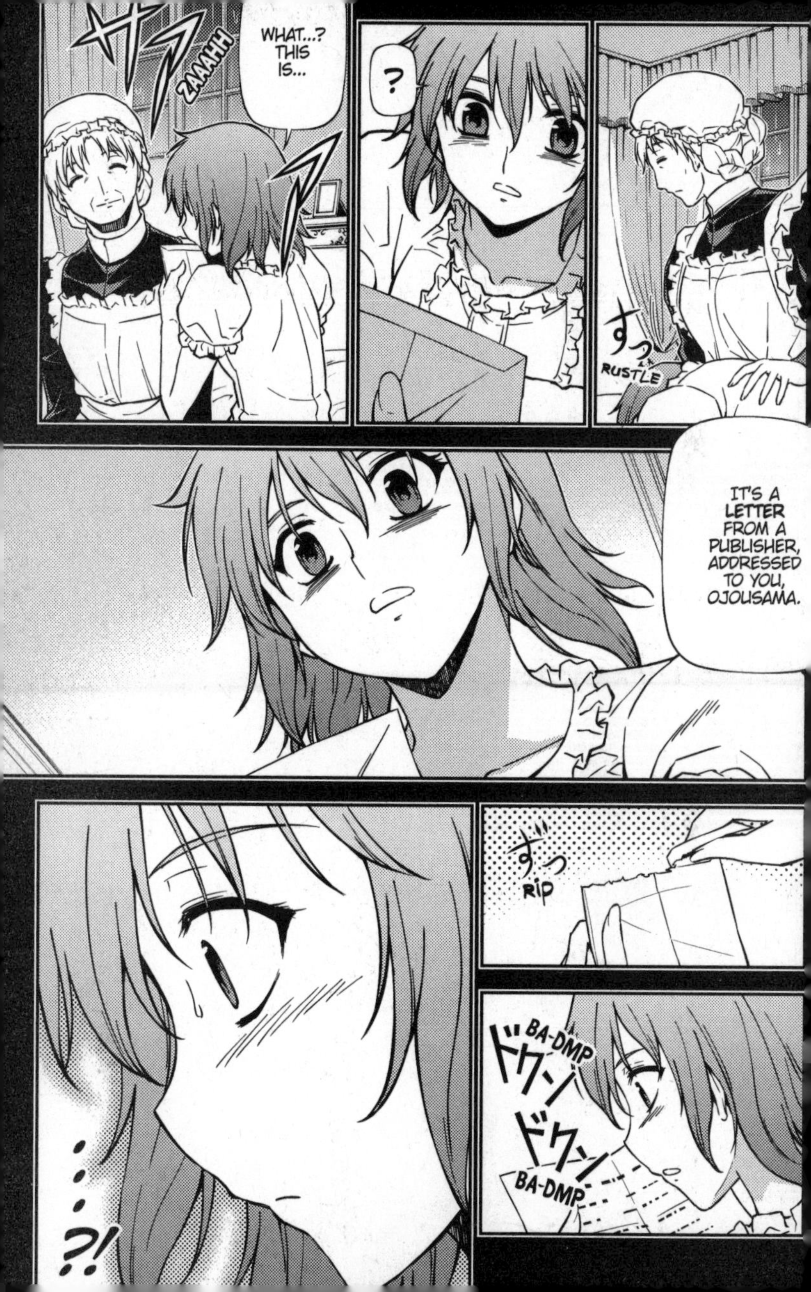
すっ
RUSTLE
?
WHAT...? THIS IS...
ZAAAHH
IT'S A LETTER FROM A PUBLISHER, ADDRESSED TO YOU, OJOUSAMA.
ずっ
RIP
ドクン
BA-DMP
ドクン
BA-DMP
......?!

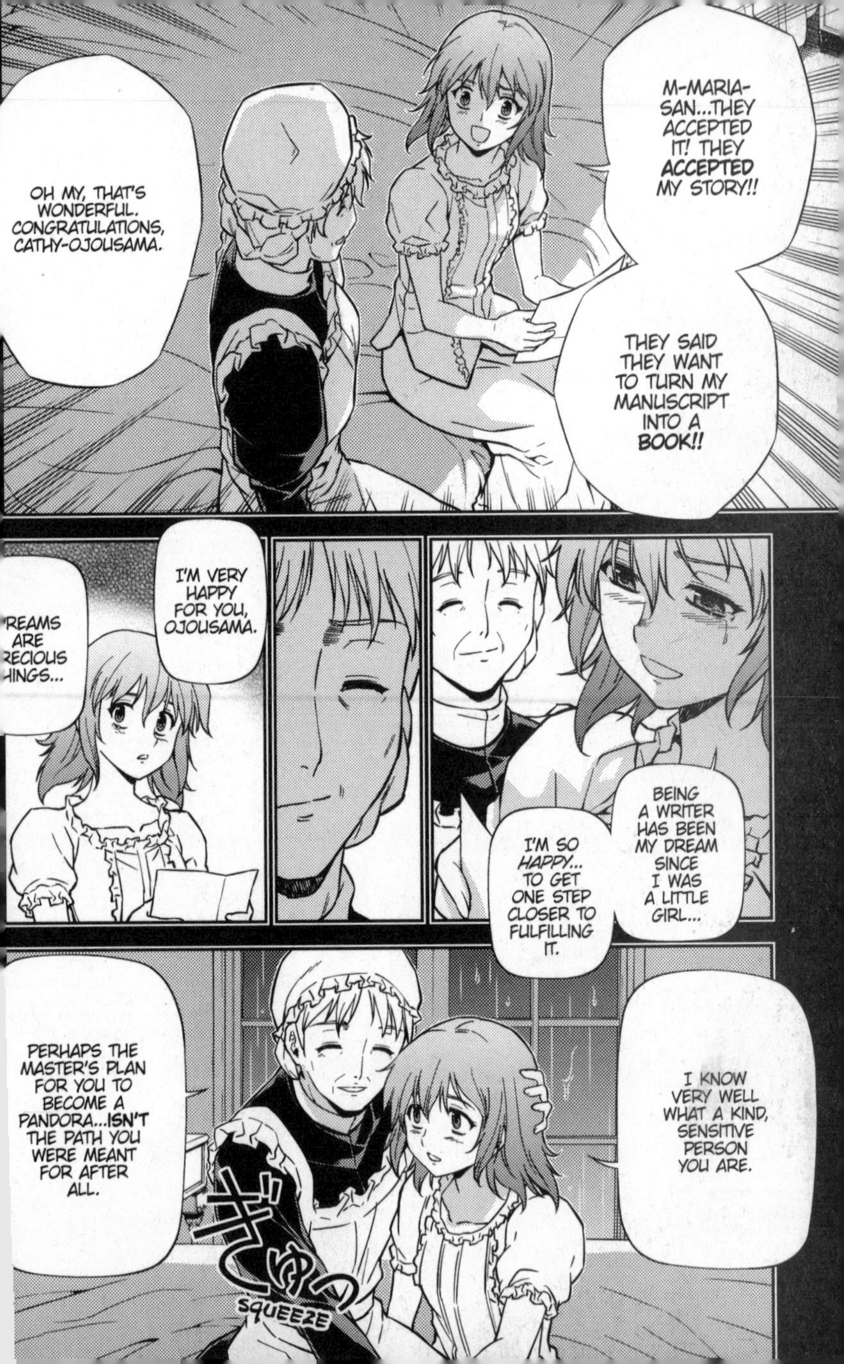
M-MARIA-SAN...THEY ACCEPTED IT! THEY ACCEPTED MY STORY!!
THEY SAID THEY WANT TO TURN MY MANUSCRIPT INTO A BOOK!!
OH MY, THAT'S WONDERFUL. CONGRATULATIONS, CATHY-OJOUSAMA.
BEING A WRITER HAS BEEN MY DREAM SINCE I WAS A LITTLE GIRL...
I'M SO HAPPY... TO GET ONE STEP CLOSER TO FULFILLING IT.
I'M VERY HAPPY FOR YOU, OJOUSAMA.
REAMS ARE RECIOUS HINGS...
I KNOW VERY WELL WHAT A KIND, SENSITIVE PERSON YOU ARE.
PERHAPS THE MASTER'S PLAN FOR YOU TO BECOME A PANDORA...ISN'T THE PATH YOU WERE MEANT FOR AFTER ALL.
ぎゅっ
SQUEEZE

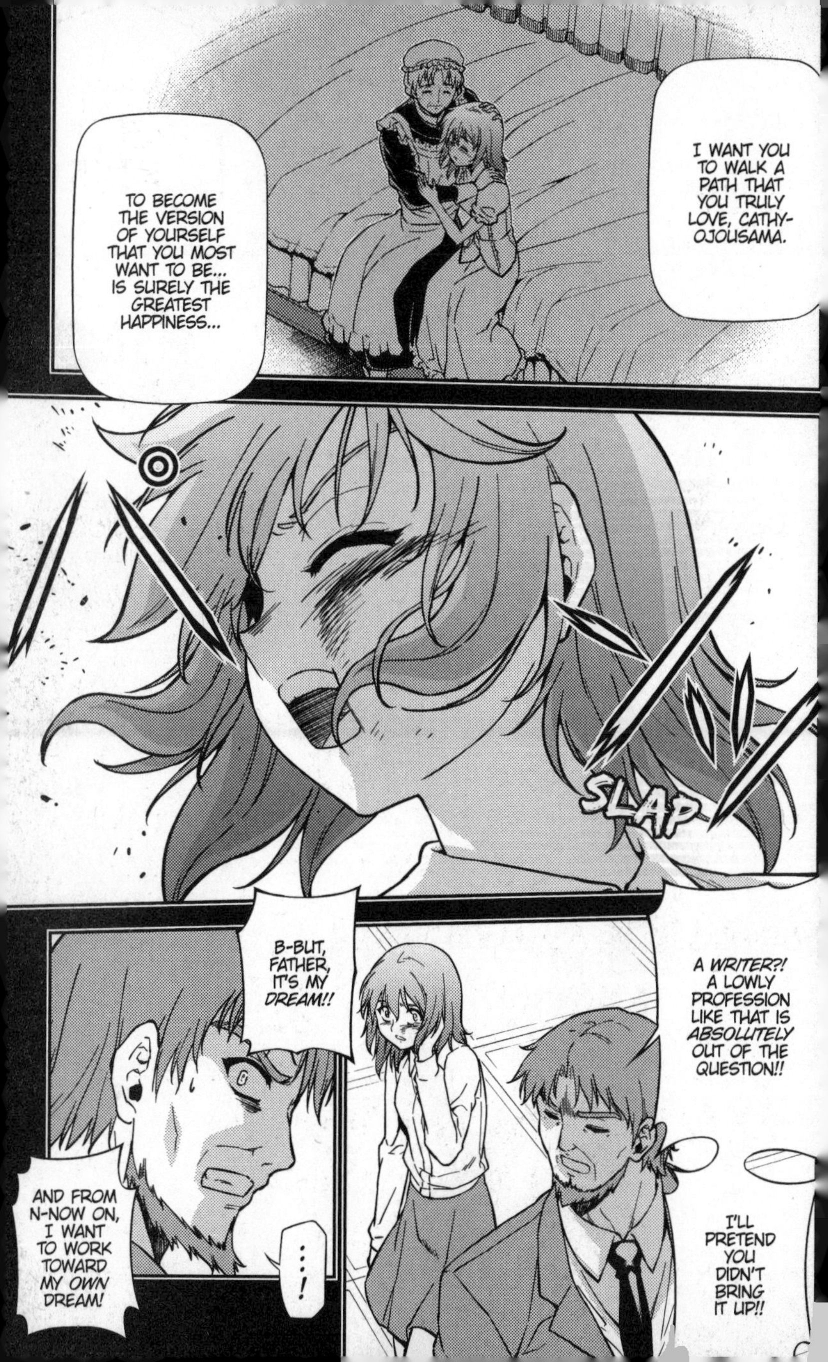
I WANT YOU TO WALK A PATH THAT YOU TRULY LOVE, CATHY-OJOUSAMA.
TO BECOME THE VERSION OF YOURSELF THAT YOU MOST WANT TO BE... IS SURELY THE GREATEST HAPPINESS...
SLAP
A *WRITER*?! A LOWLY PROFESSION LIKE THAT IS *ABSOLUTELY* OUT OF THE QUESTION!!
B-BUT, FATHER, IT'S MY *DREAM*!!
I'LL PRETEND YOU DIDN'T BRING IT UP!!
AND FROM N-NOW ON, I WANT TO WORK TOWARD MY *OWN* DREAM!
...!

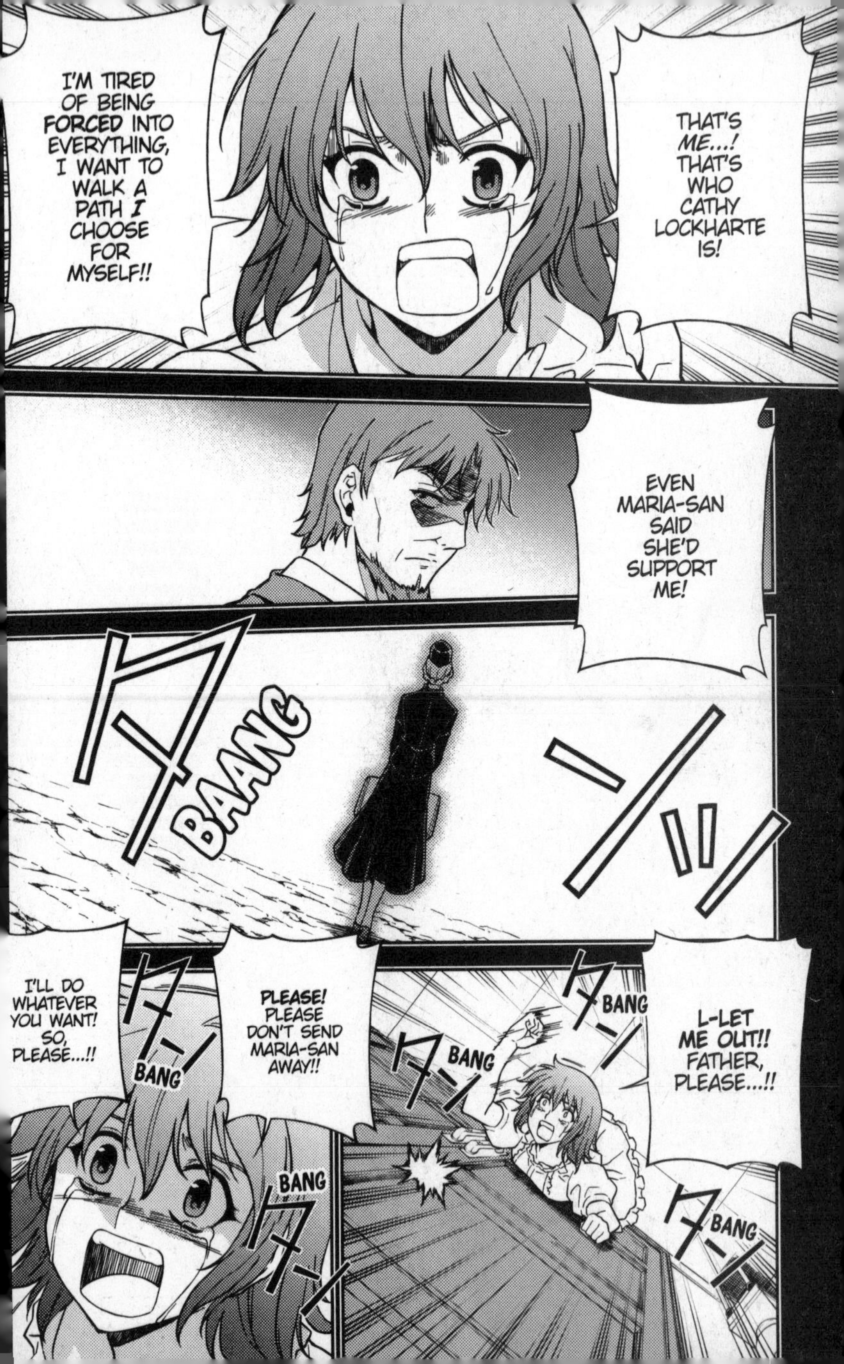
THAT'S ME...! THAT'S WHO CATHY LOCKHARTE IS!
I'M TIRED OF BEING **FORCED** INTO EVERYTHING, I WANT TO WALK A PATH *I* CHOOSE FOR MYSELF!!
EVEN MARIA-SAN SAID SHE'D SUPPORT ME!
BAANG
L-LET ME OUT!! FATHER, PLEASE...!!
BANG
BANG
BANG
PLEASE! PLEASE DON'T SEND MARIA-SAN AWAY!!
I'LL DO WHATEVER YOU WANT! SO, PLEASE...!!
BANG
BANG

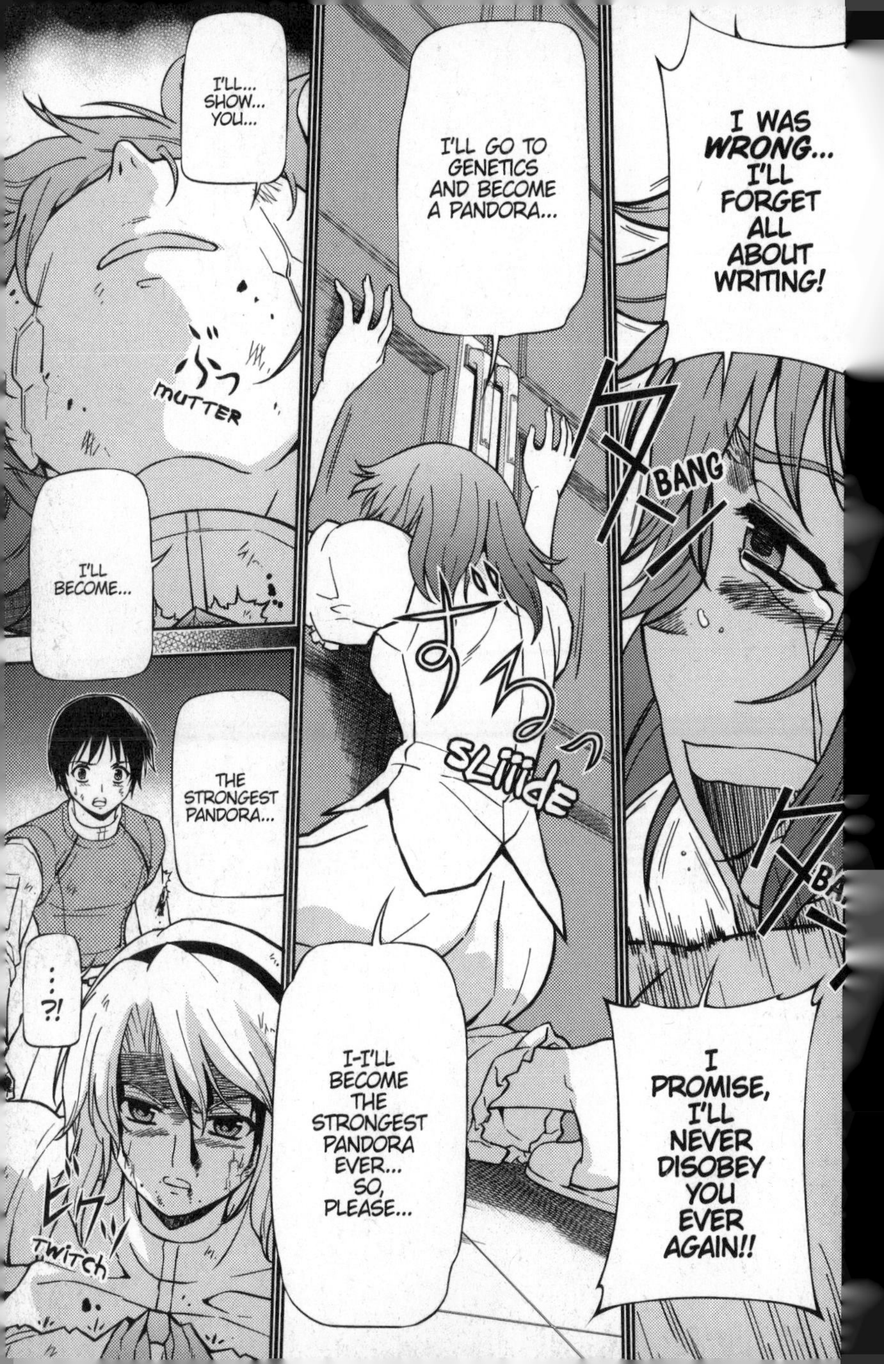
I WAS WRONG... I'LL FORGET ALL ABOUT WRITING!
BANG
I PROMISE, I'LL NEVER DISOBEY YOU EVER AGAIN!!
I'LL GO TO GENETICS AND BECOME A PANDORA...
SLIiiide
I-I'LL BECOME THE STRONGEST PANDORA EVER... SO, PLEASE...
I'LL... SHOW... YOU...
MUTTER
I'LL BECOME...
THE STRONGEST PANDORA...
...?!
TWITCH

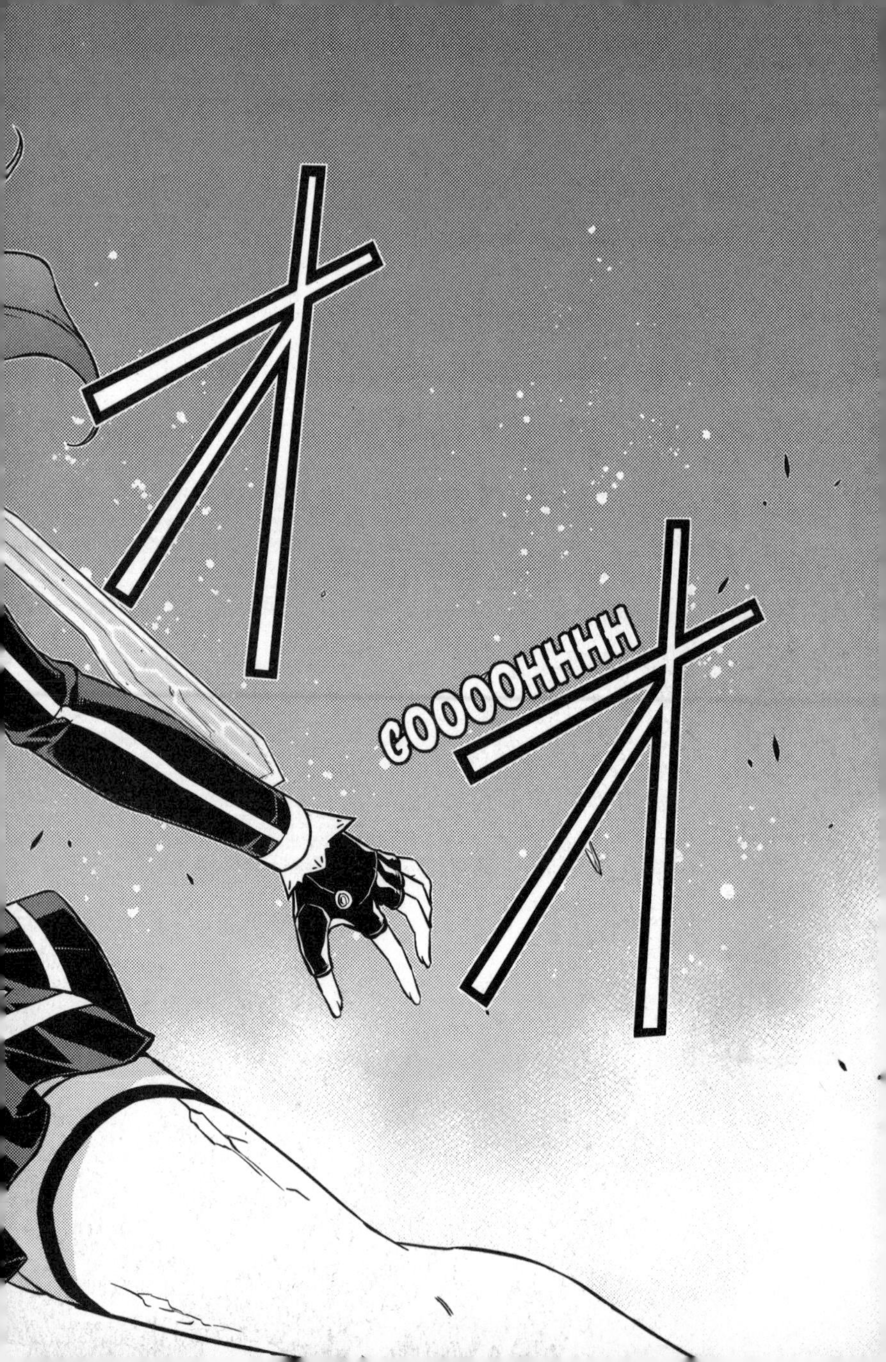
GOOOOHHHH

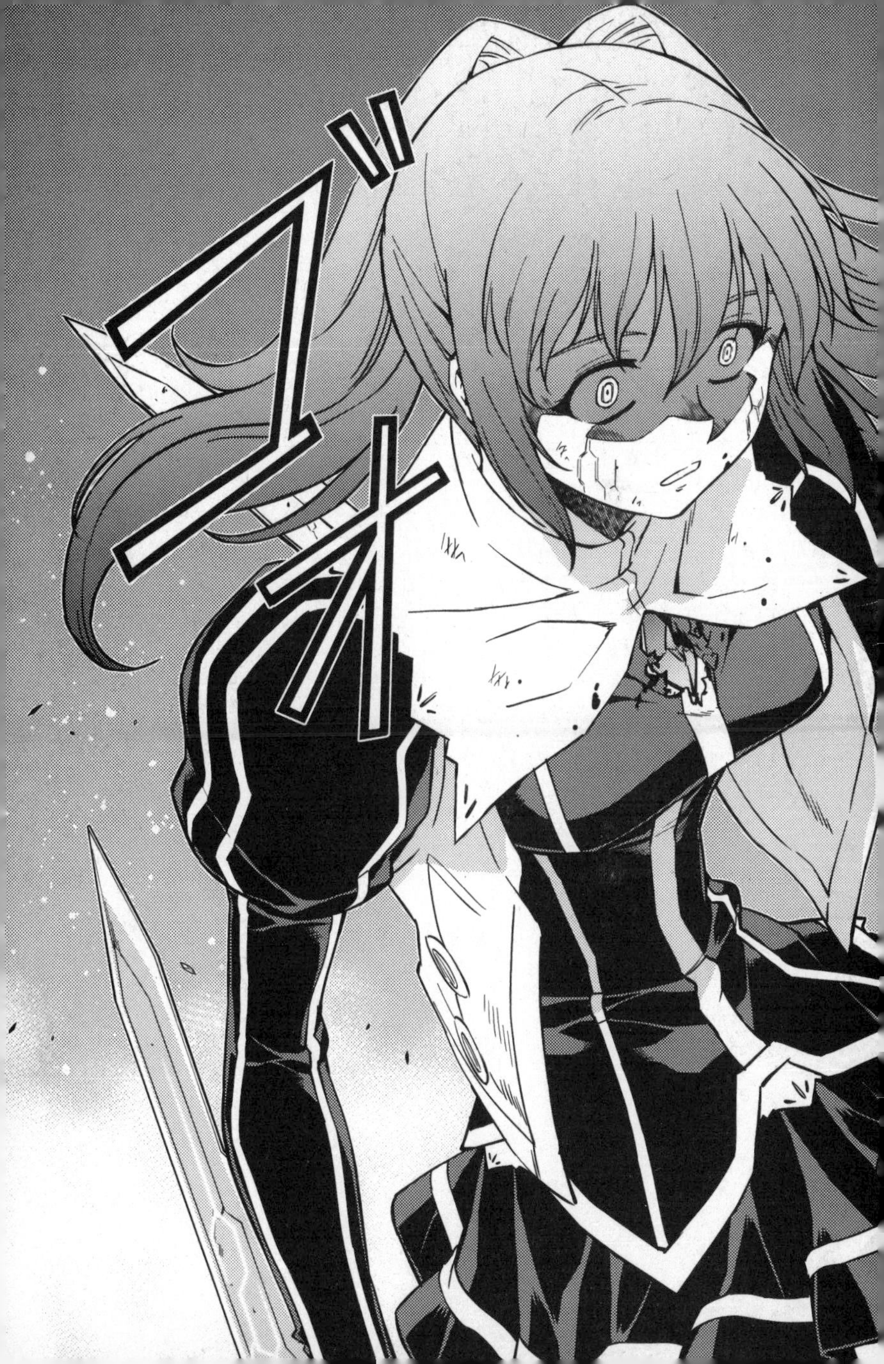

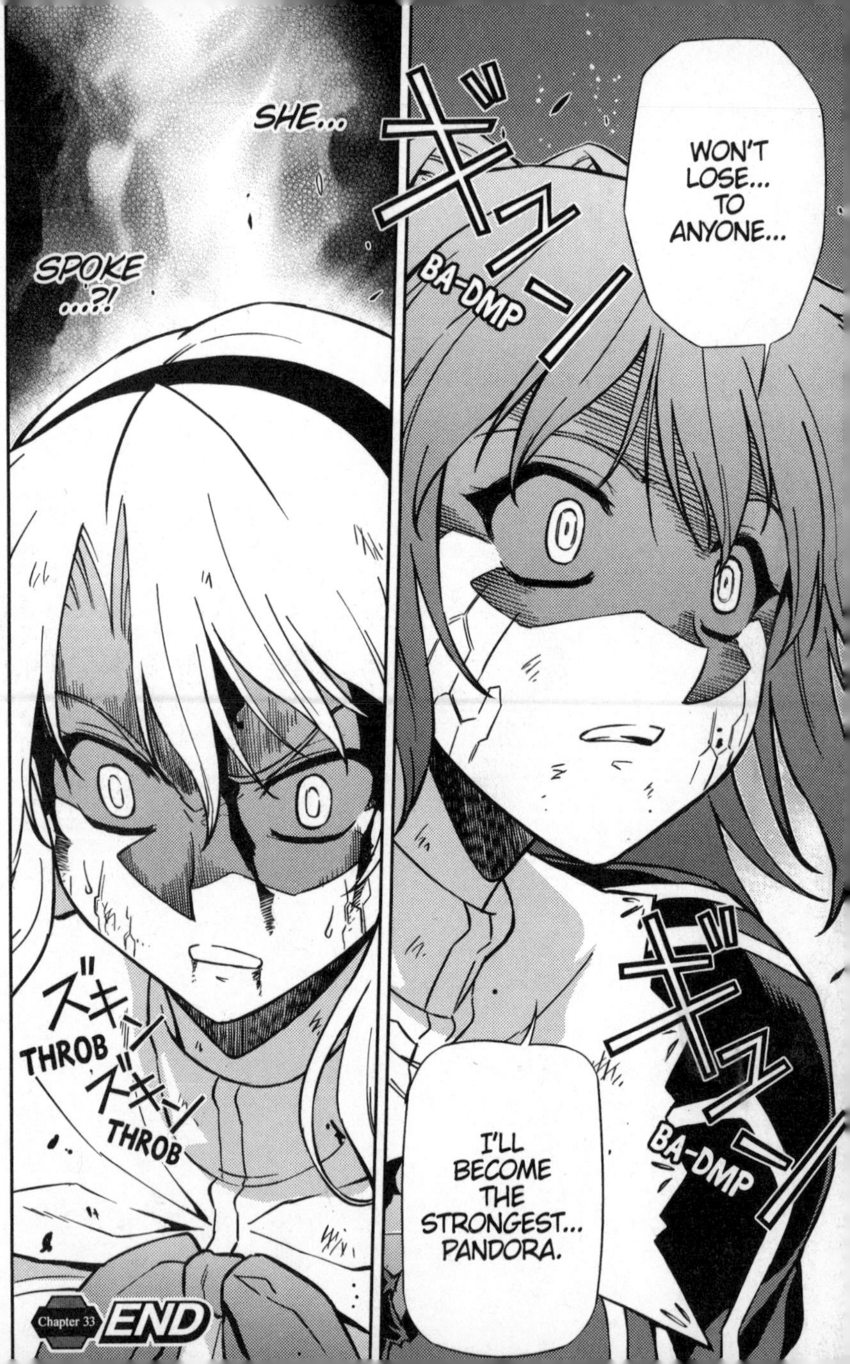
WON'T LOSE... TO ANYONE...
BA-DMP
I'LL BECOME THE STRONGEST... PANDORA.
BA-DMP
SHE...
SPOKE ...?!
ズキン
THROB
ズキン
THROB
Chapter 33 END

FREEZING VOLUME.6
HIGHLIGHT SCENE

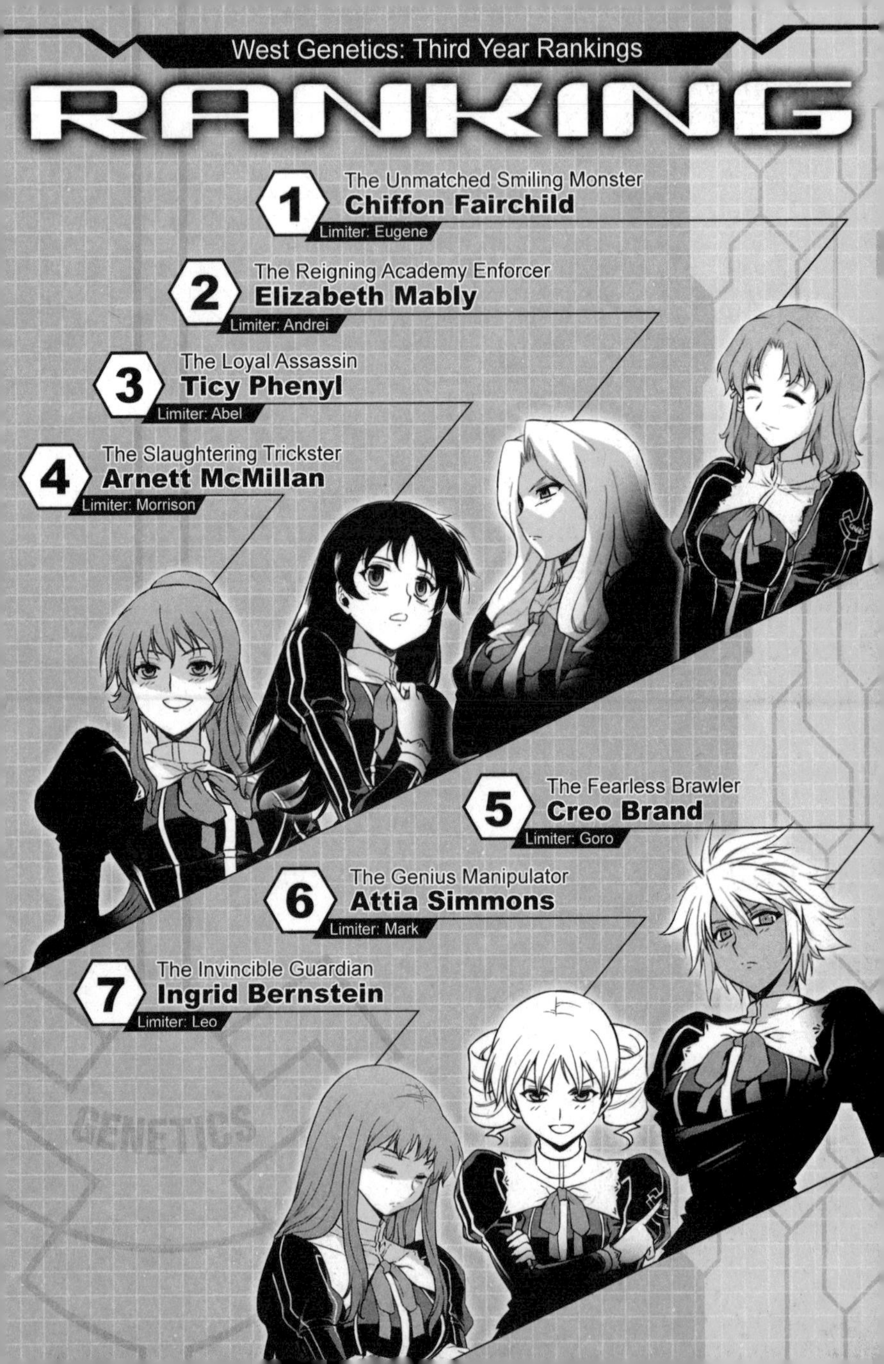
West Genetics: Third Year Rankings
RANKING
1
The Unmatched Smiling Monster
Chiffon Fairchild
Limiter: Eugene
2
The Reigning Academy Enforcer
Elizabeth Mably
Limiter: Andrei
3
The Loyal Assassin
Ticy Phenyl
Limiter: Abel
4
The Slaughtering Trickster
Arnett McMillan
Limiter: Morrison
5
The Fearless Brawler
Creo Brand
Limiter: Goro
6
The Genius Manipulator
Attia Simmons
Limiter: Mark
7
The Invincible Guardian
Ingrid Bernstein
Limiter: Leo

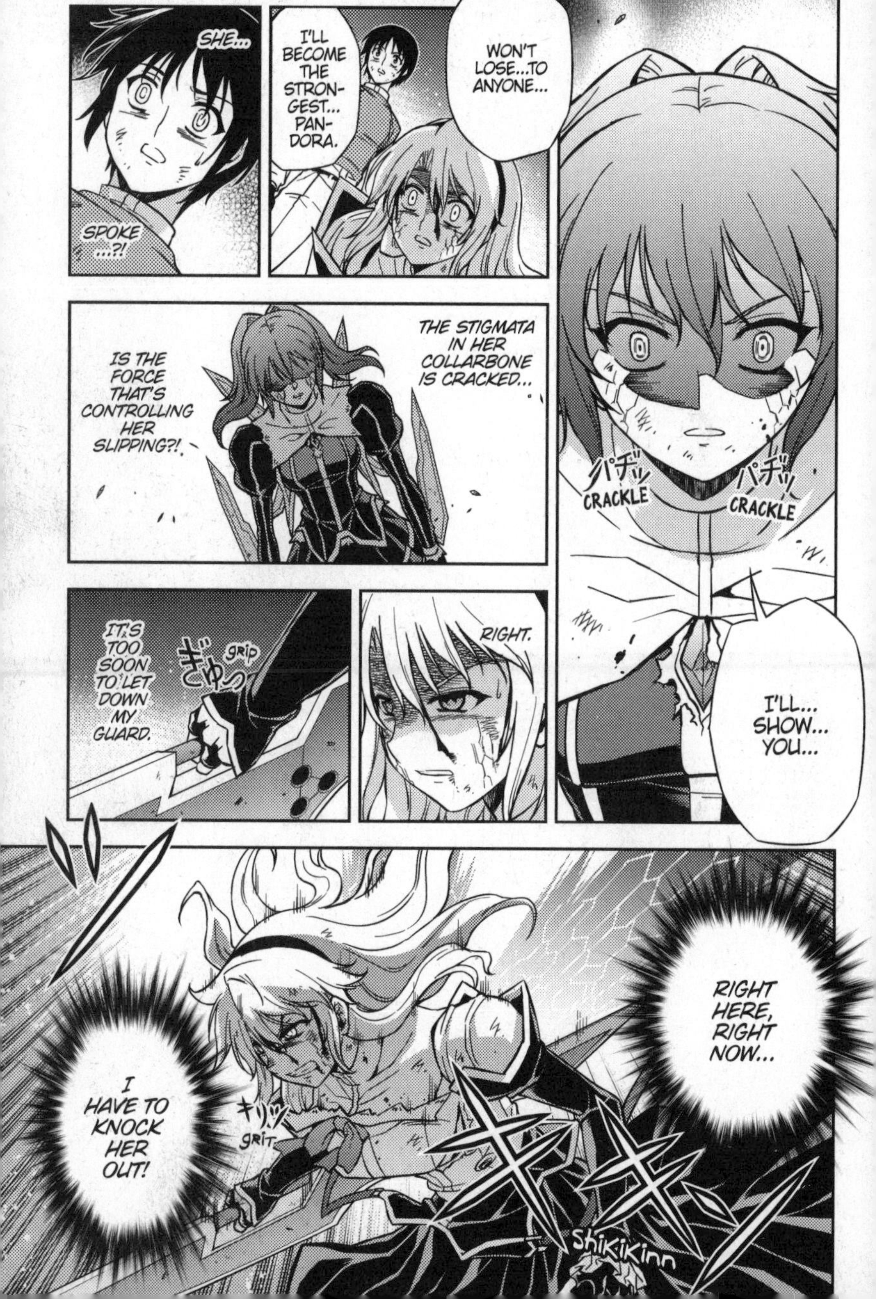
WON'T LOSE...TO ANYONE...
パチッ CRACKLE
パチッ CRACKLE
I'LL... SHOW... YOU...
I'LL BECOME THE STRONG-GEST... PAN-DORA.
SHE...
SPOKE ...?!
THE STIGMATA IN HER COLLARBONE IS CRACKED...
IS THE FORCE THAT'S CONTROLLING HER SLIPPING?!
RIGHT.
IT'S TOO SOON TO LET DOWN MY GUARD.
ぎゅっ grip
RIGHT HERE, RIGHT NOW...
I HAVE TO KNOCK HER OUT!
キリッ grit
ShiKiKinn

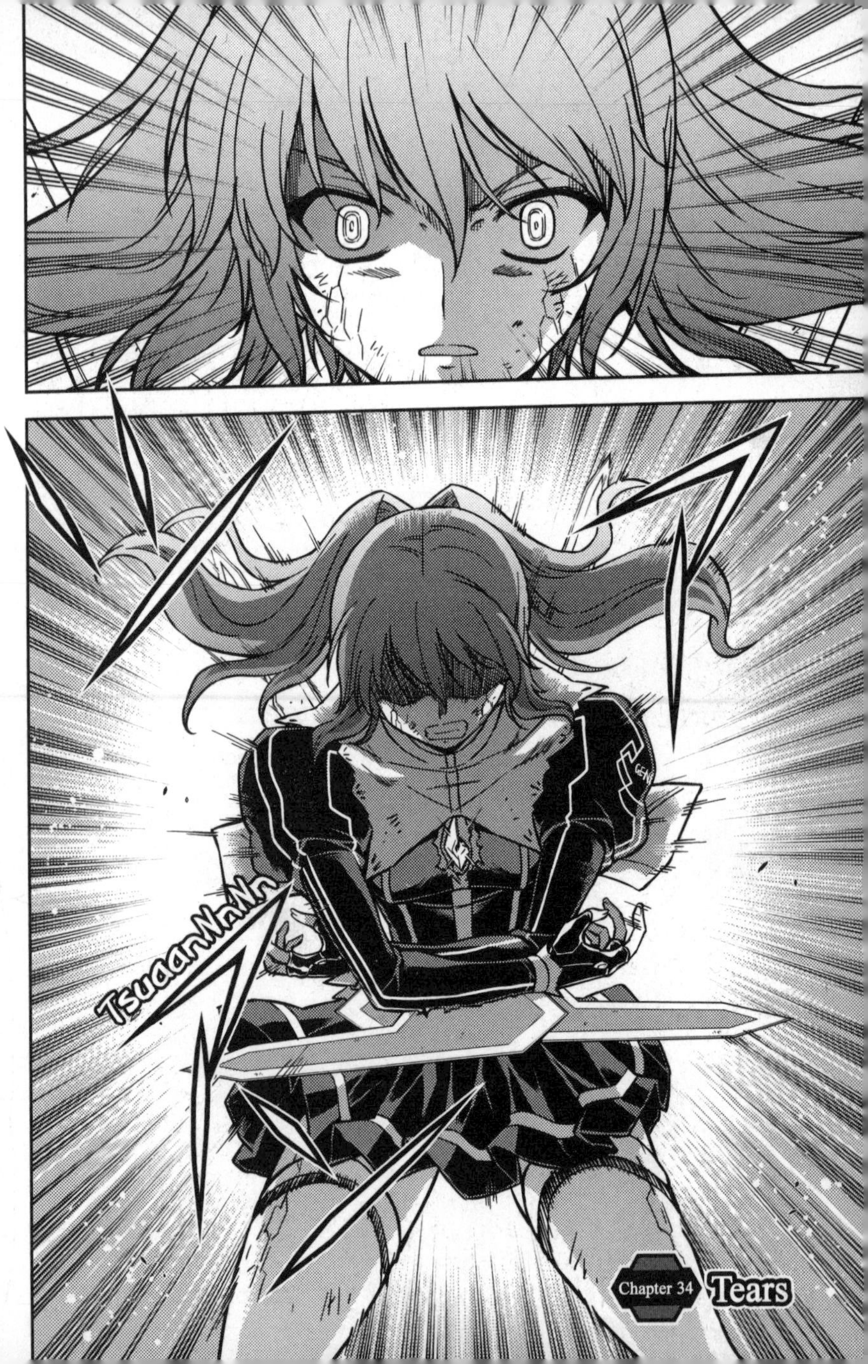
TsuaanNaNn
Chapter 34 Tears

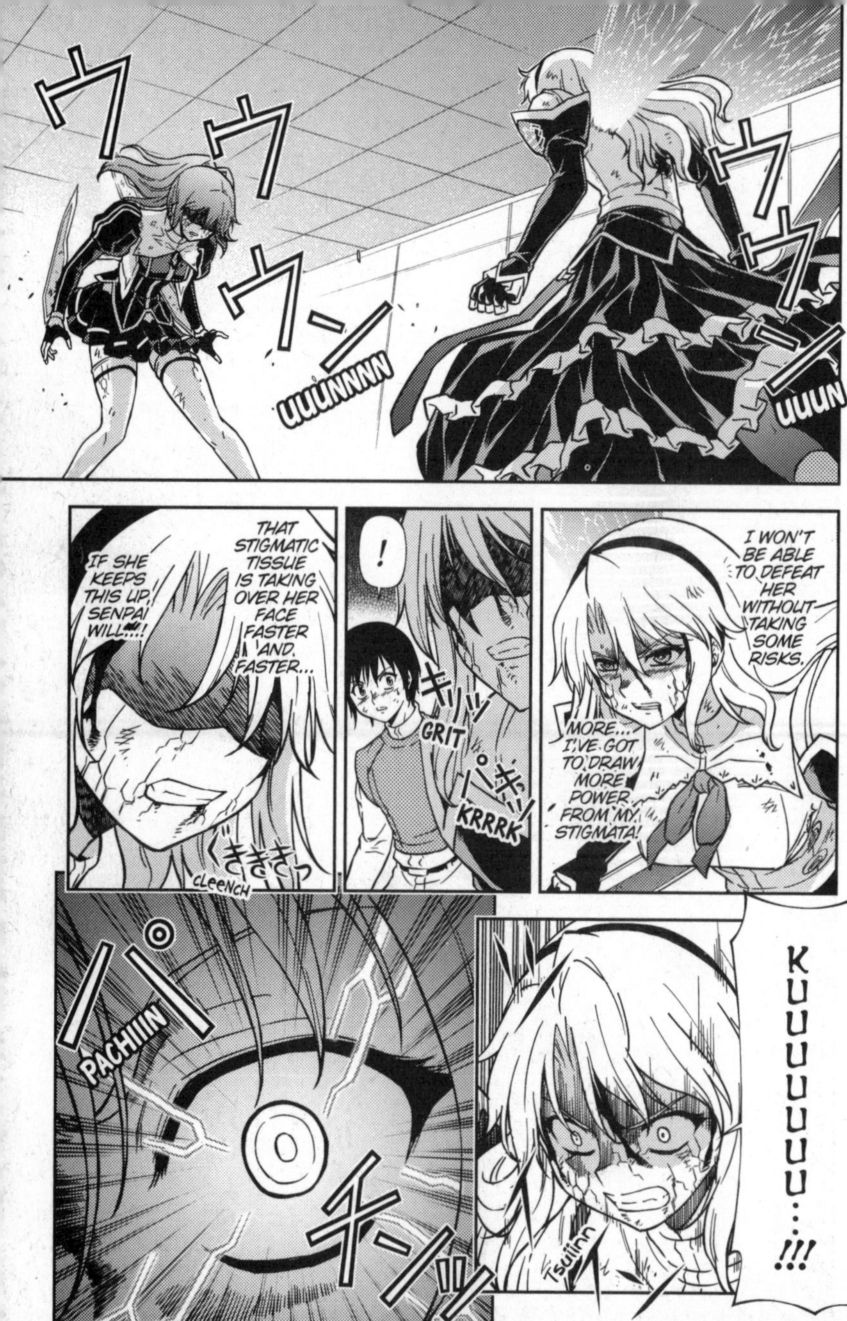
UUUN
UUUNNNN
I WON'T BE ABLE TO DEFEAT HER WITHOUT TAKING SOME RISKS.
MORE... I'VE GOT TO DRAW MORE POWER FROM MY STIGMATA!
!
GRIT
KRRRK
THAT STIGMATIC TISSUE IS TAKING OVER HER FACE FASTER AND FASTER...
IF SHE KEEPS THIS UP, SENPAI WILL...!
CLEENCH
KUUUUUUU...!!!
TSUIINN
PACHIIIN

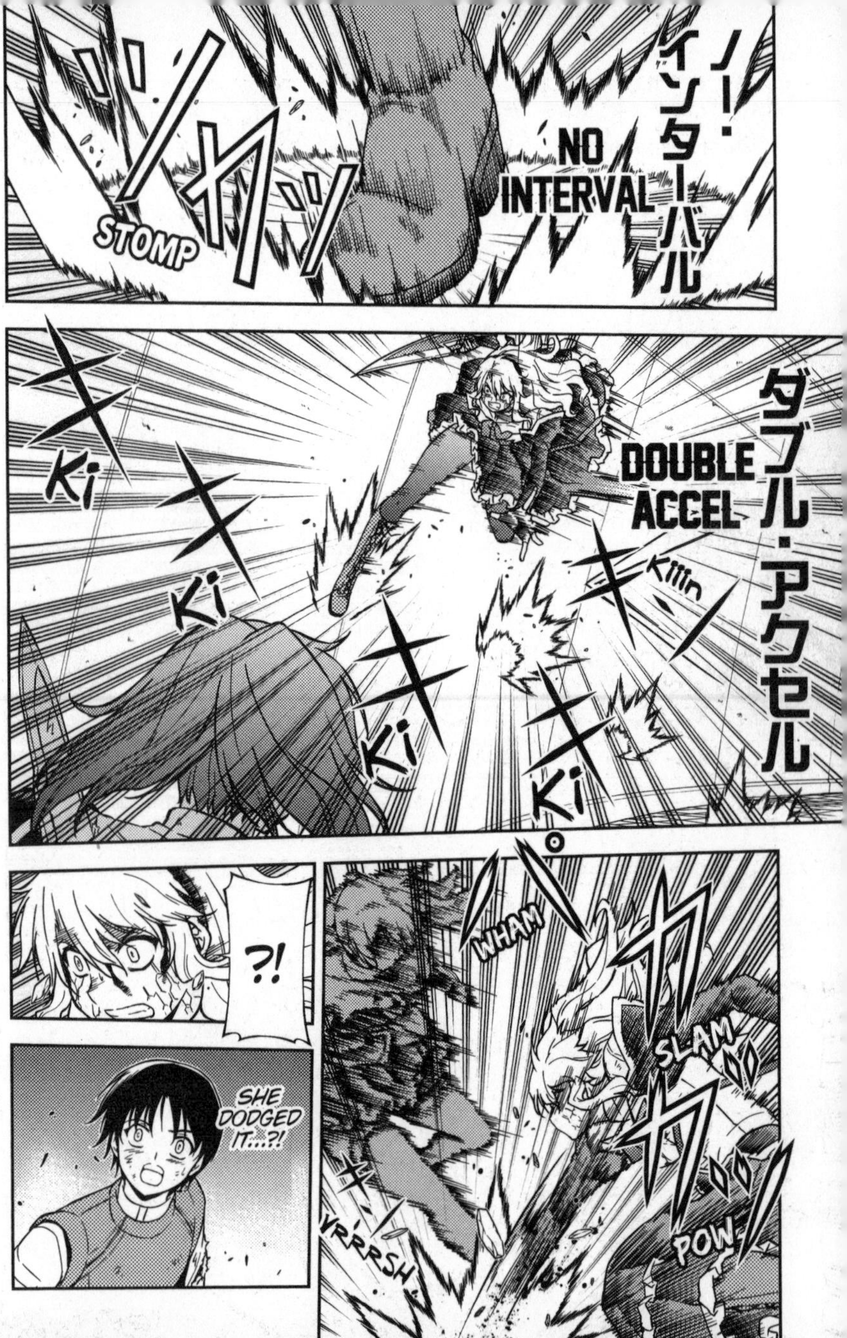
ノー・インターバル
NO INTERVAL
STOMP
ダブル・アクセル
DOUBLE ACCEL
Kiiin
Ki
Ki
Ki
Ki
WHAM
SLAM
POW
VRRRSH
?!
SHE DODGED IT...?!

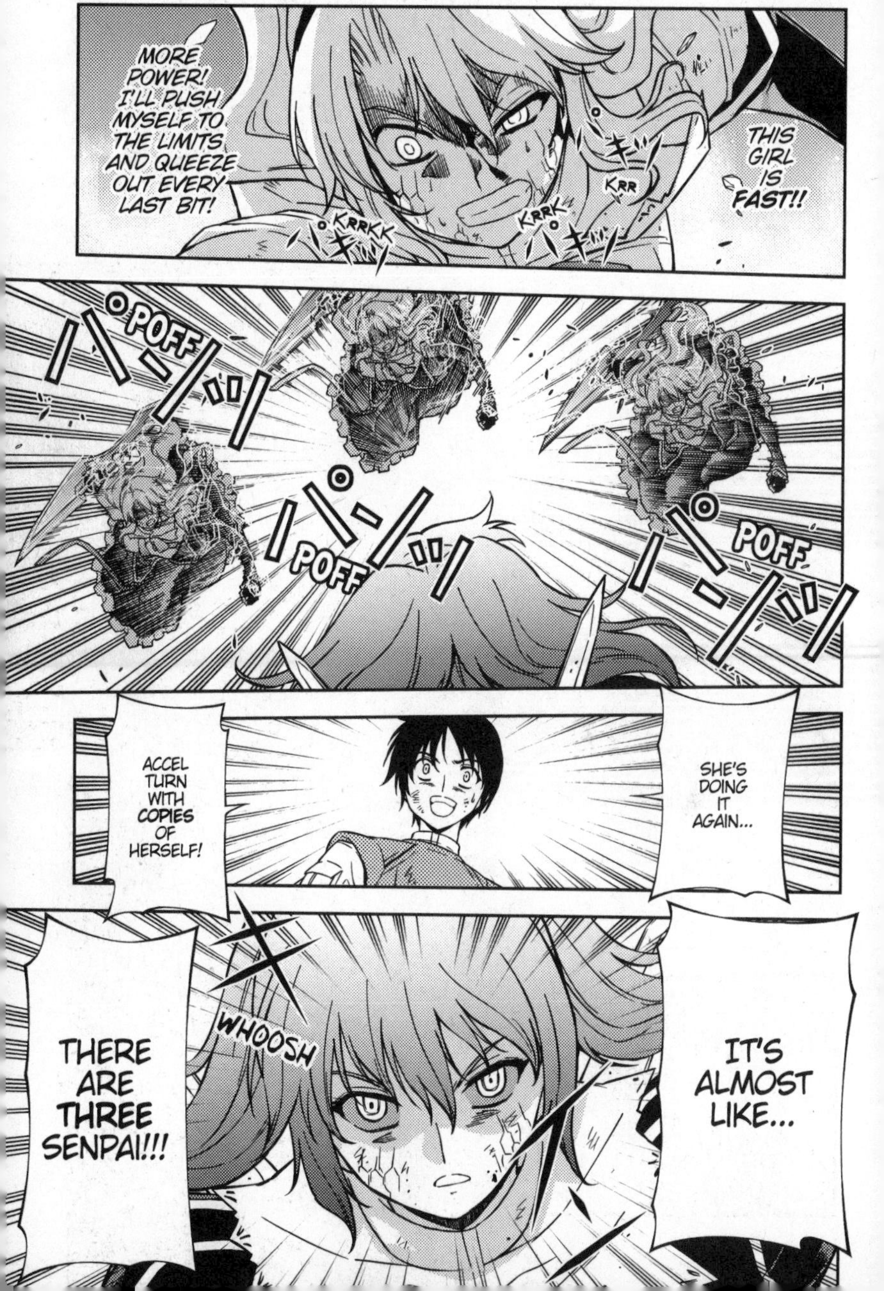
THIS GIRL IS FAST!!
KRR
MORE POWER! I'LL PUSH MYSELF TO THE LIMITS AND QUEEZE OUT EVERY LAST BIT!
KRRK
KRRKK
POFF
POFF
POFF
SHE'S DOING IT AGAIN...
ACCEL TURN WITH COPIES OF HERSELF!
IT'S ALMOST LIKE...
WHOOSH
THERE ARE THREE SENPAI!!!

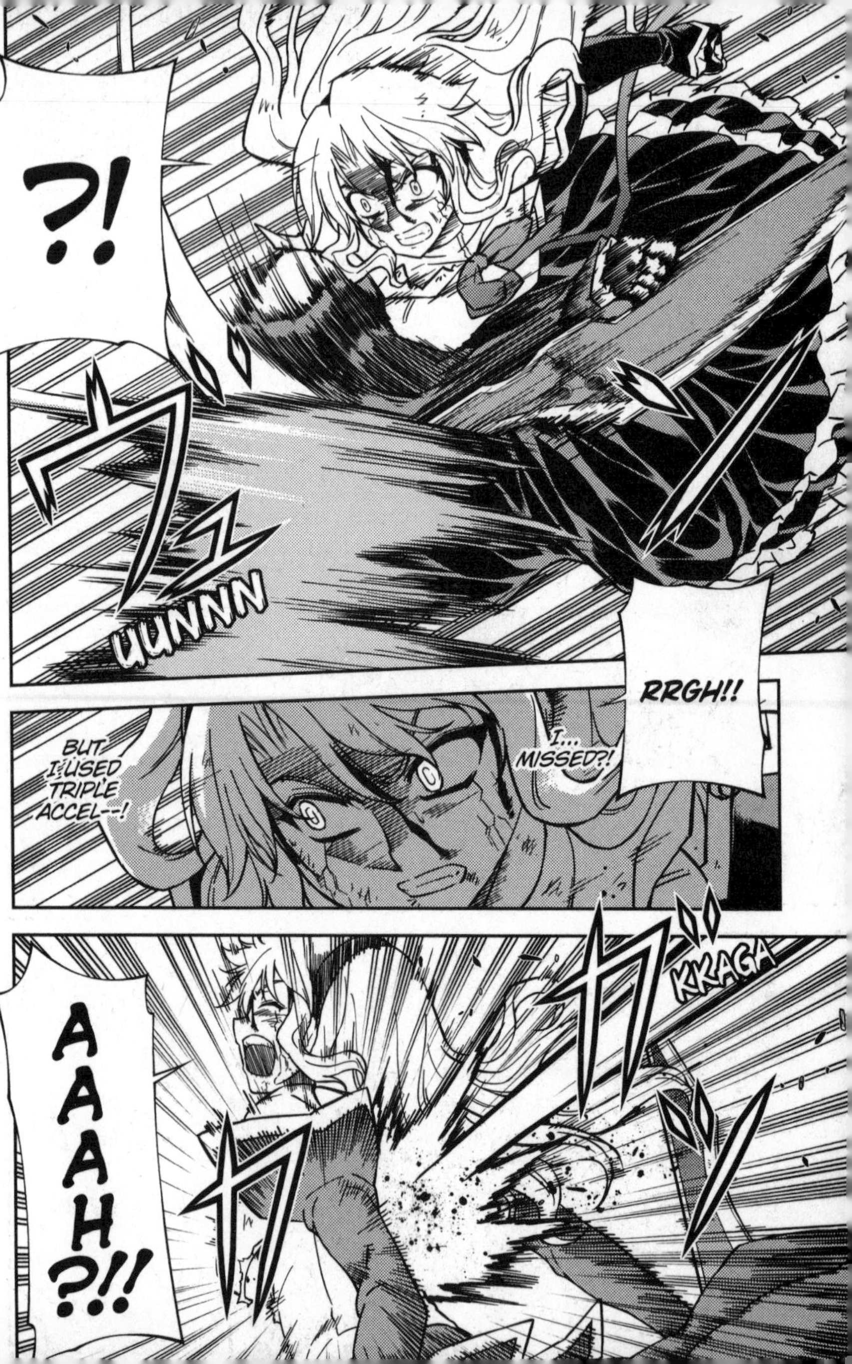
?!
UUNNNN
RRGH!!
I... MISSED?!
BUT I USED TRIPLE ACCEL--!
KKAGA
AAAH?!!

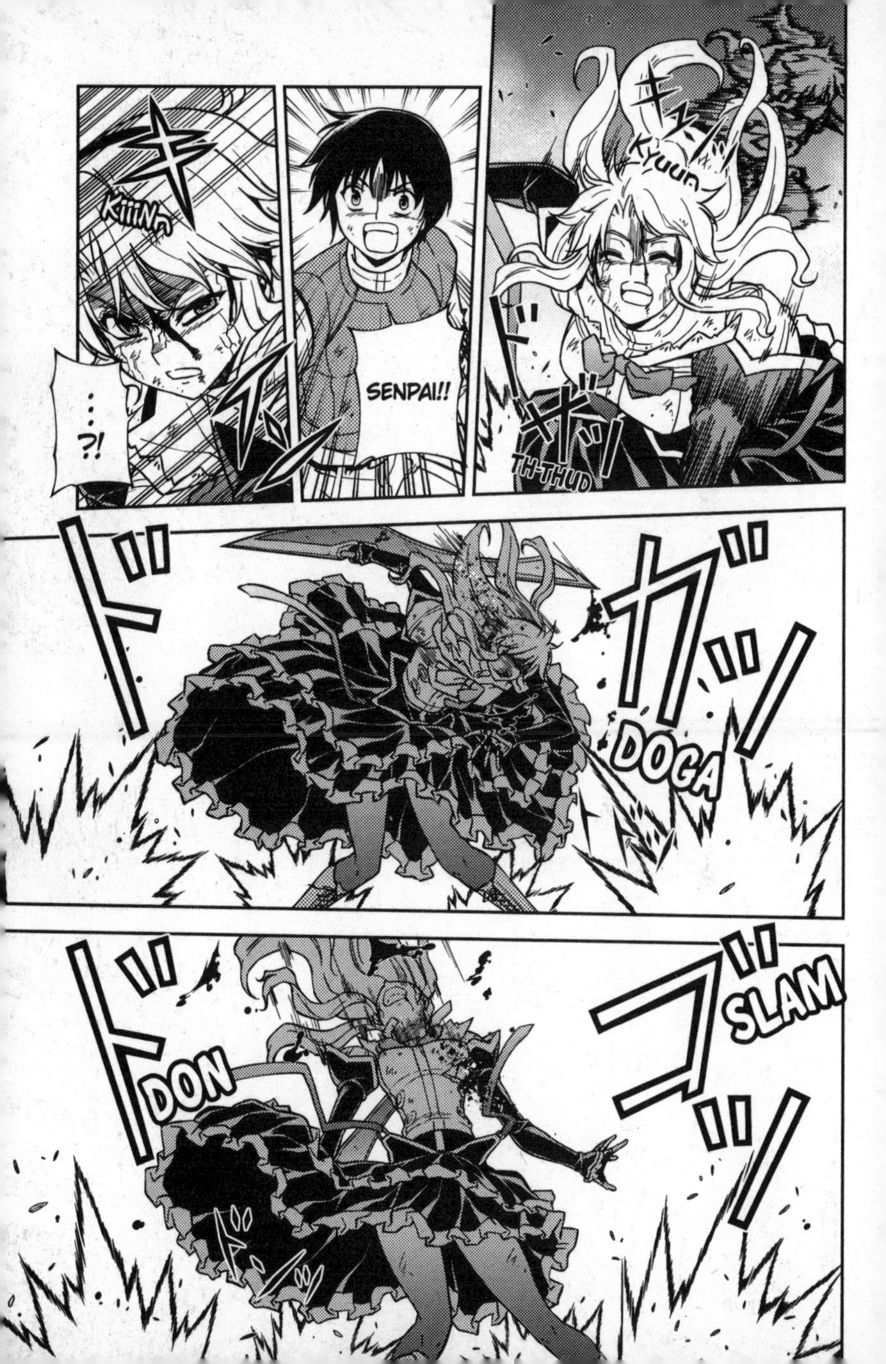
Kyuun
TH-THUD
SENPAI!!
KiiiNn
...?!
DOGA
SLAM
DON

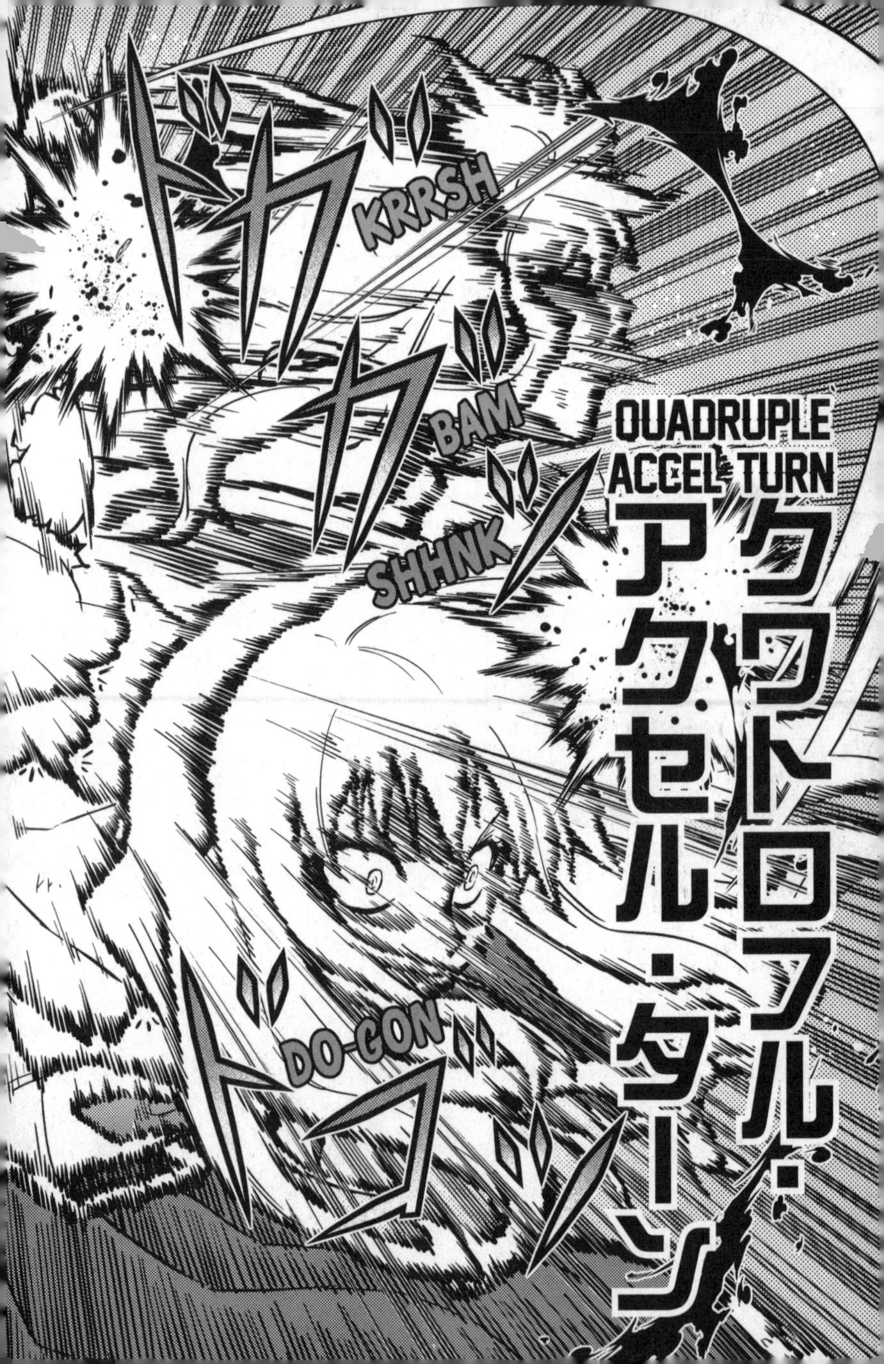
QUADRUPLE ACCEL TURN
クワトロプル・アクセル・ターン
KRRSH
BAM
SHHNK
DO-GON

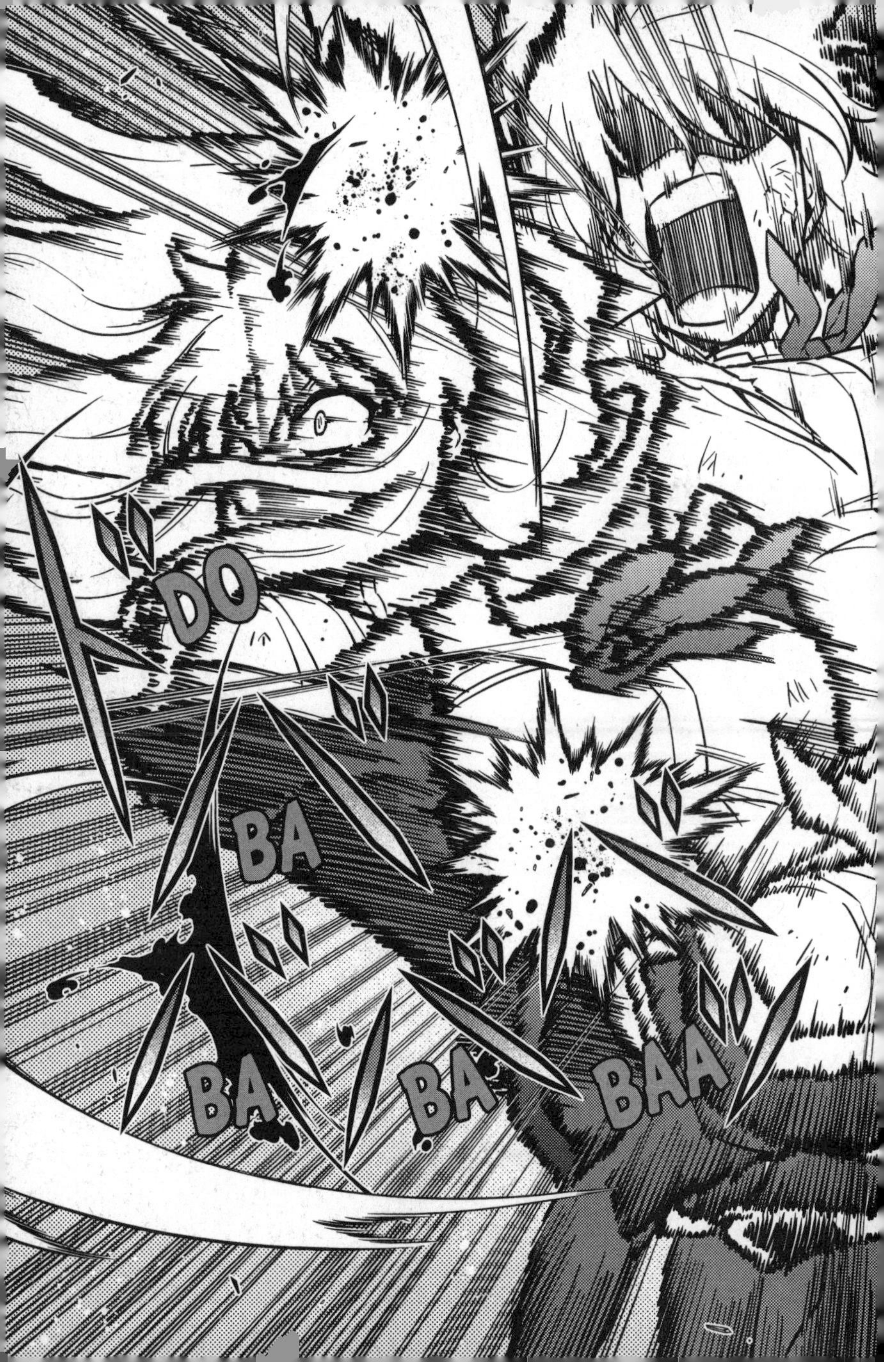
DO
BA
BA
BA
BAA

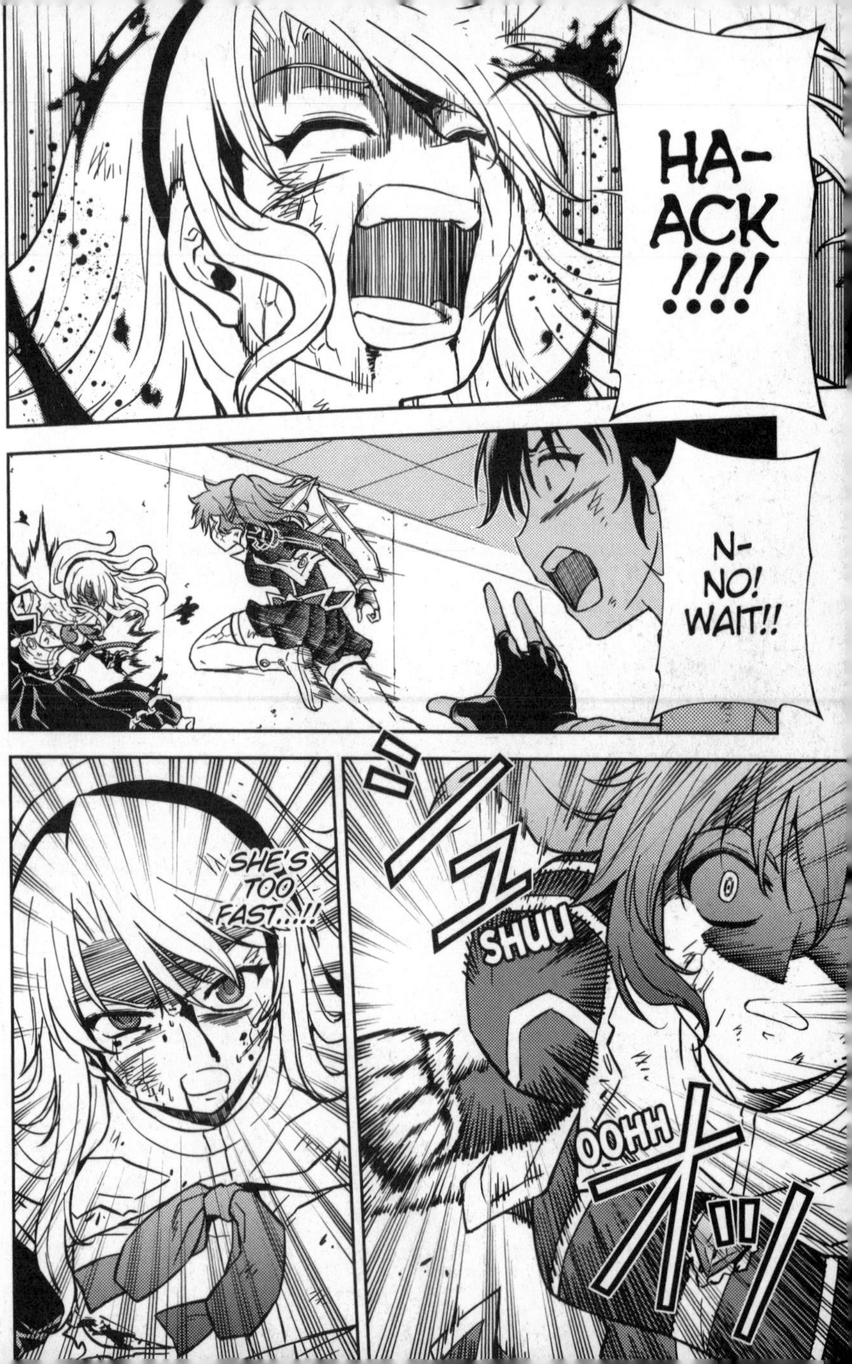
HA-ACK!!!!
N-NO! WAIT!!
SHUU
OOHH
SHE'S TOO FAST...!!

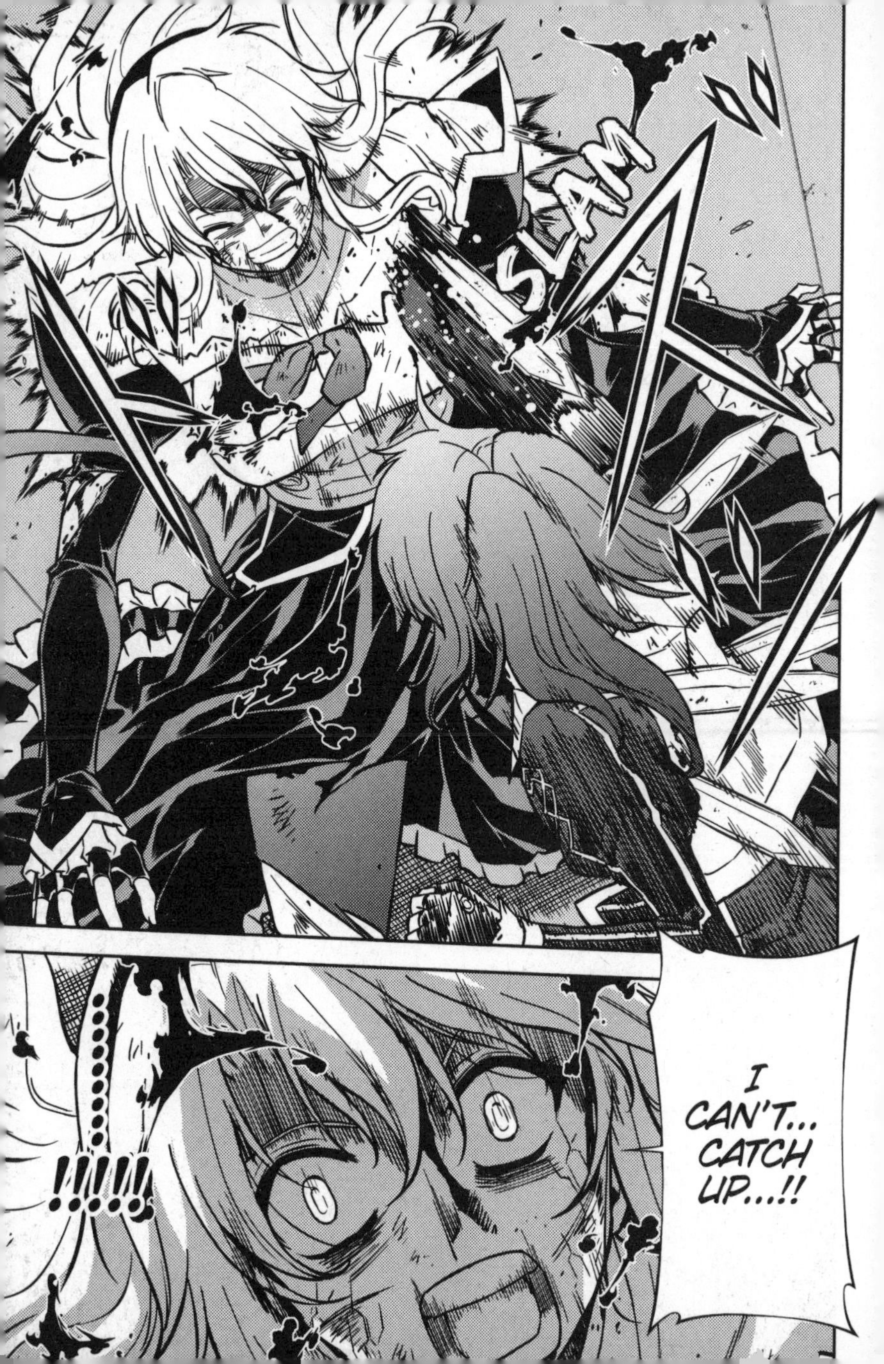
SLAM
I CAN'T... CATCH UP...!!
!!!!!!

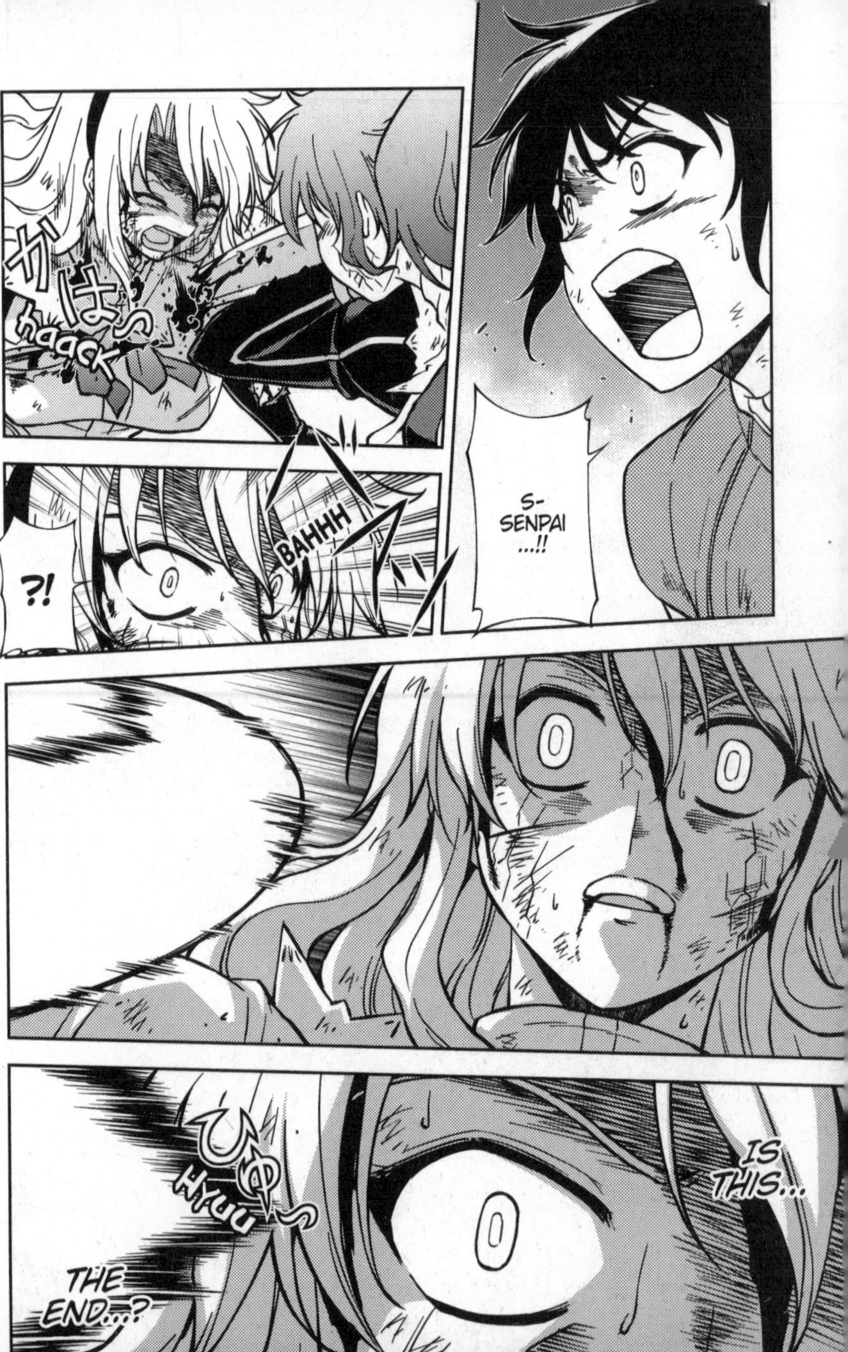
S-SENPAI ...!!
がはっ
haack
BAHHH
?!
IS THIS...
ひゅっ
Hyuu
THE END...?

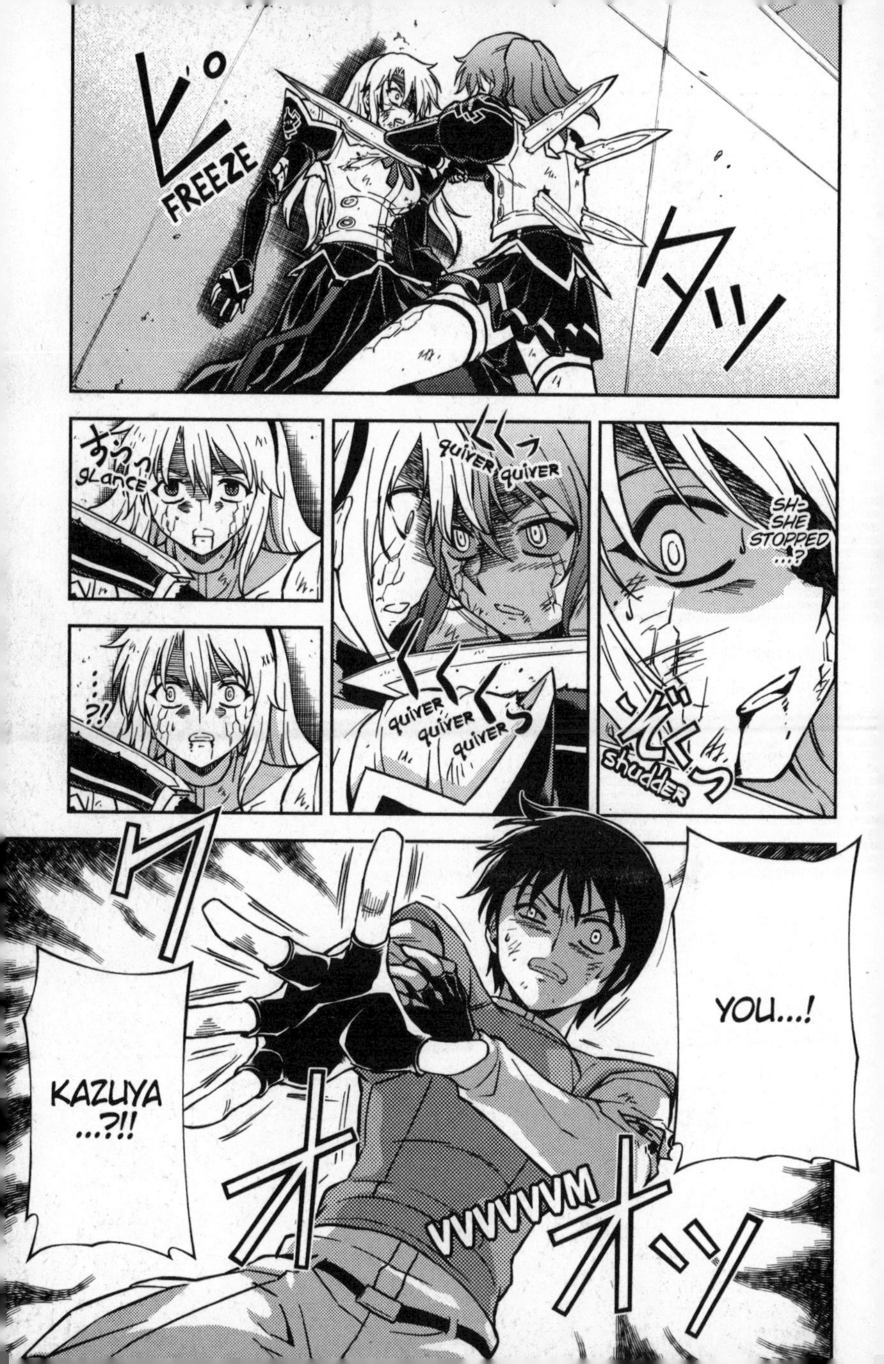
FREEZE
SH-SHE STOPPED ...?
shudder
quiver quiver
quiver quiver quiver
glance
...?!
YOU...!
KAZUYA ...?!!
VVVVVVM

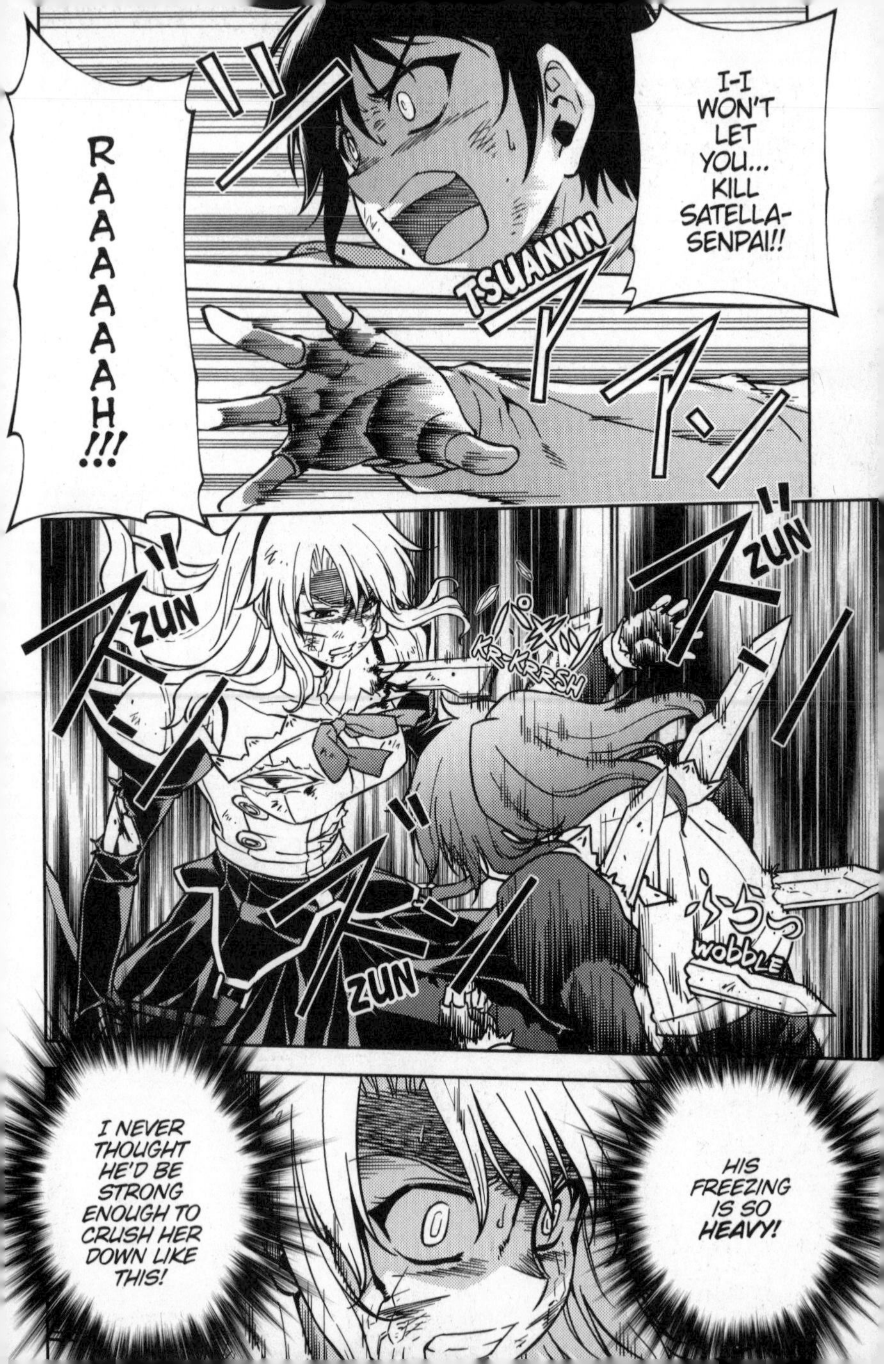

I-I WON'T LET YOU... KILL SATELLA-SENPAI!!
RAAAAAAH!!!
TSUANNN
ZUN
ZUN
KR-KRRSH
wobble
ZUN
HIS FREEZING IS SO HEAVY!
I NEVER THOUGHT HE'D BE STRONG ENOUGH TO CRUSH HER DOWN LIKE THIS!

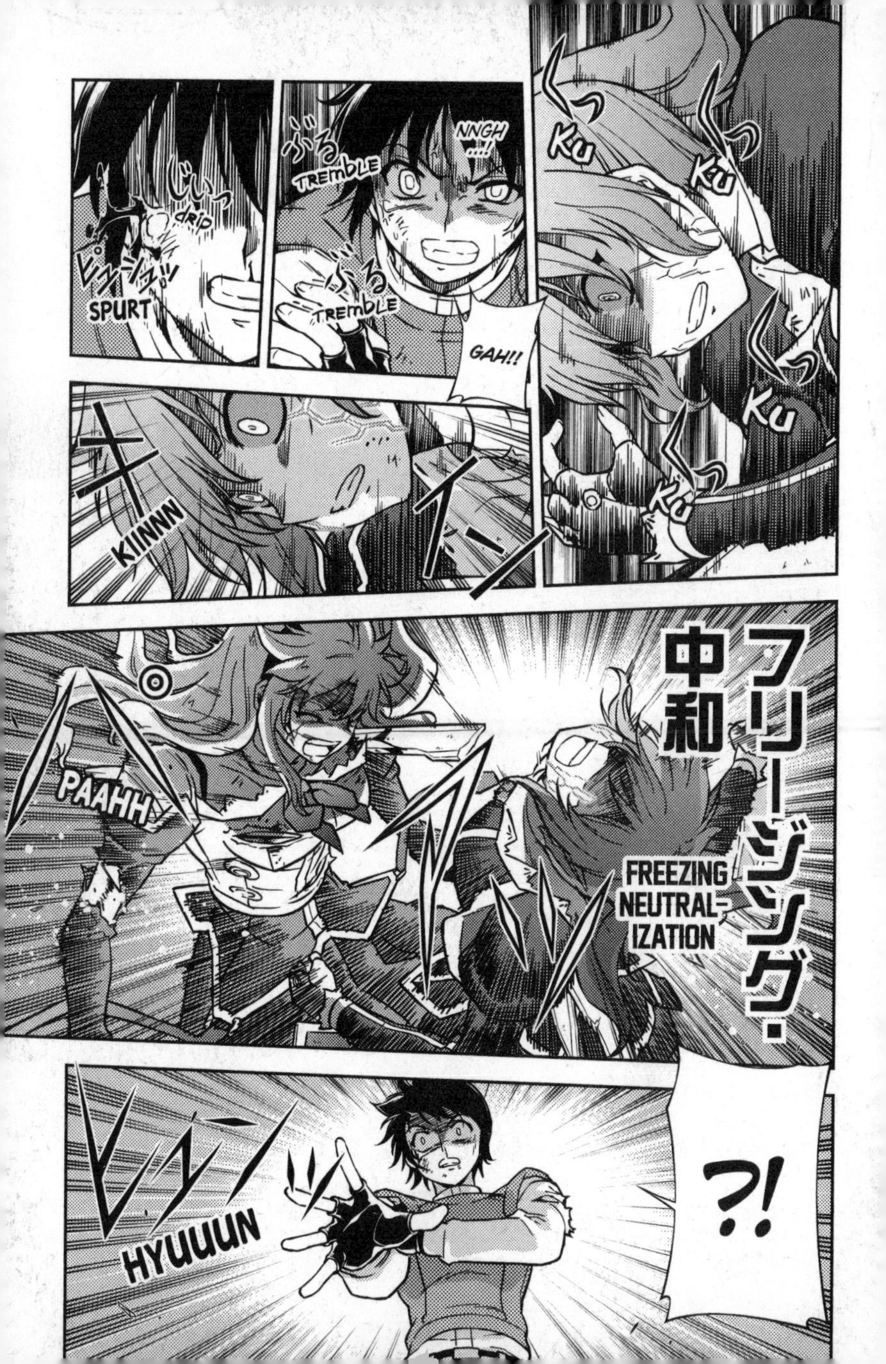

Ku
Ku
Ku
Ku
NNGH ...!!
ぶる
TREMBLE
ぶる
TREMBLE
GAH!!
drip
SPURT
KIINNN
フリージング・中和
FREEZING NEUTRALIZATION
PAAHH
?!
HYUUUN

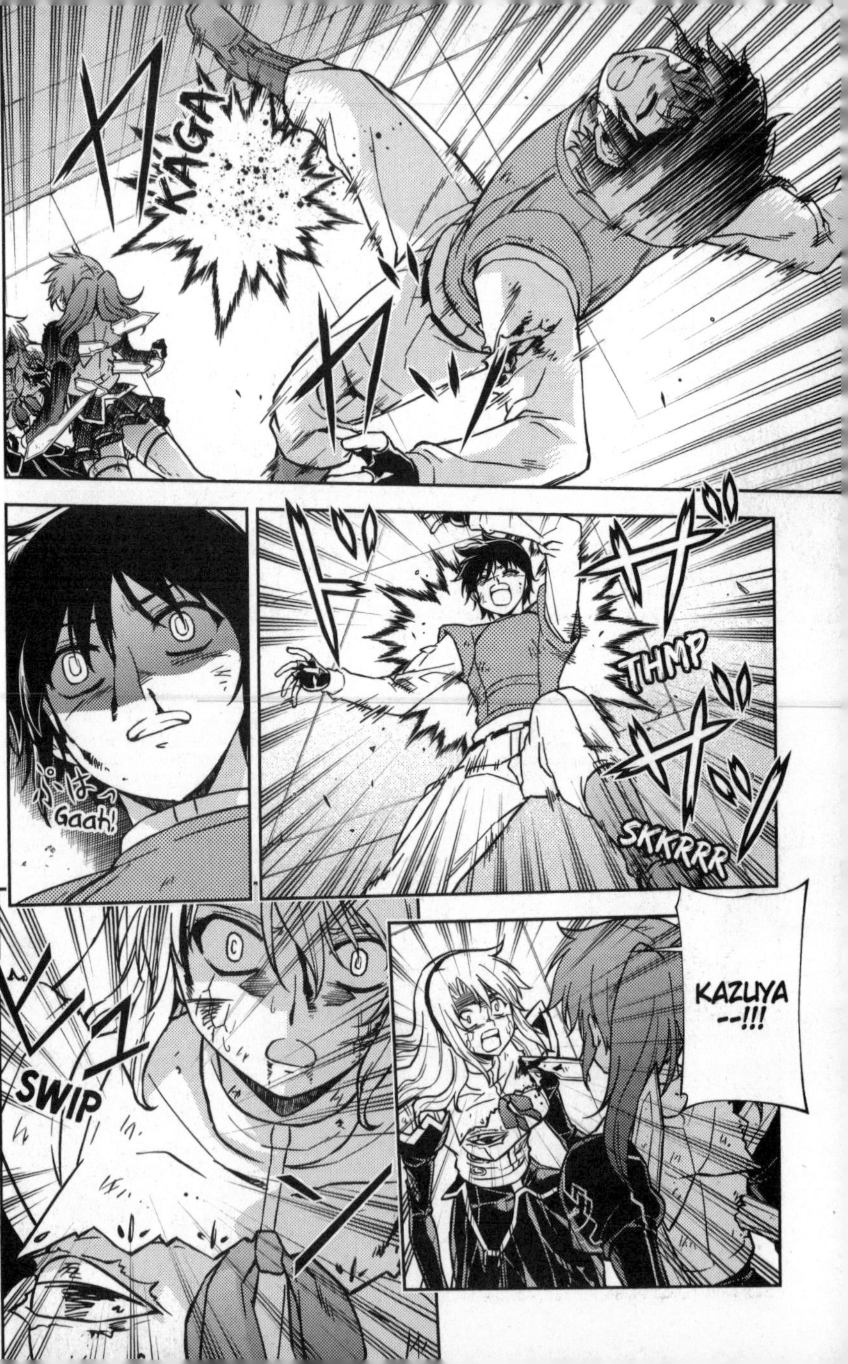
KAGA!
THMP
SKKRRR
ぷはっ
Gaah!
KAZUYA --!!!
SWIP

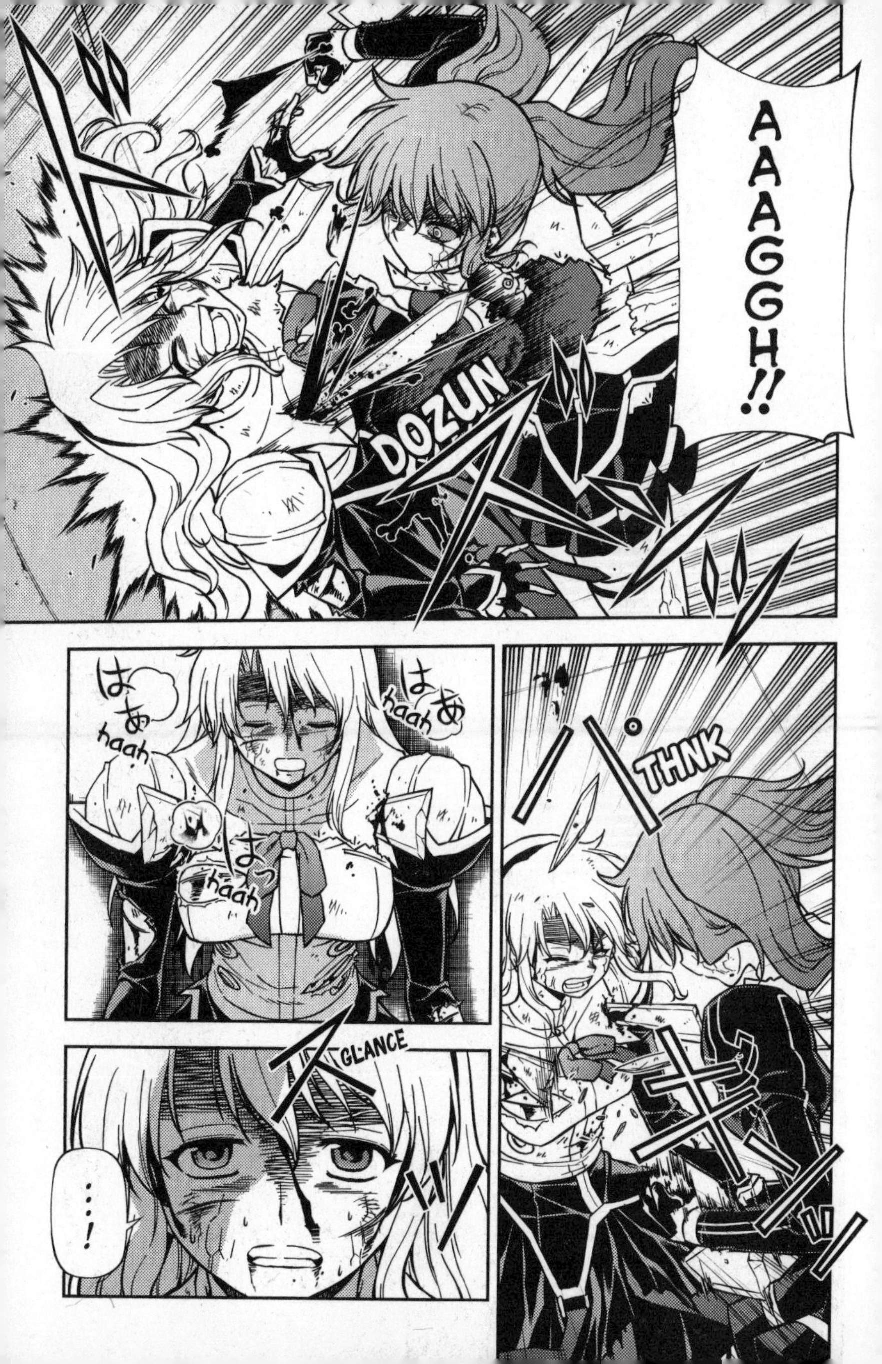
AAAGGGH!!
DOZUN
THNK
はぁ haah
はぁ haah
はっ haah
GLANCE
...!

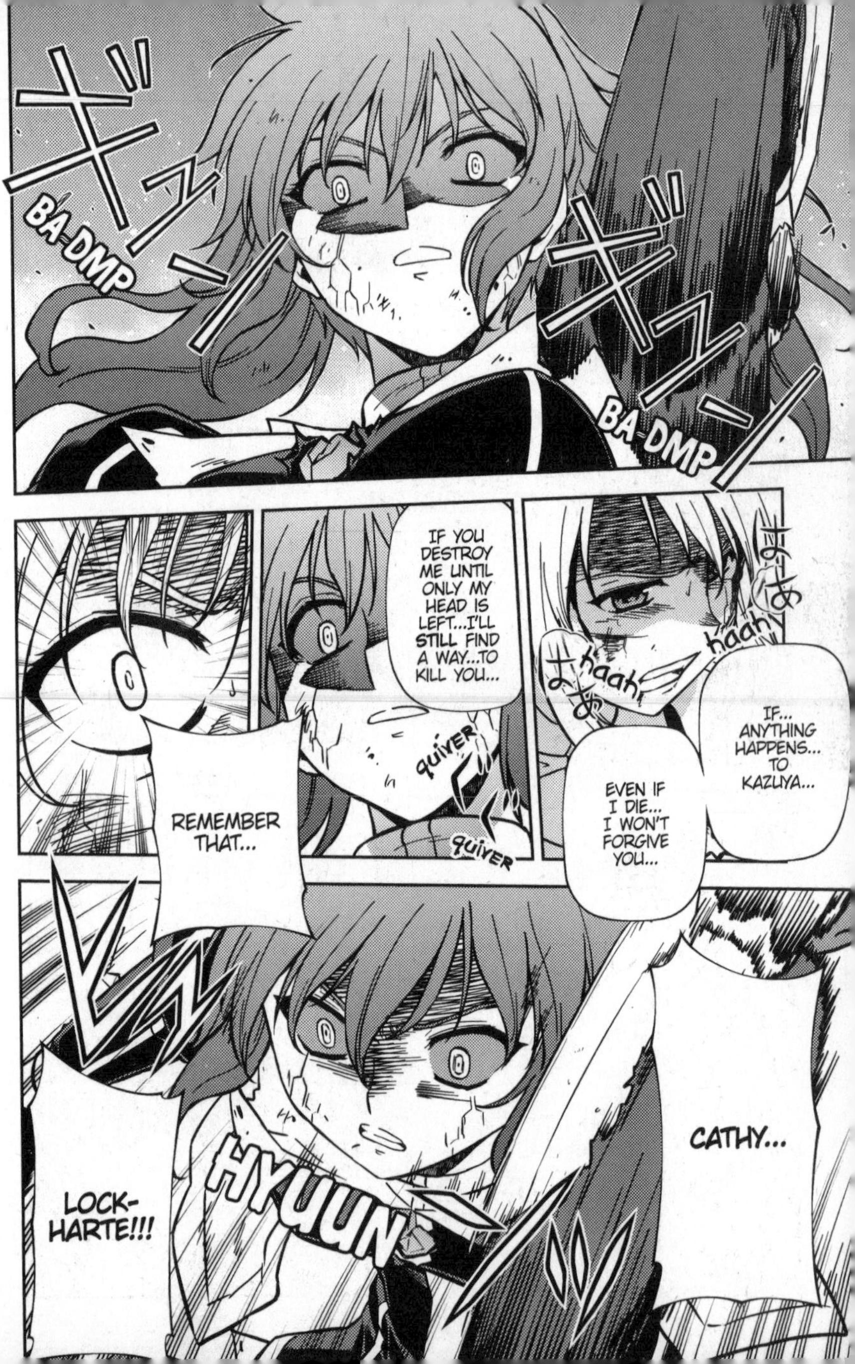
BA-DMP
BA-DMP
haah
haah
IF... ANYTHING HAPPENS... TO KAZUYA...
EVEN IF I DIE... I WON'T FORGIVE YOU...
IF YOU DESTROY ME UNTIL ONLY MY HEAD IS LEFT...I'LL STILL FIND A WAY...TO KILL YOU...
quiver
quiver
REMEMBER THAT...
CATHY...
HYUUN
LOCK-HARTE!!!

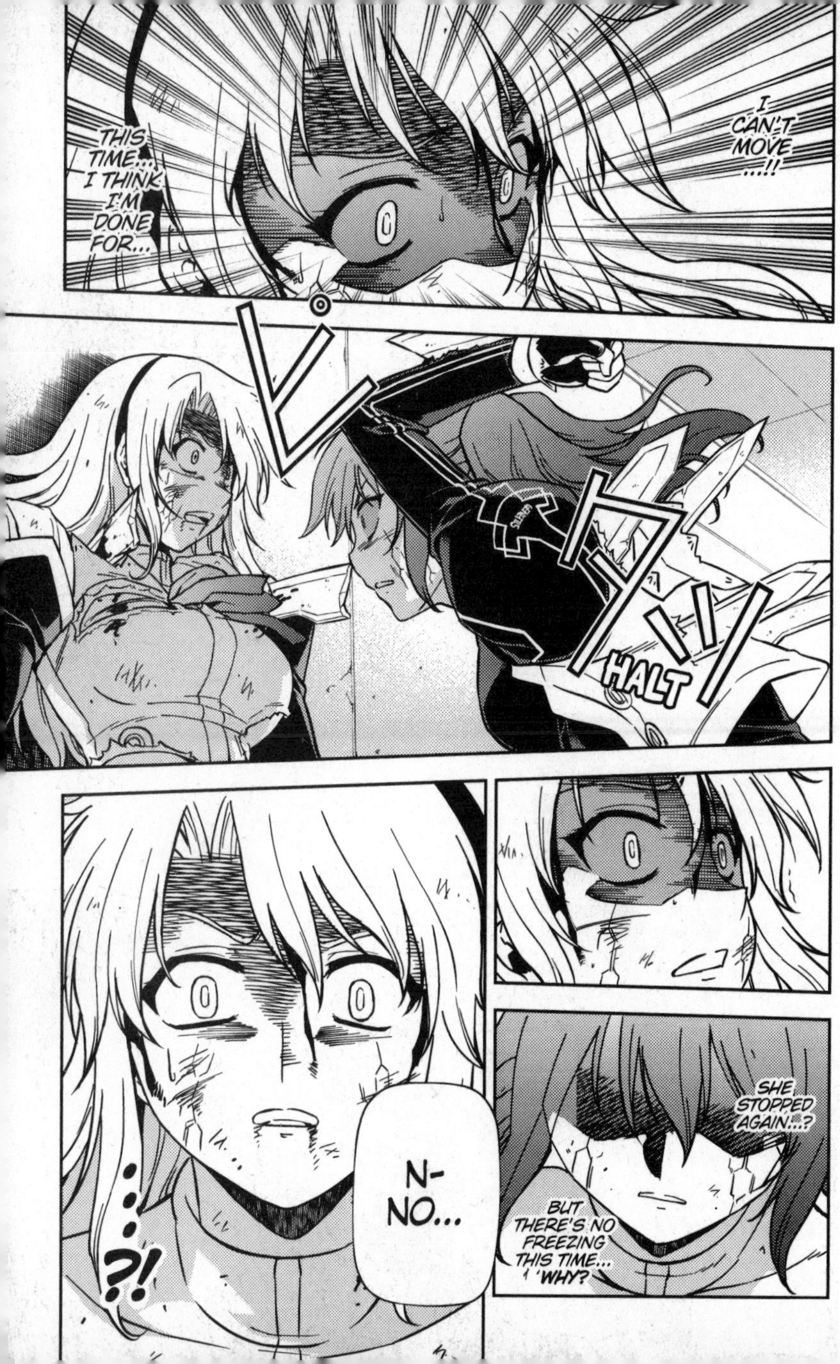
I CAN'T MOVE...!!
THIS TIME... I THINK I'M DONE FOR...
HALT
SHE STOPPED AGAIN...?
BUT THERE'S NO FREEZING THIS TIME... WHY?
N- NO...
...?!

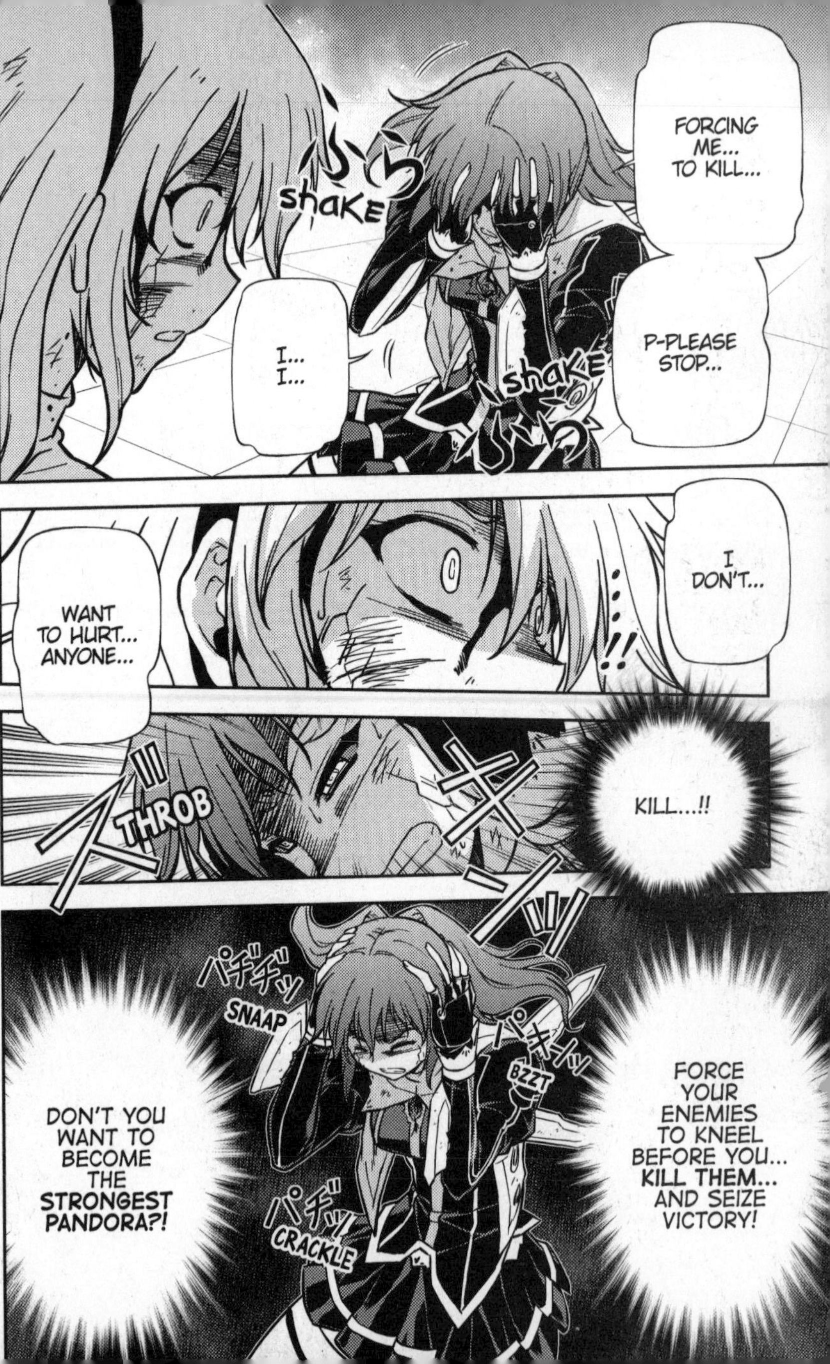
FORCING ME... TO KILL...
shake
P-PLEASE STOP...
shake
I... I...
I DON'T...
...!!
WANT TO HURT... ANYONE...
KILL...!!
THROB
FORCE YOUR ENEMIES TO KNEEL BEFORE YOU... **KILL THEM...** AND SEIZE VICTORY!
BZZT
SNAAP
DON'T YOU WANT TO BECOME THE **STRONGEST PANDORA**?!
CRACKLE

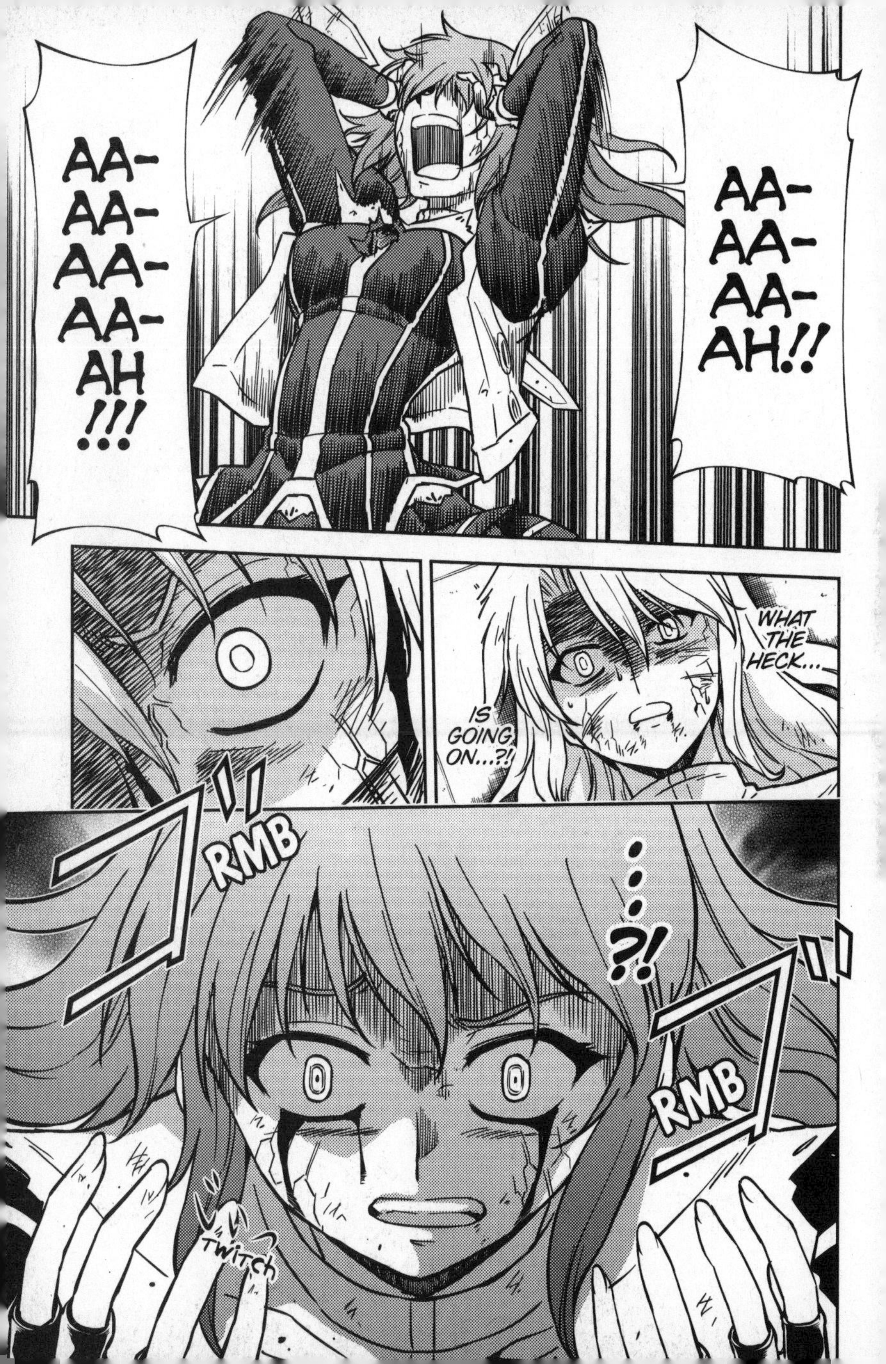
AA- AA- AA- AH!!
AA- AA- AA- AA- AH !!!
WHAT THE HECK...
IS GOING ON...?!
...?!
RMB
RMB
TWITCH

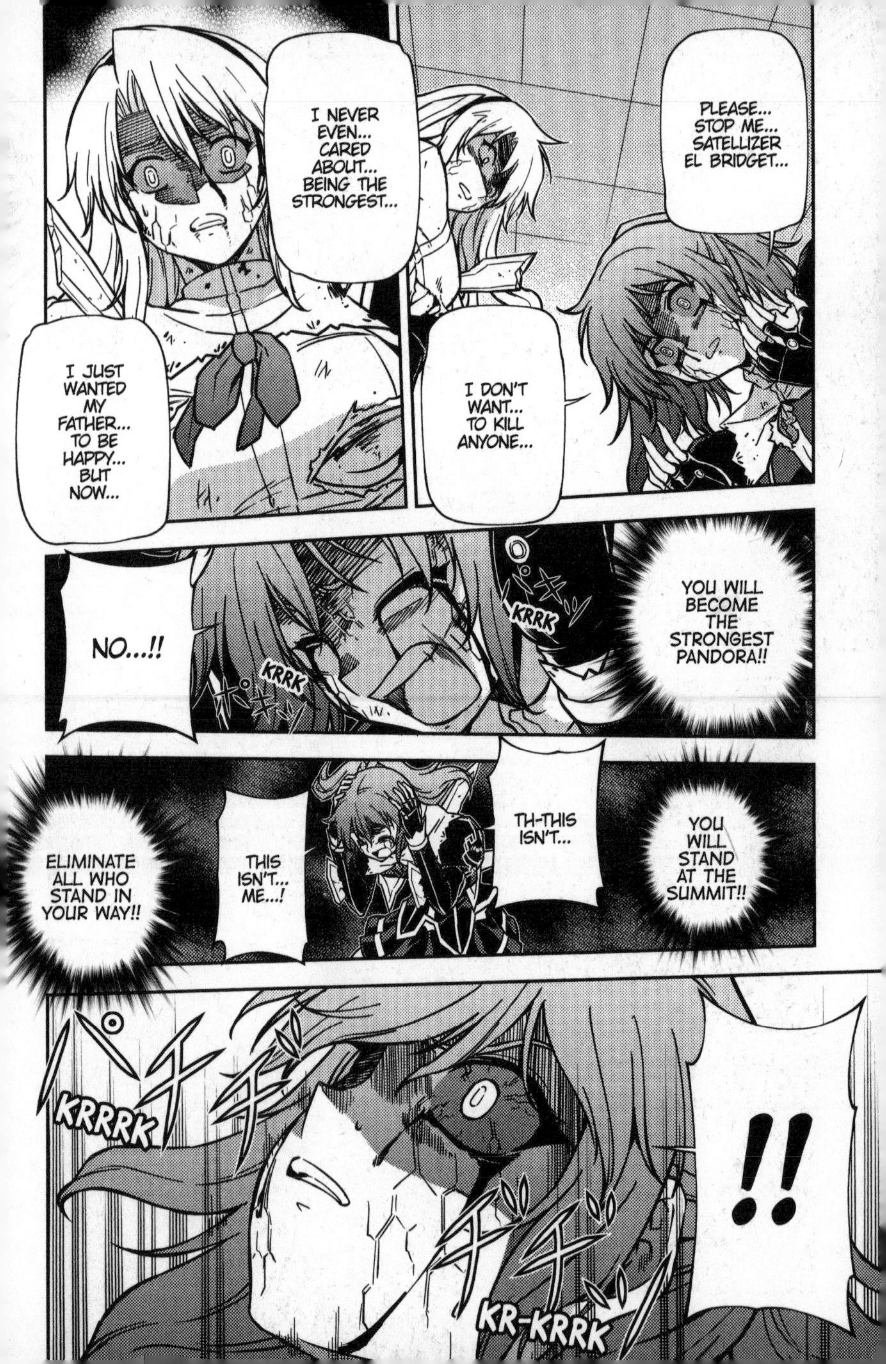

PLEASE... STOP ME... SATELLIZER EL BRIDGET...
I DON'T WANT... TO KILL ANYONE...
I NEVER EVEN... CARED ABOUT... BEING THE STRONGEST...
I JUST WANTED MY FATHER... TO BE HAPPY... BUT NOW...
YOU WILL BECOME THE STRONGEST PANDORA!!
KRRK
KRRK
NO...!!
YOU WILL STAND AT THE SUMMIT!!
TH-THIS ISN'T...
THIS ISN'T... ME...!
ELIMINATE ALL WHO STAND IN YOUR WAY!!
!!
KRRRK
KR-KRRK

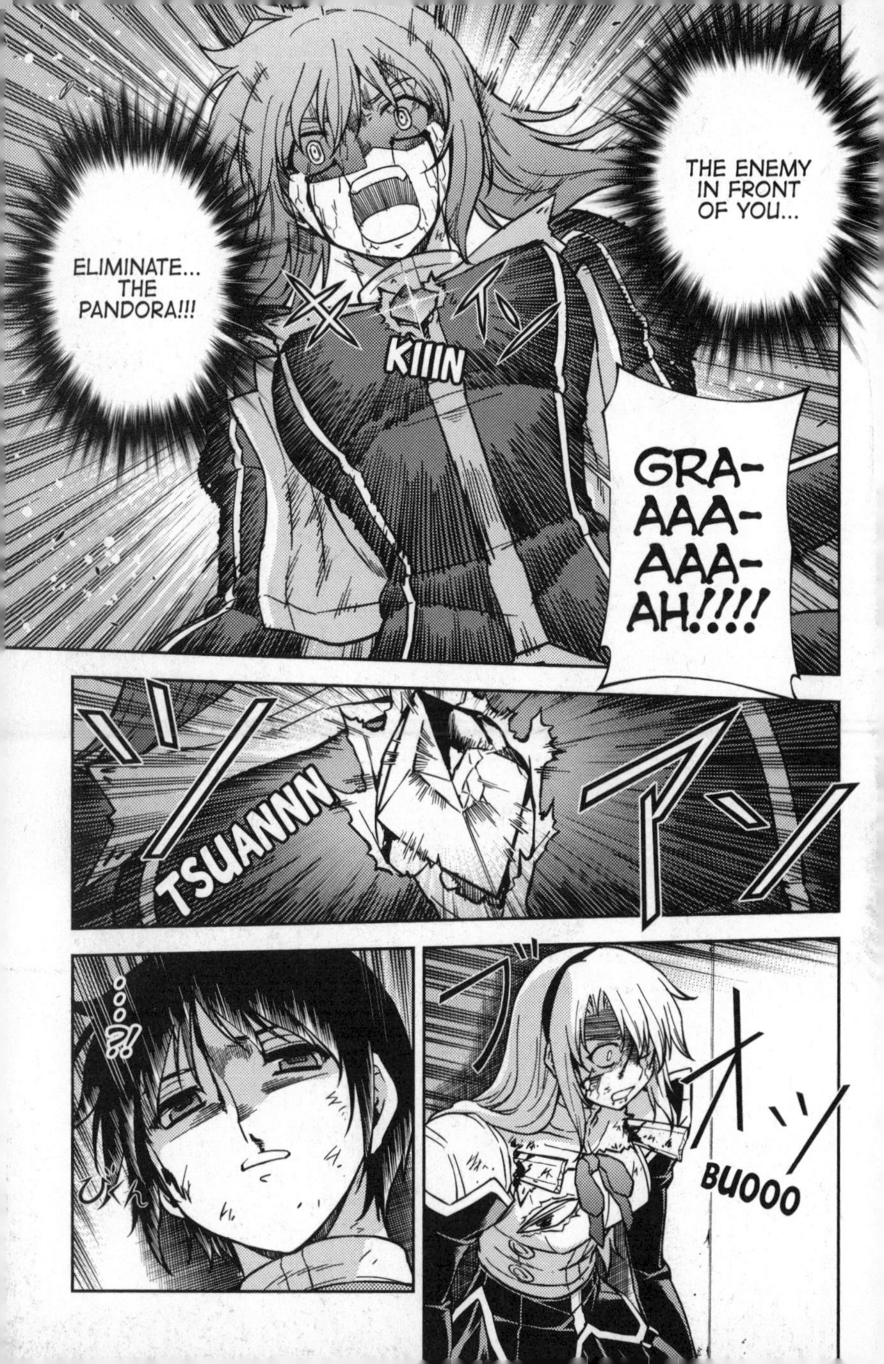
THE ENEMY IN FRONT OF YOU...
ELIMINATE... THE PANDORA!!!
KIIIN
GRA-AAA-AAA-AH!!!!!
TSUANNN
BUOOO
ooo?!

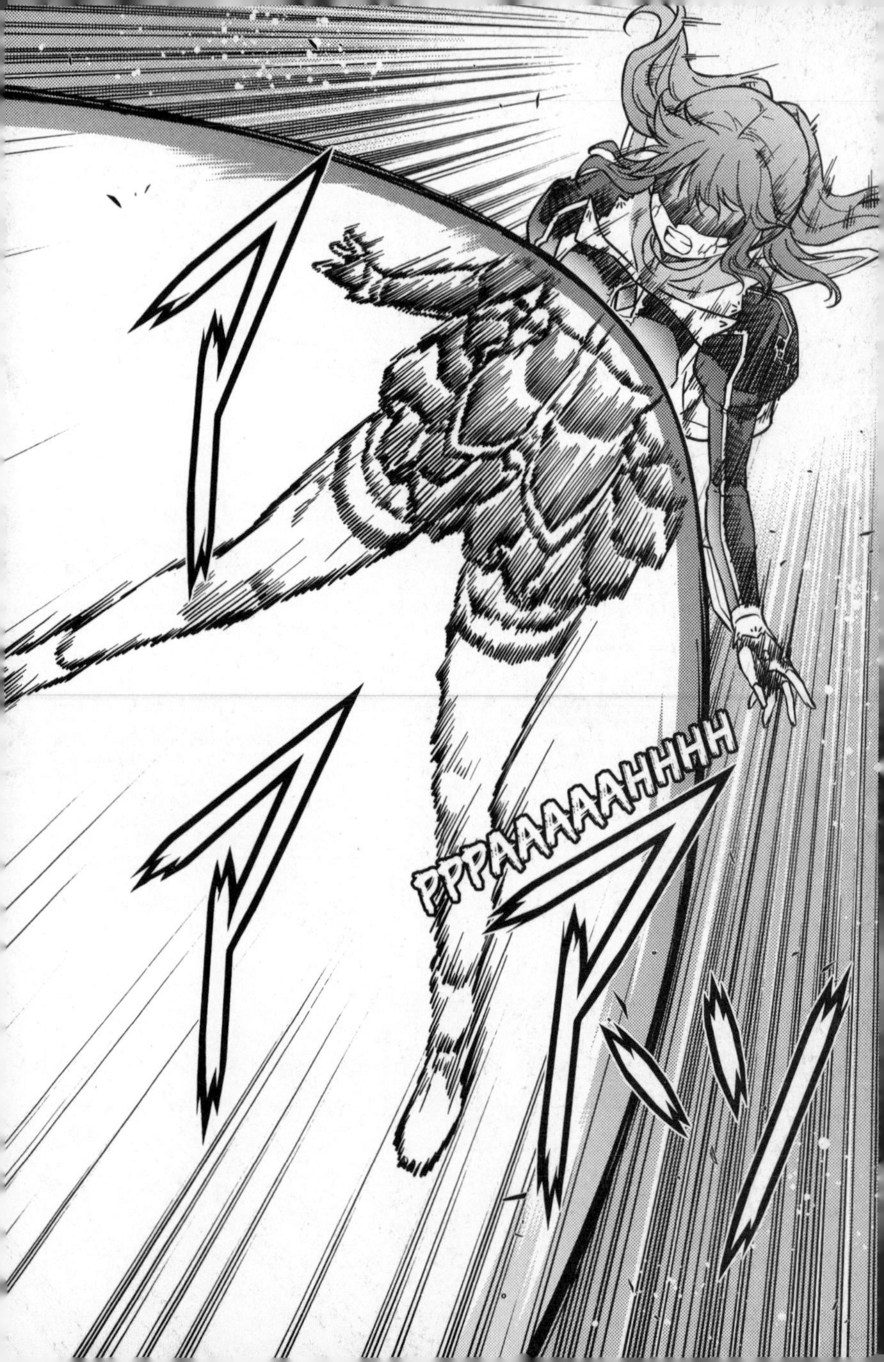
PPPAAAAAAHHHH

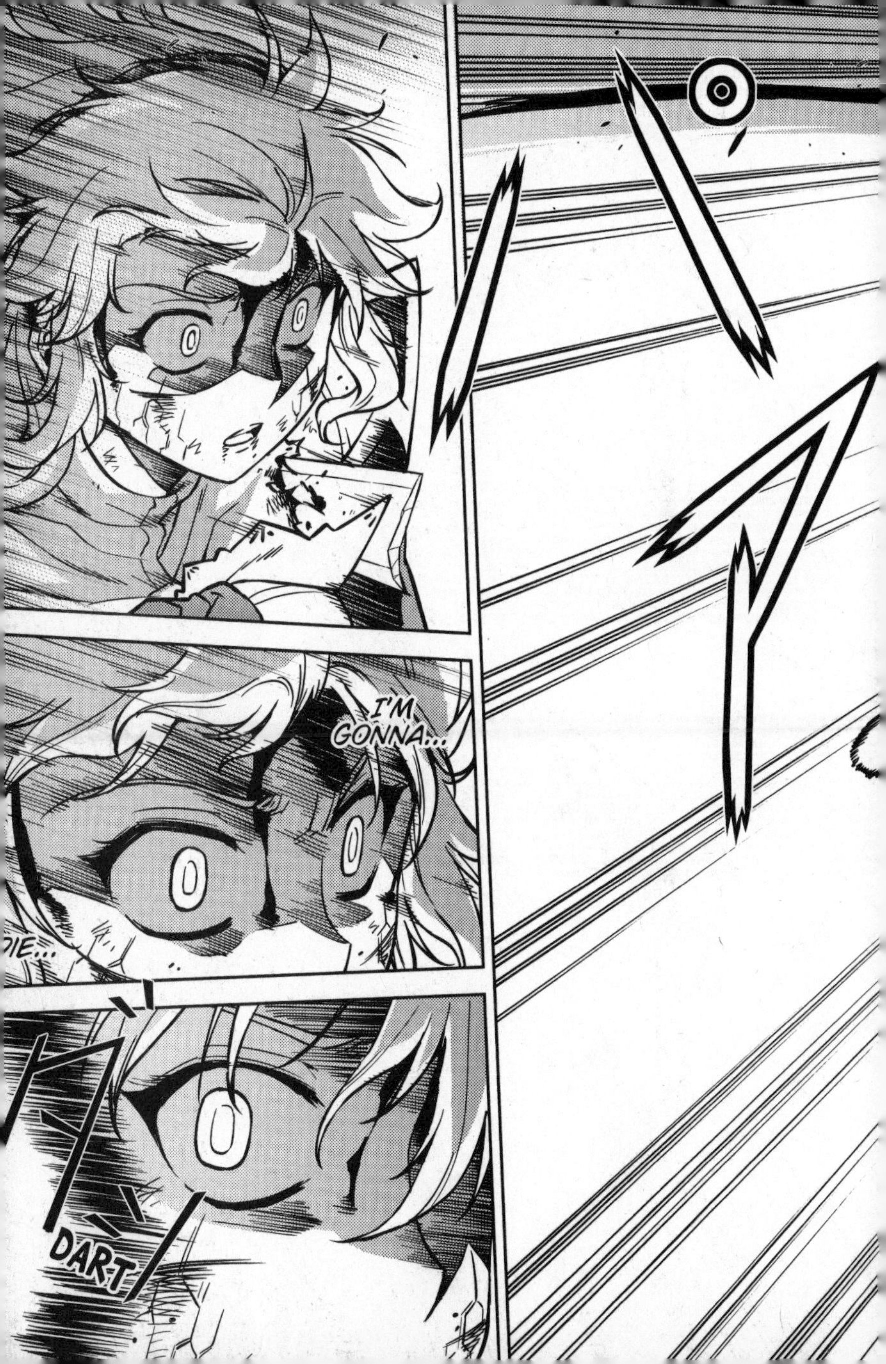
I'M GONNA...
DIE...
DART

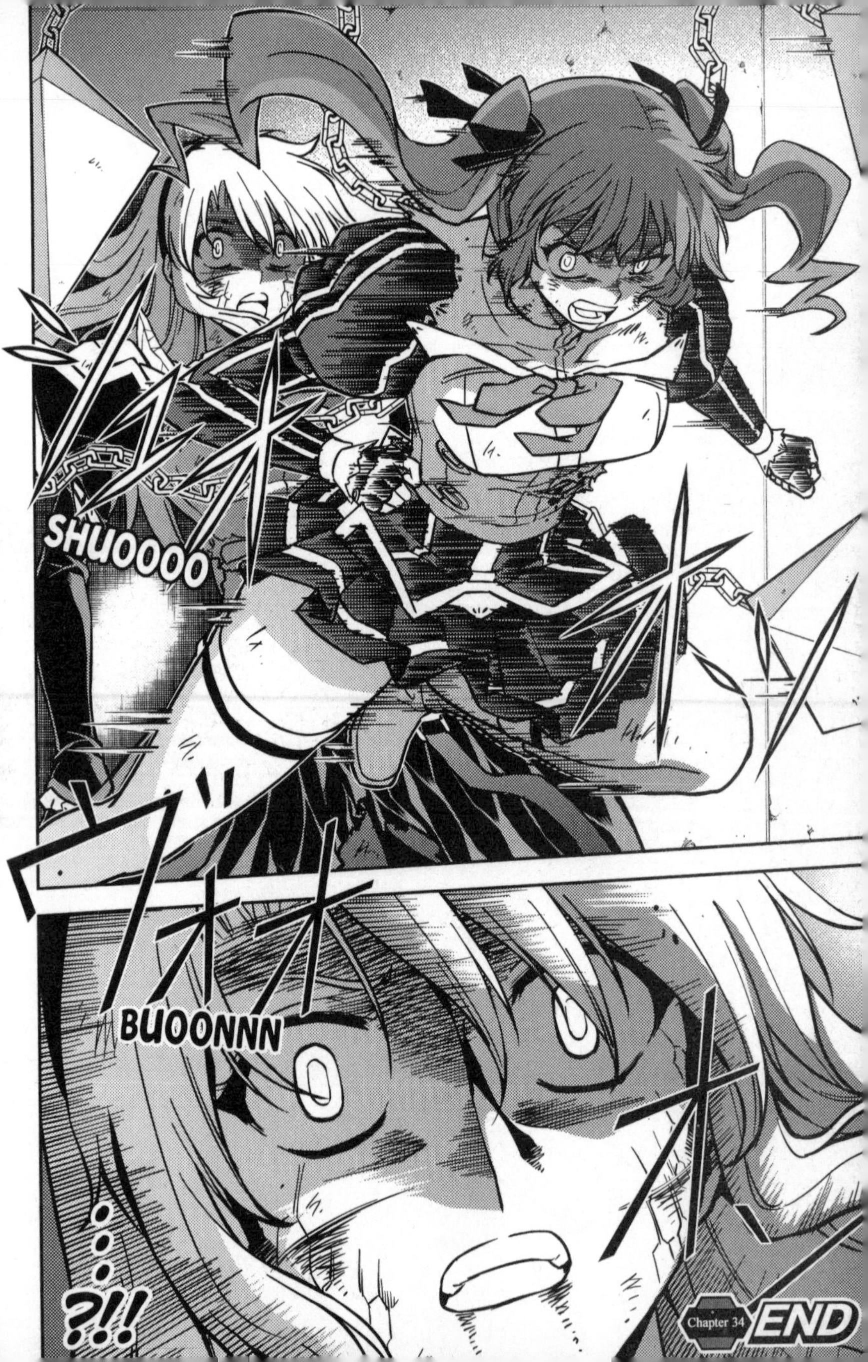
SHUOOOO
BUOONNN
...?!!
Chapter 34 END

FREEZING VOLUME.6
HIGHLIGHT SCENE

FREEZING Vol.6

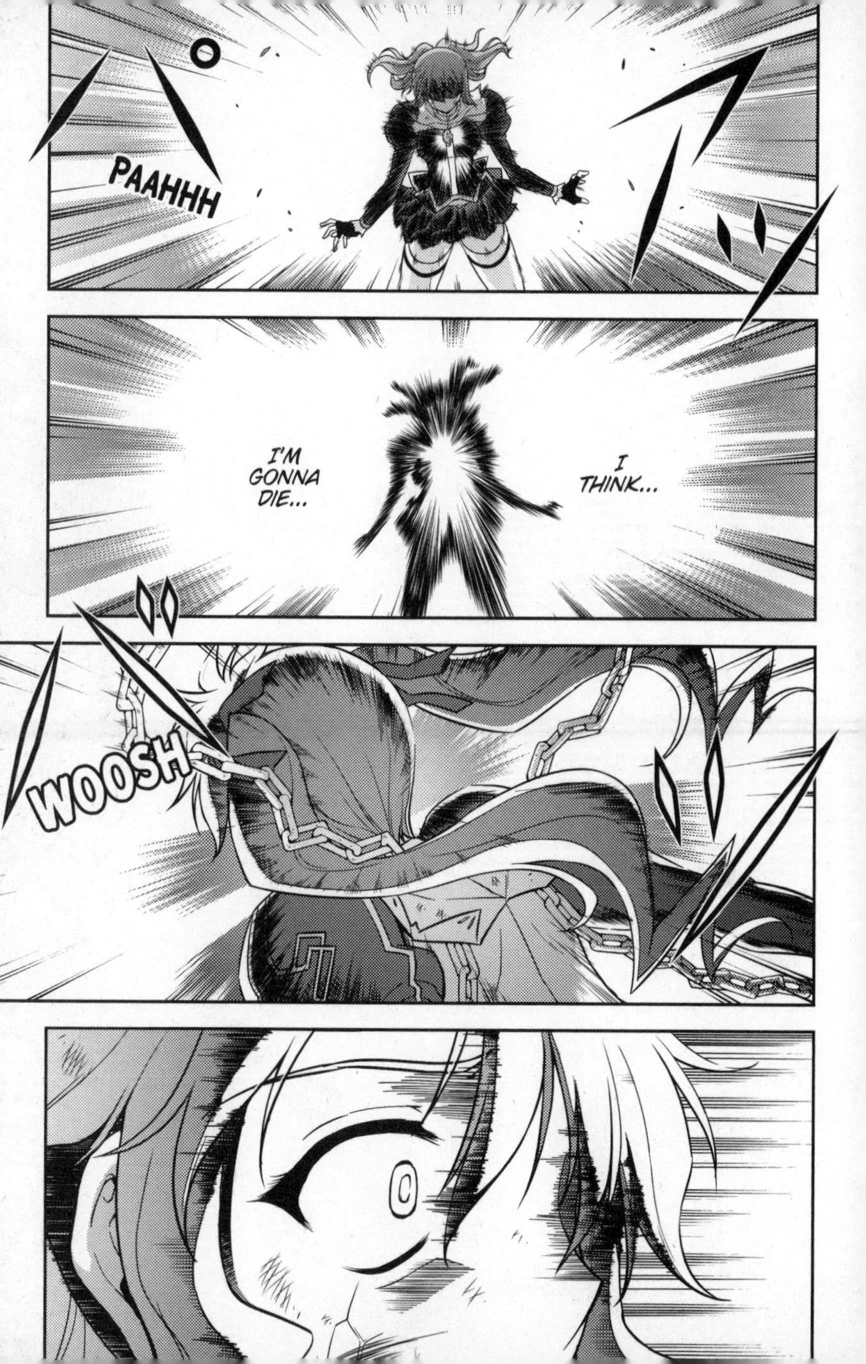
PAAHHH
I THINK...
I'M GONNA DIE...
WOOSH

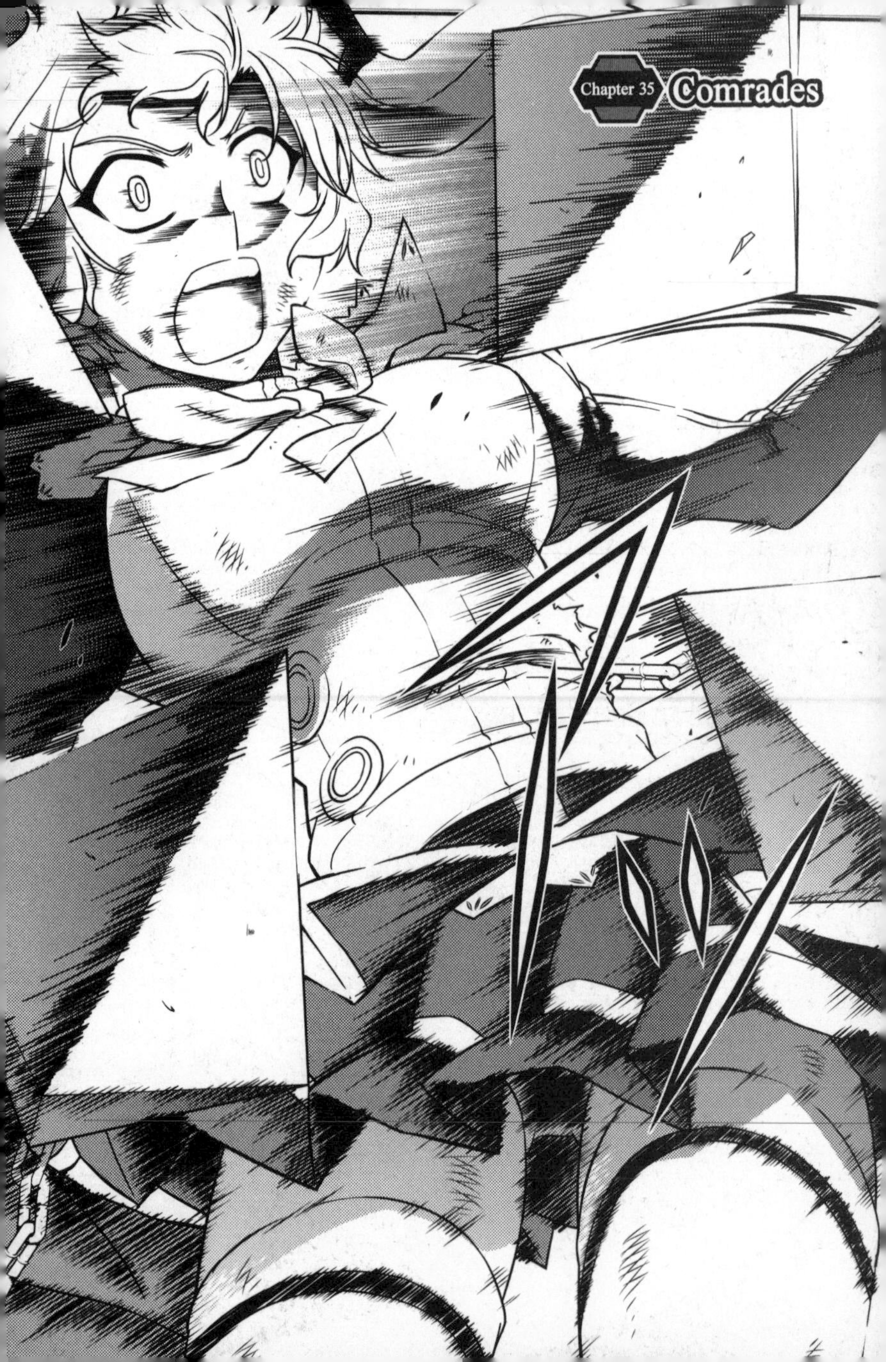
Chapter 35 Comrades

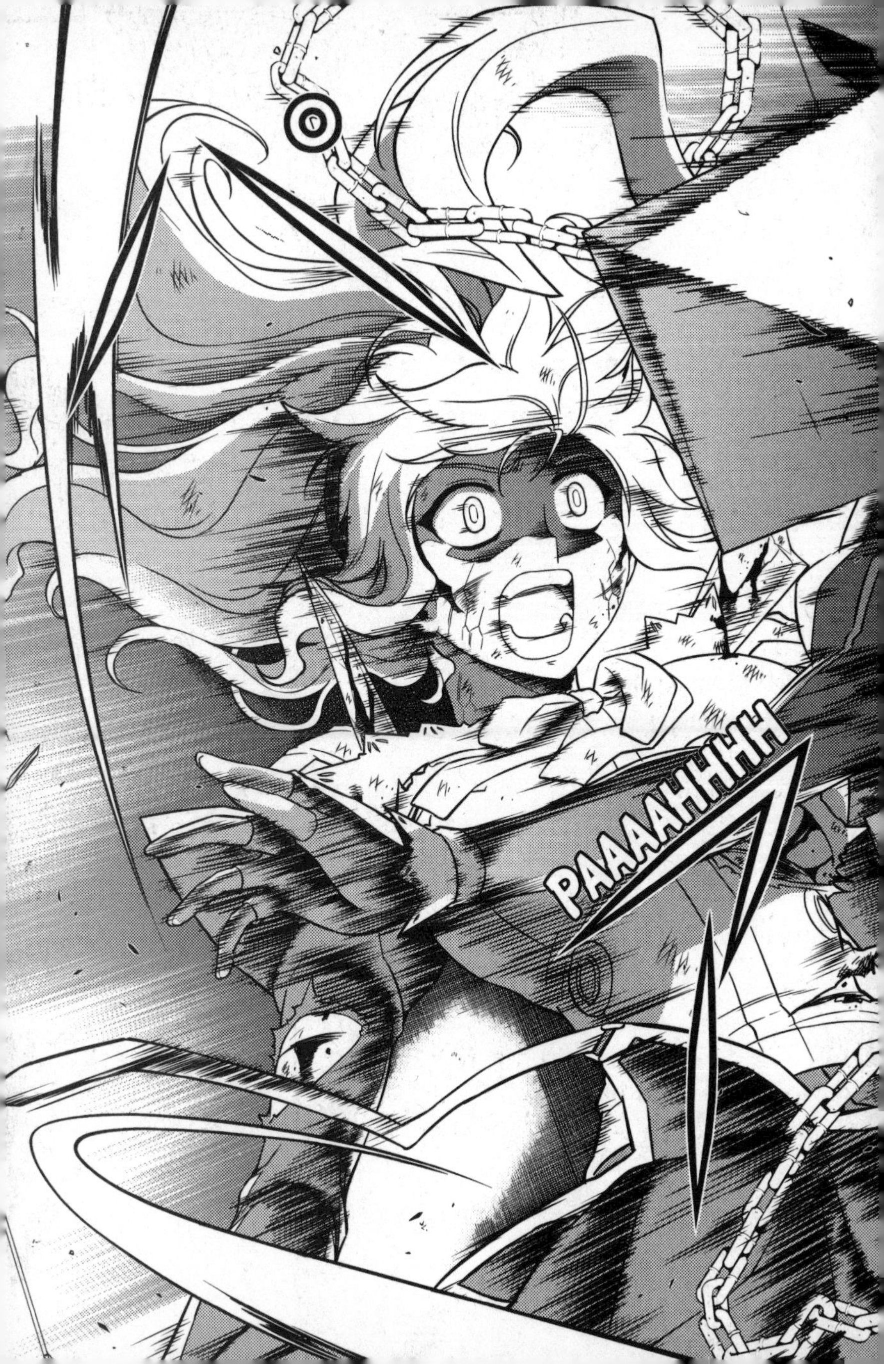
PAAAAHHHH

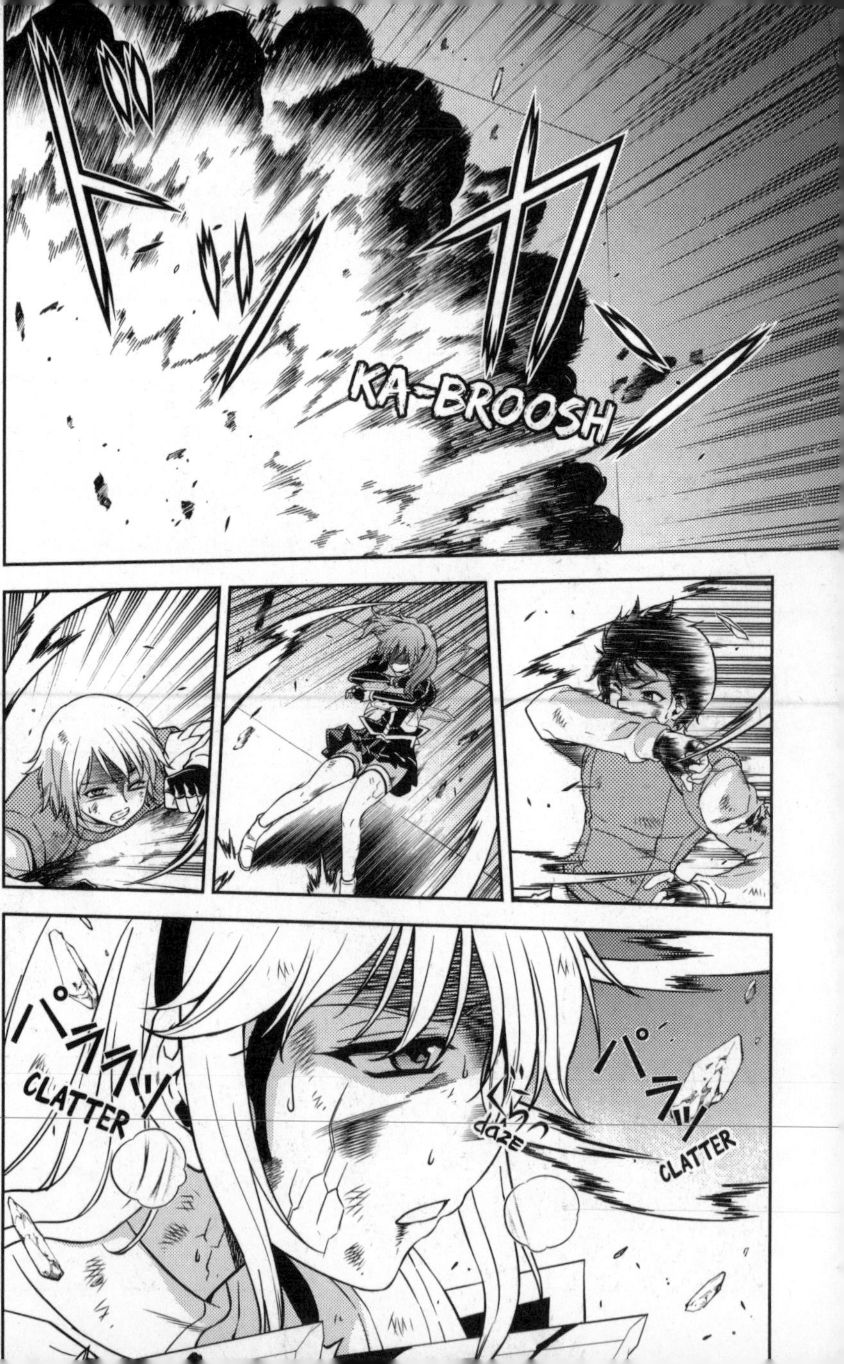
KA-BROOSH
CLATTER
daze
CLATTER

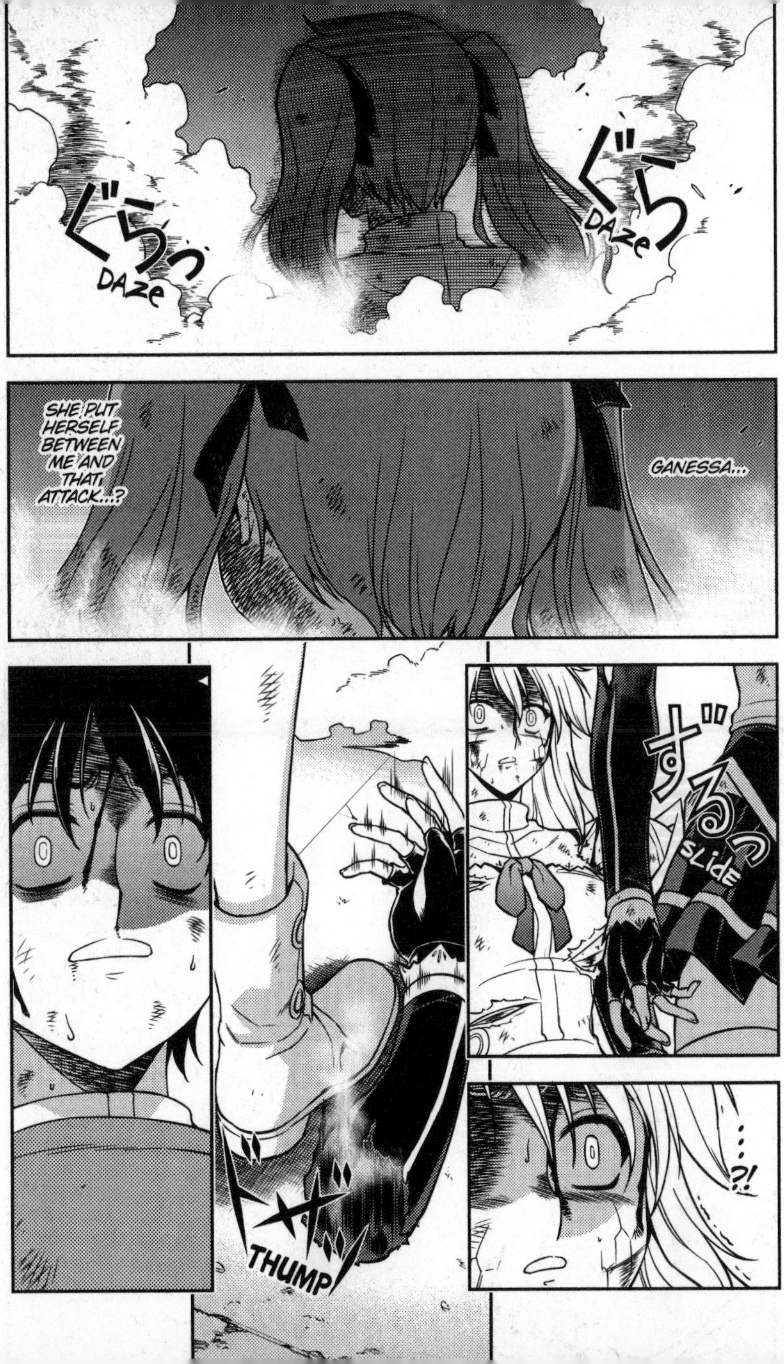
ぐら
DAZE
ぐらっ
DAZE
GANESSA...
SHE PUT HERSELF BETWEEN ME AND THAT ATTACK...?
ずるっ
SLIDE
...?!
ドザッ
THUMP

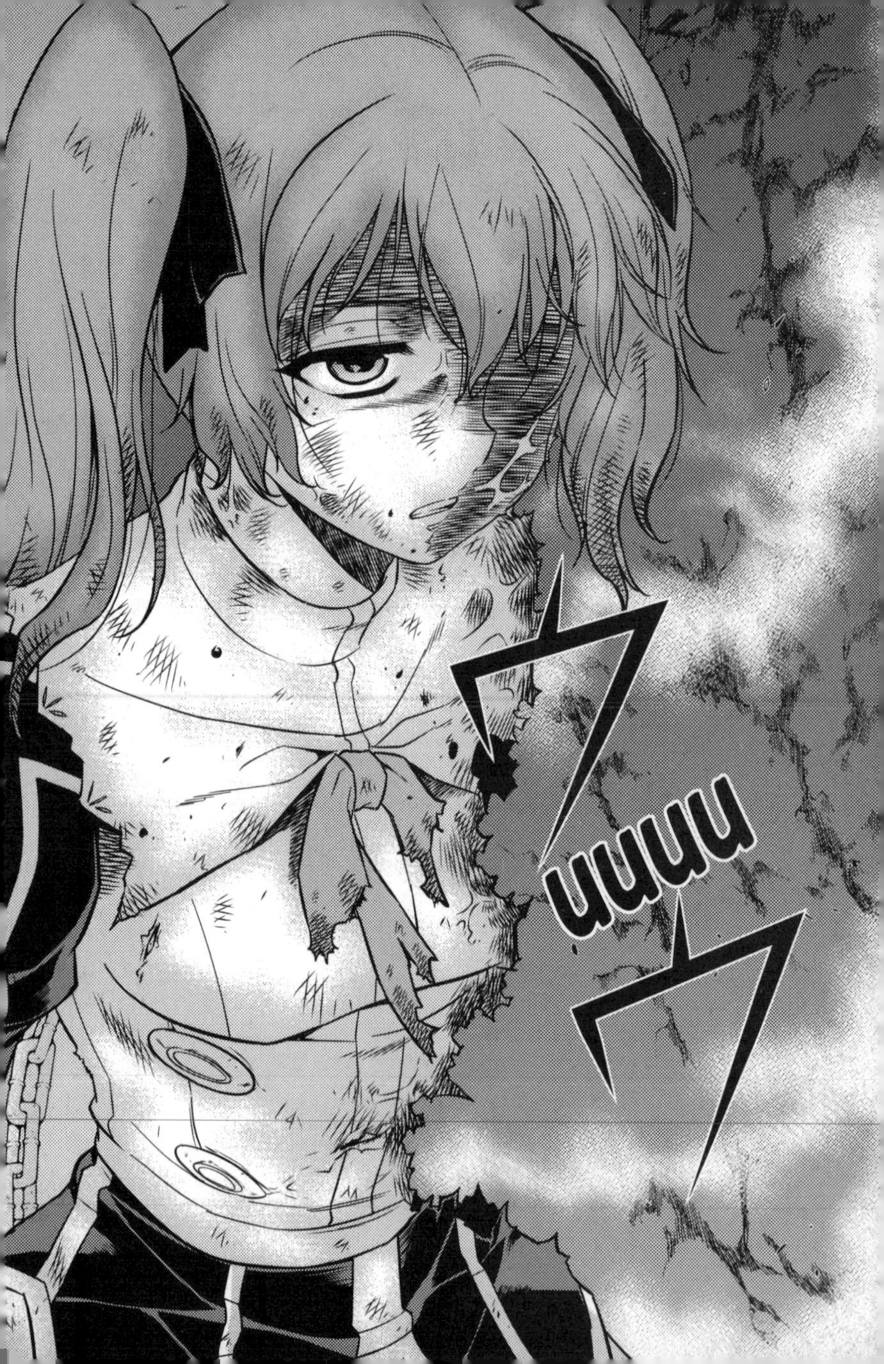
UUUUU

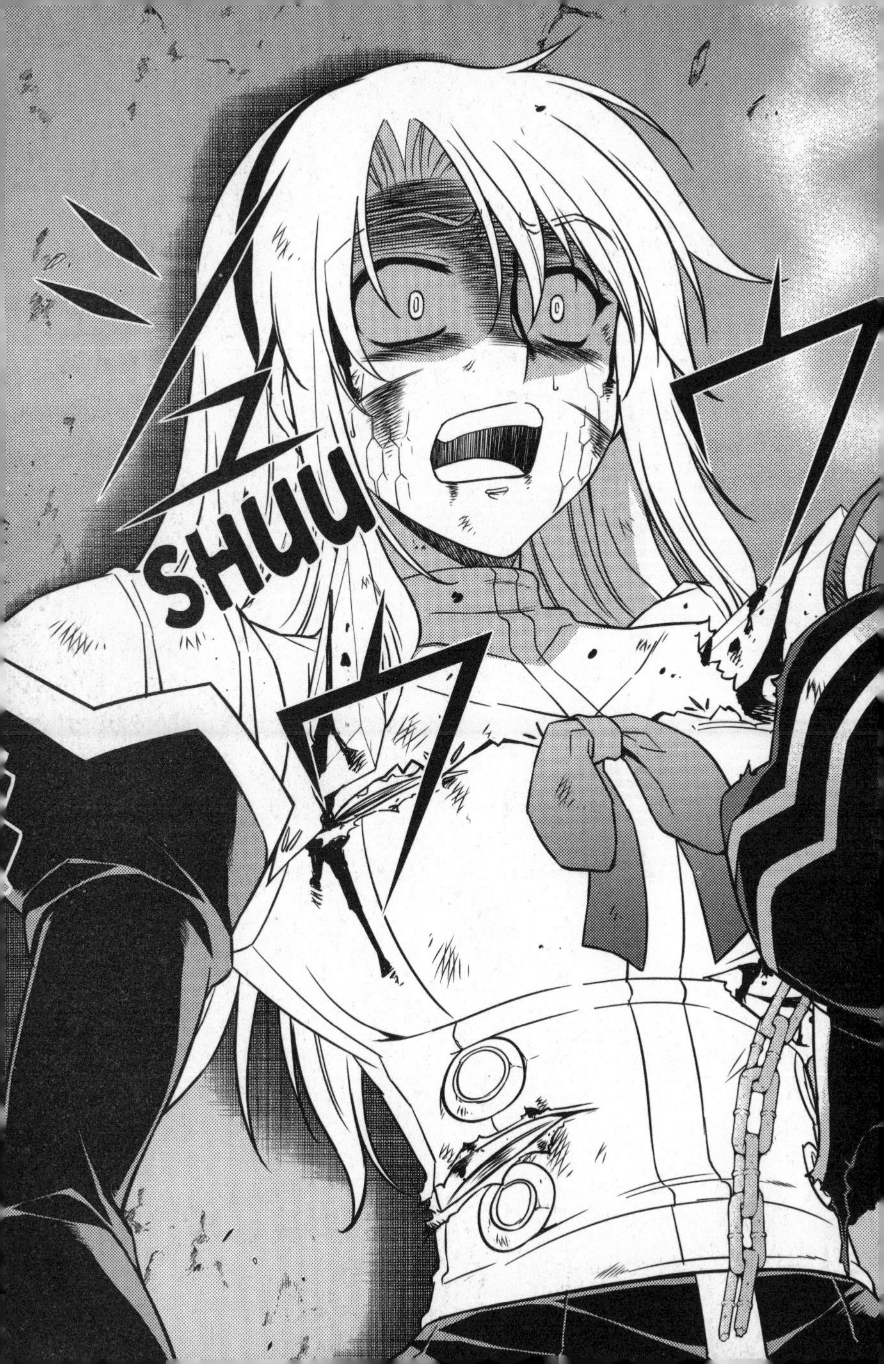
SHUU

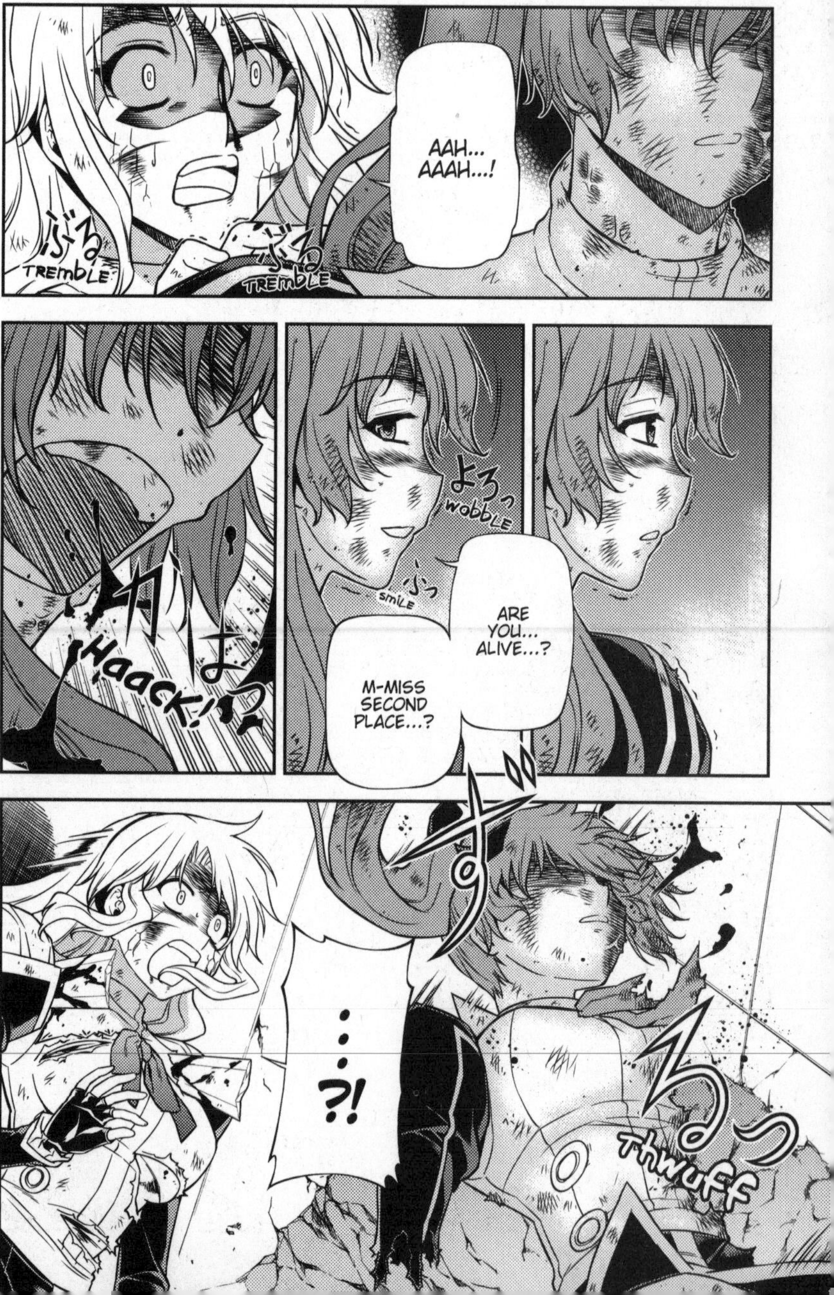
AAH... AAAH...!
ぶる TREMBLE
ぶる TREMBLE
ARE YOU... ALIVE...?
M-MISS SECOND PLACE...?
よろっ WOBBLE
ふっ SMILE
がはっ Haaack!!?
...?!
Thwuff

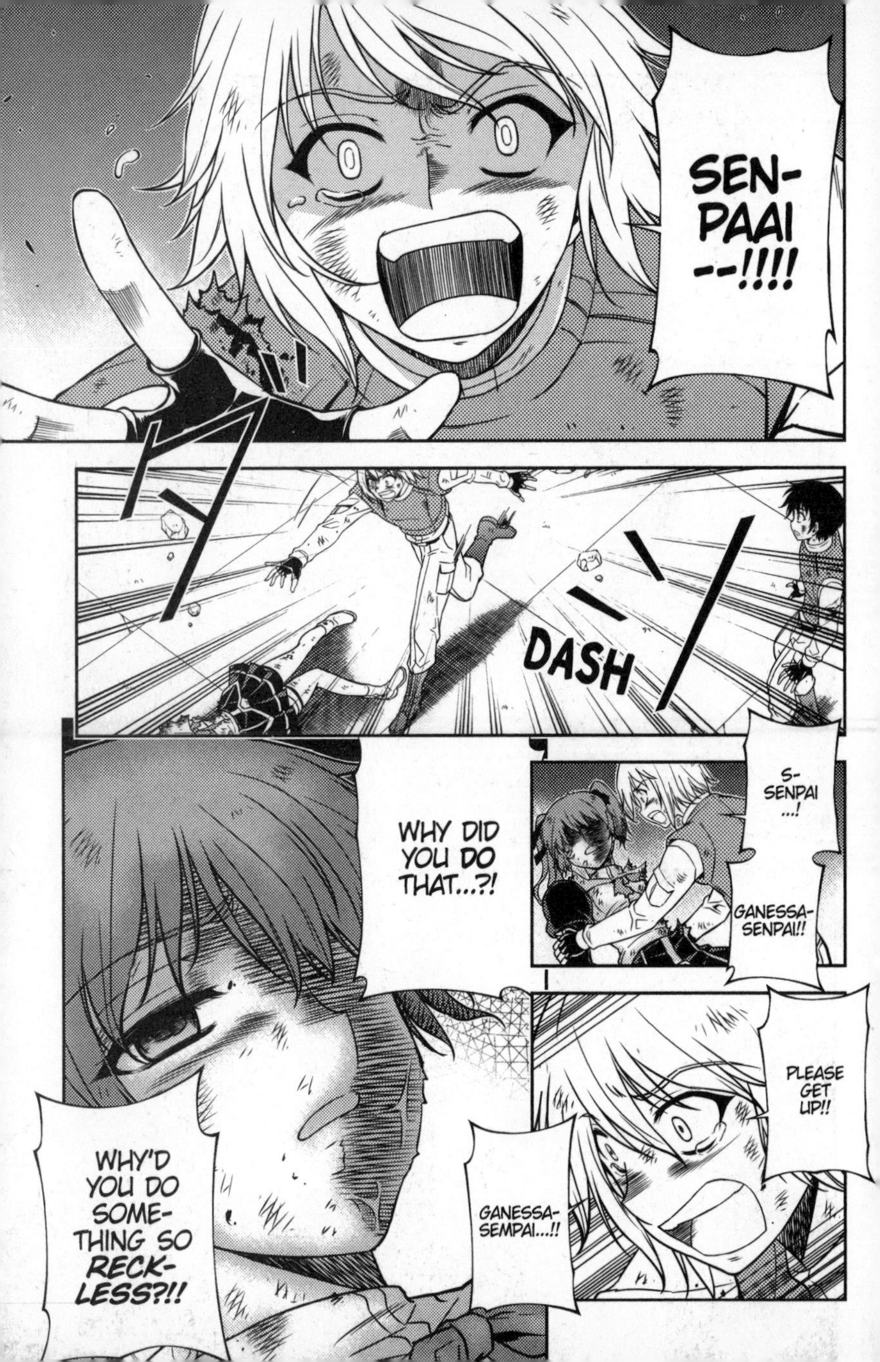
SEN-PAAI --!!!!
DASH
S-SENPAI ...!
GANESSA-SENPAI!!
PLEASE GET UP!!
GANESSA-SEMPAI...!!
WHY DID YOU DO THAT...?!
WHY'D YOU DO SOME-THING SO RECK-LESS?!!

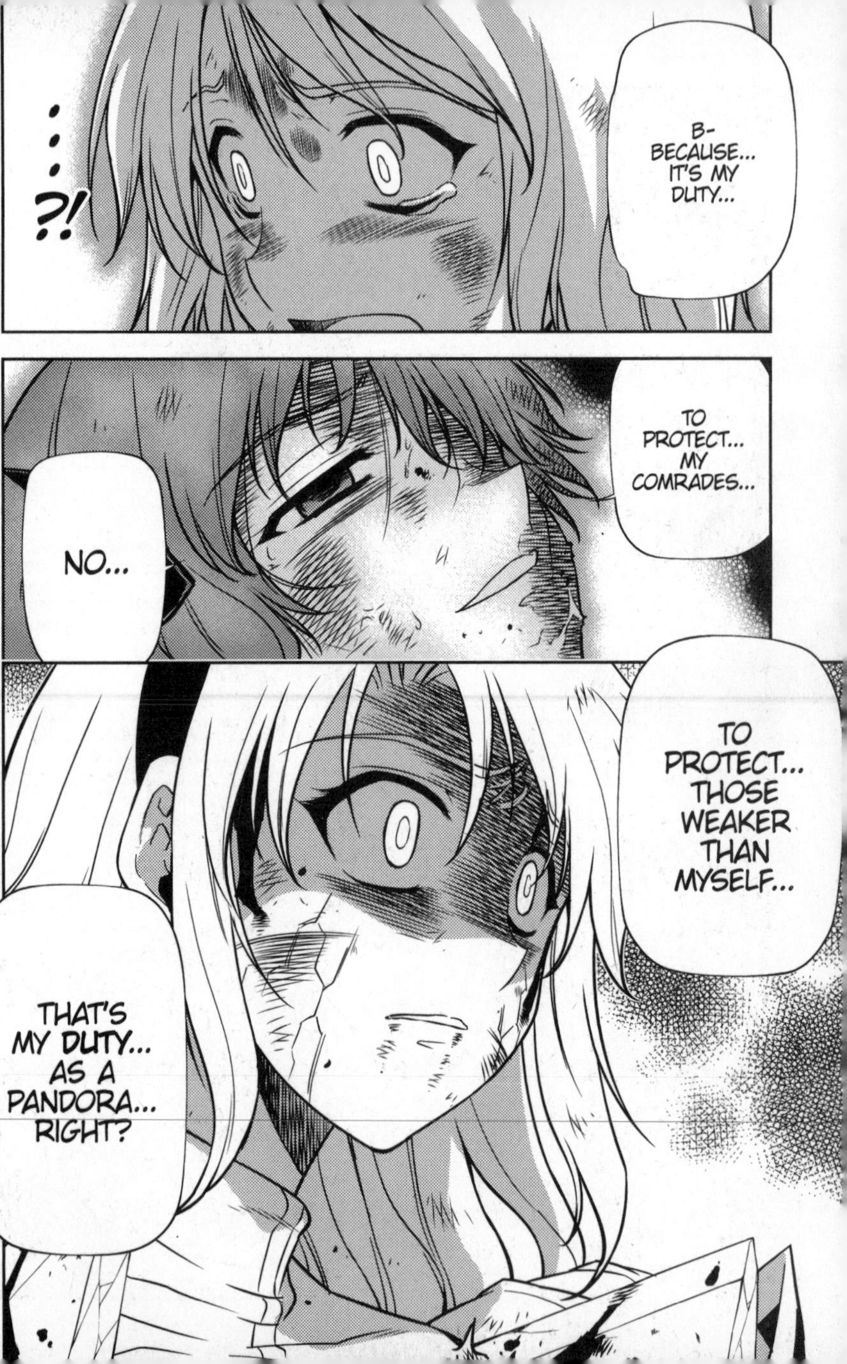
B-BECAUSE... IT'S MY DUTY...
...?!
TO PROTECT... MY COMRADES...
NO...
TO PROTECT... THOSE WEAKER THAN MYSELF...
THAT'S MY DUTY... AS A PANDORA... RIGHT?

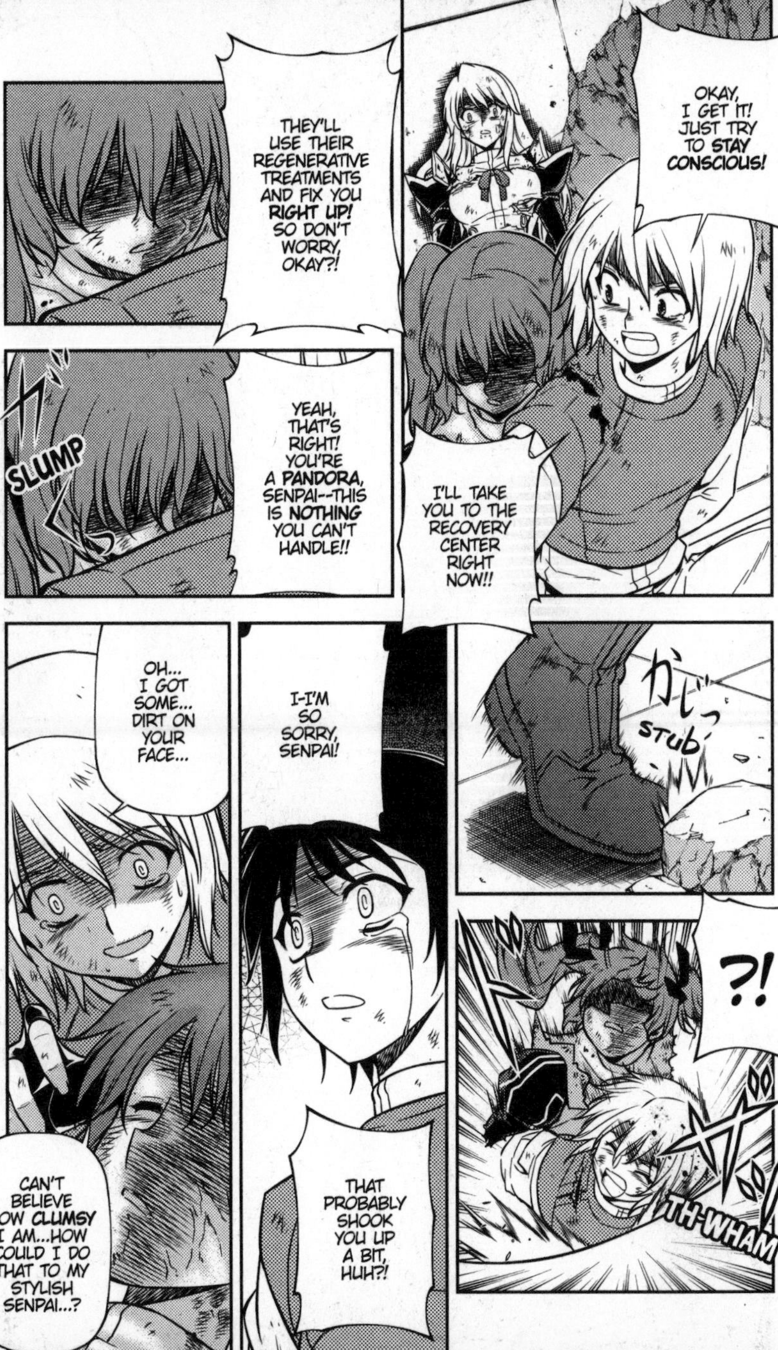
OKAY, I GET IT! JUST TRY TO STAY CONSCIOUS!
I'LL TAKE YOU TO THE RECOVERY CENTER RIGHT NOW!!
THEY'LL USE THEIR REGENERATIVE TREATMENTS AND FIX YOU RIGHT UP! SO DON'T WORRY, OKAY?!
SLUMP
YEAH, THAT'S RIGHT! YOU'RE A PANDORA, SENPAI--THIS IS NOTHING YOU CAN'T HANDLE!!
stub
?!
TH-WHAM
I-I'M SO SORRY, SENPAI!
THAT PROBABLY SHOOK YOU UP A BIT, HUH?!
OH... I GOT SOME... DIRT ON YOUR FACE...
CAN'T BELIEVE HOW CLUMSY I AM...HOW COULD I DO THAT TO MY STYLISH SENPAI...?

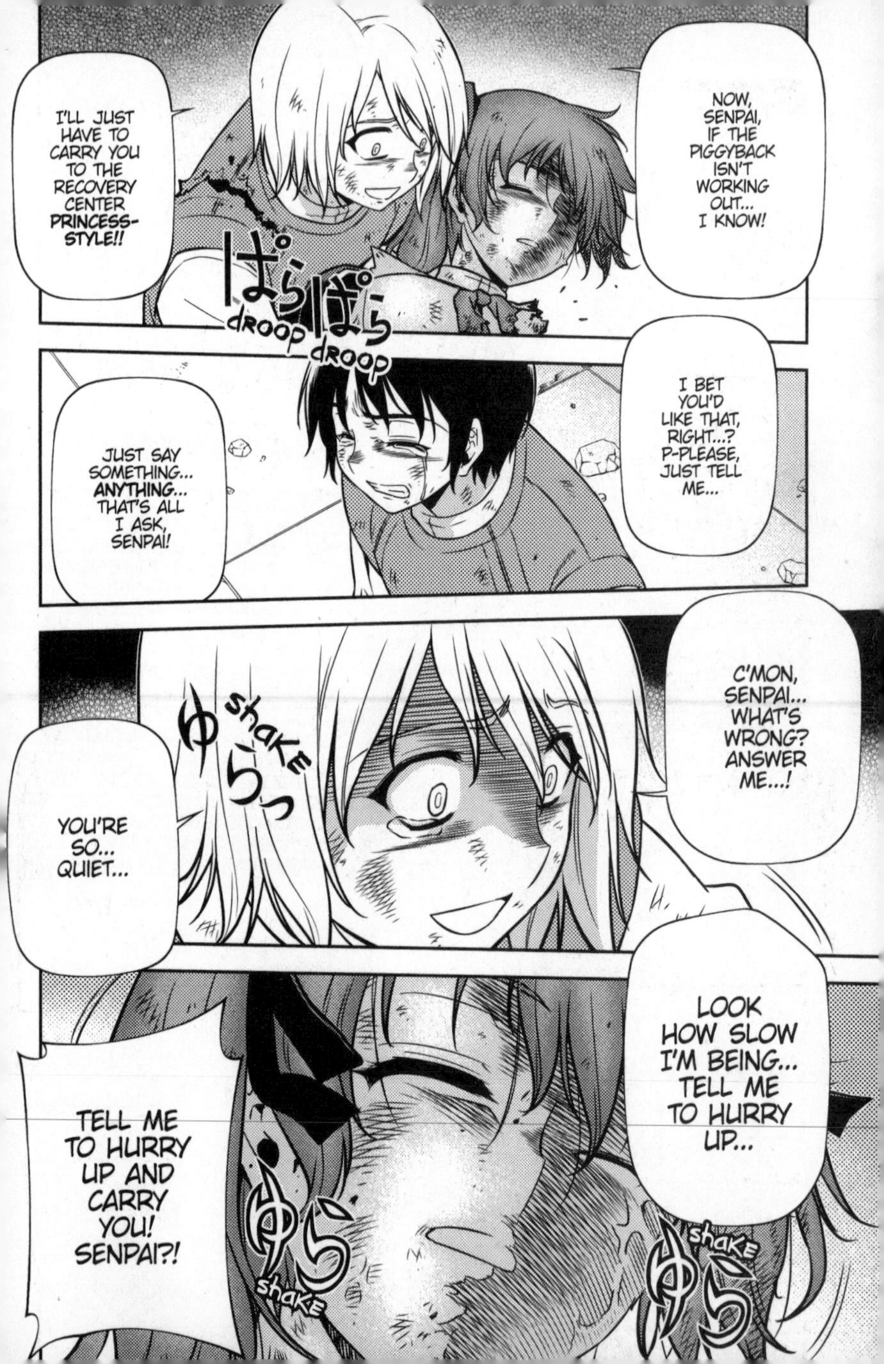
NOW, SENPAI, IF THE PIGGYBACK ISN'T WORKING OUT... I KNOW!
I'LL JUST HAVE TO CARRY YOU TO THE RECOVERY CENTER PRINCESS-STYLE!!
ぱらぱら
droop droop
I BET YOU'D LIKE THAT, RIGHT...? P-PLEASE, JUST TELL ME...
JUST SAY SOMETHING... ANYTHING... THAT'S ALL I ASK, SENPAI!
C'MON, SENPAI... WHAT'S WRONG? ANSWER ME...!
ゆらっ
shake
YOU'RE SO... QUIET...
LOOK HOW SLOW I'M BEING... TELL ME TO HURRY UP...
ゆら
shake
TELL ME TO HURRY UP AND CARRY YOU! SENPAI?!
ゆら
shake

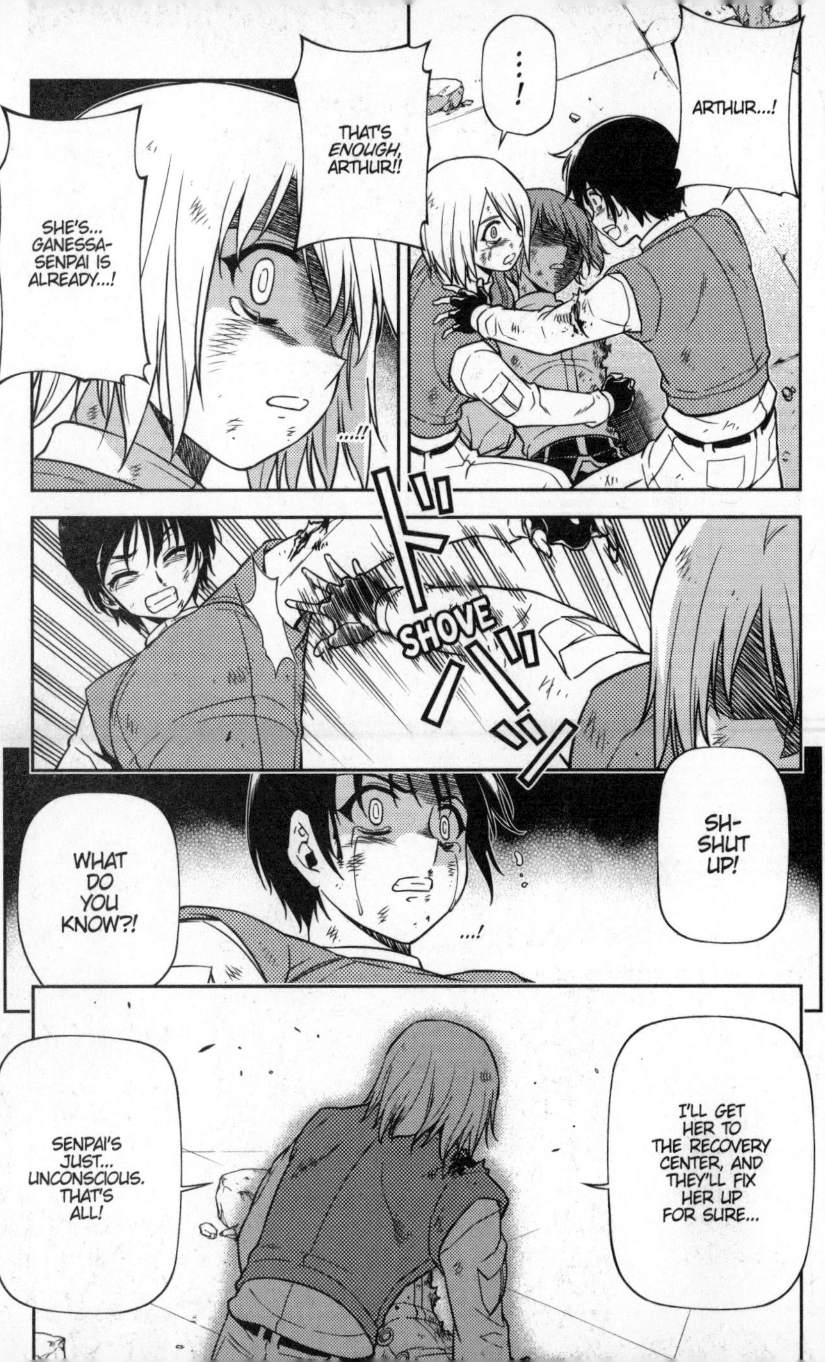
ARTHUR...!
...!
THAT'S ENOUGH, ARTHUR!!
SHE'S... GANESSA-SENPAI IS ALREADY...!
...!!
SHOVE
SH-SHUT UP!
...!
WHAT DO YOU KNOW?!
I'LL GET HER TO THE RECOVERY CENTER, AND THEY'LL FIX HER UP FOR SURE...
SENPAI'S JUST... UNCONSCIOUS. THAT'S ALL!

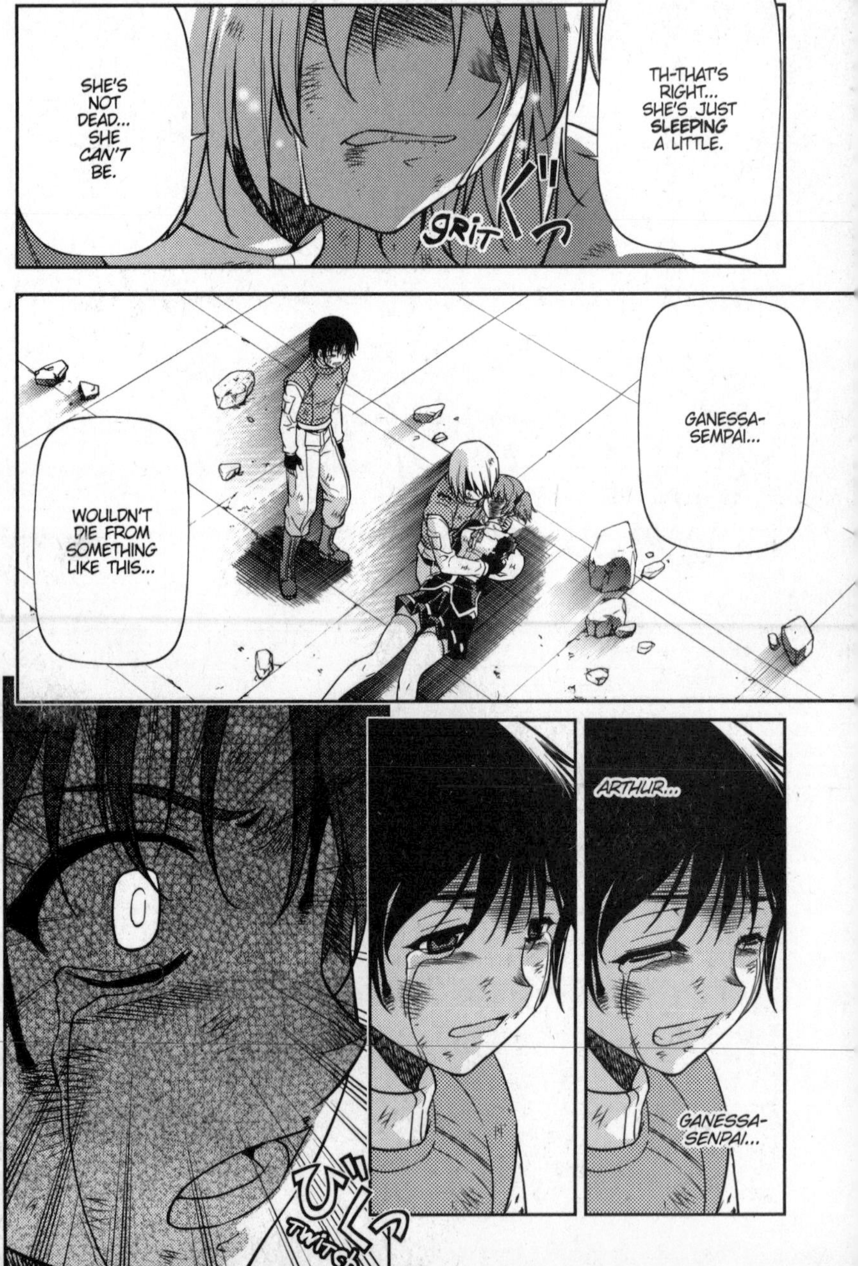
TH-THAT'S RIGHT... SHE'S JUST SLEEPING A LITTLE.
SHE'S NOT DEAD... SHE CAN'T BE.
ぐっ
grit
GANESSA-SEMPAI...
WOULDN'T DIE FROM SOMETHING LIKE THIS...
ARTHUR...
GANESSA-SENPAI...
びくっ
twitch

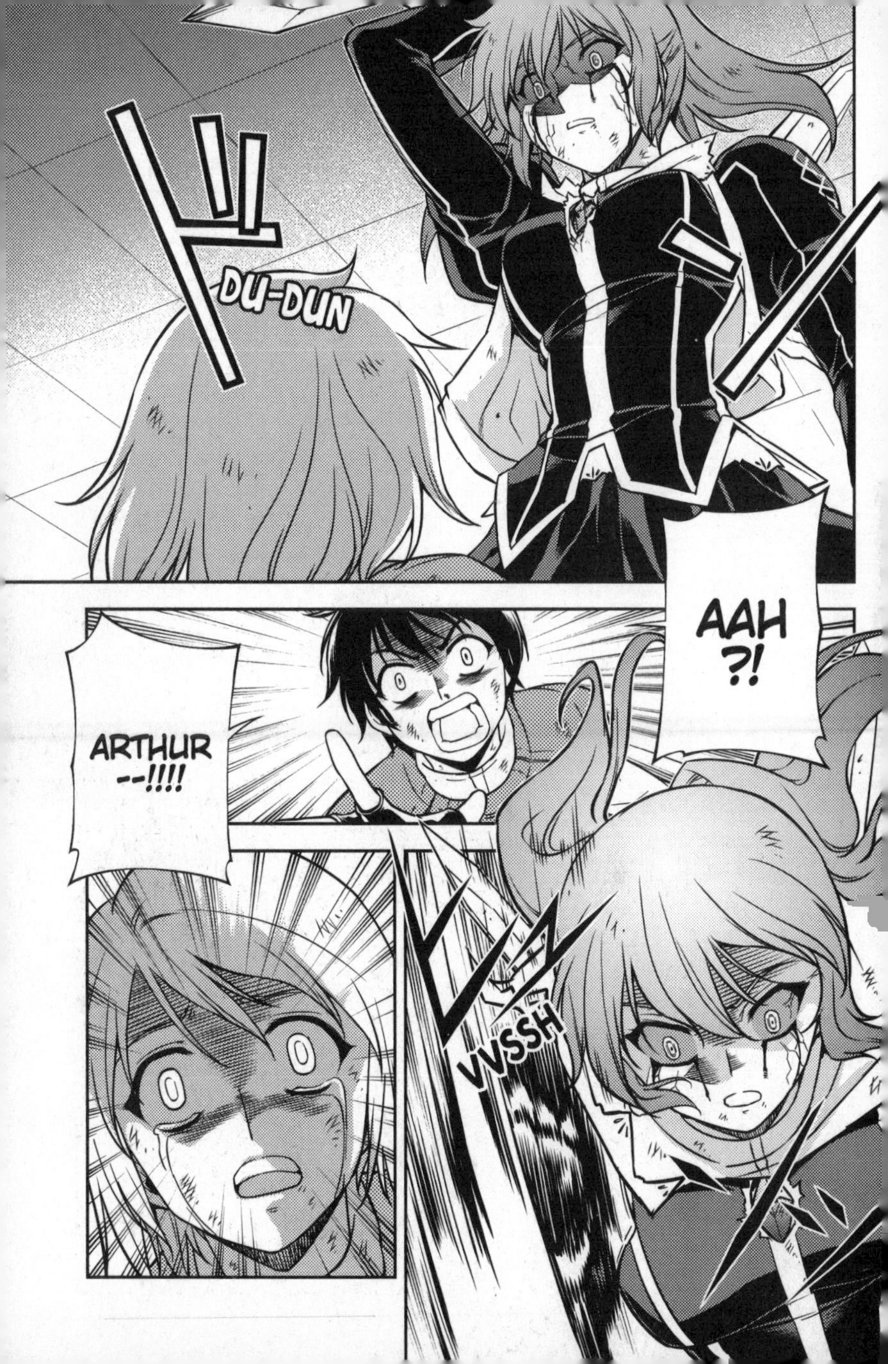
DU-DUN
AAH ?!
ARTHUR --!!!!
VVSSH

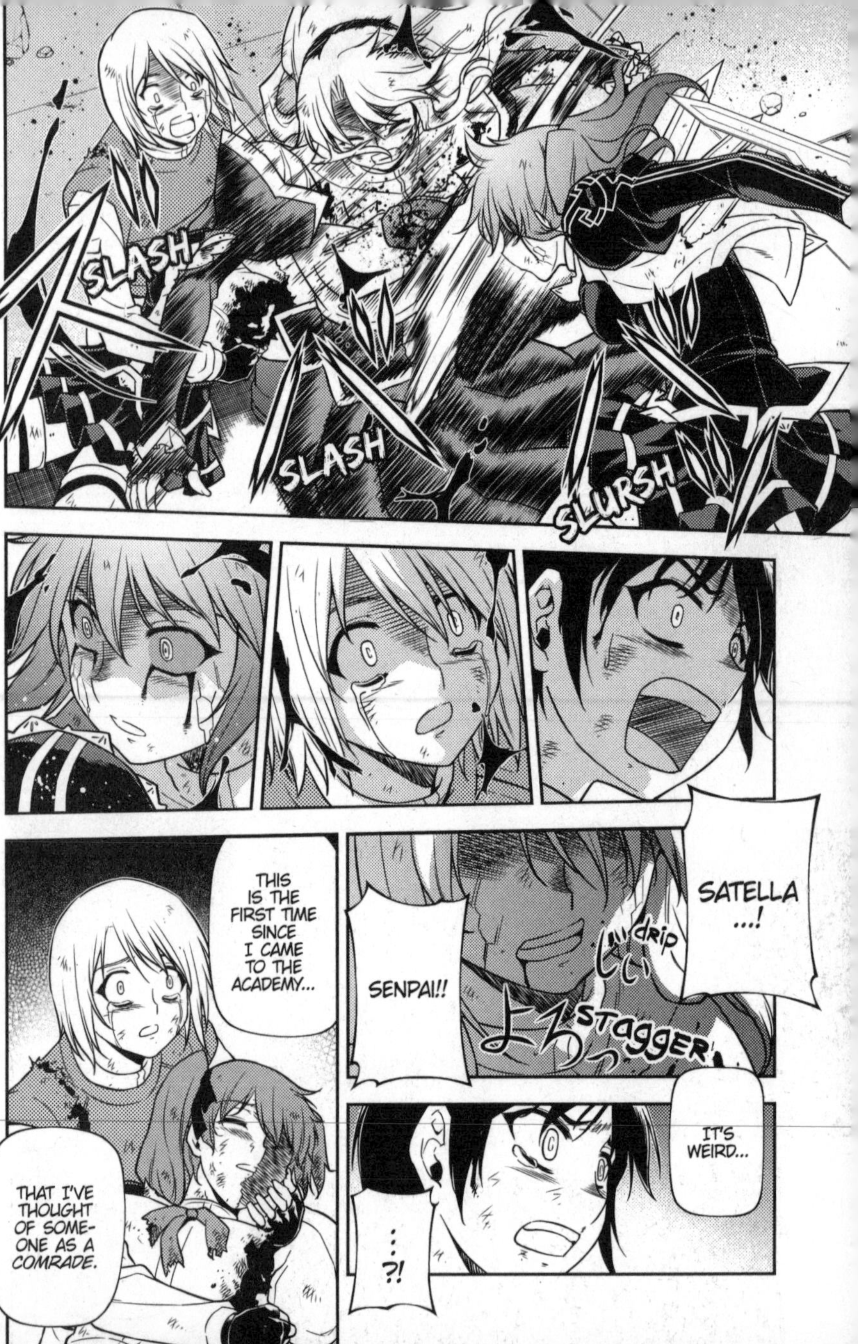
SLURSH
SLASH
SLASH
SATELLA ...!
SENPAI!!
drip
よろっ
stagger
IT'S WEIRD...
...?!
THIS IS THE FIRST TIME SINCE I CAME TO THE ACADEMY...
THAT I'VE THOUGHT OF SOME-ONE AS A COMRADE.

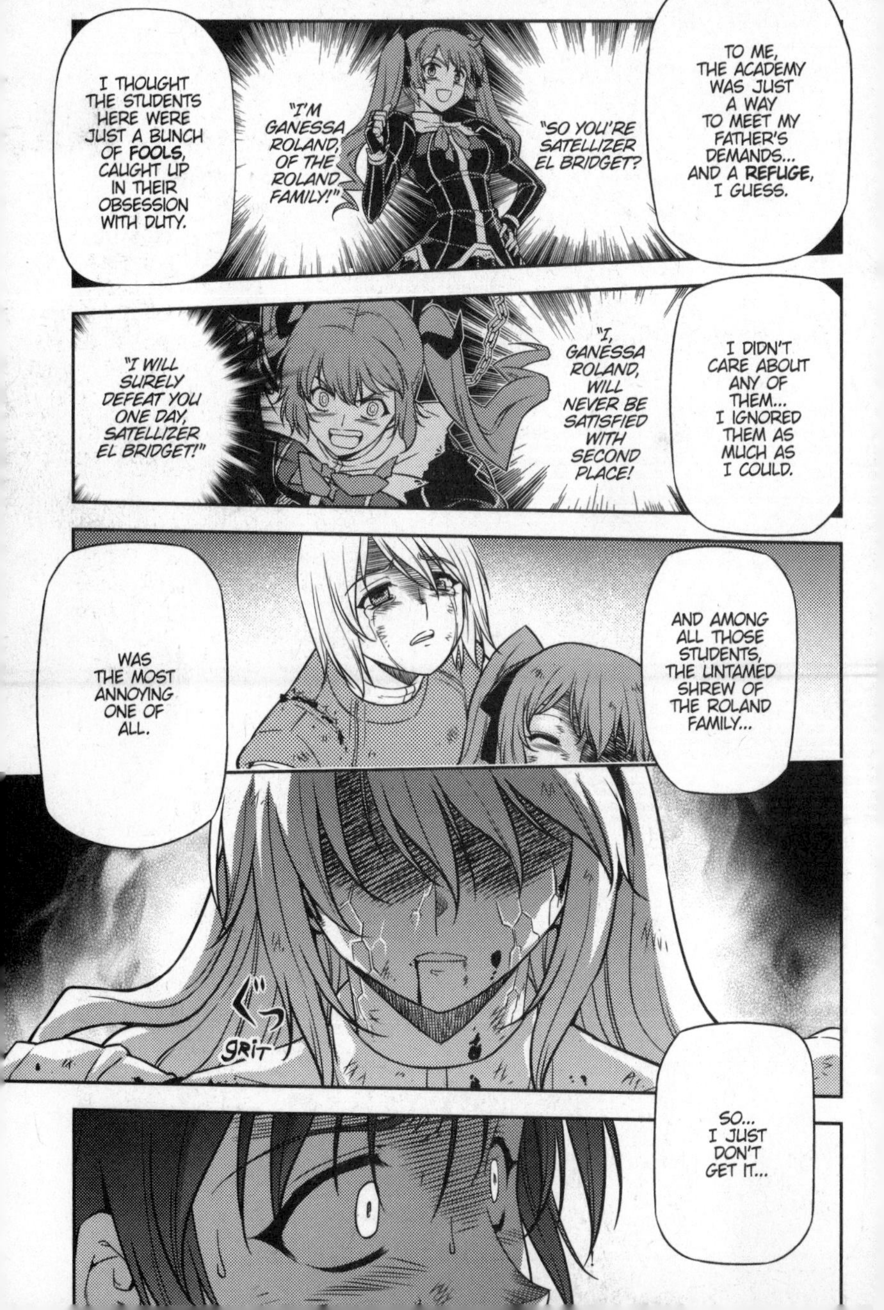
TO ME, THE ACADEMY WAS JUST A WAY TO MEET MY FATHER'S DEMANDS... AND A **REFUGE**, I GUESS.
"SO YOU'RE SATELLIZER EL BRIDGET?
"I'M GANESSA ROLAND, OF THE ROLAND FAMILY!"
I THOUGHT THE STUDENTS HERE WERE JUST A BUNCH OF **FOOLS**, CAUGHT UP IN THEIR OBSESSION WITH DUTY.
I DIDN'T CARE ABOUT ANY OF THEM... I IGNORED THEM AS MUCH AS I COULD.
"I, GANESSA ROLAND, WILL NEVER BE SATISFIED WITH SECOND PLACE!
"I WILL SURELY DEFEAT YOU ONE DAY, SATELLIZER EL BRIDGET!"
AND AMONG ALL THOSE STUDENTS, THE UNTAMED SHREW OF THE ROLAND FAMILY...
WAS THE MOST ANNOYING ONE OF ALL.
ぐっ
grit
SO... I JUST DON'T GET IT...

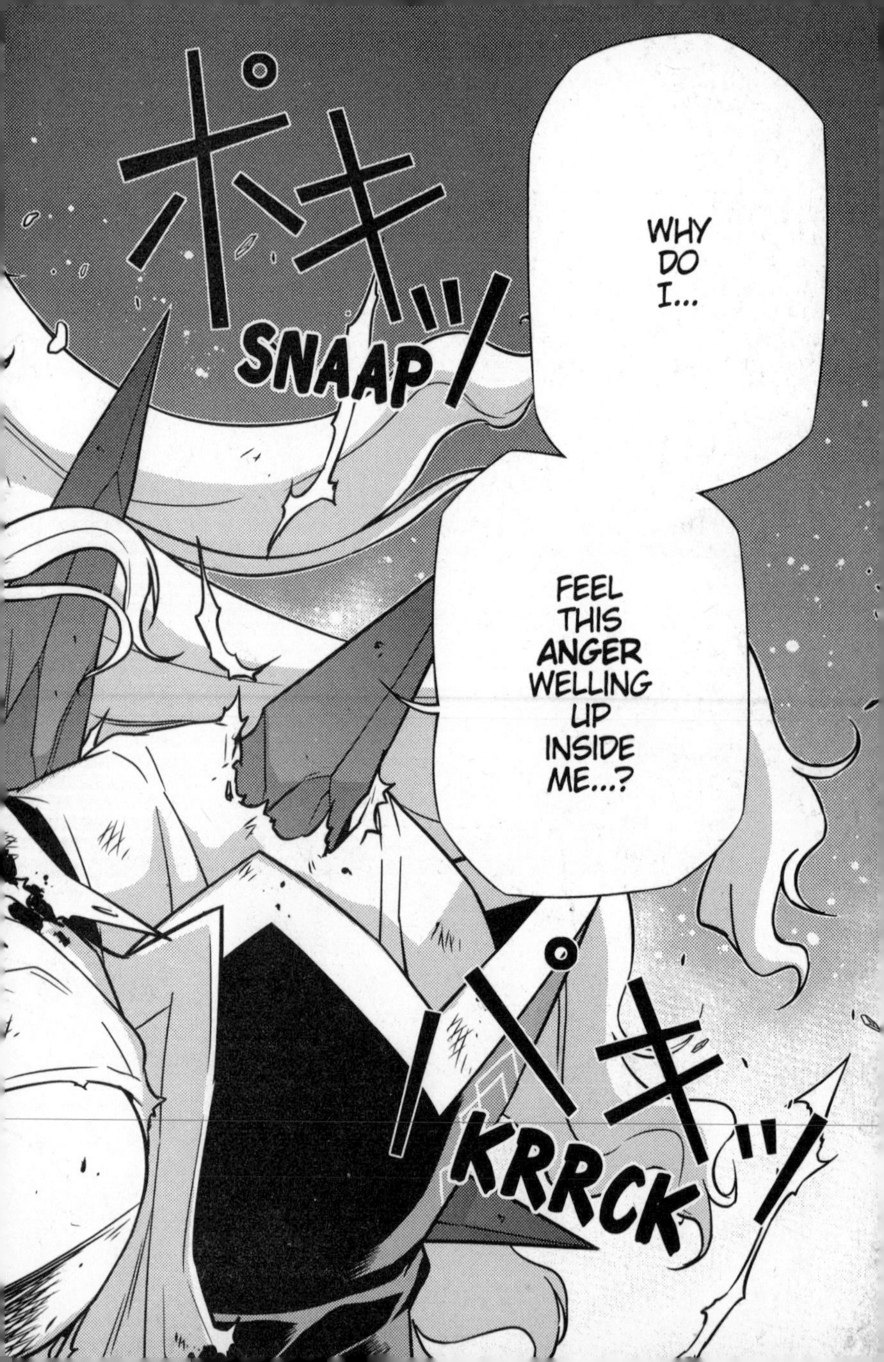
WHY DO I...
ポキッ
SNAAP
FEEL THIS ANGER WELLING UP INSIDE ME...?
ポキッ
KRRRCK

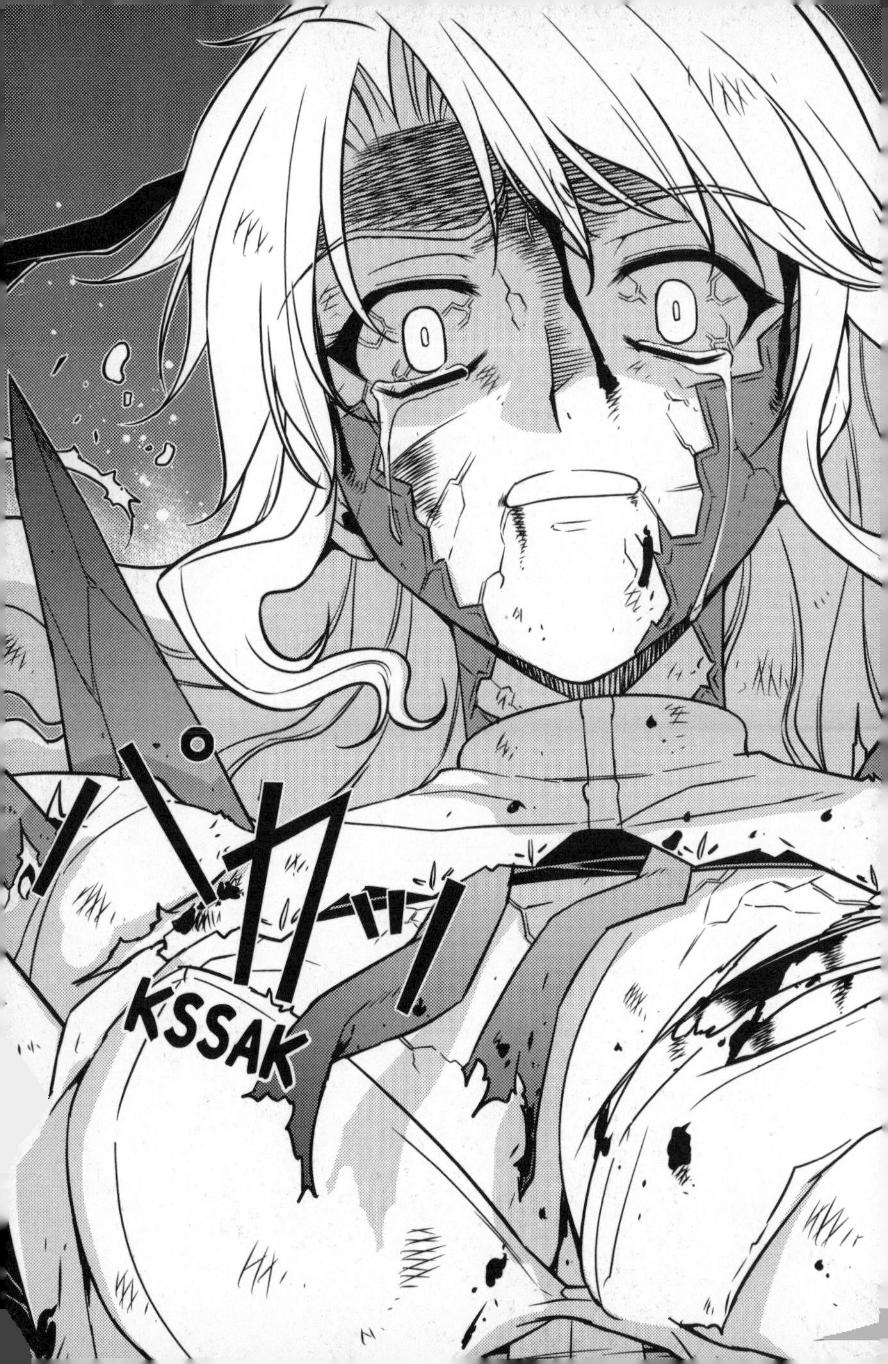
ザクッ
KSSAK

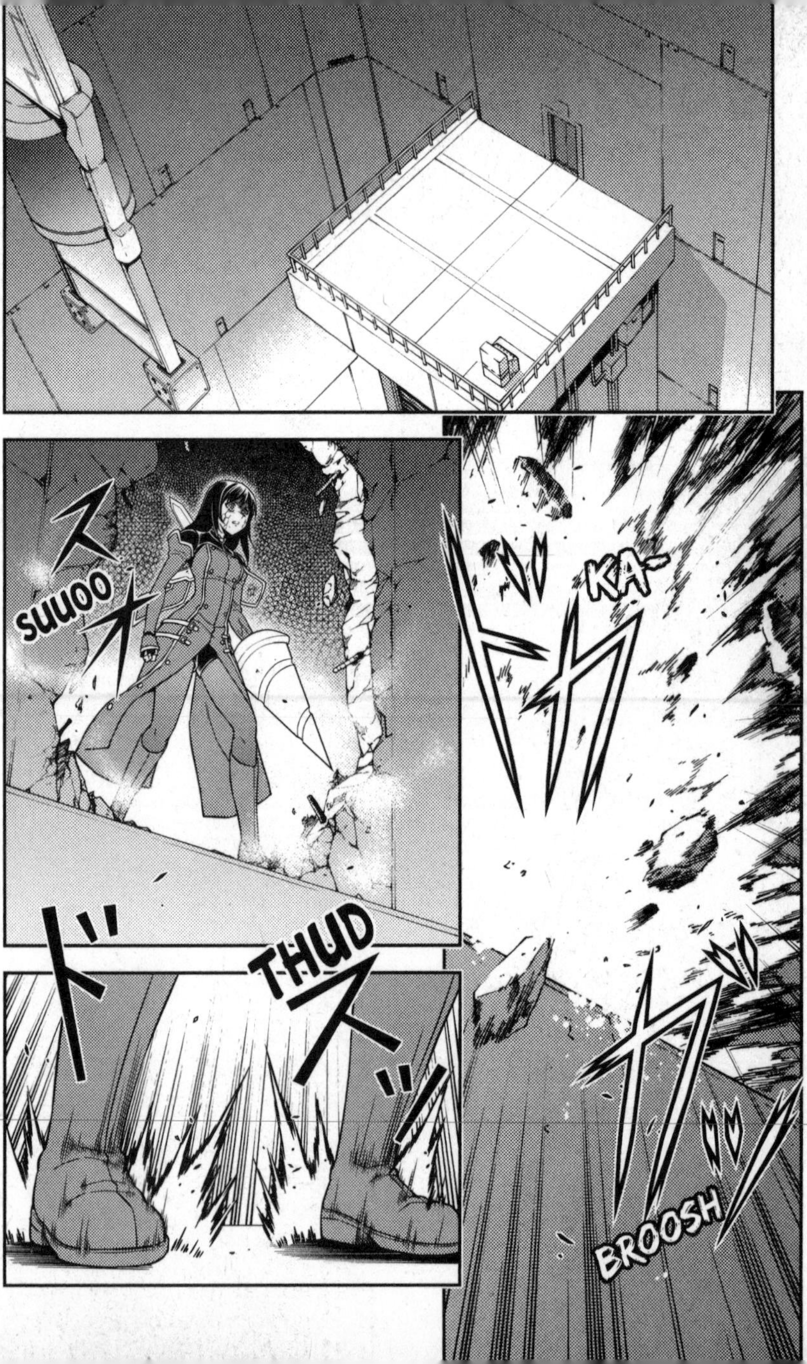
KA-
BROOSH
SUUOO
THUD

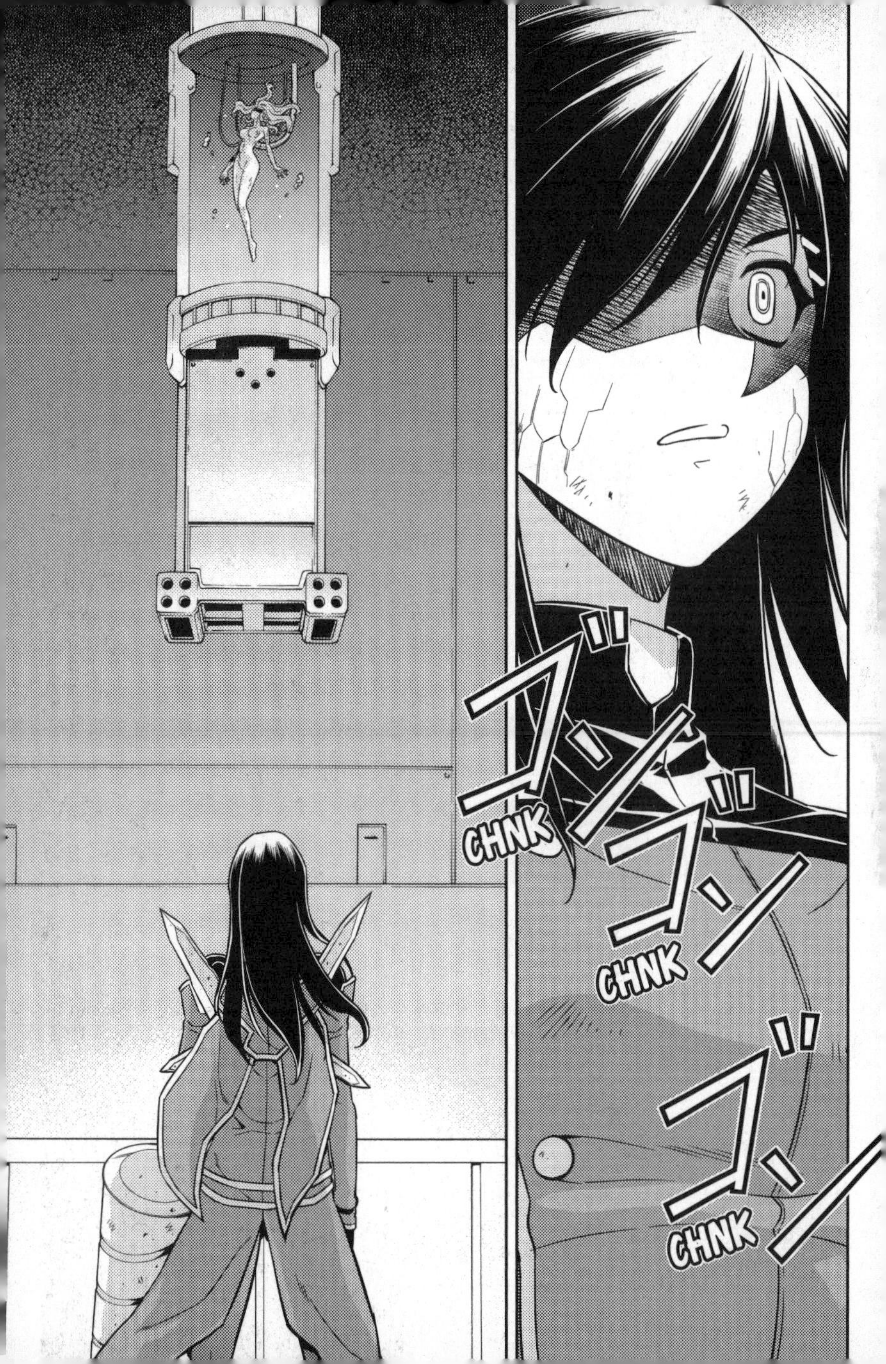
ゴゴン
CHNK
ゴゴン
CHNK
ゴゴン
CHNK

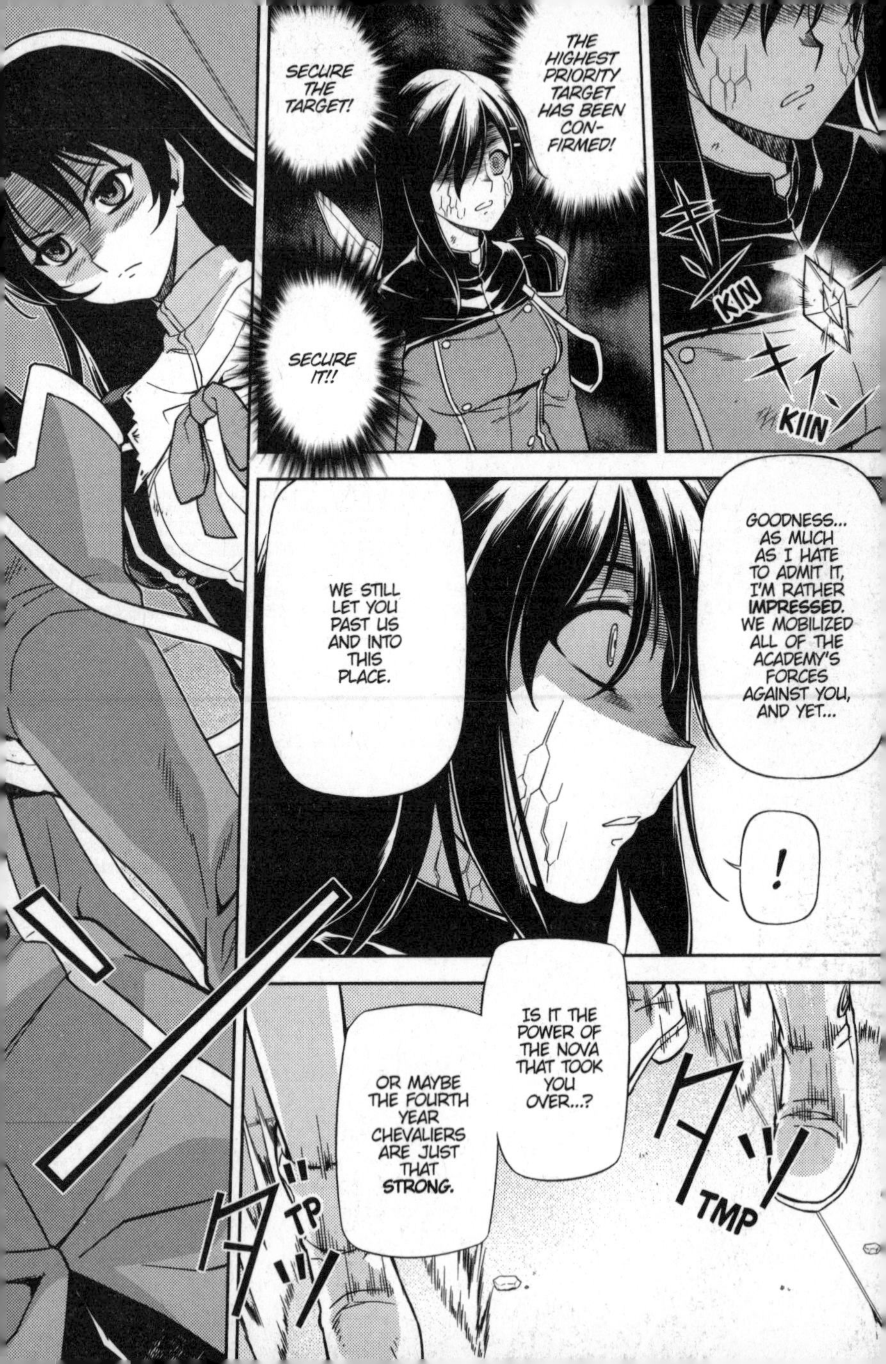
KIN
KIIN
THE HIGHEST PRIORITY TARGET HAS BEEN CON-FIRMED!
SECURE THE TARGET!
SECURE IT!!
GOODNESS... AS MUCH AS I HATE TO ADMIT IT, I'M RATHER **IMPRESSED.** WE MOBILIZED ALL OF THE ACADEMY'S FORCES AGAINST YOU, AND YET...
WE STILL LET YOU PAST US AND INTO THIS PLACE.
!
IS IT THE POWER OF THE NOVA THAT TOOK YOU OVER...?
OR MAYBE THE FOURTH YEAR CHEVALIERS ARE JUST THAT **STRONG.**
TMP
TP

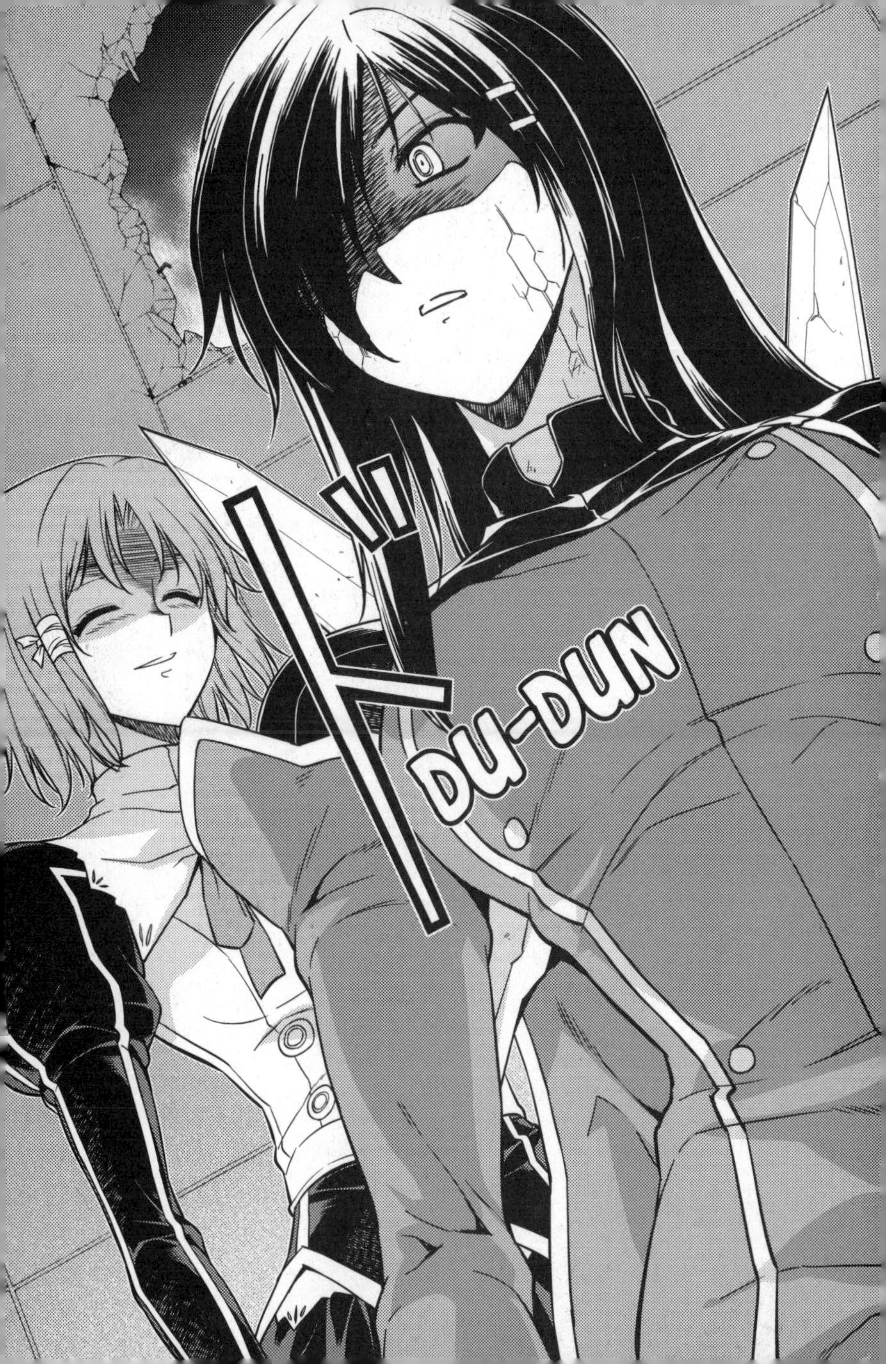
DU-DUN

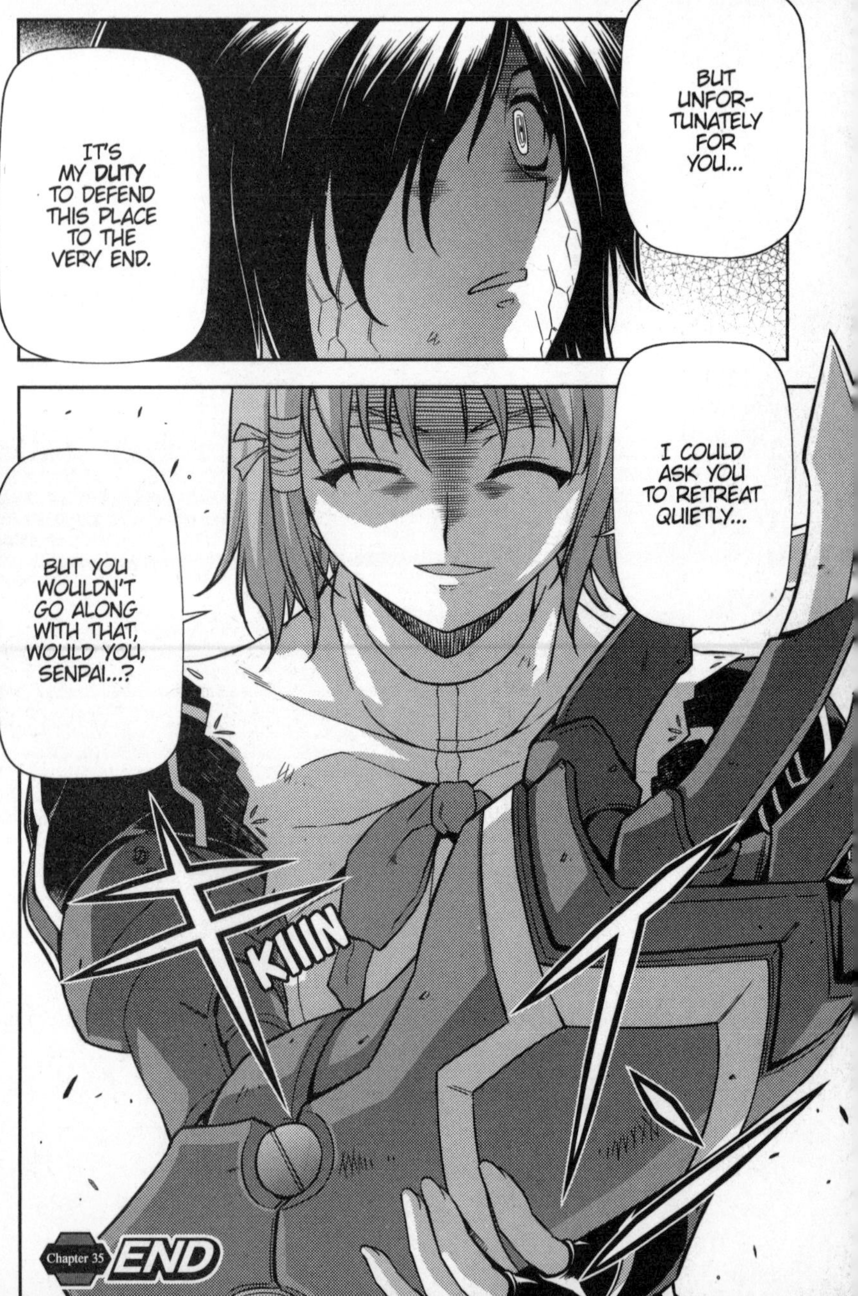
BUT UNFORTUNATELY FOR YOU...
IT'S MY DUTY TO DEFEND THIS PLACE TO THE VERY END.
I COULD ASK YOU TO RETREAT QUIETLY...
BUT YOU WOULDN'T GO ALONG WITH THAT, WOULD YOU, SENPAI...?
KIIN
Chapter 35 END

FREEZING VOLUME.6
HIGHLIGHT SCENE

FREEZING Vol.6

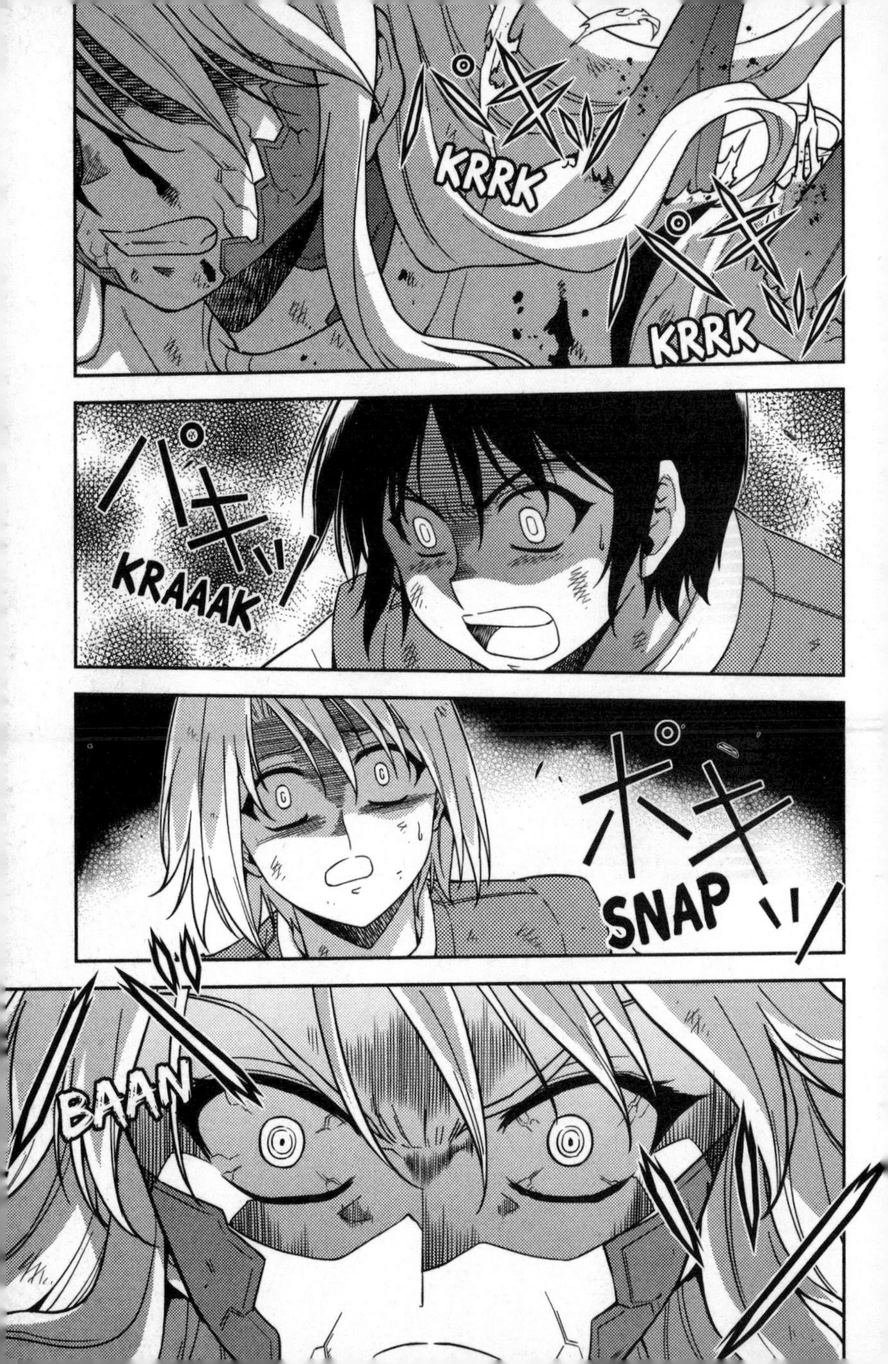
パキ
KRRK
パキ
KRRK
パキッ
KRAAAK
ポキッ
SNAP
BAAN

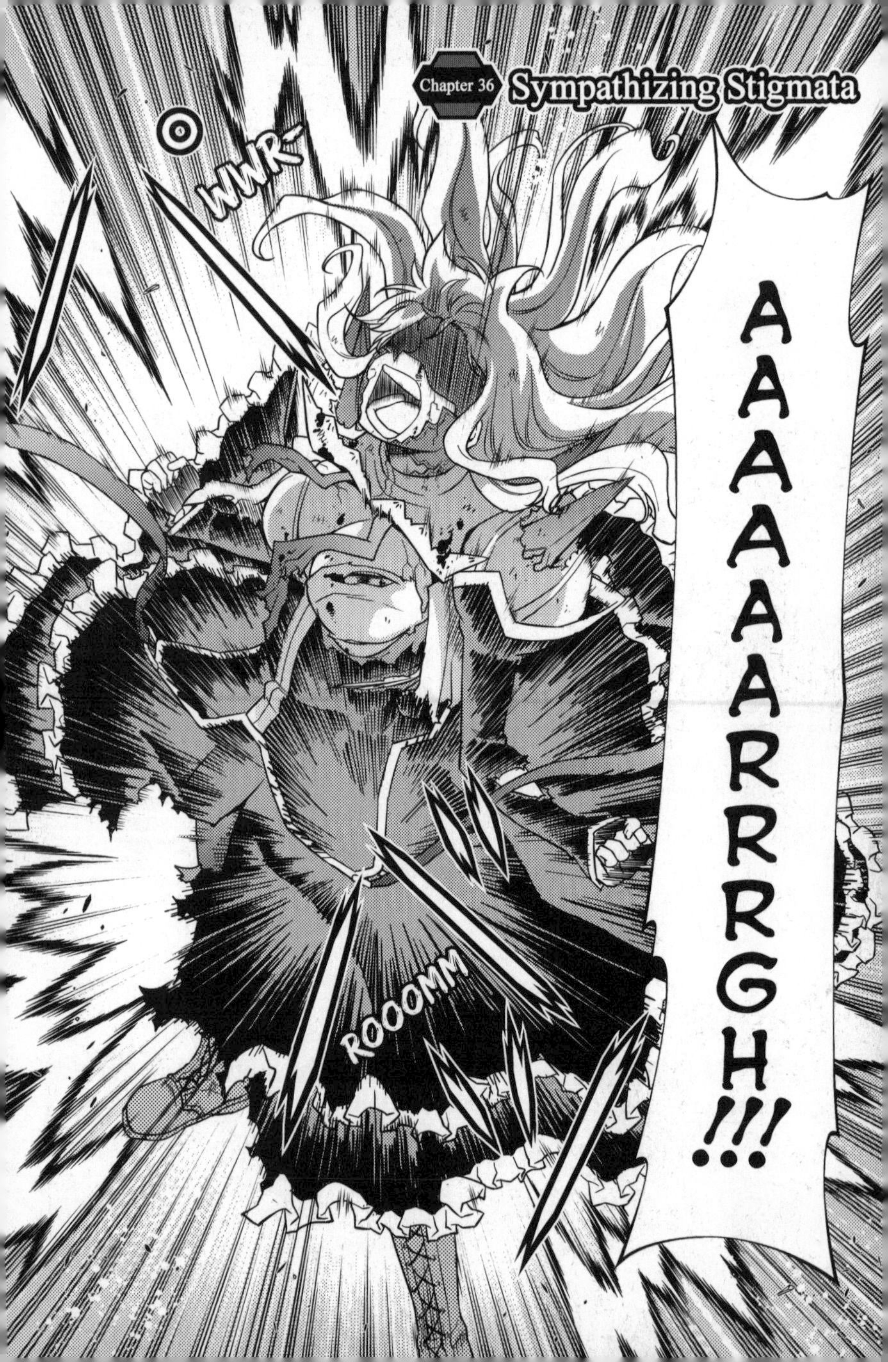
Chapter 36 Sympathizing Stigmata
AAAAARRRGH!!!
WWR
ROOOMM

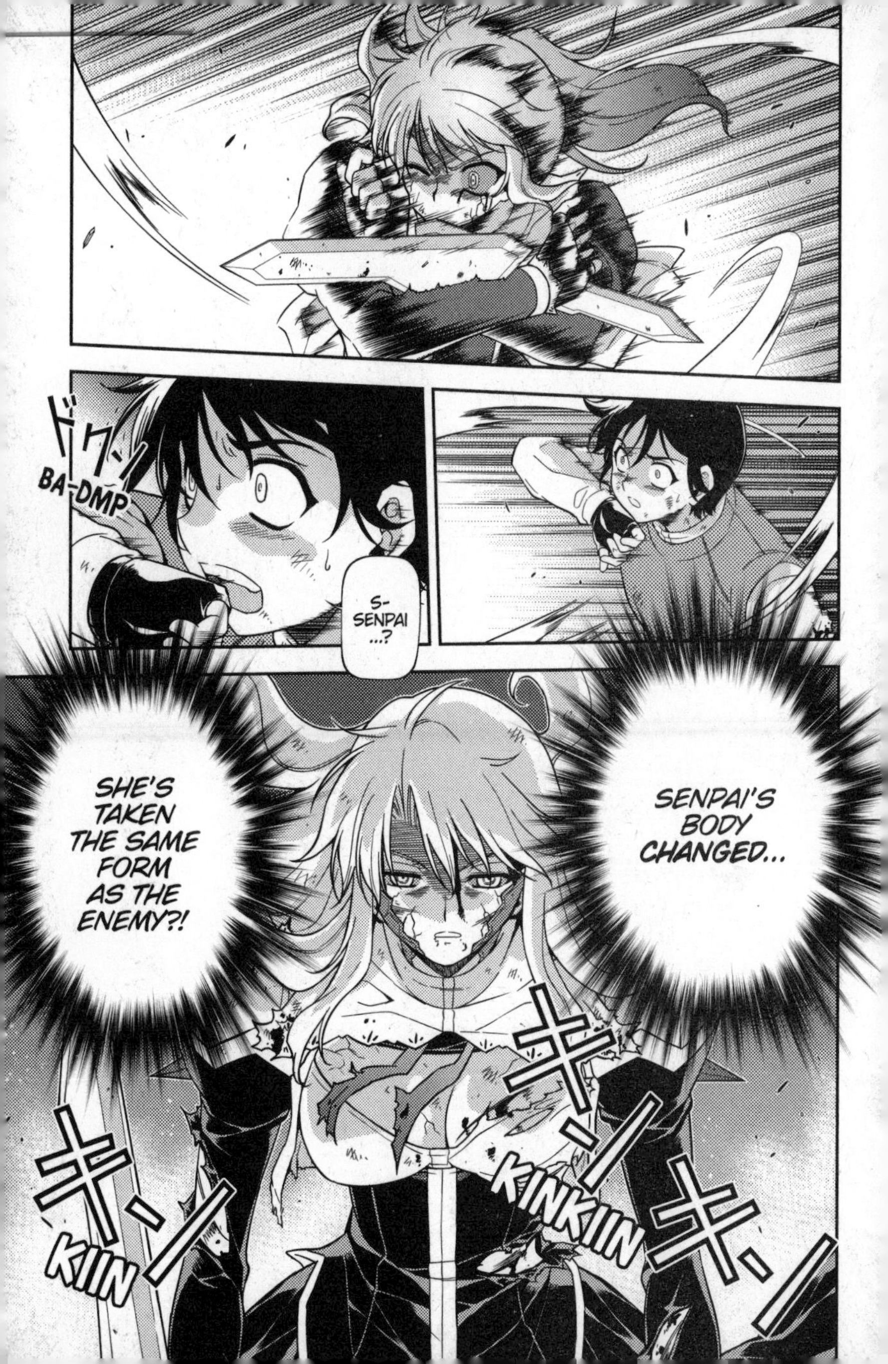

ドクン
BA-DMP
S-SENPAI ...?
SENPAI'S BODY CHANGED...
SHE'S TAKEN THE SAME FORM AS THE ENEMY?!
KINKIIN
KIIN

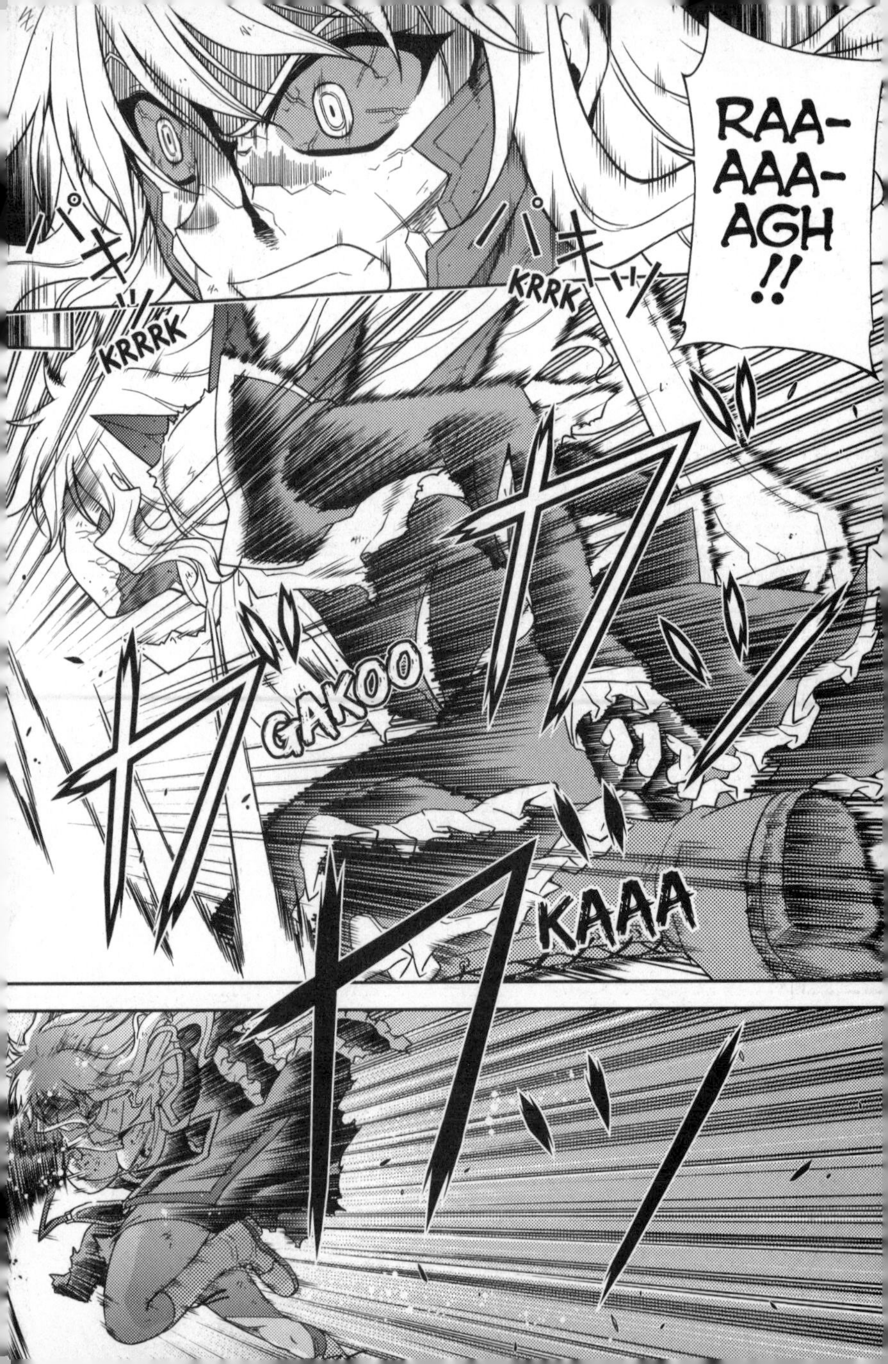
RAA-AAA-AGH!!
KRRK
KRRRK
GAKOO
KAAA

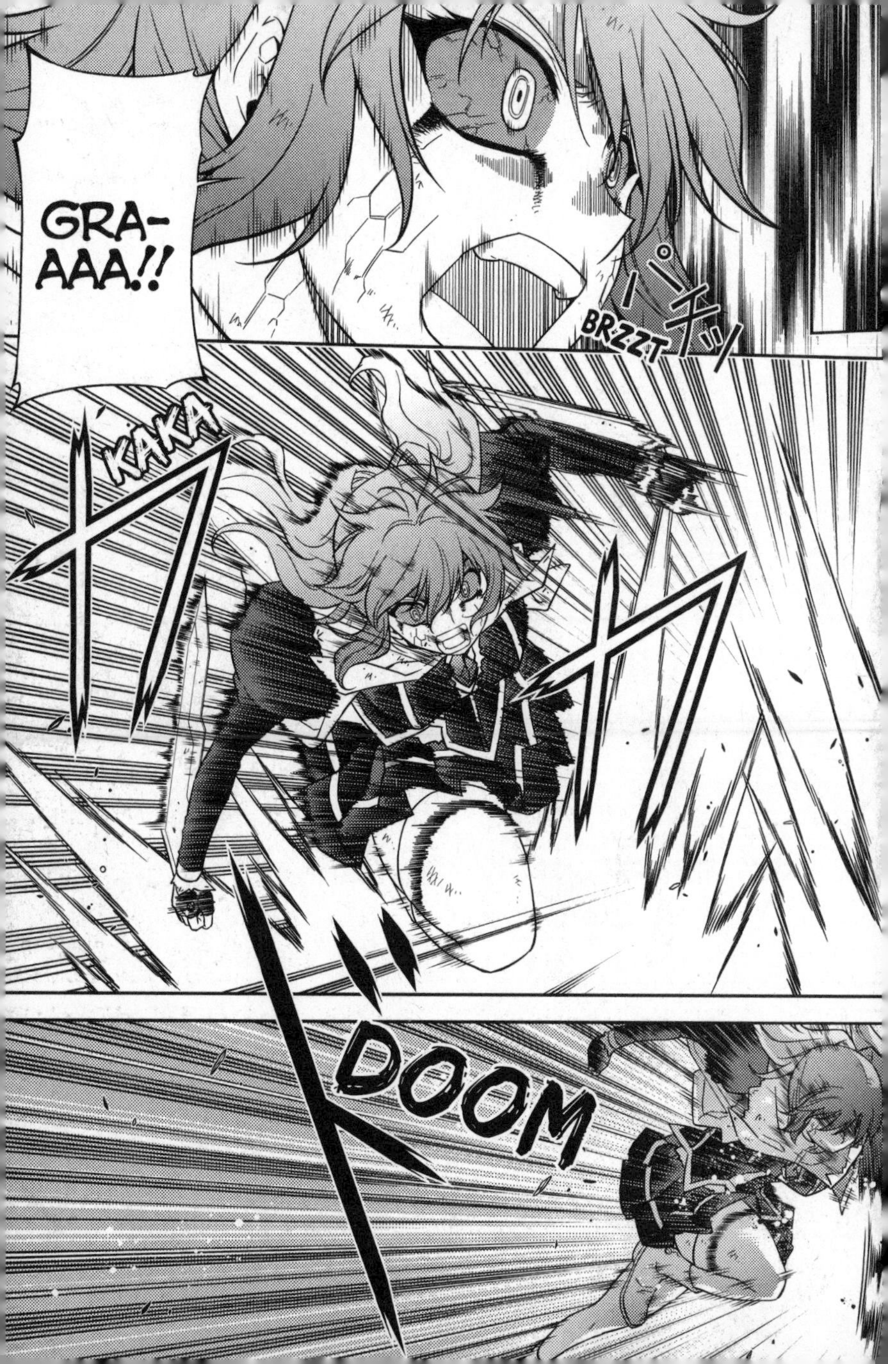
BRZZT
パチッ
GRA-
AAA!!
KAKA
DOOM

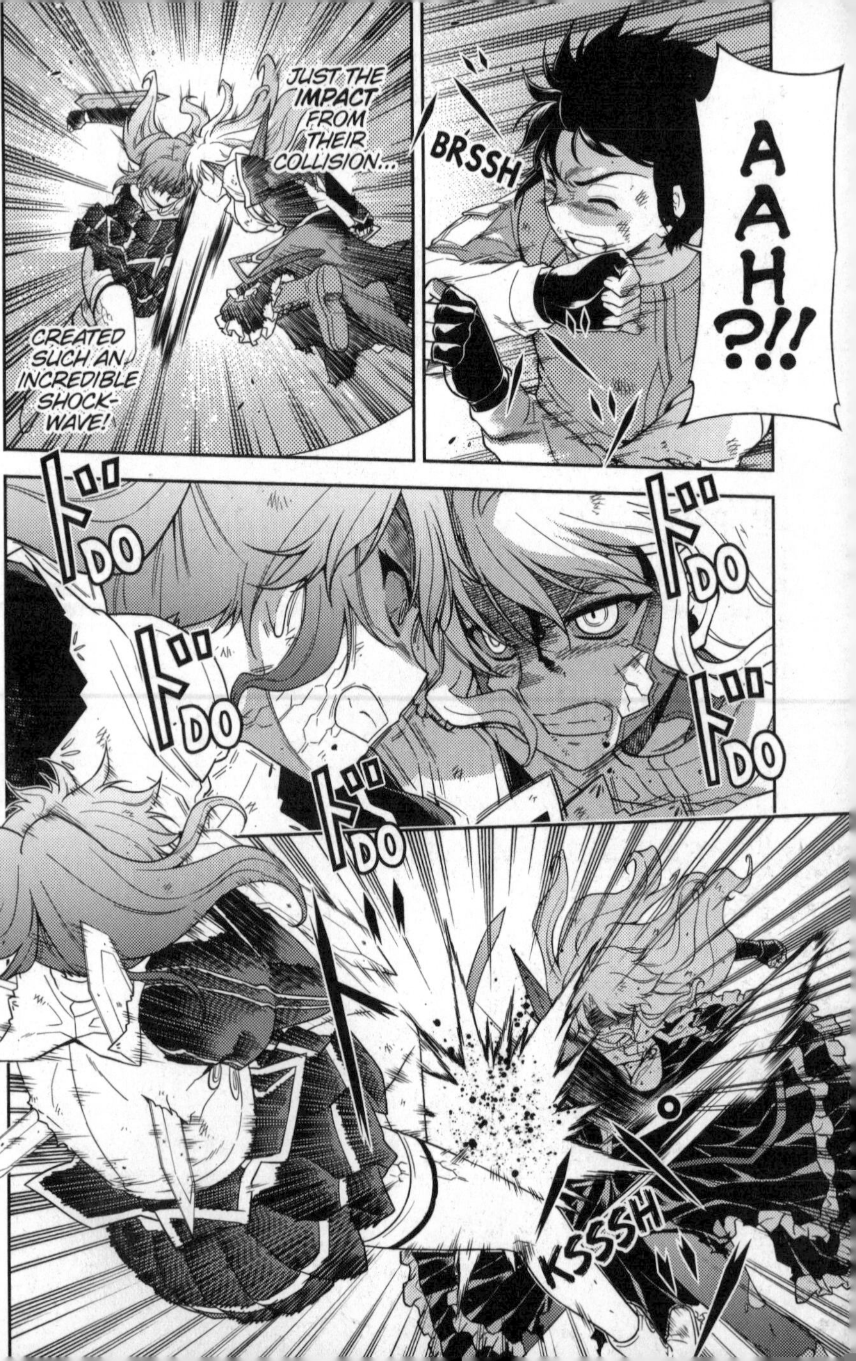
AAH?!!
BRSSH
JUST THE IMPACT FROM THEIR COLLISION...
CREATED SUCH AN INCREDIBLE SHOCK-WAVE!
ド DO
ド DO
ド DO
ド DO
ド DO
KSSSH

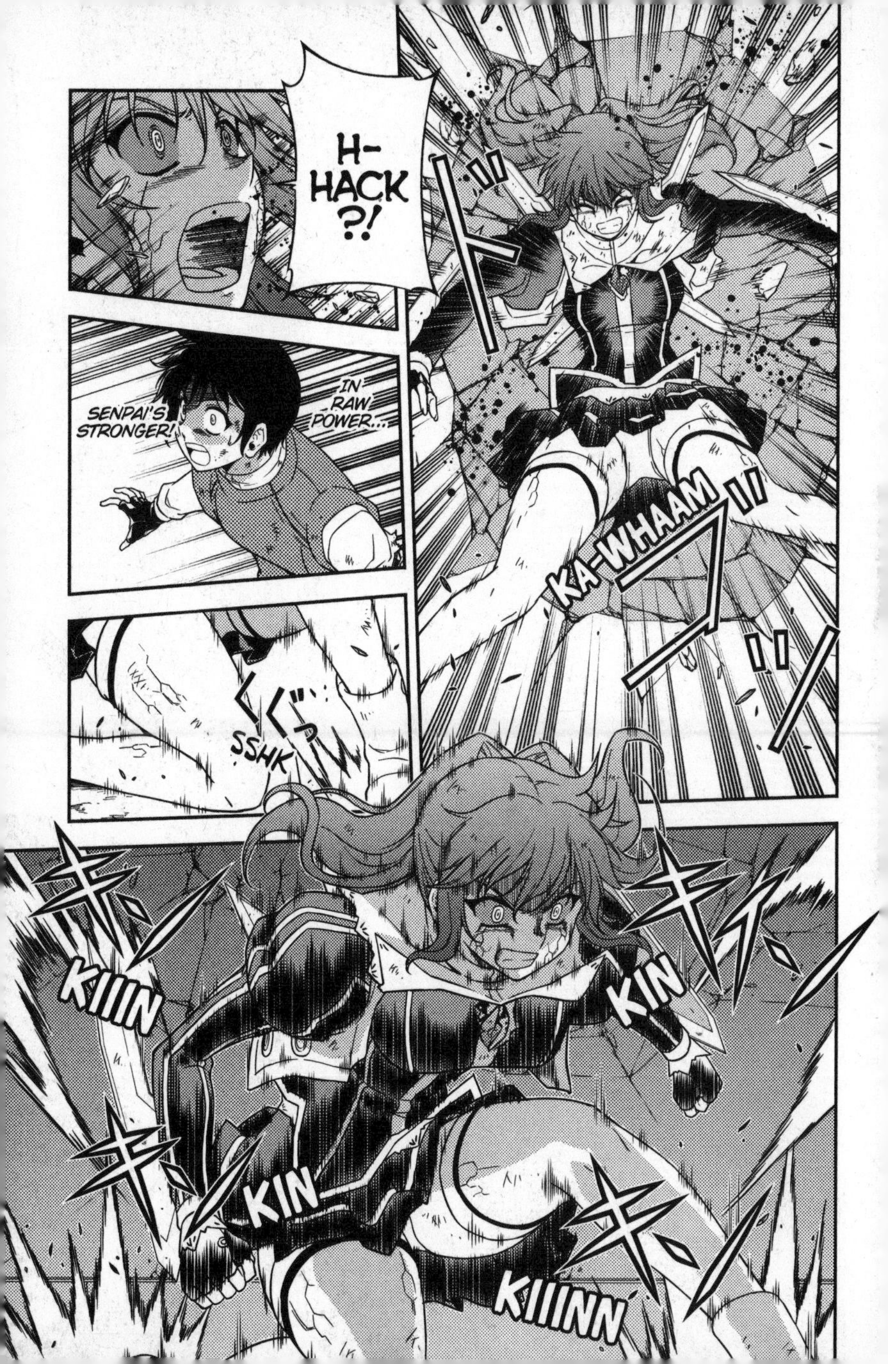
KA-WHAAM
H-HACK?!
IN RAW POWER...
SENPAI'S STRONGER!
SSHK
KIN
KIIIN
KIN
KIIINN

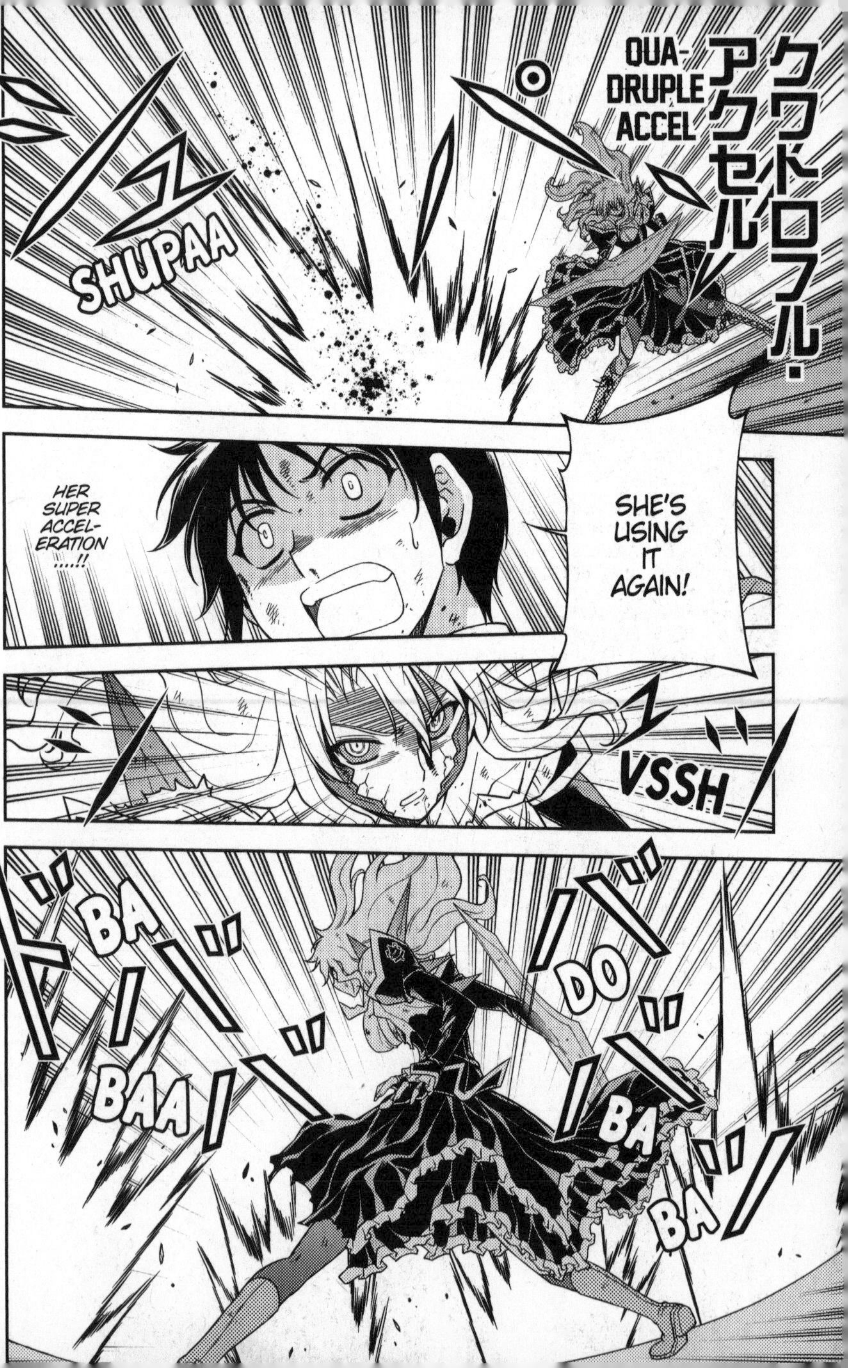
クワドロプル・アクセル
QUA-DRUPLE ACCEL
SHUPAA
SHE'S USING IT AGAIN!
HER SUPER ACCEL-ERATION .....!!
VSSH
DO
BA
BA
BA
BAA

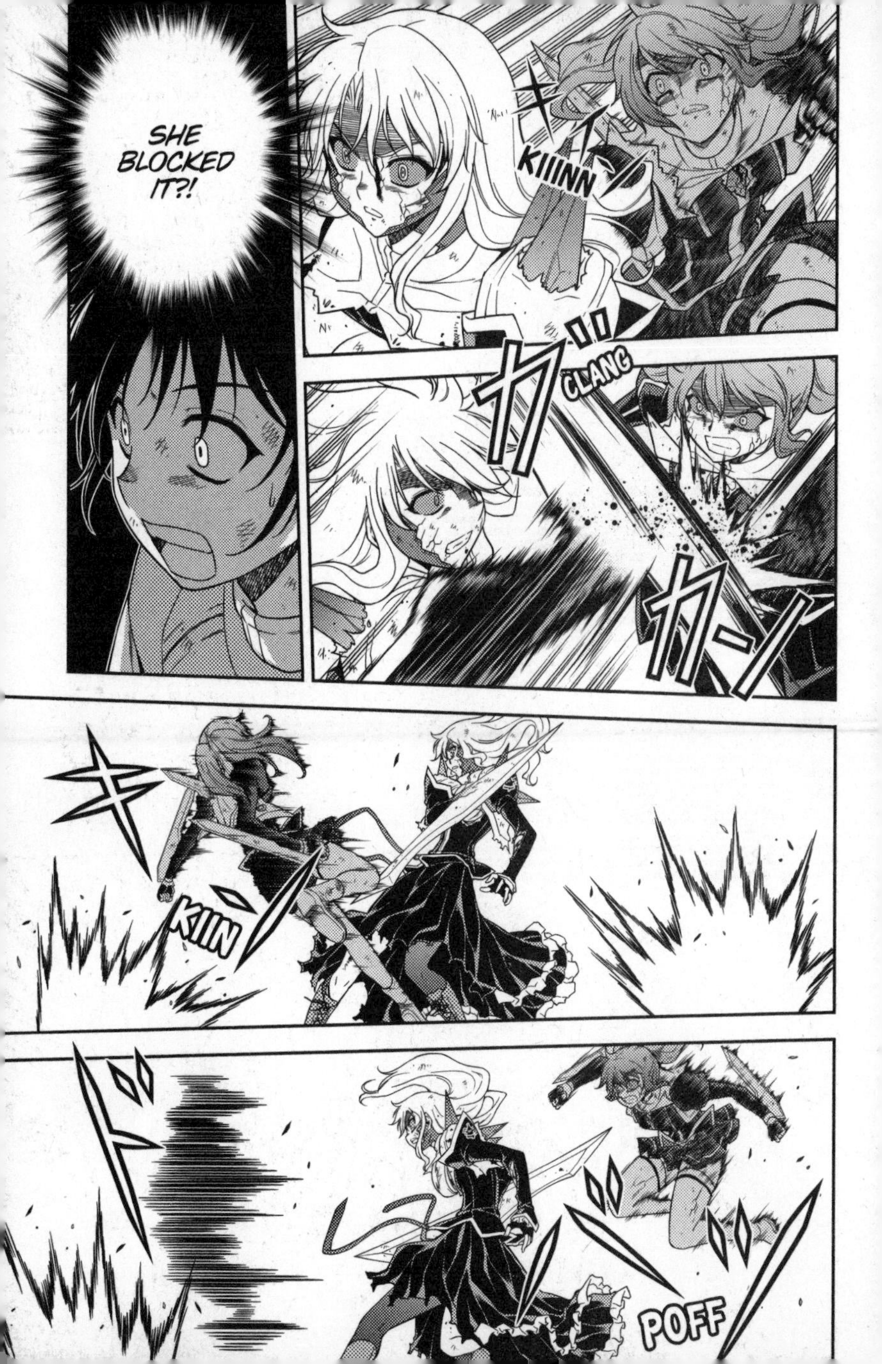
KIIINN
CLANG
カーン
SHE BLOCKED IT?!
KIIN
POFF

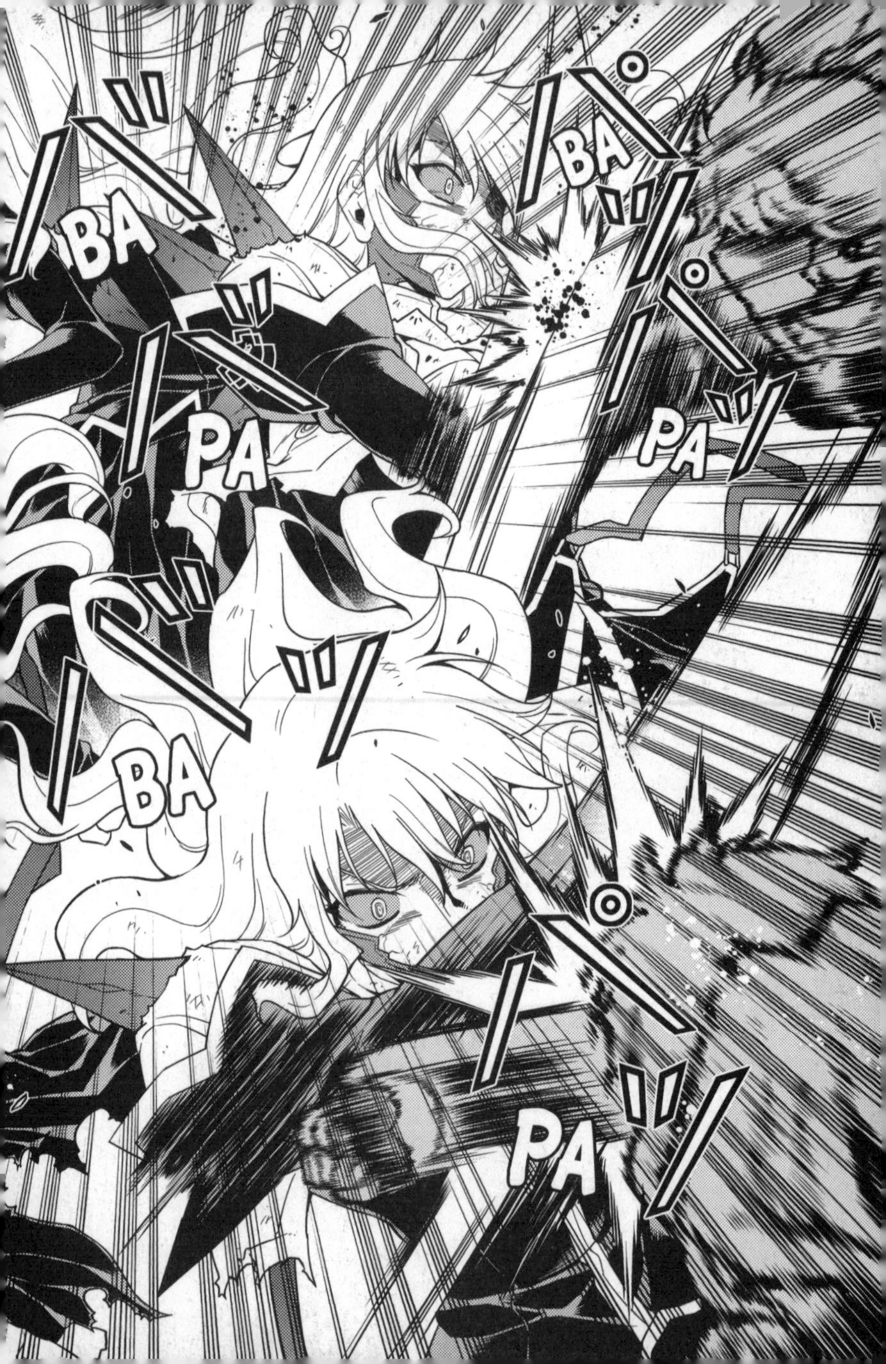
BA
PA
BA
PA
BA
PA

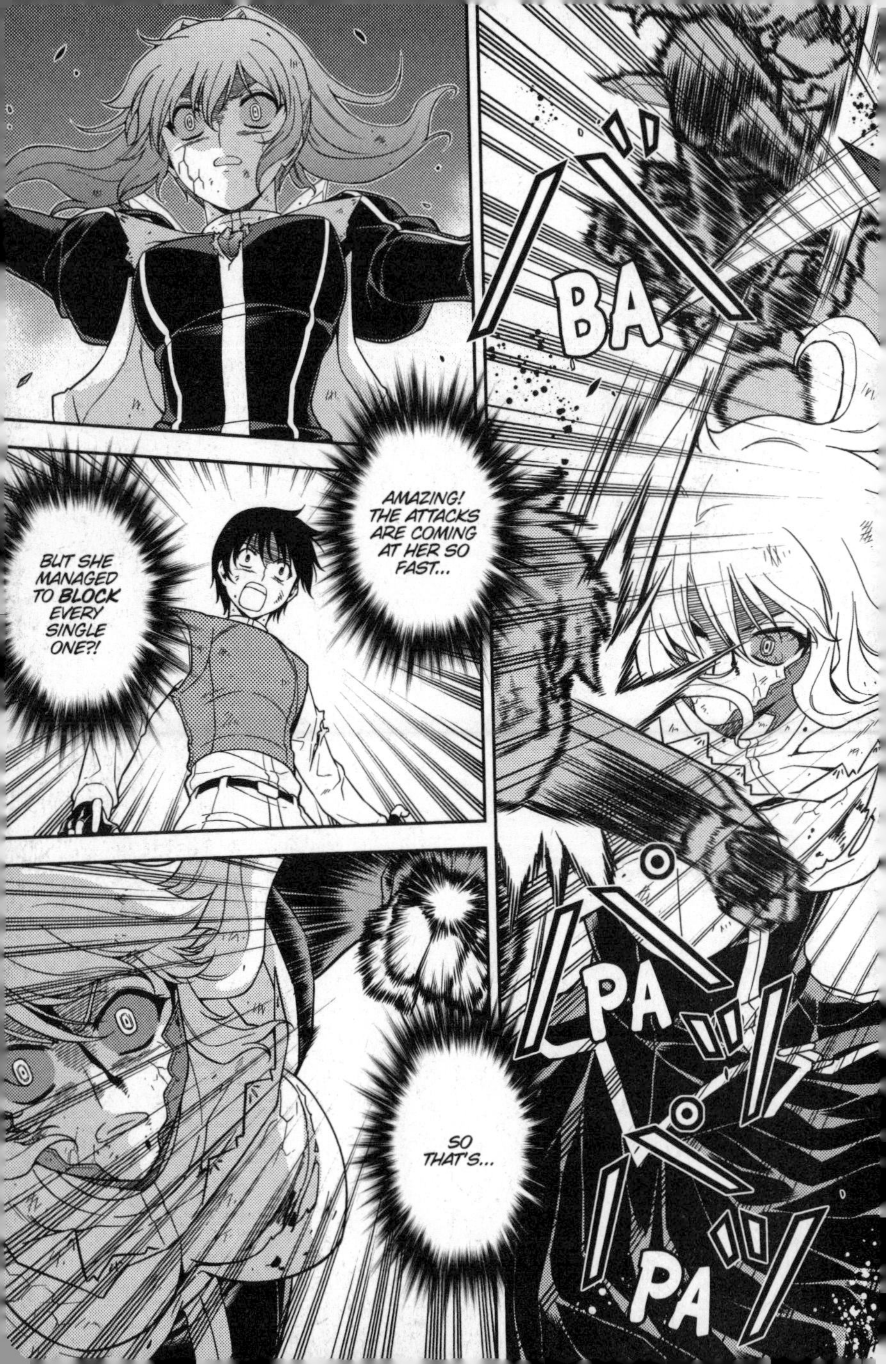
BA
PA
PA
AMAZING! THE ATTACKS ARE COMING AT HER SO FAST...
BUT SHE MANAGED TO BLOCK EVERY SINGLE ONE?!
SO THAT'S...

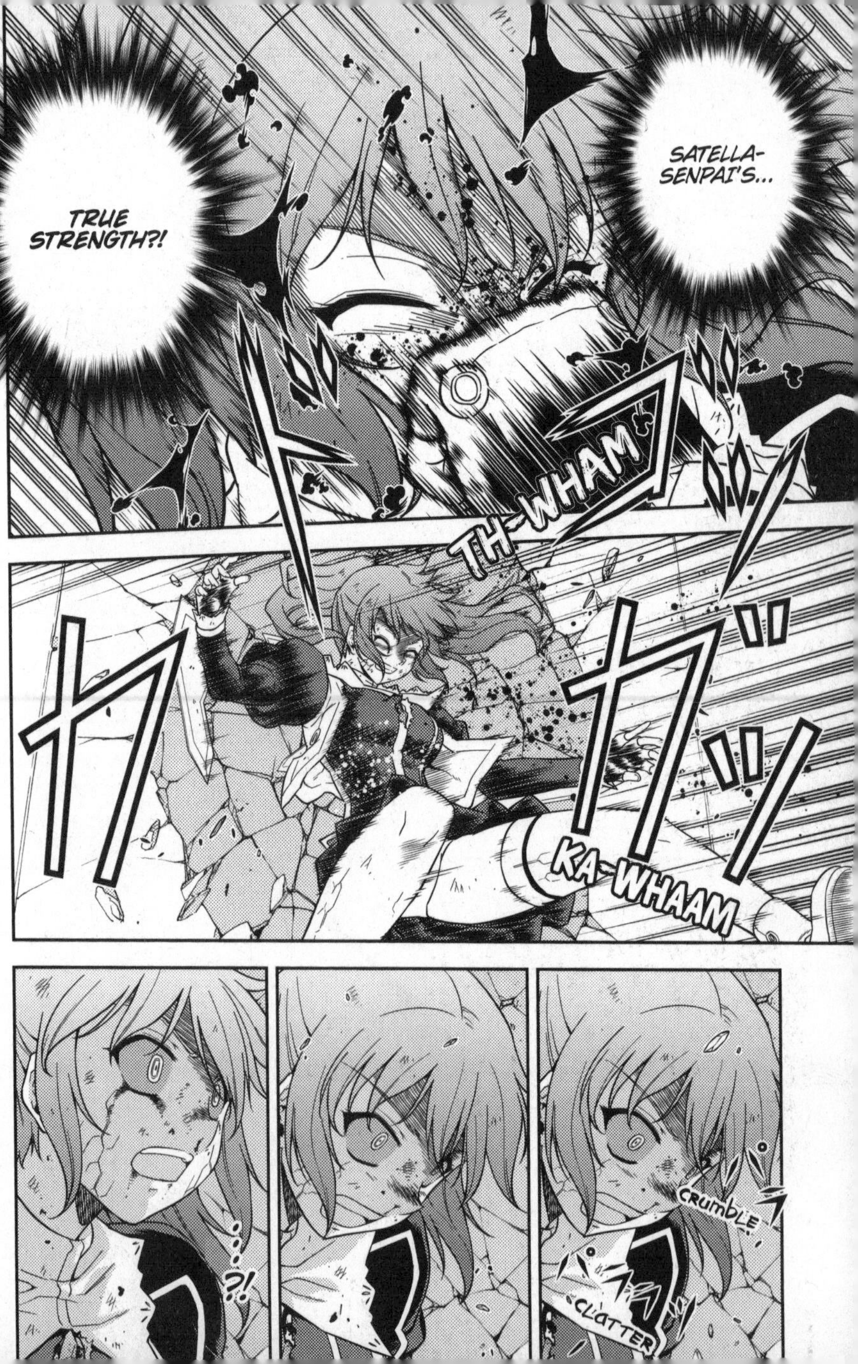
SATELLA-SENPAI'S...
TRUE STRENGTH?!
TH-WHAM
KA-WHAAM
CRUMBLE
CLATTER
...?!

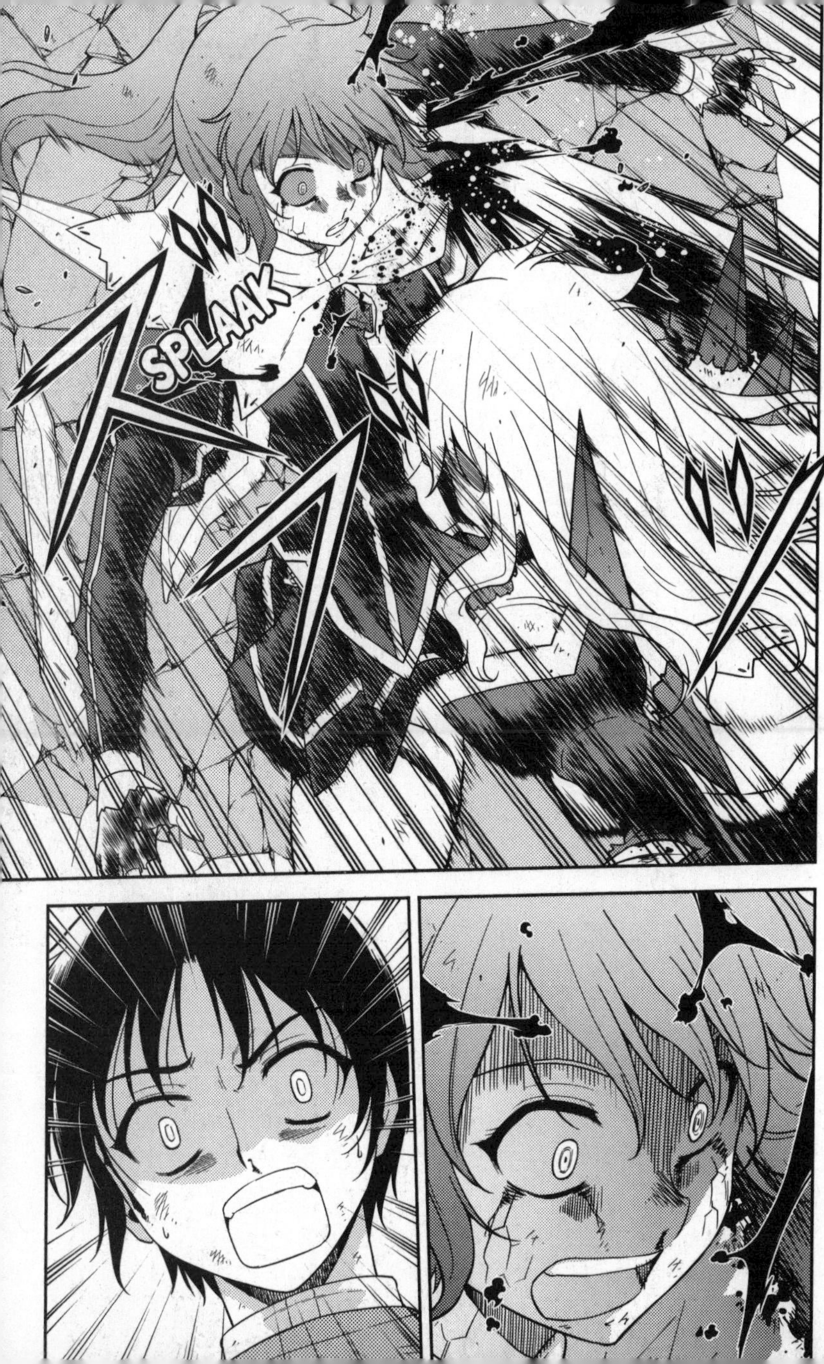
SPLAAK

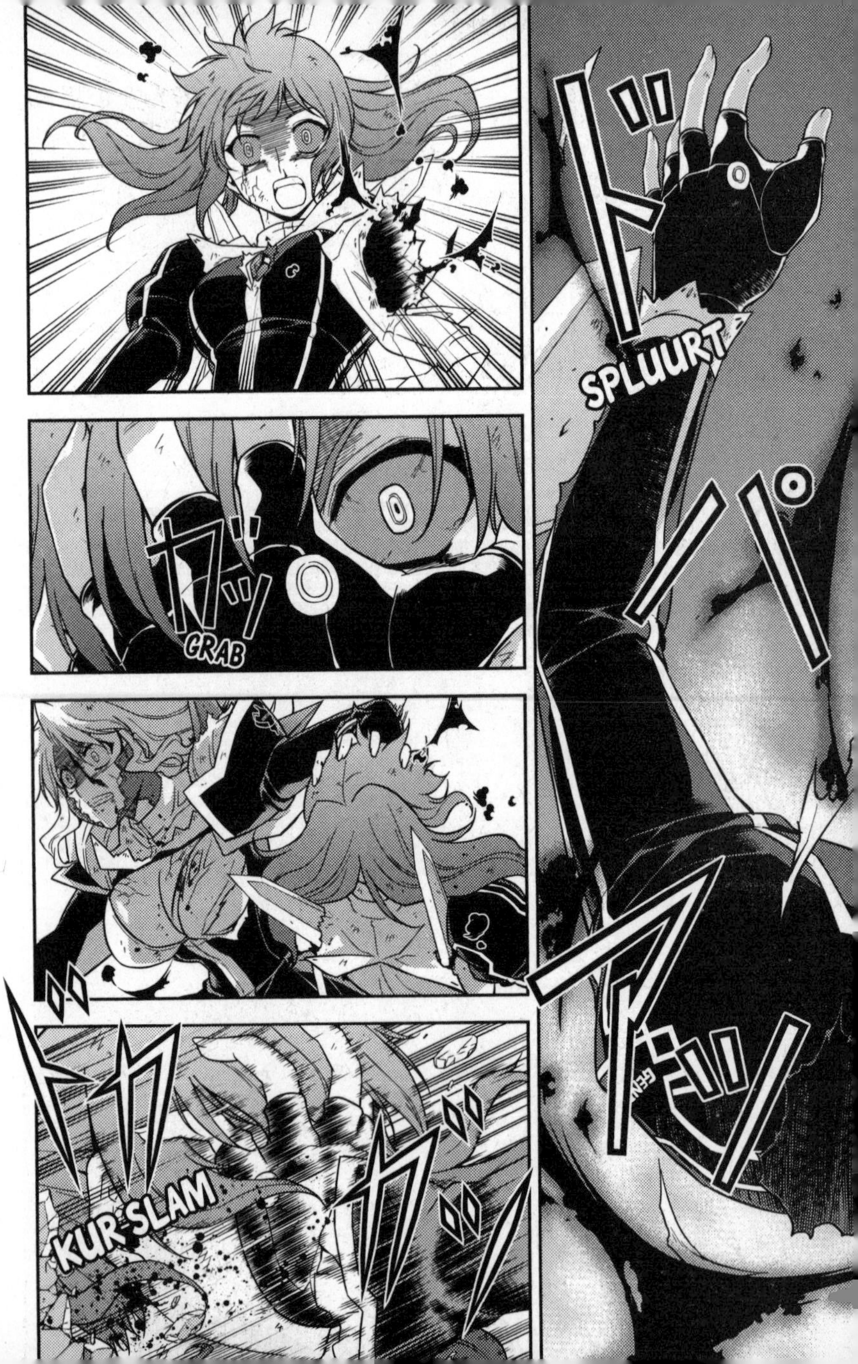
SPLUURT
GRAB
KUR-SLAM

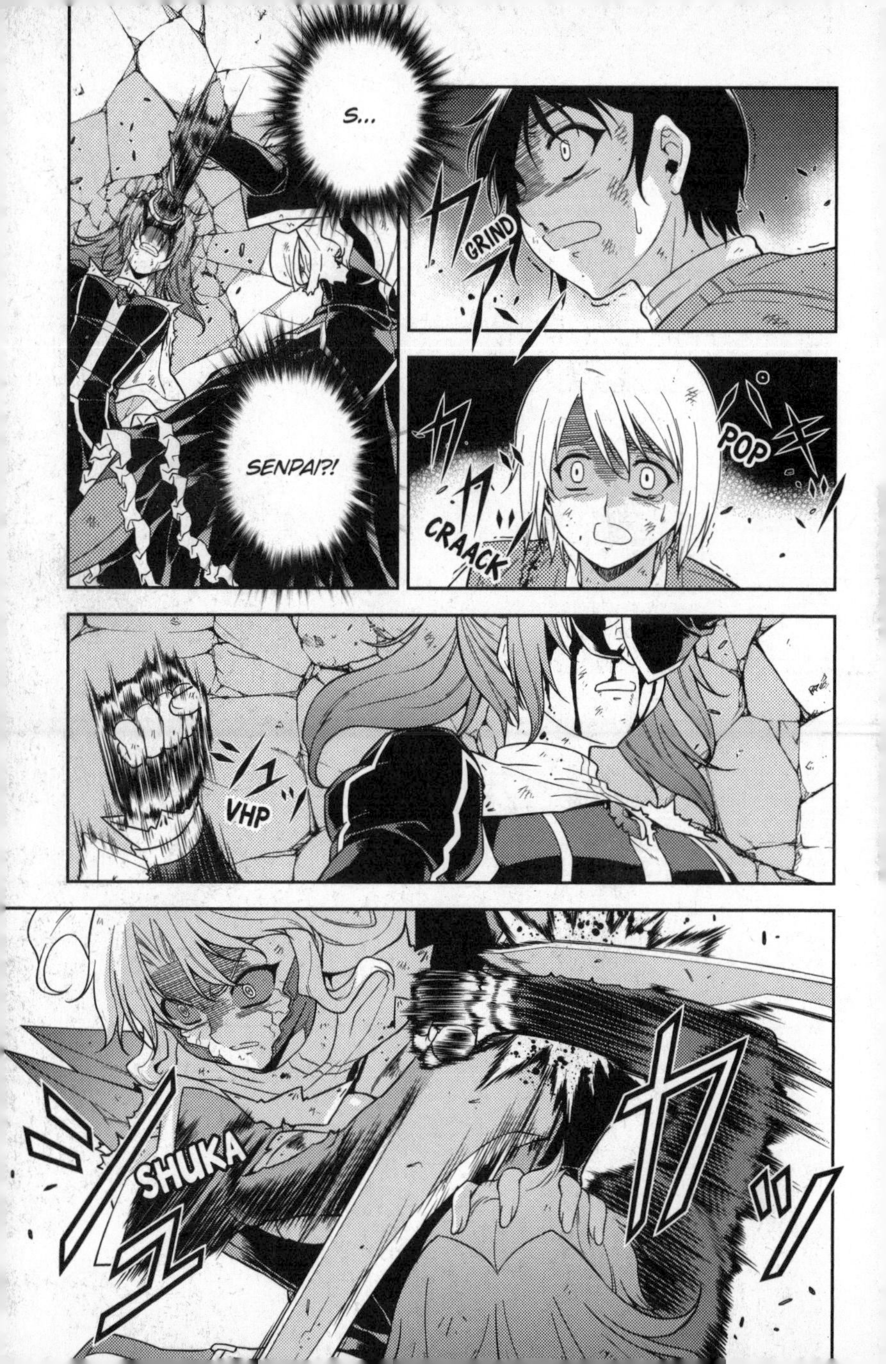
GRIND
POP
CRAACK
S...
SENPAI?!
VHP
SHUKA

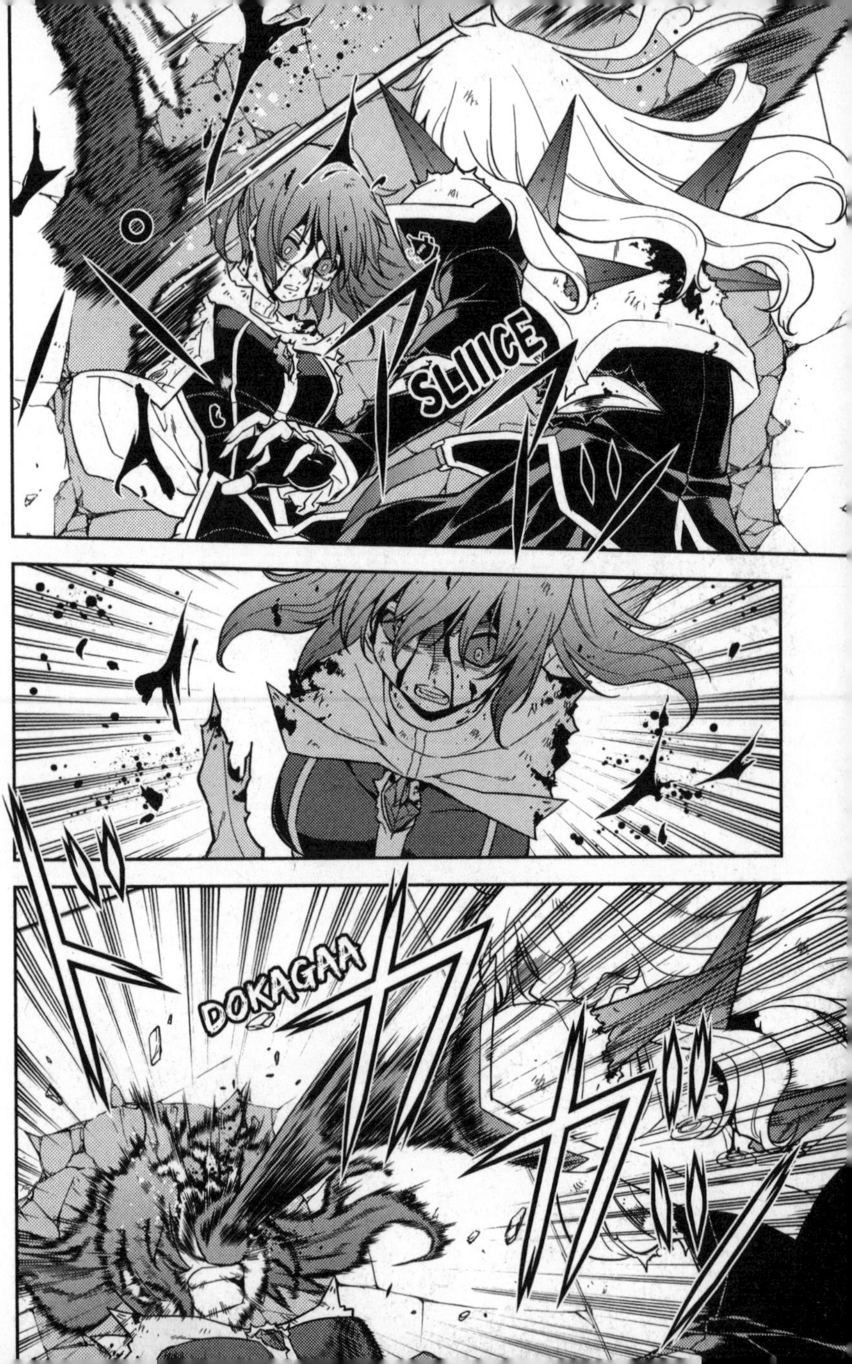
SLIICE
DOKAGAA

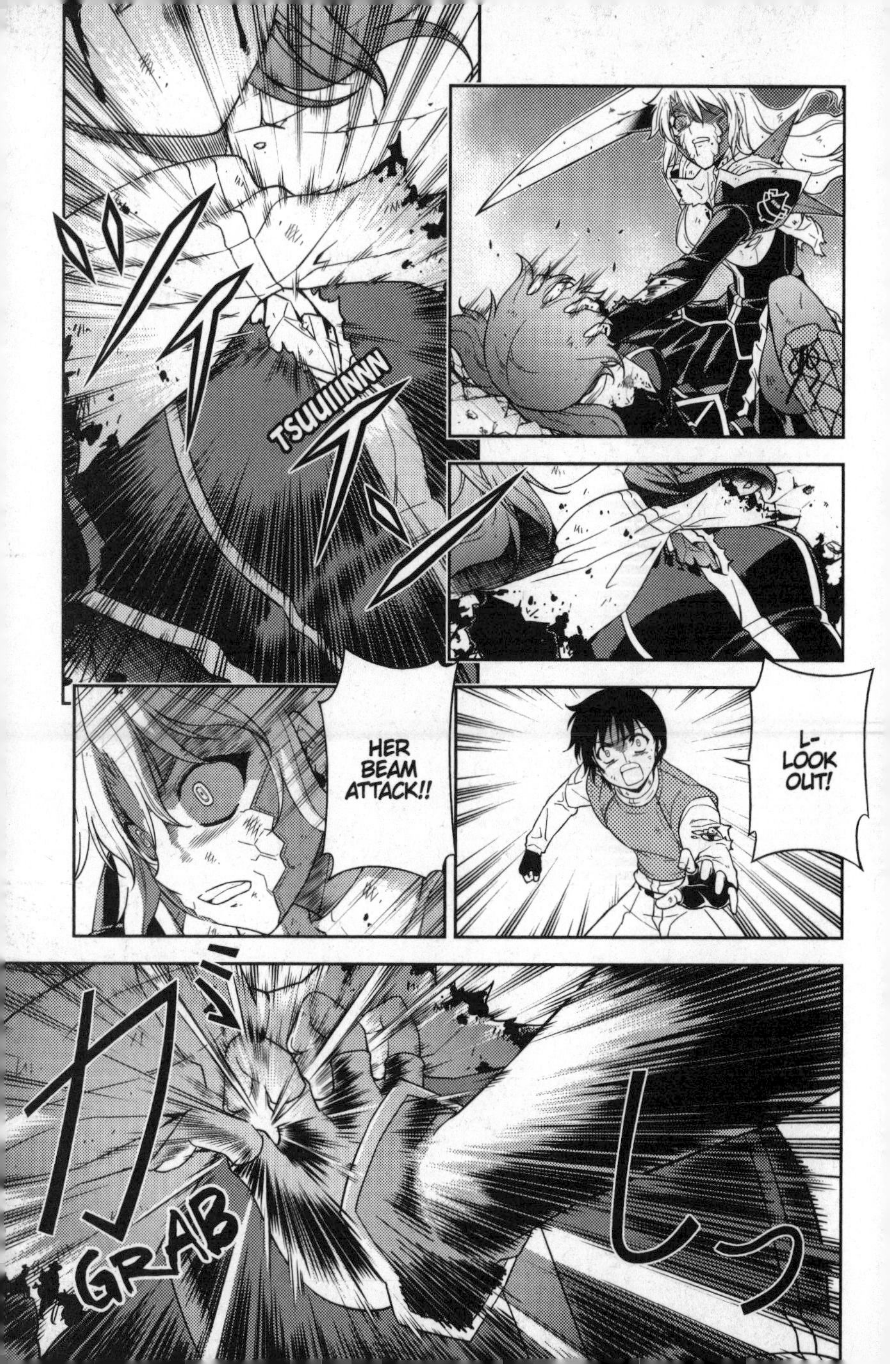
TSUUIIIINNN
L- LOOK OUT!
HER BEAM ATTACK!!
GRAB

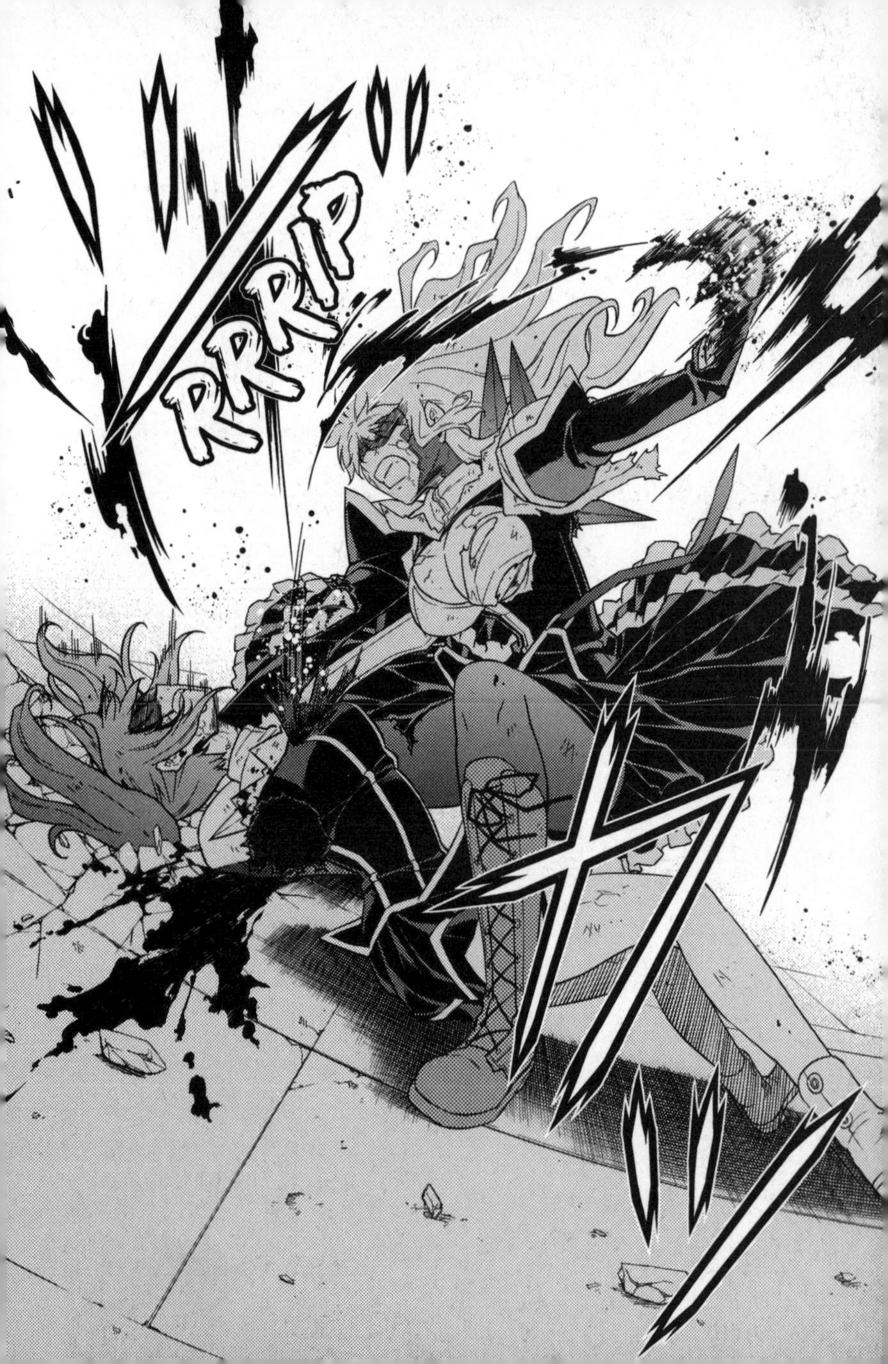
RRRIP

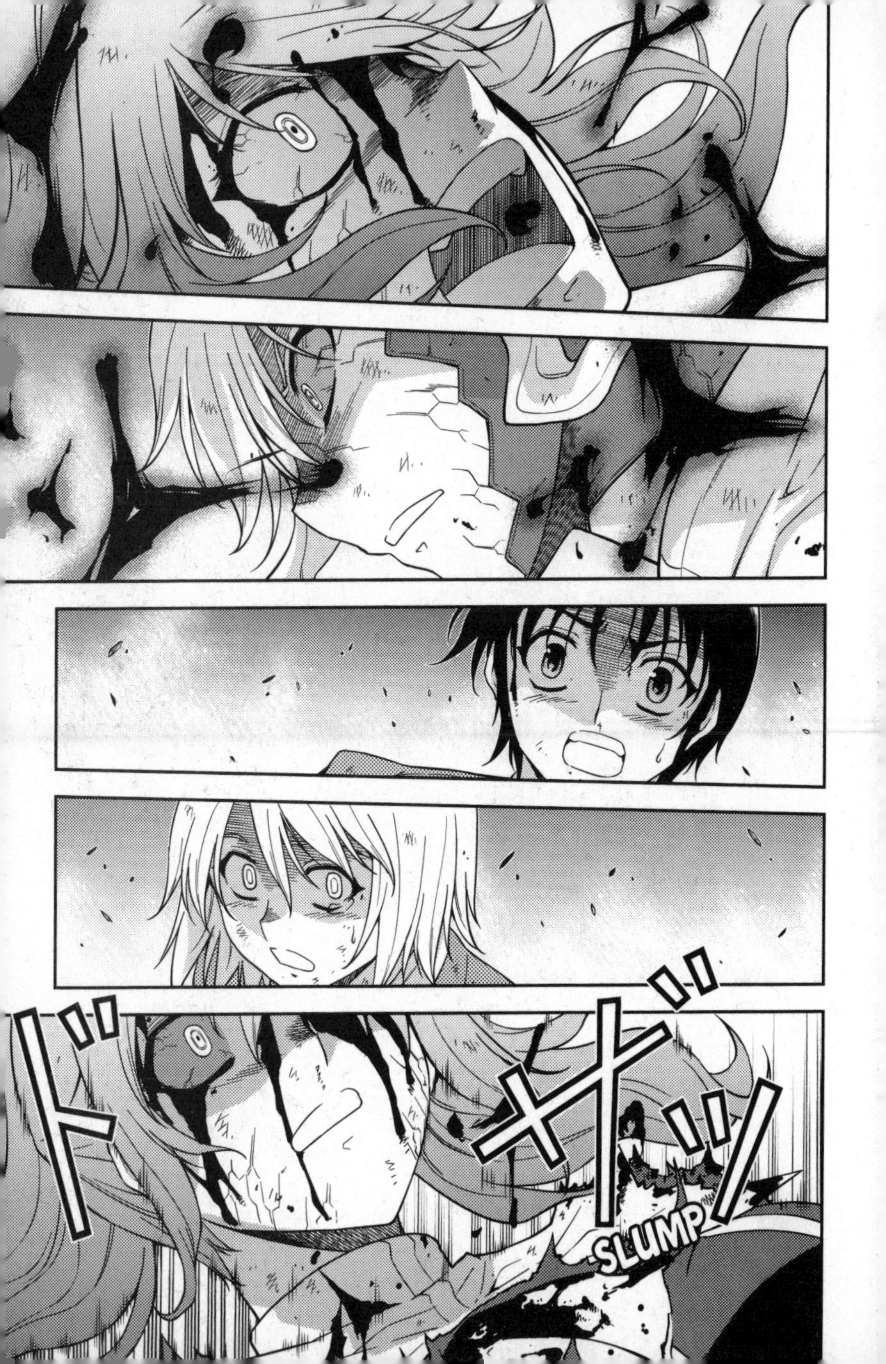
ドサッ
SLUMP

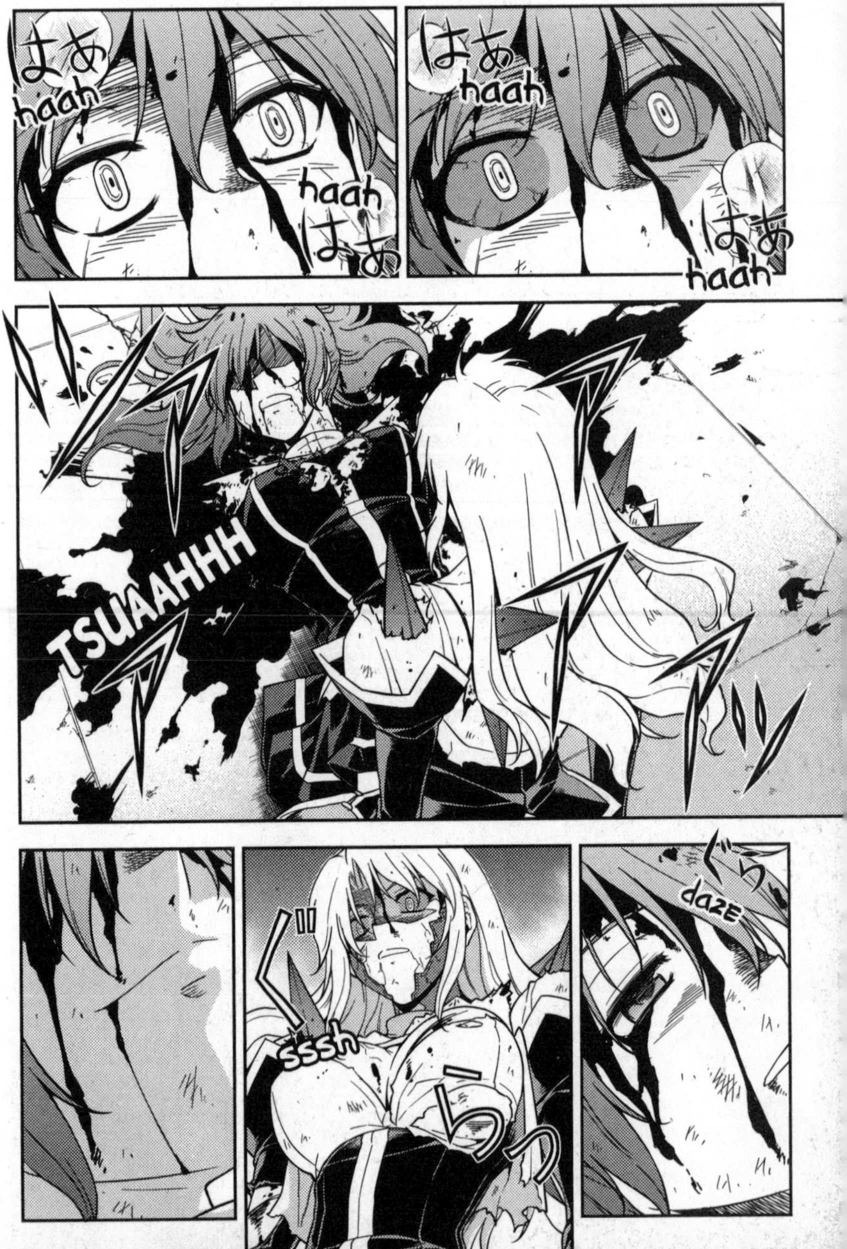
はぁ
haah
はぁ
haah
はぁ
haah
haah
はぁ
TSUAAHHH
ぐら
daze
sssh

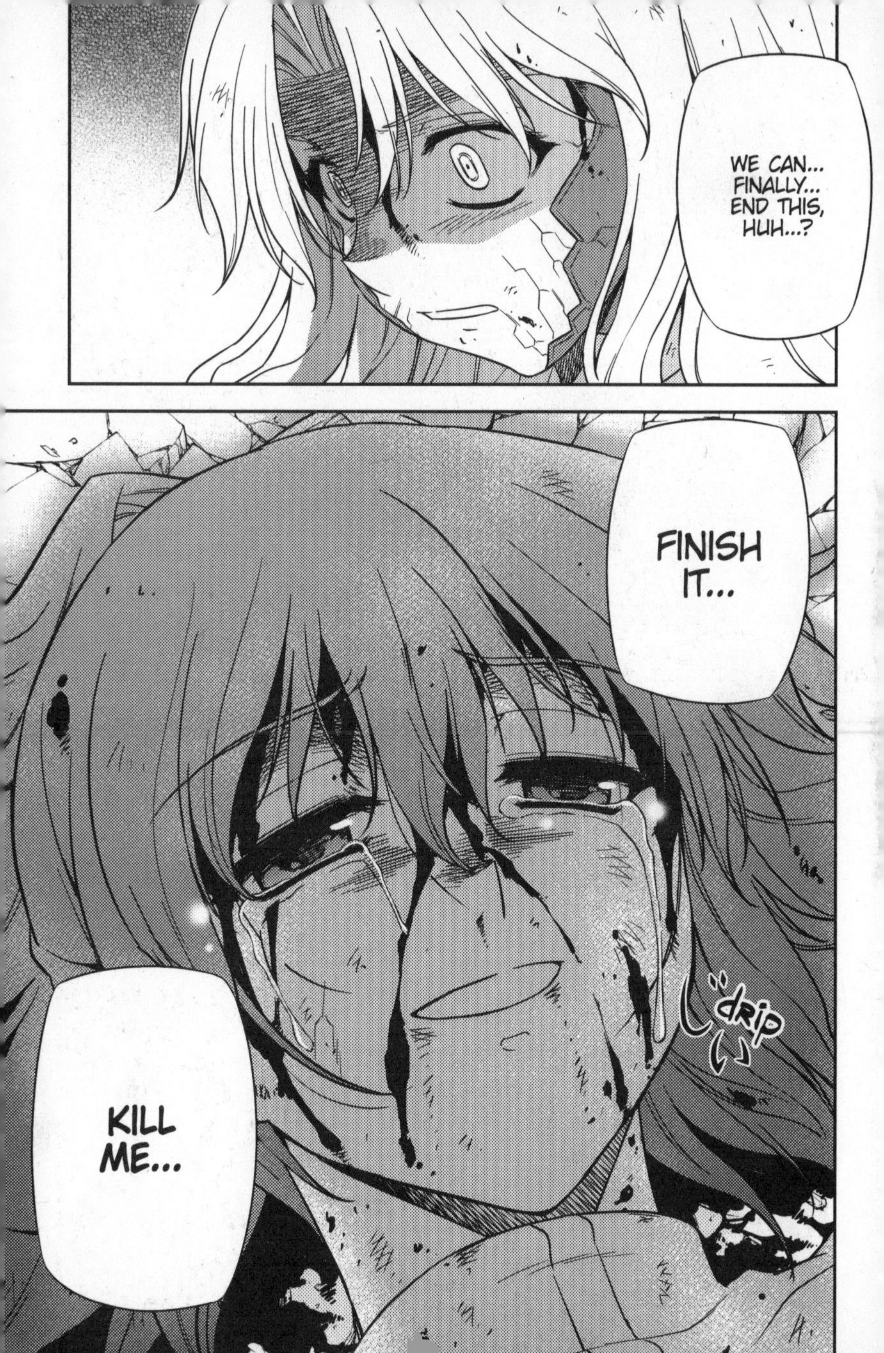
WE CAN... FINALLY... END THIS, HUH...?
FINISH IT...
じぃ drip
KILL ME...

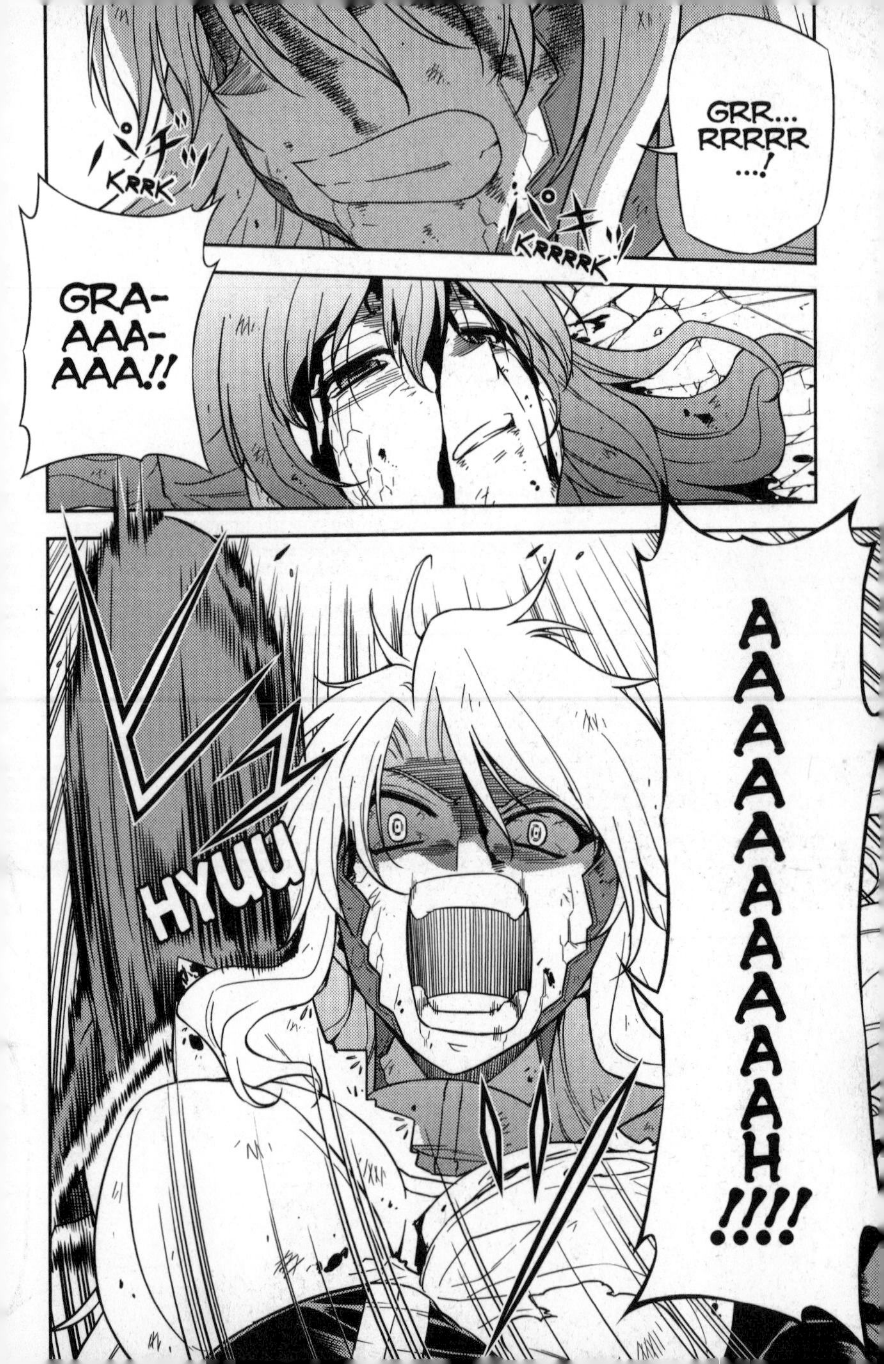
GRR... RRRRR ...!
KRRRRK
KRRK
GRA-AAA-AAA!!
AAAAAAAAAAH!!!!
HYUU

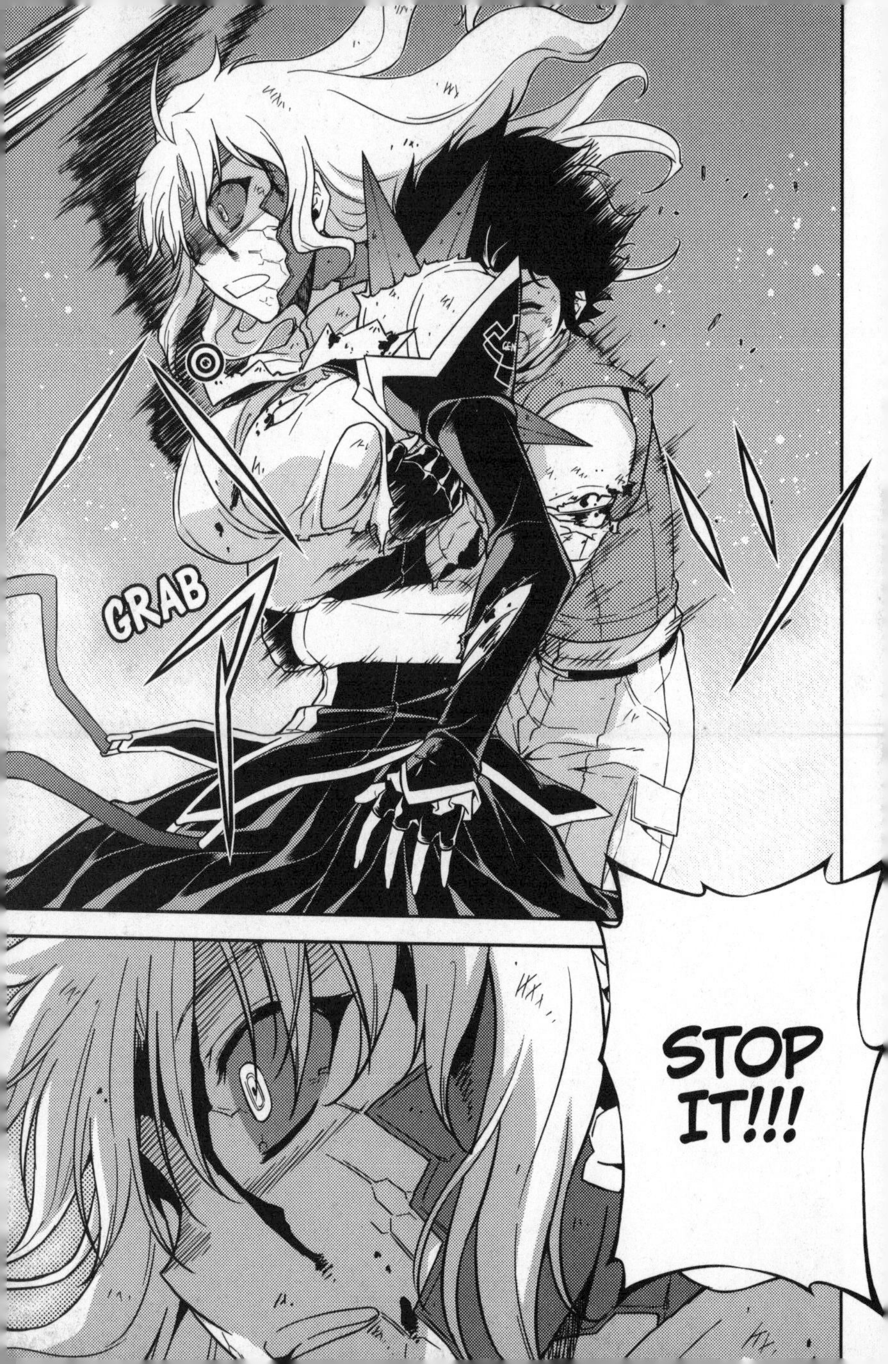
GRAB
STOP IT!!!

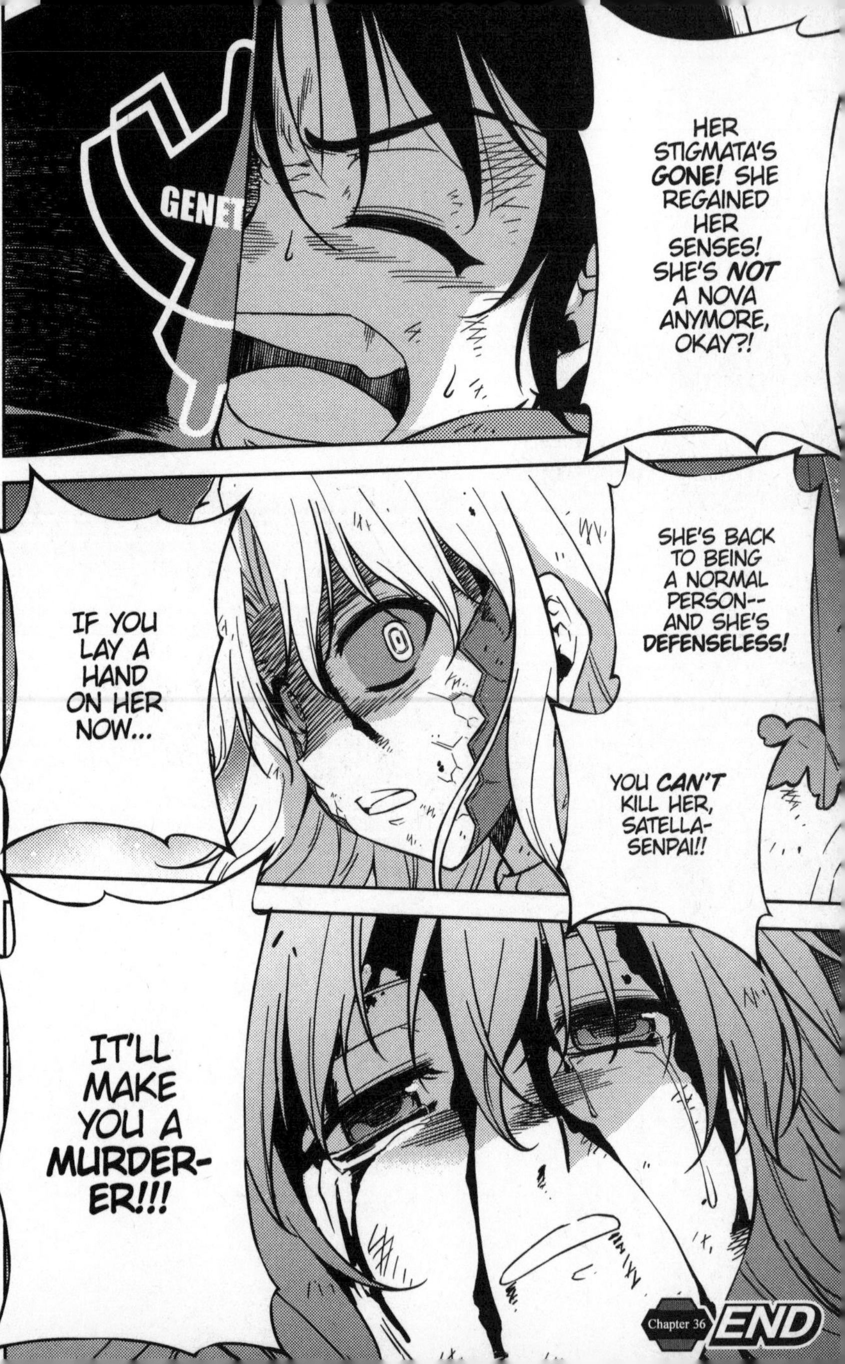
HER STIGMATA'S GONE! SHE REGAINED HER SENSES! SHE'S NOT A NOVA ANYMORE, OKAY?!
GENET
SHE'S BACK TO BEING A NORMAL PERSON-- AND SHE'S DEFENSELESS!
YOU CAN'T KILL HER, SATELLA-SENPAI!!
IF YOU LAY A HAND ON HER NOW...
IT'LL MAKE YOU A MURDER-ER!!!
Chapter 36 END

FREEZING VOLUME.6
HIGHLIGHT SCENE

FREEZING Vol.6

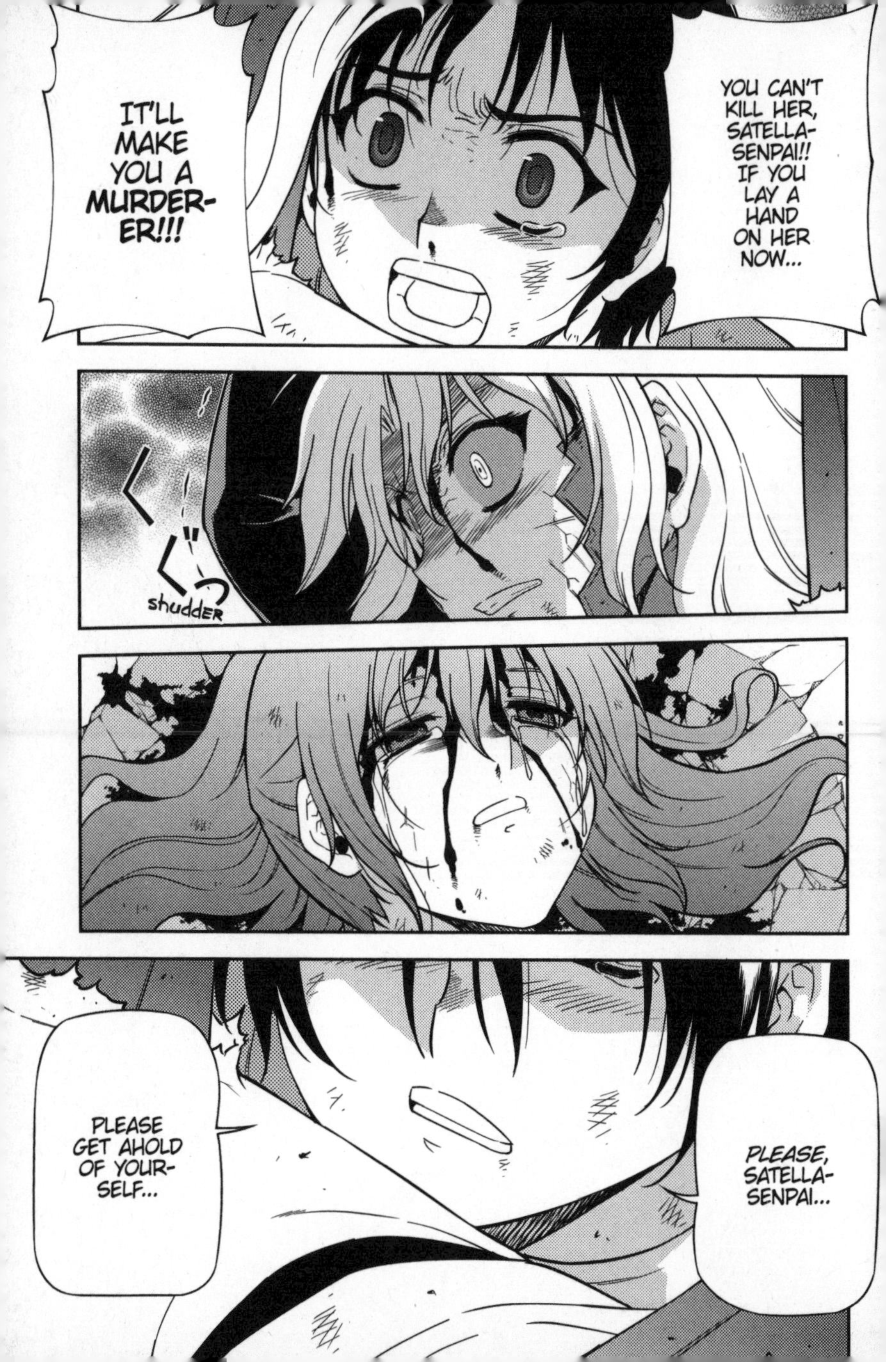
YOU CAN'T KILL HER, SATELLA-SENPAI!! IF YOU LAY A HAND ON HER NOW...
IT'LL MAKE YOU A MURDER-ER!!!
shudder
PLEASE, SATELLA-SENPAI...
PLEASE GET AHOLD OF YOUR-SELF...

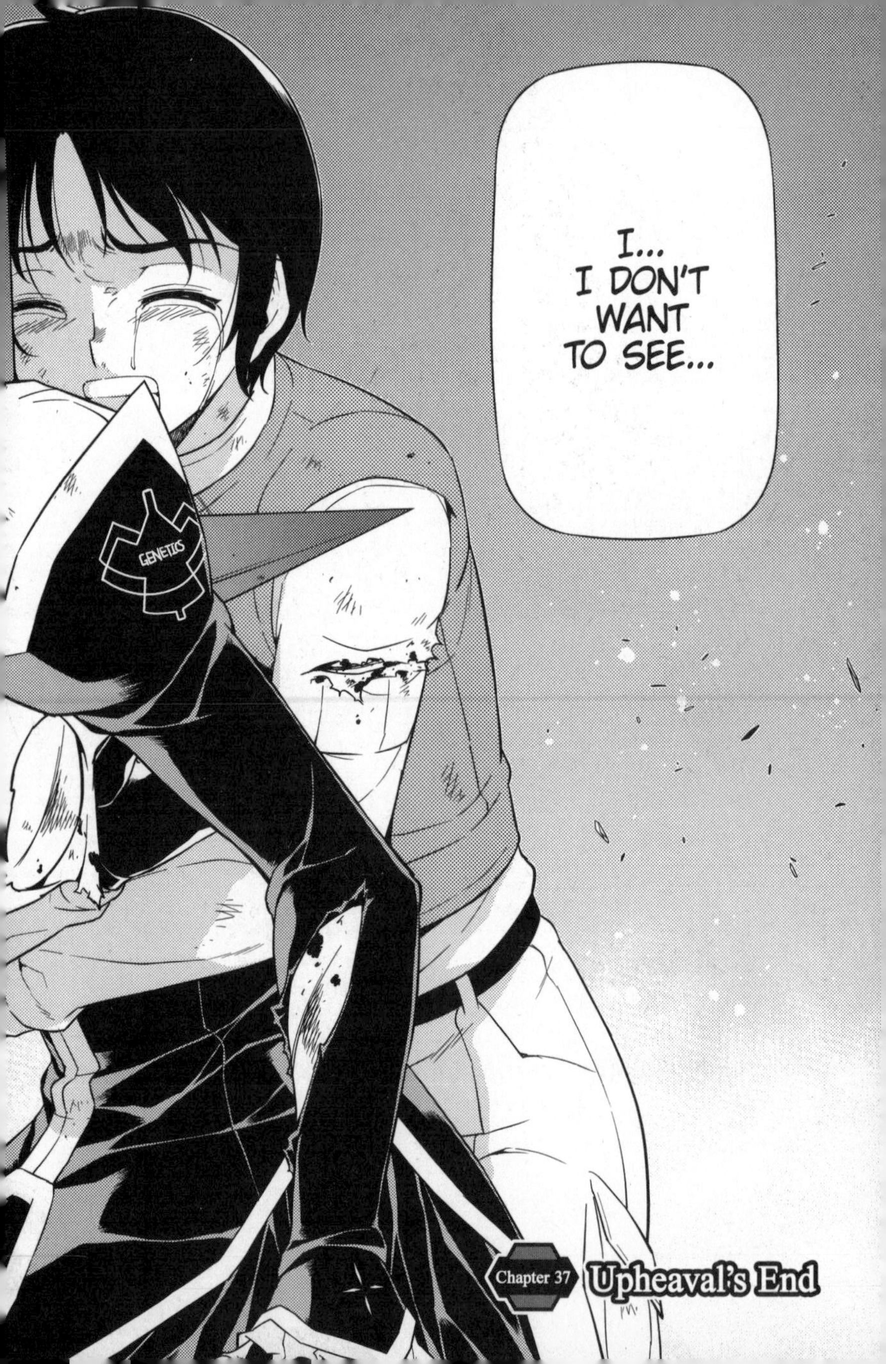
I...
I DON'T WANT TO SEE...
GENETICS
Chapter 37 Upheaval's End

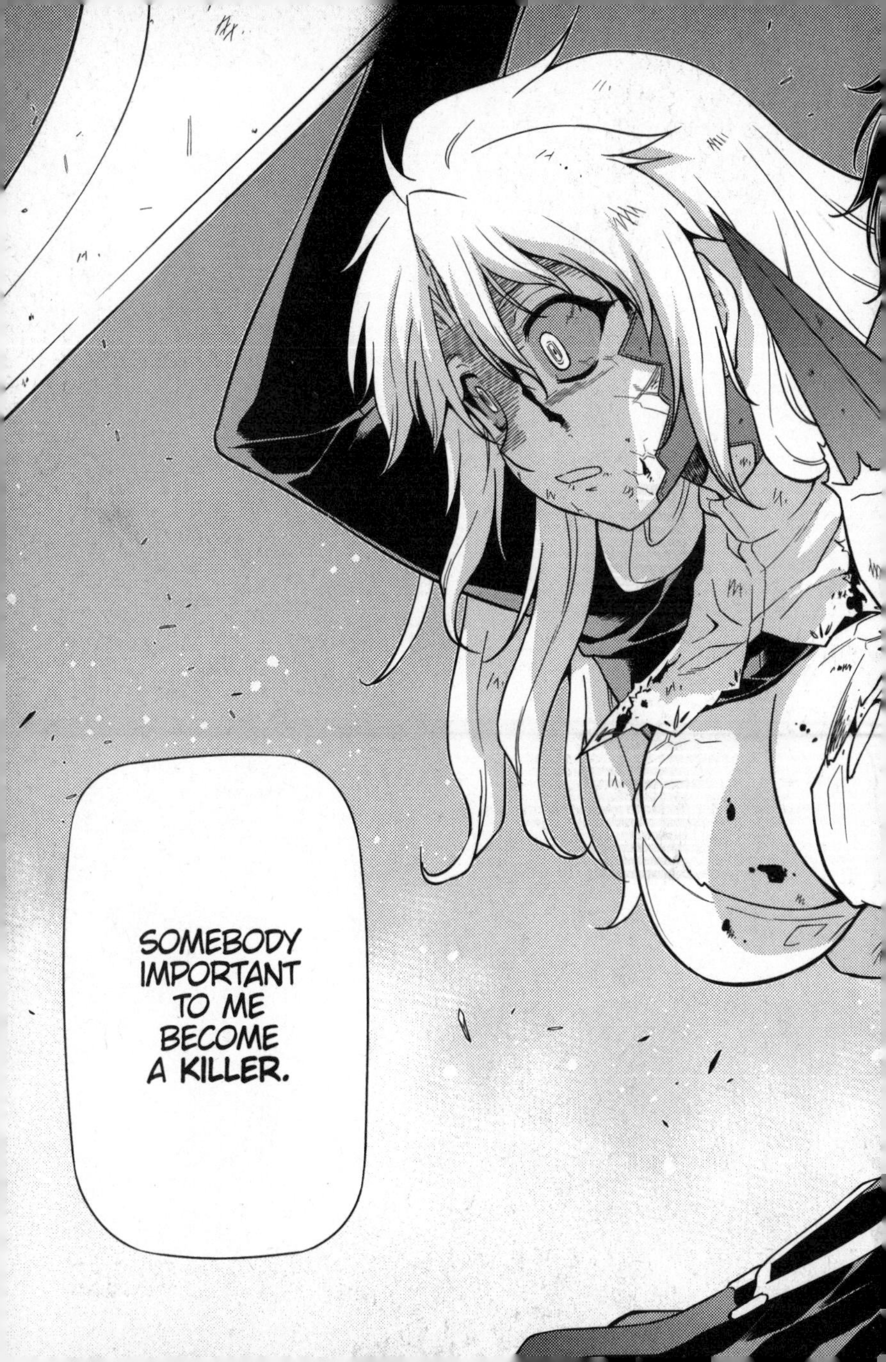
SOMEBODY IMPORTANT TO ME BECOME A KILLER.

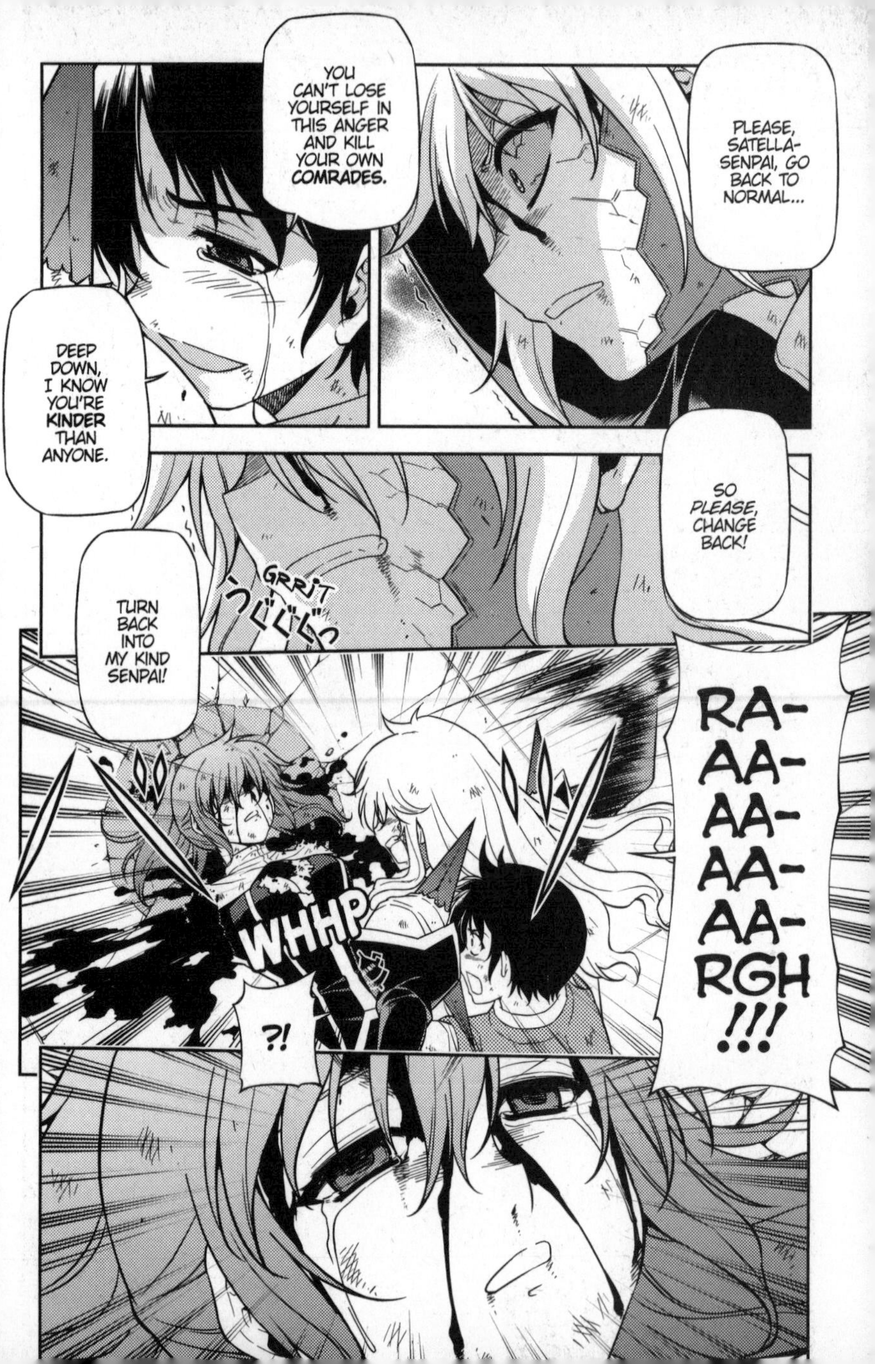
PLEASE, SATELLA-SENPAI, GO BACK TO NORMAL...
YOU CAN'T LOSE YOURSELF IN THIS ANGER AND KILL YOUR OWN COMRADES.
DEEP DOWN, I KNOW YOU'RE KINDER THAN ANYONE.
SO PLEASE, CHANGE BACK!
GRRIT
TURN BACK INTO MY KIND SENPAI!
RA-AA-AA-AA-AA-RGH!!!
WHHP
?!

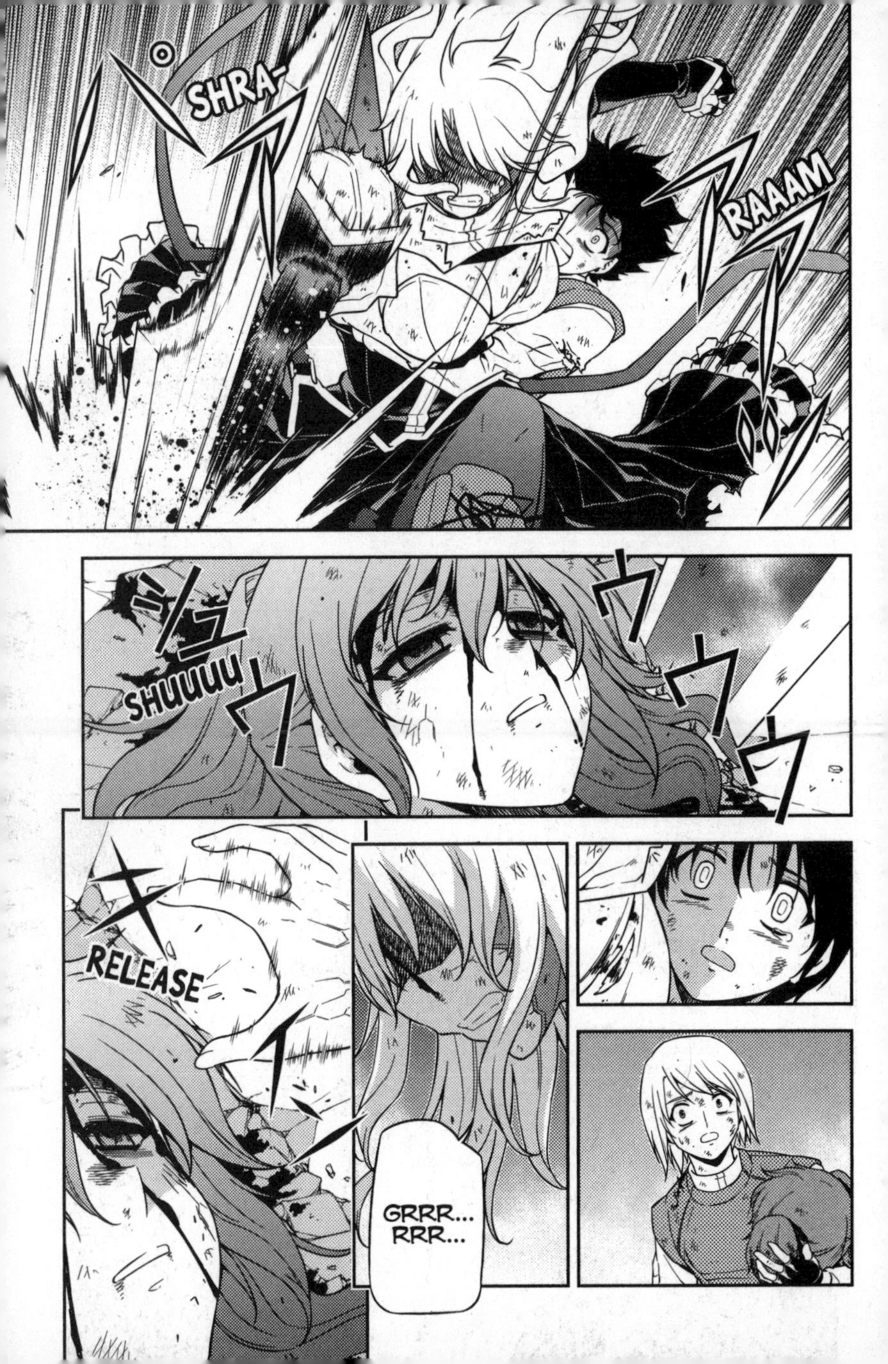
SHRA-
RAAAM
シュウウウウ
SHUUUU
GRRR... RRR...
RELEASE

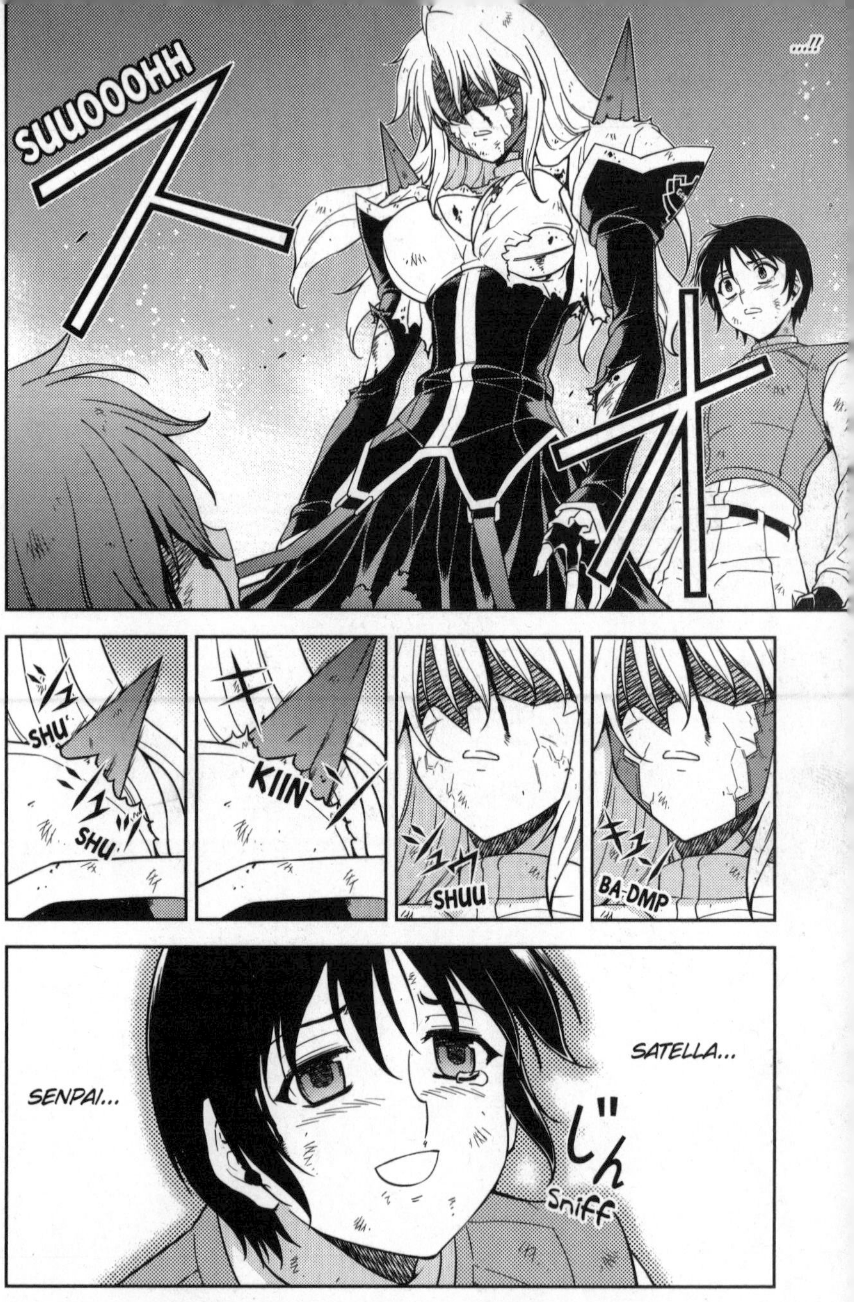

...!!
SUUOOOHH
BA-DMP
SHUU
KIIN
SHU
SHU
SATELLA...
SENPAI...
じん
Sniff

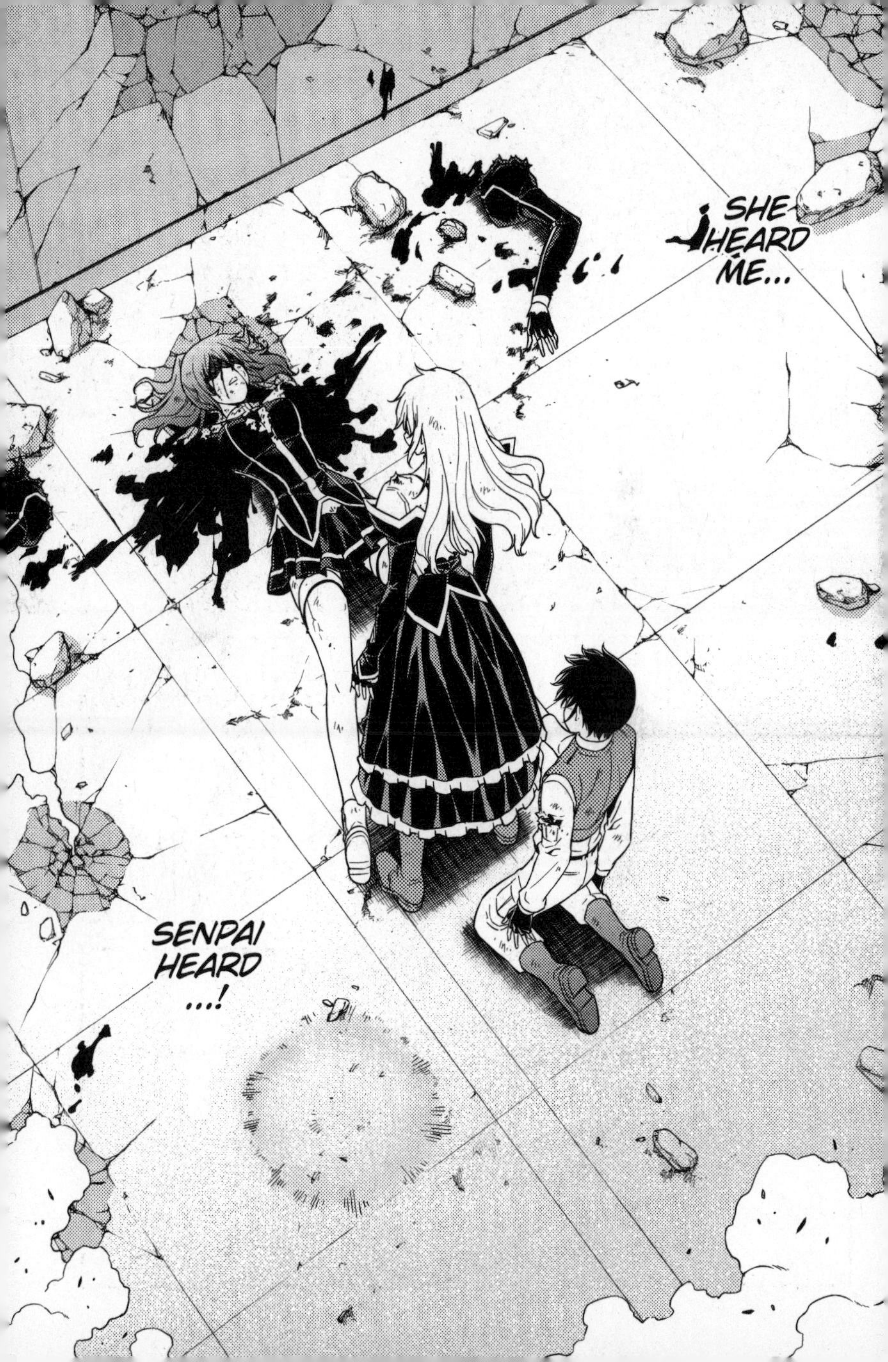
SHE HEARD ME...
SENPAI HEARD ...!

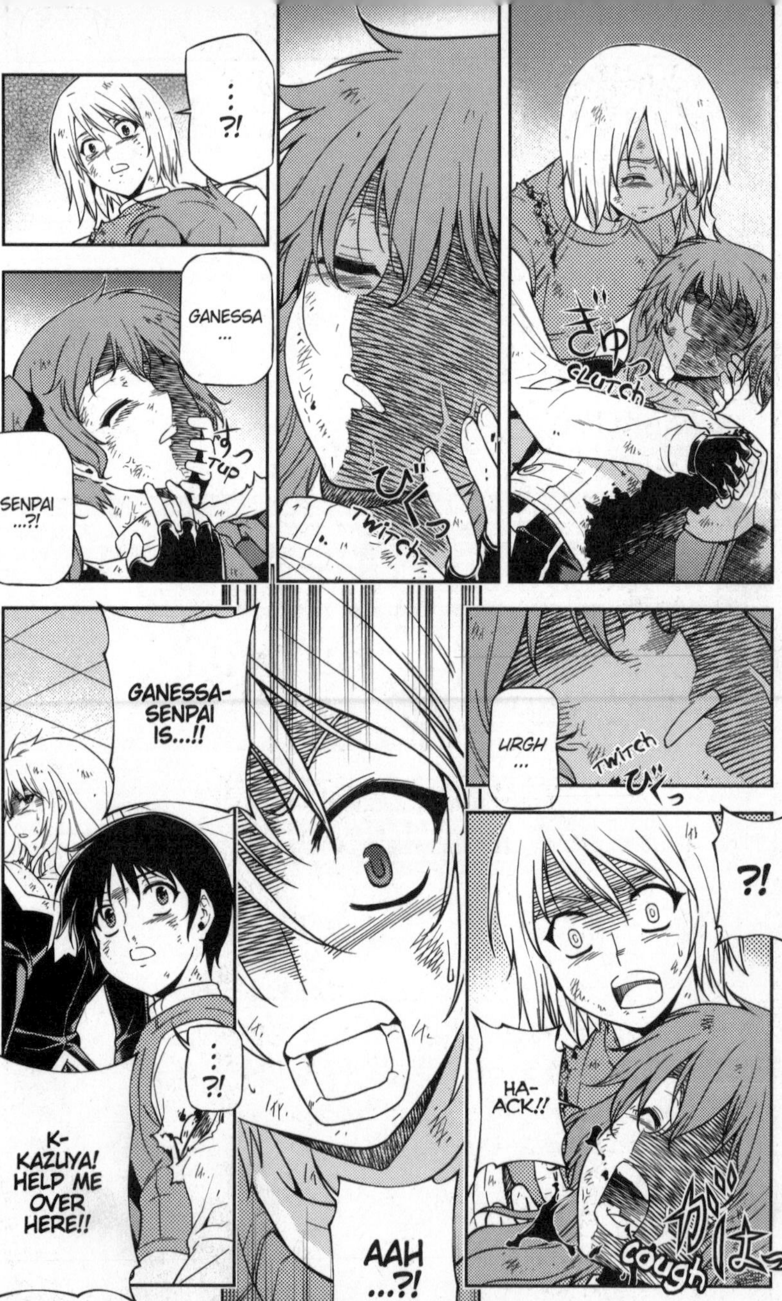

きゅっ
CLUTCH
びくっ
TWITCH
...
?!
GANESSA
...
すっ
TUP
SENPAI
...?!
URGH
...
TWITCH
びくっ
?!
HA-
ACK!!
がはっ
COUGH
GANESSA-
SENPAI
IS...!!
...
?!
K-
KAZUYA!
HELP ME
OVER
HERE!!
AAH
...?!

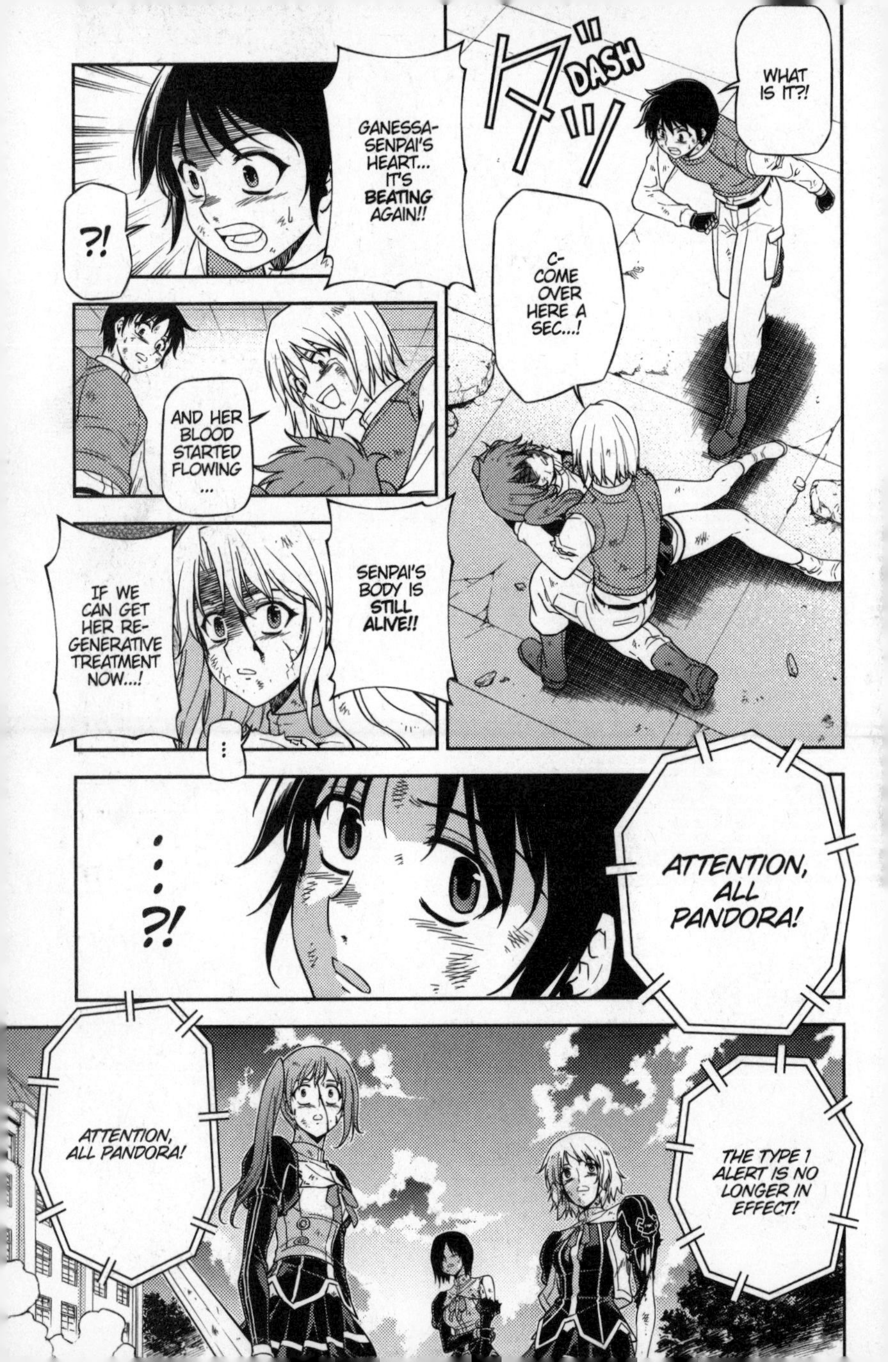
WHAT IS IT?!
DASH
C-COME OVER HERE A SEC...!
GANESSA-SENPAI'S HEART... IT'S BEATING AGAIN!!
?!
AND HER BLOOD STARTED FLOWING ...
SENPAI'S BODY IS STILL ALIVE!!
IF WE CAN GET HER RE-GENERATIVE TREATMENT NOW...!
...
ATTENTION, ALL PANDORA!
...?!
THE TYPE 1 ALERT IS NO LONGER IN EFFECT!
ATTENTION, ALL PANDORA!

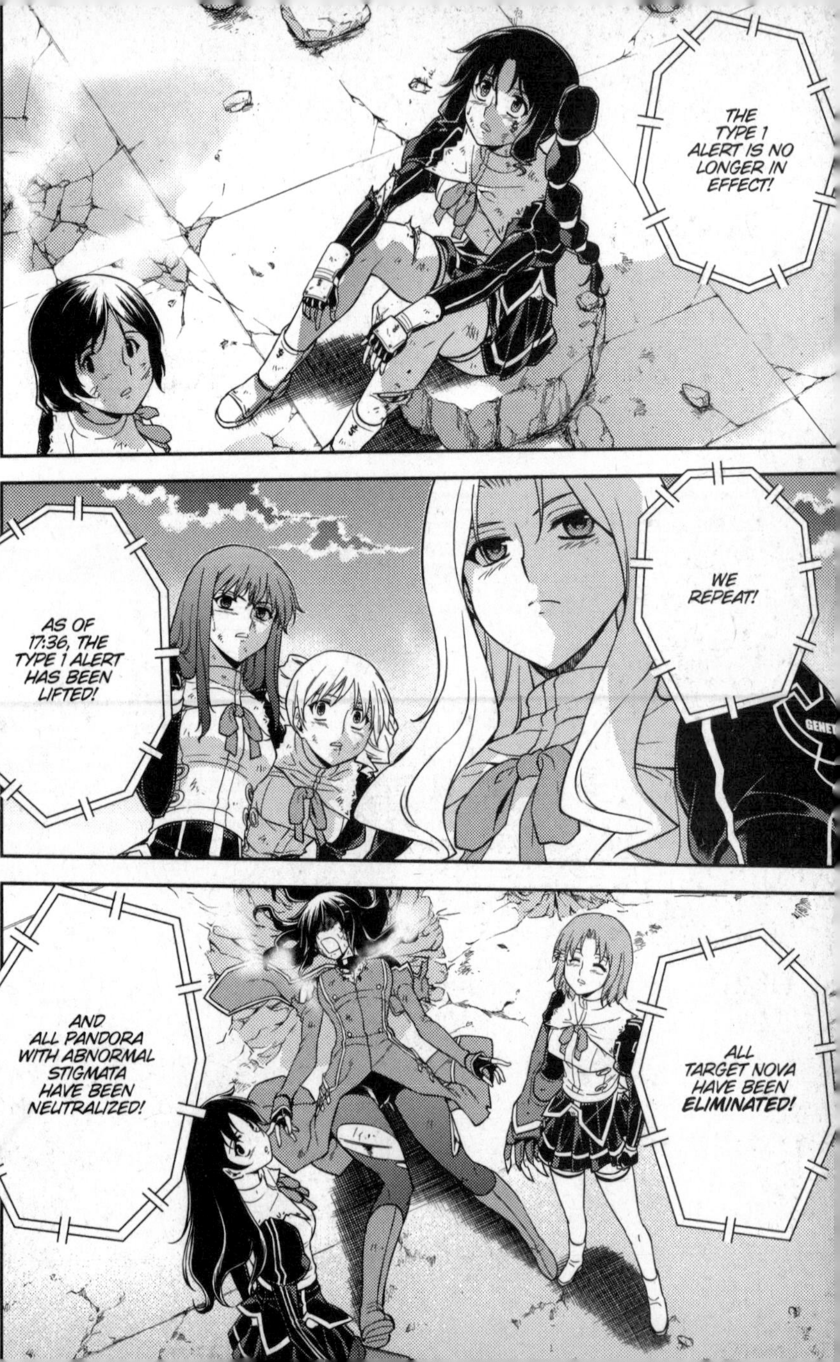
THE TYPE 1 ALERT IS NO LONGER IN EFFECT!
WE REPEAT!
AS OF 17:36, THE TYPE 1 ALERT HAS BEEN LIFTED!
ALL TARGET NOVA HAVE BEEN ELIMINATED!
AND ALL PANDORA WITH ABNORMAL STIGMATA HAVE BEEN NEUTRALIZED!

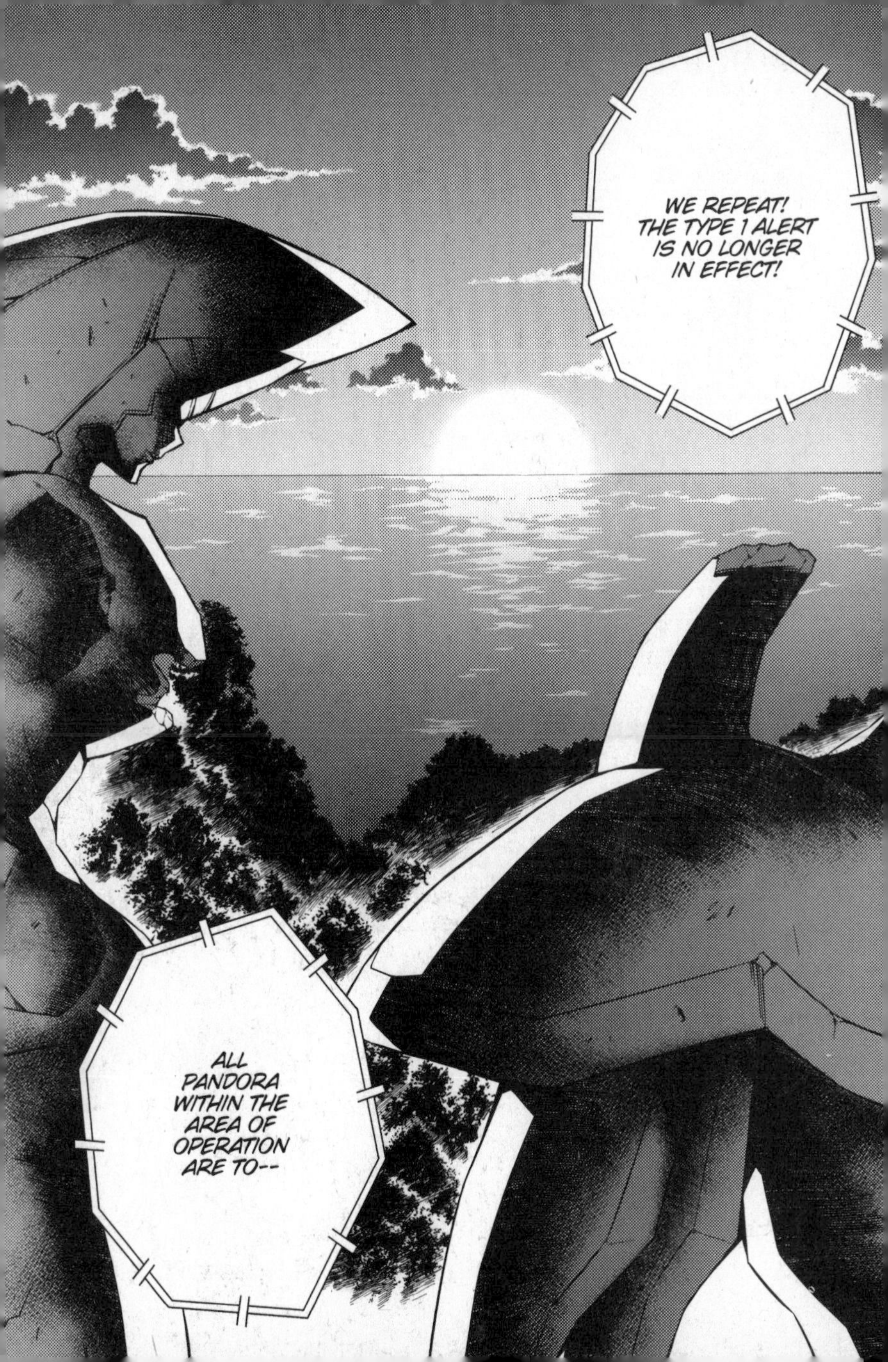
WE REPEAT! THE TYPE 1 ALERT IS NO LONGER IN EFFECT!
ALL PANDORA WITHIN THE AREA OF OPERATION ARE TO--

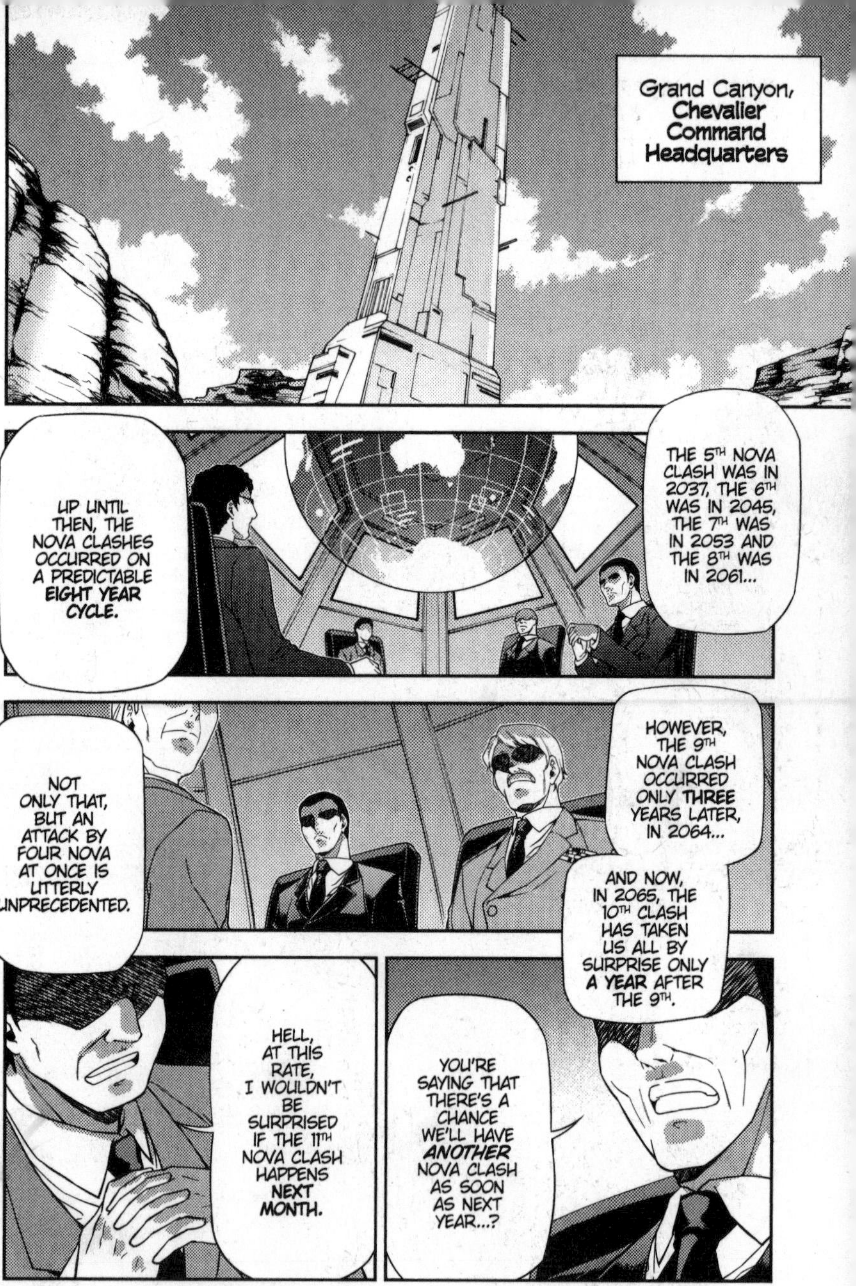
Grand Canyon, Chevalier Command Headquarters
THE 5TH NOVA CLASH WAS IN 2037, THE 6TH WAS IN 2045, THE 7TH WAS IN 2053 AND THE 8TH WAS IN 2061...
UP UNTIL THEN, THE NOVA CLASHES OCCURRED ON A PREDICTABLE **EIGHT YEAR CYCLE.**
HOWEVER, THE 9TH NOVA CLASH OCCURRED ONLY **THREE** YEARS LATER, IN 2064...
AND NOW, IN 2065, THE 10TH CLASH HAS TAKEN US ALL BY SURPRISE ONLY **A YEAR** AFTER THE 9TH.
NOT ONLY THAT, BUT AN ATTACK BY FOUR NOVA AT ONCE IS UTTERLY UNPRECEDENTED.
YOU'RE SAYING THAT THERE'S A CHANCE WE'LL HAVE ***ANOTHER*** NOVA CLASH AS SOON AS NEXT YEAR...?
HELL, AT THIS RATE, I WOULDN'T BE SURPRISED IF THE 11TH NOVA CLASH HAPPENS **NEXT MONTH.**

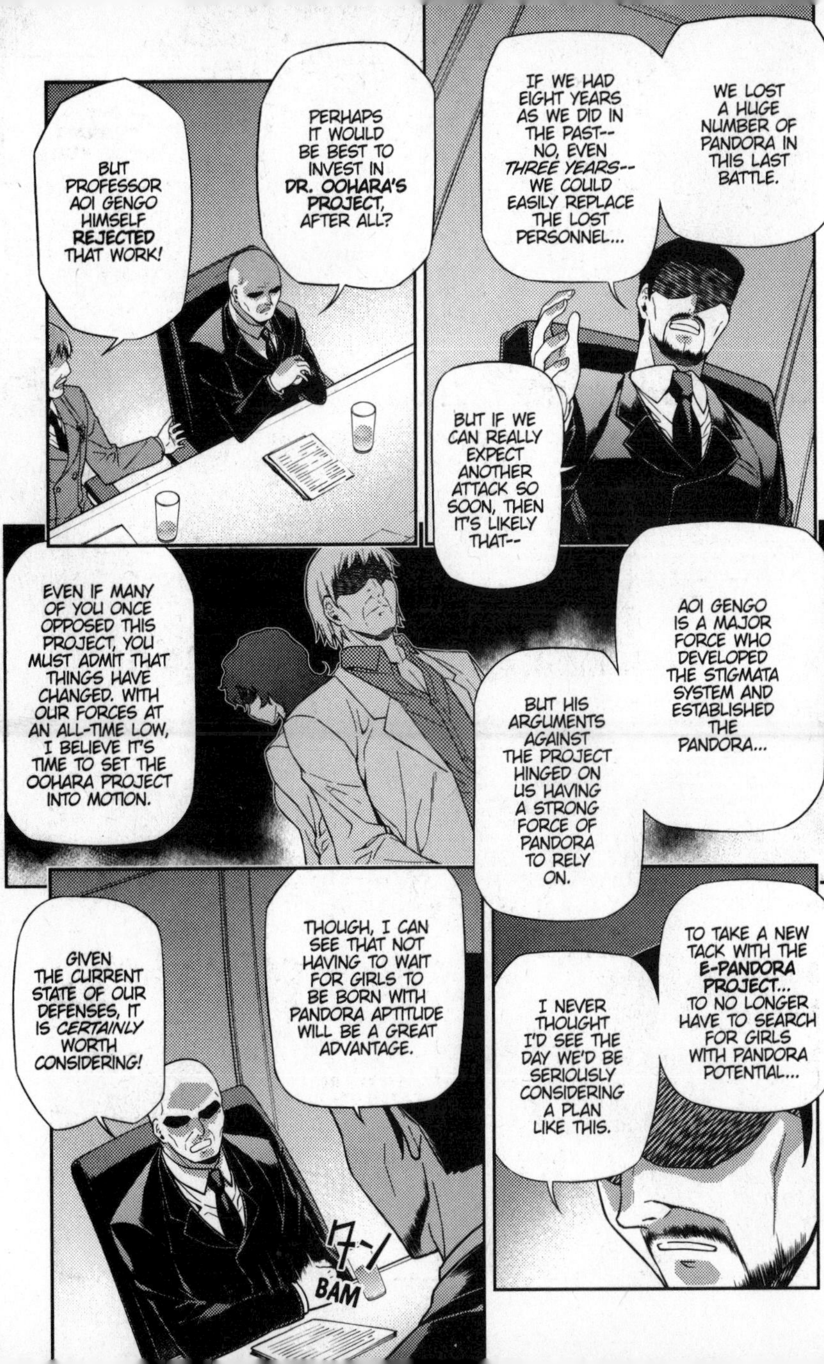
WE LOST A HUGE NUMBER OF PANDORA IN THIS LAST BATTLE.
IF WE HAD EIGHT YEARS AS WE DID IN THE PAST-- NO, EVEN *THREE YEARS*-- WE COULD EASILY REPLACE THE LOST PERSONNEL...
BUT IF WE CAN REALLY EXPECT ANOTHER ATTACK SO SOON, THEN IT'S LIKELY THAT--
PERHAPS IT WOULD BE BEST TO INVEST IN **DR. OOHARA'S PROJECT**, AFTER ALL?
BUT PROFESSOR AOI GENGO HIMSELF **REJECTED** THAT WORK!
AOI GENGO IS A MAJOR FORCE WHO DEVELOPED THE STIGMATA SYSTEM AND ESTABLISHED THE PANDORA...
BUT HIS ARGUMENTS AGAINST THE PROJECT HINGED ON US HAVING A STRONG FORCE OF PANDORA TO RELY ON.
EVEN IF MANY OF YOU ONCE OPPOSED THIS PROJECT, YOU MUST ADMIT THAT THINGS HAVE CHANGED. WITH OUR FORCES AT AN ALL-TIME LOW, I BELIEVE IT'S TIME TO SET THE OOHARA PROJECT INTO MOTION.
TO TAKE A NEW TACK WITH THE **E-PANDORA PROJECT**... TO NO LONGER HAVE TO SEARCH FOR GIRLS WITH PANDORA POTENTIAL...
I NEVER THOUGHT I'D SEE THE DAY WE'D BE SERIOUSLY CONSIDERING A PLAN LIKE THIS.
THOUGH, I CAN SEE THAT NOT HAVING TO WAIT FOR GIRLS TO BE BORN WITH PANDORA APTITUDE WILL BE A GREAT ADVANTAGE.
GIVEN THE CURRENT STATE OF OUR DEFENSES, IT IS *CERTAINLY* WORTH CONSIDERING!
BAM

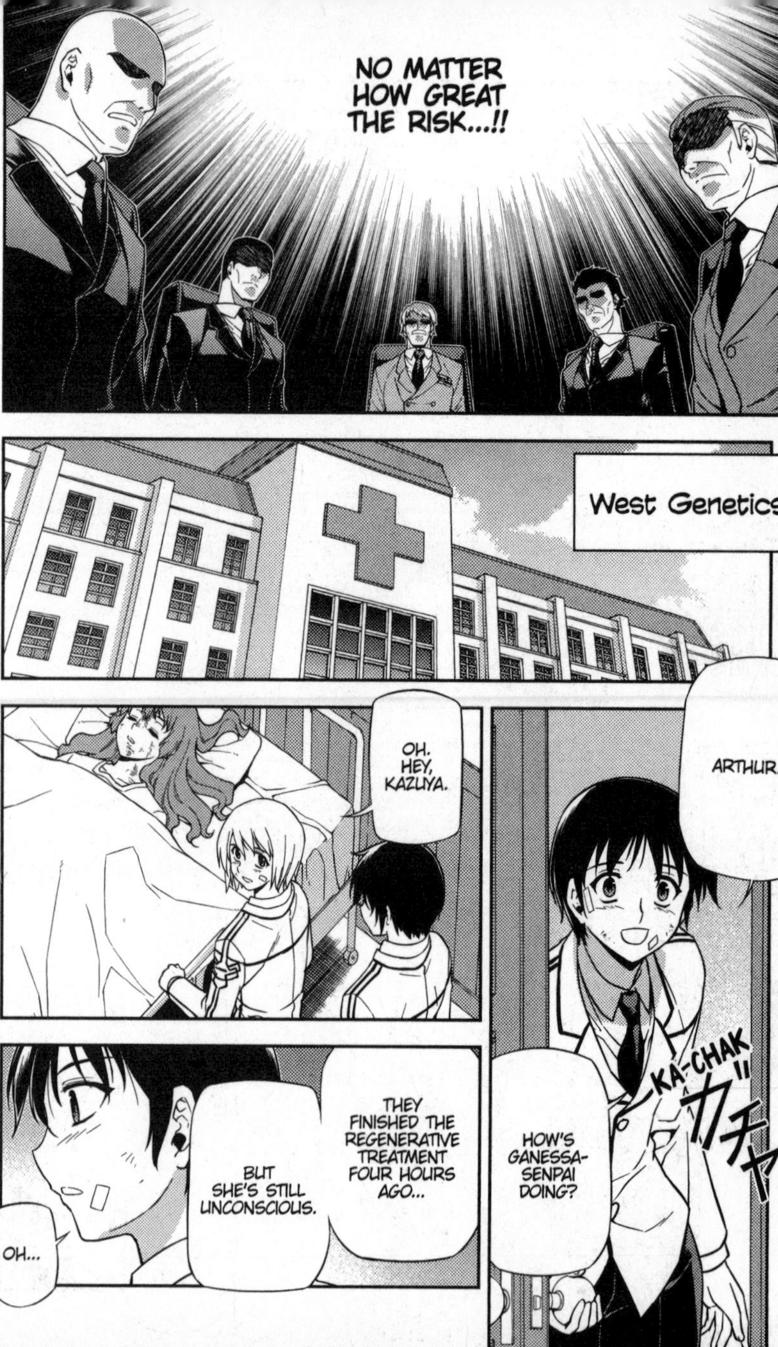
NO MATTER HOW GREAT THE RISK...!!
West Genetics
ARTHUR...
KA-CHAK
カチャ
HOW'S GANESSA-SENPAI DOING?
OH. HEY, KAZUYA.
THEY FINISHED THE REGENERATIVE TREATMENT FOUR HOURS AGO...
BUT SHE'S STILL UNCONSCIOUS.
OH...

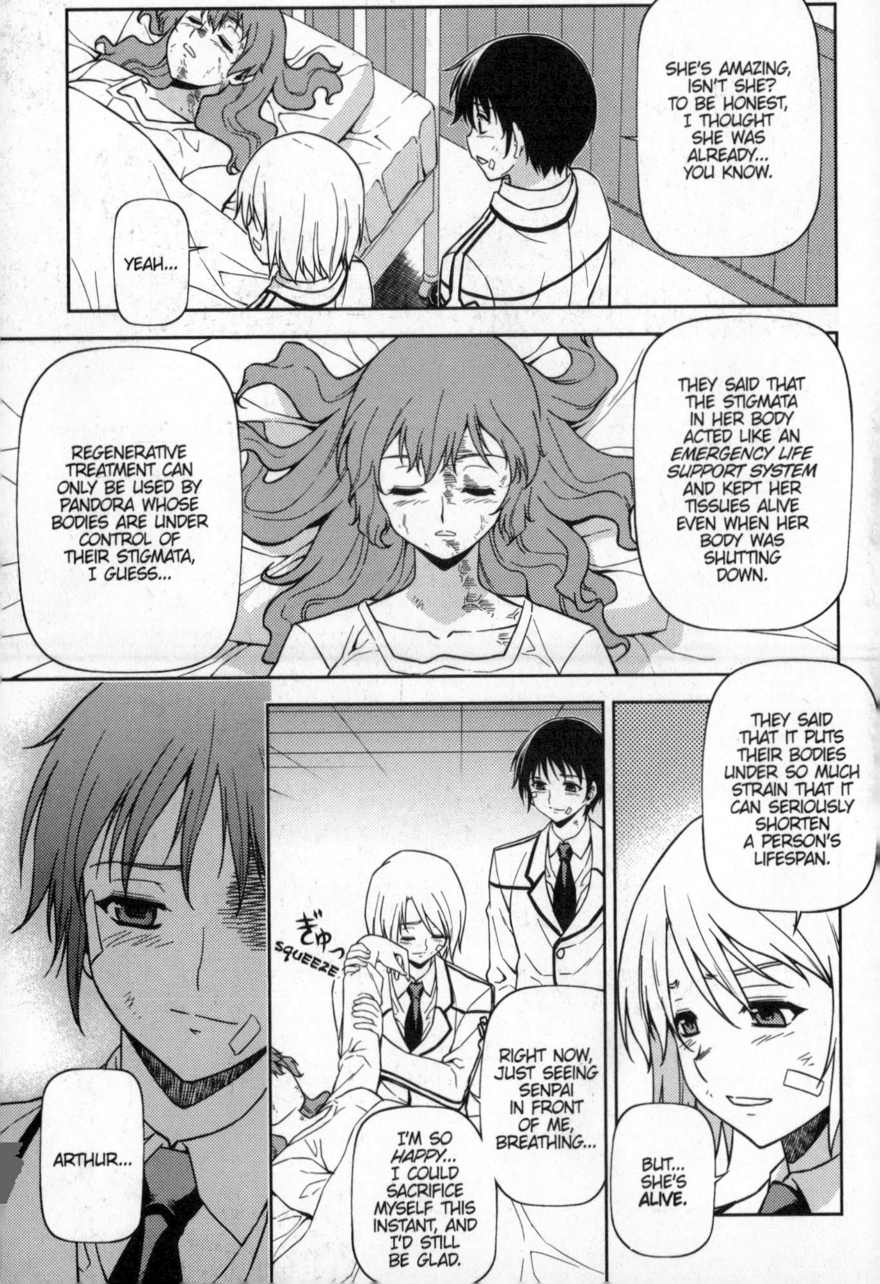
SHE'S AMAZING, ISN'T SHE? TO BE HONEST, I THOUGHT SHE WAS ALREADY... YOU KNOW.
YEAH...
THEY SAID THAT THE STIGMATA IN HER BODY ACTED LIKE AN *EMERGENCY LIFE SUPPORT SYSTEM* AND KEPT HER TISSUES ALIVE EVEN WHEN HER BODY WAS SHUTTING DOWN.
REGENERATIVE TREATMENT CAN ONLY BE USED BY PANDORA WHOSE BODIES ARE UNDER CONTROL OF THEIR STIGMATA, I GUESS...
THEY SAID THAT IT PUTS THEIR BODIES UNDER SO MUCH STRAIN THAT IT CAN SERIOUSLY SHORTEN A PERSON'S LIFESPAN.
BUT... SHE'S **ALIVE.**
ぎゅっ
SQUEEZE
RIGHT NOW, JUST SEEING SENPAI IN FRONT OF ME, BREATHING...
I'M SO *HAPPY*... I COULD SACRIFICE MYSELF THIS INSTANT, AND I'D STILL BE GLAD.
ARTHUR...

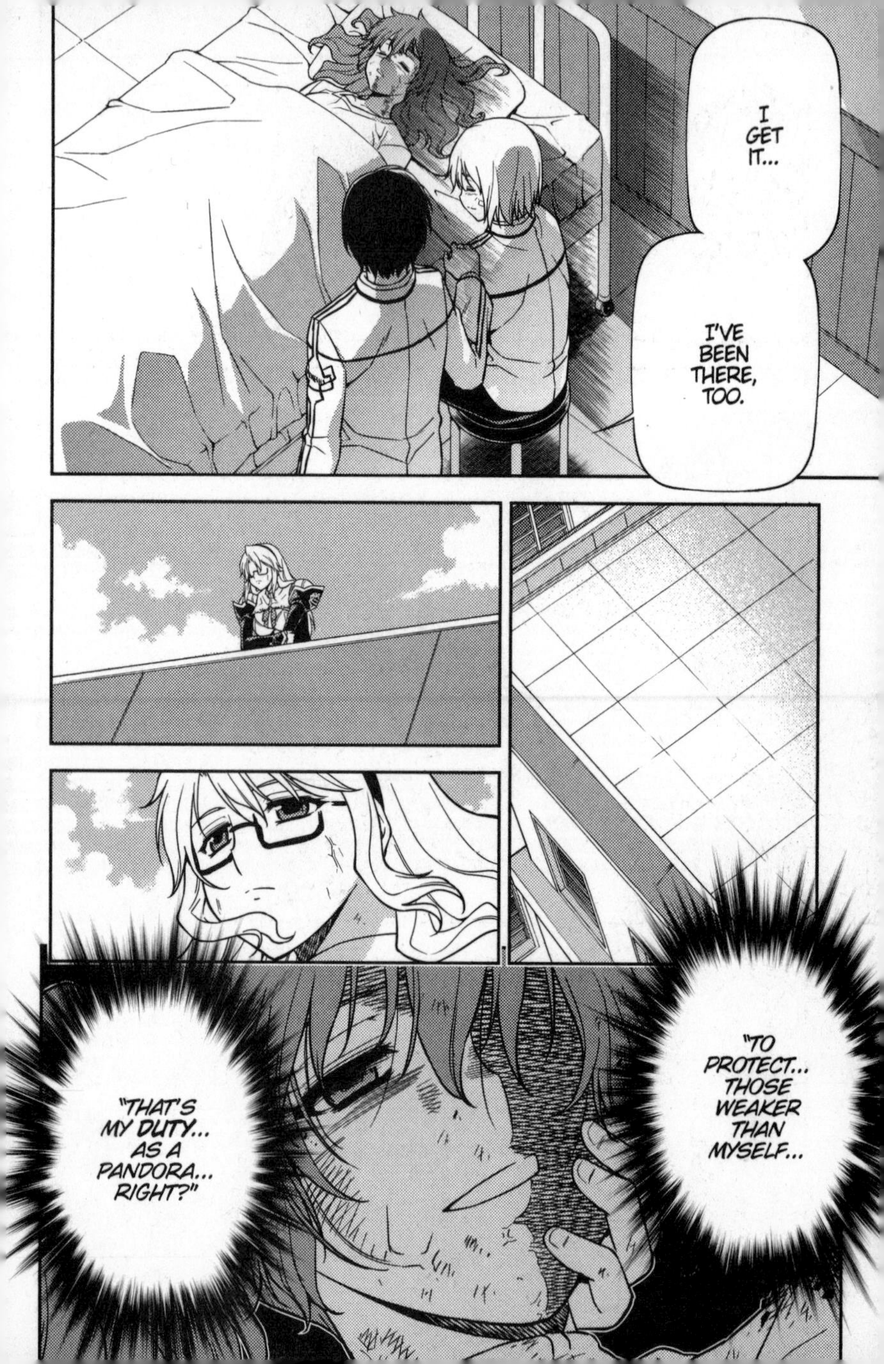
I GET IT...
I'VE BEEN THERE, TOO.
"TO PROTECT... THOSE WEAKER THAN MYSELF...
"THAT'S MY DUTY... AS A PANDORA... RIGHT?"

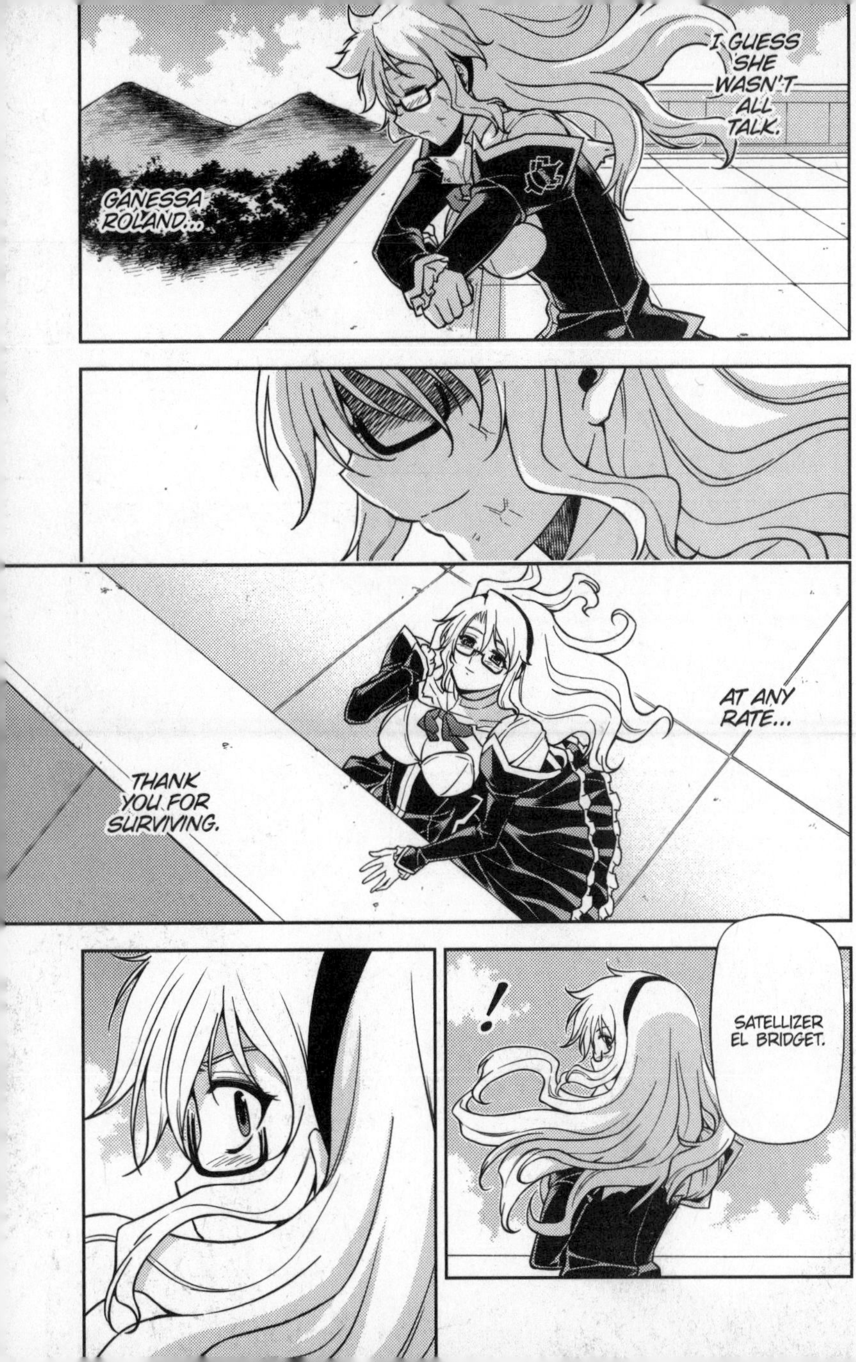
I GUESS SHE WASN'T ALL TALK.
GANESSA ROLAND...
AT ANY RATE...
THANK YOU FOR SURVIVING.
SATELLIZER EL BRIDGET.
!

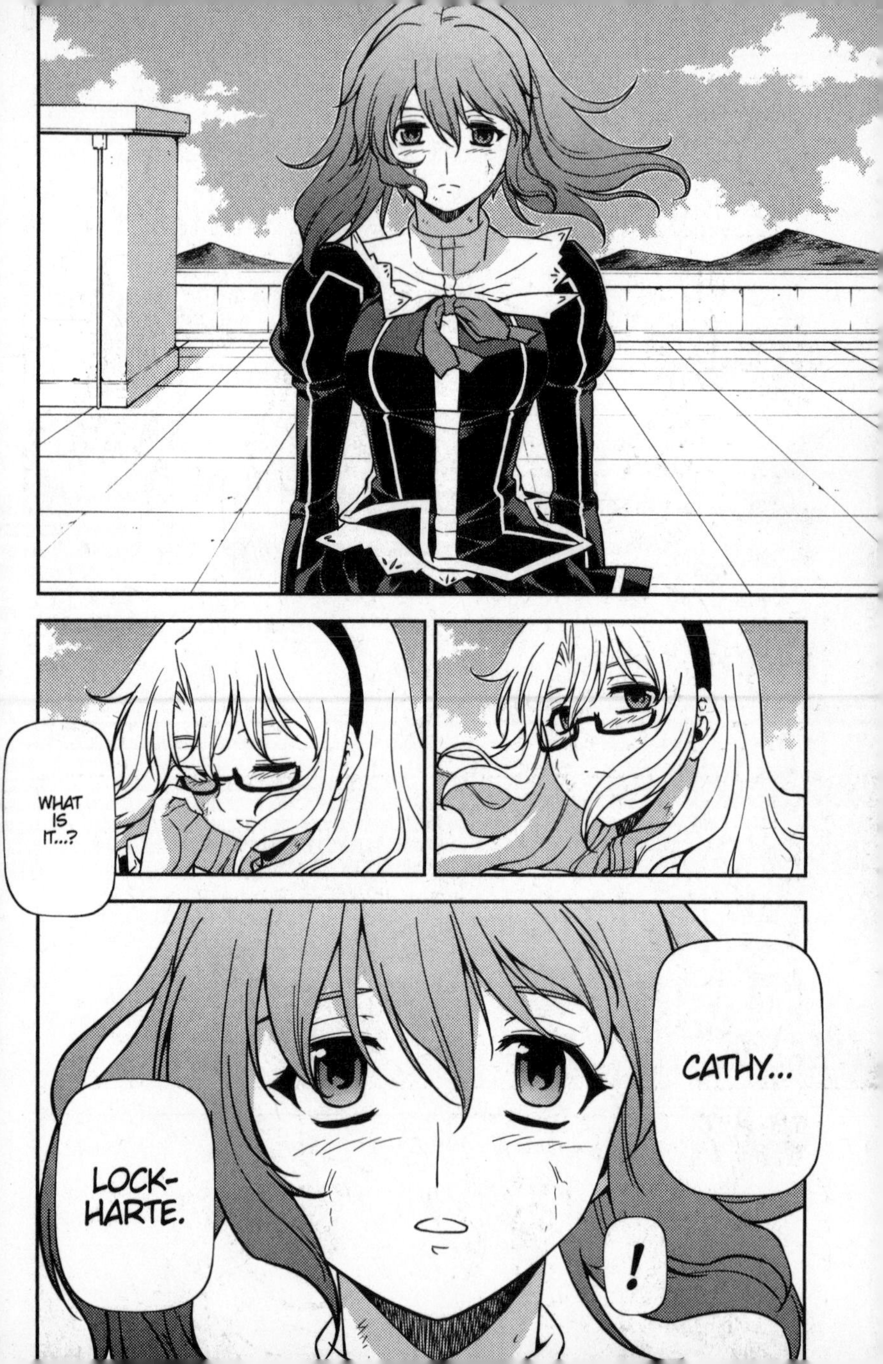
WHAT IS IT...?
CATHY...
LOCK-HARTE.
!

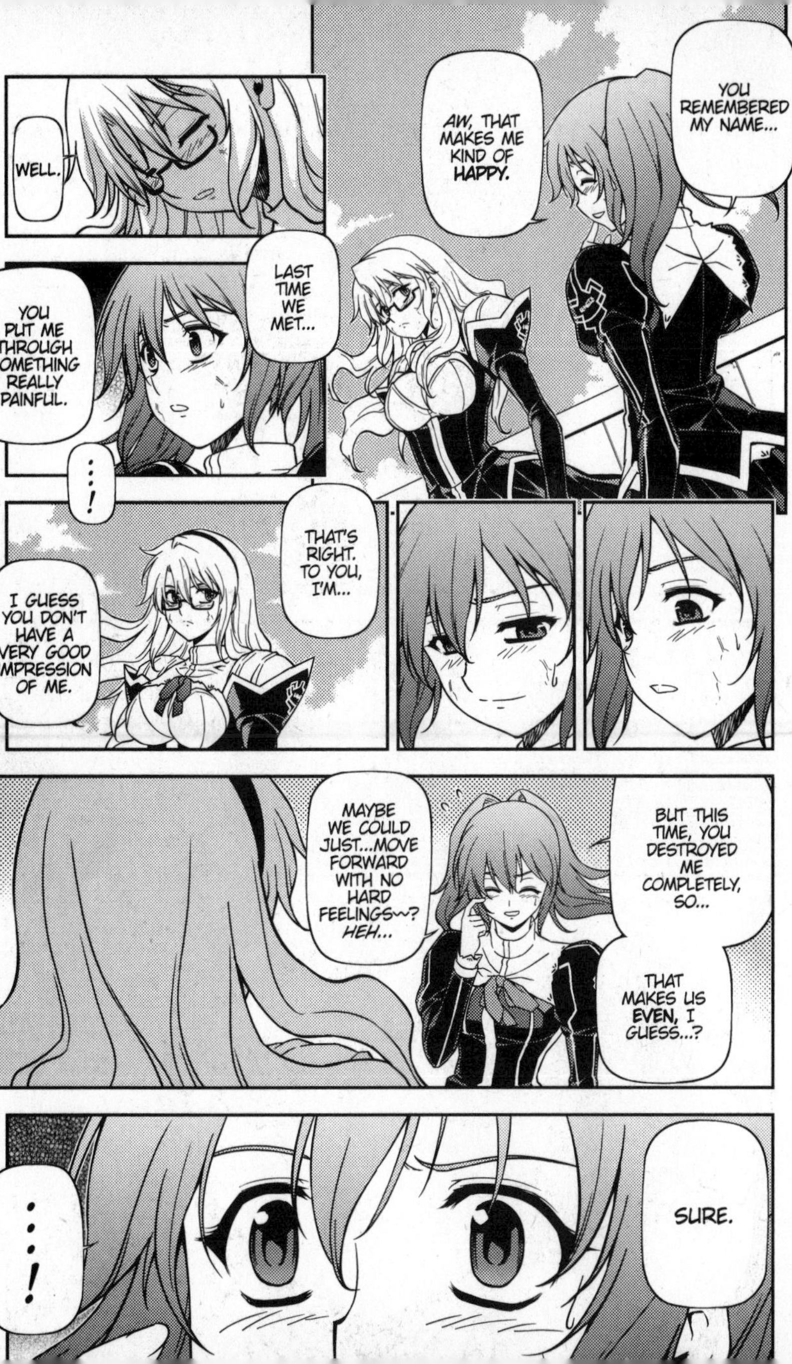
YOU REMEMBERED MY NAME...
AW, THAT MAKES ME KIND OF HAPPY.
WELL.
LAST TIME WE MET...
YOU PUT ME THROUGH SOMETHING REALLY PAINFUL.
...!
THAT'S RIGHT. TO YOU, I'M...
I GUESS YOU DON'T HAVE A VERY GOOD IMPRESSION OF ME.
BUT THIS TIME, YOU DESTROYED ME COMPLETELY, SO...
THAT MAKES US EVEN, I GUESS...?
MAYBE WE COULD JUST...MOVE FORWARD WITH NO HARD FEELINGS~? HEH...
SURE.
...!

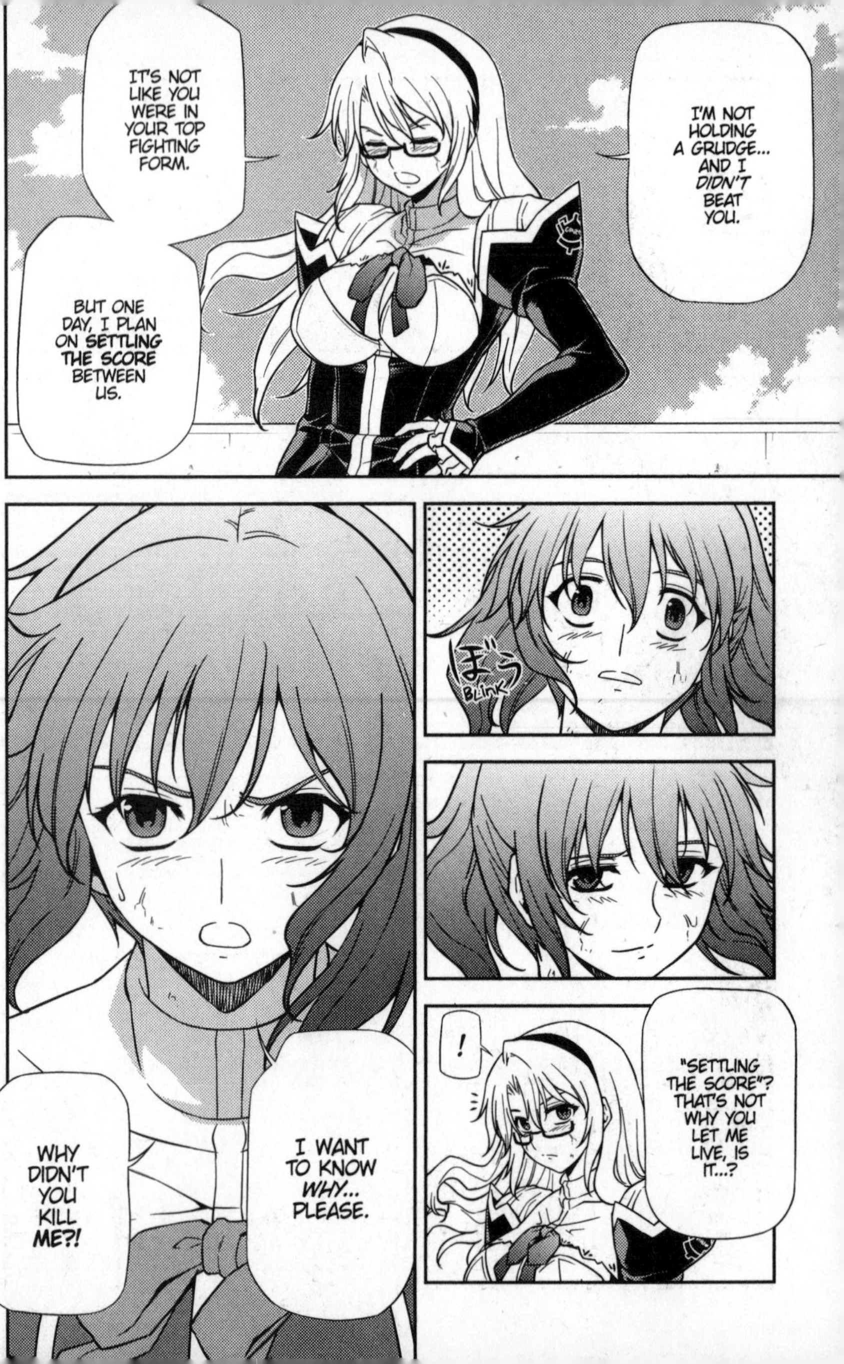
I'M NOT HOLDING A GRUDGE... AND I *DIDN'T* BEAT YOU.
IT'S NOT LIKE YOU WERE IN YOUR TOP FIGHTING FORM.
BUT ONE DAY, I PLAN ON **SETTLING THE SCORE** BETWEEN US.
BLINK
"SETTLING THE SCORE"? THAT'S NOT WHY YOU LET ME LIVE, IS IT...?
!
I WANT TO KNOW *WHY*... PLEASE.
WHY DIDN'T YOU KILL **ME?!**

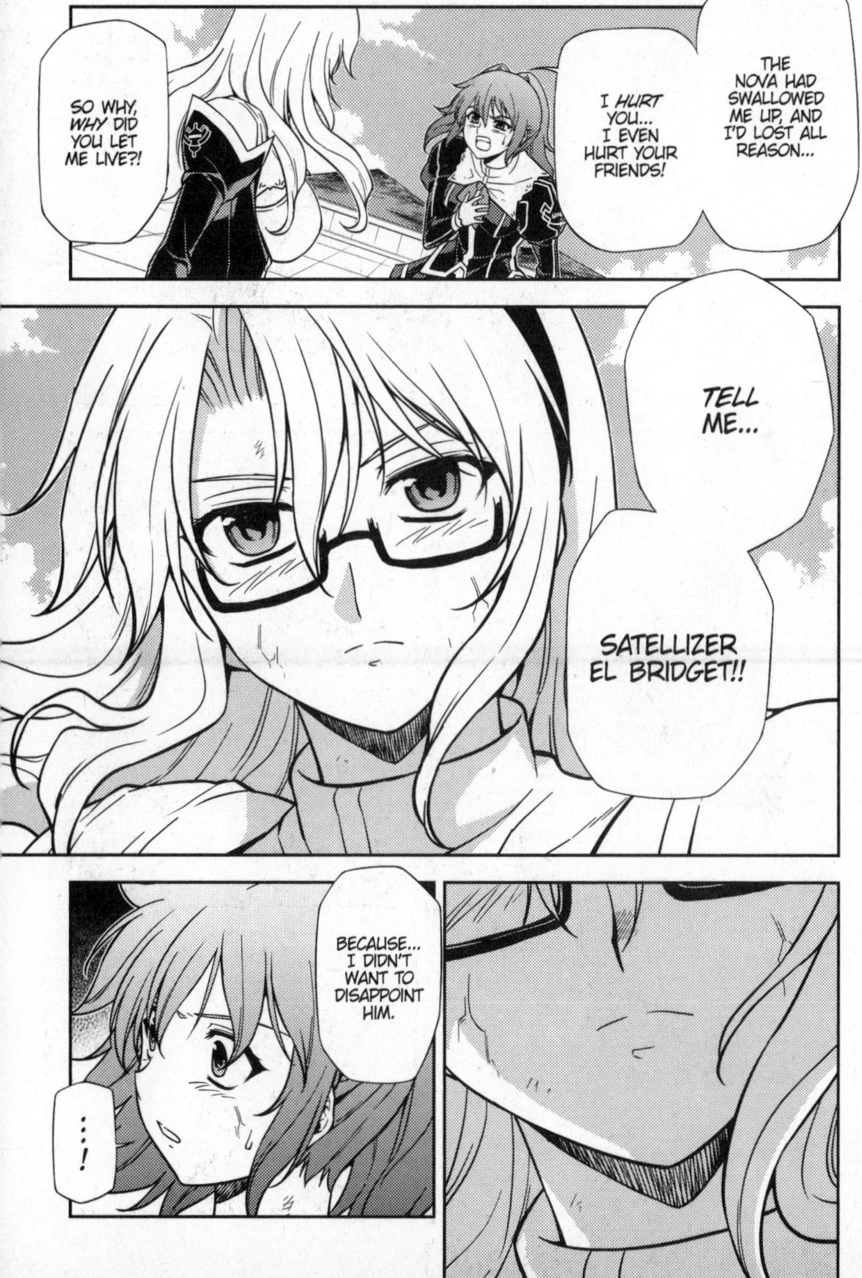
THE NOVA HAD SWALLOWED ME UP, AND I'D LOST ALL REASON...
I *HURT* YOU... I EVEN HURT YOUR FRIENDS!
SO WHY, *WHY* DID YOU LET ME LIVE?!
TELL ME...
SATELLIZER EL BRIDGET!!
BECAUSE... I DIDN'T WANT TO DISAPPOINT HIM.
...!

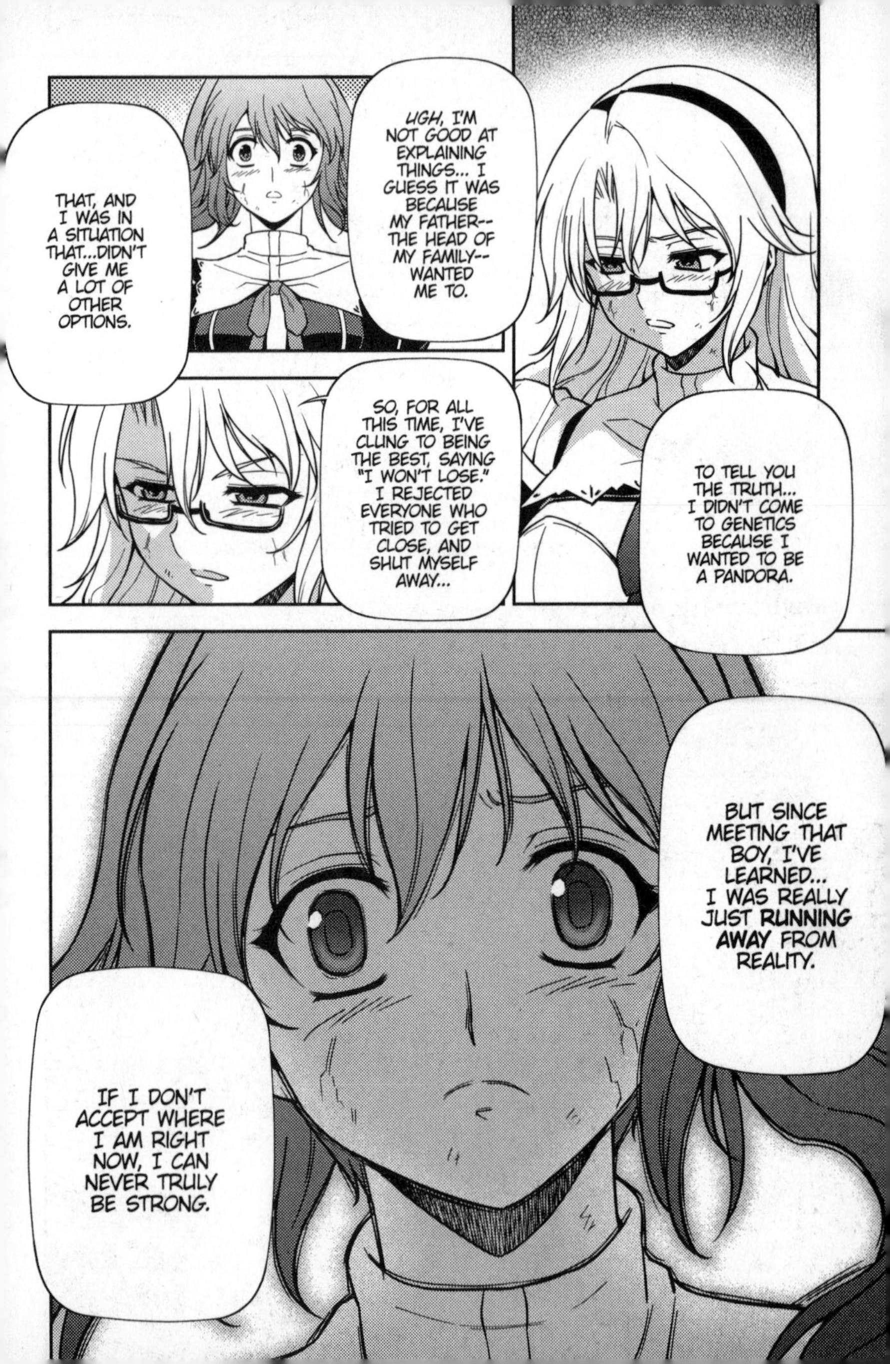
TO TELL YOU THE TRUTH... I DIDN'T COME TO GENETICS BECAUSE I WANTED TO BE A PANDORA.
UGH, I'M NOT GOOD AT EXPLAINING THINGS... I GUESS IT WAS BECAUSE MY FATHER-- THE HEAD OF MY FAMILY-- WANTED ME TO.
THAT, AND I WAS IN A SITUATION THAT...DIDN'T GIVE ME A LOT OF OTHER OPTIONS.
SO, FOR ALL THIS TIME, I'VE CLUNG TO BEING THE BEST, SAYING "I WON'T LOSE." I REJECTED EVERYONE WHO TRIED TO GET CLOSE, AND SHUT MYSELF AWAY...
BUT SINCE MEETING THAT BOY, I'VE LEARNED... I WAS REALLY JUST RUNNING AWAY FROM REALITY.
IF I DON'T ACCEPT WHERE I AM RIGHT NOW, I CAN NEVER TRULY BE STRONG.

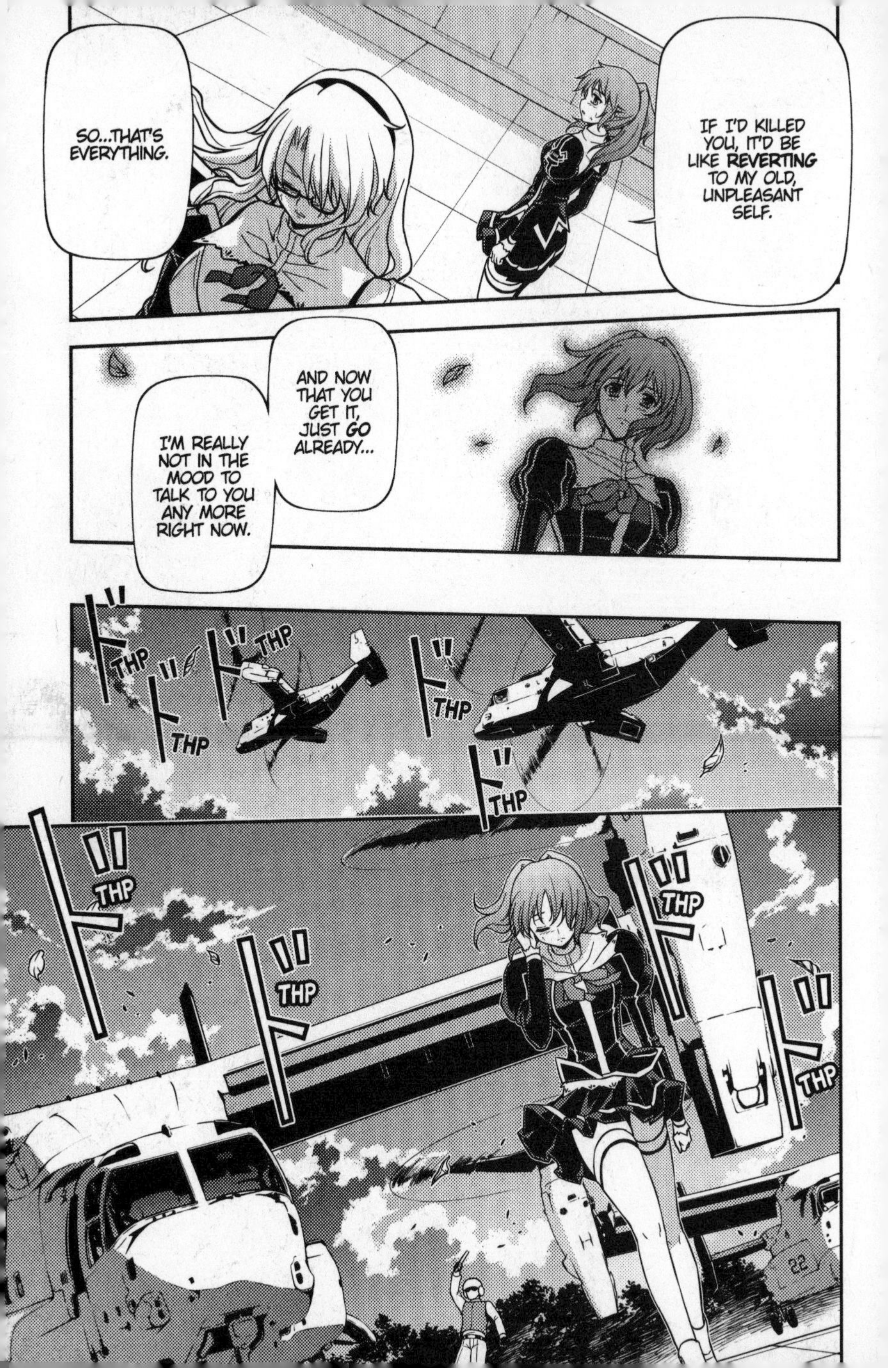
IF I'D KILLED YOU, IT'D BE LIKE REVERTING TO MY OLD, UNPLEASANT SELF.
SO...THAT'S EVERYTHING.
AND NOW THAT YOU GET IT, JUST GO ALREADY...
I'M REALLY NOT IN THE MOOD TO TALK TO YOU ANY MORE RIGHT NOW.
THP
THP
THP
THP
THP
THP
THP
THP
THP

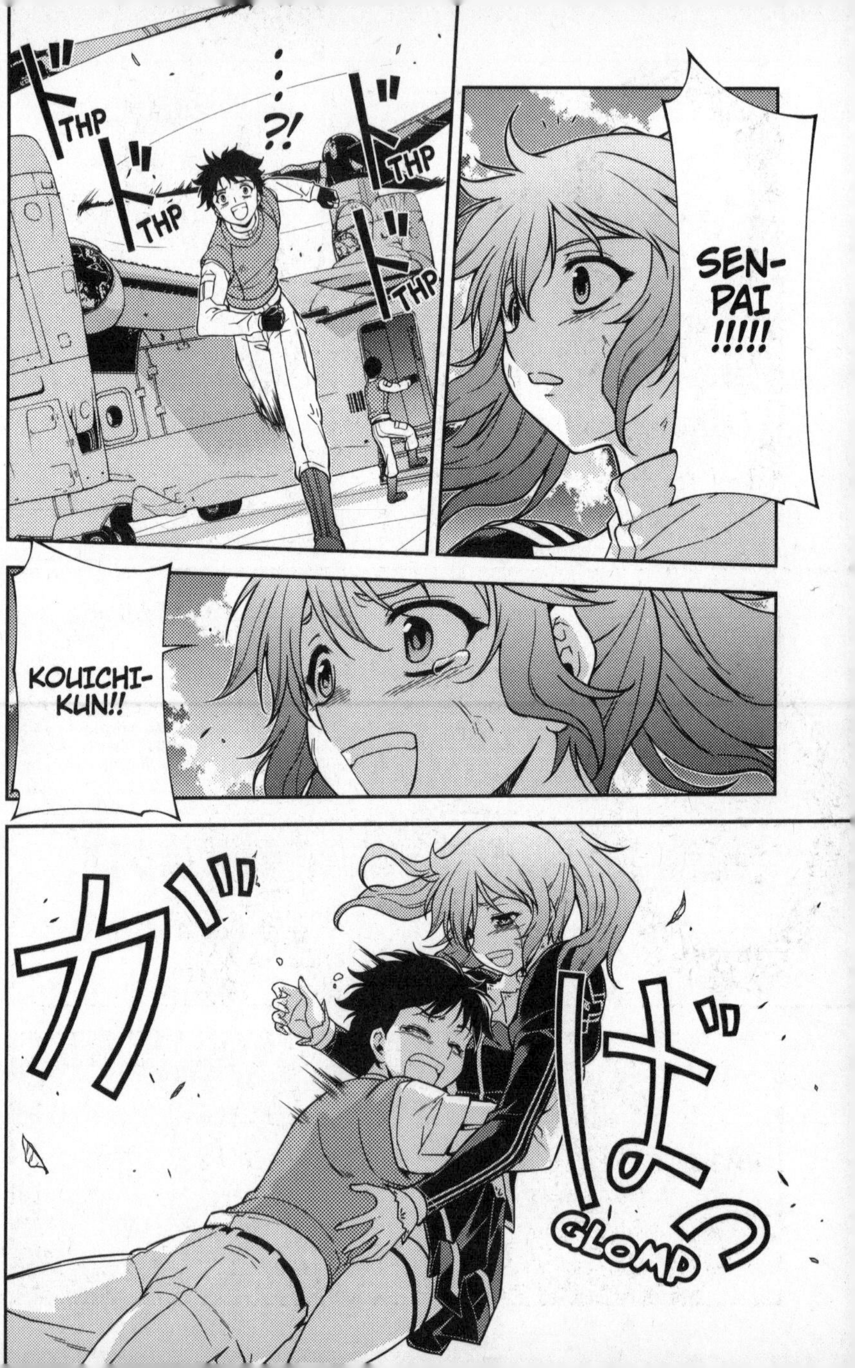
SEN-PAI!!!!!
...
?!
THP
THP
THP
THP
KOUICHI-KUN!!
GLOMP

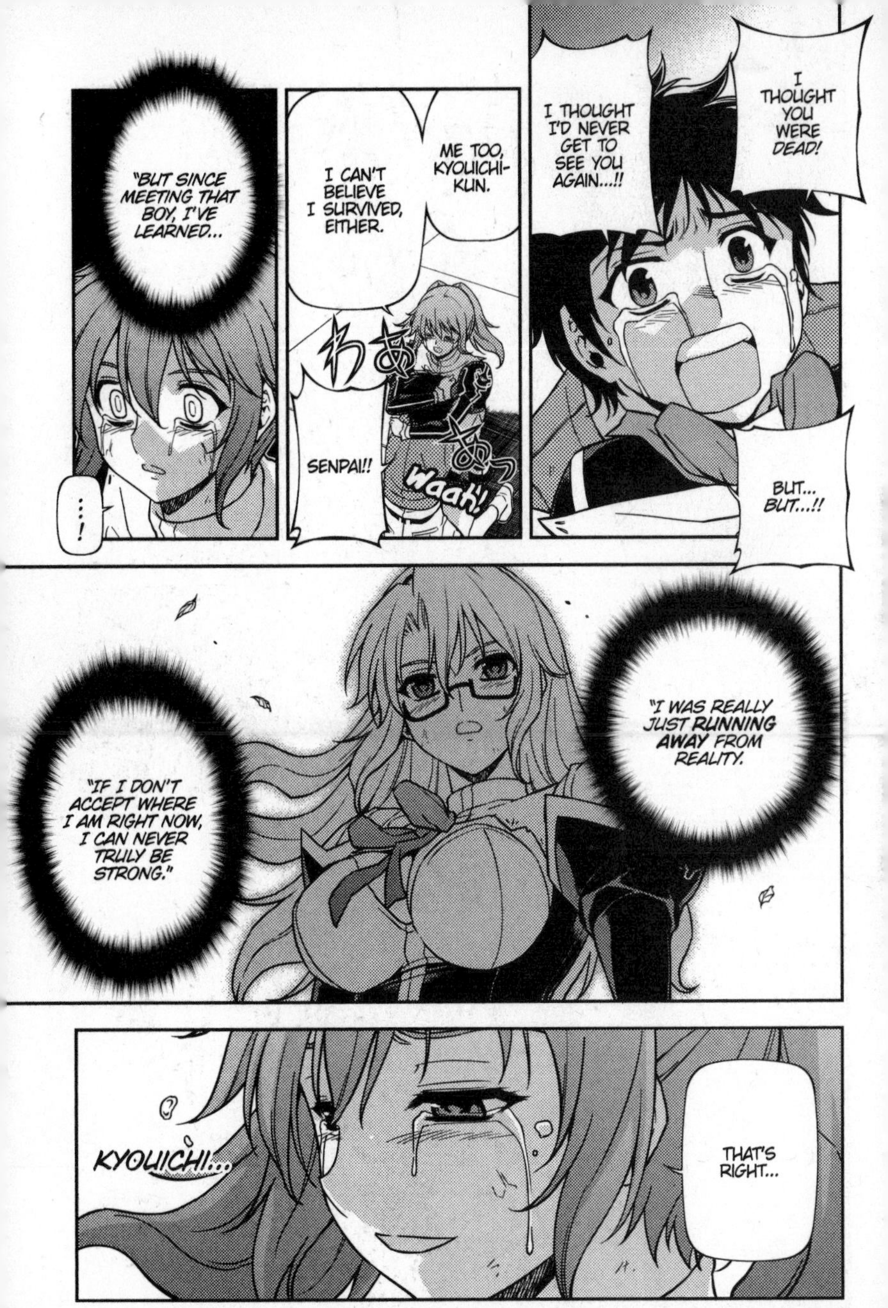
I THOUGHT YOU WERE DEAD!
I THOUGHT I'D NEVER GET TO SEE YOU AGAIN...!!
BUT... BUT...!!
ME TOO, KYOUICHI-KUN.
I CAN'T BELIEVE I SURVIVED, EITHER.
SENPAI!!
Waah!
"BUT SINCE MEETING THAT BOY, I'VE LEARNED...
...!
"I WAS REALLY JUST RUNNING AWAY FROM REALITY.
"IF I DON'T ACCEPT WHERE I AM RIGHT NOW, I CAN NEVER TRULY BE STRONG."
THAT'S RIGHT...
KYOUICHI...

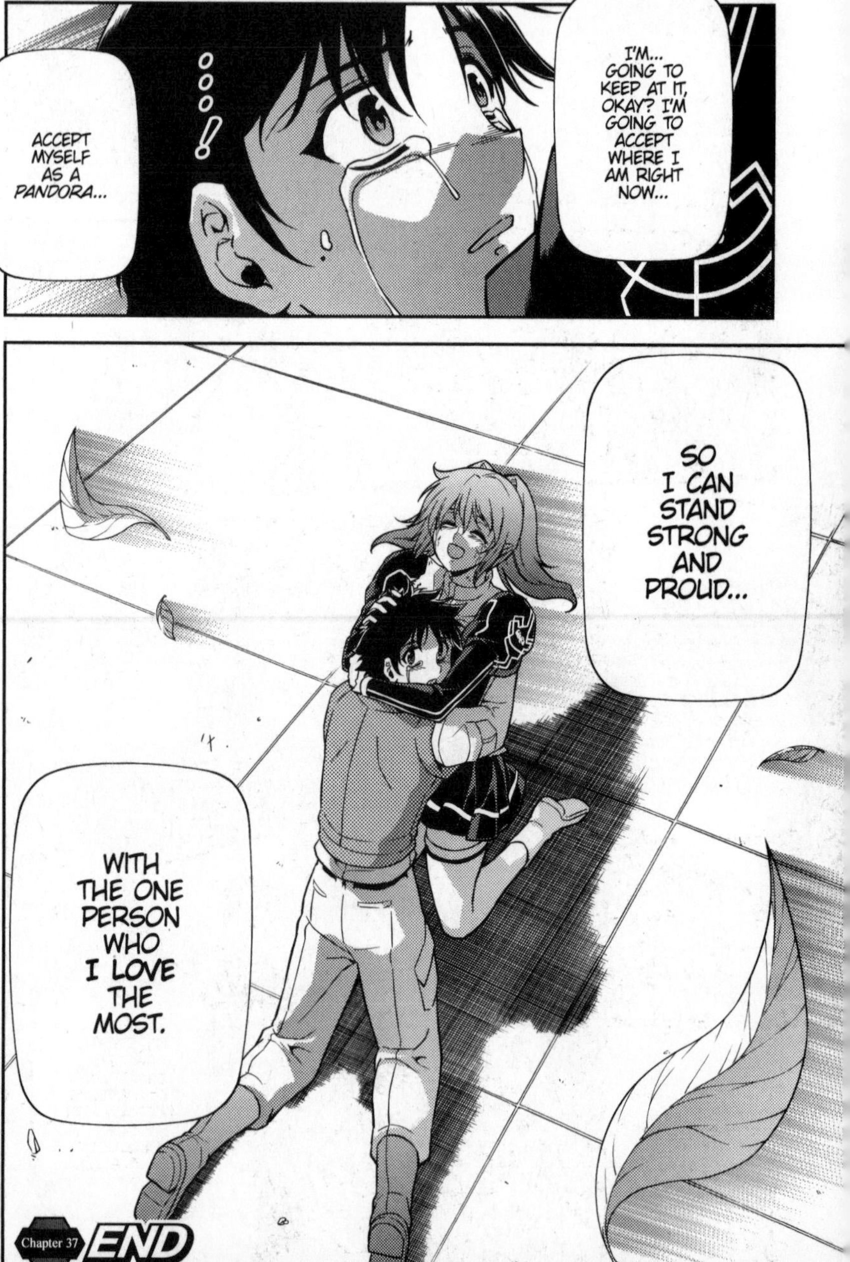
I'M... GOING TO KEEP AT IT, OKAY? I'M GOING TO ACCEPT WHERE I AM RIGHT NOW...
OOO!
ACCEPT MYSELF AS A PANDORA...
SO I CAN STAND STRONG AND PROUD...
WITH THE ONE PERSON WHO I LOVE THE MOST.
Chapter 37 END

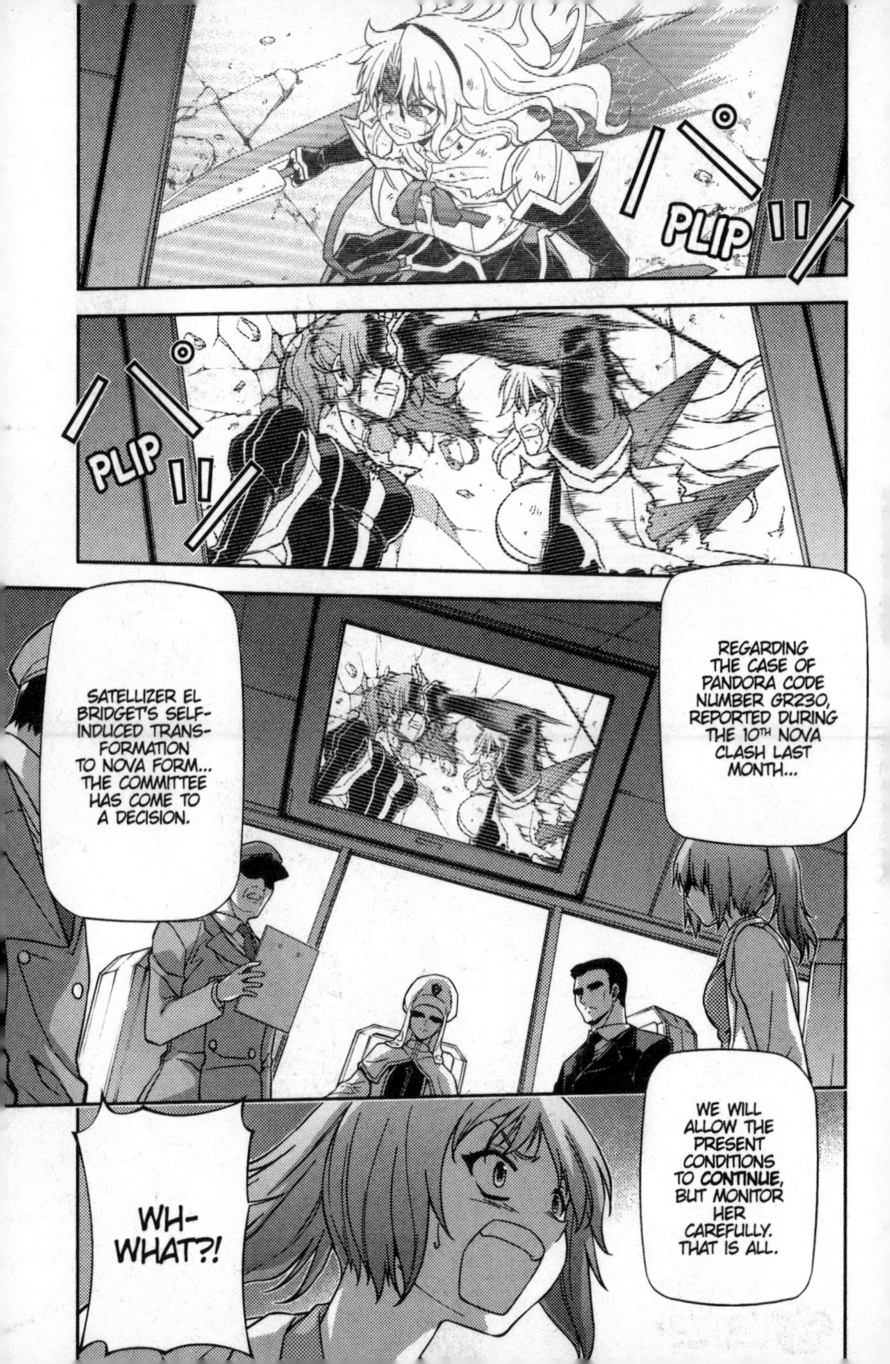

PLIP!!
PLIP!!
REGARDING THE CASE OF PANDORA CODE NUMBER GR230, REPORTED DURING THE 10TH NOVA CLASH LAST MONTH...
SATELLIZER EL BRIDGET'S SELF-INDUCED TRANSFORMATION TO NOVA FORM... THE COMMITTEE HAS COME TO A DECISION.
WE WILL ALLOW THE PRESENT CONDITIONS TO CONTINUE, BUT MONITOR HER CAREFULLY. THAT IS ALL.
WH-WHAT?!

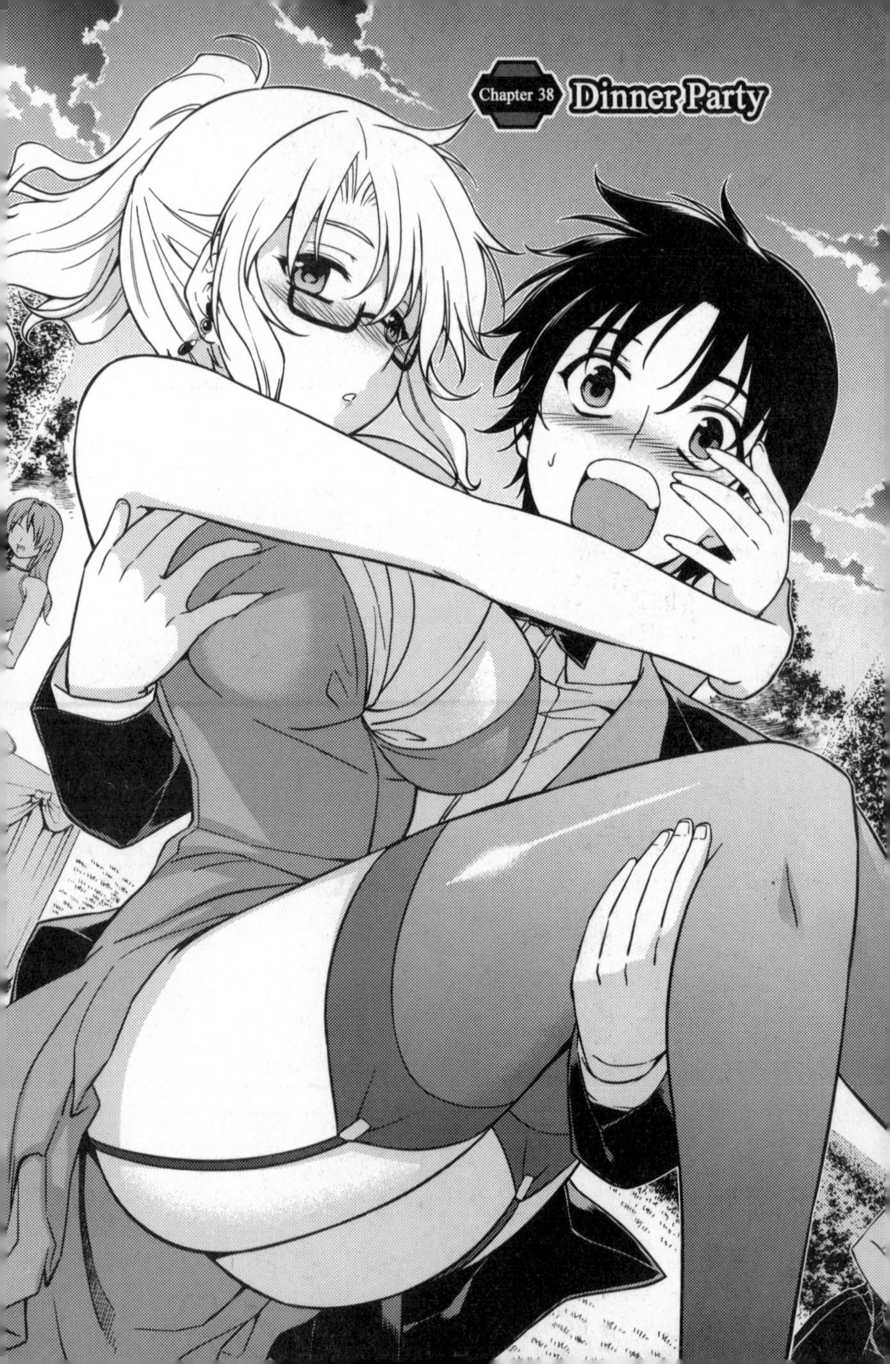
Chapter 38
Dinner Party

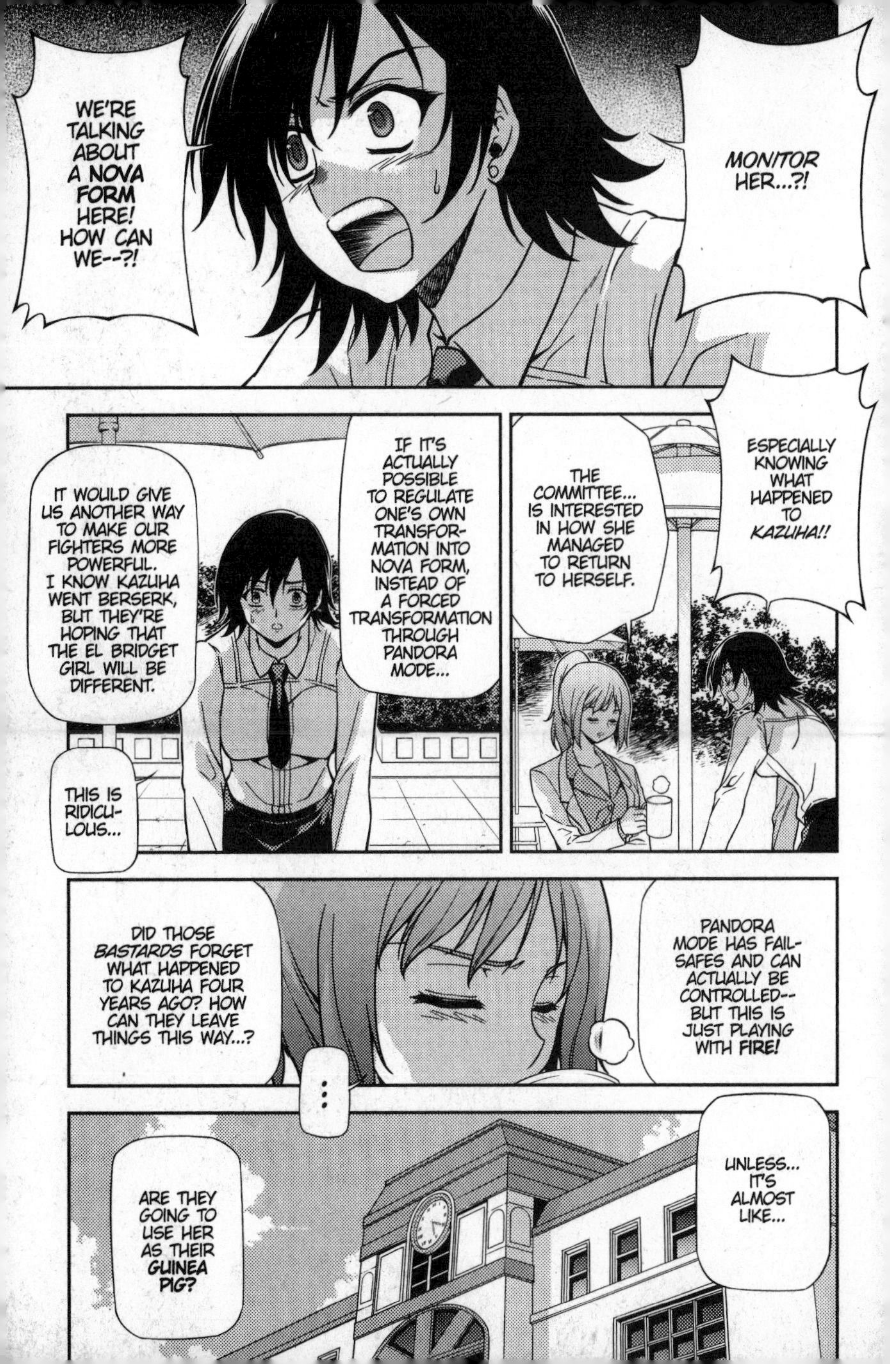
MONITOR HER...?!
WE'RE TALKING ABOUT A NOVA FORM HERE! HOW CAN WE--?!
ESPECIALLY KNOWING WHAT HAPPENED TO KAZUHA!!
THE COMMITTEE... IS INTERESTED IN HOW SHE MANAGED TO RETURN TO HERSELF.
IF IT'S ACTUALLY POSSIBLE TO REGULATE ONE'S OWN TRANSFORMATION INTO NOVA FORM, INSTEAD OF A FORCED TRANSFORMATION THROUGH PANDORA MODE...
IT WOULD GIVE US ANOTHER WAY TO MAKE OUR FIGHTERS MORE POWERFUL. I KNOW KAZUHA WENT BERSERK, BUT THEY'RE HOPING THAT THE EL BRIDGET GIRL WILL BE DIFFERENT.
THIS IS RIDICULOUS...
PANDORA MODE HAS FAIL-SAFES AND CAN ACTUALLY BE CONTROLLED--BUT THIS IS JUST PLAYING WITH FIRE!
DID THOSE BASTARDS FORGET WHAT HAPPENED TO KAZUHA FOUR YEARS AGO? HOW CAN THEY LEAVE THINGS THIS WAY...?
...
UNLESS... IT'S ALMOST LIKE...
ARE THEY GOING TO USE HER AS THEIR GUINEA PIG?

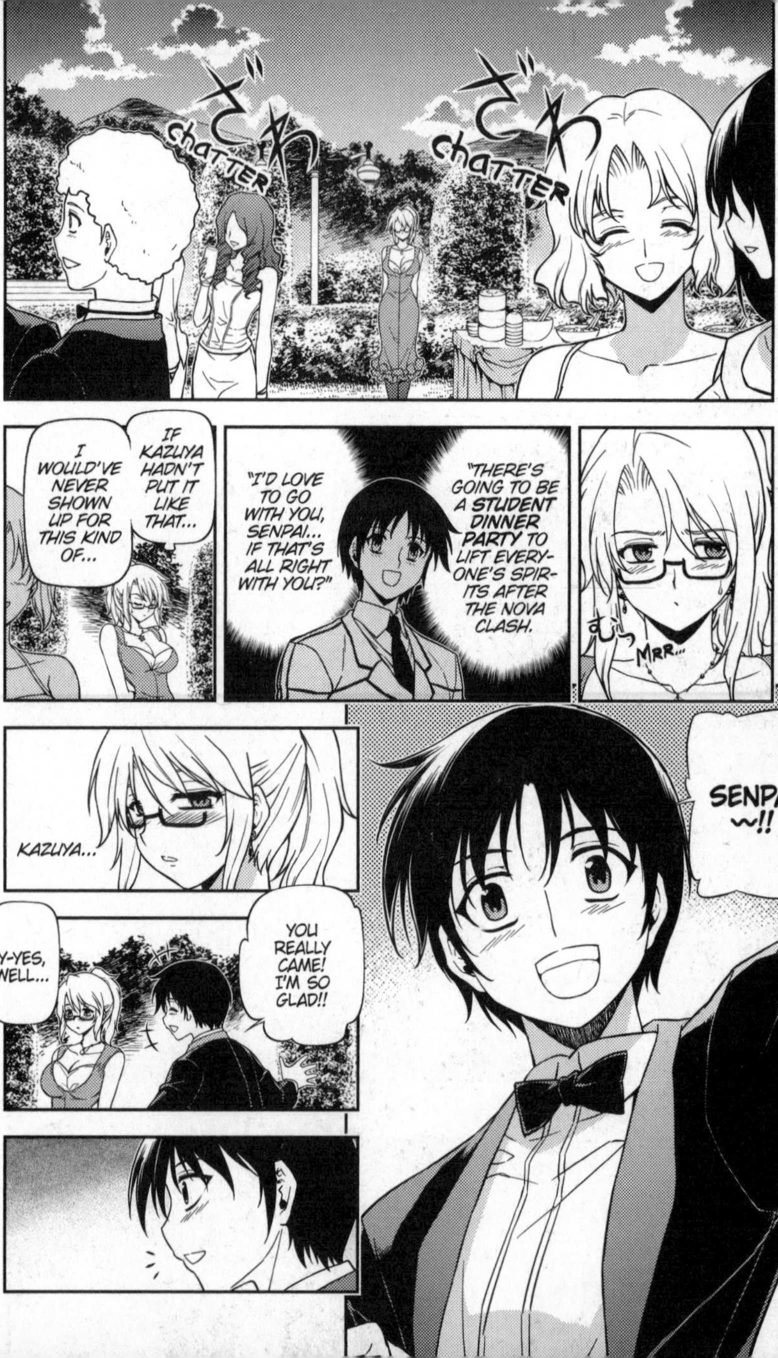
ざわ CHATTER
ざわ CHATTER
むっ MRR...
"THERE'S GOING TO BE A STUDENT DINNER PARTY TO LIFT EVERYONE'S SPIRITS AFTER THE NOVA CLASH.
"I'D LOVE TO GO WITH YOU, SENPAI... IF THAT'S ALL RIGHT WITH YOU?"
IF KAZUYA HADN'T PUT IT LIKE THAT...
I WOULD'VE NEVER SHOWN UP FOR THIS KIND OF...
SENPAI ~!!
KAZUYA...
YOU REALLY CAME! I'M SO GLAD!!
Y-YES, WELL...

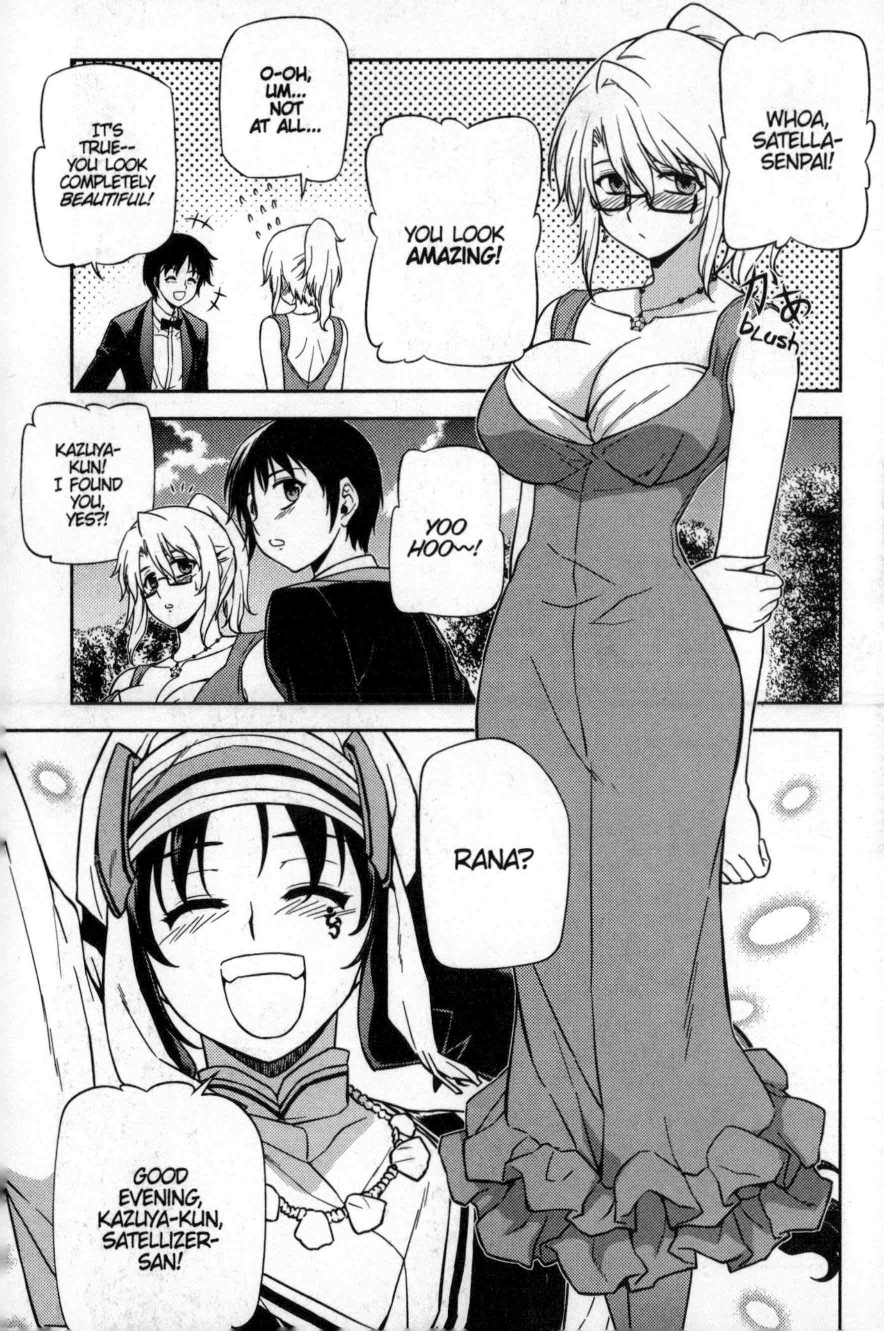
WHOA, SATELLA-SENPAI!
YOU LOOK AMAZING!
O-OH, UM... NOT AT ALL...
IT'S TRUE-- YOU LOOK COMPLETELY BEAUTIFUL!
blush
YOO HOO~!
KAZUYA-KUN! I FOUND YOU, YES?!
RANA?
GOOD EVENING, KAZUYA-KUN, SATELLIZER-SAN!

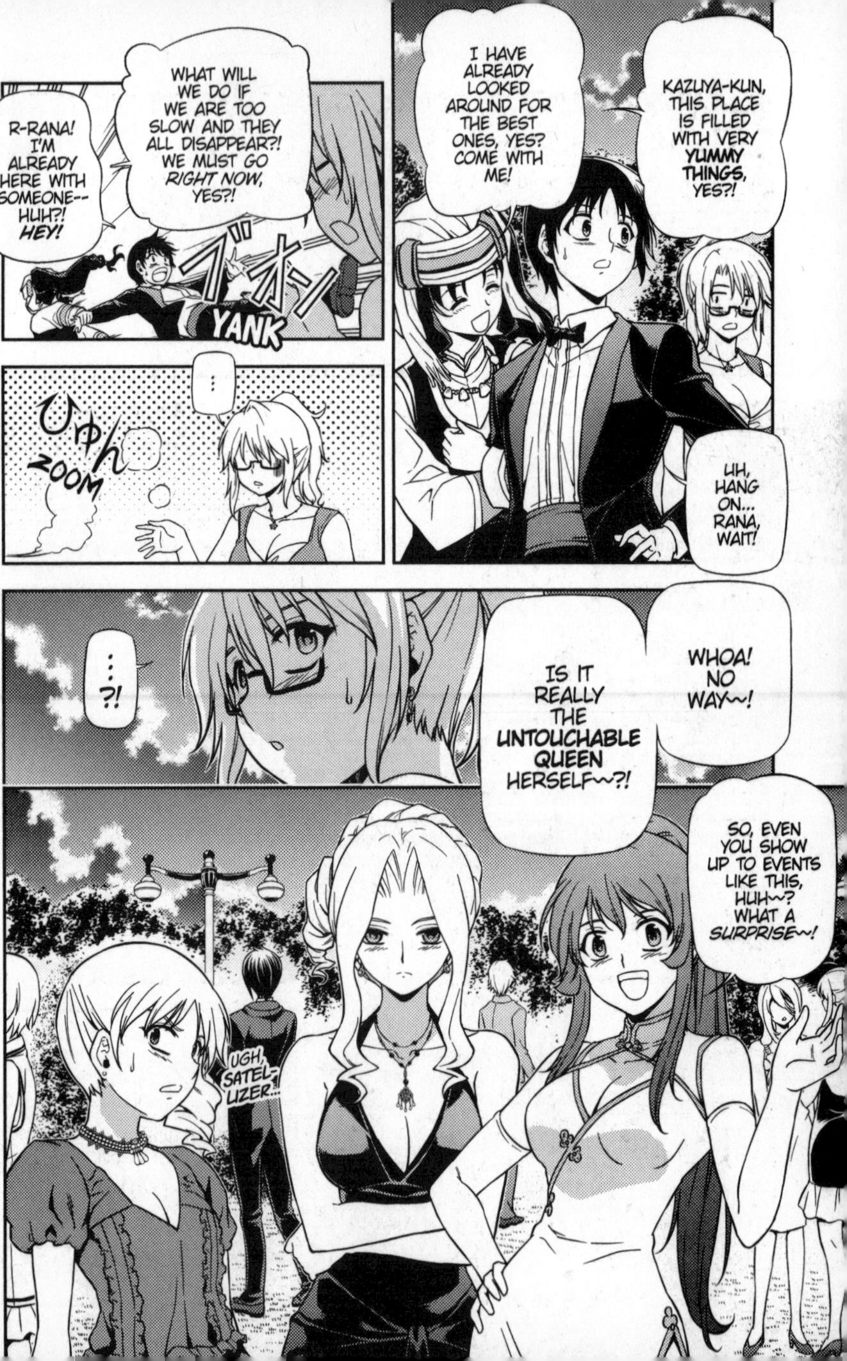
KAZUYA-KUN, THIS PLACE IS FILLED WITH VERY YUMMY THINGS, YES?!
I HAVE ALREADY LOOKED AROUND FOR THE BEST ONES, YES? COME WITH ME!
UH, HANG ON... RANA, WAIT!
WHAT WILL WE DO IF WE ARE TOO SLOW AND THEY ALL DISAPPEAR?! WE MUST GO RIGHT NOW, YES?!
R-RANA! I'M ALREADY HERE WITH SOMEONE-- HUH?! HEY!
ブオン
YANK
...
ひゅん
ZOOM
WHOA! NO WAY~!
IS IT REALLY THE UNTOUCHABLE QUEEN HERSELF~?!
...?!
SO, EVEN YOU SHOW UP TO EVENTS LIKE THIS, HUH~? WHAT A SURPRISE~!
UGH, SATEL-LIZER...

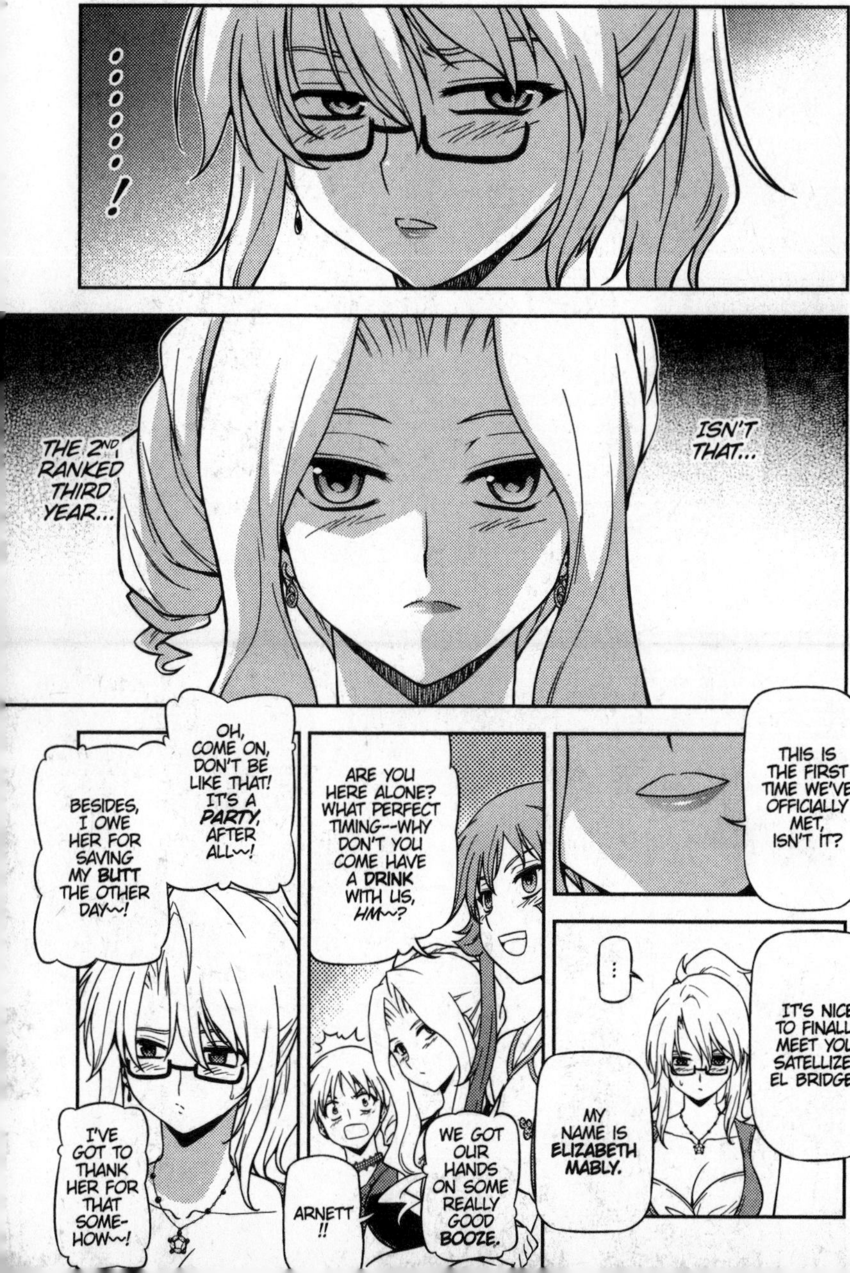
OOOOOOO!
ISN'T THAT...
THE 2ND RANKED THIRD YEAR...
THIS IS THE FIRST TIME WE'VE OFFICIALLY MET, ISN'T IT?
IT'S NICE TO FINALLY MEET YOU, SATELLIZER EL BRIDGET.
...
MY NAME IS ELIZABETH MABLY.
ARE YOU HERE ALONE? WHAT PERFECT TIMING--WHY DON'T YOU COME HAVE A DRINK WITH US, HM~?
WE GOT OUR HANDS ON SOME REALLY GOOD BOOZE.
ARNETT!!
OH, COME ON, DON'T BE LIKE THAT! IT'S A PARTY, AFTER ALL~!
BESIDES, I OWE HER FOR SAVING MY BUTT THE OTHER DAY~!
I'VE GOT TO THANK HER FOR THAT SOMEHOW~!

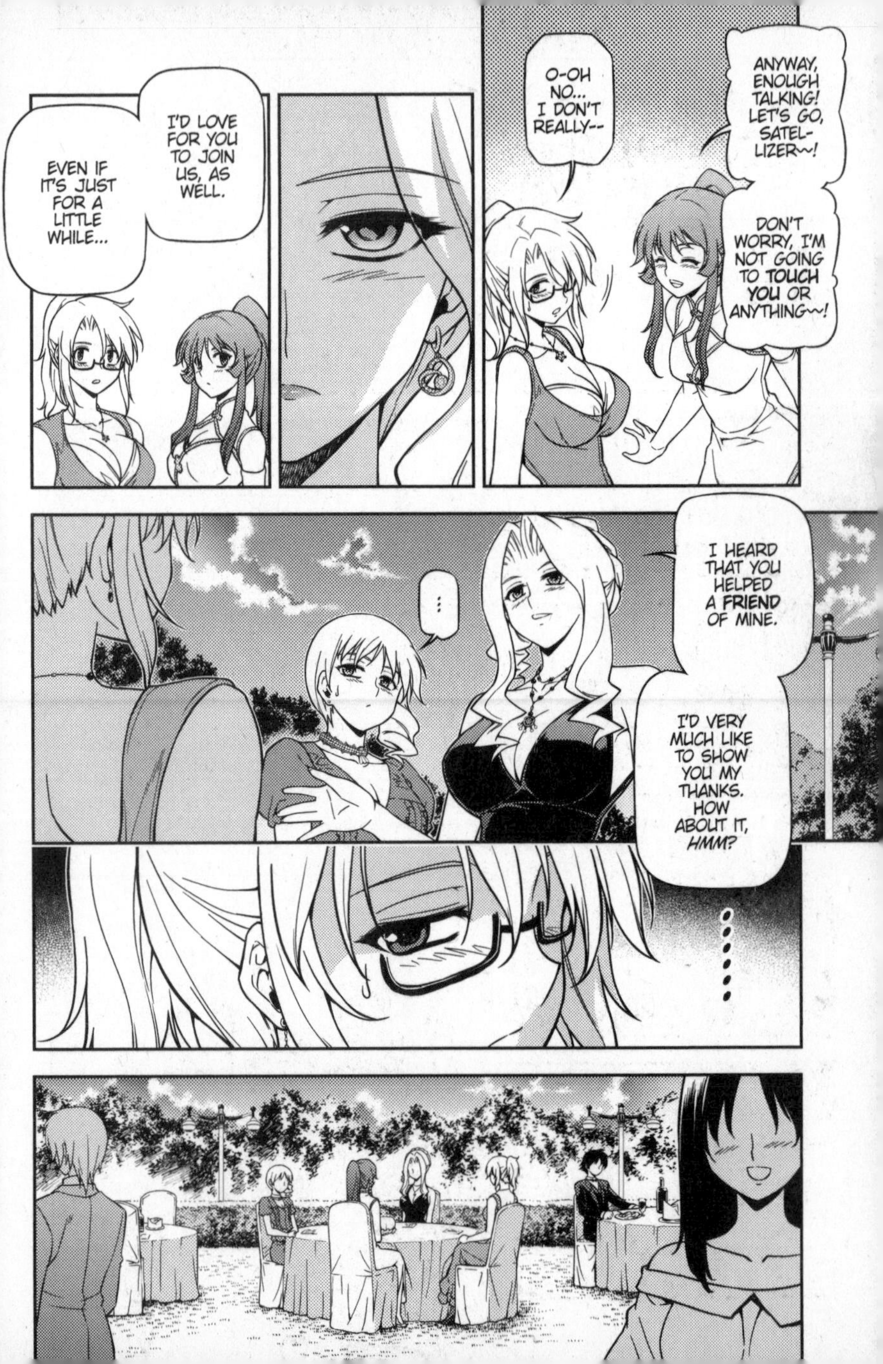
ANYWAY, ENOUGH TALKING! LET'S GO, SATEL-LIZER~!
O-OH NO... I DON'T REALLY--
DON'T WORRY, I'M NOT GOING TO **TOUCH YOU** OR ANYTHING~!
I'D LOVE FOR YOU TO JOIN US, AS WELL.
EVEN IF IT'S JUST FOR A LITTLE WHILE...
I HEARD THAT YOU HELPED A **FRIEND** OF MINE.
...
I'D VERY MUCH LIKE TO SHOW YOU MY THANKS. HOW ABOUT IT, *HMM?*
....

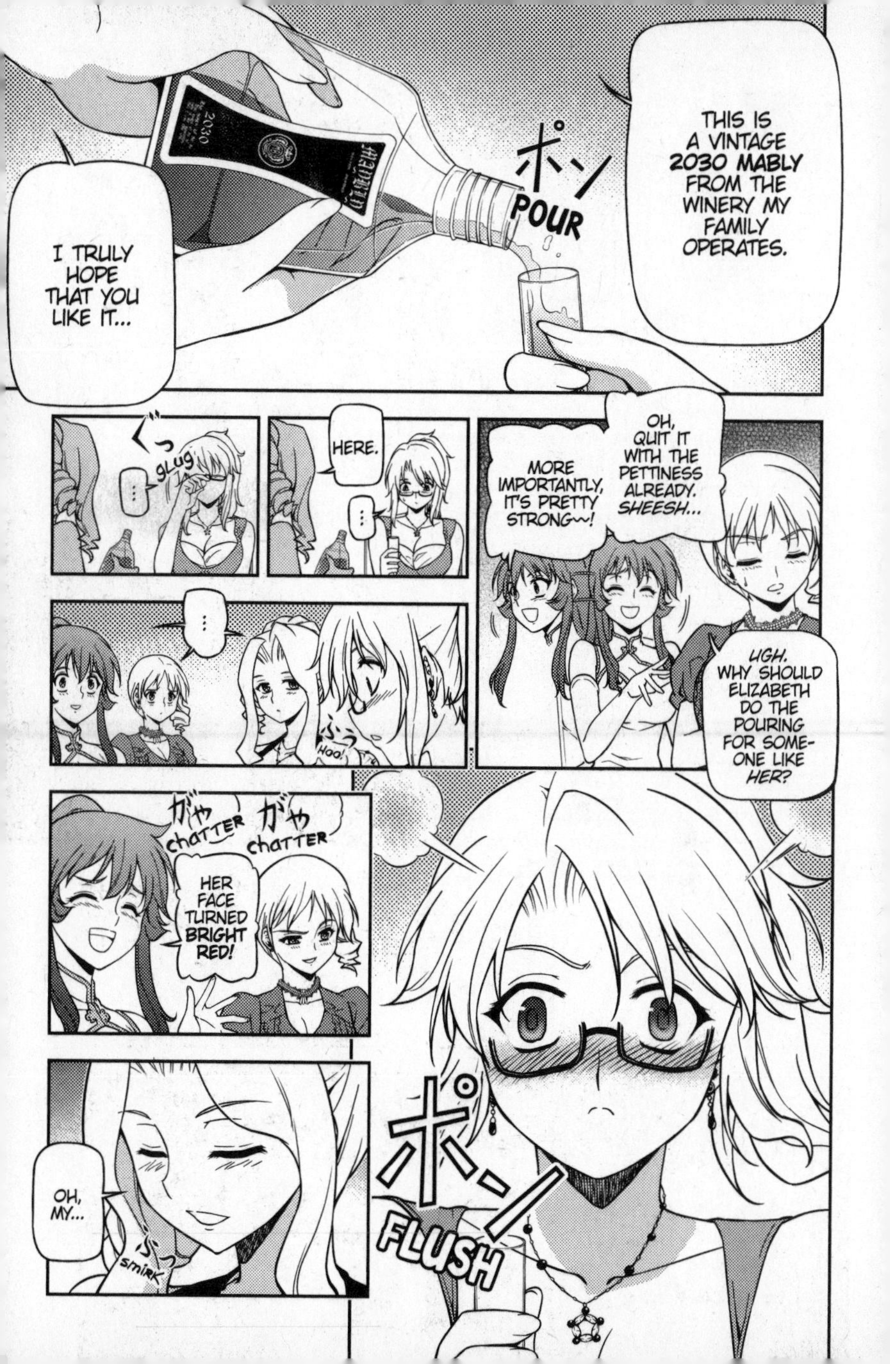
THIS IS A VINTAGE 2030 MABLY FROM THE WINERY MY FAMILY OPERATES.
ポン
POUR
I TRULY HOPE THAT YOU LIKE IT...
OH, QUIT IT WITH THE PETTINESS ALREADY. SHEESH...
MORE IMPORTANTLY, IT'S PRETTY STRONG~!
UGH. WHY SHOULD ELIZABETH DO THE POURING FOR SOME-ONE LIKE HER?
HERE.
...
ぐっ
GLUG
...
...
ふぅ
HOO!
ポ~
FLUSH
ガヤ
CHATTER
ガヤ
CHATTER
HER FACE TURNED BRIGHT RED!
OH, MY...
ふっ
SMIRK

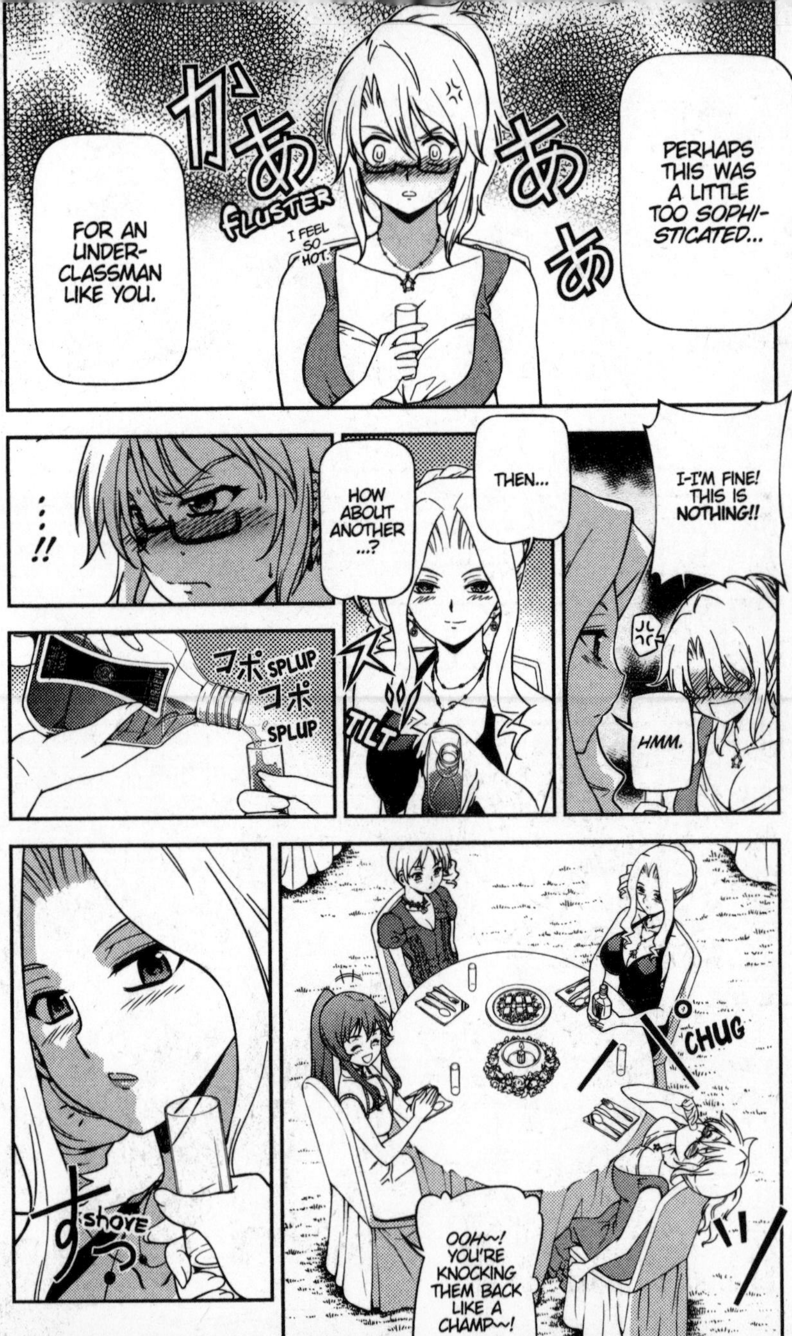
PERHAPS THIS WAS A LITTLE TOO SOPHISTICATED...
かあああ
FLUSTER
I FEEL SO HOT.
FOR AN UNDERCLASSMAN LIKE YOU.
I-I'M FINE! THIS IS NOTHING!!
HMM.
THEN...
HOW ABOUT ANOTHER ...?
TILT
...!!
コポ SPLUP
コポ SPLUP
CHUG
OOH~! YOU'RE KNOCKING THEM BACK LIKE A CHAMP~!
すっ SHOVE

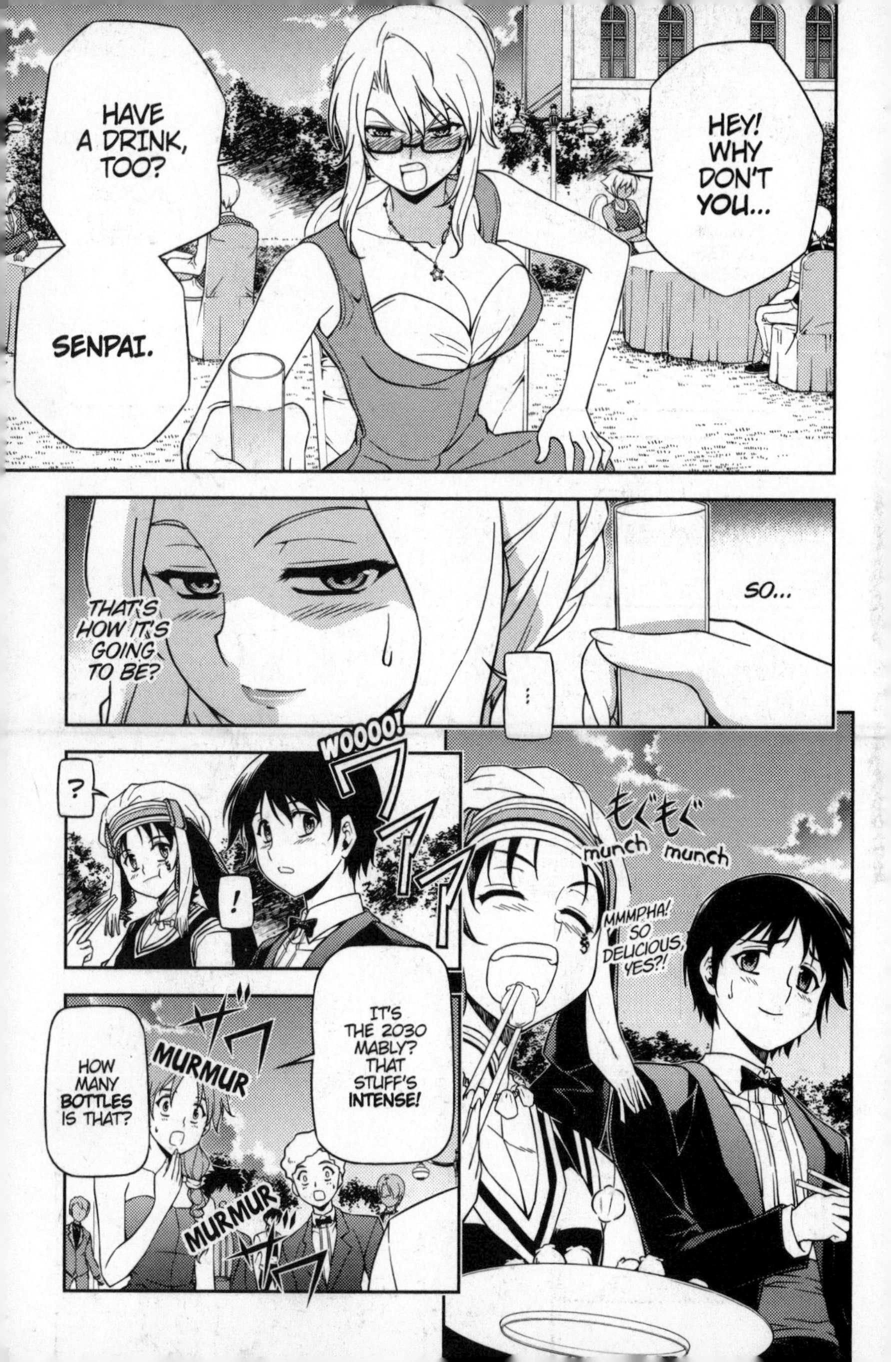
HEY! WHY DON'T YOU...
HAVE A DRINK, TOO?
SENPAI.
SO...
...
THAT'S HOW IT'S GOING TO BE?
もぐもぐ munch munch
MMMPHA! SO DELICIOUS, YES?!
WOOOO!
?
!
IT'S THE 2030 MABLY? THAT STUFF'S INTENSE!
MURMUR
HOW MANY BOTTLES IS THAT?
MURMUR

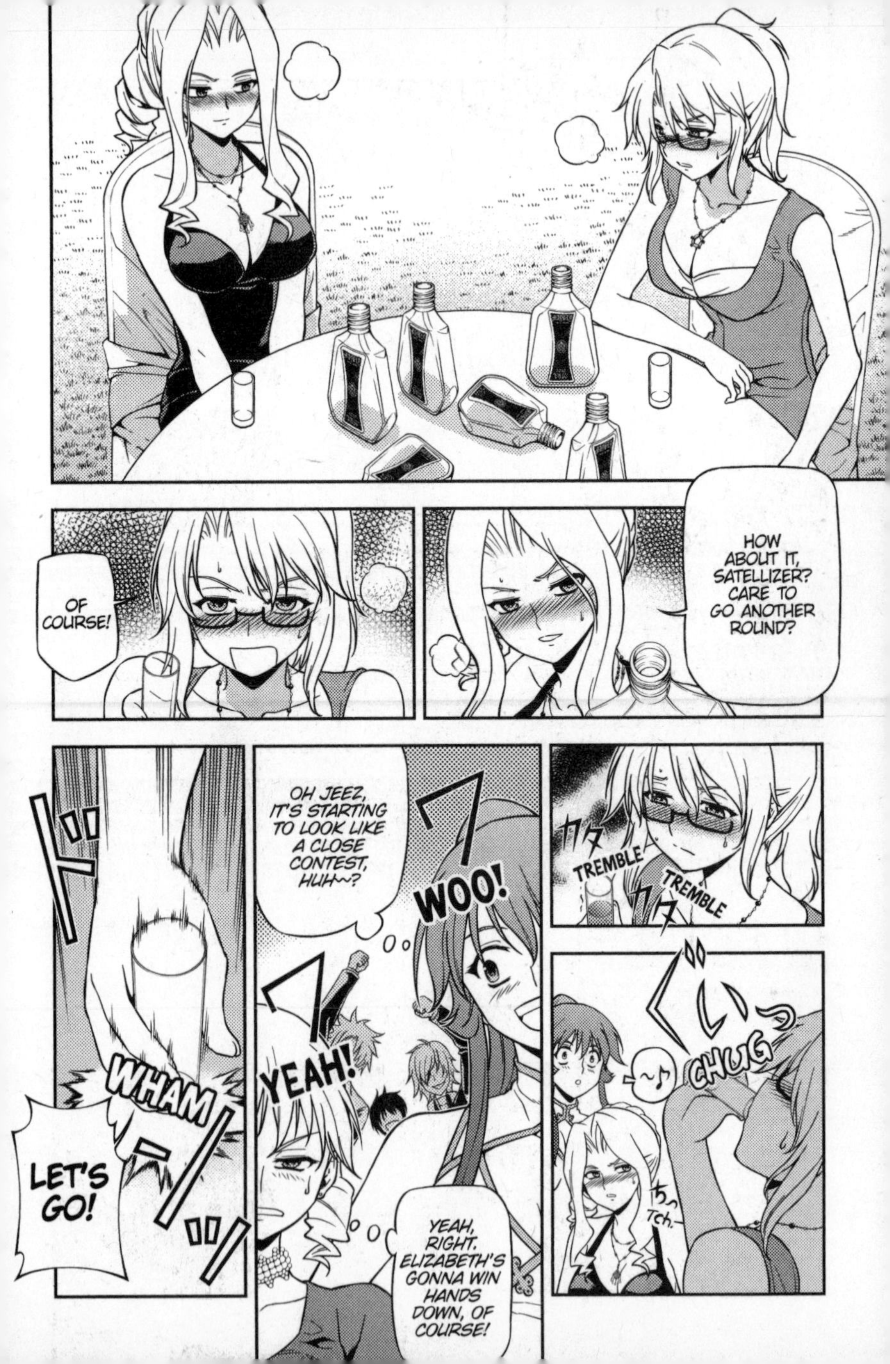
HOW ABOUT IT, SATELLIZER? CARE TO GO ANOTHER ROUND?
OF COURSE!
カタ TREMBLE
カタ TREMBLE
ぐいっ CHUG
~♪
Tch.
OH JEEZ, IT'S STARTING TO LOOK LIKE A CLOSE CONTEST, HUH~?
WOO!
YEAH!
YEAH, RIGHT. ELIZABETH'S GONNA WIN HANDS DOWN, OF COURSE!
WHAM
LET'S GO!

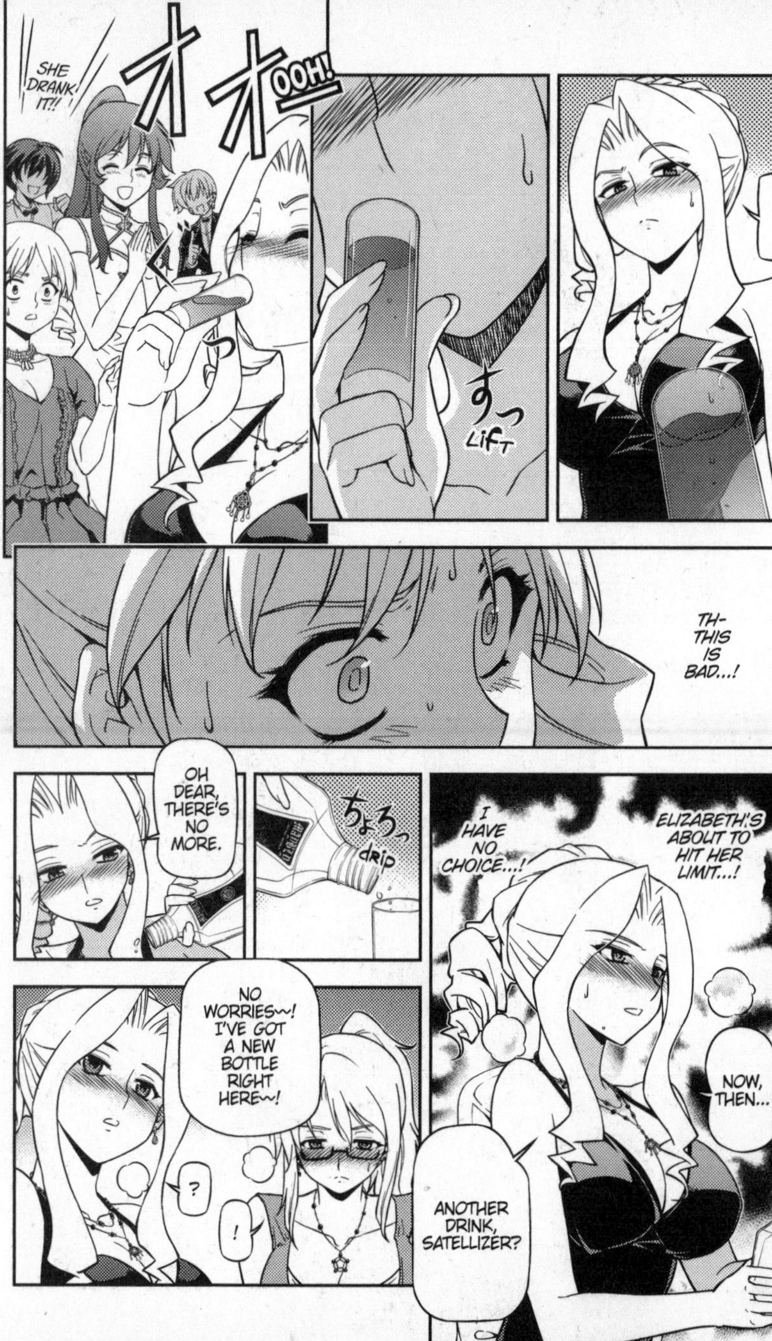
...
すっ
LIFT
SHE DRANK IT!!
オオ
OOH!
TH- THIS IS BAD...!
ELIZABETH'S ABOUT TO HIT HER LIMIT...!
I HAVE NO CHOICE...!
NOW, THEN...
ANOTHER DRINK, SATELLIZER?
ちょろっ
drip
OH DEAR, THERE'S NO MORE.
NO WORRIES~! I'VE GOT A NEW BOTTLE RIGHT HERE~!
?
!

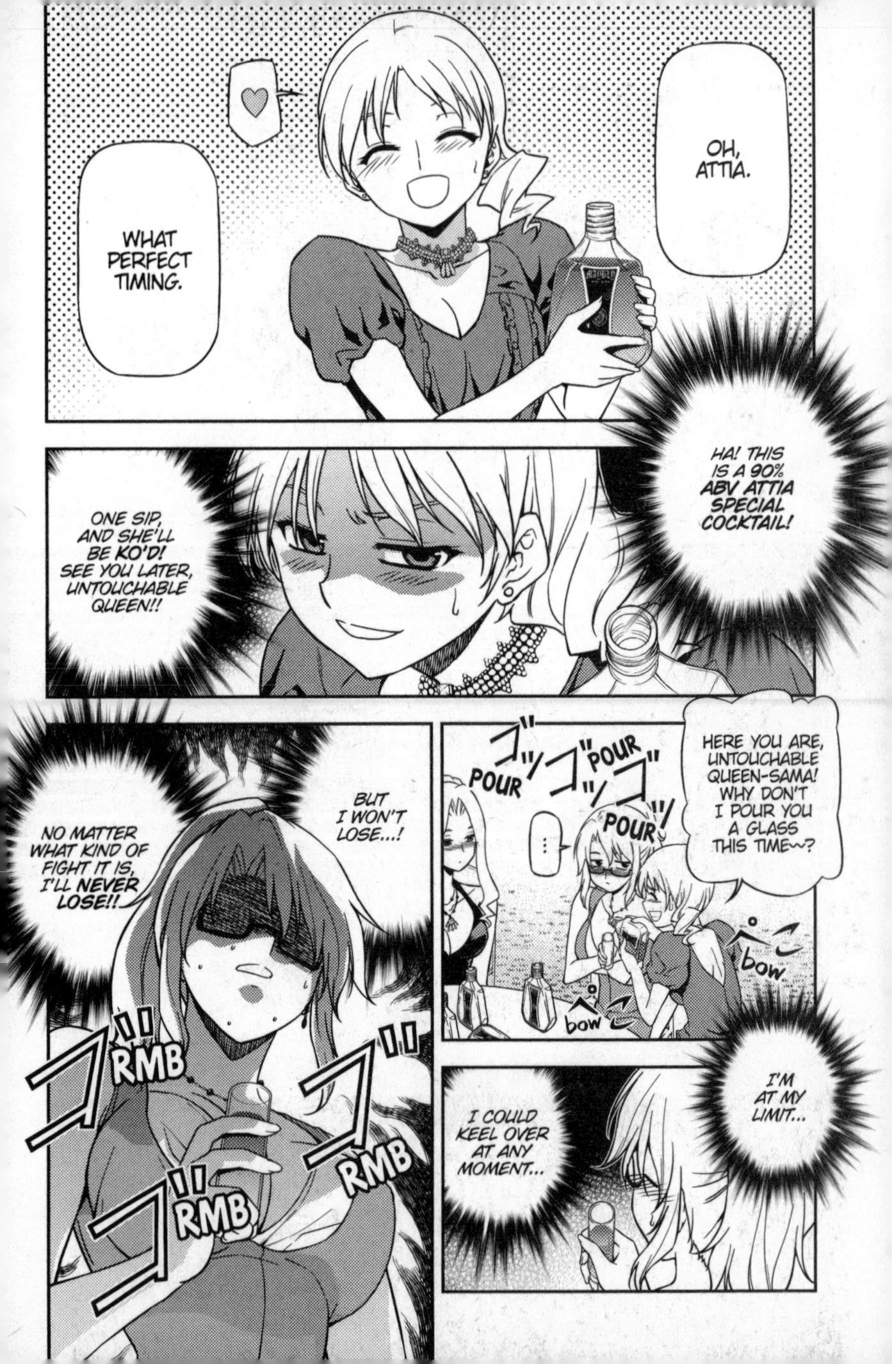

OH, ATTIA.
WHAT PERFECT TIMING.
HA! THIS IS A 90% ABV ATTIA SPECIAL COCKTAIL!
ONE SIP, AND SHE'LL BE KO'D! SEE YOU LATER, UNTOUCHABLE QUEEN!!
HERE YOU ARE, UNTOUCHABLE QUEEN-SAMA! WHY DON'T I POUR YOU A GLASS THIS TIME~?
POUR POUR POUR
...
bow bow
I'M AT MY LIMIT...
I COULD KEEL OVER AT ANY MOMENT...
BUT I WON'T LOSE...!
NO MATTER WHAT KIND OF FIGHT IT IS, I'LL NEVER LOSE!!
RMB RMB RMB

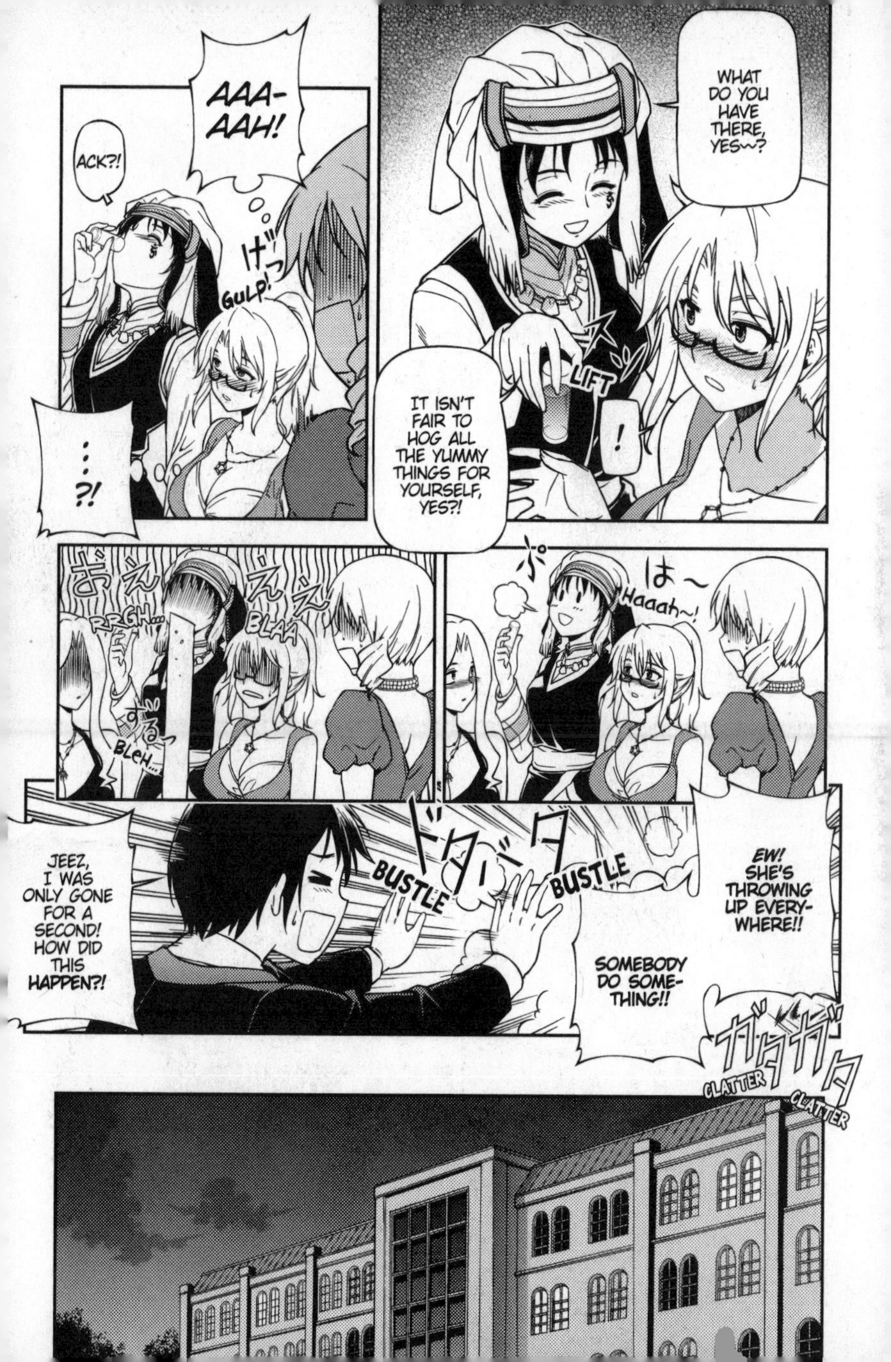
WHAT DO YOU HAVE THERE, YES~?
LIFT
!
IT ISN'T FAIR TO HOG ALL THE YUMMY THINGS FOR YOURSELF, YES?!
AAA-AAH!
ACK?!
げっ
GULP!
...?!
ぷ
は~
Haaah~!
おえええ
RRGH...
BLAA
ずる~
BLEH...
EW! SHE'S THROWING UP EVERY-WHERE!!
SOMEBODY DO SOME-THING!!
ガタガタ
CLATTER CLATTER
ドタバタ
BUSTLE BUSTLE
JEEZ, I WAS ONLY GONE FOR A SECOND! HOW DID THIS HAPPEN?!

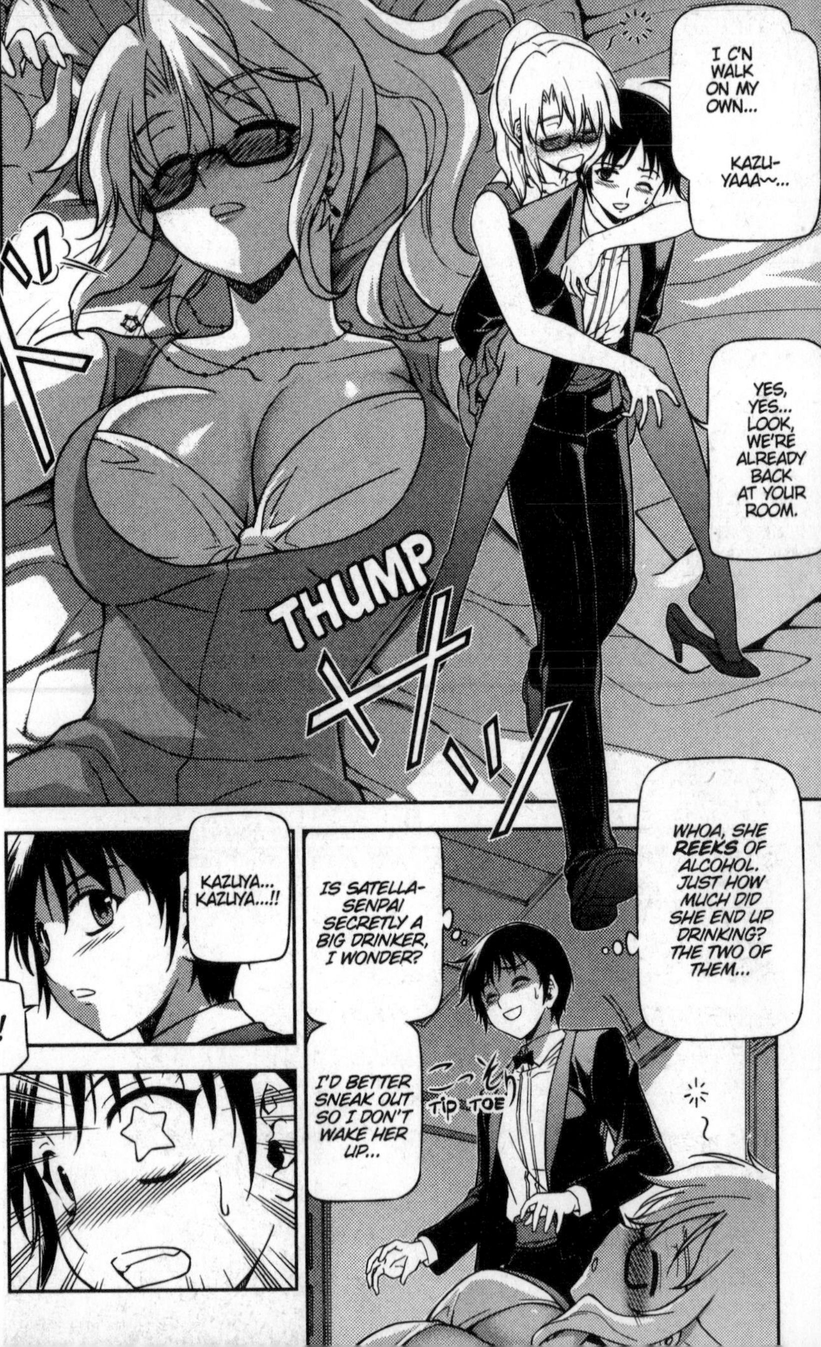
I C'N WALK ON MY OWN... KAZU-YAAA~...
YES, YES... LOOK, WE'RE ALREADY BACK AT YOUR ROOM.
THUMP
WHOA, SHE REEKS OF ALCOHOL. JUST HOW MUCH DID SHE END UP DRINKING? THE TWO OF THEM...
IS SATELLA-SENPAI SECRETLY A BIG DRINKER, I WONDER?
I'D BETTER SNEAK OUT SO I DON'T WAKE HER UP...
TIP TOE
KAZUYA... KAZUYA...!!
!

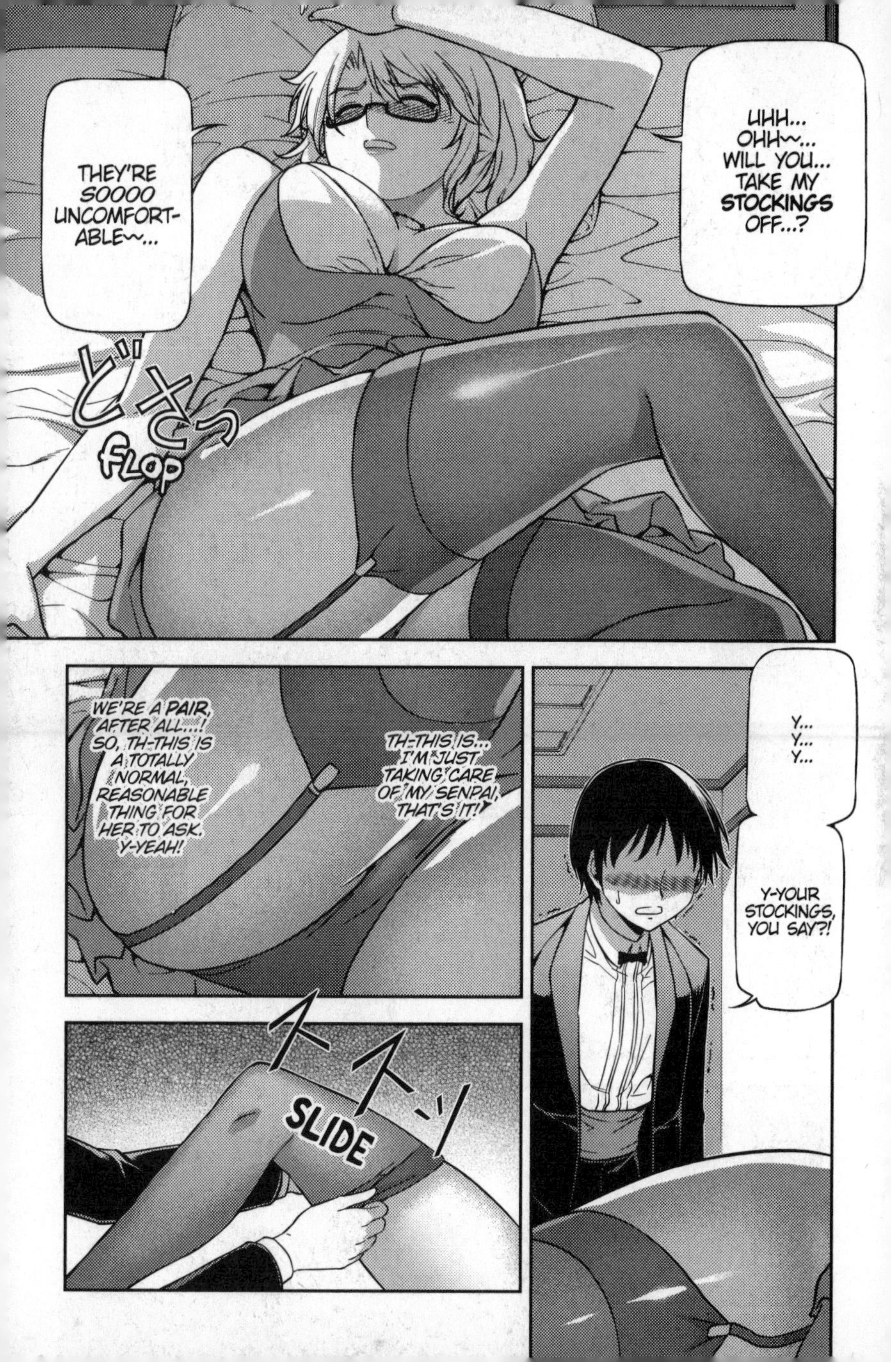
UHH... OHH~... WILL YOU... TAKE MY STOCKINGS OFF...?
THEY'RE SOOOO UNCOMFORTABLE~...
FLOP
Y... Y... Y...
Y-YOUR STOCKINGS, YOU SAY?!
TH-THIS IS... I'M JUST TAKING CARE OF MY SENPAI, THAT'S IT!
WE'RE A PAIR, AFTER ALL...! SO, TH-THIS IS A TOTALLY NORMAL, REASONABLE THING FOR HER TO ASK. Y-YEAH!
SLIDE

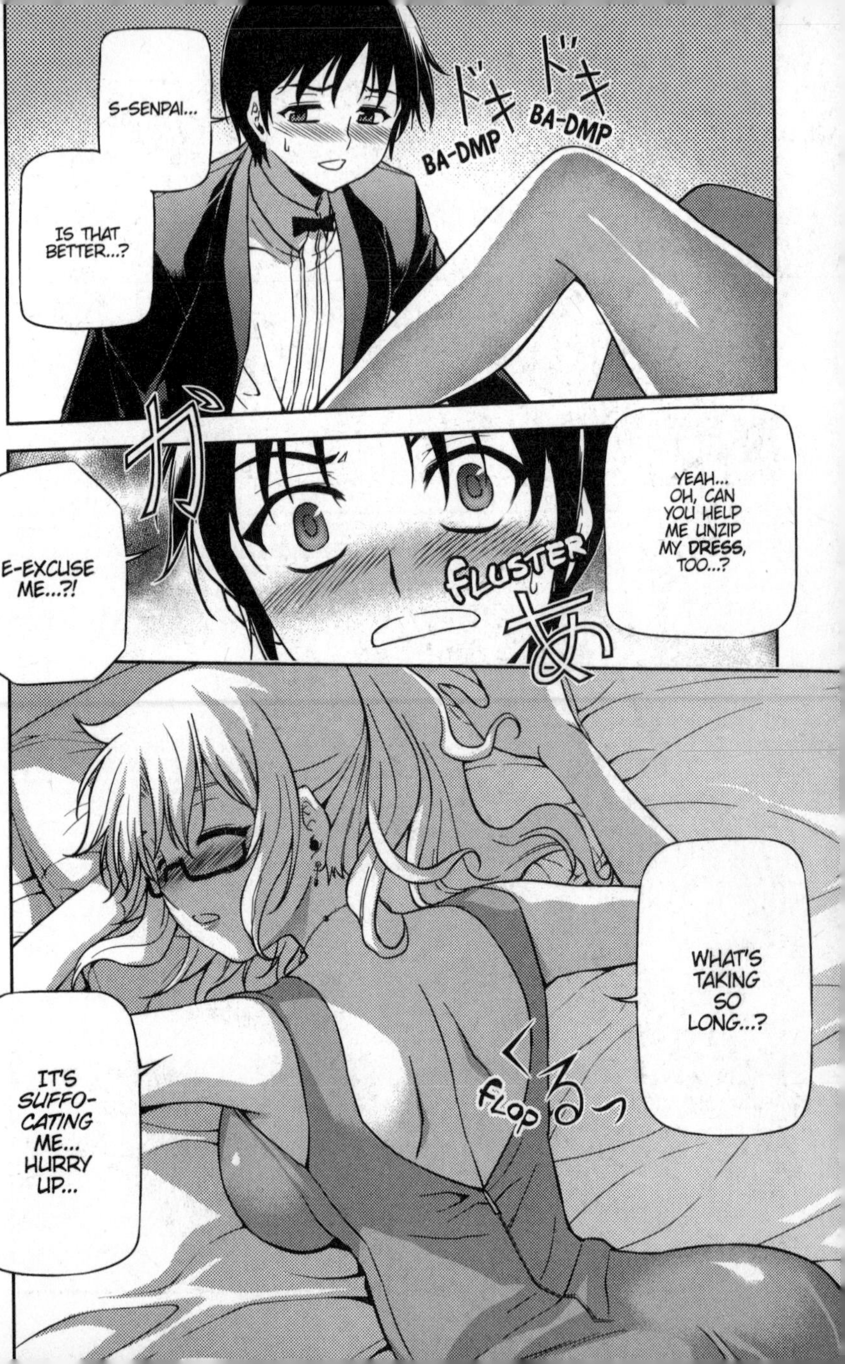
ドキ ドキ
BA-DMP BA-DMP
S-SENPAI...
IS THAT BETTER...?
YEAH... OH, CAN YOU HELP ME UNZIP MY DRESS, TOO...?
FLUSTER
E-EXCUSE ME...?!
WHAT'S TAKING SO LONG...?
FLOP
IT'S SUFFO-CATING ME... HURRY UP...

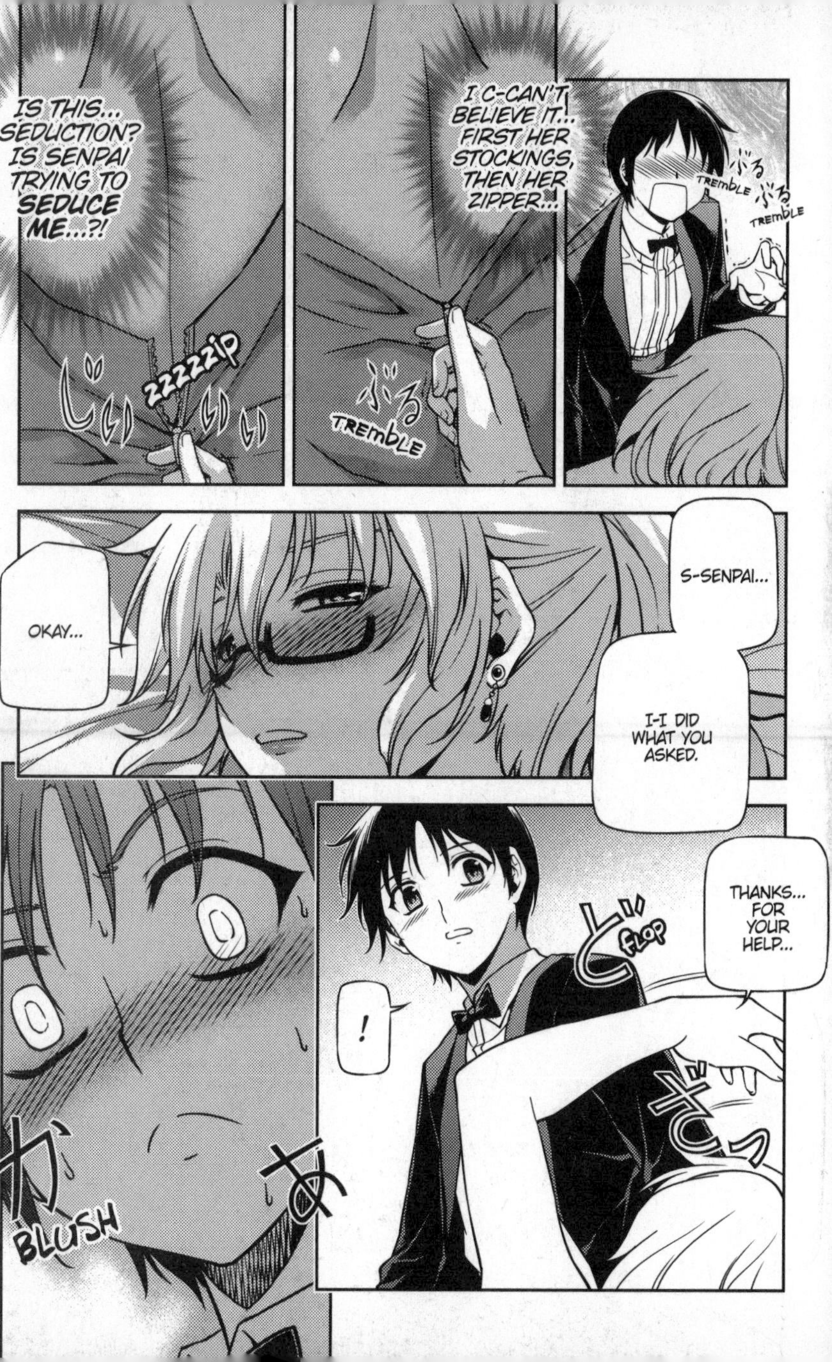

ぶる
TREMBLE
ぶる
TREMBLE
I C-CAN'T BELIEVE IT... FIRST HER STOCKINGS, THEN HER ZIPPER...
ぶる
TREMBLE
IS THIS... SEDUCTION? IS SENPAI TRYING TO SEDUCE ME...?!
zzzzzip
S-SENPAI...
I-I DID WHAT YOU ASKED.
OKAY...
THANKS... FOR YOUR HELP...
FLOP
!
BLUSH

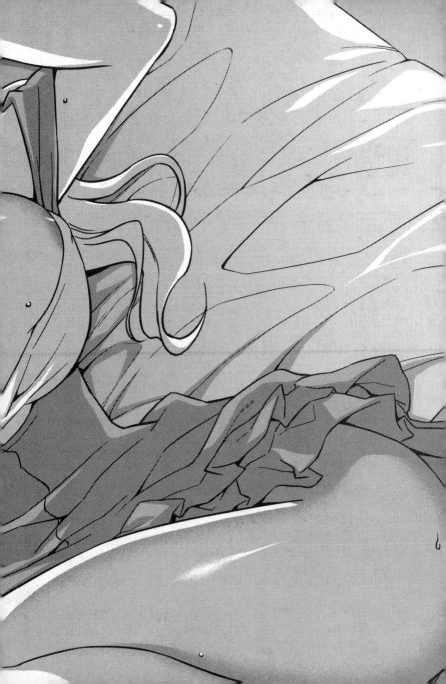

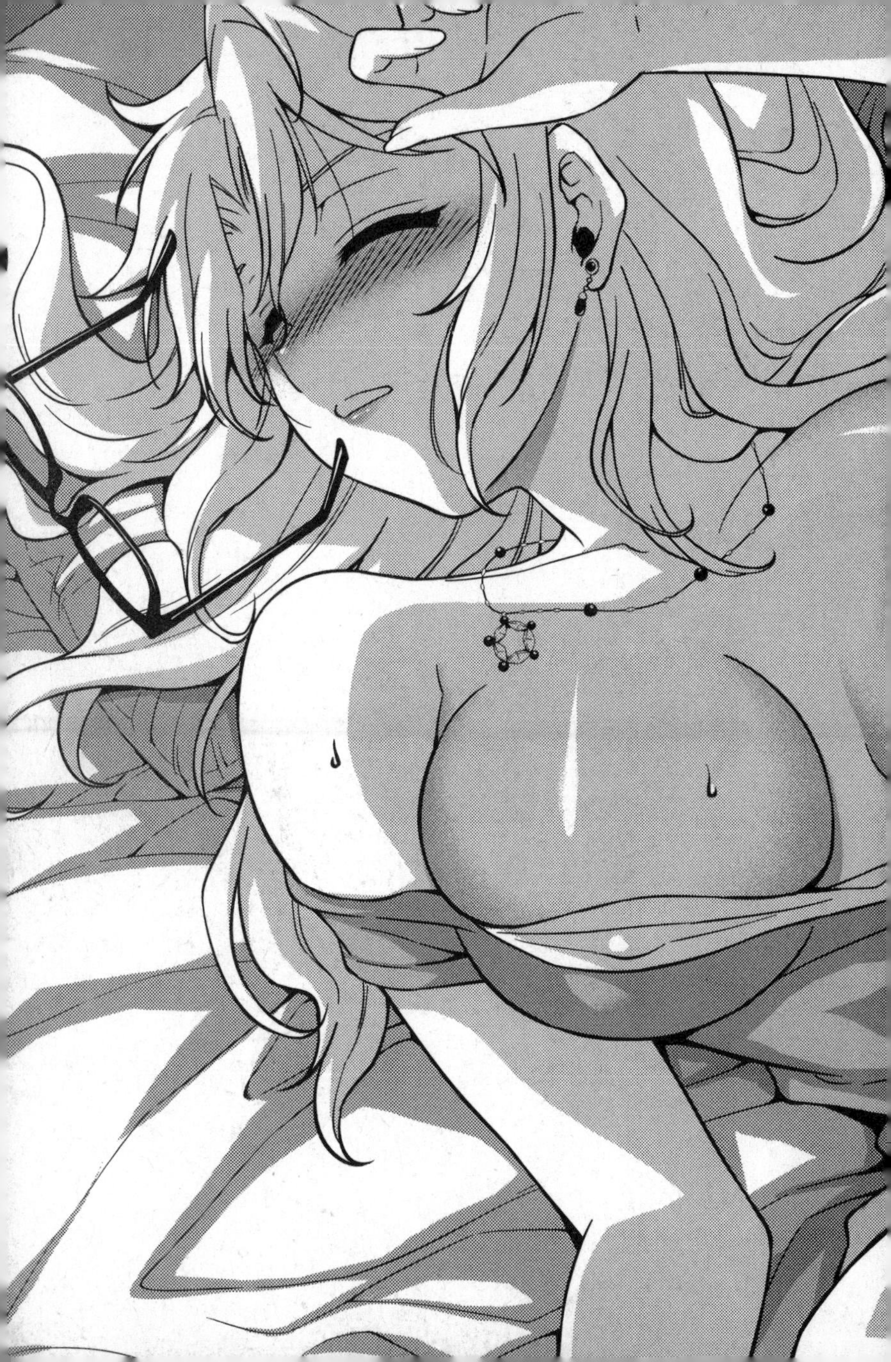

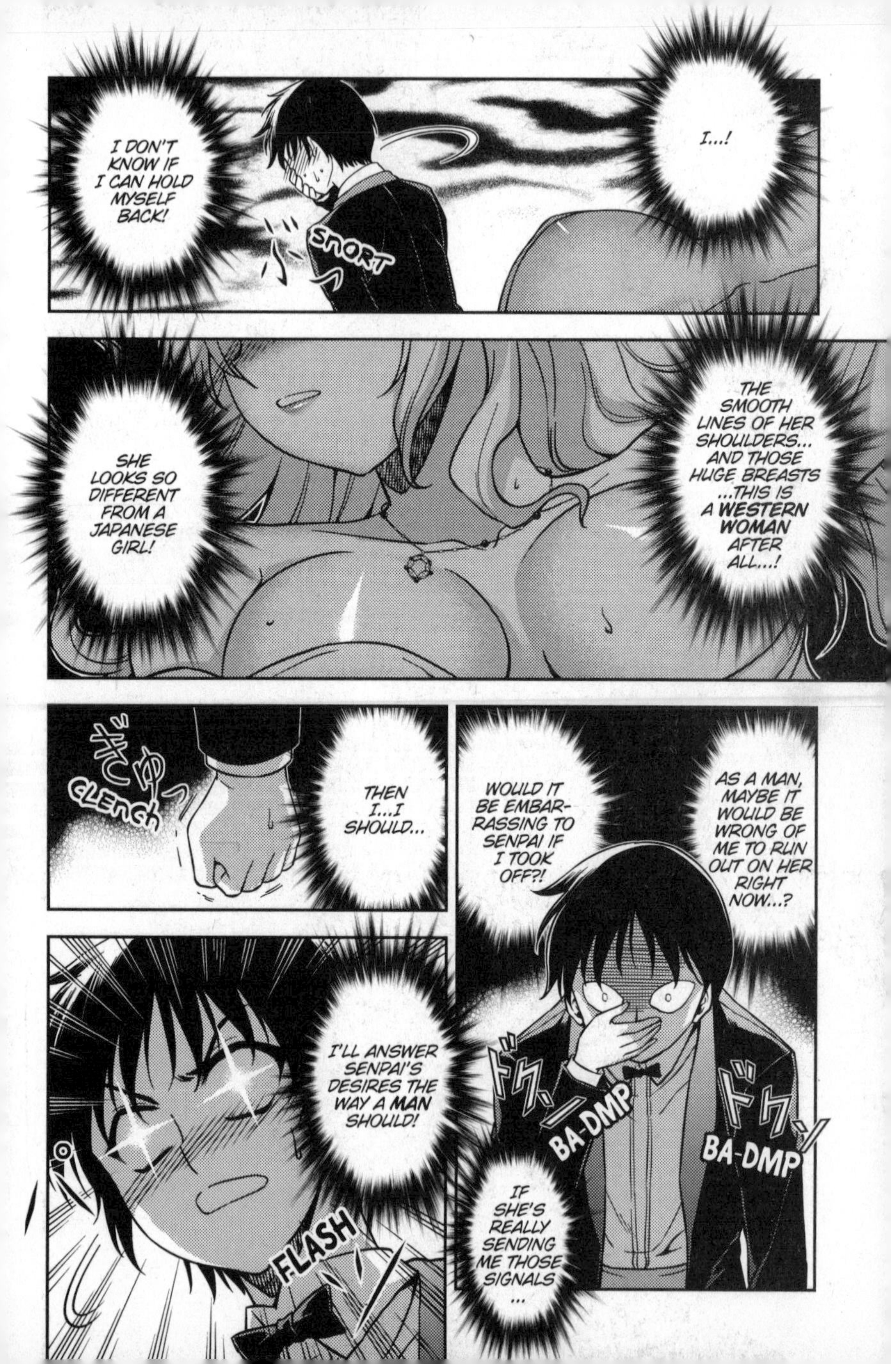
I...!
I DON'T KNOW IF I CAN HOLD MYSELF BACK!
SNORT
THE SMOOTH LINES OF HER SHOULDERS... AND THOSE HUGE BREASTS ...THIS IS A **WESTERN WOMAN** AFTER ALL...!
SHE LOOKS SO DIFFERENT FROM A JAPANESE GIRL!
AS A MAN, MAYBE IT WOULD BE WRONG OF ME TO RUN OUT ON HER RIGHT NOW...?
WOULD IT BE EMBAR-RASSING TO SENPAI IF I TOOK OFF?!
BA-DMP
BA-DMP
IF SHE'S REALLY SENDING ME THOSE SIGNALS ...
THEN I...I SHOULD...
CLENCH
I'LL ANSWER SENPAI'S DESIRES THE WAY A **MAN** SHOULD!
FLASH

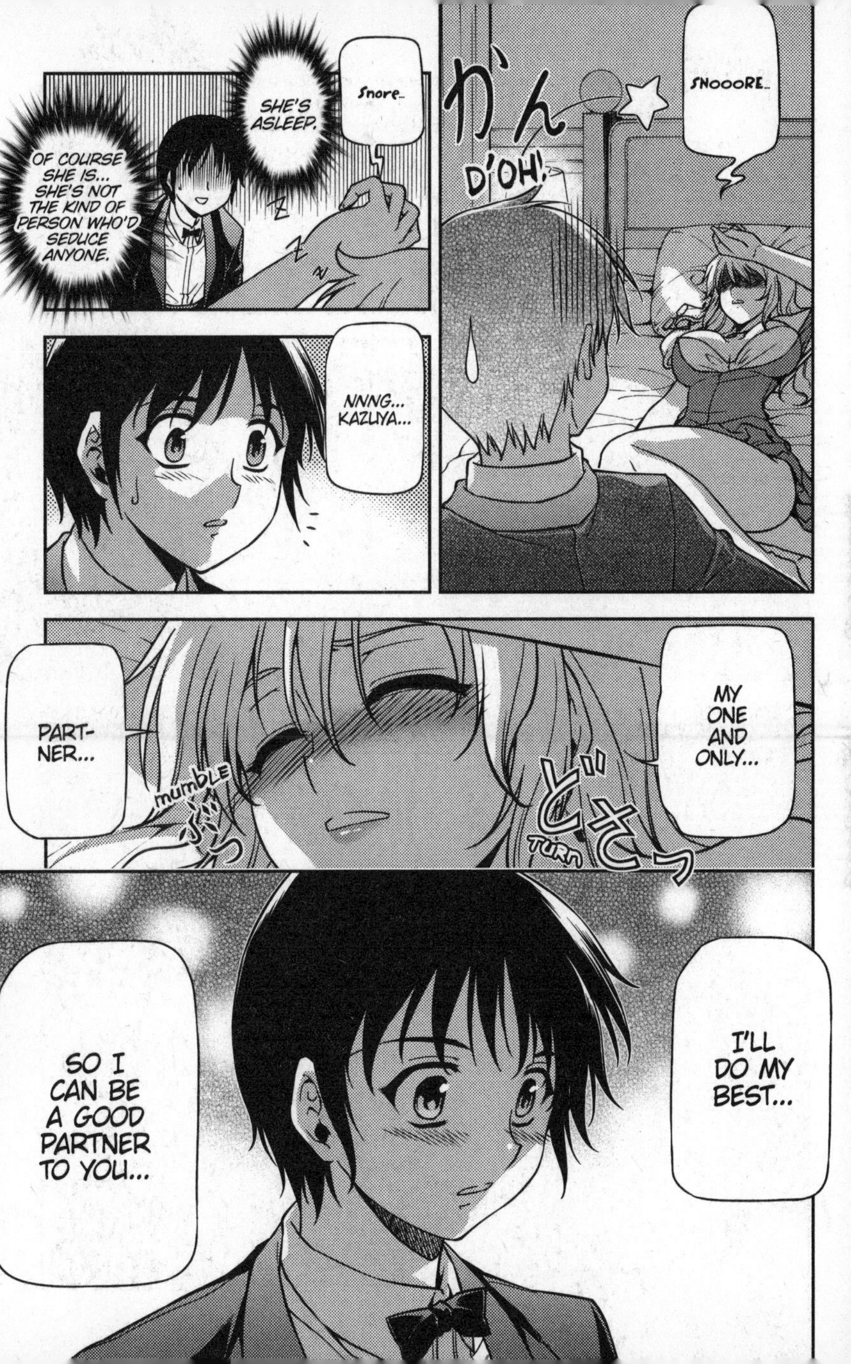
SNOOORE...
がん
D'OH!
Snore...
SHE'S ASLEEP.
OF COURSE SHE IS... SHE'S NOT THE KIND OF PERSON WHO'D SEDUCE ANYONE.
NNNG... KAZUYA...
MY ONE AND ONLY...
どさっ
TURN
ぶつ
mumble
PART-NER...
I'LL DO MY BEST...
SO I CAN BE A GOOD PARTNER TO YOU...

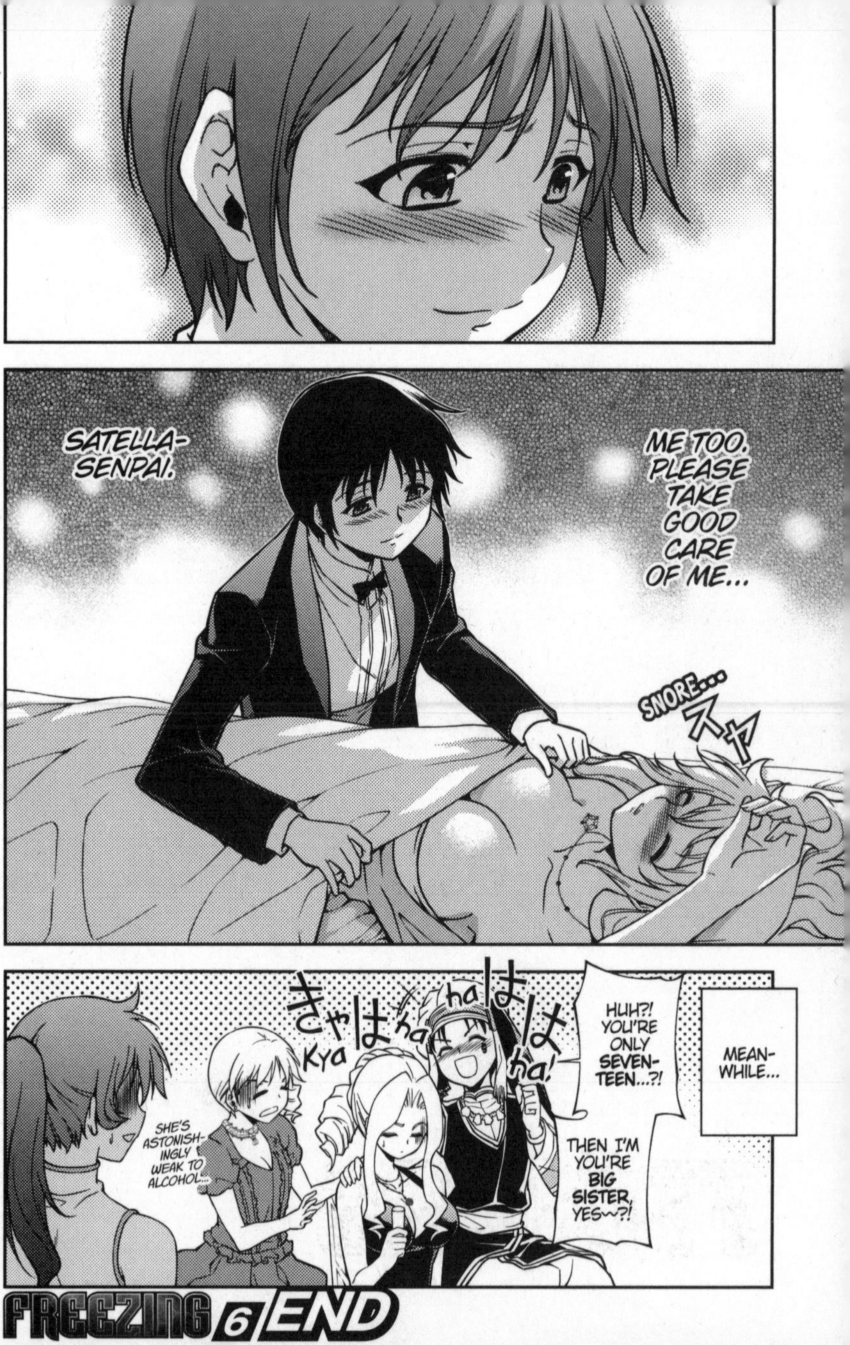
ME TOO. PLEASE TAKE GOOD CARE OF ME...
SATELLA-SENPAI.
SNORE...
スヤ
MEAN-WHILE...
HUH?! YOU'RE ONLY SEVEN-TEEN...?!
きゃははは
Kya ha ha ha!
THEN I'M YOU'RE BIG SISTER, YES~?!
SHE'S ASTONISH-INGLY WEAK TO ALCOHOL...

FREEZING 6 END

FREEZING

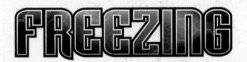

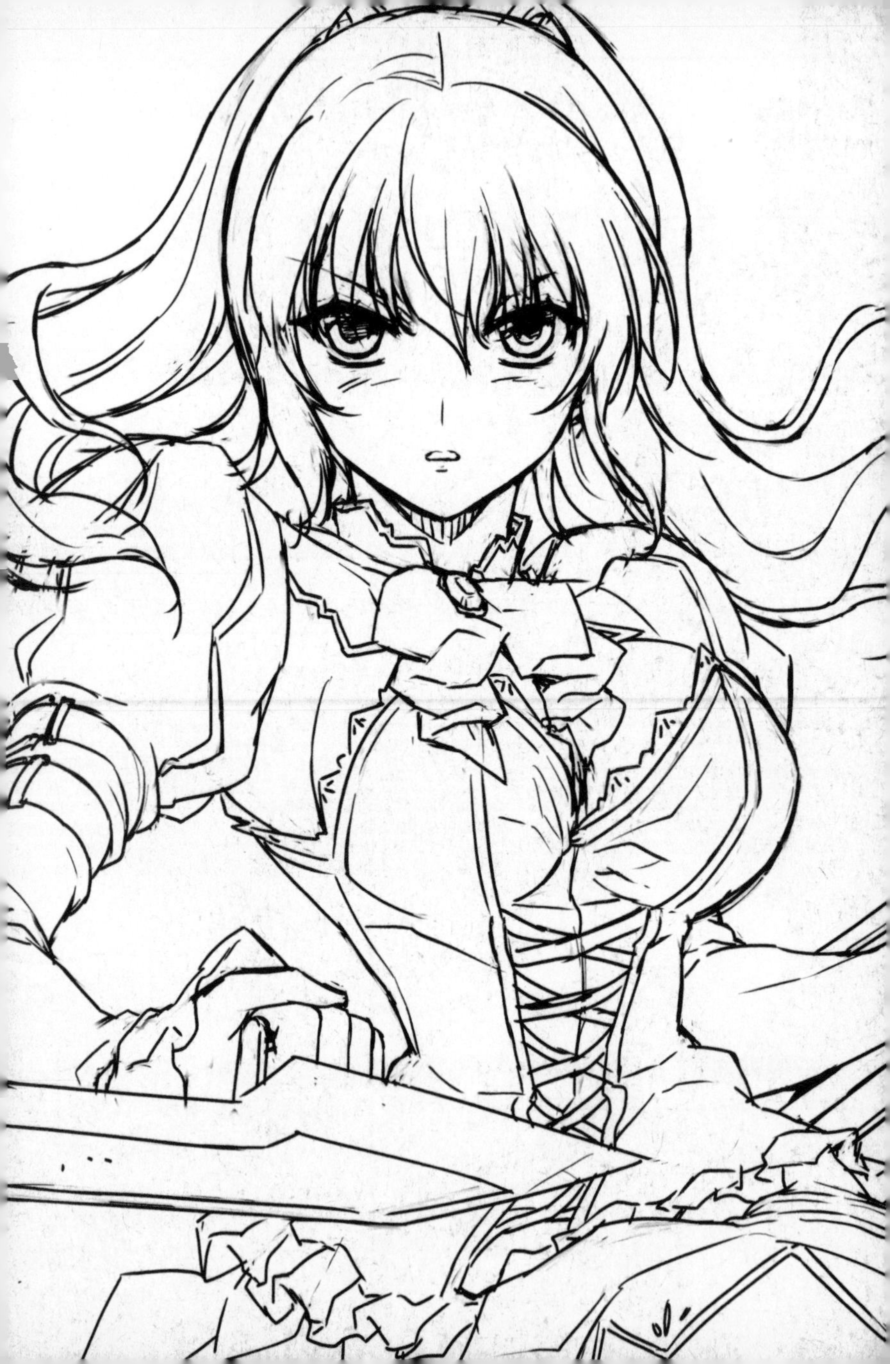

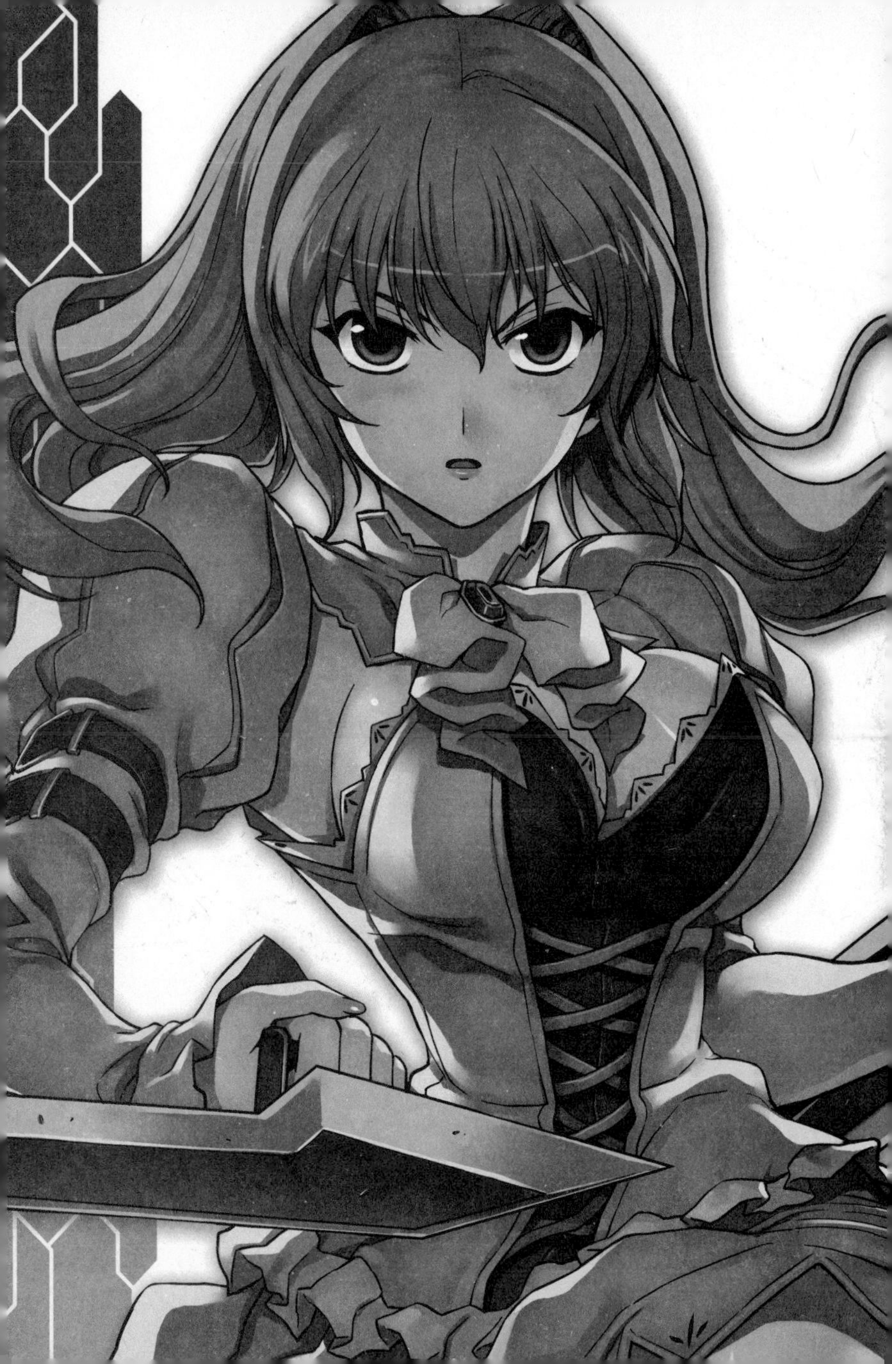

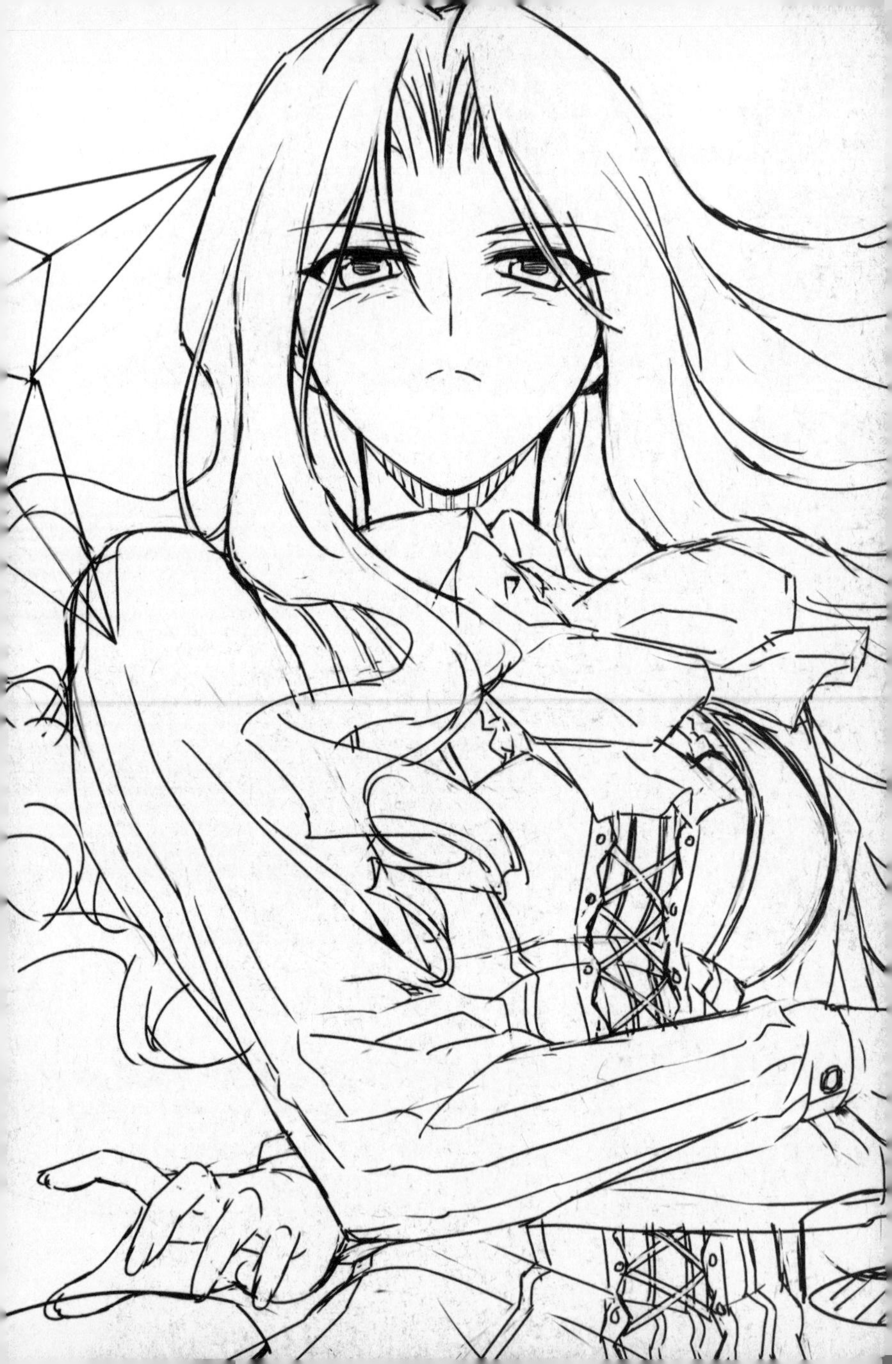

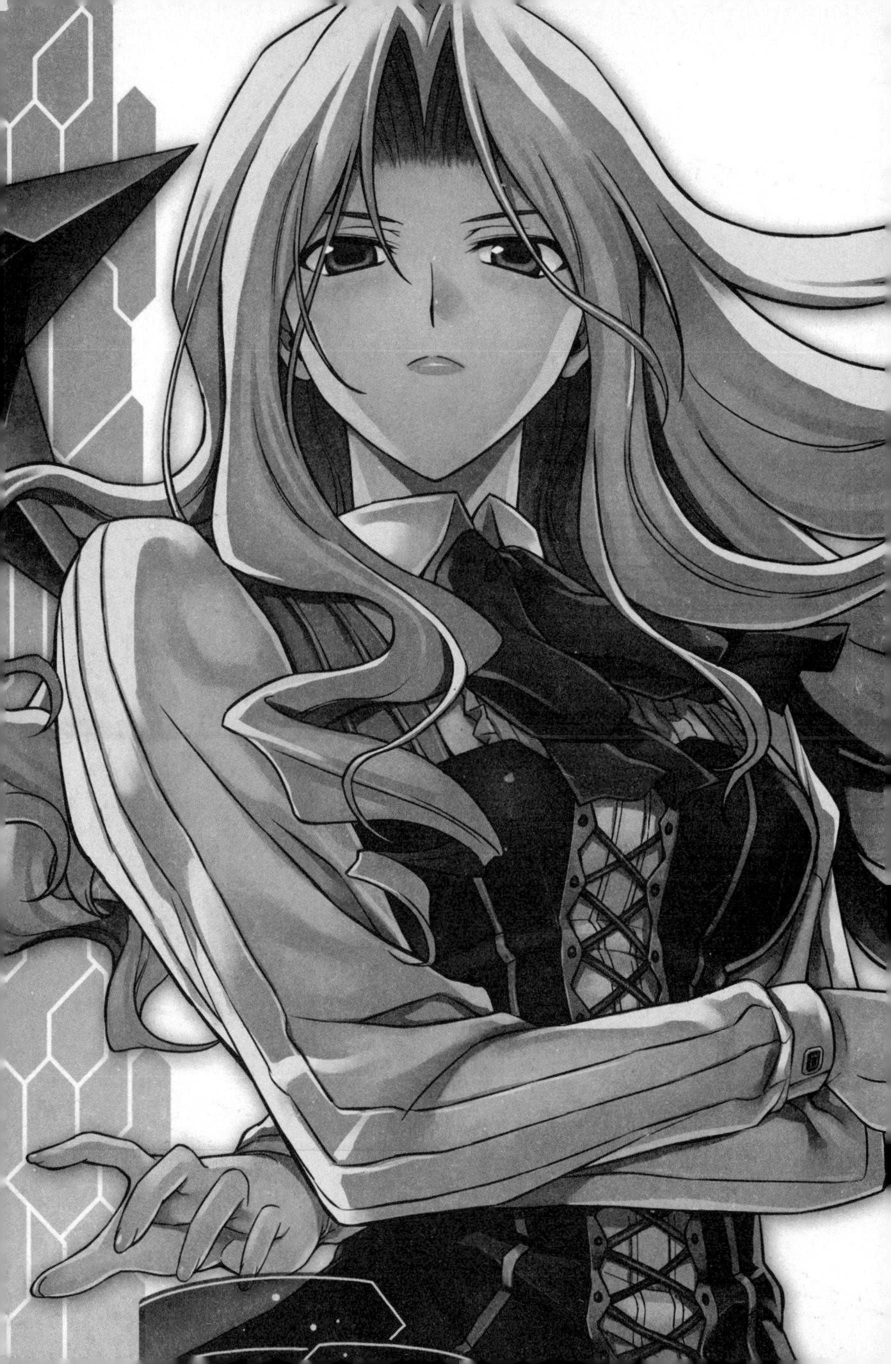

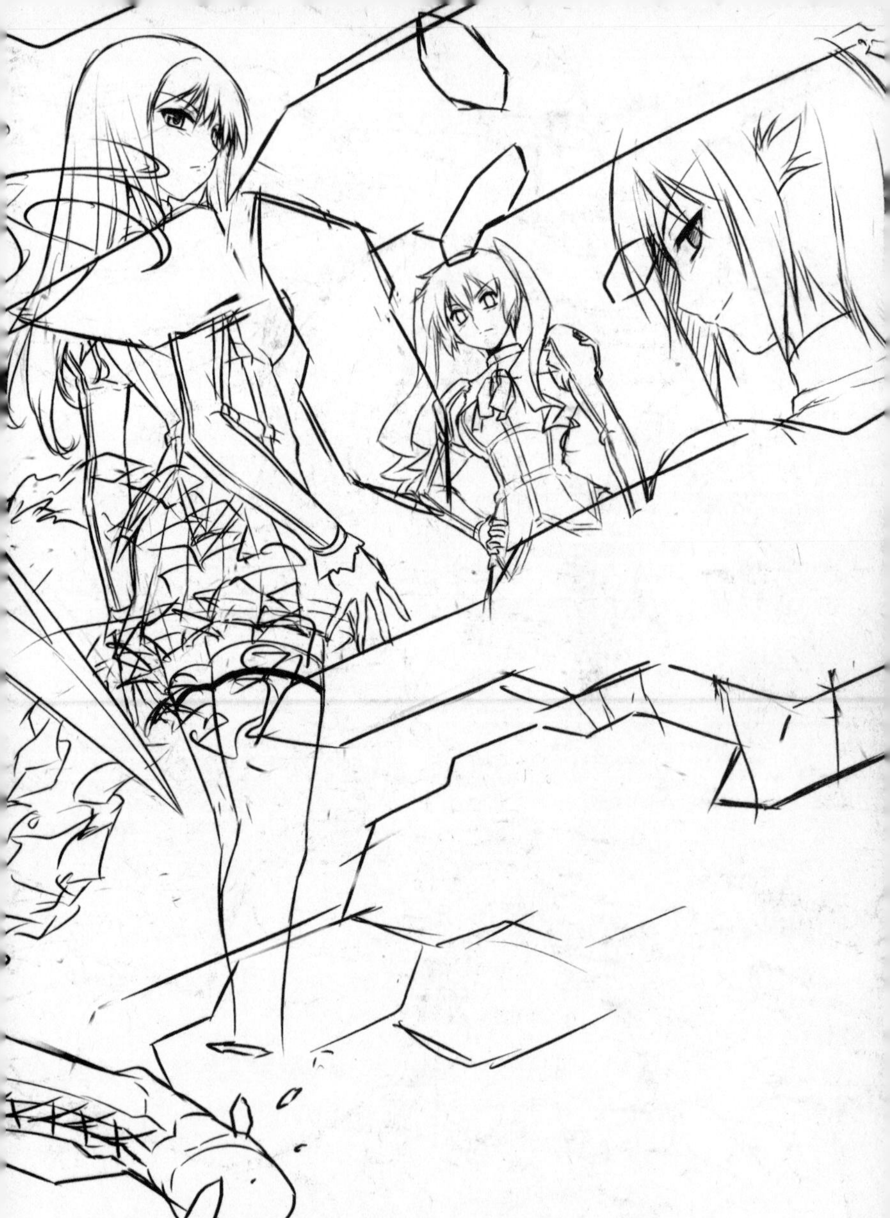

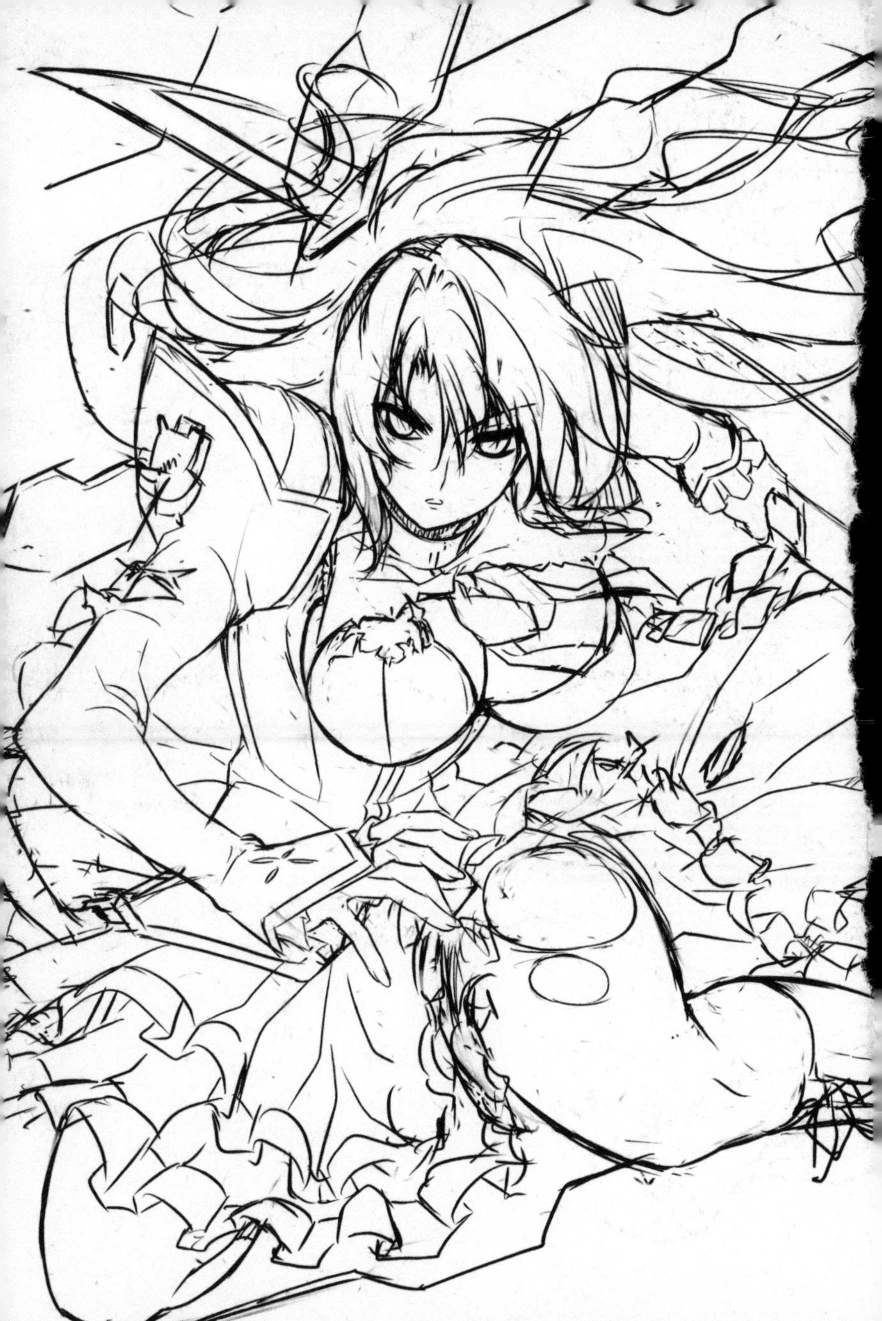

SEVEN SEAS ENTERTA[redacted]

FREEZING VOLS. 5-6

story by **DALL-YOUNG LIM** / art by **KWANG-HYUN KIM**

TRANSLATION
Nan Rymer

ADAPTATION
Rebecca Scoble

LETTERING AND LAYOUT
Alexandra Gunawan

COVER DESIGN
Nicky Lim

PROOFREADER
Patrick King

ASSISTANT EDITOR
Lissa Pattillo

MANAGING EDITOR
Adam Arnold

PUBLISHER
Jason DeAngelis

FREEZING Volumes 5-6

This edition originally published in Japan in 2009
by KILL TIME COMMUNICATION, Tokyo.
English translation rights arranged with KILL TIME COMMUNICATION
through TOHAN CORPORATION, Tokyo.

ISBN: 978-1-626922-21-1
Printed in Canada
First Printing: December 2015
10 9 8 7 6 5 4 3 2 1

FOLLOW US ONLINE: ***www.gomanga.com***

READING DIRECTIONS

This book reads from ***right to left***, Japanese style. If this is your first time reading manga, you start reading from the top right panel on each page and take it from there. If you get lost, just follow the numbered diagram here. It may seem backwards at first, but you'll get the hang of it! Have fun!!

1
2
3
4
5
6
7
8
9

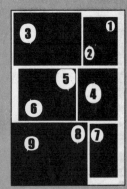